Why Do You Need This New Edition?

Think currency. Think relevancy. Think communication. The revised and updated second edition of THINK Communication includes new research, content, and strategies and skills.

1. Chapter 4 **Listening and Critical Thinking** now reflects contemporary listening research including the **HURIER Model of Listening**

2. Chapter 7 **Understanding Interpersonal Relationships** and Chapter 8 **Improving Interpersonal Communication** are completely revised and reorganized. Chapter 7 focuses on basic interpersonal principles–Strengthening Relationships, Sharing, and Expressing Emotions and Thoughts. Chapter 8 concentrates on interpersonal skills–Resolving Conflict, Assertiveness, Managing Anger, and Adapting to Culture and Gender.

3. New **Assessment Materials** in every chapter include **Communication Assessment** activities such as "How Do You Respond to Conflict?" (Chapter 8) and "Evaluate Their Speaking Style and Your Delivery" (Chapter 14); **Know Thy Self** features such as "Do You Have Poor Listening Habits?" (Chapter 4) and "What Inspires You?" (Chapter 12); and **Stop and Think** exercises such as "How's Your Netspeak, Netlingo, and leet (133t)?" (Chapter 5) and "Interpersonal Communication Online" (Chapter 7).

4. The latest content on **Social Media and Technology** appears in new features such as "The Twubble with Twitter" (Chapter 1) and "Cell Phone Conversations and Texting" (Chapter 7).

5. New **Communication in Action** features, such as "Making Sense of Our Senses" (Chapter 2) and "Just Say No" (Chapter 8), apply theory and research to everyday communication.

6. New **Communication and Culture** and **Ethical Communication** features, including "Adapt Your Gestures to Cultural Differences" (Chapter 14) and "Principles of Interpersonal Ethics" (Chapter 8), offer guiding principles *and* appropriate communication strategies.

7. Updated **Think about Theory** features, such as "Listening and Working Memory" (Chapter 4) and "Relational Dialectics Theory" (Chapter 8), analyze and apply classic and contemporary theories.

8. New **Annotated Readings** selections promote critical thinking and include "Stand by Me: Helping Bullied Victims."

9. New **photos and figures** present contemporary images that emphasize the importance of communication in today's complex and wired world.

PEARSON

THINK
COMMUNICATION

ISA N. ENGLEBERG
Prince George's Community College

DIANNA R. WYNN
Nash Community College

PEARSON

Boston   Columbus   Indianapolis   New York   San Francisco   Upper Saddle River   Amsterdam
Cape Town   Dubai   London   Madrid   Milan   Munich   Paris   Montréal   Toronto   Delhi   Mexico City
São Paulo   Sydney   Hong Kong   Seoul   Singapore   Taipei   Tokyo

Editor-in-Chief, Communication: Karon Bowers
Senior Acquisitions Editor: Melissa Mashburn
Editorial Assistant: Megan Hermida
Director of Development: Eileen Calabro
Development Editor: Erin Mulligan
Associate Development Editor: Angela Mallowes
Marketing Manager: Blair Tuckman
Senior Digital Editor: Paul DeLuca
Digital Editor: Lisa Dotson
Project Manager: Barbara Mack
Manufacturing Manager: Mary Fischer
Procurement Specialist: Mary Ann Gloriande
Project Coordination, Text Design, and Electronic Page Makeup: PreMediaGlobal
Cover Design Manager/Designer: John Callahan
Cover Photos: iPad: Shutterstock/Yuriy Kulyk; Icon images (top row): ©Dgilder/Dreamstime, ©Igor Kovalchuk/Fotolia,
©carlosseller/Fotolia, zulufoto/Shutterstock. Second row: Sukhonosova Anastasia/Shutterstock, ©maeroris/Fotolia, ©michael-
jung/Fotolia, ©Nn555/Dreamstime. Third row: Studiovision/iStockphoto, Camilo Torres/iStockphoto, ©Jiripravda/Fotolia,
dream1974/iStockphoto. Fourth row: ©Alexander Raths/Dreamstime, © jpegwiz/Fotolia, Michael DeLeon/iStockphoto,
DimaChe/iStockphoto.
Printer and Binder: Courier/Kendallville
Cover Printer: Courier/Kendallville

Credits and acknowledgments borrowed from other sources and reproduced, with permission, in this textbook appear on the
appropriate page within text or on pp. 354–355.

Library of Congress Cataloging-in-Publication Data

Engleberg, Isa N.
  Think communication / Isa N. Engleberg, Dianna R. Wynn.—2nd ed.
    p. cm.
  ISBN 978-0-205-11038-4
  1. Interpersonal communication.   2. Communication.   I. Wynn, Dianna.   II. Title.
  HM1166.E545 2013
  302—dc23
                                                                                2012004495

10 9 8 7 6 5 4 3 2 1—CRK—15 14 13 12

www.pearsonhighered.com

ISBN-13: 978-0-205-11038-4
ISBN-10:   0-205-11038-X

brief **CONTENTS**

on the cover:

▼

THINK
COMMUNICATION
ENGLEBERG • WYNN 2013

The Right Stuff
Why employers hire employees with strong communication skills

Liar, Liar
Creating, deceiving, and revealing yourself online

Public Speaking Jitters?
Understand, minimize, control your speaking anxiety

Group Decision Making
Face-to-face or cyberspace?

Listening Habits
The good, the bad, and the clueless

www.mysearchlab.com

36
Public Speaking Jitters?
Understand, minimize,
control your speaking anxiety

218
Group Decision Making
Face-to-face or cyberspace?

65
Listening Habits
The good, the bad, and the clueless

27
Liar, Liar
Creating, deceiving, and revealing yourself online

4
The Right Stuff
Why employers hire employees with
strong communication skills

detailed CONTENTS

5

6

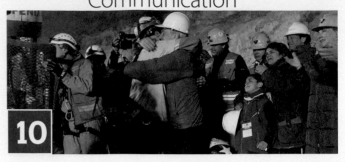

15

16

acknowledgments

The second edition of *THINK Communication* would never have seen the light of day or come out on schedule without the talent, dedication, and creativity of our publishing team. We are particularly grateful to the group of production editors, graphic designers, photo editors, copy editors, and behind-the-scenes technicians who transformed a manuscript into an engaging, cutting-edge textbook: Linda Behrens, Barbara Mack, Marie Desrosiers, Carly Bergey, Annette Linder, Sarah Bylund, and Estelle Simpson.

We extend very special thanks to Karon Bowers, our dynamic, multitasking editor in chief at Pearson whose wise advice, problem-solving ability, flexibility, creativity, and friendship have supported and sustained us through this and other textbook projects. We also welcomed and thank our new senior acquisitions editor, Melissa Mashburn, who joined us midway through this project and quickly became a valuable sounding board and conscientious manager for the rest of the journey.

Only we truly know how much credit for the second edition of *THINK Communication* goes to Erin Mulligan, our superlative development editor and muse, whose professionalism, sense of humor, inventiveness, imaginative spirit, and seemingly endless resources of new ideas and approaches made a tight, potentially terrifying set of deadlines fly by with ease.

We also thank editorial assistants Stephanie Chaisson, Megan Sweeney, and Megan Hermida as well as associate development editor Angela Mallowes for helping us expertly shepherd this textbook and its ancillaries from manuscript through to bound book. We are particularly grateful to marketing manager Blair Tuckman and the Pearson sales representatives for demonstrating the many ways in which *THINK Communication* helps students become more effective and ethical communicators.

Insightful reviewers provided many excellent suggestions that make the second edition of *THINK Communication* a better book. We salute Sarah Clements of Pulaski Technical College; Chandra K. Massner of Pikeville College; Skye Gentile of Cabrillo College; Karen Newtzie of Rappahannock Community College; Gwen Hullman of the University of Nevada, Reno; and Johh Tindell of Northampton Community College.

All things considered—and as we look at our approach to and philosophy when writing this textbook—we are particularly indebted to the students and faculty members who have shared their opinions and provided valuable suggestions and insights about our teaching and our textbooks. They are the measure of all things.

ISA ENGLEBERG, Professor Emerita at Prince George's Community College in Largo, Maryland, served as president of the National Communication Association (NCA) in 2003 and chaired the NCA Research Board from 1995 to 1998. She has written six college textbooks in communication studies, published more than three dozen articles in academic journals, and made hundreds of convention and seminar presentations. Dr. Engleberg received the Outstanding Community College Educator Award from the NCA and the President's Medal from Prince George's Community College for outstanding teaching, scholarship, and service. She has focused her professional career on improving both the content and teaching of basic communication courses at all levels of higher education as well as teaching and consulting internationally.

DIANNA WYNN is a professor at Nash Community College in Rocky Mount, North Carolina. Previously she taught at Midland College in Texas and Prince George's Community College in Maryland, where she was chosen by students as the Outstanding Teacher of the Year. She has coauthored two communication textbooks and has written articles in academic journals. She served as an officer in the Community College Section and a member of the Legislative Assembly of the National Communication Association and has participated in dozens of convention programs. In addition to teaching and college service, she has many years of experience as a trial consultant, assisting attorneys in developing effective communication strategies for the courtroom.

Human 1
COMMUNICATION

The instant you were born, you began communicating. You squirmed, cried, and even screamed when you were hungry or hurt. You smiled and gurgled when you were happy and content. And as you fussed and cooed, you also began learning how to speak and listen. From a very early age, you faced hundreds of communication challenges—and still do. Communication occupies more of your waking time than anything else you do.[1]

You communicate every day: when you greet your friends, participate in a class discussion, interact with coworkers, or shake hands with a new acquaintance. You also live in a competitive world where effective speaking allows you and your message to stand out from the rest of the crowd. Your ability to communicate, regardless of whether you're interacting with one person, a small group, or a large audience, determines how well you inform, persuade, delight, inspire, and comfort other people.

Most of the time, you communicate well, but what about when you're in the middle of a heated argument, when you can't think of what to say to a troubled friend, or when an important presentation falls short? In such situations, you need more than common sense. Like most complex processes, effective communication requires knowledge, skills, and motivation.

THINK About... and ASK YOURSELF...

1.1 Communication in Your Life | *What is communication, and how does it affect your everyday life?*

1.2 Communication Principles | *What do you need to know to become a more effective communicator?*

1.3 Communication Models | *How do communication models help you address communication challenges?*

1.4 Communication Theories, Strategies, and Skills | *How do theories help you choose effective communication strategies and skills?*

1.5 Communicating Ethically | *Why is ethical decision making essential for effective communication?*

1.1
Communication in Your Life

What is communication, and how does it affect your everyday life?

Communication is the process of using verbal and nonverbal messages to generate meaning within and across various contexts, cultures, and channels.[2] The key phrase in this definition is *generate meaning*. You generate meaning when you speak, write, act, and create visual images as well as when you listen, read, and react to messages. Although you communicate all the time, you can always learn how to do it better. And it is worth the effort. Your personal, academic, and professional success throughout your lifetime will depend on how well you communicate.[3] Personal relationships are richer and more rewarding when both parties communicate effectively. Colleagues who express respect for one another and argue constructively are more likely to enjoy productive interactions. Work group members who communicate effectively with one another are more likely to achieve their goals. And if you speak early, often, and well, you are more likely to be elected and selected for leadership roles.

According to the *Chronicle of Higher Education*, college faculty members identify speaking, listening, problem solving, interpersonal skills, working in groups, and leading groups as essential skills for every college graduate.[4] A national survey of 1,000 human resource managers concluded that oral communication skills are the *most* critical factor for obtaining jobs and advancing in a career.[5] Executives with Fortune 500 companies claim that the college graduates they employ need better communication skills as well as a demonstrated ability to work in teams and with people from diverse backgrounds.[6]

To become an effective communicator, you need to do more than learn a set of "fool-proof" rules or the "tricks of the trade." You also need to learn how to apply communication theories, strategies, and skills to multiple communication contexts. To gauge whether you communicate effectively in a variety of communication situations, ask yourself the following questions:

- *Personal.* Do I have meaningful personal relationships with close friends, relatives, and romantic partners?
- *Professional.* Do I communicate effectively within and on behalf of a business, organization, or work team?
- *Educational.* Do I demonstrate what I have learned in collegiate, corporate, and other training settings?
- *Intercultural.* Do I understand, respect, and adapt to people from diverse backgrounds?
- *Intellectual.* Do I analyze and evaluate the meaning of multiple and complex messages in an ever-changing world?
- *Societal.* Do I critically analyze and appropriately respond to public and mediated messages?
- *Ethical.* Do I apply ethical standards to personal and public communication in a variety of situations?

Know Thy Self

Do You Have the Right Stuff for the Job?

The National Association of Colleges and Employers (NACE) asked employers to rate the skills they seek in the college graduates they hire.[7] In your opinion, which of the following skills are most important to employers? Rank them in order of preference, with 1 being the most prized skill, 2 being the next most prized skill, and so on. Then ask yourself, Am I strong, moderate, or weak in terms of these skills?

Now compare your rankings to the NACE study results. Numbers indicate rankings, with 1 going to the most important skill, 2 to the next most important, and so on.

Employee Skills	Rank Order	Your Skill
a. Analytical skills		____ Strong ____ Moderate ____ Weak
b. Computer skills		____ Strong ____ Moderate ____ Weak
c. Interpersonal skills		____ Strong ____ Moderate ____ Weak
d. Leadership skills		____ Strong ____ Moderate ____ Weak
e. Oral communication skills		____ Strong ____ Moderate ____ Weak
f. Proficiency in field of study		____ Strong ____ Moderate ____ Weak
g. Teamwork skills		____ Strong ____ Moderate ____ Weak
h. Written communication skills		____ Strong ____ Moderate ____ Weak

Desired skills in college graduates: a (4); b (8); c (2); d (5); e (1); f (7); g (3); h (6)

1.2
Communication Principles
What do you need to know to become a more effective communicator?

A long time ago, in the Greek city-states of the eighth through third centuries B.C., educated citizens studied and practiced the art of oral communication. Ancient philosophers such as Plato and Aristotle discussed the role of communication in their personal and civic lives as well as its ability to help people to achieve personal goals, govern effectively, and defend freedom. Throughout Western history—in ancient Rome, in Christian Europe during the Renaissance and Enlightenment, and in our modern world—the study of communication relied on a rich intellectual foundation.[8]

In the twenty-first century, communication studies expanded beyond public speaking to encompass interpersonal and intercultural communication, group and organizational communication, and mediated and mass communication. In this book, we introduce the innovative ideas of contemporary theorists and researchers in communication studies as well as the enduring wisdom of historically significant philosophers, speakers, and communication scholars.

The rich history of communication studies has endured and evolved in part because communication is a *process* rather than a simple *activity* or unchanging *thing*. David Berlo, a twenty-first century communication pioneer, described a *process* as something that is constantly moving and in which the elements interact with one another to bring about a result.[9] Thus, the characteristics of other communicators can affect your purpose, your choice of message content can affect your style of speaking, and your personal values can determine how you adapt to the context in which you communicate.

Consider, for example, what happens when you look at photos from a

wedding or party. How do you interpret an image of a guest holding up a broken wineglass? Although the person in the photo is captured in a moment of communication, the picture tells you very little about the background, complexity, and outcome of the communication situation. Why is the glass broken? Does the context of the situation tell you more? What can you learn from examining the person's facial expression and posture?

In scientific disciplines such as physics, chemistry, or biology, you learn "laws" that explain predictable outcomes that occur under the *same* conditions. For example, you learn that if you raise the temperature of water to 212 degrees Fahrenheit under standard conditions at sea level, it will boil.

In communication studies, we do not have such strict "laws" because we cannot predict communication outcomes with such certainty. At best, we can explain how communication works in general under *similar* conditions. Rather than following strict laws, we apply accepted principles about the nature of human communication.

The Seven Key Elements and Guiding Principles of Effective Communication graphic on this page represent critical decision points in the communication process. When you communicate effectively, you make many strategic decisions about how to present your *self* and how to connect with *others*. You communicate for a *purpose* in a specific *context*, both of which affect the *content*, *structure*, and *expression* of your message.

The **7** Key Elements and Guiding Principles of Effective Communication

1 SELF Know thy SELF

2 OTHERS Connect with OTHERS

3 PURPOSE Determine your PURPOSE

4 CONTEXT Adapt to CONTEXT

5 CONTENT Select Appropriate CONTENT

6 STRUCTURE STRUCTURE your message

7 EXPRESSION Practice skillful EXPRESSION

Much like a set of interacting gears, the decisions you make about each key element affect the others. But unlike a linear process that follows an established pathway or a set of predictable steps, communication is a psychological and behavioral process that asks you to make multiple, interdependent decisions about how you will use verbal and nonverbal messages to generate meaning.

1 Know Thy Self

The first effective communication guideline is to *know thy self*. Communication is personal: Each of you communicates in your own unique way. Your genetic code is one of a kind among the billions of genetic codes on earth. Your communication abilities and instincts are also one of a kind. Therefore, make sure you understand how *your* characteristics and attitudes affect the way you communicate.

2 Connect with Others

Regardless of whether you are talking to one person or a large audience, always consider and *connect with others*. Communication is relational;

the nature of your relationship with others affects what, when, where, why, and how you communicate. An invitation such as "Let's grab a drink after work" can mean one thing coming from your best friend, but it can mean something entirely different coming from your manager or a colleague who would like to start dating you. The nature of your relationship with another person affects your choice of specific communication strategies and skills.

Cultural diversity plays a critical role in communication. We use the term **culture** to describe "a learned set of shared interpretations about beliefs, values, norms, and social practices which affect the behaviors of a relatively large group of people."[10] Given this definition, a rancher from Texas and an advertising executive from New York can have different cultural perspectives about how to greet an acquaintance, as can a Nigerian, an Indonesian, and a Navajo tribal member. Consider what happens when you share a message with or respond to someone whose race, age, gender, religious beliefs, political attitudes, or educational level differs from yours.

SELF: Why Are *You* a One-of-a-Kind Communicator?

- How do *your* characteristics, traits, skills, needs, attitudes, values, and self-concept influence your communication goals and style?

- How well do you suspend your personal needs and attitudes when you listen to others?

- What are your ethical responsibilities as a communicator?

OTHERS: How Well Do You Connect?

- With whom are you communicating? How do their characteristics, traits, skills, needs, attitudes, and beliefs affect the way they listen and respond?

- How can you better understand, respect, and adapt to others when you communicate with them?

- How well do you listen when interacting with others?

COMMUNICATION&CULTURE

DOES EVERYONE COMMUNICATE THE SAME WAY?

Do the differences between people outweigh what they have in common? How do these differences affect the way we communicate with one another? Carefully consider the following questions and answer *yes* or *no*.

Now think about how you responded to each of these questions. Why did you respond this way? After reading Chapter 3, "Adapting to Others," return to this survey and think about whether you would change any of your answers. If so, why? If not, why not?

Yes No

☐ ☐ 1. Is the U.S. culture the most individualistic (independent, self-centered, me-first) culture in the world?

☐ ☐ 2. Are Asian American students smarter than African American and Latino American students?

☐ ☐ 3. Do women talk more than men?

☐ ☐ 4. Are racial classifications based on significant genetic differences?

3 Determine Your Purpose

When you communicate with another person or a group of people, you usually have a reason for interacting with them. That reason, or goal, can be as weighty as proposing marriage, securing a lucrative business contract, or resolving a world crisis or as simple as asking for the time. *Determining your purpose*—what you and others are trying to accomplish by communicating—is essential when deciding what, when, and how to communicate.

Even when you're not fully conscious of your intentions, your communication is purposeful. When you say, "Hi, how ya doin'?" as you pass a friend in the hallway, unconsciously nod as someone talks to you, or touch the arm of a colleague who has received bad news, you are maintaining and strengthening your friendships and working relationships. Even when

---

PURPOSE: What's the Point?

- What do you want others to know, think, believe, feel, or do as a result of communicating with them?
- How might others misunderstand or misinterpret your purpose?
- Can you correctly identify the purpose of other communicators?

---

you have no intention of communicating, someone else may perceive that you have sent a purposeful message. For example, if Fred overhears you talking about a good film you have seen, have you communicated with Fred? If you see your boss frowning, should you assume that she wants you to know she is unhappy, worried, or angry? In a very general sense, some communication occurs whether we intend it or not.

4 Adapt to the Context

All communication occurs within a **context**, the circumstances and setting in which communication takes place. Although this definition may appear simple—after all, communication must occur somewhere—context is anything but simple. Effective communicators analyze and *adapt to the context*. Consider, for example, how various contexts affect the implied meaning of the question "Why are you here?" In addition to the contexts shown in the images shown below, there are countless other meanings for the phrase that change as the context changes. A mother asking her teenage daughter, "Why are you here?" at home in the morning may mean, "You are late for school and need to get going." A person asking, "Why are you here?' at a funeral could be saying, "Tell me how you knew Gloria." In a workplace

conference room, "Why are you here?" means, "We need to determine how your department will contribute to and benefit from this meeting."

There are four types of interrelated communication contexts: psychosocial, logistical, interactional, and mediated.

Psychosocial Context Psychosocial **context** refers to the psychological and cultural environment in which you live and communicate. For example, consider your relationship with other communicators, their personality traits, and the extent to which they share cultural attitudes, beliefs, values, and behaviors. Consider their age, gender, race, ethnicity, religion, sexual orientation, levels of ability, and socioeconomic class.

The psychosocial context also includes *your* emotional history, personal experiences, and cultural background. Thus, if you have a history of conflict with a work colleague, your feelings, experience, and culture may influence your response to a suggestion made by that colleague.

Logistical Context Logistical context refers to the physical characteristics of a particular communication situation and focuses on a specific time, place, setting, and occasion. Are you talking to your friend privately or in a busy hallway? Are you speaking informally to colleagues in a staff meeting or welcoming guests

---

"WHY ARE YOU HERE?" THE EFFECTS OF CONTEXT

In the classroom

"Why are you here?" (Meaning: I can help you achieve your goals if I know why you have enrolled in this course.)

At the doctor's office

"Why are you here?" (Meaning: Tell me how you're feeling.)

On the Job

"Why are you here?" (Meaning: How will each of you contribute to this project?)

to an important celebration? Can your PowerPoint slides be seen in the back row?

Interactional Context **Interactional context** refers to whether the interaction is between two people, among group members, or between a presenter and an audience. We label these interactions as interpersonal, group, and presentational contexts.

Interpersonal communication occurs when a limited number of people, usually two, interact for the purpose of sharing information, accomplishing a specific goal, or maintaining a relationship. Chapters 7 through 9 focus on the fundamentals of interpersonal communication and strategies for effective communication in personal and professional relationships.

Group communication refers to the interaction of three or more interdependent people who interact for the purpose

Psychosocial Context

Logistical Context

Interactional Context

of achieving a common goal. A group is more than a collection of individuals who talk to one another; it is a complex system in which members depend on one another. Family members and friends, work groups, neighborhood associations, self-help groups, social clubs, and athletic teams engage in group communication. Chapters 10 and 11 focus on understanding how groups work and discuss strategies for effective group participation, leadership, decision making, and problem solving.

Presentational communication occurs between speakers and their audience members.[11] Presentational communication comes in many forms, from formal commencement addresses, campaign speeches, and conference lectures to informal class reports, staff briefings, and training sessions. You will make many presentations in your lifetime—at school, at work, at family and social gatherings, or at community or public events. Chapters 12 through 16 explain how to apply the key elements of effective communication to ensure the successful preparation and delivery of presentations.

Mediated Context When you communicate in a **mediated context**, "something" exists between communicators. That something is usually some type of technology. Personal forms of mediated communication include phone calls, social media posts, and email messages. Forms that occur between a person and a large, often unknown audience are classified as **mass communication**. Radio, television, film, blogs, and websites are forms of mass communication, as are newspapers, magazines, and books.

Usually, the person who shares a message using mass communication cannot see or hear how audience members react as they look and listen. All

CONTEXT: Does Context Really Matter?

- What role are you assuming in this setting or situation?

- How do you behave in different psychological and interactional contexts?

- How well do you adapt to the logistics of the place where you will communicate and the occasion?

THINK ABOUT THEORY

Media Richness Theory

Media Richness Theory examines how the qualities of different media affect communication. The theory also helps explain why your physical presence makes a significant difference in how well you communicate. Let's say you have a message you want to share with a group of people.

You can share that message in several ways: face-to-face, on the telephone, through email or text messages, by sending a personal letter, or by posting a notice.

Face-to-face communication (be it in a conversation, group meeting, or presentation) is the richest communication medium because you can (1) see and respond instantly to others, (2) use nonverbal communication (body movement, vocal tone, and facial expression) to clarify and reinforce messages, (3) use a natural speaking style, and (4) convey your personal feelings and emotions. In contrast, text-based communication channels such as email are quite

the opposite. Readers have to rely exclusively on printed words and illustrations to interpret the sender's meaning. In short, face-to-face communication engages more of our senses and sensibilities than any other form of communication.[12]

---

mass communication is mediated, but not all mediated communication—text messages, letters, or greeting cards—is intended for the masses.

5 Select Appropriate Content

Although both animals and humans can send and receive messages, human beings are "unique in [their] ability to communicate or convey an open-ended volume of concepts."[13] Put another way, our language is symbolic; we have the distinct ability to generate meaning by combining letters and/or sounds. We can invent new words, say sentences that have never been said before, and communicate creative ideas.

Effective communicators enlist the power of good ideas and language by *selecting appropriate content.*

A symbol is something that represents something else. In language, a **symbol** is an *arbitrary* collection of sounds or letters that in certain combinations stand for a concept but do not have a direct relationship to the things they represent.

Symbols are *not* the things they represent. There is absolutely nothing in the letters C, A, and T that looks, smells, sounds, or feels like a cat. And even though dictionaries may define *cat* as a carnivorous mammal domesticated as a catcher of rodents and as a pet, you would be hard pressed to imagine what a cat looks, smells, sounds, or feels like if you had never seen one.

Since there is no tangible relationship between a symbol, the thing it represents, and how you may feel about it, there is always the potential for misunderstanding. For example, what does it mean to you if someone says that it's cold outside? If you live in the far north, "cold" can mean more than 40 degrees below zero. If you live at sea level near the equator, "cold" can mean 40 degrees above zero.

6 Structure Your Message

Once you address the challenges of developing an appropriate and purposeful message, you face the additional challenge of *structuring your message* in a way that others will understand.

The word *structure* refers to how the components or parts of something are assembled and arranged to form a whole. You would not build a house without knowing something about who will live in it, the location and setting, and the materials needed to assemble it. House construction involves putting all of these elements together into a well-designed, durable structure. The same is true in communication. **Structure** involves organizing message content into a coherent and purposeful order.

7 Practice Skillful Expression

When two children argue on a playground, one child may yell, "Take it back!" while the other might shriek, "I will not!" Whether you say something you regret or hit the Send button on your email before you're ready, you can't undo communication. At best, you can attempt to clarify what you've said or try to repair unintended consequences. You can sincerely apologize to someone about something you've said, but you can't literally "take it back." Because communication is irreversible, you must express your message skillfully and thoughtfully. Effective communicators prepare for and *practice skillful expression*.

Communication **channels** are the various physical and electronic media through which we express messages. You can transmit messages using one or more of your sensory channels: sight, sound, touch, taste, and smell.

Although we use sight and sound most frequently when we speak and listen to others, do not dismiss the power of the other three senses. Perfumes and colognes are designed to communicate attractiveness or mask offensive odors. A carefully prepared dinner or an expensive restaurant meal to which you have been specially invited can communicate a great deal about how the other person feels about you. A warm hug or a rough shove can exhibit intense emotions.

In addition, the communication channels you use today extend well beyond a face-to-face environment into the far reaches of cyberspace. The personal computer is also an interpersonal computer. Technology

enables you to enlist a variety of electronic media: telephones, television, personal computers, portable electronic communication devices, and the World Wide Web. Whether you're engaged in an online chat or participating in a videoconference, the media you choose and use affect the nature and outcome of your communication.

GETTING IN **GEAR**

The seven guiding principles of effective communication just described apply to all types of communication, regardless of whether you are talking to a friend, delivering a speech to a large audience, planning a business meeting, or participating in a videoconference. No matter how well you structure the content of your message, you won't achieve your purpose if you do not think carefully about the other factors involved in the communication process. If you offend your listeners or use words they don't understand, you won't achieve your purpose. If you dress perfectly for a job interview but fail to speak clearly and persuasively, you may lose out on a career opportunity. If you hug someone who dislikes being touched, you've chosen the wrong communication channel.

What forms of expression are represented in this photo? How many different communication channels are being used?

The Twubble with Twitter

In the first edition of THINK *Communication*, the following headline introduced this topic: *Is Twittering the Next New Frontier?* We noted that although social network sites such as Facebook and MySpace were popular ways of communicating with others near and far, Twitter had grabbed the spotlight and was poised to be the next new communication frontier.

Although the company does not release the number of active accounts on Twitter, the Nielsen.com blog ranked Twitter as the fastest-growing site in online services in February 2009 with a monthly growth of 1,382 percent![14] As is the case with most new technology, Twitter's growth will not continue at this pace. Eventually Twitter will join the ranks of email, blogs, Facebook, and MySpace as another useful—but not unique—communication channel in cyberspace.

In our first edition, we also reported that Twitter started out as a way to let others in on the events of your daily life but became a valuable channel for up-to-the-minute citizen reporting and public expression. Many people thought this was the case in 2009, when Iranian citizens took to the streets to protest the reelection of President Mahmoud Ahmadinejad. During this incident, the U.S. State Department asked Twitter to delay scheduled maintenance to avoid disrupting communications among protesters. An Iranian American activist claimed that because Iran was restricting the movement of foreign reporters, "the predominant information is coming from Twitter." News agencies dubbed what was happening in Iran as a "Twitter revolution."[15]

Perhaps we all jumped to conclusions about Twitter's power too quickly. Researchers who have taken a closer look at the role of Twitter have drawn a very different picture. "It is time to get Twitter's role in the events in Iran right," Golnaz Esfaniari wrote in *Foreign Policy*. "Simply put: There was no Twitter Revolution inside Iran."

Apparently, English-speaking journalists were tweeting one another rather than communicating directly with Iranians in the streets. Esfaniari asks why "no one seemed to wonder why people trying to coordinate protests in Iran would be writing in any language other than Farsi."[16]

Twitter has its critics on other fronts as well. Probably the biggest complaint about Twitter is that many tweets are "dumb" or "empty." Who cares that you bought a new pair of shoes or that you're tired? Do we really need to know that you're tweeting during a boring biology class? A second criticism is that it wastes a lot of time. However, Darren Rowse, a popular blogger, puts this complaint in perspective, writing. He asserts that twittering is no less a waste of time than blogging, attending conferences, social messaging, or talking on the phone. "I would

> **❝Did you Tweet today?❞**

argue," he concludes, "that there's never been a type of communication invented that can't be used in a way that is a waste of time."[17]

Twitter may soon be overshadowed by Tumblr. The "About" section of the Tumblr website quotes the news website Telegraph.co.uk, which describes this technology as the next great social media tool:

> **❝Twitter is a waste of time, unless you use it in a way that isn't. ❞**
> Darren Rowse

"Weblogs? Been there, done that. Facebook? It's full of kids. Twitter? That's so 2006, darling. No, the smart thing to be doing online these days is tumblelogging, which is to weblogs what text messages are to email—short, to the point, and direct. Tumblr lets you effortlessly share anything. Post text, photos, quotes, links, music, and videos, from your browser, phone, desktop, email, or wherever you happen to be. You can customize everything, from colors, to your theme's HTML."[18]

Who knows? Rather than picking on Twitter, in our next edition we may title a box "The Twubble with Twumblr."

Evan Williams, Twitter co-founder and former CEO

Communication Models

How do communication models help you address communication challenges?

When we discuss the nature of communication, we sometimes use **communication models**. Communication scholars Rob Anderson and Veronica Ross write that "a model of communication—or any other process, object, or event—is a way of simplifying the complex interactions of elements in order to clarify relevant relationships, and perhaps to help predict outcomes."[19] Communication models

- identify the basic components in the communication process,
- show how the various components relate to and interact with one another, and
- help explain why a communicative act succeeds or fails.

Early Communication Models

The earliest type of communication model, a **linear communication model**, functions in only one direction: a source creates a message and sends it through a channel to reach a receiver. Linear models identify several important components but do not address the interactive nature of human communication.

Communication theorists next devised **interactive communication models**, which include the concepts of noise and feedback to show that communication is not an unobstructed or one-way street. When feedback is added, each communicator becomes both the source *and* the receiver of messages. When noise is added, every component becomes susceptible to disruption.

Feedback Feedback is any verbal or nonverbal response you can see or hear from others. A person giving feedback may smile or frown, ask questions or challenge your ideas, listen intently, or tune out. If you accurately interpret feedback, you can assess how well your message is being received and whether it is likely to achieve your purpose.

A president of a New York marketing and design company told us how much she relies on feedback: "You *know* when they are with you." Expert communicators are sensitive to listener reactions. They use feedback—whether positive or negative—to evaluate whether and how well they are achieving their purpose, and then they adjust their message accordingly.

Noise Interactive communication models also recognize obstacles that can prevent a message from reaching its receivers as intended; in communication studies, this is referred to as **noise**. Noise can be external or internal. **External noise** consists of physical elements in the environment that interfere with effective communication. Noise is often an audible problem: heavy vehicle traffic outside the window, a soft-speaking voice, or a difficult-to-understand accent. However, noise is not limited to just the sounds you hear. An uncomfortably warm room, an unpleasant odor, or even bright and distracting wall designs can interfere with your ability to be an attentive and effective communicator.

While external noise can be any distracting element in your environment, internal noise is a mental distraction within yourself. **Internal noise** consists of thoughts, feelings, and attitudes that interfere with your ability to communicate and understand a message as it was intended. A listener preoccupied with personal thoughts can miss or misinterpret a message. As a speaker, you may be distracted and worried about how you look during a presentation instead of focusing on your message and your audience. Or you may be thinking about your upcoming vacation rather than listening to a coworker's instructions. Such preoccupations can inhibit your ability to speak and listen effectively.

Encoding and Decoding In most of the early models, communicators have two important functions: they serve as both the source and the receiver of messages. The communication **source** is a person or group of people who create a message intended to produce a particular response. Your message has no meaning until it arrives at a **receiver**, another person or group of people who interpret and evaluate your message. These two actions, sending and receiving, are called *encoding* and *decoding*.

When you communicate with others, you *encode* your ideas: you transform them into verbal and nonverbal messages, or "codes." Thus, **encoding** is the decision-making process by which you create and send **messages** that generate meaning.

Decoding converts a "code" or message sent by someone else into

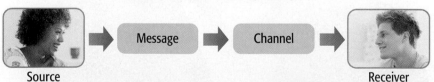

Linear Communication Model

Source → Message → Channel → Receiver

Interactive Communication Model

Source / Channel / Message / Feedback / Source / Receiver / Channel / Receiver / Noise

a form you can understand and use. Decoding is the decision-making process you use to interpret, evaluate, and respond to the meaning of verbal and nonverbal messages. Certainly, your own unique characteristics and attitudes influence the decoding process.

Transactional Communication Models

Communication is more complex than the processes depicted in linear or interactive models. In reality, communication is a *simultaneous* transaction in which we continuously exchange verbal and nonverbal messages, and share meanings. Transactional communication is also fluid, not a "thing" that happens. **Transactional communication models** recognize that we send and receive messages simultaneously within specific contexts. Even when we listen to someone, our nonverbal reactions send messages to the speaker.

Recall the seven key elements and guiding principles of effective communication. In an ideal communication transaction, you have a clear purpose in mind. You have adapted your message to others and the context. Your message contains appropriate and well-structured content as it is expressed through one or more channels with a minimum of interfering noise. Effective communicators accept the fact that they may never create or deliver a perfect message, but they never stop trying to reach that ideal.

Transactional Communication Model

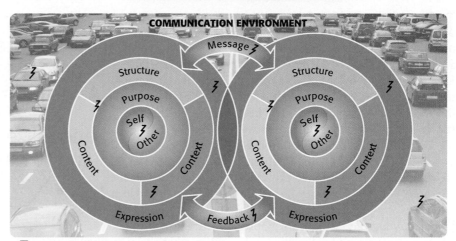

⚡ = Noise

STOP&THINK

How Noisy Can It Get?

Noise can affect *every* aspect of the communication process, threatening or preventing you from achieving the intended outcome of your message. For each type of noise described below, add a second example.

- *Noise and Self:* Personal problems and anxieties: (1) Because Katya was worried about her grade, she had trouble concentrating during her class presentation.

  (2)_____.

- *Noise and Others:* Failure to analyze the characteristics, culture, and opinions of others: (1) When Michelle asked Gerald to work on Saturday morning, she forgot that he goes to synagogue that day.

  (2)_____.

- *Noise and Purpose:* Unclear thinking: (1) When no one donated $25 to buy Jill's present, Jack realized he was asking for too much money.

  (2)_____.

- *Noise and Context:* Distraction within and outside a room: (1) When police and fire trucks came screaming down the street, everyone stopped talking and listening.

  (2)_____.

- *Noise and Content:* Invalid research, unclear explanations, or inappropriately chosen words: (1) When Lex began swearing about the group's lack of progress, members

decided they would rather stop working than listen to Lex and his foul language.

(2)_____.

- *Noise and Structure:* A poorly organized message: (1) Caleb's stories can be entertaining except for when he rambles on and on without making a point or coming to some sort of conclusion.

  (2)_____.

- *Noise and Expression:* A weak voice, defensive posture, or poor graphics: (1) Wanda made a poor impression when she kept twirling her hair and taking her glasses on and off during her presentation.

  (2)_____.

Communication Theories, Strategies, and Skills

How do theories help you choose effective communication strategies and skills?

Most of us would laugh if someone tried to become a champion tennis player, a professional airline pilot, or a gourmet chef just by reading a book. Likewise, no textbook or classroom lecture alone can teach you to become a more effective communicator. The best way to study communication is to apply an understanding of communication theories to appropriate strategies and skills. Mastering isolated skills will not help you resolve a conflict, lead a discussion, or plan a presentation. Understanding the relationship among theories, strategies, and skills will.

Learn About Theories

Theories are statements that explain how the world works. They describe, explain, and predict events and behavior.

Communication theories have emerged from extensive observation, empirical research, and rigorous scholarship. They help you understand *what* is happening when you communicate and *why* communication is sometimes effective and sometimes ineffective.

Learning about theories in isolation will not make you a more effective communicator. Theories do not necessarily tell you what to do or what to say. Nevertheless, without theories, we would have difficulty understanding why or how a particular strategy works or how strategies and skills interact.

Choose Appropriate Strategies

Strategies are the specific plans of action you select to help you communicate. The word *strategy* comes from the Greek word *strategia* and refers to the office of a military general. Like great generals, effective communicators marshal their "forces" to achieve a specific purpose: to comfort a friend, resolve a conflict, lead a group

discussion, or deliver an informative presentation.

However, learning about strategies is not enough. Effective strategies are based on theories. If you don't understand theory, you won't know why strategies work in one situation and fail in another. Strategies based on theory help you understand when, where, why, and how to use a particular strategy most effectively.

Develop Effective Skills

Communication **skills** refer to your ability to accomplish communication goals through interactions with others. Communication skills are the tools or techniques you use to collaborate with a colleague, prepare a meeting agenda,

> **❝Theories are nets to catch what we call 'the world': to rationalize, to explain, and to master it.❞**
>
> Karl R. Popper, philosopher,[20]

and speak loudly enough to be heard by a large audience. Throughout this book, you will read about and practice many communication skills: how to be more assertive, how to think critically, how to resolve conflicts, how to speak clearly, how to organize a message, and how to explain complex concepts or persuade others.

Like strategies, skills are most effective when grounded in theory. Without theories, you may not understand when and why to use a particular strategy or skill to its best advantage. For example, in the hope of improving group morale, you may be tempted to forgo using a well-structured, problem-solving agenda at a critical meeting when, in fact, group morale is low because your approach

Adapt to others

Prepare and deliver a presentation

COMMUNICATION SKILLS

Improve your personal relationships

Improve your professional relationships

Collaborate with colleagues

to problem solving is disorganized and wastes their time. However, if you are familiar with group communication theory, you will know that using a standard agenda helps a group to follow a series of practical steps to solve problems. In our eagerness to communicate effectively, we may grab ready-made, easy-to-use "tricks of the trade" that are inappropriate or ineffective. Enlisting skills without an understanding of theories and strategies can make communication inefficient and ineffective as well as frustrating for everyone.

Skilled speakers and listeners have made effective communication into an enduring habit. As Stephen Covey notes, a habit has three components: knowledge, skills, and desire. Knowledge plays a role similar to theories and strategies: it describes *what* to do and *why* to do it. Skills represent *how* to do it. And desire is the motivation to communicate effectively and ethically: you *want* to do it. Effective and ethical communication relies as much on your attitude (*wanting* to do it) as it does on your knowledge and skills.

Learning to communicate is a complex challenge that requires a great deal more than simple rules and superficial imitation. Highly successful communicators internalize the knowledge, skills, and motivation they need to communicate effectively and ethically.

MAKE EFFECTIVE COMMUNICATION AN ENDURING HABIT

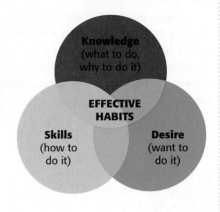

STEPHEN COVEY is the author of *The 7 Habits of Highly Effective People*, one of the most popular self-help/business books ever published. Covey presents a principle-centered approach for solving personal and professional problems. He claims that effective people transform these principles into enduring habits. We believe the same is true about the principles of communication. Effective communicators transform communication principles into enduring habits, things you do so frequently and for so long that you've stopped thinking about why, when, how, and whether you do them. In the following excerpts from *The 7 Habits of Highly Effective People*, Covey uses a communication example to demonstrate this transformation:

"For our purposes, we will define a habit as the intersection of *knowledge, skill,* and *desire*. Knowledge is the theoretical paradigm, the *what to do* and the *why*. Skills represent *how* to do it. And desire is the motivation, the *want to do*. In order to make something a habit in our lives, we have to have all three... .

I may be ineffective in my interactions with my work associates, my spouse, or my children because I constantly tell them what I think, but I never really listen to them. Unless I search out correct principles of human interaction, I may not even *know* I need to listen.

Even if I do know that in order to interact effectively with others I really need to listen to them, I may not have the skill. I may not know *how* to really listen deeply to another human being.

But knowing I need to listen and knowing how to listen is not enough. Unless I *want* to listen, unless I have the desire, it won't be a habit in my life. Creating a habit requires work in all three dimensions."[21]

Communicating Ethically

Why is ethical decision making essential for effective communication?

How would you feel if you learned that

- a corporate executive hid lavish, personal expenditures while laying off employees?
- a teacher gave higher grades to students he liked and lower grades to students who annoyed him?
- a close friend shared your most intimate secrets with people you don't know or don't like?
- a politician used a racial slur in private to describe a disgruntled group of constituents?

Most of these behaviors are not illegal. They are, however, unethical.

Theories answer *why* (Why does communication work this way?), strategies answer *what* (What should work in this communication situation?), and skills answer *how* (How should I express myself?). An effective communicator also must be able to answer the *whether* questions, that is, whether you should communicate as planned: Is it right? Is it fair? Is it deceptive?[22]

Ethical issues arise whenever we communicate because communication has consequences. What we say and do can help or hurt others. Sadly, the theories, strategies, and skills in this textbook can and have been used for less-than-ethical purposes. Unscrupulous speakers have misled trusting citizens and consumers. Bigots have used hate speech to oppress and discriminate against those who are "different." Self-centered people have destroyed the reputations of their rivals by spreading cruel rumors among friends and colleagues.

Ethics requires an understanding of whether communication behaviors meet agreed-on standards of right and wrong.[23] The National Communication Association (NCA), which is the largest professional association of communication scholars, researchers, educators, students, and practitioners in the world, provides a Credo for Ethical Communication. In Latin, the word *credo* means "I believe." Thus, the NCA Ethics Credo is a set of belief statements about what it means to be an ethical communicator.

ETHICAL COMMUNICATION

The National Communication Association Credo for Ethical Communication[24]

Questions of right and wrong arise whenever people communicate. Ethical communication is fundamental to responsible thinking, decision making, and the development of relationships and communities within and across contexts, cultures, channels, and media. Moreover, ethical communication enhances human worth and dignity by fostering truthfulness, fairness, responsibility, personal integrity, and respect for self and others. We believe that unethical communication threatens the well-being of individuals and the society in which we live. Therefore we, the members of the National Communication Association, endorse and are committed to practicing the following principles of ethical communication:

- We advocate truthfulness, accuracy, honesty, and reason as essential to the integrity of communication.
- We endorse freedom of expression, diversity of perspective, and tolerance of dissent to achieve the informed and responsible decision making fundamental to a civil society.
- We strive to understand and respect other communicators before evaluating and responding to their messages.
- We promote access to communication resources and opportunities as necessary to fulfill human potential and contribute to the well-being of families, communities, and society.
- We promote communication climates of caring and mutual understanding that respect the unique needs and characteristics of individual communicators.
- We condemn communication that degrades individuals and humanity through distortion, intimidation, coercion, and violence, and through the expression of intolerance and hatred.
- We are committed to the courageous expression of personal conviction in pursuit of fairness and justice.
- We advocate sharing information, opinions, and feelings when facing significant choices while also respecting privacy and confidentiality.
- We accept responsibility for the short- and long-term consequences of our own communication and expect the same of others.

Are You an Effective Communicator?

How can you become a more effective communicator? Use the five-point scale below to rate the following competencies in terms of their importance. Circle only one number for each item.

Competencies	Extremely Important	Very Important	Somewhat Important	Not Very Important	Not at All Important
1. Reduce your speaking anxiety	5	4	3	2	1
2. Influence the attitudes and behavior of others	5	4	3	2	1
3. Use humor appropriately	5	4	3	2	1
4. Listen effectively to others	5	4	3	2	1
5. Develop good interpersonal relationships	5	4	3	2	1
6. Hold an interesting conversation	5	4	3	2	1
7. Use your voice effectively	5	4	3	2	1
8. Resolve interpersonal conflicts	5	4	3	2	1
9. Use gesture, movement, and eye contact effectively	5	4	3	2	1
10. Interview for a job	5	4	3	2	1
11. Adapt to people from different cultures	5	4	3	2	1
12. Lead a group or work team	5	4	3	2	1
13. Present visual aids and slides effectively	5	4	3	2	1
14. Tell stories skillfully	5	4	3	2	1
15. Chair or conduct a meeting	5	4	3	2	1
16. Gain audience or listener attention and interest	5	4	3	2	1
17. Prepare and deliver an effective presentation	5	4	3	2	1
18. Explain complex ideas to others	5	4	3	2	1
19. Inspire or motivate others	5	4	3	2	1
20. Assert your ideas and opinions	5	4	3	2	1
21. Participate effectively in a group discussion	5	4	3	2	1
22. Organize the content of a presentation	5	4	3	2	1
23. Begin and end a presentation	5	4	3	2	1
24. Use appropriate and effective words	5	4	3	2	1
25. Develop strong, valid arguments	5	4	3	2	1
26. Interact in business and professional settings	5	4	3	2	1
27. Support and comfort others	5	4	3	2	1

Review your ratings: Circle the competency item numbers next to the skills that you scored as fives—skills that, in your opinion, are the most important and essential for effective communication. Why did you select these items?

1.1
Communication in Your Life

What is communication, and how does it affect your everyday life?

- Communication is the process of using verbal and nonverbal messages to generate meaning within and across various contexts, cultures, and channels.

- Effective communication helps you achieve your personal, professional, educational, intercultural, intellectual, societal, and ethical goals.

1.2
Communication Principles

What do you need to know to become a more effective communicator?

- Effective communicators make critical decisions about the seven guiding principles of human communication represented by the key elements *self*, *others*, *purpose*, *context*, *content*, *structure*, and *expression*.

- The four types of communication context are psychosocial, logistical, interactional, and mediated.

- The three interactional contexts are interpersonal, group, and presentational communication.

1.3
Communication Models

How do communication models help you address communication challenges?

- Unlike linear and interactional communication models, the transactional model depicts communication as a *simultaneous* transaction in which we continuously exchange verbal and nonverbal messages and share meanings.

- In a communication transaction, communicators encode and decode messages at the same time.

- The components of a transactional communication model include all seven elements of effective communication as well as message, feedback, and noise.

1.4
Communication Theories, Strategies, and Skills

How do theories help you choose effective communication strategies and skills?

- Your choices of communication strategies and skills are most effective when they are grounded in theory. Without theory, you may not understand when and why to use a particular strategy or skill to its best advantage.

- Make communication an enduring habit by knowing what to do and why to do it (knowledge), knowing how to do it (skills), and wanting to do it (desire).

1.5
Communicating Ethically

Why is ethical decision making essential for effective communication?

- Questions of right and wrong arise whenever people communicate. Ethical communication is fundamental to responsible thinking, decision making, and the development of relationships and communication within and across contexts, cultures, and channels.

- The National Communication Association Credo for Ethical Communication endorses principles of ethical communication for all communicators.

MySearchLab®

TEST YOUR KNOWLEDGE

1.1 What is communication, and how does it affect your everyday life?

1 The textbook defines *communication* as the process of using verbal and nonverbal messages to generate meaning within and across various contexts, cultures, and channels. Which term in this definition refers to the various physical and electronic media through which we express messages?
- a. messages
- b. meaning
- c. contexts
- d. cultures
- e. channels

2 Which of the following skills received the *lowest* ranking in the study of skills employers seek in college graduates?
- a. computer skills
- b. written communication skills
- c. oral communication skills
- d. leadership
- e. proficiency in field of study

1.2 What do you need to know to become a more effective communicator?

3 Which communication principle seeks an answer to the following question: How well do you suspend *your* personal needs and attitudes when you listen?
- a. Know Thy Self
- b. Connect with Others
- c. Determine Your Purpose
- d. Adapt to the Context
- e. Structure Your Message

4 Which communication principle seeks an answer to the following question: How can I adapt to the psychological circumstances and physical setting of the communication situation?
- a. Know Thy Self
- b. Select Appropriate Content
- c. Connect with Others
- d. Adapt to the Context
- e. Structure Your Message

5 The logistical context of communication refers to
- a. the cultural environment in which you live.
- b. your emotional history, personal experiences, and cultural background.
- c. the time, place, setting, and occasion in which you will interact with others.
- d. whether communication occurs one to one, in groups, or between a speaker and an audience.
- e. interpersonal, group, and presentational communication.

1.3 How do communication models help you address communication challenges?

6 Linear models of communication
- a. include the concepts of noise and feedback.
- b. function in only one direction: a source creates a message and sends it through a channel to reach a receiver.
- c. recognize that we send and receive messages simultaneously.
- d. illustrate the interrelationships among the key elements of human communication.
- e. all of the above

7 The encoding process can be described as
- a. the way you feel about others.
- b. the process of minimizing internal noise.
- c. effective listening.
- d. converting a "code" sent by someone else into a meaningful message.
- e. the decision-making process you use to create messages that generate meaning.

1.4 How do theories help you choose effective communication strategies and skills?

8 Stephen Covey defines a habit as the intersection of
- a. theories, strategies, and skills.
- b. theories, methods, and tools.
- c. knowledge, cognition, and intellectual skills.
- d. knowledge, skill, and desire.
- e. preparation, practice, and performance.

9 Theories answer *why*, strategies answer *what*, skills answer *how*, and ethics answers *questions* of
- a. who
- b. where
- c. when
- d. whether
- e. all of the above

1.5 Why is ethical decision making essential for effective communication?

10 Which principle in the NCA Credo for Ethical Communication is violated if a close friend shares your most intimate secrets with people you don't know or don't like?
- a. We advocate truthfulness, accuracy, honesty, and reason as essential to the integrity of communication.
- b. We strive to understand and respect other communicators before evaluating and responding to their messages.
- c. We promote access to communication resources and opportunities as necessary to fulfill human potential.
- d. We advocate sharing information, opinions, and feelings when facing significant choices while also respecting privacy and confidentiality.
- e. We are committed to the courageous expression of personal conviction in pursuit of fairness and justice.

Answers found on page 366.

Key Terms

Channels	**Interactive**	**Presentational**
Communication	**communication model**	**communication**
Communication	**Internal noise**	**Psychosocial context**
models	**Interpersonal**	**Receiver**
Context	**communication**	**Skills**
Culture	**Linear communication**	**Source**
Decoding	**model**	**Strategies**
Encoding	**Logistical context**	**Structure**
Ethics	**Mass communication**	**Symbol**
External noise	**Media Richness Theory**	**Theories**
Feedback	**Mediated context**	**Transactional**
Group communication	**Messages**	**communication model**
Interactional context	**Noise**	

19

THINK
COMMUNICATION

Communication
Knowledge for Communicating Well *Currents*

N C A

A Publication of the National Communication Association

Volume 5, Issue 3 - June 2010

Examining Communication

Our communication practices are among the most human of all human behavior. We use words to create messages, and we create meanings from those messages. Humans are social creatures, making the need to communicate essential to our survival, development, and happiness. Too often, communication is thought of as just something we do. However, to fully appreciate communication, let's examine it more closely.

Communication is functional. Communication allows us to create things we need. For example, an organization does not exist until we talk one into existence. For an organization to survive, we must talk about the culture we want to create and develop procedures for procuring and providing products and services. In large organizations and communities, communication can be more difficult as time and geography separate us. For example, you call the utility company to report a disruption of service and get "press 1 for . . ." In this case, what is functional for the utility company (and the people who represent it) is different than your idea of functionality. Often the ways in which we use communication to accomplish a function or do something complicates the conversations we have.

Communication is social. Communication allows us to create and manage relationships with one another. You don't have a boyfriend until you have the talk about being boyfriend and girlfriend. You can't get a divorce until you (or the lawyer and judge) talk one into existence. Relationships between people are negotiated from talk. Formal relationships become solidified as you accept your role as manager and talk as a manager to your subordinates. The relationship between husband and wife is also negotiated—think of the number of couples who disagree over what is said in their wedding vows. You can't just say, "I do." This simple phrase has to be said after what you vow to do, and after it is said in front of others (or at least a justice of the peace). Informal relationships, such as friendships, are derived from talk that shares personal information. Somewhere in those conversations, acquaintances turn to friendships—but you really don't know you are friends until he or she introduces you with, "Say hello to my friend Jeff."

Communication is symbolic. Communication is not water that can be turned on or off. Its symbolic nature is fluid and dynamic, and, as a result, meanings are not necessarily fixed. Communicators can't give meaning, rather meaning is negotiated through talk with others. This is why your meaning and my meaning can differ, although we agree that you sent me a specific message. "Mowing the grass" said

To what extent does this short statement support the definition of communication in Chapter 1: "Communication is the process of using verbal and non-verbal messages to generate meaning within and across various contexts, cultures, and channels"?

Identify other examples of how companies use communication in ways that work for them, but not necessarily for the people who work in the organization or use its services?

Besides terms such as boyfriend and girlfriend, are the appropriate terms for unmarried couples who have been living together for 20 years? When parents divorce or one parent dies and the other remarries, does the term "stepparent" apply to both new "parents"?

Many words used in political contexts have multiple and potentially very different meanings. Depending on your political views, your feelings about liberals, conservatives, socialist, and labor unions may be positive or negative. New words and phrases such as Tea Party and birther have "created" new political perspectives.

by my dad, I soon learned, did not mean simply pushing the lawnmower around the yard. Rather, through negotiated talk (okay, yelling), I came to understand that mowing the lawn meant (in this order): picking up trash and sticks in the yard, mowing the grass, sweeping grass clippings off the driveway and walk, cleaning the mower, and, finally, returning the mower to where it was stored. Over time, I forgot about the negotiation and was able to use his "mowing the grass" message for this set of tasks. Imagine my surprise when many years later I hired someone to "mow my grass" and he did exactly that. I had failed to negotiate what "mowing the grass" meant.

Communication is cultural. Obviously, we have flattened the world through travel and the use of technology. Beyond these obvious national differences in culture, cultural differences also exist locally. The culture of neighborhoods and regions, age and sex, race and religion, and politics and philosophy complicate communication. We often argue and disagree because our fundamental views of the world are at odds with one another. I announce to my colleagues that I have to go home and "get the kids." I use this phrase even though my kids are dogs. Why? Because it's acceptable to leave the meeting to pick up your children from school, but less acceptable to leave to let the dogs out of the house.

Communication is functional, social, symbolic, cultural, and complicated—whether it is face to face or mediated. However, sometimes we need to accomplish something by communicating, and yet we do not always want to expose ourselves too much to the other person. For example, having a courteous interaction with a retail clerk is sufficient. I do not need to establish a relationship more explicit than clerk-customer with him or her. Saying "yes" to the clerk's "Did you find everything you need?" is all that is needed (whether I found everything or not).

Sometimes, we don't have the words or messages to express ourselves fully. Not all feelings can be easily labeled; not all experiences can be easily translated. I may feel that something is not right about our relationship, but cannot find a way to express it to you that sounds genuine. After all, communication often appears to be linear, yet feelings, experiences, and meanings can be simultaneously layered: "I love you, but I can't stand you."

Sometimes, we fail to take the time to talk with others in a meaningful way. Time is a precious commodity. When I'm in a hurry, "please" and "thank you" interfere in my making a meeting on time. You come to my office to talk over a problem with me, but I have only 15 minutes before I must be somewhere else. When communication is strained by time and other pressures, people communicate less effectively because they talk at rather than talk with others.

Communication is complicated. Communication scholars have studied these complexities, and are learning more about how to communicate more effectively.

ABOUT THE AUTHORS
Joann Keyton is a professor of Communication at North Carolina State University, Raleigh, North Carolina. She is the founding editor of *Communication Currents* (Volumes 1 through 5). This essay appeared in the June 2010 issue of *Communication Currents,* a publication of the National Communication Association.

What strategies do you use when you communicate with someone whose race, age, gender, religious beliefs, political attitudes, or educational level differs from yours?

Recall these statements from Chapter 1: "Communication occupies more of your time than anything else you do" and "like most complex processes, effective communication requires knowledge, skills, and motivation."

Enlist the seven basic elements and guiding principles of communication (self, others, purpose, context, content, structure, and expression) in order to adapt to the complex challenge of generating meaning within and across a wide range of contexts, cultures, and channels.

In light of what you've read in Chapter 1, what should you focus on to communicate more effectively? What specific strategies and skills will help you achieve this goal?

Understanding
YOUR SELF
2

On June 25, 2009, the world learned that the man regarded as one of the "greatest entertainers of our time" had died. Thousands upon thousands of grieving fans from New York to Tokyo swarmed the Web to Tweet, Facebook, and Google—crashing Twitter's servers and slowing the Internet down to a snail's pace. Almost everyone who had ever heard him sing or watched him dance wanted to know: Was the King of Pop really gone?

As his death had such a profound effect, we are compelled to ask, "Who was Michael Jackson?" According to *Newsweek*'s David Gates, "He was a music legend and a legendary oddball. . . . He was the king of pop."[1] For many of us, when we think of Michael Jackson, we remember the five-year-old superstar who started singing and dancing with his brothers in the Jackson Five; and we remember the 18-time Grammy Award–winning solo artist he would eventually become.

But from the 1990s, when Jackson's career and personal life began its sad decline, we also remember a troubling and tragic side to this former child star. Rumors of his "sleepovers" with young children at his Neverland ranch led to allegations of child abuse. He contracted vitiligo, an autoimmune disease that turned his skin from brown to white.[2] Quite literally, Jackson changed before our eyes. Eventually, his physical and emotional problems led to prescription drug dependence and ultimately his death.

Trying to answer the question, "Who was Michael Jackson?," British blogger *hysperia* writes that he was "a man who couldn't be known and who, most likely, could not know himself."[3] While reflecting on Michael Jackson and his life, we must acknowledge the importance of knowing one's own *self*. All communication begins with *you*. Who you are and how you think determines how you interact with others and how others interact with you.

Who Are You?

How do your characteristics, perceptions, self-concept, and level of confidence affect the way you communicate?

Your **self-concept** represents the sum total of beliefs you have about yourself. It answers two simple questions: "Who are you?" and "What makes you *you*?" Not only are you defined by characteristics such as your age, nationality, race, religion, and gender (as in "I am a 30-year-old, African American, Catholic female"), your life experiences, attitudes, and personality traits also influence your opinion of yourself.

Your self-concept changes as you change; you are always *becoming*. A physically awkward child may eventually grow into a confident and graceful dancer. A middle school student with poor grammar may eventually become a celebrated author.

Sources of Self-Concept

Where does your self-concept come from? You certainly aren't born with one. Infants only begin to recognize themselves in a mirror between 18 and 24 months of age. Only then do they begin to express the concept of "me."[4] Although many factors influence how you develop a self-concept, the following are among the most significant: self-awareness, the influence of others, past experiences, and cultural perspectives.

Self-Awareness Self-awareness is an understanding of your core identity.[5] It requires a realistic assessment of your traits, thoughts, and feelings. In his best-selling book *Emotional Intelligence*, Daniel Goleman identifies self-awareness as the first and most fundamental emotional competency: the keystone of emotional intelligence.[6] He also claims that "the ability to monitor feelings from moment to moment is crucial to psychological insight and self-understanding. An inability to notice our true feelings leaves us at their mercy."[7]

Awareness of your thoughts and feelings is referred to as **self-monitoring**. Effective self-monitoring helps you

realize, "This is anger I'm feeling." It gives you the opportunity to modify or control anger rather than allowing it to hijack your mind and body. Self-monitoring also helps you differentiate emotional responses: love versus lust, disappointment versus depression, and anxiety versus excitement. By becoming aware of your thoughts and feelings, you can avoid mistaking lust for everlasting love, avoid letting minor

problems trigger depression, and avoid mistaking fear for anger. People who are *high self-monitors* constantly watch other people, what they do, and how they respond to the behavior of others. They are also self-aware, like to "look good," and usually adapt well to differing social situations. On the other hand, *low self-monitors* are often oblivious to how others see them and may "march to their own, different drum."[8]

❝ People with greater certainty about their feelings are better pilots of their lives, having a surer sense of how they really feel about personal decisions from whom to marry to what job to take.❞

—Daniel Goleman[9]

The Influence of Others Although self-awareness may be the keystone of emotional intelligence, the influence of other people is a more powerful determinant of your self-concept. Influences include significant others, the groups to which you belong, the roles you assume, and the rewards you receive from others (as shown below).

Past Experiences Without past experiences and personal memories, you would have little basis for a coherent self-concept. For example, vivid memories of traumatic events—the death of a loved one, the 9/11 attacks, a serious automobile accident, or life-threatening combat—can affect how you interpret and react to current events and personal circumstances. Who would you be if you could not remember the past experiences that define you?[10]

It is not surprising that you (and everyone else) have a tendency to distort memories. You tend to remember the past as if it were a drama in which you were the leading player.[11] When asked about high school, many people describe it as "terrible" or "wonderful" when they really mean it *seemed* terrible or wonderful *to them*. When we tell stories about the past, we cast ourselves at the center of action rather than as bit players or observers.

Cultural Background Culture plays a significant role in determining who you are and how you understand your self. Intercultural communication scholar Min-Sun Kim explains that cultures have "different ways of being, and different ways of knowing, feeling, and acting."[12] For example, Western cultures emphasize the value of independence and self-sufficiency,

> Who would you be if you could not remember your parents or childhood playmates, your successes and failures, the places you lived, the schools you attended, the books you read, and the teams you played for?

whereas East Asian cultures emphasize the value of group memberships. The "self" generally is not perceived outside its relationship to the "other." Chapter 3, "Adapting to Others," focuses on how the characteristics and cultures of others affect how we communicate.

THE **INFLUENCE** OF **OTHERS**

Significant others are people whose opinions you value, such as family members, friends, coworkers, and mentors. What do such people tell you about yourself? Equally important, how do they behave around you?

Roles are adopted patterns of behaviors associated with an expected function in a specific context or relationship. Your behavior often changes when you shift to a different role. For example, how does your public role (student, teacher, mechanic, nurse, manager, police officer) affect your view of yourself? How do your private roles (child, parent, spouse, lover, best friend) shape your self-concept? Not surprisingly, you learn how to behave in a role largely by modeling others in that role. For example, for better or worse, you learn the parenting role from your parents.

Reference groups are groups with whom you identify. Think about a high school clique to which you may have belonged (popular, smart, artistic, geeky, athletic). How did that membership affect your self-concept and interaction with others? How do your current group memberships (work team, church group, civic association, professional organization, social or campus club) affect the way you see yourself?

Rewards are recognitions received from others at home, at school, on the job, or in a community for good work (academic honor, employee-of-the-month award, job promotion, community service prize). Praise and words of encouragement from others affect your self-concept. Consider how you might feel about yourself if you never received positive feedback.

Assessing Yourself

Self-appraisals are evaluations of your self-concept in terms of your abilities, attitudes, and behaviors. "I'm not popular" or "I'm an excellent basketball player" are examples of self-appraisals. It is not surprising that when your appraisals are positive, you are more likely to succeed. Positive beliefs about your abilities can make you more persuasive when asking for a promotion or when dealing with rejection. At the same time, your mind may try to protect you from potentially hurtful or threatening feedback from others. These ego-defense mechanisms can mislead us into forming a distorted self-image:[13] "What's the big deal about being late to a meeting? She's just obsessed with time and took it out on me. It's no big deal."

> **❝Of all the judgments we** pass in life, **none is as important as the ones we pass on ourselves.❞**
> —Nathaniel Branden[14]

Examining and understanding self-concept is difficult because we tend to view ourselves favorably—often more favorably than we deserve. In his book *The Varnished Truth: Truth Telling and Deceiving in Ordinary Life*, David Nyberg writes, "Human self-deception is one of the most impressive software programs ever devised."[15] Most of us seem to be "wired" to fool ourselves about ourselves, often deceiving ourselves about things we want to be true (but aren't).[16] To minimize this kind of self-deception, you should enlist two forms of self-appraisals—actual performance and social comparison.

Actual Performance Your actual performance or behavior is the most influential source of self-appraisals.[17] If you repeatedly succeed at something, you are likely to evaluate your performance in that area positively. For example, if you were an "A" student in high school, you probably expect to be a good student in college. Thus, you may be disappointed or distressed if you receive a low grade and, as a result, doubt your academic and intellectual abilities.

Social Comparison According to social psychologist Leon Festinger, **social comparison** is the process of evaluating yourself in relation to the others in your reference groups.[18] The notion of "keeping up with the Joneses" is an example of our need to compare favorably with others. If you are the only one in the class who receives a failing grade on a test, you may conclude that you are less intelligent, less prepared, or less capable than your classmates. On the other hand, if everyone does poorly on the test, comparing yourself with your class-mates may make you feel better about yourself because it means you did just as well as everyone else. We also compare ourselves with others in terms of appearance and physical ability. When people compare themselves with fashion models, alluring movie stars, and professional athletes, however, they have chosen an almost impossible ideal.

Self-Concept Continuum
RATE YOURSELF

Attractive	Unattractive
Respected	Not respected
Successful	Unsuccessful
Confident	Anxious
Good	Bad
Intelligent	Unintelligent
Humorous	Humorless

Fashion models are a poor choice for social comparison because their looks are unrepresentative of society as a whole

Creating, Deceiving, and Revealing Yourself Online

Researchers disagree about whether online communication harms or promotes the development of a self-concept. Some suggest that the endless number of social media communities with constantly changing contexts, significant others, and reference groups make it difficult for anyone to develop a stable self-identity.[19] Others argue that social media provide opportunities to experiment with identities. For example, shy teenagers may feel more confident and comfortable communicating online than in face-to-face interactions. As they "try on" different selves online, positive feedback from virtual others can help them develop a stronger self-concept and a healthier self-esteem.[20]

Unfortunately, the absence of *real*, face-to-face interactions makes it easier to distort aspects of your self, as well as to fabricate a false identity. A study of personal characteristics described by participants in online dating services uncovered gender-based misrepresentations. Men were more likely to misrepresent

"Who are you Online?"

their personal assets (job status, income, intelligence, education). Women were more likely to misrepresent their weight as lower; men were more likely to misrepresent their age as older.[21]

Many people have been betrayed or seriously hurt by online deceptions—as in the tragic case of Megan Meier, who committed suicide after falling victim to the cruel torment of and rejection by a boy named Josh Evans, someone she'd met on MySpace. It turned out that Josh was actually a fictitious character created by Lori Drew, the mother of a former friend of Megan's. Drew, who created this false identity as a way of humiliating and punishing Megan for supposedly spreading rumors about Drew's daughter, was indicted on misdemeanor charges in November 2008. In July 2009, a federal judge threw out Drew's conviction and acquitted her of all charges.[22]

In numerous other cases, people have been betrayed and hurt by online revelations. Tyler Clementi, an 18-year-old college freshman, posted a suicide message on his

Facebook page before jumping to his death from a bridge. He took his own life after his roommate, Dharun Ravi, used a webcam to videotape Clementi having sex with a man in his dorm room. In addition to videostreaming the encounter on the Internet, the roommate posted Twitter messages about Clementi: "I saw him making out with a dude. Yay." and "Found out my roommate was gay." This public persecution may have precipitated Tyler Clementi's suicide. A Grand Jury indicted Dharun Ravi on 15 counts including invasion of privacy, bias intimidation, tampering with physical evidence, witness tampering, and hindering apprehension or prosecution.[23]

When you share aspects of yourself online—be they your opinions, your personal feelings, your photos, or the story of your wild summer vacation—remember that once you've hit the Send button, your communication is irreversible. Always ask yourself, Can this message embarrass or hurt me now or in the future? Will it hurt someone else? Would I want my family or a potential employer to read or see this posting?

How We Make Ourselves **LOOK GOOD**

In Order to Maintain a Positive Self-Concept, We Tend to:

➡ attribute successes to our own abilities and blame our failures on external factors.

➡ view evidence depicting us unfavorably as flawed.

➡ forget negative feedback and remember positive feedback.

➡ compare ourselves to others who make us look good.

➡ overestimate how many people share our opinions and underestimate how many people share our abilities.

➡ believe our good traits are unusual while our faults are common.

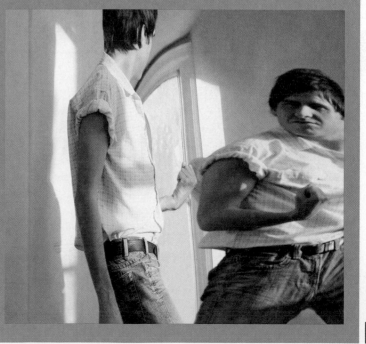

2.2
Building Self-Esteem
What communication strategies and skills can improve your self-esteem?

Now that you know something about your self-concept, how do you *feel* about yourself? Are you satisfied, discouraged, delighted, optimistic, surprised, or troubled? **Self-esteem** represents your judgments about yourself. Nathaniel Branden puts it this way: "Self-esteem is the reputation we acquire with ourselves."[24] Not surprisingly, your personal beliefs, behavior, and performance influence your level of self-esteem.

Studies consistently find that people with high self-esteem are significantly happier than people with low self-esteem. They are also less likely to be depressed. One especially compelling study surveyed more than 13,000 college students. High self-esteem emerged as the strongest factor in overall life satisfaction.[25]

If your self-esteem isn't very high, you can take steps to improve it by self-monitoring and learning new ways of communicating with others. There are several specific strategies you can try as well. Keep in mind that engaging in these practices requires persistence and effort.

Beware of Self-Fulfilling Prophecies

A prophecy is a prediction. A **self-fulfilling prophecy** is "an impression formation process in which an initial impression elicits behavior . . . that conforms to the impression."[27] More simply, it is a prediction you make that you cause to happen or become true. For example, if young girls are told that boys do better in mathematics, they may believe it and stop trying to succeed. As a result, they won't do as well in math as boys, just as predicted.

Factors that Affect YOUR SELF-ESTEEM

YOUR BELIEFS

Beliefs about yourself: "I am competent/incompetent."

Beliefs about your emotions: "I am happy/sad."

YOUR BEHAVIOR

Positive behavior: "I am assertive and appropriately ask for what I need or want."

Negative behavior: "I'll start some juicy rumors that Gregory's been cutting out of work early."

YOUR PERFORMANCE

Skills: "I am a good writer and feel proud of that."

Character: "I am a good person and enjoy helping others."

"I think the answers to a lot of issues come from self-esteem. Young girls and women have to believe they are worth something more, they have to see opportunities for themselves beyond a relationship or beyond what's right there in front of them."

—Michelle Obama

Know Thy SELF

Assess Your Self-Esteem

The statements below describe different ways of thinking about your self. Read them carefully and choose the phrase that indicates how much you agree with each statement.[26]

Strongly Disagree (SD), Disagree (D), Agree (A), Strongly Agree (SA)

Scoring: Score items 1, 2, 6, 8, and 10 in a positive direction (i.e., strongly agree = 4, agree = 3, and so on) and items 3, 4, 5, 7, and 9 in a negative direction (i.e., strongly agree = 1, agree = 2, and so forth). The highest possible score is 40 points; the lowest possible score is 10 points. Higher scores indicate higher self-esteem. Please note that there are no good or bad scores; rather, the scale measures how you *perceive* your level of self-esteem.

_____ 1. I feel that I'm a person of worth, at least on an equal plane with others.

_____ 2. On the whole, I am satisfied with myself.

_____ 3. I wish I could have more respect for myself.

_____ 4. I certainly feel useless at times.

_____ 5. At times I think I am no good at all.

_____ 6. I feel that I have a number of good qualities.

_____ 7. All in all, I am inclined to feel that I am a failure.

_____ 8. I am able to do things as well as most other people.

_____ 9. I feel that I do not have much to be proud of.

_____ 10. I take a positive attitude toward myself.

STRATEGIES TO IMPROVE Your Self-Esteem[28]

STRATEGY	EXCEPTION
Practice self-acceptance ☑ **Self-acceptance** means recognizing, accepting, and "owning" your thoughts, feelings, and behavior. You may not like your actions, but be willing to accept them as part of who you are. No one is perfect.	**But not as an excuse** ☒ Self-acceptance is not an excuse for bad behavior. If a manager shouts at employees and justifies it by saying, "I'm a very emotional man. If you can't take it, quit," the concept of self-acceptance has been taken to extremes.
Practice self-responsibility ☑ **Self-responsibility** means taking responsibility for your own happiness and for achieving your goals. If you assume responsibility for what you do, you are more likely to be happy and satisfied.	**But don't try to control everything** ☒ Resist the urge to control everything so you don't end up feeling overburdened, frustrated, and angry with others. Ask for and accept help when you need it.
Practice assertiveness ☑ Stand up for yourself in appropriate ways to satisfy your needs and pursue your goals. Don't become obsessed with getting approval from others.	**But respect the needs of others** ☒ Be assertive, not aggressive, when you pursue your goals. Don't stand in the way of others when you stand up for yourself.
Practice personal integrity ☑ **Personal integrity** means behaving in ways that are consistent with your values and beliefs. Don't simply think about what you should do; instead actually do "the right thing."	**But understand and respect others** ☒ "The right thing" for you may not be "the right thing" for someone else. Make sure your actions do not offend or hurt others.
Practice positive self-talk ☑ **Self-talk** represents the silent statements you make to yourself about yourself. Replace negative, self-defeating statements with more positive and productive statements.	**But listen to others, too** ☒ Listening to yourself should never substitute for or prevent you from listening to others.

In one study, researchers administered a math test to different groups of women. Before taking the test, one group of women was told that men and women do math equally well. Another group was told that there is a genetic difference in math ability that explains why women are not as good at math as men. The women in the first group got nearly twice as many right answers as those in the second group. The researchers concluded that people tend to accept genetic explanations as powerful and permanent, which can lead to self-fulfilling prophecies.[29]

In her commencement address at Mount Holyoke College in 2009, the president of Ireland, Mary McAleese, said, "When I was in my mid-teens, I announced at home that I had decided to become a lawyer. The first words I heard in response were, 'You can't because you are a woman.'"[30] President McAleese did not let these words and her parents' beliefs become a self-fulfilling prophecy.

High self-esteem will not solve all your personal problems, nor will it automatically improve your ability to communicate effectively and ethically. Educators have learned this lesson, much to the detriment of students. For example, some well-meaning school systems tried to raise the self-esteem of disadvantaged

Avoid the Self-Fulfilling Prophecy Trap

To minimize the chances of falling into the self-fulfilling prophecy trap, ask yourself the following questions:

- What prediction am I making about my own and/or the behavior of others?
- Why am I making this prediction? Is it justified?
- Am I doing anything to elicit the predicted response?
- What alternative behaviors could help avoid fulfilling my prophecy?

The school bully's overinflated self-esteem demonstrates his sense of superiority over Calvin.

and failing students by passing them to the next grade. Unfortunately, such efforts have had no positive effects and demonstrated that "artificially boosting self-esteem may lower subsequent academic performance.[31]

Researchers once assumed that people acted violently toward others because they suffered from low self-esteem; rather, the opposite seems to be true. Violent people often act the way they do because they suffer from *high* but unrealistic self-esteem. Violent criminals often describe themselves as superior to others. Even playground bullies regard themselves as superior to other children. Low self-esteem is found among the victims of bullies but not among bullies themselves. In fact, most violent groups generally have belief systems that emphasize their superiority over others.[32] Someone with an overinflated sense of self-esteem may be a braggart, bully, or tyrant rather than a person with a healthy self-concept. Someone with lower self-esteem but a secure and confident sense of self can be a model of humility and goodness.

STOP&THINK

Practice Positive Self-Talk

Read the example of negative self-talk and its corresponding example of positive self-talk below. Then provide two examples of negative self-talk and corresponding examples of positive self-talk.

Negative Self-Talk

⊖ Example: *I won't be able to work as quickly as the other group members.*

Your example:_____

_____

Your example:_____

_____

Positive Self-Talk

⊕ Example: *I'll do my best and ask for help if I need it.*

Your example:_____

_____

Your example:_____

_____

2.3

The Power of Perception

How do your perceptions affect the way you select, organize, and interpret the world around you?

Why does one person experience great satisfaction in a job while another person in the same job dreads it? Why do you find a speech inspiring while another person finds it offensive? The answer to these questions lies in one word: *perception*. Imagine that you and a colleague are chatting after a meeting. You say, "That was a good session. We got through all the issues and ended early." Your friend responds with "Are you kidding? Didn't you notice that Lynn rushed us through the agenda to avoid any serious discussion or disagreement?" What happened here? You both attended the same meeting, but each of you perceived the experience quite differently.

From a communication point of view, we define **perception** as the process through which you select, organize, and interpret sensory stimuli in the world around you. The accuracy of your perceptions determines how well you interpret and evaluate experiences and the people you encounter. At the same time, once you reach a conclusion, it's often difficult to change your perception.

Generally, we trust our perceptions and treat them as accurate and reliable. We say things such as, "Seeing is believing," "I call it as I see it," or "I saw it with my own eyes." However, as shown to the right, we can't always rely on what we see. Police officers know very well that three witnesses to a traffic accident may provide three different descriptions of the cars involved, the

Old Woman or Young Woman?

What you see depends on how your eyes select graphic details, how you organize that information, and how you interpret the results.

estimated speed they were traveling, and the physical characteristics of the drivers. In fact, eyewitness testimony, although persuasive, is often the least reliable form of courtroom evidence.

Even though you run the risk of drawing incorrect conclusions, you would be lost in a confusing world without your perceptions. Not only does perception help you make sense out of other people's behavior, but it also helps you decide what you will say or do. For example, suppose you notice that your boss keeps track of employees who arrive late and leave early, and that she rarely grants these employees the special privileges given to those who put in full workdays. These perceptions tell you that it is a good idea to arrive early and stay late if you want a positive evaluation or a future promotion.

There are three components to perception: selection, organization, and interpretation.

Selection

You use your senses (sight, sound, taste, smell, and touch) to notice and choose from the many stimuli around you. Your needs, wants, interests, moods, and memories largely determine which stimuli you will select. For example, when your eyes and ears detect something familiar or potentially interesting as you flip through television channels, you stop. Or you may be daydreaming in class, but when your professor says, "The following chapters will be covered on the next test," you find yourself paying full attention again.

According to the **figure–ground principle** of perception: people focus on certain features (the figure) while deemphasizing less relevant background stimuli (the ground).[33] Thus, while walking down the street, if you notice someone standing against a building, that's what you would see first: a person standing against a building, not a building with a person-shaped hole in it.[34] When communicating, your friend may smile and tell you that everything is okay. However, you focus your attention

COMMUNICATION IN *ACTION*

Making Sense of Our Senses

Neuroscientists have discovered that what you see can influence what you taste. In other words, your senses "talk" to and influence one another because your brain "glues" your senses together.[35] Here are a few examples of how the boundaries between your senses are blurred:

- If you put red food coloring in a glass of white wine, some of the most accomplished wine experts will believe they're drinking red wine.

- If you show a friend a single flash on a computer screen while playing two beeps, she may swear she saw two flashes.

- If you ask someone to rub his hands together while listening to an audiotape of rubbing dry skin, his skin may feel rough and parched to him.

- If you dye a delicious strawberry blue, it's likely to smell strange as well as taste strange.

Neuroscientists have also observed that what you touch can change how you feel and how you interact with other people. For example, when you're holding a hot cup of coffee, you're more likely to view others as caring and generous. Sit in a comfy chair (rather than a hard one), and you may be more open to a compromise. Below are a few more examples of how different physical sensations affect your perceptions of people *and* their perceptions of you.[36]

Types of Touch	How Touch Affects Perceptions
Soft Touch	Touching something soft can make you more open to suggestion. When people touch smooth surfaces, they feel a sense of ease.
Rough or Smooth Touch	Rough textures are associated with friction. Smooth surfaces, such as a soft blouse or a soft leather binder, can influence a meeting outcome more positively than if you wear or bring along something with a rough surface.
Warm Feelings	When you're warm, you're more likely to both trust others and be trustworthy yourself. Heated rooms promote more social connections than cold rooms do.
Cold Feelings	The old phrase "She gave me the cold shoulder" now makes new sense. When people were asked to choose a gift for either themselves or a friend, those made to feel chilled were 75 percent more likely to give themselves the gift; those who felt warm were 54 percent more apt to offer it to a friend.
Hard or Soft Hearted	Research subjects who held hard blocks and met someone in the role of an employee judged the employee to be stricter than those same employees were judged to be by research subjects who were holding soft blankets.
Heavy Weight	Heaviness implies seriousness, importance, and status. Choosing heavier paper for your correspondence can give the impression that you're "weighty" and therefore more serious.

on her red and swollen eyes, suspect that she has been crying, and conclude that she is upset. Her smile and verbal assurances are relegated to the background. Ultimately, what you select to focus on will affect how you organize and interpret the events around you *and* how well you communicate in those situations.

Organization

Suppose you see a middle-aged woman wearing a suit walking across campus. You conclude that she is a professor. You also observe a young man entering a classroom wearing a school sweatshirt and carrying a backpack that appears to be loaded with books. You assume that he is a student. You took the information, or stimuli, you observed and categorized it into "professor" and "student." What these two scenarios demonstrate is how *context* influences the way you organize information. For example, you could conclude that a woman in a suit on campus is a professor, but in a different context, you might conclude that she is a business executive. You may conclude that a young man wearing a school sweatshirt and carrying books on campus is a student, but backstage in a theater, you may decide that he is an actor or stagehand.

You sort and arrange the sensory stimuli you select into useful categories based on your knowledge and past experiences with similar stimuli. Four principles influence how you organize or categorize information: the **proximity principle**, the **similarity principle**, the **closure principle**, and the **simplicity principle**.[37]

The Proximity Principle The closer objects, events, or people are to one another, the more likely you will perceive them as belonging together.[38] You go to a restaurant to eat lunch alone, and another person whom you do not know gets in line behind you. The host asks, "Two for lunch?" When you don't want to be perceived as associated with an individual, you may move away from that person to create greater physical distance.

The Similarity Principle Similar elements or people are more likely to be perceived as part of a group. When two individuals share one characteristic or trait, you may conclude that they also have other things in common. For example, you meet a person from Texas and assume that she enjoys

country music because other Texans you know listen to that kind of music. Unfortunately, the similarity principle can lead to stereotyping and inaccurate conclusions. Your new acquaintance may dislike country music but love jazz.

The Closure Principle We often fill in missing elements to form a more complete impression of an object, person, or event. Look, for example, at the above figure.

The Simplicity Principle We tend to organize information in a way that provides the simplest interpretation. For example, on a cloudy day, you look out the window and see that the sidewalk is wet and think that it must have rained. This is a reasonable and simple conclusion. There may be other explanations for the wet sidewalk, like automatic sprinklers or a leak in a water pipe, but you chose the simplest one first.into categories.

How Many Triangles Do You See?

Some people see as many as 11 triangles in this drawing. However, given that a triangle is a figure with three attached sides, there are no triangles. If you saw triangles, you mentally filled in or "closed" the image's elements.

COMMUNICATION&CULTURE

WEST IS WEST AND EAST IS EAST

The mental process of perception is the same across cultures. Everyone selects, organizes, and interprets stimuli. Psychologist Richard Nisbett argues that each culture can "literally experience the world in very different ways."[39] Look, for example, at the three objects depicted on your right. Which two objects would you pair together?

People from Western cultures are more likely to put the chicken and cow together because they are both animals. East Asians, however, are more likely to pair the cow and the grass because cows eat grass. According to Nisbett, East Asians perceive the world in terms of relationships, whereas westerners are inclined to

Your culture influences what you notice, how you organize that information, and how you interpret information and situations.

see objects that can be grouped into categories. As Chapter 3, "Adapting to Others," explains, many cultures—and East Asian cultures in particular—are more sensitive to the context in which communication takes place. As Rudyard Kipling wrote in *The Ballad of East and West*, "Oh, East is East, and West is West, and never the twain shall meet."

Perception-Checking Guidelines:
The Martha and George Dilemma

Perception checking enlists the seven key elements of effective communication to assess and improve your ability to select, organize, and interpret sensory stimuli into more accurate perceptions. Read the following scenario carefully. Then examine how the perception-checking guidelines and application examples help a communicator respond fairly and appropriately to this particular situation.

Your best friend, Martha, has lived with George for three years. Everyone had been expecting them to get married, so you were shocked when Martha told you they'd broken up. Martha explained that she could no longer live with a man who made fun of her "menial" job as a receptionist, comparing it unfavorably to his as a senior marketing manager. When he insisted that he control all their finances and refused to tell her how he was spending their money, she couldn't take it anymore and left him. Yesterday, you learned that George has been hired as a consultant to develop a marketing plan for your office. Whether you like him or not, you will have to work with him for the next four weeks.

Communication Elements	Perception-Checking Guidelines	Applying Perception-Checking Guidelines
1 SELF	How could factors such as your personal biases, level of self-awareness, cultural background, or the influence of others affect your perceptions?	How do my feelings about Martha, my biases, my past experiences with George, and my gender affect my perceptions of their breakup and George's character?
2 OTHERS	Do you perceive a situation the same way others do? If not, how can you adapt to their perceptions?	Although I was shocked at George's behavior, I know there are usually two sides to every story.
3 PURPOSE	How does the way you select, organize, and interpret information affect the way you communicate?	When I work with George, I may pay more attention to his mistakes or suggestions I don't like rather than to the job we need to do. I need to be aware of and guard against such assumptions and behavior.
4 CONTEXT	How could the psychological, logistical, and interactional communication context affect your perceptions and the perception of others?	In the office environment, I will do my best to put aside my feelings about George and work with him to get the job done in a professional way.
5 CONTENT	How could your perceptions affect the content you choose for a message?	I won't make comments about Martha. Certainly, I need to avoid commenting about menial jobs, receptionists, and personal finances.
6 STRUCTURE	How could your perceptions affect the way you organize ideas and information in a message? Will others interpret your meaning differently based on the way you organize your content?	I will put the job first and, if George begins talking about Martha, I will tell him that discussing personal matters is inappropriate at work.
7 EXPRESSION	How could your perceptions affect the way you express your messages and choose communication channels?	I will try to avoid engaging in negative nonverbal behavior such as frowning, avoiding eye contact, or putting more distance between us.

Interpretation

A number of factors influence your interpretation of experiences. Suppose a friend asks you to volunteer your time over the weekend to help build a house for Habitat for Humanity. The following factors may affect your interpretation and reaction to your friend's request:

- *Past experiences.* After volunteering at a soup kitchen last year, you felt really good about yourself.
- *Knowledge.* You spent a summer working as a house painter and have a useful skill to contribute.
- *Expectations.* It sounds like fun, and you might meet some interesting people.
- *Attitudes.* You believe that volunteering in the community is important.
- *Relational involvement.* This work is really important to your friend.

These same factors may also lead to inaccurate perceptions. For example, suppose you once volunteered at a homeless shelter and had a terrible experience. The coordinator assigned you the task of washing the sheets and towels every morning and cleaning the bathrooms. As a result, you didn't use your counseling skills and rarely talked to a homeless person.

Clearly, your previous experience may have created an unfair or erroneous perception of volunteer work.

Perception Checking

Psychologists Richard Block and Harold Yuker point out that "perception often is a poor representation of reality. Yet it is important to recognize that a person's behavior is controlled less by what is actually true, than what the person believes is true. Perceptions may be more important than reality in determining behavior!"[40]

You can improve the accuracy of your perceptions by pausing to check the basis for your conclusions. **Perception checking** involves noticing and analyzing how you select, organize, and interpret sensory stimuli, whether you consider alternative interpretations, and whether you try to verify your perceptions with others.[41]

In the *Martha and George Dilemma* on the previous page, you learned how perception checking can help you assess and make appropriate responses in a difficult communication situation. However, perception checking is just as valuable in everyday life. Much like the paraphrasing skills we describe in Chapter 2, "Listening and Critical Thinking," perception checking helps you decode messages more accurately, reduce the likelihood of misunderstanding or conflict, and respond fairly and appropriately to others.

ETHICAL COMMUNICATION

The Golden Rule Does Not Always Apply

The Golden Rule, "Do to others what you would have them do to you," comes from the New Testament (Matthew 7:12).[42] However, what *you* would do is not necessarily what another person wants you to do. In his *Maxims for Revolutionists*, playwright George Bernard Shaw wrote, "The golden rule is that there are no golden rules.... Do not do unto others as you would that they should do unto you. Their tastes may not be the same."[43] If you wish to follow the Golden Rule, keep in mind these two cautions:

- Consider how another person may perceive the situation differently than you do
- Look for solutions that would be appropriate and fair from someone else's point of view or culture

2.4
Communicating with Confidence
How do you become a more confident communicator?

Your self-concept and level of self-confidence directly affect how successfully you communicate.[44] Most of us see ourselves as bright and hardworking. At the same time, all of us have occasional doubts and insecurities. If you lack confidence, you are less likely to share what you know or voice your opinions. On the other hand, when you feel good about yourself, you can engage in a conversation with ease, defend your ideas in a group, and give successful presentations.

Most people experience some anxiety when they are in an important communication situation. In fact, that "keyed-up" feeling is a positive and normal reaction and demonstrates that you care about what you have to say.

Communication Apprehension

The anxiety you may experience when speaking to others is referred to by many names: *communication apprehension, speech anxiety,* and *stage fright.* **Communication apprehension** is "an individual's level of fear or anxiety associated with either real or anticipated communication with another person or persons."[45] It occurs in a variety of communication contexts, such as group discussions, meetings, interpersonal conversations, public speaking, and job interviews.

Communication apprehension is not just "in your head"; it is a type of stress that manifests in real physiological responses. Physical reactions such as sweaty palms,

Preparation changes the unfamiliar into something familiar.

Communication Apprehension

Since the early 1970s, the study of communication apprehension has been a major research focus in the communication discipline. Leading researcher James C. McCroskey explains that "it permeates every facet of an individual's life," including major decisions such as career and housing choices, as well as affects the quality of our communication behavior in a variety of interpersonal, small group, social, educational, work, and public settings.[46]

In the beginning, when McCroskey began studying communication apprehension, he believed that it was a "learned trait, one that is conditioned through reinforcements of the child's communication behavior."[47] More recently, he has argued that a person's environment or situation has only a small effect on that person's level of anxiety. He now believes that communication apprehension is a personality trait, "an expression of principally inborn neurobiological functioning."[48]

Communication apprehension, concludes McCroskey, can be reduced by a variety of methods and has already [been] so reduced for literally thousands of individuals."[49] In the remainder of this chapter we provide a deeper understanding of communication apprehension and a variety of methods for reducing its effects.

---

perspiring, a fast pulse, shallow breathing, cold extremities, flushed skin, nausea, trembling hands, quivering legs, or "butterflies" in the stomach are the body's response to the release of hormones such as adrenaline.[50]

Surveys have discovered that fear of snakes and fear of speaking in public are the top two common fears among North Americans, way ahead of fear of heights, anxieties about financial problems, and even fear of death.

Strategies for Becoming a Confident Communicator

Always remember that in most cases, your anxiety is invisible. We can't see your pounding heart, upset stomach, cold hands, or worried thoughts. Most of us think we display more anxiety than listeners report noticing. However, the fact that your anxiety is often invisible to others does not make it feel any less real to you. Fortunately, there are a number of strategies to reduce your anxiety and help you become a more confident communicator.

Prepare Although you may not be able to predict unexpected situations or anticipate the nature of everyday conversations, you can prepare for many of the communication situations you encounter. For instance, you can prepare for a job interview or performance appraisal, a staff meeting or professional seminar, and a public speech or presentation. When you are prepared, you know a great deal about the ideas you wish to discuss, the others who will be involved, the context of the situation, the content and structure of your message, and how you will express yourself.

Relax, Rethink, Re-vision By learning to relax your body, you can reduce your level of communication apprehension. However, physical relaxation is only half the battle; you also need to change the way you think about communication.[51] When you have confident thoughts ("I know I can persuade this group to join the Animal Rescue League"), you begin to feel more confident. Three strategies can help you rethink your attitudes, visualize your message, and relax your body:

- **Cognitive restructuring** is a method for reducing anxiety by replacing negative, irrational thoughts with more realistic, positive self-talk. The next time you feel anxious, repeat any one of these positive statements: "My message is important" or "I am a well-prepared, skilled communicator," "I know more about this than the audience does," or "I've done this before, so I'm not going to be as nervous as I've been in the past."

Sources of **COMMUNICATION APPREHENSION**

The process of managing communication apprehension begins with recognizing why you feel anxious when speaking to an individual, group, or audience. Although everyone has personal reasons for nervousness, researchers have identified some of the key fears that underlie communication apprehension.[52]

FEAR OF **FAILURE**

Many researchers claim that the fear of a negative evaluation is the number one cause of communication anxiety.[53] When you focus your thoughts on the possibility of failure, you are more likely to fail. Try to shift your focus to the positive feedback you see from others—a nod, a smile, or an alert look. When you sense that a listener likes you and your message, you may gain the extra confidence you need.

FEAR OF **OTHERS**

Do you get nervous when interacting with people who have more status or power, education or experience, fame or popularity? Fear of others can be heightened when talking to a powerful person, an influential group, or a large audience. Usually, this fear is based on an exaggerated feeling of being different from or inferior to others. If you don't know much about the people around you, you are more likely to feel apprehensive. Learning more about your listeners can decrease your anxiety. You may have more in common with them than you realize.

FEAR OF **BREAKING THE RULES**

"Three strikes and you're out" works in baseball, and "What goes up must come down" makes sense in physics, but the rules of communication are not hard and fast and should not be treated as though they are enforceable laws. For example, novice speakers sometimes overrehearse to the point of sounding robotic for fear of saying "uh" or "um" in a presentation. Good communicators learn not to "sweat the small stuff" and that, sometimes, "rules" should be bent or broken.

FEAR OF **THE UNKNOWN**

Most people fear the unknown. Performing an unfamiliar or unexpected role can transform a usually confident person into a tangle of nerves. If you are attending an event as an audience member and suddenly are called on to introduce a guest to the audience, you can become very unsettled. Similarly, most people feel stressed when interviewing for a job in an office they've never been to and with a person they hardly know.

FEAR OF **THE SPOTLIGHT**

Although a little attention may be flattering, being the center of attention makes many people nervous. Psychologist Peter Desberg puts it this way: "If you were performing as part of a choir, you'd probably feel much calmer than if you were singing a solo."[54] The more self-focused you are, the more nervous you become. This is especially true when giving a presentation to an audience. Try to stay focused on your purpose and message rather than allowing yourself to be distracted by the spotlight.

associated with stressful situations.[55] You start with deep muscle relaxation. In this relaxed state, you then imagine yourself in a variety of communication contexts ranging from very comfortable to highly stressful. By working to remain relaxed while visualizing various situations, you gradually associate communication with relaxation rather than nervousness.

Focus One of the best ways to build confidence is to concentrate on your message. Anxiety only draws your attention away from your message and directs it to your fears. When you focus on getting your message across, you don't have time to think about how you might look or sound.

Practice The best way to become good at something is to practice, regardless of whether it's cooking, serving a tennis ball, or communicating. You can practice wording a request or expressing an emotion to another person, answering questions in an interview, stating your position at a meeting, or making a presentation to an audience.

In addition to enhancing your confidence, practice stimulates your brain in positive ways. As Daniel Goleman notes in *Social Intelligence*, "Simulating an act is, in the brain, the same as performing it."[56] Practicing communication mentally and physically is as important as practicing the piano or a gymnastics routine. At the very least, communicators should practice what they intend to say to others before they say it.

Even successful and experienced rock stars like Sting practice meditation and other relaxation techniques to transform nervousness and anxiety into calmness and confidence.

- **Visualization** is a powerful method for building confidence, and it allows you to imagine what it would be like to communicate successfully. Find a quiet place, relax, and imagine yourself walking into the room with confidence and energy. Think about the smiles you'll receive as you talk, the heads nodding in agreement, and the look of interest in the eyes of your listeners. By visualizing yourself communicating effectively, you are mentally practicing the skills you need to succeed while also building a positive self-image.

- **Systematic desensitization** is a relaxation and visualization technique developed by psychologist Joseph Wolpe to reduce the anxiety

Personal Report of Communication Apprehension

The Personal Report of Communication Apprehension (PRCA)[58] is composed of 24 statements. Indicate the degree to which each statement applies to you by marking whether you (1) strongly agree, (2) agree, (3) are undecided, (4) disagree, or (5) strongly disagree. Work quickly; record your first impression.

_____ 1. I dislike participating in group discussions.

_____ 2. Generally, I am comfortable while participating in group discussions.

_____ 3. I am tense and nervous while participating in group discussions.

_____ 4. I like to get involved in group discussions.

_____ 5. Engaging in a group discussion with new people makes me tense and nervous.

_____ 6. I am calm and relaxed while participating in a group discussion.

_____ 7. Generally, I am nervous when I have to participate in a meeting.

_____ 8. Usually, I am calm and relaxed while participating in a meeting.

_____ 9. I am very calm and relaxed when I am called on to express an opinion at a meeting.

_____ 10. I am afraid to express myself at meetings.

_____ 11. Communicating at meetings usually makes me feel uncomfortable.

_____ 12. I am very relaxed when answering questions at a meeting.

_____ 13. While participating in a conversation with a new acquaintance, I feel very nervous.

_____ 14. I have no fear of speaking up in conversations.

_____ 15. Ordinarily, I am very tense and nervous in conversations.

_____ 16. Ordinarily, I am very calm and relaxed in conversations.

_____ 17. While conversing with a new acquaintance, I feel very relaxed.

_____ 18. I'm afraid to speak up in conversations.

_____ 19. I have no fear of giving a speech.

_____ 20. Certain parts of my body feel very tense and rigid while I am giving a speech.

_____ 21. I feel relaxed while giving a speech.

_____ 22. My thoughts become confused and jumbled when I am giving a speech.

_____ 23. I face the prospect of giving a speech with confidence.

_____ 24. While giving a speech, I get so nervous I forget facts I really know.

Scoring: As you score each subcategory, begin with a score of 18 points. Then add or subtract from 18 based on the following instructions:

Subscores	Scoring Formula
Group discussions	18 + scores for items 2, 4, and 6; – scores for items 1, 3, and 5
Meetings	18 + scores for items 8, 9, and 12; – scores for items 7, 10, and 11
Interpersonal conversations	18 + scores for items 14, 16, and 17; – scores for items 13, 15, and 18
Public speaking	18 + scores for items 19, 21, and 23; – scores for items 20, 22, and 24

To obtain your total score for the PRCA, add your four subscores together. Your score should range between 24 points and 120 points. Then examine your score for each of the subcategories. If, for example, your score for the Group subcategory is 20 (which is higher than average), you are probably more anxious than most other people when participating in a group discussion.

Norms for PRCA

	Mean	Standard Deviation
Total score	65.5	15.3
Group	15.4	4.8
Meetings	16.4	4.8
Interpersonal	14.5	4.2
Public speaking	19.3	5.1

communication assessment

2.1
Who Are You?
How do your characteristics, perceptions, and confidence affect the way you communicate?

- Your self-concept is determined by your level of self-awareness, the influence of other people, past experiences, and your cultural perspectives.

- People-based factors (significant others, reference groups, your roles, and the rewards you receive from others) are powerful determinants of your self-concept.

- Beware of self-fulfilling prophecies, which are predictions that directly or indirectly cause themselves to become true.

- You can minimize self-deception and trust your view of yourself by objectively assessing your own behavior and by comparing yourself to others.

2.2
Building Self-Esteem
What communication strategies and skills can improve your self-esteem?

- You can improve your self-esteem by practicing self-acceptance, self-responsibility, self-assertiveness, personal integrity, and self-talk.

- Practice converting negative self-talk about yourself into positive self-talk.

2.3
The Power of Perception
How do your perceptions affect the way you select, organize, and interpret the world around you?

- Perception is the process through which you select, organize, and interpret sensory stimuli in the world around you.

- Your needs, interests, moods, wants, and memories largely determine which stimuli you will select.

- Four principles that influence how you organize information are the proximity, similarity, closure, and simplicity principles.

- Your past experiences, knowledge, expectations, attitudes, and relationships affect how you interpret and react to people and events.

- When you engage in perception checking, apply pereception-checking guidelines and skills linked to the seven key elements of effective communication to the specific situation.

2.4
Communicating with Confidence
How do you become a more confident communicator?

- *Communication apprehension* refers to an individual's level of fear or anxiety associated with real or anticipated communication with another person or persons.

- Sources of communication apprehension include fear of failure, fear of the unknown, fear of the spotlight, fear of others, and fear of breaking the supposed rules.

- Strategies for reducing your level of communication apprehension include (1) preparation, (2) physical relaxation, (3) cognitive restructuring, (4) visualization, (5) systematic desensitization, (6) focus, and (7) practice.

MySearchLab®

TEST YOUR KNOWLEDGE

2.1 How do your characteristics, perceptions, and confidence affect the way you communicate?

1 Most infants begin to recognize themselves in a mirror _____ months of age.
   a. by 6
   b. between 6 and 12
   c. between 12 and 18
   d. between 18 and 24
   e. after 24

2 If your parents or teachers tell you that you'll never become a doctor because you're not a good science student, you may not pursue this career goal. Which aspect of self-concept may be responsible for your decision?
   a. self-awareness
   b. self-monitoring
   c. self-assertiveness
   d. self-fulfilling prophecy
   e. self-disclosure

2.2 What communication strategies and skills can improve your self-esteem?

3 Which of the following techniques for improving self-esteem can help you stop blaming others for your failures?
   a. self-talk
   b. personal integrity
   c. self-assertiveness
   d. self-responsibility
   e. self-acceptance

4 As a member of the varsity team, Selena believes that she's a better soccer player than anyone on the intramural teams. What factor has influenced Deidre's Selena about her self?
   a. Reference groups
   b. Significant others
   c. Rewards
   d. Personal memories
   e. Actual performance

2.3 How do your perceptions affect the way you select, organize, and interpret the world around you?

5 Your textbook uses the example of eyewitness testimony to illustrate
   a. the power of self-concept.
   b. the inaccuracies in human perception.
   c. the role of selection in the perception process.
   d. the role of organization in the perception process.
   e. the role of interpretation in the perception process.

6 A mother sees blood on her daughter's sleeve and assumes that her daughter has been badly hurt in an accident. This is an example of
   a. the proximity principle.
   b. the similarity principle.
   c. the closure principle.
   d. the simplicity principle.
   e. the complexity principle.

7 Which guiding principle helps you check your perceptions?
   a. Know Thy Self
   b. Connect with Others
   c. Determine Your Purpose
   d. Select Appropriate Content
   e. all of the above

8 Why doesn't the Golden Rule always work?
   a. Because you have to get to know your neighbor very well before you can "love thy neighbor as thyself."
   b. Because "turning the other cheek" may not help you understand another person's motives.
   c. Because sacrificing yourself for the sake of others may help the other person but be very detrimental to you.
   d. "Honoring thy father and mother" all of the time may prevent you from realizing your own potential.
   e. Because if you "do to others as you would have them do unto you," you may discover that the other person may not want the same things you do.

2.4 How do you become a more confident communicator?

9 Which communication scholar has done the most research on communication apprehension?
   a. Hermann Rorschach
   b. Daniel Goleman
   c. James McCroskey
   d. Min-Sun Kim
   e. Leon Festinger

10 Which strategy for reducing your level of communication apprehension involves replacing negative, irrational thoughts with more realistic, positive self-talk?
   a. Be prepared.
   b. Use cognitive restructuring.
   c. Imagine what it would be like to experience an entire communication act successfully.
   d. Use systematic desensitization.
   e. Focus on your message and practice that message.

Answers found on page 366.

Key Terms

Closure principle	Reference groups	Self-responsibility
Cognitive restructuring	Rewards	Self-talk
Communication Apprehension	Role	Significant others
Figure–ground principle	Self-acceptance	Similarity principle
	Self-appraisals	Simplicity principle
Perception	Self-awareness	Social comparison
Perception checking	Self-concept	Systematic desensitization
Personal integrity	Self-esteem	
Proximity principle	Self-fulfilling prophecy	Visualization
	Self-monitoring	

A U.S. Air Force Major touches noses with a New Zealand Maori warrior during the sacred welcoming ceremony known as *hongi*. When pressing noses and heads, greeters exchange the breath of life.

3 Adapting to **OTHERS**

ot that many years ago, a white American business*man* could predict the gender, race, average age, and even religion of his neighbors, friends, and colleagues: They would look like him, speak like him, and share many of the same attitudes, beliefs, and values. Today, corporations are global communities in which a 35-year-old woman from India might be a CEO, a salesperson, an attorney, or a building engineer.

Not that many years ago, an African American could be denied a room or a table at a "white" hotel or restaurant and be ordered to sit at the back of the bus. Interracial couples who married could be jailed for "mixing races." Same-sex couples hid—and in some cases, still hide—the fact that they are more than "just friends" in order to be welcomed by their families and to avoid verbal and physical harassment. But, in 2009, the son of an African immigrant and a white American woman became the forty-fourth president of the United States. And just as the laws and attitudes against interracial marriage took many years to change,[1] the laws and attitudes about same-sex marriages are also slowly changing. Gay couples are openly and legally married in states such as Massachusetts, Connecticut, New York, and Iowa. The "other" we thought we knew now defies our expectations. Now, more than ever, we must understand, respect, and adapt to the many others we encounter every day.

THINK About... and **ASK YOURSELF**...

3.1
The Many Faces of Others

How has the "changing face" of the United States affected your daily interactions?

The increasing diversity of the U.S. population affects us in many ways—socially, economically, artistically, and spiritually. According to the 2010 Census, the "face" of the United States continues to change in significant ways. More than half the growth in the total U.S. population between 2000 and 2010 was due to increases in the Hispanic population—from 13 to 16 percent of the population. Of all population groups, Asians had the fastest rate of growth and the non-Hispanic whites experienced the slowest growth. The Census also projects that 82 percent of the increase in the U.S. population from 2005 to 2050 will be due to immigration.[2] Soon after the middle of this century, white Americans will become one of the many minority groups living in the United States.[3]

Defining Culture

When some people hear the phrase *cultural diversity*, they think about skin color and immigrants. Words such as *nationality*, *race*, and *ethnicity* are often used synonymously with the term *culture*. However, culture comprises much more than a country of origin, race, or ancestral heritage. In Chapter 1, we defined *culture* as "a learned set of shared interpretations about beliefs, values, and norms which affect the behaviors of a relatively large group of people."[4]

Within most cultures, there are also groups of people—members of **co-cultures**—who coexist within the mainstream society yet remain connected to one another through their cultural heritage.[5] In the United States, American Indian tribes are co-cultures, as are African Americans, Hispanic/Latino Americans, Asian Americans, Arab Americans, Irish Americans, and members of large and small religious groups. Given our broad definition of culture, a Nebraska rancher and a Boston professor can have very different cultural perspectives, as would a native Egyptian, a Brazilian, an Indonesian, and a Chippewa tribal member.

Know Thy SELF

What Do *You* Believe Is Culturally "Normal"?

Respond to each of the following items by putting a check mark in the column that indicates your evaluation of behaviors or customs on a continuum from "quite ordinary" to "quite strange."

Behaviors	Quite Ordinary	Ordinary	Neutral	Strange	Quite Strange
1. A man wearing a skirt in public					
2. A woman breast-feeding her child in public					
3. Talking with a person who does not look you in the eye					
4. A woman refusing to shake hands with a man					
5. A family taking a communal bath					
6. A man who stands so close you can smell his breath					
7. People who will not eat the food in your home					

Review your ratings. All seven behaviors are customary *and* normal in another culture or country. What are some of *your* culture's ordinary behaviors, and why might others consider them unusual or strange?[6]

3.2
Barriers to Understanding Others

How do ethnocentrism, stereotyping, prejudice, discrimination, and racism affect communication?

Learning to communicate effectively in the global village that characterizes life in the twenty-first century can be a significant challenge. In order to become a more effective and ethical communicator in a multicultural nation and world, you must avoid or overcome five obstacles that can inhibit your understanding of others: ethnocentrism, stereotyping, prejudice, discrimination, and racism.

Ethnocentrism

Ethnocentrism is the mistaken belief that your culture is a superior culture with special rights and privileges that are or should be denied to others.

Ethnocentric communicators offend others when they imply that they come from a superior culture with superior values. As an ethical and culturally sensitive communicator, you

BARRIERS
to Understanding Others

Ethnocentrism
Stereotyping
Prejudice
Discrimination
Racism

should examine your own ethnocentric beliefs. Begin by investigating how your culture and your culture-based perspectives may differ from others. Then complete the GENE (Generalized Ethnocentrism) Scale at the end of this chapter to assess your level of ethnocentrism.

Stereotyping

Stereotypes are generalizations about a group of people that oversimplify the group's characteristics. When we stereotype others, we rely on exaggerated beliefs to make judgments about an entire group of people. Unfortunately, stereotyping usually attributes negative traits to all group members when, in reality, only a few people may possess those traits. A study of college students found that, even in the mid-1990s, African Americans were stereotyped as lazy and loud, and Jews were described as shrewd and intelligent.[7] Comments such as "Athletes are poor students," "Old people are boring," and "Latinos are always late" express stereotypical sentiments.

In addition to negative stereotypes, we may hold positive ones. Comments such as "Women are more

COMMUNICATION IN *ACTION*

How Does Language Shape Stereotypes?

Intercultural communication scholars Stella Ting-Toomey and Leeva C. Chung claim that the nature of our language creates many stereotypes. Paired words, for example, encourage either/or thinking: *straight* or *gay*, *us* or *them*, *female* or *male*, *black* or *white*, *rich* or *poor*, *old* or *young*, *red state* or *blue state*. Such either/or perceptions lead us to interpret the social world as either good or bad, normal or abnormal, and right or wrong. When you think in either/or terms, you may overlook the fact that a person may not be old *or* young but somewhere in between or that there are blue voters in red states and red voters in blue states.[8]

Highlighting a cultural detail about someone while sharing a personal story can also contribute to stereotyping. Such

details are usually superfluous and, rather than strengthening a point, promote a biased view, as in the following example:

> Corrine: You know I have such a bad sense of direction, but I must look like I know where I'm going because people are always coming up to me to ask for directions. Last week, I was shopping in downtown Portland and this young—(Corrine pauses at this point to lean in to her friend, raise her hand up to partially cover her mouth, and whisper) *black* guy came up to me and asked for directions to Powell's Books.

Clearly, the point of Corrine's story is that despite her poor sense of direction, people often ask her for directions. So, why did Corrine mention the race of the man who approached her? And why announce his race in such hushed tones? The extraneous details and the manner

in which Corrine expresses those details perpetuate stereotypes. Pay careful attention to your word choices—what you say, why you say it, and the way you say it.

compassionate than men" and "Gays dress with style" make positive but all-inclusive generalizations. Although positive stereotypes may not seem harmful, they can lead to unfair judgments and prevent you from seeing people's individual strengths and characteristics. Believing that all Asian students excel in science may overlook someone's interest or talent in the arts.

Prejudice

Stereotypes lead to **prejudices**: positive or negative attitudes about an individual or cultural group based on little or no direct experience with that person or group. The word

The Characteristics of PREJUDICE

- Biased beliefs about group members that are not based on direct experience and firsthand knowledge[9]
- Irrational feelings of dislike and even hatred for a group
- A readiness to behave in negative and unjust ways toward members of a group

prejudice has two parts: *pre*, meaning "before," and *judice*, as in "judge." When you believe or express a prejudice, you are making a judgment about someone before you get to

know that person and learn whether your opinions and feelings are justified. Although prejudices can be positive—"He must be brilliant if he went to Yale"—most prejudices are negative. Statements such as "I don't want a disabled person working on our group project" or "He's too old to understand cutting edge technology" are examples of prejudice based on stereotypes.

Discrimination

Discrimination is how we act out and express prejudice. When we discriminate, we exclude groups of people from opportunities granted to others: employment, promotion, housing,

STOP&THINK

Is There Such a Thing as Race?

According to many anthropologists, biologists, geneticists, and ethicists, race is "a social construct, not a scientific classification," and a "biologically meaningless" concept.[10] They emphasize that 99.9 percent of DNA sequences are common to all humans.[11] Extensive research clearly establishes that pure races never existed and that all humans belong to the same species, *Homo sapiens*, which originated in Africa.

Before the human genome was decoded, most systems of race classification were based on characteristics such as skin color. The genetic definition of race, however, has absolutely nothing to do with any physical or behavioral characteristics.[12]

So what does all of this mean? Is there such a thing as race? The word *race* certainly has meaning and is very real to all of us. Those who believe that one race (depending on their ethnicity or background) is superior to another have an erroneous, misguided, or biased view of race. Rather, **race** should be viewed as a socially constructed concept *and* understood as the outcome of ancient population shifts that left their mark in our genes. When race is viewed in social and genetic contexts, it becomes a neutral human characteristic.

How have human genome research and biological studies affected beliefs about race?

ETHICAL COMMUNICATION

Acknowledge Unconscious Biases

The National Communication Association's *Credo for Ethical Communication* includes the following principle: "We condemn communication that degrades individuals and humanity through distortion, intimidation, coercion, and violence, and through the expression of intolerance and hatred."[13] Practicing this principle, however, is often more difficult than it seems. Despite claims of "I'm not prejudiced," most of us have positive and negative attitudes about cultural groups based on little or no direct experience with that group.

Two Harvard researchers, Mahzarin Banaji and Brian Nosek, have developed an implicit association test you can take for free on Harvard's website at http://implicit.harvard.edu. The results indicate that the majority of Americans, including people of color and other minorities, show a variety of biases they believe they do *not* have. Banaji and Nosek recommend that when it comes to prejudice, it is less important how biased you are and more important how willing you are to confront your unconscious thoughts about others. When you acknowledge your unconscious biases, you can take steps to confront them.[14]

Two bullet holes in a glass door of the United States Holocaust Memorial Museum mark a hate-crime shooting that left a security officer dead and the gunman wounded.

---

political expression, equal rights, and access to educational, recreational, and social institutions.

Sadly, discrimination comes in many forms: discrimination against racial, ethnic, religious, and gender groups; discrimination based on sexual orientation, disability, age, and physical appearance; and discrimination against people from different social classes and political ideologies.

Racism

Racism emerges from ethnocentrism, stereotyping, prejudice, and discrimination. Racist people assume that a person with a certain inherited characteristic (often something superficial such as skin color) also has negative characteristics and abilities. Racists also believe in the superiority of their own race above all others. In his book *Privilege, Power, and Difference*, Allan Johnson points out that racism is built into the system that people live and work in. It goes beyond the personal and becomes a pattern of privilege and oppression within a society.[15]

Racism usually leads to the abuse of power. When racists acquire power, they may dominate, restrain, mistreat, and harm people of other races. In its cruelest form, racism results in the torture, humiliation, and extermination of others—the abuse of black slaves in the Americas by white slave owners, the brutality of the Nazis against Jews and other ethnic minorities in Europe, or the genocide in Rwanda in which hundreds of thousands of Tutsi people were murdered by Hutu militia groups and gangs.

Extreme racism can and has led to a rise of hate crimes and hate groups. For example, on June 10, 2009, an 88-year-old gunman stepped through the doors of the U.S. Holocaust Memorial Museum in Washington, D.C., and fatally shot a black security guard. The gunman, James W. von Brunn, was a white

> **Racism** is an attitude, a collection of stereotypes, a bad intention, a desire or need to discriminate or do harm, a form of hatred.
>
> —Allan Johnson, *Privilege, Power, and Difference*[16]

supremacist who hosted a racist, anti-Semitic website and wrote a book titled *Kill the Best Gentiles*, alleging a Jewish "conspiracy to destroy the white gene pool."[17] In 2011, Norway's Anders Breivik justified his brutal massacre of 76 people in an online manifesto that described his hatred for Muslims and multiculturalism.[18]

The gunmen in these cases were described as loners, but their virulent hatred of "others" reflects the views of many hate groups. "Hate group membership," writes Judith Warner, of *The New York Times*, "has been expanding steadily over the course of the past decade—fueled largely by anti-immigrant sentiment. But after President Barack Obama's election, it spiked. The day after the election, the computer servers of two major white supremacist groups crashed, because their traffic went through the roof."[19]

barriers to understanding others

47

Understanding Cultural Diversity

Why is understanding cultural diversity so important?

Each one of us has an ethnicity, gender, age, religious belief (including atheism), socioeconomic position, sexual orientation, and abilities. We also live in or have come from a certain region or country. Consider the following examples:

- A sixth-generation, female, Lutheran teacher whose family still lives in the same midwestern town
- A 55-year-old Jewish male scientist living in New York whose family emigrated from Russia
- An Islamic, African American female working as a researcher for the federal government in Washington, D.C.

All these characteristics contribute to our **social identity**: our self-concept as derived from the social categories to which we see ourselves belonging.[20] Many of us, however, although we may identify ourselves as Irish, Korean, Ethiopian, or Sioux, have lost touch with our family history and culture.

Understanding *Your* Culture

Culture affects your life in both obvious and subtle ways. The first step in understanding others is to understand your own culture. You derive a significant part of your social identity from the cultural groups to which you belong as well as the groups to which you do *not* belong: "I know who I am and that I am *not* you." This is a thoroughly natural feeling. However, we often divide our world into distinct and very opposite social groups (men and women, rich and poor, black and white, young and old, American and foreign) in a way that sets us in opposition to others. A more constructive approach is to explore your own social identity and compare it to people with different kinds of identity.

For example, many white people in the United States don't think of their behavior as characteristic of a culture. Because whiteness is a historical norm in the United States, it is difficult to classify it as a culture. Yet as Dr. Rita Hardiman wrote,

> Like fish, whose environment is water, we are surrounded by Whiteness and it is easy to think that what we experience is reality rather than recognizing it as the particular culture of a particular group. And like fish who are not aware of water until they are out of it, White people sometimes become aware of their culture only when they get to know, or interact with, the cultures of people of color.[21]

Understanding *Other* Cultures

If you believe you can live a life in which you avoid people from other cultures, you are fooling yourself. Even many remote towns have been transformed by major influxes of migrant workers (Mexican laborers in Garden City, Kansas), immigrant populations (Hmong communities in Manitowoc County, Wisconsin), and religious groups (Orthodox Jews in Postville, Iowa).

Religion is also a very important aspect of a culture, but what some people forget is that in many countries and for many groups, the religion *is* the culture, such as Buddhism in Tibet and Islam in Iran. Occasionally, when religious groups attempt to practice their culture in a secular country, they encounter intolerance. In France, for example, religious attire, including head scarves for Muslim girls, skullcaps for Jewish boys, and crosses for Christian children, has been banned from public high schools.[22] Regardless of your individual religious beliefs, "you must remember that people feel strongly about their religion, and that differences between religious beliefs and practices do matter."[23]

You live in a pluralistic society; the more knowledge you gain about the people around you and the more you learn to respect others, the better you will be able to communicate. On a practical level, your willingness and ability to work in a diverse environment will likely increase your chances of career advancement.

In *Avatar*, ex-Marine Jake Sully is transformed from a human into a Na'vi cat person. After infiltrating the cat people to gather intelligence for a military invasion, he falls in love with a cat woman. A "race traitor" to his fellow humans, Sully leads the cat people to victory over the human invaders. Are the Na'vi just blue versions of oppressed people of color or do they represent something more significant?

Questions of Faith

According to Stephen Prothero, professor of religion at Boston University, many of us are illiterate about our own and others' religions. He defines **religious literacy** as "the ability to understand and use the religious terms, symbols, images, beliefs, practices, scripture, heroes, themes, and stories that are employed in American public life."[24] Test your knowledge about a few of the world's major religions by selecting "True," "False," or "I Don't Know" (?) for each of the items below:[25]

T	F	?	1.	Muslims believe in Islam and the Islamic way of life.
T	F	?	2.	Judaism is an older religion than Buddhism.
T	F	?	3.	Islam is a monotheistic religion (belief in one God) just like Christianity and Judaism.
T	F	?	4.	A Christian Scientist believes that disease is a delusion of the carnal mind that can be cured by prayer.
T	F	?	5.	Jews fast during Yom Kippur; Muslims fast during Ramadan.
T	F	?	6.	Jesus Christ was Jewish.
T	F	?	7.	Roman Catholics throughout the world outnumber all other Christians combined.
T	F	?	8.	Sunni Muslims compose about 90 percent of all adherents to Islam.
T	F	?	9.	Hindus believe in the idea of reincarnation.
T	F	?	10.	The Ten Commandments form the basis of Jewish religious laws.
T	F	?	11.	Mormonism is a Christian faith founded in the United States.[26]
T	F	?	12.	The Protestant reformer Martin Luther labeled the beliefs of Muslims, Jews, and Roman Catholics as false.
T	F	?	13.	One-third of the world's population is Christian.
I	F	?	14.	One-fifth of the world's population is Muslim.
T	F	?	15.	Hinduism is the oldest of the world's major religions, dating back more than 3,000 years.

Answers: All of the statements are true.

3.4

The Dimensions of Culture

What cultural dimensions affect the way you communicate with others?

We owe a great deal to social psychologist Geert H. Hofstede and anthropologist Edward T. Hall for identifying several important dimensions of culture. Hofstede's groundbreaking research on cultural characteristics has transformed our understanding of others. He defines **intercultural dimension** as "an aspect of a culture that can be measured relative to other cultures."[27] His work on cultural variability identifies several dimensions that characterize cultural groups. Here we look at three of those dimensions—individualism/ collectivism, power distance, and masculine/feminine values—because they have received more research attention and support than the others. Hall adds a fourth and fifth dimension: high-context/low-context cultures and monochronic/polychronic time.

Individualism/Collectivism

Individualism/collectivism may be the most important factor distinguishing one culture from another.[28] According to Hofstede and many contemporary researchers, while most North Americans traditionally value **individualism**,

5 DIMENSIONS OF CULTURE

1 Individualism/Collectivism

2 Power Distance

3 Masculine/Feminine Values

4 High/Low Context

5 Monochronic/Polychronic Time

- ■ "I" is important.
- ■ Independence is worth pursuing.
- ■ Personal achievement should be rewarded.
- ■ Individual uniqueness is valued.

COLLECTIVIST
Characteristics[34]

- ■ "We" is important.
- ■ The needs, beliefs, and goals of the "in-group" (e.g., family, community members) are emphasized above those of the individual.
- ■ Achievements that benefit and foster cooperation in the group should be rewarded.
- ■ Individual uniqueness is not considered important.

70 percent of the world's population values interdependence or **collectivism**.[29] For instance, once children have completed high school or higher education in the United States, many parents encourage them to strike out on their own—to pursue a career and find their own place to live. However, in many Asian countries, parents encourage their children to stay at home and work until they marry and, once they do, to work for the benefit of the immediate *and* extended family. Figure 3.1 ranks the top countries in each category.[30]

Despite the fact that the United States ranks highest in terms of individualism, not all Americans are individualistic. In fact, many African Americans, Asian Americans, and

Latino co-cultures have the characteristics of collectivist societies. The focus on individual achievement and personal rewards in the United States can make interaction with people from collectivist cultures and co-cultures quite difficult. The typical U.S. communicator's style and behavior may be viewed as arrogant, antagonistic, power hungry, ruthless, and impatient. Interestingly, as poor nations gain wealth, they begin to shift toward greater individualism.[31]

Power Distance

Is it easy to make a personal appointment with the president of your college or university? Can you simply walk into your boss's office, or do you have to navigate your way through an army of secretaries and administrative assistants? Does our society truly believe in the sentiments expressed in the U.S. Declaration of Independence that all people are created equal? These are the questions addressed in Hofstede's power distance dimension. **Power distance** refers to the physical and psychological distance between those who have power and those who do not in relationships, institutions, and organizations. It also represents "the extent to which the less powerful person in society accepts inequality in power and considers it normal."[32]

In cultures with **high power distance**, individuals accept differences in power as normal. It is accepted that all people are *not* created equal. In such cultures, the privileged have

MOST **INDIVIDUALISTIC**
COUNTRIES

1. United States
2. Australia
3. Great Britain
*4/5. Canada/
     The Netherlands

MOST **COLLECTIVIST**
COUNTRIES

1. Guatemala
2. Ecuador
3. Panama
4. Venezuela
5. Colombia

*Tied rankings.

Figure 3.1 Individualism and Collectivism

much more power and use it to guide or control the lives of people with less power. In a high-power-distance culture, you accept and do not challenge authority. Parents have total control over their children. Husbands may have total control over their wives. And government officials, corporate officers, and religious authorities dictate rules of behavior and have the power to ensure compliance.

In cultures with **low power distance**, power distinctions are minimized: supervisors work with subordinates, professors work with students, elected officials work with constituents. Figure 3.2 ranks the top countries in each category of this dimension. Despite the fact that the United States claims to be the greatest democracy on earth and an equal opportunity society, it is sixteenth on the list after low-power-distance countries such as Finland, Switzerland, Great Britain, Germany, Costa Rica, Australia, the Netherlands, and Canada.[35]

Power distance has enormous implications for communication. For example, in Australia (a low-power-distance country), students and professors are often on a first-name basis, and lively class discussions are the norm. However, in Malaysia (a high-power-distance country), students show up and are seated *before* class begins; almost no one comes late. Students are polite and appreciative but rarely challenge a professor's claims. In a high-power-distance culture, you do not

openly disagree with teachers, elders, bosses, law enforcement officials, or government agents.

If you compare Figures 3.1 and 3.2, you will notice a strong correlation between collectivism and high power distance and between individualism and low power distance. If you are individualistic and strongly encouraged to express your own opinion, you are more willing to challenge authority. If, on the other hand, your culture is collectivist and your personal opinion is subordinate to the welfare of others, you are less likely to challenge the collective authority of your family, your employer, or your government.

Masculine/Feminine Values

Hofstede uses the terms *masculine* and *feminine* to describe whether masculine or feminine traits are *valued* by a culture. The terms are used to describe a societal perspective rather than individuals.

In **masculine societies**, men are supposed to be assertive, tough, and focused on material success, whereas women are supposed to be more modest, tender, and concerned with the quality of life. In **feminine societies**, gender roles overlap: Both men and women are supposed to be modest, tender, and concerned with the quality of life.[36] Figure 3.3 ranks countries in terms of masculine/feminine values.[37]

Hofstede ranks the United States as fifteenth in terms of masculine values but still less masculine than Australia, New Zealand, and Greece. In masculine societies, personal success, competition, assertiveness, and strength are admired. Unselfishness and nurturing may be seen as weaknesses or feminine. Although women have come a long way from the rigid roles of past centuries, they have miles to go

U.S. Secretary of State Hillary Clinton and the president of the Republic of Tatarstan, Russia, congratulate newlyweds at an Islamic mosque. How does Secretary Clinton demonstrate her understanding and respect for this country and its peoples' values?

before they achieve genuine equality in cultures with high masculine values.

High/Low Context

In Chapter 1, we defined *context* as the psychosocial, logistical, and interactional environment in which communication occurs. Edward T. Hall sees context as the information that surrounds an event, inextricably bound up with the meaning of the event. He claims that a message's context—in and of itself—may hold more meaning than the actual words in a message.[38] Like Hofstede's dimensions, we can place cultures on a continuum from high context to low context.

In a **high-context culture**, very little meaning is expressed through words. In contrast, gestures, silence, and facial expressions, as well as the relationships among communicators, have meaning. In high-context cultures, meaning can also be conveyed through status (age, gender, education, family background, title, and affiliations) and through an individual's informal network of friends and associates.

In a **low-context culture**, meaning is expressed primarily through language. As members of a low-context culture, people in North America tend to speak more, speak more loudly, and speak more rapidly than a person from a high-context culture. Americans and Canadians

HIGHEST **POWER-DISTANCE** COUNTRIES
1. Malaysia
*2/3. Guatemala
    Panama
4. Philippines
*5/6. Mexico/Venezuela

LOWEST **POWER-DISTANCE** COUNTRIES
1. Austria
2. Israel
3. Denmark
4. New Zealand
5. Ireland
*Tied rankings.

Figure 3.2 Power Distance

51

Figure 3.3 Masculine and Feminine Values

"speak up," "spell it out," "just say no," and "speak our mind." Figure 3.4 contrasts the characteristics of high- and low-context cultures.[39]

High-context communication usually occurs in collectivist cultures in which members share similar attitudes, beliefs, and values. As a result, spoken communication can be indirect, implied, or vague because everyone *gets* the meaning by understanding the context, the person's nonverbal behavior, and the significance of the communicator's status.

Shirley van der Veur, a former Peace Corps volunteer and now a university professor, relates the following illustration of this concept: A scholar from Kenya was invited to dinner at an American colleague's home. Even though he ate ravenously, not leaving a morsel of food on his plate, the American hosts were not convinced that he liked his dinner because he had not *said* so. In Kenya, if his hosts saw him appreciatively eating his meal, they would know that he was enjoying it without necessarily needing him to express his pleasure verbally.[40]

Monochronic/ Polychronic Time

In most parts of northern Europe and North America, time is a very valuable commodity. As a result, we fill our days and nights with multiple commitments and live a fast-paced life. However, the pace of life in India, Kenya, and Argentina, for example, is driven less by a need to "get things done" than by a sense of participation in events that create their own rhythm.[41]

Edward T. Hall classifies time as a form of communication and claims that cultures treat time in one of two ways: as monochronic or polychronic.[42] In **monochronic time**, or M-time, events are scheduled as separate items—one thing at a time. M-time people like to concentrate on one job before moving to another and may become irritated when someone in a meeting brings up a personal topic unrelated to the purpose of the meeting.

In **polychronic time**, or P-time, schedules are not as important and are frequently broken. People in polychronic cultures are not slaves to time and are easily distracted and tolerant of interruptions. P-time people are frequently late for appointments or may not show up at all.[43] If you are a P-time person, you probably find it stimulating to think about several different problems at the same time and feel comfortable holding two or three conversations simultaneously.

Hall maintains that these two time orientations are incompatible. When monochronic and polychronic people interact, the results can be frustrating. Hall notes that monochronic North Americans become distressed by how polychronic people treat appointments. Being on time in some countries simply doesn't have the same significance as it does in the United

Figure 3.4 Characteristics and Examples of High- and Low-Context Cultures

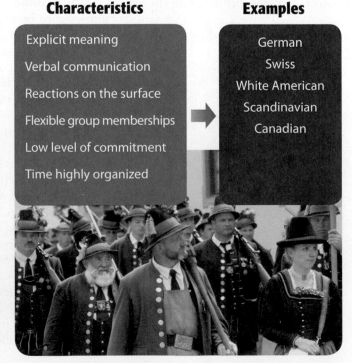

HIGH-CONTEXT CULTURES

Examples	Characteristics
Chinese	Implicit meaning
Japanese	Nonverbal communication
South Korean	Reserved reactions
Native American	Strong in-group bonds
African American	High level of commitment
Mexican American and Latino	Time open and flexible

LOW-CONTEXT CULTURES

Characteristics	Examples
Explicit meaning	German
Verbal communication	Swiss
Reactions on the surface	White American
Flexible group memberships	Scandinavian
Low level of commitment	Canadian
Time highly organized	

Muted Group Theory

Cheris Kramarae's **Muted Group Theory** observes that powerful, wealthy groups at the top of a society determine who will communicate and be listened to. For this reason, women, the poor, and people of color may have trouble participating and being heard.[44] The following three assumptions in muted group theory explain how women's voices are subdued or silenced in many cultures:

1 Women perceive the world differently than men because of traditional divisions of labor. Examples: Homemaker versus breadwinner, nurse versus doctor.

2 Women's freedom of expression is limited by men's dominance in relationships and institutions. Examples: Women in the United States only gained the right to vote in 1920. The "glass ceiling" still prevents women from achieving professional advancement.

3 Women must transform their thinking and behavior to participate fully in society. Example: Women have become politically active and even militant to make sure that sexual harassment, date and marital rape, and spousal abuse are seen as serious crimes rather than practices that may be excused or tolerated.

Although muted group theory focuses on women, its assumptions apply to many groups. The voices of people of color, recent immigrants, the disabled, and the poor are also muted.

States. For P-time people, schedules and commitments, particularly plans for the future, are not firm, and even important plans may change right up to the last minute.[45]

If you are an M-time person, you can try to modify and relax your obsession with time and scheduling. If you are a P-time person, you can do your best to respect and adapt to a monochronic person's need for careful scheduling and promptness. Figure 3.5 depicts several differences between monochronic and polychronic perspectives and cultures.

Figure 3.5 Monochronic and Polychronic Time: Characteristics and Cultures

MONOCHRONIC CULTURES

Examples
German
Austrian
Swiss
White American

Characteristics
Do one thing at a time
Concentrate on the job
Take all time commitments (deadlines, schedules) seriously
Adhere to plans
Emphasize promptness
Engage in short-term relationships

POLYCHRONIC CULTURES

Characteristics
Do many things at once
Are easily distracted
Take time commitments less seriously
Often change plans
Base promptness on the importance of a relationship
Build lifetime relationships

Examples
Latin American
Arab
African
African American

3.5
Intercultural Communication Strategies

What strategies can help you understand, respect, and effectively communicate with "others"?

As a way of understanding the perspectives of "others," intercultural communication trainers often urge their trainees to "see the world through other people's eyes."

The fundamental purpose of understanding others—seeing the world as others see it—is to minimize miscommunication and prejudice. Of course learning about and adapting to the many "others" you encounter every day may require changes in long-standing habits of thought and action.

Be Mindful

Mindfulness is both a very old and a very new concept. The ancient concept can be traced back to the first millennium b.c. to the foothills of the Himalayas, when it is believed that Buddha attained enlightenment through mindfulness.[46] **Mindfulness** involves being fully aware of the present moment without making hasty judgments.

Before explaining mindfulness in more detail, let's take a look at its opposite: mind*less*ness. **Mindlessness** occurs when you allow rigid categories and false distinctions to become habits of thought and behavior.[47] For example, you approach a sales counter and say "Excuse me" to the salesperson. Why did you say that? Did you really mean to beg their pardon, or were you apologizing for interrupting someone who should have been paying more attention to you in the first place? All of us engage in some mindless behavior without any serious consequences. But when mindlessness occurs in a sensitive situation, the results can be detrimental to a relationship or damaging to an important project. For example, after the 9/11 tragedy, many patriotic Muslim Americans suffered mindless stereotyping, prejudice, and discrimination as a result of a larger ignorance about the Islamic faith and culture. If you are mindless, you are trapped in an inflexible, biased world in which your religion is always right and good; people from other cultures are inferior and untrustworthy; boys will always be boys, and girls will always be girls; and change is a terrible and scary thing.[48]

Mind*ful*ness, in contrast, requires paying attention to how you and another person communicate. It asks you to observe what is happening as it happens, without forming opinions or taking sides as you learn more about someone else.[49] When you are mindful, you recognize stereotypical thinking and prejudices and try to overcome them. Mindfulness gives you the freedom and motivation to understand, respect, and adapt to others.

Mindful communicators understand what they experience *inside themselves* (body, mind, heart, spirit) and pay full attention to what is happening *around them* (people, the natural world, surroundings, events).[50]

Be Receptive to New Information Mindful communicators learn more about others and their cultures by being open to new information. Too often, we dismiss another person's belief or behavior as irrational or bizarre when more information about that belief or behavior would help us understand it. Once you learn why observant Muslims and Jews won't eat pork products or why Hindus won't eat the meat of sacred cows even under famine conditions, you may become more mindful and tolerant of their customs.

Respect Others' Perspectives In addition to being open to new information, mindful communicators are open to other points of view. Psychologist Richard Nisbett credits a graduate student from China with helping him understand such differences. When he and the student were trying to work and communicate with each other, his Chinese student said, "You know, the difference between you and me is that I know the world is a circle, and you think it's a line. The Chinese believe in constant change, but with things always moving back to some prior state . . . Westerners live in a simpler world . . . and they think they can control events because they know the rules that govern the behavior of objects."[51]

When you cling to one way of seeing a person or interpreting an event, you have stopped being mindful. Every idea, person, or object can be many things, depending on the perspective from which it is viewed. A cow is steak to a rancher, a sacred creature to a Hindu, a collection of genes and proteins to a biologist, and a mistreated animal to members of PETA (People for the Ethical Treatment of Animals).[52]

Adapt to Others

You probably feel most comfortable when you "fit in" with the people around you. To fit in, you may modify the way you talk to family members, friends, colleagues, authority figures, and strangers. For example, two people may be from different areas of the country, one from Maine and the other from Alabama. When they go "home," their dialects, vocabulary, sentence structure, rate of speech, and even volume change to accommodate their home culture. Yet, in professional settings, their speech may be more formal in style and substance.

RANGE OF THINKING

WESTERN

Focuses on discovering the basic and predictable nature of objects and events

Tries to control objects, events, and environments

Puts things in discrete categories

Uses formal logical rules

Insists on the correctness of one belief vs. another

EAST ASIAN

Focuses on the interacting, unpredictable relationships among events

Doubts that objects, events, and environments are controllable

Describes relationships and connections, not categories

Accepts contractions and dissimilar beliefs

COMMUNICATION & CULTURE

WHY DON'T HUNGRY HINDUS EAT SACRED COWS?

Among India's Hindus, cows are a sacred symbol of life. There is no greater sacrilege for a Hindu than killing a cow. At first, this belief may seem irrational, particularly in light of India's food shortage and poverty. If you have visited or seen pictures of India, you've seen cows wandering city streets and sidewalks, highways and railroad tracks, gardens, and agricultural fields. You've also seen pictures of extreme poverty and hunger.

In his book *Cows, Pigs, Wars, and Witches: The Riddles of Culture*, Marvin Harris offers an explanation for Hindus' treatment of cows.[53] Cows give birth to oxen, which are the principal source for plowing fields. Unfortunately, there are too few oxen for India's 60 million farms. Without oxen to plow fields, farmers cannot farm, food shortages result, and people go hungry. If you

kill a cow, you eliminate your source of oxen. During the worst famines, killing a cow only provides temporary relief. Once a cow is killed, there will be no more oxen to plow the field in future years. The long-term effect may be a much more devastating famine. Harris offers this conclusion:

> What I am saying is that cow love is an active element in a complex, finely articulated material and cultural order. Cow love mobilizes the latent capacity of human beings to persevere in a low-energy ecosystem in which there is little room for waste or indolence.[54]

In light of Harris's anthropological explanation, you can begin to understand and respect why hungry peasants in India refuse to eat the cows that surround them.

Professor Howard Giles explores these adaptive tendencies in **Communication Accommodation Theory**,[55] which states that in every communication situation, we compare ourselves with speakers from other groups. If we believe that another group has more power or has desirable characteristics, we tend to "accommodate" our conversations to the accepted speech behaviors and norms of that group. According to communication accommodation theory:

1. *Communication similarities and differences exist in all conversations.* Whether you talk to an international student or your grandmother, you will encounter differences.
2. *The manner in which we perceive the communication of others will determine how we evaluate our interaction with others.* Effective communicators avoid stereotyping by carefully listening to others and attentively observing what they do.
3. *Language and behavior convey information about social status and group membership.* Usually, the person or group with more status and power establishes the "accepted" type of talk and behavior. For example, if you are being interviewed for a job by someone who behaves formally, you are likely to behave the same way.
4. *Accommodation varies in its degree of appropriateness, and norms guide the accommodation process.* When a situation is awkward, you will try to accommodate the behavior of the group in that situation. Thus, if you interact with a culture that respects its elders, you may hesitate questioning the views of an older person or senior official. Or when you learn that a particular behavior is *inappropriate*, you will not engage in that behavior. For example, if you and your colleagues are on a deadline at work and they decide to leave the office before they complete the project, you may not leave with them.

Actively Engage Others

Direct, face-to-face interaction with people from culturally diverse backgrounds benefits everyone. You and others may transform long-held negative beliefs about each other's cultures into positive opinions.

One of the most interesting and exciting ways to actively engage others is to travel. Within the United States, visits to San Francisco, New Orleans, Miami, and New York will put you in touch with, literally, different worlds. Traveling abroad is just as engaging and has long-term benefits. A survey of students who studied abroad found a positive link to career success, a more tolerant worldview, and increased self-confidence. When questioned about their intercultural development and understanding, 98 percent reported that study abroad helped them to better understand their own cultural values and biases.[56]

If you succeed in minimizing your level of anxiety and uncertainty when encountering others, you may discover new worlds with fascinating people who can enrich your life. The fact is, regardless of culture, nationality, gender, religion, age, and ability, all of us share the traits unique to the amazing human condition.

Communication Traits ALL PEOPLE SHARE[57]

We **SMILE** when happy.

We **WAVE** as a greeting.

We **LAUGH** when amused.

We **BLUSH** when embarrassed.

We **CRY** when sad or in pain.

We **FROWN** when concerned or ill at ease.

We adopt a **FETAL POSITION** when dejected, cold, or in a hopeless situation.

We **SHRUG** to express "I don't know."

We **SLUMP** when dejected or tired.

We **STAND STRAIGHT** when alert or confident.

The Generalized Ethnocentrism (GENE) Scale[58]

Read the following statements concerning your feelings about your and others' cultures. In the space provided, indicate how each statement applies to you by marking whether you (5) strongly agree, (4) agree, (3) are undecided, (2) disagree, or (1) strongly disagree. There are no right or wrong answers. Some of the statements may seem very similar. Remember, everyone experiences some degree of ethnocentrism. Be honest. Work quickly and record your first response.

_____ 1. Most other cultures are backward compared with my culture.

_____ 2. My culture should be the role model for other cultures.

_____ 3. People from other cultures act strangely when they come to my culture.

_____ 4. Lifestyles in other cultures are just as valid as those in my culture.

_____ 5. Other cultures should try to be more like my culture.

_____ 6. I'm not interested in the values and customs of other cultures.

_____ 7. People in my culture could learn a lot from people in other cultures.

_____ 8. Most people from other cultures just don't know what's good for them.

_____ 9. I respect the values and customs of other cultures.

_____ 10. Other cultures are smart to look up to our culture.

_____ 11. Most people would be happier if they lived like people in my culture.

_____ 12. I have many friends from different cultures.

_____ 13. People in my culture have just about the best lifestyles anywhere.

_____ 14. Lifestyles in other cultures are not as valid as those in my culture.

_____ 15. I am very interested in the values and customs of other cultures.

_____ 16. I apply my values when judging people who are different.

_____ 17. I see people who are similar to me as virtuous/good.

_____ 18. I do not cooperate with people who are different.

_____ 19. Most people in my culture just don't know what is good for them.

_____ 20. I do not trust people who are different.

_____ 21. I dislike interacting with the values and customs of other cultures.

_____ 22. I have little respect for the values and customs of other cultures.

To determine your ethnocentrism score, complete the following four steps:

1. Add your responses to items 4, 7, and 9.

2. Add your responses to items 1, 2, 5, 8, 10, 11, 13, 14, 18, 20, 21, and 22.

3. Subtract the sum from step 1 from 18 (i.e., 18 minus step 1 sum).

4. Add results from step 2 and step 3. This is your generalized ethnocentrism score. Scores of more than 55 points indicate high ethnocentrism.

3.1
The Many Faces of Others

How has the "changing face" of the United States affected your daily interactions?

- Effective communicators learn how to understand, respect, and adapt to cultural diversity.
- By 2050 there will be no majority culture in the United States.
- Culture is a learned set of shared interpretations about beliefs, values, and norms that affect the behaviors of a relatively large group of people.
- Co-cultures exist within the mainstream of society yet remain connected to one another through their cultural heritage.

3.2
Barriers to Understanding Others

How do ethnocentrism, stereotyping, prejudice, discrimination, and racism affect communication?

- Ethnocentrism is a belief that your culture is superior to others; stereotypes are generalizations about a group of people that oversimplify their characteristics.
- Stereotypes lead to prejudices, which are positive or negative attitudes about an individual or cultural group based on little or no direct experience.
- Prejudice leads to discrimination, the exclusion of groups of people from opportunities granted to others.
- In the extreme, prejudice and discrimination lead to racism, which justifies dominating and mistreating people of other races.

3.3
Understanding Cultural Diversity

Why is understanding cultural diversity so important?

- When we view race as a socially constructed concept, it becomes a very neutral and natural characteristic.
- Many people are not literate about others' religions or about their own religion. This lack of knowledge can affect their ability to communicate effectively with others.

3.4
The Dimensions of Culture

What cultural dimensions affect the way you communicate with others?

- The individualism/collectivism cultural dimension contrasts independence and personal achievement with interdependence and group values.
- The power distance cultural dimension examines the physical and psychological distance between those with power and those without power.
- The masculine/feminine values cultural dimension contrasts an assertive and tough perspective with a more modest and tender perspective.

- The high-/low-context cultural dimension focuses on whether meaning is expressed in words or through nonverbal communication and the nature of personal relationships.
- The monochronic/polychronic time cultural dimension contrasts cultures that value time and concentrate on one job at a time and cultures that are not slaves to time and are easily distracted by interruptions.

3.5
Intercultural Communication Strategies

What strategies can help you understand, respect, and effectively communicate with "others"?

- Effective communicators are mindful; that is, they are receptive to new information and are responsive to and respectful of other perspectives.
- Communication accommodation theory provides principles to help understand, respect, and successfully adapt to others without stereotyping.
- Finding ways to interact and actively engage people who are different than you are can help you be a better communicator.

MySearchLab®

3.1 *How has the "changing face" of the United States affected your daily interactions?*

1 According to the U.S. Census, between 2000 and 2010, _____ had the fastest rate of population growth and _____ had the slowest rate of growth.
   a. Non-Hispanic whites; Hispanic whites
   b. Latinos; Asians
   c. Asians; non-Hispanic whites
   d. Hispanic whites; Immigrants
   e. Immigrants; Latinos

3.2 *How do ethnocentrism, stereotyping, prejudice, discrimination, and racism affect communication?*

2 Jack sincerely believes that most people would be better off if their government and country were more like the United States. Which barrier to understanding others does Jack exemplify?
   a. ethnocentrism
   b. stereotyping
   c. prejudice
   d. discrimination
   e. racism

3 When the courts examined a supermarket's hiring record, they found that the company never hired nonwhite applicants for the better-paying job of working cash registers. Which barrier to understanding others does this example exemplify?
   a. ethnocentrism
   b. stereotyping
   c. prejudice
   d. discrimination
   e. racism

4 When James W. von Brunn fatally shot a black security guard at the U.S. Holocaust Memorial Museum in Washington, D.C., his actions were described as the consequences of _____.
   a. ethnocentrism
   b. stereotyping
   c. prejudice
   d. discrimination
   e. racism

5 A study in the 1990s found that many college students described African Americans as lazy and loud and Jews as shrewd and intelligent. Which barrier to understanding others is demonstrated by the responses this study?
   a. ethnocentrism
   b. stereotyping
   c. prejudice
   d. discrimination
   e. racism

3.3. *Why is understanding cultural diversity so important?*

6 Which of the following contributes to your social identity?
   a. ethnicity
   b. socioeconomic position
   c. sexual orientation
   d. gender
   e. all of the above

3.4 *What cultural dimensions affect the way you communicate with others?*

7 Which of the following countries exhibits the most individualism?
   a. Australia
   b. Indonesia
   c. Taiwan
   d. Peru
   e. Pakistan

8 There is a strong correlation between collectivist cultures and cultures in which there is _____.
   a. individualism
   b. high power distance
   c. low power distance
   d. high-context communication
   e. monochronic time

9 Which behavior is characteristic of a society with feminine values?
   a. Men are assertive, tough, and focused on success, whereas women are more modest and tender.
   b. Men's and women's gender roles overlap.
   c. Women assume most homemaking and child-rearing responsibilities.
   d. Men assume most homemaking and child-rearing responsibilities.
   e. Women are assertive, tough, and focused on success, whereas men are more modest and tender.

3.5 *What strategies can help you understand, respect, and effectively communicate with "others"?*

10 Which behavior demonstrates mindfulness when communicating with people from other cultures?
   a. You pay attention to how you and another person are communicating.
   b. You recognize your personal prejudices and try to overcome them.
   c. You understand and respect different cultural values.
   d. You are receptive to new ideas and respect other people's perspectives.
   e. You do all of the above

Answers found on page 366.

Key Terms

Co-cultures	High-context culture	Muted Group Theory
Collectivism	Individualism	Polychronic time
Communication	Intercultural dimension	Power distance
Accommodation	Low power distance	Prejudices
Theory	Low-context culture	Race
Discrimination	Masculine societies	Racism
Ethnocentrism	Mindfulness	Religious literacy
Feminine societies	Mindlessness	Social identity
High power distance	Monochronic time	Stereotypes

THINK
COMMUNICATION

Communication
Knowledge for Communicating Well
Currents

N C A

A Publication of the National Communication Association

Volume 3, Issue 1 - February 2008

> Remember that the majority of the world's cultures are collectivist in nature.

Culture and Deception:
Moral Transgression or Social Necessity?

> In what way does this statement relate to the differences between individualistic and collectivist cultures in Chapter 3, pp. 49–50.

Lies, dishonesty, trickery, fraud, duplicity, betrayal—these words are often entangled together in the proverbial web of deceit. But does lying receive an unnecessary bad rap? Recent cross-cultural research suggests that deceptive communication can actually serve more functional purposes than our society generally wishes to acknowledge.

People choose to lie for a variety of reasons. Motives for not telling the truth typically fall into two categories: lies to benefit the self and lies to benefit the other. People will often tell lies in pursuit of personal gain, to escape punishment, or to make themselves appear better than their characteristics actually deserve. At other times, people will lie to protect another's image, to avoid hurting the other, or to avoid unwanted relational trauma. It is no secret that lies have indeed spared many a person from unnecessary distress and possible harm.

While people may have their own motives for avoiding the truth, the pervasive influence of culture is less often recognized as a key factor affecting one's ultimate decision to tell the truth. Results of a recent cross-cultural study conducted by researchers of the University of Hawai'i revealed that a person's motivation to deceive is clearly influenced by his or her cultural self-identity. They also found that one's cultural identity greatly influenced whether or not a message was perceived to be deceptive.

Employing samples from Hong Kong, Hawai'i and mainland U.S., the study revealed that people who strongly valued their own independence and individuality over the social relationships in which they are embedded reported having a lower overall motivation to deceive. By contrast, people who possessed cultural self-identities which emphasize placing group needs over the individual reported having a greater overall motivation to avoid telling the truth.

An interesting twist, however, is that when people were presented with a scenario in which deception would serve to benefit them personally, those who valued their independence were more willing to use deception than in cases where deception would benefit someone else. People who valued social relationships over individuality, however, reported a greater willingness to use deception to benefit others rather than for self-serving purposes.

How does one go about explaining these particular findings? Western as well as European cultures have long been noted to cultivate members who value their individuality and prefer more explicit and direct styles of communicating in order to emphasize their uniqueness. In this case, being a moral and ethical human being would require avoiding any type of communication that would jeopardize one's own personal integrity. Lying is a form of communication that could possibly compromise that integrity.

> How do such findings account for the fact that people from collectivist cultures often stereotype U.S. communicators as selfish, arrogant, and greedy?

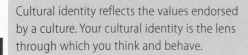

> Cultural identity reflects the values endorsed by a culture. Your cultural identity is the lens through which you think and behave.

Review the differences between high-context and low-context cultures in Chapter 3, pp. 51–52.

By comparison, East Asian cultures have been well-known for endorsing more indirect styles of communication in order to protect the image of the other and promote trouble-free relationships. In this regard, deceptive communication has and continues to serve as a useful tool in the maintenance and preservation of significant social relationships.

It should not come as a surprise then that when people of varying cultural backgrounds were asked to rate the deceptiveness of different types of deceptive responses, highly independent people rated messages that departed from the truth as highly deceptive, while highly interdependent people viewed the exact same deceptive responses as not deceptive. For example, when asked to comment on a co-worker's repulsive style of dress, those high in independent cultural orientation rated the "When is lunch?" evasive response as highly deceptive, whereas those high in interdependent orientation rated the same response as not at all deceptive.

How would you rate this response to the way a person is dressed? Are deception and evasion the same?

Just as cultures differ in their regard for the value of the individual versus the group, cultural influences are likely to impress upon the meaning of morality. Cultures in which the needs of the group take precedence over the individual tend to regard morality strictly as a social phenomenon that takes into account the needs and expectations of group members. Being a moral human being in the collective sense requires protecting the image and welfare of others in the group. If avoiding the truth will serve to achieve this end, then telling a lie would be the most moral choice. In light of this fact, it is not surprising that those with high regard for social relationships would be more inclined to avoid the truth to escape potential conflict with others.

Name five collectivist cultures that focus more on the needs and expectations of group members than on the needs of individuals.

Costly misunderstandings can arise from an interaction in which the truth was told when a less than true response was expected, or vice versa. A poignant illustration is one in which Americans and Japanese conduct business together. A Japanese businessperson, who is highly *interdependent* in cultural orientation, asks his American colleague, who is highly *independent* in cultural orientation to comment on his less than average performance on a presentation. The American, being a person of integrity, might respond with an honest "It was really disorganized. What happened?" despite the Japanese colleague's expectation of a more socially acceptable and less face-threatening response. This can potentially lead to strained relations between the two which can, in turn, have detrimental effects on the business.

Alternatively, if the American businessperson were to ask her Japanese colleague to comment on her less than average performance on a presentation, the Japanese counterpart might respond with what she regards as a less face-threatening response: "Well, you tried your best and that's what really counts." However, the American colleague, expecting an honest and candid evaluation, now doubts that her Japanese colleague can be trusted to give an honest evaluation. Cross-cultural misunderstandings of this nature are commonplace. Damages to significant social relationships as a result of these misunderstandings can run the gamut from trivial to severe.

What would you think if someone responded this way to you? Would you feel hurt, or would you appreciate the person's honest assessment?

In the final analysis, the various motivations for and perceptions that people hold about deception are greatly influenced by dominant cultural values. From greater awareness comes greater cultural sensitivity; from greater sensitivity comes a greater ability to adapt one's communication styles to the other. The result is more effective intercultural interactions and more satisfying intercultural relationships.

ABOUT THE AUTHORS

Karadeen Y. Kam is Instructor of Speech at Honolulu Community College. **Min-Sun Kim** and **William F. Sharkey** are Professors in the Department of Speech at the University of Hawaii at Manoa. **Theodore M. Singelis** is Professor in the Department of Psychology at California State University, Chico. This essay is based on Kim, M. S., Kam, K. Y., Sharkey, W. F., & Singelis, T. M. (2008). "Deception: Moral transgression or social necessity? Cultural-relativity of deception motivations and perceptions of deceptive communication." *Journal of International and Intercultural Communication*, 1, pp. 23–50. The *Journal of International and Intercultural Communication* and *Communication Currents* are publications of the National Communication Association.

How would you feel if someone responded this way to you? Would you distrust the other person, or would you just assume the person is trying to be nice by not wanting to hurt your feelings?

culture and deception: moral transgression or social necessity?

LISTENING and Critical THINKING

Y ou're walking down the street with a friend when she sees a man she knows. Your friend waves at him and pulls you over to meet him. You extend your hand and smile while your friend introduces the two of you, and says each of your names clearly. After a couple of minutes, you realize that you cannot recall his name. You don't want to appear rude by asking for his name again, especially because he's said your name several times during the conversation. Two weeks later, you bump into him and he greets you by name. You cannot return the honor.

Why do so many of us forget names? In *How to Start a Conversation and Make Friends*, Don Gabor suggests that it is because we're not *listening* effectively. We're too busy thinking about ourselves, what we're going to say, whether we will make a good impression, and how other people will react to us.[1]

Remembering names—as well as the many more complex messages you hear every day—requires two communication skills: effective listening *and* critical thinking. When you listen effectively, you do much more than hear and recognize the words in a message. Regardless of why, where, when, and to whom you listen, you should always think critically about what you hear. After all, if no one will listen to you, why communicate? And if you have not given serious thought to your message, why *should* anyone listen?

THINK About... and **ASK YOURSELF**...

4.1
The Nature of Listening
Why is listening critical for effective communication?

The International Listening Association defines **listening** as "the process of receiving, constructing meaning from, and responding to a spoken and/or nonverbal message."[2] This definition describes what effective listeners *do*; however, it does not explain *how* the listening process works. Listening—just like speaking, reading, and writing—is a complex process that goes beyond "you speak, I listen." Because many people do not appreciate this complexity, listening may appear to be easy and natural. In fact, just the opposite is true. Hearing only requires physical ability; listening requires complex thinking ability.

Listening is our number one communication activity. A study of college students that accounted for Internet and social media use found that listening occupies more than half of their communicating time.[3] Additionally, effective listening skills are a significant factor in predicting a student's academic success and survival.[4] On the flip side, poor listening is a significant factor in predicting student failure. Although percentages vary from study to study, Figure 4.1 shows how most people divide up their daily communicating time.

In the business world, many executives devote more than 60 percent of their workdays to listening to others.[5] Moreover, listening is often cited as the communication skill most lacking in new employees.[6]

How Well Do You Listen?

In *The Lost Art of Listening*, Michael Nichols writes that "Listening is so basic that we take it for granted. Unfortunately most of us think of ourselves as better listeners than we really are."[7] For example, immediately after listening to a short talk, most of us cannot accurately report 50 percent of what was said. Without training, we listen at about 25 percent efficiency.[8] And of that 25 percent, most is distorted or inaccurate.[9]

A study of Fortune 500 company training managers concludes that "ineffective listening leads to ineffective performance or low productivity." These same problems also appear in studies of sales professionals, educators, health practitioners, lawyers, and religious leaders.[10]

Listening at home is just as—or more—important. In families the common cry "Nobody around here listens to me!" may come from a frustrated mother, father, or any of the children. But good parenting necessitates good listening. Michael P. Nichols notes that "adolescents need their parents to listen to their troubles, their hopes, and ambitions, even some of their farfetched plans."[12]

Effective listening is hard work. Researchers note that active listeners register an increase in blood pressure, a higher pulse rate, and even more perspiration.[13] Active listeners try to understand what a speaker is saying, the emotions behind the content, and the conclusion the speaker is making without stating it openly.[14] Effective listening requires the kind of preparation and concentration required of attorneys trying a case and psychologists counselling a client.

Assess Your Listening Habits

In Chapter 1 we highlighted Stephen R. Covey's claim that an enduring habit must have three components: *knowledge*, *skills*, and *desire*. Here we briefly summarize how he applied this claim to listening:

1. *Knowledge*. Unless you understand the principles of human interaction, you may not even know you need to listen.
2. *Skills*. Even if you know you need to listen, you may not have the skill.
3. *Desire*. Knowing you need to listen and knowing how to listen are not enough. Unless you *want* to listen, listening won't be an enduring habit.

An interesting study expands and applies Covey's listening competencies to college students and people working in organizational settings. Research by Lynn Cooper and Trey Buchanan identified the "big five" of listening competencies. Notice how they reflect Covey's criteria for an enduring habit:[15]

1. Openness or willingness to listen
2. Ability to read nonverbal cues
3. Ability to understand verbal cues
4. Ability to respond appropriately
5. Ability to remember relevant details

> Although most of us can *hear*, we often fail to *listen* to what others say.

Listening
40–70%

Speaking
20–35%

Reading
10–20%

Writing
5–10%

Figure 4.1 How Communication Time is Spent[11]

Do You Have Poor Listening Habits?[16]

Examine the poor listening habits below and circle the response that best reflects how you listen. Notice that we have not included a "never" option because no one is a perfect listener 100 percent of the time.

Poor Listening Habits	How Frequently Do You Listen This Way?		
Defensive Listening. Do you feel threatened or humiliated by critical remarks from others? Do you focus on how to respond to or challenge another person's questions and criticisms rather than listening objectively?	Often	Sometimes	Rarely
Disruptive Listening. Do you interrupt others while they're speaking? Do you exaggerate your responses by sighing audibly, rolling your eyes, shaking your head in a *no*, or obviously withholding your attention?	Often	Sometimes	Rarely
Pseudolistening. Do you fake attention or pretend to listen when your mind is elsewhere, you're bored, or you think it pleases the speaker? Do you nod or smile even though your response has nothing to do with the message?	Often	Sometimes	Rarely
Selective Listening. If you don't like or agree with someone, do you avoid listening or look for faults in what that person says? Do you avoid listening to complex or highly technical information?	Often	Sometimes	Rarely
Superficial Listening. Do you pay more attention to the way other people look or how they speak rather than to what they say? Do you draw conclusions about others' intentions or claims before they've finished talking?	Often	Sometimes	Rarely

If you answered with an honest *rarely* to all of the questions, you are probably a good listener. If you answered *often* or *sometimes*, you have a lot to learn about listening.

4.2
The Listening Process

What are the key components of the listening process?

Listening researchers, cognitive scientists, and neurologists describe listening as a complex phenomenon. To address the complexity of listening, Judi Brownell, a leading listening researcher and author, presents a six-component HURIER listening model. The letters in HURIER represent six interrelated listening processes: **H**earing, **U**nderstanding, **R**emembering, **I**nterpreting, **E**valuating, and **R**esponding. Brownell links each of these six components to appropriate listening attitudes, relevant listening principles, and methods for improving your listening skills[17] (see Figure 4.2).

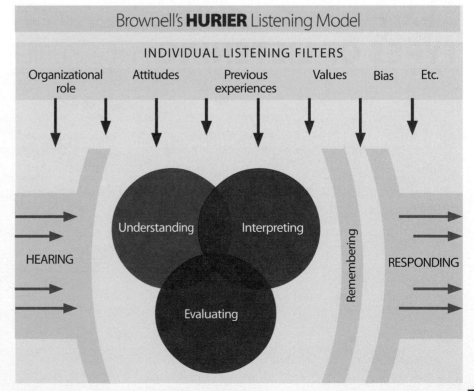

Figure 4.2 The HURIER Model of Listening.

The HURIER model "recognizes that you are constantly influenced by both internal and external factors that color your perceptions and subsequent interpretations." These listening filters include your attitudes, values, biases, and previous experiences.[18] For example, if you know that your instructor's exams include questions based on her lectures, you are more likely to listen attentively to what she says.

The HURIER model also recognizes that different listening skills become more or less important depending on both your purpose and the communication context.[19] For instance, when you're listening to a topic expert, you may be "all ears" and be open to learning and agreeing. In contrast, you may listen more critically when a less informed speaker presents a poorly structured proposal for solving a problem. And if you are listening to someone in a hot, noisy room at a late hour of the day, it may be very difficult to focus your attention and energy on the task.

Brownell's HURIER listening model highlights six types of listening to ensure that you accurately and appropriately hear, understand, remember, interpret, evaluate, and respond to spoken and/or nonverbal messages. In this section, we take a more detailed look at the different kinds of listening in the HURIER model to help you decide which ones best meet your own and others' listening needs and abilities.

Listening to Hear

Hearing, the ability to make clear, aural distinctions among the sounds and words in a language, is the "prerequisite to all listening."[20] Your hearing ability also determines whether you can detect the meaning of non-word sounds such as a groan or a laugh.

Hearing ability differs from person to person. According to the National Institute on Deafness and Other Communication Disorders, about 36 million American adults report some degree of hearing loss. Given that hearing loss is usually gradual and cumulative throughout your life, older adults have greater hearing losses than children and young adults. However, "approximately 15 percent (26 million) of Americans between the ages of 20 and 69 have high frequency hearing loss due to exposure to loud sounds or noise at work or in leisure activities."[21] Researchers at Gallaudet University report that about 2 to 4 of every 1,000 people in the United States are "functionally deaf," though more than half became deaf relatively late in life.[22] Later in this chapter, we describe the ways in which people with hearing loss listen.

Answering the following questions can help you understand why hearing is the gateway to effective listening.

- Do you often ask others to repeat what they've said or misunderstand what they've said because you did not hear them accurately?
- Do you notice nonverbal messages expressed in people's facial expressions, gestures, posture, movement, and vocal sounds (sighs, groans, laughter, gasps)?

Listening to Understand

Listening to understand, also known as comprehensive listening, focuses on accurately grasping the *meaning* of someone's spoken and nonverbal messages. After all, if you don't understand what someone means, how can you respond in a reasonable way? For example, an after-class discussion might begin as follows: "Let's have a party on the last day of class," says Geneva. If you are listening to understand, you may wonder whether Geneva means that (1) we should have a party instead of an exam, (2) we should ask the instructor whether we can have a party, or (3) we should have a party *after* the exam. Misinterpreting the meaning of Geneva's comment could result in an inappropriate response.

TYPES OF LISTENING in the HURIER Listening Model

TYPE OF LISTENING	DEFINITION	EXAMPLE
Hearing	Your ability to make clear, aural distinctions among the sounds and words in a language	I sometimes have trouble hearing a soft-spoken person, particularly if there's background noise.
Understanding	Your ability to accurately grasp the *meaning* of someone's spoken and nonverbal messages	When you say *wait*, do you mean we should wait a few more minutes or wait until Caleb gets here?
Remembering	Your ability to store, retain, and recall information you have heard	Hi George. I remember meeting you last month. Did you end up selling your old truck?
Interpreting	Your ability to empathize with another person's feelings without judging the message	It must be frustrating and discouraging to have such an unsympathetic instructor.
Evaluating	Your ability to analyze and make a judgment about the validity of someone's message	I see two reasons why that proposal won't work. They are …
Responding	Your ability to respond in a way that indicates you fully understanding someone's meaning	You seem to be saying that it's not a good time to confront Mercedes. Am I right?

Asking questions is one of the best ways to make sure you understand the meaning of someone's words and nonverbal behavior.[23] The strategies in the figure to the right about asking good questions constitutes a blueprint for determining what a person means.

Listening to Remember

How good is your memory? How well do you store, retain, and recall information? Do you ever forget what you're talking about during a discussion? Can you remember a person's name or a phone number if you haven't written it down? Occasionally, everyone experiences memory problems. As we noted earlier in this chapter, most people cannot recall 50 percent of what they hear immediately after hearing it. At the same time, your ability to remember directly affects how well you listen.

When we ask students "How good is *your* memory?" they often answer,

Ask **GOOD QUESTIONS** to Ensure Understanding

1. **Have a plan.** Make sure your question is clear and appropriate so it will not be misunderstood or waste time.
2. **Keep the questions simple.** Ask one question at a time and make sure it's relevant to the message.
3. **Ask nonthreatening questions.** Avoid questions that begin with "Why didn't you … ?" or "How could you … ?" because they can create a defensive climate in responders.
4. **Ask permission.** If a topic is sensitive, explain why you are asking the question and ask permission before continuing. "You say you're fearful about telling Sharon about the mistake you made. Would you mind helping me understand why you're so apprehensive?"
5. **Avoid biased or manipulative questions.** Tricking someone into giving you the answer you want can destroy trust. There's a big difference between "Why did we miss the deadline?" and "Who screwed up?"
6. **Wait for the answer.** In addition to asking good questions, respond appropriately to the response you receive. After you ask a question, give the other person time to think and then wait for the answer.

"It depends." For example, if you're very interested in what someone's saying you're more likely to remember the conversation, discussion, or presentation. However, if you're under a lot of stress or preoccupied with personal problems, you may not remember anything. Here are just a few

THINK ABOUT THEORY

Listening and Working Memory

People with more working memory capacity are more likely to **understand** what others mean, to **analyze** complex issues and discussion threads, to **track** relevant and irrelevant interactions, and to **develop** appropriate responses.

Early studies of listening focused on understanding **short-term memory**, the content you remember immediately after listening to a series of numbers or words. Psychologist Samuel Wood and colleagues note that this kind of "short-term memory has a very limited capacity—about seven (plus or minus two) different items or bits of information at one time. This is just enough for phone numbers and ordinary zip codes."[24] We use something much more complex than short-term memory to engage in effective listening.

Working memory theory recognizes that listening involves more than the ability to tap your short-term memory. Listening engages your **working memory**. Psychologists define working memory as the memory subsystem we use to comprehend, remember, and form a mental image of what is going on around us; we use working memory to learn new things, solve problems, and form and act on goals.[25] Listening researcher Laura Janusik describes working memory as "a dual-task system involving processing and storage functions. The processing function is synonymous with attention, and the storage function is synonymous with memory. Attention is allocated, and resources not used for attention are available for storage."[26] Your working memory does more than store what you've heard; it allows you to shift what you've heard and understood "from and into long-term memory" as a way to create new meanings.[27]

Peter Desberg, author of *Speaking Scared Sounding Good*, describes working memory as a clearinghouse where you have fewer than 30 seconds to decide if the information is worth keeping and storing in your long-term memory. If your brain is preoccupied or doesn't take the time to process the information, the information disappears.[28]

suggestions that, with practice, can improve your memory:

- **Repeat.** Repeat an important idea or piece of information after you hear it; say it aloud if you can. For example, if you've just learned that your class project group report is due on the 22nd, use this date in a sentence several times ("Let's see how many meetings we need to have before the 22nd"; "We'll need to have our first draft done a week ahead of time—22 minus 7 is 15"). If you're in a situation where it's not appropriate to do this aloud, repeat the information in your mind.

- **Associate.** Associate a word, phrase, or idea with something that describes it. For example, when you meet someone whose name you want to remember, associate the name with the context in which you met the person (Jamal in biology class) or with a word beginning with the same letter that describes the person (Blonde Brenda).

- **Visualize.** Visualize a word, phrase, or idea. For example, when a patient was told she might need to take calcium channel blockers, she visualized a swimmer trying to cross the English Channel filled with floating calcium pills.

- **Use mnemonics.** A *mnemonic* is a memory aid that is based on something simple like a pattern or rhyme. For example, the HURIER in Brownell's Model of Listening is an acronym (the first letters for the six components of listening). Many people remember which months of the year have 30 days with the poem that begins "Thirty days hath September . . . ." For instance, by rearranging the above memory suggestions, you might be able to remember MARV (mnemonics, associate, repeat, visualize).

Remembering Names

At the beginning of this chapter, we described the frequent challenge of recalling a new acquaintance's name even a few minutes after hearing it. In *How to Start a Conversation and Make Friends*, Don Gabor suggests six strategies for remembering someone's name:

> **"I'm sorry, I forgot your name."**

poet who wrote the *Iliad* and *Odyssey*. If you meet someone who looks like a childhood friend, teachers, relative, or even celebrity with the same name, associate the new person with the name of that person.

1. Focus on the moment of introduction—rather than on yourself.

2. Don't think about what to say—listen for the name and information about the person.

3. Repeat the name out loud when you hear it.

4. Think of someone you know or someone famous with the same name. For example, if you meet someone named Homer, think about Homer Simpson or the epic

5. Link the person's name to a unique characteristic such as a word that begins with the same letter (Strong Sergio, Laughing Lewis, Cooking Cathy), a characteristic word that rhymes with the person's name (Curley Shirley, Slim Jim), or a word that reminds of you of an event (Tom's Toe because you met him the night he broke his toe).

6. Use the name during and at the end of the conversation.[29]

Listening to Interpret

Judi Brownell equates the ability to interpret what someone says as "a primary factor in empathic listening, where your ability to recognize and respond appropriately to emotional meanings is critical."[30] Empathic listening answers this question: How does the other person feel? **Empathic listening** goes beyond comprehending what a person means; it involves focusing on understanding someone's situation, feelings, or motives. Can you see the situation through the other person's eyes? How would you feel in a similar situation?

By not listening for feelings, you may overlook the most important part of a message. Even if you understand every word a person says, you can still miss the anger, enthusiasm, or frustration in someone's voice. As an empathic listener, you don't have to

> **"[Listening] involves learning how to suspend your own emotional agenda and then realizing the rewards of genuine empathy."**
>
> —Michael Nichols, *The Lost Art of Listening*.[31]

agree with or feel the same way as others, but you do have to try to understand the type and intensity of feelings they are experiencing. For example, the after-class discussion mentioned earlier might continue as follows: "A class party would be a waste of time!" exclaims Kim. An empathic listener may wonder whether Kim means that

(1) she has more important things to do during exam week, (2) she doesn't think the class or the instructor deserves a party, or (3) she doesn't want to attend such a party.

Empathic listening is difficult, but it also is "the pinnacle of listening" because it demands "fine skill and exquisite tuning into another's mood and feeling."[32]

Answering the following questions can help you understand the scope of empathic listening:

- Do you show interest and concern about the other person?

- Does your nonverbal behavior communicate friendliness and trust?

- Do you avoid highly critical reactions to others?

- Do you avoid talking about your own experiences and feelings when someone else is describing theirs?[33]

Apply the Golden Listening Rule

The **golden listening rule** is easy to remember: *Listen to others as you would have them listen to you.* Unfortunately, this rule can be difficult to follow. It asks you to suspend your own needs and opinions to listen to someone else's.[34]

The golden listening rule is also an ethical listening practice. It reflects a principle in the National Communication Association's Credo for Ethical Communication: "We strive to understand and respect other communicators before evaluating and responding to their message."[35] When you follow the golden listening rule, you communicate your interest, patience, and open-mindedness.

The golden listening rule is not so much a "rule" as it is a positive listening attitude. If you aren't motivated to listen, you won't listen. Effective listeners have made listening an enduring habit by recognizing the importance of good listening, learning effective listening skills, and—perhaps most important of all—*wanting* to listen. An appropriate listening attitude does not mean that you know exactly what another person thinks or feels. Rather, it requires a strong motivation to listen and discover.[36] The six positive listening attitudes that follow have six negative counterparts:[37]

How Positive Is Your Listening Attitude?

Positive Listening Attitudes	Negative Listening Attitudes
Interested	Uninterested
Responsible	Irresponsible
Group-centered	Self-centered
Patient	Impatient
Equal	Superior
Open-minded	Closed-minded

Listening to Evaluate

Evaluative listening requires that you employ critical thinking skills to analyze what someone says. Once you are sure you've comprehended the meaning of a message, ask yourself whether your reasoning is sound and the conclusion is justified. Evaluative listeners understand why they accept or reject someone's ideas and suggestions. They make judgments based on their evaluation of another person's message: Is the speaker right or wrong, logical or illogical? Should I accept or reject the speaker's ideas and suggestions? Evaluative listeners are open-minded. They put aside biases or prejudices about the speaker or message when they analyze what they hear in order to arrive at a rational conclusion or decision.

Recognizing that someone is trying to persuade—rather than merely inform—is one of the first steps in improving your evaluative listening. Ask yourself the following questions to determine your ability to listen and evaluate what you hear:[38]

- Do you recognize persuasive communication strategies?

- Can you tell when someone is appealing to your emotions and/or to your critical thinking ability?

- Can you assess the quality and validity of arguments and evidence?

The ability to think critically as you listen and carefully evaluate what someone is saying is a difficult but learnable skill. The final section of this chapter focuses on the critical thinking skills you need to enhance the quality of communication and to separate the valid from invalid claims you hear.

Listening to Respond

When you listen to others (and especially if you listen to hear, understand, remember, interpret, and evaluate), you are likely to respond verbally and/or nonverbally. You may ask a question, provide support, offer advice, or share your opinion. You may frown, smile, laugh, shrug, or look confused. Fortunately, there is a critical responding skill that can help you make sure you fully understand someone else's meaning. That skill is called paraphrasing, and it is critical to becoming a highly effective listener.

The Nature of Paraphrasing Paraphrasing is the ability to restate what people say in a way that indicates you understand them. When you paraphrase, you go beyond the words you hear to understand the feelings and underlying meanings that accompany the words. Too often, we jump to conclusions and incorrectly assume that we know what a speaker means and feels.

Paraphrasing is a form of feedback—a listening check—that asks, "Am I right—is this what you mean?" Paraphrasing is not repeating what a person says; it requires finding *new* words to describe what you have heard.

Functions of PARAPHRASING

- To ensure comprehension before evaluation
- To reassure others that you want to understand them
- To clear up confusion and ask for clarification
- To summarize lengthy comments
- To help others uncover their own thoughts and feelings
- To provide a safe and supportive communication climate
- To help others reach their own conclusions[39]

> Effective paraphrasing requires mindful listening. Paraphrasing says, "I want to hear what you have to say, and I want to understand what you mean."

Type of Paraphrase	Effective Paraphrase Example	Ineffective Paraphrase Example
Susan: "I never seem to get anywhere on time and I don't know why."		
Paraphrase Content: Find new words to express the same meaning. Paraphrase, don't parrot.	"Sounds as though you've tried to figure out the reasons why you're often late but can't. Is that what you're saying?"	"Ah, so you don't know why you never seem to get anywhere on time?" Susan's response: "Yeah, that's what I just said."
Susan: "People, including my boss, bug me about being late, and sometimes I can tell that they're pretty angry."		
Paraphrase Depth: Match the emotions to the speaker's meaning. Avoid responding lightly to a serious problem and vice versa.	"When you say that people are angry, you sound as though it's become serious enough to put your job at risk or damage your relationships with your boss and coworkers; is that right?"	"In other words, you worry that other people are upset by your lateness."
Susan: "I really don't know . . ."		
Paraphrase Meaning: Match the overall meaning. Avoid adding unintended meaning or completing the speaker's sentences.	"Let me make sure I understand what you're saying. Is it that you don't know why you're always late, or that you wish you had a better idea of how to manage your time?"	". . . how to manage your time?" (Susan was intending to finish her sentence with "what to do.")
Susan: "So I still can't figure out why I'm always late getting to the office."		
Paraphrase Language: Use clear, simple language to ensure the person's understands your paraphrase.	"It sounds as though being late has become a big problem at work and you're looking for ways to fix it. Right?"	"Ahh, your importunate perplexities about punctuality are inextricably linked." Susan's response: "Huh?"

Figure 4.3 Types of Paraphrasing

The Complexities of Paraphrasing Paraphrasing is difficult. Not only are you putting aside your own interests and opinions, but you are also finding *new* words that best match someone else's meaning. Figure 4.3 above shows how a paraphrase can vary in four critical ways: content, depth, meaning, and language.[40]

Paraphrasing says, "I want to hear what you have to say, and I want to understand what you mean." If you paraphrase accurately, the other person will appreciate your understanding and support. Even if you don't get the paraphrase right, your feedback provides another opportunity for the speaker to explain.[41]

STOP&THINK

Paraphrase This

Read the following three statements and write a response that paraphrases their meaning, as demonstrated in the following example:

Group member: "I get really annoyed when André yells at one of us during our meetings."

Paraphrase: *"You sound as though you become very upset when André shouts at you or other group members. Is that what's bothering you?"*

1. **Friend:** I have the worst luck with computers. The computer I have now has crashed again, and I lost all of my documents. Maybe I'm doing something wrong. Why me?

   Paraphrase: _____

2. **Colleague:** I dislike saying *no* to anyone who asks for help, but then I have to rush or stay up late to get my own work done. I want to help, but I also want to do my own job.

   Paraphrase: _____

   _____

3. **Classmate:** How on earth am I going to get an A on this exam if I can't even find time to read the textbook?

   Paraphrase: _____

   _____

Listening Strategies and Skills

What listening strategies and skills can help you communicate more effectively?

At this point, you should know *why* good listening is essential for effective and ethical communication. You should also have some ideas about how to better hear, understand, remember, interpret, evaluate, and respond appropriately to others. In this section, we introduce several general listening strategies and skills that can improve your listening ability in most contexts and help you develop effective listening habits. When and how you use these strategies depends, in part, on whether you are the speaker or the listener (or both) and whether you are speaking to one person or a large group of people.

Use Your Extra Thought Speed

Most people talk at about 125 to 150 words per minute. But most of us can *think* at three to four times that rate.[42] Thus, we have about 400 extra words of spare thinking time during every minute a person talks to us.

Thought speed is the speed (words per minute) at which most people can think compared with the speed at which they can speak. Poor listeners use their extra thought speed to daydream, engage in side conversations, take unnecessary notes, or plan how to confront a speaker. Conscientious listeners use their extra thought speed to enhance all types of listening.

You can use your extra thought speed to:

- make sure you **hear** what someone says.
- determine the **meaning** of a message.
- identify and summarize **key ideas**.
- **remember** what someone says.
- **empathize** with a person's expressed **feelings**.
- **analyze** and **evaluate** arguments.
- determine the most appropriate way to **respond** to what you hear.

How to Use Your THOUGHT SPEED

- Identify and summarize key ideas and opinions
- Pay extra attention to the meaning of nonverbal behavior
- Analyze the strengths and weaknesses of arguments
- Assess the relevance of a speaker's message

Listen to Feedback

One of the most important and challenging communication skills is listening to and providing appropriate feedback to others during a conversation, meeting, or presentation. Feedback, the verbal and nonverbal responses others communicate as they listen, reveals how listeners react—negatively or positively—to you and your message.

All listeners react in some way. They may smile or frown or nod "yes" or "no." They may break into spontaneous applause or not applaud at all. They may sit forward at full attention or sit back and look bored.

> ... next to the words you say, your face is the primary source of information about you and the meaning of your message.
>
> —Mark Knapp and Judith Hall[43]

Analyzing your listeners' feedback helps determine how you and your message affect others. As you speak, look and listen to the ways in which people react to you. Do they look interested or uninterested, pleased or displeased? If you can't see or hear reactions, ask for feedback. You can stop in the middle of a conversation, meeting, or presentation to ask whether others understand you. Soliciting feedback helps you adapt to your listeners and tells your listeners that you are interested in their reactions. It also helps others focus their attention and listen more effectively to your message.

Listen to Nonverbal Behavior

Very often, another person's meaning is expressed through nonverbal behavior (see Chapter 6). For example, a change in vocal tone or volume may be another way of saying, "Listen up! This is very important." A person's sustained eye contact may mean, "I'm talking to you!" Facial expressions can reveal whether a person is experiencing joy, skepticism, or fear. Nonverbal behavior also reveals others' intentions. A recent study found that children as young as three are less likely to help a person at a later point in time after seeing them harm someone else. What's intriguing about this finding is that "the toddlers judged a person's intention" by observing their nonverbal behavior. In other words— just like most three-year-olds— most of us can determine others'

intentions without hearing them say a single word.[44]

Gestures express emotions that words cannot convey. For example, at the moment during a trial when an attorney makes his final argument to the jury that his client should be acquitted, one juror, almost imperceptibly, moves her head back and forth, signifying "no." When the attorney states that his client had no idea that a crime had been committed, another juror raises one eyebrow with a look that says, "Okay, you've done your best to defend your client, but you and I know he's guilty as sin." In the end, the jury finds the defendant guilty as charged.

Listen Before You Leap

Ralph Nichols, often called the "father of listening research," counsels listeners to make sure they understand a speaker's message *before* reacting, either positively or negatively. This strategy requires taking time to bring your emotions under control. You may comprehend a speaker perfectly but be infuriated or offended by what you hear. If an insensitive speaker refers to women in the room as "chicks" or a minority group as "those people," you may need to count to 20 to collect your thoughts and refocus your attention on comprehensive listening.

The Personal Listening Styles Controversy

Communication research on listening is dynamic and continues to evolve. In 1995, communication researchers Kittie Watson, Larry Barker, and James Weaver theorized that each of us prefers and uses one or more of four distinct listening styles. They claimed that by understanding your preferred listening style or styles, you "can explore other styles and learn how to adapt [your] behaviors accordingly to maximize communication."[45]

In 2010 and 2011, researchers Graham Bodie, Debra Worthington, and Christopher Gearhart analyzed the personal listening styles concept proposed by Watson, Barker, and Weaver and concluded that the four styles cannot be validated as distinct or separate from one another and do not represent a reliable explanation of listening styles.[46] They also provided substantive evidence supporting an alternative set of listening styles as well as a statistically validated instrument to measure those styles. The table in this box lists each set of listening styles.

At first glance, these two sets of listening style may seem very similar. What makes them different is the way in which each listening style is defined

Which style or styles do you generally prefer and use when listening to others?

and the instruments used to uncover and measure each style. In light of the original research by Watson, Barker, and Weaver and the analysis by Bodie, Worthington, and Gearhart do your best to answer the following questions:

1. If you have a preferred listening style or styles, what are the positive and negative characteristics of that style?
2. How, if at all, can understanding these four styles help you adapt to others?
3. Which of the two lists makes the most sense to you? How can continued research help us better understand the complex task of listening to others?

Personal Listening Styles Research

Watson, Barker, and Weaver	Bodie, Worthington, and Gearhart
Action-oriented: Focuses on objectives and results; prefers clear and structured messages; focuses on what will be done and who will do it	**Task Listening:** Focuses on completing simple communication transactions effectively and efficiently; describes listeners who need structure
Time-oriented: Focuses on the clock; time and listening are organized in neat segments; wants short answers to question	**Critical Listening:** Focuses on noting inconsistencies and errors when others speak; listens to evaluate what others say
People-oriented: Focuses on feelings, emotions, and understanding others; responds with "we" statements; Interested in understanding, not criticizing	**Relational Listening:** Focuses on understanding emotions and connecting with others; empathic listening
Content-oriented: Focuses on what is said, not who says it; not concerned about feelings; interested in facts, evidence, logic, and complex ideas	**Analytical Listening:** Focuses on withholding judgment about others' ideas in order to consider all sides of an issue before responding

> **"We must always withhold evaluation until our comprehension is complete."**
>
> —Ralph Nichols[47]

What are students "telling" this instructor (who is reading from his lecture notes)?

If a speaker tells an offensive joke, you may react with both anger at the speaker and disappointment with those who laughed. Try to understand the effects of offensive comments and emotion-laden words without losing your composure or concentration.

When you listen before you leap, you are using your extra thought speed to decide how to react to controversial, prejudiced, or offensive comments. Listening before you leap gives you time to adjust your reaction and to clarify and correct a statement rather than offend, disrupt, or infuriate others.

Minimize Distractions

Have you ever attended a lecture where the room was too hot, the seats were uncomfortable, or people in the hallway were talking loudly? Distractions such as loud and annoying noises, poor seating arrangements, foul odors, frequent interruptions, and unattractive décor can make listening very difficult.[48] Other forms of distraction include a speaker's delivery that is too soft, fast, slow, or monotone; an accent that is unfamiliar; or mannerisms and appearance that appear unconventional or distracting.

You can help people listen better by taking action to overcome distractions. For example, when a distraction is physical, you are well within your rights as a listener or speaker to shut a door, open a window, or turn on more lights. In large groups, you may want to ask permission to improve the group's surroundings. Depending on the circumstances and setting, you can also take direct action to reduce behavioral distractions. If someone is talking or fidgeting while the speaker is addressing the audience, ask that person to stop. After all, if someone is distracting you, he or she is probably distracting others. If someone is speaking too quietly, kindly ask the presenter to speak more loudly.

Take Relevant Notes

Given that most of us only listen at 25 percent efficiency, why not take notes and write down important facts and big ideas? Research has found that note takers recall messages in more detail than non–note takers.[49]

Taking notes makes a great deal of sense but *only* if it is done skillfully. If you are like most listeners, only one-fourth of what is said may end up in your notes. Even if you copy every word you hear, your notes will not include the nonverbal cues that often tell you more about what a person means and feels. And if you spend all your time taking notes, when will you put aside your pen and ask or answer an important question?

Ralph Nichols summarizes the dilemma of balancing note taking and listening when he concludes that "there is some evidence to indicate that the volume of notes taken and their value to the taker are inversely related."[50] This does not mean you should stop taking notes, but you should learn how to take useful notes—the key to which is adaptability. Effective listeners adjust their note taking to the content, style, and organizational pattern of a speaker.

If someone tells stories to make a point, jot down a brief reminder of the story and its point. If a professor lists tips, dos and don'ts, or recommendations, include those lists in your notes. If someone asks and answers a series of questions, your notes should reflect that pattern. If someone describes a new concept or explains a try to paraphrase the meaning in your notes or jot down questions you want to ask.

Good listeners are flexible and adaptable notetakers.

4.4
Listening to Gender and Culture

How do gender and culture affect the way we listen?

Understanding and adapting to the diverse listening skills, types, and levels of others can be a challenging task, particularly when gender and cultural differences are taken into account. Keep in mind that there are many exceptions to the research summaries we present about listening differences. As you read, you may say, "But I know women who don't listen this way." The existence of exceptions does not mean that the general claim is false. Diversity research provides useful insights that help explain common differences in listening behavior.

Gender and Listening

The listening behaviors of women and men often differ. In general, men are more likely to listen to the content of what is said, whereas women focus on the relationship between the speaker and listener. Males tend to hear the facts, whereas females are more even aware of the mood of the communication. In other words, men generally focus on comprehensive and analytical listening, whereas women are more likely to be empathic and appreciative listeners.

Culture and Listening

In Chapter 3, "Adapting to Others," we introduced the concept of high- and low-context cultures. In comparision to low-context countries, in high-context countries such as Japan, China, and Korea and in African American, American Indian, and Arab cultures, not all meaning is expressed through words. Much more attention is given to nonverbal cues and the relationships among the communicators. As a result, listeners from high-context cultures "listen" for meanings in your behavior and in who you are rather than in the words you say. However, most listeners from Germany, Switzerland, Scandinavia, and the United States focus on words. They expect speakers to be direct. When high-context speakers talk to low-context listeners—and vice versa—misunderstanding, offense, and even conflict may result. In many Asian cultures, the amount of time spent talking and the value placed on talking are very different than they are in the United States and Latin America.

COMMUNICATION IN *ACTION*

How Men and Women Listen to Each Other

Many women complain that their male partners and colleagues don't listen to them. Interestingly, men sometimes make the same complaint about women. Linguist Deborah Tannen explains that the accusation "You're not listening" often means "You don't understand what I said" or "I'm not getting the response I want."[51]

Tannen offers an explanation for why it may *seem* that men don't listen. Quite simply, many men don't *show* they are listening, whereas women do. In general, women provide more feedback when listening: They provide listening responses, like *mhm, uh-huh,* and *yeah.* And women respond more positively and enthusiastically by nodding and laughing. To a man (who expects a listener to be quiet and attentive), a woman giving off a stream of feedback and support will seem to be "talking" too much for a listener. To a woman (who expects a listener to be active and show interest, attention, and support),

> **"It sounds like a typical "he said/she said" situation."**

a man who listens silently will seem to have checked out of the conversation. The bottom line is this: Women may get the impression that men don't listen when, in fact, they are listening. Unfortunately, there are also men who really don't want to listen because they believe that it puts them in a subordinate position to women.[52]

Researchers also note that men often tune out things they can't solve or wonder why they should even listen if there isn't a problem to solve. Women may become more involved and connected to the speaker and see listening as something important to do for the other person.[53] Although men use talk to establish status, women are more likely to use listening to empower others. Unfortunately, people who listen much more than they talk are often viewed as subordinate and subservient rather than powerful.[54]

4.5

The Nature of Critical Thinking

How does critical thinking enhance the quality of communication?

Critical thinking is the thought process you use to analyze what you read, see, or hear to arrive at a justified conclusion or decision. It is a conscious process that, when effective, can result in a conclusion, decision, opinion, or behavior.[56] It can also result in a more meaningful conversation, group discussion, or presentation. Good critical thinkers know how to develop and defend a position on an issue, ask probing questions, be open-minded, and draw reasonable conclusions.[57] They are also highly skilled listeners who know how to accurately hear, understand, remember, interpret, and evaluate messages as well as appropriately respond to others.

The rest of this chapter focuses on critical thinking strategies and skills to help you analyze the claims, facts, inferences, arguments, and thinking errors you encounter every day.

Critical Thinking About Claims

A **claim** is a statement that identifies your belief or position on a particular issue or topic. For example, claims answer the question "What am I trying to explain or prove?" In Chapter 16, you will learn how to create strong **arguments** by providing persuasive evidence or reasons for accepting a strong claim. Here, we describe several types of claims, as shown below. You might claim that something is true or

TYPE OF CLAIM	FUNCTION	EXAMPLE
FACT	States that something is true, that an event occurred, that a cause can be identified, or that a theory correctly explains a phenomenon.	• Obese children are at risk for heart disease, diabetes, and kidney failure in early adulthood. • Viruses, not bacteria, cause the common cold.
CONJECTURE	Suggests that something will or will not happen in the future.	• The economy will improve next year. • By 2050, whites will be one of many minority groups in the United States.
VALUE	Asserts the worth of something—good or bad, right or wrong, best, average, or worst.	• Ben is the best applicant. • Plagiarism is unethical.
POLICY	Recommends a course of action or solution to a problem.	• Our state should ban smoking in all public places. • All college students should take a communication course.

false, probable or improbable, good or bad, or reasonable or unreasonable.

Critical Thinking About Facts and Inference

In addition to understanding the different types of claims, critical thinkers know how to separate claims of fact (a statement that can be proved true or false) from inferences. An **inference** is a conclusion based on claims of fact. For example, "Julia has been late to the last three project meetings" is a claim of fact. You can document the truth of this statement. However, the statement "Julia does not care about our team's project" is an inference that may or may not be true.

Critical thinking helps you separate verifiable facts from questionable inferences. When you accept an inference as a fact, you are jumping to conclusions that may not be justified. When you assume that an inference is true, you may be led down a path that leads to a poor decision. Julia's tardiness might instead be the result of car trouble, unreliable child care, or the needs of an elderly parent. More facts are needed to make a justifiable inference.

Critical Thinking About Fallacies

If you listen effectively and think critically about the content of conversations and quarrels, group discussions and meetings, speeches and presentations, media reports, and books, you will encounter valid and invalid claims. One way to recognize invalid arguments is to look for fallacies. A **fallacy** is an error in thinking that has the potential to mislead or deceive others. Fallacies can be intentional or unintentional.

After you've learned to identify a variety of fallacies, don't be surprised if you begin noticing them everywhere—in television commercials, in political campaigns, on talk radio, and in everyday conversations. As you learn about fallacies, ask yourself what is fallacious about advertisers' claims that "no other aspirin is more effective for pain than ours" and appeals to "buy America's best-selling pickup truck"? Are fallacies involved when a political candidate talks about an opponent's past as an antiwar protester or a recovering alcoholic? We highlight six of the most common fallacies below.

Attacking the Person The fallacy of **attacking the person** also has a Latin name—*ad hominem*—which means "against the man." An *ad hominem* argument makes irrelevant attacks against a person rather than against the content of a person's message. Responding to the claim "Property taxes should be increased" with "What would you know? You don't own a home!" attacks the person rather than the argument. Name-calling, labeling, and attacking a person rather than the substance of an argument are unethical, *ad hominem* fallacies. Political campaign ads are notorious for attacking candidates in personal ways rather than addressing their positions on important public issues.

> When an unethical communicator misuses evidence or reasoning or when a well-meaning person misinterprets evidence or draws erroneous conclusions, the result is still the same— inaccuracy and deception.

COMMON **FALLACIES**

FALLACY	DEFINITION	EXAMPLE
ATTACKING THE PERSON	Claiming that a person's opinions and arguments are wrong or untrue by attacking the person rather than what they are saying	Of course, she supports universal health care for everyone—she's a socialist!
APPEAL TO AUTHORITY	Basing a claim on the opinion of a supposed expert who has no relevant experience on the issues being discussed	Look at all the celebrities who support him for governor. He must be the best candidate.
APPEAL TO POPULARITY	Claiming that an action is acceptable or excusable because many people are doing it	The Kindle is much better than the Nook because more people buy Kindles.
APPEAL TO TRADITION	Claiming that a certain course of action should be followed because it has always been done that way in the past	Grandma says that drinking brandy with a little honey is the best way to cure a cold.
FAULTY CAUSE	Claiming that a particular situation or event is the cause of another event before ruling out other possible causes	In our family we rarely get sick because we drink brandy with honey when we feel a cold coming on.
HASTY GENERALIZATION	Claiming that something is true based on too little evidence or too few experiences	My neighbor told me that vaccines cause autism and other disabilities in children.

STOP&THINK

Can You Tell a Fact from an Inference?[59]

Read the story carefully and assume that all the information presented is accurate and true while understanding that the story has ambiguous parts purposely designed to lead you astray. Then read the statements about the story and for each, select one of the following options:

T: The statement is definitely true on the basis of the information presented.

F: The statement is definitely false.

?: The statement may be true or false, but it is unclear from the information available.

Answer each statement in order, and do not go back to change previous answers. Once you have completed and counted the number of correct answers you have, take time to analyze the answers you selected and why.

STORY: A businessman had just turned off the lights in the store when a man appeared and demanded money. The owner opened the cash register. The contents of the cash register were scooped up and the man sped away. A member of the police force was notified promptly.

Statements About the Story:

T	F	?	1. A man appeared after the owner had turned off his store lights.
T	F	?	2. The robber was a man.
T	F	?	3. The man who appeared did not demand money.
T	F	?	4. The man who opened the cash register was the owner.
T	F	?	5. The store owner scooped up the contents of the cash register and ran away.
T	F	?	6. Someone opened the cash register.
T	F	?	7. After the man who demanded the money scooped up the contents of the cash register, he ran away.
T	F	?	8. While the cash register contained money, the story does not state how much.
T	F	?	9. The robber demanded money of the owner.
T	F	?	10. A businessperson turned off the lights when a man appeared in the store.
T	F	?	11. It was broad daylight when the man appeared.
T	F	?	12. The man who appeared opened the cash register.
T	F	?	13. No one demanded money.
T	F	?	14. The story concerns a series of events in which only three persons are referred to: the owner of the store, a man who demanded money, and a member of the police force.
T	F	?	15. The following events occurred: someone demanded money, a cash register was opened, its contents were scooped up, and a man dashed out of the store.

Answers: (1) ?, (2) ?, (3) F, (4) ?, (5) ?, (6) T, (7) ?, (8) ?, (9) ?, (10) ?, (11) ?, (12) ?, (13) F, (14) ?, (15) ?.

Appeal to Authority So-called expert opinion is often used to support arguments. However, when the supposed expert has no relevant experience on the issues being discussed, the fallacy of **appeal to authority** occurs, as in "I'm not a doctor, but I play one on TV, and I recommend Nick's Cough Syrup." Unless the actor has expert credentials on medical issues, the argument is fallacious. You see television and magazine advertisements in which celebrities praise the medicines they use, the companies that insure them, and the beauty products that make them look young and attractive. Just because someone is a good actor or good looking does not make her or him an expert on these topics.

Appeal to Popularity An **appeal to popularity** claims that an action is acceptable or excusable because many people are doing it. "Most of your neighbors have agreed to support the rezoning proposal" is an appeal to popularity. Just because a lot of people hold a particular belief or engage in an action does not make it right. If most of your friends overindulge on alcohol, should you? If lots of people tell you that penicillin can cure a common cold, should you demand a prescription from your doctor? Unfortunately, appeals to popularity have also been used to justify discrimination, unscrupulous financial schemes, and dangerous behavior.

Appeal to Tradition Claiming that a certain course of action should be followed because it was done that way in the past is an **appeal to tradition**. "We must have our annual company picnic in August because that's when we always schedule it" appeals to tradition. Just because a course of action has been followed for a time does not mean it is the best option.

Faulty Cause "We are losing sales because our sales team is not working hard enough." This statement may overlook other causes for low sales, such as a price increase that made the product less affordable or a competitor's superior product. The **faulty cause** fallacy occurs when you claim that a particular situation or event is the cause of another event before ruling out other possible causes. Will you catch a cold if you don't bundle up when you go outside? Will you have bad luck if you break a mirror? If you answer yes to either of these questions, you are not thinking critically. *Viruses* cause colds, although a chill can weaken your immune system. Beliefs about breaking a mirror or walking under a ladder or allowing a black cat to cross your path are nothing more than superstitions.

Hasty Generalizations You commit a **hasty generalization** fallacy when

Superstitions are faulty cause fallacies.

you jump to a conclusion based on too little evidence or too few experiences. The fallacy argues that if it is true for some, it must be true for all. "Don't go to that restaurant. I went once and the service was awful" is a hasty generalization. One negative experience does not mean that other visits to the restaurant would not be enjoyable.

Oprah Winfrey is viewed as an authority by her fans. When her talk show was still on the air and she chose a book for her Book Club, it sold millions. When she talked about her favorite products, stores were swamped with eager shoppers. When she raved about a film, it became a hit.

STOP&THINK

Do Emotions Matter in Critical Thinking?

Sometimes, emotions trigger a response that defies rational thinking. In such cases, instincts may be more reliable than a conclusion based on detailed analysis. Antonio Damasio, a neurologist, maintains that emotions play a crucial role in critical thinking. In his studies of patients with damage to the emotional centers of their brains, Damasio found that a lack of feelings actually impaired rational decision making.[60]

Emotions, gut feelings, instincts, hunches, and practical wisdom can help you make good decisions. They help you understand how decisions affect others and provide a way of assessing value when considering competing options.

Although you should pay attention to your emotions, they can also act as a barrier to critical thinking and decision making. Your intuitions and hunches are not always correct. For this reason, emotions must be balanced with critical thinking. Think about these popular sayings: "Opposites attract" and "Absence makes the heart grow fonder." Are these statements true? As much as your personal experiences or conventional wisdom may confirm both of these maxims, social science research suggests that both are usually wrong.

Student Listening Inventory[61]

Use the following numbers to indicate how often you, as a student, engage in the following listening behaviors. The "speaker" can refer to the instructor or another student.

1 = almost never   2 = not often   3 = sometimes   4 = more often than not   5 = almost always

Scoring: Add up your scores to assess how well you think you listen.

Listening Behavior

1. When someone is speaking to me, I purposely block out distractions such as side conversations and personal problems.   _____

2. I ask questions when I don't understand something a speaker has said.   _____

3. When a speaker uses words I don't know, I jot them down and look them up later.   _____

4. I assess a speaker's credibility while listening.   _____

5. I paraphrase and/or summarize a speaker's main ideas in my head as I listen.   _____

6. I concentrate on a speaker's main ideas rather than the specific details.   _____

7. I try to understand people who speak both directly and indirectly.   _____

8. Before reaching a conclusion, I try to confirm fully with the speaker my understanding of the message.   _____

9. I fully concentrate when a speaker is explaining a complex idea.   _____

10. When listening, I devote my full attention to a speaker's message.   _____

11. I apply what I know about cultural differences when listening to someone from another culture.   _____

12. I watch a speaker's facial expressions and body language for meaning.   _____

13. I give positive nonverbal feedback to speakers—nods, eye contact, vocalized agreement.   _____

14. When listening to a speaker, I establish eye contact and stop doing nonrelated tasks.   _____

15. I avoid tuning out speakers when I disagree with or dislike their message.   _____

16. When I have an emotional response to a speaker or the message, I try to set aside my feelings and continue listening to the message.   _____

17. I try to match my nonverbal responses to my verbal responses.   _____

18. When someone begins speaking, I focus my attention on the message.   _____

19. I try to understand how past experiences influence the ways in which I interpret a message.   _____

20. I attempt to eliminate outside interruptions and distractions.   _____

21. When I listen, I look at the speaker, maintain some eye contact, and focus on the message.   _____

22. I avoid tuning out messages that are complex, complicated, and challenging.   _____

23. I try to understand the other person's point of view when it is different from mine.   _____

24. I try to be nonjudgmental and noncritical when I listen.   _____

25. As appropriate, I self-disclose personal information similar to the information the other person shares with me.   _____

Score	Interpretation
0–62	You perceive yourself to be a poor listener.
63–86	You perceive yourself to be an adequate listener.
87–111	You perceive yourself to be a good listener.
112–125	You perceive yourself to be an outstanding listener.

4.1
The Nature of Listening
Why is listening essential for effective communication?

- We spend most of our communicating time engaged in listening.
- Most people cannot accurately recall 50 percent of what they hear after listening to a short talk. Without training, we listen at about 25 percent efficiency.

4.2
The Listening Process
What are the key components of the listening process?

- The six types of listening in the HURIER listening model—hearing, understanding, remembering, interpreting, evaluating, and responding—call for unique listening skills.
- Effective paraphrasing involves restating what others say in a way that indicates you understand their meaning.
- Asking well-planned, appropriate questions can help you understand another person's meaning.
- Working memory is your brain's processing center for deciding if information is worth keeping and storing in your long-term memory.
- The golden listening rule is: Listen to others as you would have them listen to you.

4.3
Listening Strategies and Skills
What listening strategies and skills can help you communicate more effectively?

- Conscientious listeners use their extra thought speed to enhance listening.
- Effective communicators skillfully listen to feedback and nonverbal behavior while also making sure that they withhold evaluation until their comprehension is complete.
- Effective listeners avoid and minimize distractions to themselves and others.
- Adaptability and flexibility are keys to listening and taking useful notes.

4.4
Listening to Gender and Culture
How do gender and culture affect the way we listen?

- Adjusting to diverse listening styles, particularly those involving differences in gender, culture, and hearing ability, is a challenging task that requires an understanding, respect, and adaptation to others.

4.5
The Nature of Critical Thinking
How does critical thinking enhance the quality of communication?

- Critical thinking is the kind of thinking you use to analyze what you read, see, or hear to arrive at a justified conclusion or decision.
- Critical thinking requires an understanding of the nature and types of claims, including claims of fact, conjecture, value, and policy.
- Critical thinkers understand and can separate verifiable facts from unsubstantiated inferences.
- Effective communicators identify and avoid using fallacies such as attacking the person, appeal to authority, appeal to popularity, appeal to tradition, faulty cause, and hasty generalizations.
- In addition to thinking critically, emotional responses in the form of gut feelings, instincts, hunches, and practical wisdom can help you make good decisions.

MySearchLab®

TEST YOUR KNOWLEDGE

4.1 Why is listening essential for effective communication?

1 In general, we spend 40 to 70 percent of our communicating time engaged in _____.
- a. writing
- b. speaking
- c. reading
- d. listening
- e. reading and writing

2 Immediately after listening to a short talk or lecture, most people cannot accurately report _____ percent of what was said.
- a. 10
- b. 30
- c. 40
- d. 50
- e. 70

4.2 What are the key components of the listening process?

3 Listening to interpret refers to
- a. how accurately you understand the meaning of another person's message.
- b. your ability to distinguish auditory and/or visual stimuli in a listening situation.
- c. how you act out ethnocentrism and stereotyping of others.
- d. your ability to evaluate the validity of a message.
- e. how well you focus on understanding and identifying with a person's situation, feeling, or motives.

4.3 What listening strategies and skills can help you communicate more effectively?

4 Read the following statement and a listener's paraphrase that follows. What characteristic of paraphrasing has the listener failed to take into account?

Grace: My whole family—parents, sisters, and Aunt Ruth—bug me about it, and sometimes I can tell they're very angry with me and how I'm overdrawn at the bank.

Listener: In other words, your family is angry because you're overdrawn at the bank; am I right?
- a. The listener is not mindful.
- b. The listener is not using new words to express Grace's message.
- c. The listener has not heard Grace's words correctly.
- d. The listener has not asked for confirmation.
- e. all of the above

5 Which of the following listening strategies involves using your extra thought speed productively?
- a. Identify the key ideas in a message.
- b. Pay attention to the meaning of a speaker's nonverbal behavior.
- c. Analyze the strengths and weaknesses of arguments.
- d. Assess the relevance and ethics of a speaker's comments.
- e. all of the above

4.4 How do gender and culture affect how we listen?

6 In general, men are more likely to listen comprehensively and analytically, whereas women are more likely to listen _____.
- a. only comprehensively
- b. empathically
- c. empathically and appreciatively
- d. appreciatively and comprehensively
- e. only emotionally

4.5 How does critical thinking enhance the quality of communication?

7 "The economy will improve next year" is an example of which type of argumentative claim?
- a. fact
- b. conjecture
- c. value
- d. policy
- e. emotion

8 Which of the following statements is an inference?
- a. I must have the flu.
- b. It is now flu season.
- c. I have a fever and ache all over.
- d. Both of my sisters had the flu two weeks ago.
- e. No one in my immediate family has had a flu shot.

9 What fallacy is committed in this statement: "John went outside in the cold without his hat or gloves. No wonder he has a cold."
- a. attacking the person
- b. appeal to authority
- c. appeal to popularity
- d. appeal to tradition
- e. faulty cause

10 What fallacy is committed in this statement: "Congestion and nausea! Oh, my God. John must have the swine flu!"
- a. hasty generalization
- b. appeal to authority
- c. attacking the person
- d. appeal to tradition
- e. faulty cause

Answers found on page 366.

Key Terms

Appeal to authority	Empathic listening	Listening to Remember
Appeal to popularity	Fallacy	Listening to Respond
Appeal to tradition	Faulty cause	Listening to Understand
Argument	Golden listening rule	Mnemonic
Attacking the person	Hasty generalization	Paraphrasing
Claims	Hearing	Short-term memory
Claims of Conjecture	Inference	Thought speed
Claims of Fact	Listening	Working memory
Claims of Policy	Listening to Evaluate	Working Memory Theory
Claims of Value	Listening to Hear	
Critical thinking	Listening to Interpret	

VERBAL
Communication

There is no denying the power of language, but it also comes with potential hazards. Once the words are out of your mouth, you cannot take them back. For example, President Bill Clinton's words—"I've had no sexual relations with that woman, Miss Lewinski"—came back to haunt him during the 1998 impeachment hearings. When, during a drunk driving arrest, actor Mel Gibson's words to the arresting officer—"F***ing Jews. . . . The Jews are responsible for all the wars in the world. . . . Are you a Jew?"—were made public, they became part of the long list of "the terrible things Mel Gibson has said."[1]

A survey of college students enrolled in basic communication courses ranked "choosing appropriate and effective words" as one of the top ten speaking skills. When asked to justify their rankings, students explained, "I'm afraid that right in the middle of speaking, I'll have trouble finding the words I need." "Sometimes, when someone asks me a question at work, I fumble with the answer—not because I don't know the answer but because I can't find the right words to explain what I know." "When someone disagrees with me, I can't seem to explain my position. I can't find the right words."[2]

Well-chosen words lie at the heart of electrifying, memorable presentations and at the core of meaningful and long-lasting interpersonal relationships. The right words explain, teach, support, comfort, persuade, inspire, and delight.

5.1
Human Language
What makes human language unique?

Humans do not share the remarkable sensory skills of many animals. You cannot track a faint scent through a forest trail or camouflage your skin color to hide from a predator. Many mammals do a much better job of interpreting body movement than you do.[3] Yet you can do something that no other animal can: You can speak.

Even though other animals use sophisticated communication systems, they do not use a language as complex and powerful as the one you are reading right now. The ability to learn words and to combine, invent, and give meaning to new words makes humans unique among animals.[5]

Researchers estimate that the first humans to speak language as we know it lived in East Africa about 150,000 years ago.[6] In a 100,000-year-old skull, anthropologists found a modern-shaped hyoid bone, which fits right at the top of the windpipe and resembles part of the modern apparatus we need to speak. Fully modern language probably evolved only 50,000 years ago.[7] Thus, the ability to speak is relatively new given that our earliest known ancestors lived about 3.3 million years ago in what is now Ethiopia.[8]

Our early ancestors also walked upright rather than hunched over like apes. Standing upright made it possible for humans to use their hands to carry things, make tools, and gesture in complicated ways. Equally important, it contributed to physiological changes in the larynx, lungs, throat, and vocal cavity that enabled speech. As a result, we are the only species whose anatomy allows for speech and complex language development.[9]

Human **language** is a system of arbitrary signs and symbols used to communicate thoughts and feelings. Every language spoken on this planet is a *system*: an interrelated collection of words and rules employed to construct and express messages that generate meaning. In addition to determining the meanings of words, all languages impose a grammar that arranges words in a meaningful way. "The went store he to" makes no sense until you rearrange the words: "He went to the store." And although "Him go to store" may be understandable, it breaks several grammatical rules.

> **"The difference between the almost right word and the right word is really a large matter—'tis the difference between the lightning bug and the lightning."**
> —Mark Twain[4]

A *Wall Street Journal* article warns that you risk "derailing your career" when you use language incorrectly. This claim is supported by the following anecdotes:

A recruiter refused to recommend a financial manager for a chief financial officer position in another company because he often said "me and so-and-so," followed by the wrong verb form.

The president of a publishing company rejects sales and editorial candidates because they exhibit grammatically incorrect speech. The president complained that such behavior "reflects a low level of professionalism."[10]

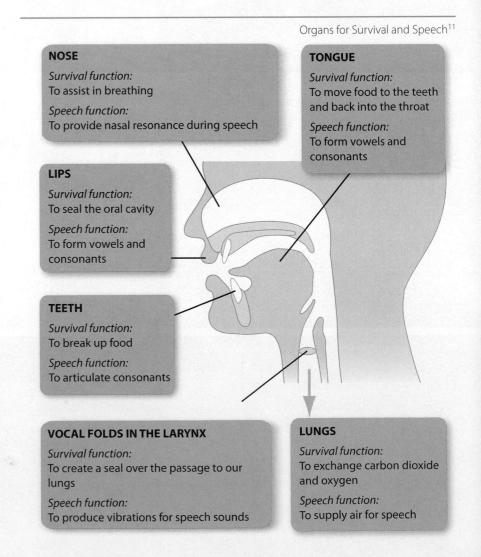

Organs for Survival and Speech[11]

NOSE
Survival function:
To assist in breathing

Speech function:
To provide nasal resonance during speech

TONGUE
Survival function:
To move food to the teeth and back into the throat

Speech function:
To form vowels and consonants

LIPS
Survival function:
To seal the oral cavity

Speech function:
To form vowels and consonants

TEETH
Survival function:
To break up food

Speech function:
To articulate consonants

VOCAL FOLDS IN THE LARYNX
Survival function:
To create a seal over the passage to our lungs

Speech function:
To produce vibrations for speech sounds

LUNGS
Survival function:
To exchange carbon dioxide and oxygen

Speech function:
To supply air for speech

Well-chosen words lie at the heart of effective communication, whether you are chatting with a friend, leading a group, addressing an audience, or writing a novel. In this chapter, we focus on **verbal communication**—the ways in which we use the words in a language to generate meaning, regardless of whether we communicate face-to-face, fax-to-fax, cell-phone-to-cell-phone, or email-to-email.[13] In the following chapter (Chapter 6), we focus on nonverbal communication—the ways in which we use message components *other than words* to generate meaning.

5.2
Language and Meaning

How do the characteristics of language affect meaning?

When you don't know the meaning of a word, you may look it up in a dictionary. Depending on the word, however, you may find several definitions. Likewise, no two people share exactly the same meaning of the same word.

Words do not have meanings; people have meanings for words.[14]

Signs and Symbols

As noted earlier, all languages are human inventions composed of signs and symbols: The words we speak or write, and the system that underlies their use, have all been made up by people.[15] A **sign** stands for or represents something specific and often looks like the thing it represents. Thus, it has a visual relationship to that thing. For example, the graphic depictions of jagged lightning and dark clouds on a weather map are signs of a storm.

Unlike signs, **symbols** do *not* have a direct relationship to the things they represent. Instead, they are an *arbitrary* collection of sounds

The Many Meanings of **LOVE**

Consider the many ways in which people define the word *love*.

Romantic **love**

Love for family and friends

Love for a pet

Love for a hobby or sport

Love of country

that in certain combinations stand for concepts. Nothing in the compilation of letters that make up the word *lightning* looks or sounds like lightning. The letters making up the word *cloud* are neither white and puffy nor dark and gloomy. You cannot be struck by the word *lightning* or get wet from the word *rain*.

When you see or hear a word, you apply your knowledge, experience, and feelings to decide what the word means. For example, if someone talks about a steak dinner, you may have very different reactions to the word *steak* depending on whether you are a rancher, a gourmet chef, a vegetarian, or an animal rights activist.

Language scholars C. K. Ogden and I. A. Richards provide an explanation of this phenomenon. They employ a triangle to explain the three elements of language: the thinking person, the symbol (or sign) used to represent something, and the actual thing, idea, or feeling being referenced.[16] The triangle does not have a solid base because the symbol and the referent are *not* directly related. The symbol must be mentally processed before it has meaning.

Denotative and Connotative Meaning

One of the great myths about language is that every word has an exact meaning. The truth is just the opposite: Just as no two communicators or communication contexts are exactly alike, no two word meanings can ever be the same.[17]

Two linguistic concepts—denotation and connotation—help explain the elusive nature of word meanings. **Denotation** refers to the specific and objective-dictionary-based meaning of

THOUGHT
The mental process of connecting the symbol and the referent

Yum... A well-done steak!

TRIANGLE OF MEANING

REFERENT
The thing or action the word represents.

SYMBOL
The word

"steak"

Ogden and Richards's Triangle of Meaning[18]

a word. For example, most of us would agree that a *snake* is a scaly, legless, sometimes venomous reptile with a long, cylindrical body. Plumbers have their own version of a *snake*—a flexible metal wire or coil used to clean out pipes. Each of these "snakes" has a denotative meaning.

❝CONNOTATION is the aura of feeling, pleasant or unpleasant, that surrounds practically all words.❞[19]
—S. I. Hayakawa, semanticist

Connotation refers to the emotional response or personal thoughts connected to the meaning of a word. Connotation, rather than denotation, is more likely to influence your response to words. For example, just the thought of a snake is enough to make some people who have a fear of snakes

Common **SIGNS**

Rain

Rain and Lightning

Partly Cloudy

STOP&THINK

What's in a Name?

HELLO
my name is

Ifeyinwa

Our ability "to name" is uniquely human. It has been considered a holy privilege as well as a magical gift. According to Judaism and Christianity, the first honor God confers on Adam is that of naming the animals.[20]

Many names also have interesting histories as well as special meanings. For example, the English name *Dianna* is probably derived from an old Indo-European root meaning "heavenly" and "divine" and is related to Diana, the Roman goddess of the moon, hunting, forests, and childbirth.

The name *John* comes from the Greek name meaning "gracious." This name owes its popularity to John the Baptist and the apostle John in the New Testament. All cultures have their own naming traditions. Consider, for example, the story of a Nigerian student named Ifeyinwa:

> In Africa, back in the days when my grandparents were alive, names meant many things and people named their children from events or circumstances. When my father was about six years old, his mother gave birth to twin babies. They did not survive because they were put in a special clay pot and left in the fields until they died. That was the tradition of the land then. It was taboo for a woman to give birth to more than one child at a time. My father named me after this ordeal. My name Ifeyinwa means "child is supreme" and "precious." He knows a child is a precious gift from God and each child is unique in his or her own special ways. I have always loved my name but even more after learning its meaning. I wish to live up to my father's expectations of me and the meaning of my name.[21]

Now consider *your* name. Why did your parents choose this name? Does their choice say something about your family's history or your culture? How has your name affected your life?

---

tremble. Others may immediately think of the snake in the Garden of Eden, who lured Adam and Eve to eat forbidden fruit. Yet a serpentologist—a scientist who studies snakes—would try to convince you that snakes are among the most intriguing and magnificent of animals.

For most people, a word's connotation has much more significance than its denotation. Whereas you may tell someone that a *cop* pulled you over and gave you an undeserved ticket, a *police officer* may have helped you with a flat tire. What seems like a neutral word to you can have strong connotations to others.

the serpent   the plumbing tool

Concrete and Abstract Words

Your choice of concrete or abstract words significantly affects whether and how well others understand the intended meaning of your message. **Concrete words** refer to specific things you perceive with your senses—things you can smell, taste, touch, see, or hear. The words *table*, *Paris*, *giraffe*, and *red rose* are concrete because, unlike *furniture*, *city*, *animal*, and *flower*, they narrow the number of possible meanings and decrease the likelihood of misinterpretation. **Abstract words** refer to ideas or concepts that usually cannot be observed or touched and often require interpretation. The word *animal* is more abstract than *giraffe* because there are a huge number of different kinds of animals. Moreover, you can see a giraffe in your mind, but what image does an animal conjure up? Both a crayfish and a giraffe are animals. Similarly, words such as *fairness*, *freedom*, and *evil* can have an almost endless number of meanings and don't specifically refer to something you can see, hear, smell, taste, or touch. The more abstract your language is, the more likely it is that your listeners may interpret your meaning other than the way you intended.[22]

Language has three general levels of meaning that range from highly

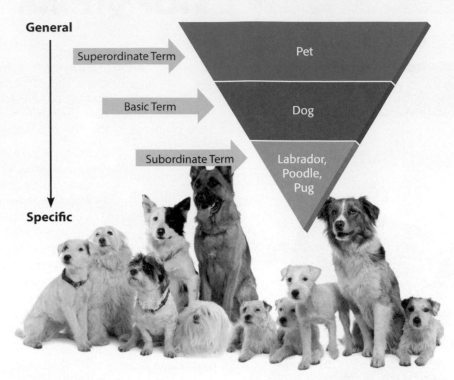

Three Levels Of MEANING

General → Superordinate Term → **Pet**

Basic Term → **Dog**

Subordinate Term → **Labrador, Poodle, Pug**

Specific

abstract to very concrete.[23] **Super-ordinate terms** group objects and ideas together very generally; *vehicle*, *animal*, or *location* are superordinate terms. **Basic terms** further describe a superordinate term, such as *car*, *van*, *truck*; *cat*, *chicken*, *mouse*; or *New England*, *Deep South*, *Appalachia*.

Subordinate terms offer the most concrete and specialized descriptions. The vehicle parked outside is not just a *car*. It is a 1988 red Mercedes sports car convertible. The cat purring on your lap is not just a cat; it is a blue-eyed male Siamese cat named Gatsby.

5.3

Language and Culture

How do language and culture affect one another?

"Tall half-skinny half-1 percent hot quad shot latte with whip, please."

There are approximately 5,000 to 6,000 languages spoken in the world, all of them with different vocabularies and rules of grammar.[24] Have you ever tried to talk to or understand someone who speaks very little English? The experience can be frustrating, comical, enlightening, or even disastrous.

In one of Tony Hillerman's mystery novels, a Navaho tribal police officer explains to an FBI agent who cannot come up with anything better than the word *rocks* to describe a murder scene, "It's said the Inuits up on the Arctic Circle have nine words for snow. I

The Whorf Hypothesis

One of the most significant and controversial language theories attempts to explain why people from different cultures speak and interpret messages differently from one another. Linguist Edward Sapir and his student Benjamin Whorf spent decades studying the relationship between language, culture, and thought. Whorf's most controversial theory contends that the structure of a language *determines* how we see, experience, and interpret the world around us. For example, if you don't have a word for *red*, will you be able to see red or separate it from other colors you do recognize?

In English, we understand the grammatical differences between "I saw the girl," "I see the girl," and "I will see the girl." Whorf observed that the Hopi Indians of Arizona make no past-, present-, and future-tense distinctions in their language. Therefore, he concluded, they must perceive the world very differently. He also noted that the Hopi have a single word, *masa'ytaka*, for everything that flies, from insects to airplanes. Does that mean the Hopi cannot think about tomorrow and cannot see the differences between an airplane and a fly? Originally, many linguists believed that the answer was *yes*. Now linguists understand that the Hopi *do* think about tomorrow, even if they may lack a word for it.

Like many controversial theories, the Whorf hypothesis (also referred to as

> While language does not determine everything we think, it does influence the way we perceive others and the world around us.[25]

the Sapir-Whorf hypothesis) has been accepted, rejected, resurrected, and amended—several times. Today, most linguists accept a more moderate version of the **Whorf hypothesis**: Language *reflects* cultural models of the world, which in turn influence how the speakers of a language come to think, act, and behave.[26] For example, in English, terms that end with *man*, such as *chairman*, *fireman*, and *policeman*, may lead us to view certain roles and jobs as only appropriate for men. Substituting words such as *chairperson*, *firefighter*, and *police officer* may change perceptions about who can work in these careers.

---

guess, living in our stony world, we're that way with our rocks."[27] The words in a language often reflect what is important to the people in a specific culture. Just as there are dozens of words used to describe camels in Arabic languages and snow in Eskimo languages, there are hundreds of English words to describe the many kinds of vehicles driven in the United States, as well as for coffee drinks served at a Starbucks. In many countries, there are significant regional differences in vocabulary. For example, a sandwich on a large roll with a variety of meats and cheeses on it may be a *grinder*, a *hero*, a *sub*, a *hoagie*, or a *po'boy*, depending on the region of the country.[28]

Pronouns

As we noted in Chapter 3, individualism-collectivism is the most significant cultural dimension and the factor that best distinguishes one culture from another. Individualistic cultures have an "I" orientation; collectivist cultures have a "we" orientation.

Interestingly, "English is the only language that capitalizes the pronoun *I* in writing. English does not, however, capitalize the written form of the pronoun *you*."[29] By contrast, people of the Athabaskan-speaking community in Alaska speak and think in a collective plural voice. The word for *people*, *dene*, is used as a kind of *we*, and is the subject for almost every sentence requiring a personal pronoun.[30]

When speaking to others, pay attention to the individualistic or collectivist tendencies in the way they use languages. Although frequent use of the words *I*, *me*, and *you* may be common for a group of ambitious and individualistic corporate executives in the United States, the word *we* and *us* might be heard more frequently from African Americans or people from Central and South America, who are more collectivist.

Verbal Directness

Most people living in the United States have a low-context, direct way of speaking. In the eyes of other cultures, we get to the point with blunt, straight talk. When we say no, we mean no! Many other cultures view this direct use of language as a disregard for others that can lead to embarrassment and injured feelings.[31] For example, at a news conference, President George W. Bush acknowledged that his all-American speaking style may have been too direct when dealing with the leaders of other nations. "'I explained to the prime minister [Tony Blair of Great Britain] that the policy of my government is the removal of Saddam.' Catching himself, Bush added: 'Maybe I should be a little less direct and be a little more nuanced, and say we support regime change.'"[32]

Most North Americans learn to say yes or no when expressing their opinions; however, a Japanese person may say yes to a suggestion or business proposal because it is what she or he believes you want to hear when, in fact, the real response may be no.

5.4
Language and Gender
How does language reflect gender differences?

Most languages reflect a gender bias. These differences can be minor or major depending on the language and context in which communication takes place.[33] In English, we struggle with the words *he* and *she*. For many years, the pronoun *he* was used to refer to an unspecified individual. Older English textbooks used sentences such as:

Every speaker should pay attention to his words. Other languages have gender-related challenges as well. French, for example, has separate third-person plurals: masculine and feminine versions of *they*. Japanese distinguishes gender in both the first and the second person; they use a different version of *you* for men and women. The language of Finland may have the best solution. All pronouns are gender neutral; there is a single word that means both *he* and *she*.[34]

Although some languages, such as Finnish, make very few distinctions between men and women, English favors men over women. Most gender-related word pairings begin with the male

> How do you talk about a couple when using their first names?
> Is it Juliet and Romeo or Romeo and Juliet Adam and Eve or Eve and Adam?

term: male and female, boys and girls, husband and wife, Jack and Jill, Romeo and Juliet, Mr. and Mrs.[35] If you doubt this preference, think about the married couples you know. Would you address a letter to Mrs. and Mr. Smith?

Unfortunately, because of the male bias in English and in American society, female terms tend to take on demeaning connotations. The connotations of the second word in the following pairings are negative or outdated for women: *governor/governess*, *master/mistress*, and *sir/madam*. Women are also compared with animals: *chick, bitch, fox, cow, shrew, dog.* One study lists more than 500 English slang terms for *prostitutes* but only 65 for the men who are their willing clients.[36]

Robin Lakoff, one of the first linguists to write about gender differences, in *Language and Woman's Place*, contends that women tend to use language that expresses uncertainty, lack of confidence, and excessive deference or politeness.[37] For example, women tend to use questions tagged onto sentences to gain approval, such as "don't you agree?" and

> When the communication goal is significant and personally important, *both* men and women use highly powerful language.

Strategies for AVOIDING GENDER BIAS WITH PRONOUNS

- **Use plural forms.** Instead of saying, "Every speaker should pay attention to his words," consider, "All speakers should pay attention to their words."

- **Avoid using any pronoun.** Instead of using a pronoun at all, consider, "Good speakers pay careful attention to language."

- **Use variations on the phrase "he or she" as well as "his and hers."** Instead of saying, "Every speaker should pay attention to his or her words," consider, "Every speaker should pay attention to her or his words."

"haven't you?" They are more likely to avoid direct requests, using super-polite phrases instead such as "Could you please close the door?" or "Would you mind closing the door?" Women's speech is also described as more tentative, using such hedges or "fillers" as *like, you know, well,* and *kind of.*

We would be guilty of stereotyping if we didn't note the exceptions to such tendencies. Certainly, many men speak tentatively and cooperatively, and many women speak directly and assertively.

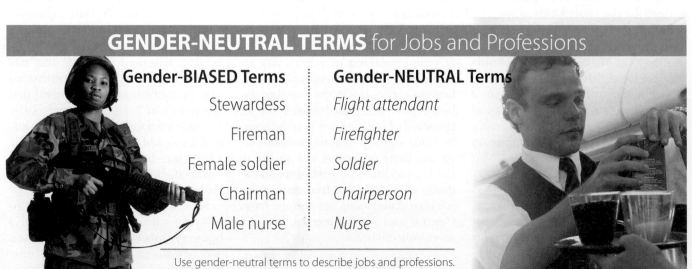

GENDER-NEUTRAL TERMS for Jobs and Professions

Gender-BIASED Terms	Gender-NEUTRAL Terms
Stewardess	*Flight attendant*
Fireman	*Firefighter*
Female soldier	*Soldier*
Chairman	*Chairperson*
Male nurse	*Nurse*

Use gender-neutral terms to describe jobs and professions. In the theater and film industries, for example, the word *actor* is replacing actress for female performers.

COMMUNICATION & CULTURE

DO WOMEN TALK MORE THAN MEN?

One language myth is that women talk more than men. This belief is neither new nor confined to the United States.[38] Most research studies, however, paint a different picture. A recent study of 400 college students found that the number of words uttered by males and females were virtually the same. An analysis of 63 studies of gender differences in talkativeness found that men actually "yakked slightly more than women, especially when interacting with spouses or strangers and when the topic was non-personal." Women talked more with classmates, with parents and children, and in situations where the topic of conversation required disclosure of feelings.[39]

In work settings, men do most of the talking. Even when women hold influential positions, they often find it hard to contribute to a discussion as much as men do. This pattern is also evident in educational settings (from kindergarten through university), where males usually dominate classroom talk. Sadly, when women talk as much as men do, they may be perceived as talking "too much."[40]

When linguist Janet Holmes answers the question "Do women talk more than men?" she concludes, "It depends." It depends on the social context, the kind of talk, the confidence of the speaker, the social roles, and the speaker's expertise. Generally, men are more likely to dominate conversation in formal, public contexts where talk is highly valued and associated with status and power. Women, on the other hand, are likely to contribute more in private, informal interactions, when talk functions to maintain relationships and in situations where women feel socially confident.[41]

5.5
Language and Context

How does context affect language choices?

What kind of language would you use in a college classroom, at a family member's funeral, at a critical job interview, at a political or pep rally, at home with your parents, or at a party with your friends? There would be subtle and not-so-subtle differences in your choice of words and grammar. We naturally change the way we use language based on our relationships with other communicators, their psychological traits and preferences, and the extent to which they share our cultural attitudes, beliefs, values, and behaviors.

The phrase *code switching* refers to a common strategy for adapting to the many contexts in which we communicate. If you can speak more than one language, you already code switch as you move from one language to another. Here we use the term **code switching** in a broader sense: to describe how we modify our verbal and nonverbal communication in different contexts.

Effective communicators learn to adapt their language to the communication context. Although a swear word would never pass your lips at a job interview, during a church service, or in a formal public speech, you may curse in the company of close friends and like-minded colleagues. In his book *Word on the Street*, linguist John McWhorter notes that many middle-class African Americans typically speak both Black English (the language they may speak at home) and Standard English (the language they may speak among white people), switching constantly between the two, often in the same sentence.[42] For example, a Black English speaker may use double negatives ("He don't know nothing") and delete *to be* verbs ("She fine") within statements made in Standard English. McWhorter also notes that African Americans usually code switch between Standard and Black English when the topic or tone is informal, lighthearted, or intimate. As a result, African Americans are competent in two sophisticated dialects of English.[43]

How do context and culture affect the way we choose and use language?

5.6
Overcoming Common Language Barriers

How do bypassing, exclusionary language, and offensive language affect communication?

CHAPTER 5 | verbal communication

Despite our best efforts to understand the complex relationship between language and meaning, misunderstandings are inevitable. Three common language barriers to effective communication are bypassing, exclusionary language, and offensive language.

Bypassing

When two people assign different meanings to the same word or phrase, they risk bypassing each other. **Bypassing** is a form of miscommunication that occurs when people "miss each other with their meanings."[44] If you have ever found yourself saying, "But, that's not what I meant," you have experienced bypassing.

Note the problem created in the following example of bypassing: A high school graphic design teacher wrote a letter to Randy Cohen, a former "ethicist" for *The New York Times Magazine*. The teacher explained that students were assigned the task of creating a guitar using Photoshop. A few asked if they could use an online tutorial. The teacher said *yes*, assuming and quite sure they'd merely consult it for help. Three students handed in identical work because they'd carefully followed the tutorial to the letter. The teacher wanted to give each student a C on the assignment because the other students created their

work from scratch. Thus his question: Should he give them the C, or is he bound by having given them the okay to use the tutorial?

The ethicist wrote back, saying, "There's something not quite right about penalizing these students for doing what you explicitly permitted them

> Remember that it's not what words mean to *you*, but what others mean when they use those words.

to do. It's a teacher's obligation to be clear about what is and what is not acceptable."[45] The students clearly believed they had permission to use the tutorial to create the guitar graphic, whereas the teacher assumed they would only consult the tutorial for help.

COMMUNICATION IN *ACTION*

Tiptoeing Around Words

When you use a **euphemism**, you substitute a bland, mild, vague, or unobjectionable word or phrase for one considered too direct, indecent, harsh, offensive, or hurtful. Rather than say someone has died, we may say he or she has "passed away." In Victorian England, the word *limb* was used for *leg*, a word that had sexual connotations. Even a chair leg wasn't referred to as such because it might spark thoughts of sexuality. In U.S. restaurants, we usually ask for directions to the restroom rather than the toilet.[46] Some euphemisms also substitute letters in a word to make it less offensive.

You frequently hear people say "jeeze" instead of "Jesus," "darn" instead of "damn," and "heck" rather than "hell." Can you "translate" the following words and phrases into their non-euphemistic meaning: *doggone*, *freaking*, *oh my goodness*, and *shoot*?

Euphemisms, however, can be used to mask the truth. The Pentagon referred to the information-seeking techniques Americans used on Iraqis in the Abu Ghraib prison as *interrogation*, whereas many critics described these techniques (food and sleep deprivation, water boarding, stress positioning, hooding, and attacking with dogs) as *torture*.[47]

What Slanguage Do You Speak?

Slanguage is the language of slang, which is nothing new. It's been around since we began creating and speaking words. Although there is disagreement about the origins of the word **slang**, most linguists agree that slang is a short-lived, group-related, ever-changing, creative and innovative, often playful and metaphorical, colloquial language variety that is below the level of stylistically neutral language.[48] Huh? In other words, slang consists of informal, nonstandard words or phrases that tend to originate in subcultures (such as teenagers, musicians, athletes, inner-city gangs, railroad workers, prisoners) within a society.

Slang helps language change and renew itself.[49] Many words that began as slang—cool; Uncle Tom and Mr. Charley; booze; bread and dough; and lots of words for toilet (john, head, can, loo)—have ended up in standard usage dictionaries. Just about every surviving slang word has an interesting history. Why, for example, do people say "I have to use the john?" Could it be that the inventor of the first toilet in a home (as opposed to an outhouse) was Sir John Harrington, a member of Queen Elizabeth I's court in England?[50]

Most slang, however, doesn't last long. As Kathryn Lindskoop writes in *Creative Writing*, "It looks foolish when it gets old, when it is slightly misused, and when it is used by the wrong people in a futile attempt to sound hip."[51] In other words, we see nothing wrong with using slang in the right place at the right time with the right people and for the right reasons.

Shown here is a survey of the slang used by students on the campus of the University of North Carolina at Pembroke. The list of words is based on common slang terms generated by students. Athletes, sororities, fraternities, and student club members contributed words that had meaning for their specific groups. The most commonly slang term in this study was "What's up?"[52]

> ## Slang is language which takes off its coat, spits on its hands—and goes to work.
> —Carl Sandburg, American poet[53]

Of the 25 terms referred to as slang by the University of North Carolina at Pembroke students, check the category that best describes your use of these words.

SLANG TERMS	Never	Seldom	Sometimes	Frequently
1. Chill				
2. Cool				
3. Da bomb				
4. Floss				
5. For real				
6. Grub				
7. Kick it				
8. Like				
9. My bad				
10. Phat				
11. Playa				
12. Stoked				
13. Tight				
14. Trip/trippin/trip out				
15. Wack				
16. What's up?				
17. Whatever				
18. Yo				

Now answer the following questions:

- Have you heard friends and fellow students use these slang terms? If not, why not? Is it because your geographic location is different, because you're not an 18- to 21-year-old college student, or because (given the time it takes to write and publish a textbook) the terms are already dated?

- What would you add to this list? What other slang terms do you and your friends use?

- Which term or terms do you believe is the most frequently used slang term on your campus or in your neighborhood?

William Haney, an organizational communication scholar, maintains that effective "communicators who habitually look for meanings in the people using words, rather than in the words themselves, are much less prone to bypass or be bypassed."[54]

Exclusionary Language

Exclusionary language uses words that reinforce stereotypes, belittle other people, or exclude others from understanding an in-group's message. Exclusionary language widens the social gap by separating the world into *we* (to refer to people who are like you) and *they* or *those people* (to refer to people who are different from you). Such terms can offend others. You don't have to be excessive about being "politically correct," using *vertically challenged* for *short*, but you should avoid alienating others and use language that includes rather than excludes. Specifically, avoid mentioning anything about age, health or mental and physical abilities, sexual orientation, or race and ethnicity unless these characteristics are relevant to the discussion.

- **Age.** Instead of *old lady*, use *older woman* or just *woman*.

- **Health and Abilities.** Rather than use terms such as *cripple* or *head case*, use *physically disabled* and *person with an emotional illness*. Never use the word *retarded* in reference to *mental ability* or *physical ability*.

- **Sexual Orientation.** Never assume that the sexual orientation of others is the same as your own. *Homo*, *fairy*, *fag*, *butch*, and *dyke* are unacceptable; instead, use *gay* or *lesbian*.

- **Race and Ethnicity.** Avoid using stereotypical terms and descriptions based on a person's race, ethnicity, or region, such as *hick*. Use the names people prefer to describe their racial or ethnic affiliations, such as black, African American, Latino/a, Hispanic, and Asian. Rather than saying "That Polish guy down the block owns several repair shops," say instead, "That man down the block owns several repair shops."

If you doubt that people still use exclusionary language, consider the 2010 election campaign for U.S. Senate in West Virginia. The National Republican Senatorial Committee put out a casting ad calling for "hicky"-looking blue-collar actors to play everyday West Virginians. The democratic opponent, Joe Manchin, put out his own ad in response calling the GOP portrayal "insulting" and asserting that Republican candidate John Raese "thinks we're hicks." When the story broke, the Republican committee pulled their ad.[55]

In addition to stereotyping others, exclusionary language can prevent some people from participating in or joining a discussion that relies on specialized jargon. **Jargon** is the specialized or technical language of a profession or homogeneous group. English professor William Lutz points out that groups use jargon as "verbal shorthand that allows members to communicate with each other clearly, efficiently, and quickly."[56] In some settings and on some occasions, such as at a meeting of psychiatrists, attorneys, information technology professionals, or educators, the ability to use jargon properly is a sign of group membership, and it speeds communication among members.

Some speakers use jargon to impress others with their specialized knowledge. For example, a skilled statistician may bewilder an audience by using unfamiliar terms to describe cutting-edge methodologies for establishing causality. In other situations, people use jargon when they have nothing to say; they just string together a bunch of nonsense and hope no one notices their lack of content.[57] Such tactics fail to inform others and often result in misunderstandings and resentment.

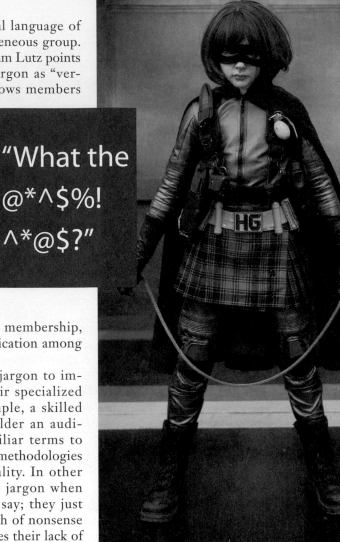

"What the @*^$%! ^*@$?"

Cursing and using sexually explicit language were once taboo on television and not considered "ladylike." Although some women now believe swearing is "liberating," it remains a stigma in many contexts—for both women *and* men. Pictured here is the foul-mouthed character Hit Girl from the cult film *Kick-Ass*.

ETHICAL COMMUNICATION

Sticks and Stones May Break Your Bones, but Words Can Hurt Forever

Movie director Spike Lee rejects being labeled as a "black" filmmaker. "I want to be known as a talented filmmaker. That should be first. But the reality today is that no matter how successful you are, you're black first."

Two problems occur when you label someone or accept a label you hear or see. First, you reduce an entire person into a label: black filmmaker, dumb blonde, female doctor, or rich uncle. Second, the label can affect your perceptions or relationship with that person. For example, if you label a person as inconsiderate, you may dismiss an act of kindness: "I wonder what prompted her to do that?" When you label someone as near perfect, you may go to great lengths to justify or explain less-than-perfect behavior: "Nicole is still the best player on the softball team; she's just having an off year." Labels also influence how we interpret the same behavior:

- I'm energetic; you're overexcited; he's out of control.
- I'm laid-back; you're untidy; she's a slob.
- I'm smart; you're intelligent; Chris is brilliant!

Offensive Language and Swearing

During the first half of the twentieth century, many words were considered inappropriate, particularly those that referred to private body parts and functions. Women went to the *powder room* and men to the *lavatory*. Even the word *pregnant* was once considered improper. Instead, a woman was "in a family way" or "with child." In 1952, Lucille Ball became the first pregnant woman to appear on a television show. The scripts called her an "expectant mother," never using the word *pregnant.* All of the *I Love Lucy* scripts were reviewed by a priest, a rabbi, and a minister to make certain they were in good taste.[58] Not that long ago, swear words were literally unheard of on radio and television. Today you may hear dozens of swear words on cable television shows, and you might easily witness steamy sexual scenes that would have given the *I Love Lucy* censors heart attacks. And then there's the Internet, where swearing and pornography are only a few clicks away.

Researchers who study the evolution of language report that swearing or cursing is a human universal.[59]

How would you define swearing? Is it bad language, embarrassing language, profane language? **Swearing** refers to using words that are taboo or disapproved of in a culture that should *not* be interpreted literally and can be used to express strong emotions and attitudes.[60] When we use swear words, we rarely wish that someone would literally "go to hell" or be "damned." Rather, we are using the words as a coping mechanism to express a strong emotion or to release stress.[61] In some cases, swearing may be signs of a neurological disorder, as is the case with the small percent of people with Tourette's syndrome, who cannot control their tendency to swear.[62]

There are good reasons to stop swearing or, at least, to control where, when, and with whom you use such language. For example, swearing

STOP&THINK

How's Your Netspeak, Netlingo, and leet (133t)?

Netspeak, Netlingo, and leet are three types of Internet slang. Unless you are a *n00b* (newbie—as in new and inexperienced or uninformed), you're probably familiar with the new language forms used in email, text messages, and increasingly in everyday writing.

David Crystal, who writes about language, claims that "Netspeak is a development of millennial significance. A new medium of linguistic communication does not arrive very often in the history of the [human] race."[63] Check out these brief descriptions of three of these languages, Netspeak, Netlingo, and leet:

NETSPEAK includes common typographic strategies used to achieve a more sociable, oral, and interactive communication style:

- *Letter homophones.* Examples: RU (are you); OIC (oh, I see); CUL8R (see you later)
- *Capitalization or other symbols used for emphasis.* Examples: YES, * yes *
- *Sound-based and/or stylized spelling.* Examples: cooooool, hahahahahah
- *Keyboard-generated emoticons.* Examples: :-) = smiley; @>—;— = rose; ;-) = winking; ;-o = shocked, uh-oh, oh-no

NETLINGO refers to a variety of language forms used in Internet communication, such as the familiar FYI (for your information) and FAQ (frequently asked questions):

- *Compounds and blends.* Examples: shareware, netiquette, e- and cyber- anything
- *Abbreviations and acronyms.* Examples: BTW = by the way; THX = thanks; IRL = in real life; F2F = face to face; IMHO = in my humble opinion; GMTA = great minds think alike; BBL = be back later; WDYT = what do you think?
- *Less use of capitalization, punctuation, and hyphenation.* Examples: internet and email
- *Less use of traditional openings and closings.* Examples: *Hi* or *Hey* instead of *Dear* or using no greeting phrase at all[64]

LEET, also known as *eleet* or *leetspeak*, uses an alternative alphabet to create words. In many cases the new alphabet's symbols visually resemble our standard alphabet. So *leet* can become 133t, or 1337. *Leetspeak* becomes 133tspeek. Leet also uses common misspellings or letters and symbols that correspond to the sound of a word as in *skillz* or skills as well as a variety of symbols for sounds as c@tL0vr, c@(47 £0v3r, and (@ L0\/3r for cat lover.

Here's an explanation of leet in leet. See if you can translate this example *before* reading the provided translation.[65]

1t'5 4 v4r14t10n 0f t3h w0rd 3l1t3 u53d by 14m3r5 wh0 th1nk th3y 4r3 3l1t3 . . . 0ft3n us3d w1th 4r3 v4r1at10n 0f d1g1t5 1n5t34d 0f l3tt3r5 . . . 0ft3n u53d by 5cr1pt k1dd135 t0 d35cr18e th31r 5k1ll.

Translation: It's a variation of the word *elite*, used by lamers who think they are *elite* . . . often used with are variation of digits instead of letters . . . often used by script kitties to describe their skill.

Be careful when using netlingo, netspeak, and especially leet. Some readers may not "get it" and will become confused or exasperated. The changing trends in internet language even have some people in their 20s feeling old or slightly out of touch. As a 23-year-old technology consultant complained about his 12- and 19- year-old siblings' messages, "I have no idea what they're saying. . . . I may not text in full sentences, but at least there's punctuation to get my point across. I guess I'm old school."[66]

If you send difficult-to-understand netspeak, netlingo, or leet messages to people who will have to translate your "words" into recognizable English, they may not make the effort or ignore what you're saying. Don't load your messages with unnecessary or "show-off" symbols. Too many in one message can make reading difficult and annoying, as well as make you and your writing appear immature.[67]

frequently offends others. One study reported that 91 percent of respondents ranked foul language as "the most ill-mannered type of workplace behavior."[68] People who do *not* swear are seen as more intelligent (because they can find more accurate and appropriate words) and more pleasant (because they don't offend anyone). They are also perceived as effective communicators who have greater control over their emotions.

If swearing is a problematic habit of speech for you, you can take steps to break it. Like any habit—biting your nails, overeating, or abusing alcohol—you must *want* to stop doing it. When you feel like swearing, use a euphemism such as *darn* or *good grief*. Look for better, more interesting words. Rather than saying "This place looks likes *&%#!" try something like "This place looks like an infantry company camped here *and* partied."

> **"Every language, dialect or patois ever studied, living or dead, spoken by millions or by a small tribe, turns out to have its share of forbidden speech."**
> —Natalie Angier, science writer for *The New York* Times[69]

5.7
Improving Your Way with Words
What strategies can improve your way with words?

In the previous section, we emphasized what *not* to do if you want to be understood and respected by others. Here we take a more positive approach by examining five ways in which you can use language to express messages clearly and appropriately: expand your vocabulary, use oral language, use active language, use *I* and *you* pronouns wisely, and know your grammar.

Expand Your Vocabulary

How many words do you know? By the age of five, you probably knew about 10,000 words, which means that you learned about 10 words a day. Children have an inborn ability for learning languages that diminishes at around age 12 or 13. Although children can learn a second or third language with relative ease, adults struggle to become fluent in a second language.[70]

By the time you are an adult, your vocabulary has expanded to include tens of thousands of words. Not surprisingly, finding the "right" word is a lot easier if you have many words from which to choose. When your only ice cream choices are vanilla or chocolate, you miss the delights of caramel butter pecan, mocha fudge swirl, and even simple strawberry. When you search for words in the English language, you have more than a million choices.

As you learn more words, make sure you understand their meaning and usage. For example, you should be able to make distinctions in meaning among the words in the following groups:[71]

- Absurd, silly, dumb, ridiculous, ludicrous, idiotic
- Pretty, attractive, gorgeous, elegant, lovely, cute, beautiful

Remember, the difference between the almost-right word and the right word is significant. You may not mind being called "silly" but may have serious objections to being called "idiotic." Improving your vocabulary is a lifelong task—and one that will be much easier if you are an avid reader.

Use Oral Language

Usually, there is a big difference between the words we use for written documents and the words we use orally in conversations, group discussions, and presentations. In his book *How to Win Any Argument*, Robert Mayer writes, "The words you'll craft for a listener's ears are not the same as the words you'll choose for a reader's eyes. Readers can slow their pace to reread, to absorb, and to understand—luxuries listeners don't have."[72]

Use Active Language

Effective communicators use active language: vivid, expressive verbs rather than passive forms of the verb *to be* (*be, am, is, are, was, being, been*). Consider the difference between "Cheating is a violation of the college's plagiarism rules" and "Cheating violates the college's plagiarism rules." The second sentence is stronger and draws attention to the subject.

Voice refers to whether the subject of a sentence performs or receives

Know Thy SELF

How Broad Is Your Vocabulary?

We generally assume that most of you know and can define the words we use in this textbook. We also understand that this may not always be the case. Consider the following, non–key term words from this chapter. Can you write a coherent definition of each and use it in a sentence? If you cannot, we urge you to look up and learn the words you do not know.

Arbitrary	**Demeaning**	**Nuanced**
Causality	**Hypothesis**	**Regime**
Colloquial	**Impeachment**	**Semanticist**
Deference	**Linguist**	**Stigma**

Crafting Language **FOR THE EAR**

Oral Style	When You Speak, Say This	Do Not Say This
Shorter, familiar words	Large	Substantial
Shorter, simple sentences	He came back.	He returned from his point of departure.
Contractions	I'm not going and that's that.	I am not going and that is that.
Informal, colloquial expressions	Give it a try.	You should attempt it first.
Incomplete sentences	Old wood, best to burn; old wine, best to drink	Old wood burns the best, and old wine is best to drink.

Say what you mean by speaking the way you talk, not the way you write.

Instead, they shift responsibility from themselves to others by using the word *you*. **You** language can express judgments about others. When the judgments are positive—"You did a great job" or "You look marvelous!"—there's rarely a problem. When *you* is used to accuse, blame, or criticize, however, it can arouse defensiveness, anger, and even revenge. Consider the following statements: "You make me angry." "You embarrass me." "You drive too fast."

When you use *you* language, you are saying that another person makes you feel a certain way rather than accepting that you control how you feel. To take personal responsibility and decrease the probability of defensive reactions, use *I* language even when your impulse tells you to use *you*.

The following examples demonstrate how the three components of *I* language listed to the lower left can help you express yourself by describing someone's behavior and explaining how it affects you. Also note that the *you* statements are short. The *I* statements are longer because they offer more information to explain the speaker's feelings.

You versus I

You **Statement**
You embarrassed me last night.

I **Statement**
I was really embarrassed last night when you interrupted me in front of my boss and contradicted what I said. I'm afraid she'll think I don't know what I'm doing.

You **Statement**
What a stupid thing to do!

I **Statement**
When you turn on the gas grill and let it run, I'm afraid that it will blow up in your face when you light it.

the action of the verb. If the subject performs the action, you are using an **active voice**. If the subject receives the action, you are using a **passive voice**. A strong, active voice makes your message more engaging, whereas a passive voice takes the focus away from the subject of your sentence. "The *Iliad* was read by the student" is passive. "The student read the *Iliad*" is active. Because an active voice requires fewer words, it also keeps sentences short and direct. Simply state who is doing what, not what was done by whom.

Less committed and confident speakers often have trouble using the active voice because they worry about sounding too direct. Look at the differences in these sentences:

Active verb: Sign this petition.

Passive verb: The petition should be signed by all of you.

The more passive the sentence, the less powerful the message.

Use *I* and *You* Language Wisely

The pronouns you use can affect the quality and meaning of your verbal communication. Understanding the nature and power of pronouns can help you improve your way with words.

When you use the *I* **Language**, you take responsibility for your own feelings and actions: *I* feel great. *I* am a good student. *I* will not vote for someone who cuts spending on education. Some people avoid using the word *I* because they think it may seem like they are showing off, being selfish, or bragging. Other people use the word *I* too much and appear self-centered or oblivious to those around them.

Unfortunately, some people avoid *I* language when it is most important.

The Three Components of *I* Language

1. Identify your feelings.
2. Describe the other person's behavior.
3. Explain the potential consequences.

improving your way with words

Gobbling Gobbledygook

Semanticist Stuart Chase defines **gobbledygook** (the sound of which imitates the nonsense gobbling of a turkey) as "using two or three or ten words in place of one, or using a five-syllable word where a single syllable would suffice." He cites the example of the single word "now" being replaced by the five-word, 17-letter phrase "at this point in time."[73]

In his book *Say What You Mean*, Rudolf Flesch contends that long words are a curse, a special language that comes between a speaker and listener.[74]

To demonstrate the value of clear, plain language, John Strylowski of the U.S. Department of the Interior and a frequent speaker at plain language seminars offers several recommendations:

- Never write a sentence with more than 40 words.
- Cover only one subject per sentence.
- Don't include information just because you know it. Think about what the reader [or listener] needs.
- Use shorter words and phrases such as "now" rather than "at the present time."[75]

If you doubt the need for plain language, try to decipher the gobbledygook used by former Secretary of Defense Donald Rumsfeld:

Reports that say something hasn't happened are always interesting to me, because as we know, there are known knowns; there are things we know we know. We also know there are known unknowns; that is to say, we know there are some things we do not know. But also unknown unknowns—the ones we don't know we don't know.[76]

Use Grammatical Language

In his book *If You Can Talk, You Can Write*, Joel Saltzman notes that when you're talking to someone, you rarely worry about grammar or let it stand in the way of getting your point across. You probably never say to yourself, "Because I don't know if I should use *who* or *whom*, I won't even ask the question." According to Saltzman, when you're talking, 98 percent of the time, your grammar is fine and not an issue. For the 2 percent of time your grammar is a problem, many of your listeners won't even notice your mistakes.[77]

We are not saying that grammar isn't important. However, worrying about it all the time may make it impossible for you to write or speak. If you have questions about grammar, consult a good writing handbook or website. Although most listeners miss or forgive a few grammatical errors, consistent grammatical problems can distract listeners and seriously harm your credibility. Your ability to use grammar correctly makes a public statement about your education, social class, and even intelligence.

Writing Apprehension Test (WAT)[78]

Writing apprehension is the fear or anxiety associated with writing situations and topic-specific writing assignments. The following statements will help you to gauge how you feel about writing. Indicate the degree to which each statement applies to you by marking whether you (1) strongly agree, (2) agree, (3) are uncertain about, (4) disagree, or (5) strongly disagree with the statement. Although some of these statements may seem repetitious, take your time and try to be as honest as possible.

_____ 1. I avoid writing.

_____ 2. I have no fear of my writing being evaluated.

_____ 3. I look forward to writing down my ideas.

_____ 4. My mind seems to go blank when I start to work on a composition.

_____ 5. Expressing ideas through writing seems to be a waste of time.

_____ 6. I would enjoy submitting my writing to magazines for evaluation and publication.

_____ 7. I like to write my ideas down.

_____ 8. I feel confident in my ability to express my ideas clearly in writing.

_____ 9. I like to have my friends read what I have written.

_____ 10. I'm nervous about writing.

_____ 11. People seem to enjoy what I write.

_____ 12. I enjoy writing.

_____ 13. I never seem to be able to write down my ideas clearly.

_____ 14. Writing is a lot of fun.

_____ 15. I like seeing my thoughts on paper.

_____ 16. Discussing my writing with others is an enjoyable experience.

_____ 17. It's easy for me to write good compositions.

_____ 18. I don't think I write as well as other people write.

_____ 19. I don't like my compositions to be evaluated.

_____ 20. I'm not good at writing.

Scoring: To determine your score on the WAT, complete the following steps:

1. Add the scores for items 1, 4, 5, 10, 13, 18, 19, and 20.
2. Add the scores for items 2, 3, 6, 7, 8, 9, 11, 12, 14, 15, 16, and 17.
3. Determine your score using the following formula:

   WAT score = 48 – total from step 1 + total from step 2
   Your score should be between 20 and 100 points. If your score is less than 20 or more than 100 points, you have made a mistake in computing the score. The higher your score, the more apprehension you feel about writing.

Score	Level of Apprehension	Description
20–45	Low	Enjoys writing; seeks writing opportunities
46–75	Average	Some writing creates apprehension; other writing does not
76–100	High	Troubled by many kinds of writing; avoids writing in most situations

5.1
Human Language
What makes human language unique?

- The ability to learn words and to combine, invent, and give meaning make humans different from other animals.
- Language is a system of arbitrary signs and symbols used to communicate with others.

5.2
Language and Meaning
How do the characteristics of language affect meaning?

- Whereas signs often look like the thing they represent, symbols are arbitrary collections of sounds that in certain combinations stand for concepts.
- Words have both denotative and connotative meanings and also differ in terms of whether they are concrete or abstract.

5.3
Language and Culture
How do language and culture interact with one another?

- The Whorf hypothesis claims that the nature of your language reflects your culture's view of the world.
- Individualistic cultures have an "I" orientation, whereas collectivist cultures have a "we" orientation.
- People living in low-context cultures rely on words to convey meaning. In high-context, collectivist cultures, people rely on nonverbal behavior and the relationship between communicators to generate meaning.

5.4
Language and Gender
How does language reflect gender differences?

- Most languages have a gender bias that privileges men more than women.
- Men tend to talk more than women even though many people believe the opposite.
- Avoid gender bias by avoiding male and female pronouns when possible.

5.5
Language and Context
How does context affect language choices?

- Code switching refers to modifying verbal and nonverbal communication during interaction with people from other cultures.

5.6
Overcoming Common Language Barriers
How do bypassing, exclusionary language, and offensive language affect communication?

- Communicators who look for meaning in words rather than in the people using words are more likely to bypass and be bypassed.
- Exclusionary language uses words that reinforce stereotypes, belittle other people, or exclude others from understanding an in-group's message.
- People who rarely swear or use offensive language are seen as more intelligent, more pleasant, and more skilled at controlling their emotions.

5.7
Improving Your Way with Words
What strategies can improve your way with words?

- You can improve your way with words by expanding your vocabulary, using oral language when you speak, speaking in an active voice, using the pronouns *I* and *you* wisely, and avoiding gobbledygook.
- An excessive number of grammatical errors in your speech can derail a career or create a negative personal impression.

TEST YOUR KNOWLEDGE

5.1 What makes human language unique?

1 _____ are an arbitrary collection of sounds that in certain combinations stand for concepts.
   a. Signs
   b. Symbols
   c. Denotations
   d. Connotations
   e. Vocalized grunts

5.2 How do the characteristics of language affect meaning?

2 Which of the following words is a superordinate term?
   a. liquid
   b. water
   c. rain
   d. ocean
   e. Caribbean Sea

5.3 How do language and culture affect one another?

3 Approximately how many languages are currently spoken on planet Earth?
   a. 50–60
   b. 500–600
   c. 5,000–6,000
   d. 50,000–60,000
   e. 500,000–600,000

4 According to the more modern version of the Whorf hypothesis,
   a. people without a word for "airplane" cannot see airplanes.
   b. primitive people, even with training, cannot understand modern technology.
   c. language reflects cultural models and influences how people think and act.
   d. people without a word for "tomorrow" or "future" cannot plan.
   e. all of the above

5 The only language that capitalizes the first-person singular pronoun is
   a. English
   b. Finnish
   c. French
   d. Hopi
   e. Korean

5.4 How does language reflect gender differences?

6 Which of the following demonstrates the male bias in the English language?
   a. Grammar books advising using the pronoun "he" to describe both men and women.
   b. Words such as *stewardess* instead of *flight attendant* and *mankind* instead of *human beings*.
   c. Gender word pairings such as *Mr. and Mrs., men and women,* and *husband and wife*.
   d. Word pairings such as *wizard and witch* as well as *master and mistress*.
   e. all of the above

5.5 How does context affect language choices?

7 Which cultural group may use code switching?
   a. African Americans
   b. Hispanic Americans
   c. Asian Americans
   d. Italian Americans
   e. all of the above

5.6 How do bypassing, exclusionary language, and offensive language affect communication?

8 All of the following are examples of exclusionary language except:
   a. The man who served us at lunch was very professional.
   b. A little old lady tipped the young man.
   c. Even though she's a cancer victim, she has a very positive attitude.
   d. What do you expect from such a right-wing nut?
   e. Asian women are quiet and polite.

9 Which of the following strategies can help you control cursing?
   a. When you feel like swearing, bite your tongue until it hurts.
   b. Ask a friend to hold her nose if she hears you swearing.
   c. Do not participate in an argument or a heated exchange with others.
   d. Describe what you see or hear rather than swearing.
   e. Swear in another language so no one understands what you are saying.

5.7 What strategies can improve your way with words?

10 Effective oral language
   a. uses shorter, familiar words.
   b. uses shorter, simpler sentences.
   c. uses an informal speaking style.
   d. uses colloquial expressions.
   e. uses all of the above.

Answers found on page 366.

Key Terms

Abstract word	Exclusionary language	Slang
Active voice	Gobbledygook	Subordinate terms
Basic terms	Jargon	Superordinate terms
Bypassing	Language	Swearing
Code switching	Leet	Symbol
Concrete word	Netlingo	Verbal communication
Connotation	Netspeak	Whorf Hypothesis
Denotation	Passive voice	Writing apprehension
Euphemism	Sign	*You* language

THINK
COMMUNICATION

This article from *Communication Currents* has been slightly edited and shortened with permission from the National Communication Association.

Communication Currents
Knowledge for Communicating Well

N C A

A Publication of the National Communication Association

Volume 4, Issue 2 - April 2009

Language Convergence; Meaning Divergence

We've probably all begun a conversation with, "But I thought we said" or "I thought we agreed." It usually occurs after people leave a conversation thinking that they have reached agreement. Later, they are surprised by the other person's interpretation of the interaction. This example illustrates a new theory of communication called *language convergence/meaning divergence.* The theory emerged during a study attempting to identify the difference between how people define flirting and sexual harassment.

We began our study hoping to discover how people differentiate flirting from sexual harassment in the workplace. We were not so much interested in the legal definitions, as we were interested in the practical definitions people use to distinguish between the two concepts. To accomplish this, we interviewed 14 men and 14 women in a variety of occupations. We asked them for their definitions of each term and for examples of each that they had either seen or experienced. We also specifically asked them what distinguishes flirting from sexual harassment. What we found surprised us.

To understand the findings of our study, it is first necessary to understand the difference between language and meaning. Language is quite simply the words that we use. People who speak a common language typically use the same words. Meaning, on the other hand, constitutes the underlying definition of a given word. Words are necessarily a shortcut for meanings. Conversations would be exhausting if we had to define each word. Unfortunately, language as a conversational shortcut can also create the illusion of a shared meaning—in other words, it makes people think they agree when they really don't.

We discovered that people use the same words but with different meanings. For example, the study participants all used the word *flirting,* but with different meanings. Sometimes meanings were radically different; sometimes the meanings were subtly different. To illustrate, we provide radically different examples of flirting from two women who participated in the study.

Susan: "You know, the men were always just making inappropriate comments to the girls. Um, we had one manager in particular who all this happened with. His sales name was Cloud. Huge um, I don't know maybe a 350 pound guy. He was a very, he was an intimidating kind of guy and definitely used that to his power. Um, you know and there was an incident where we were all out at a, it wasn't at work but it was a work function, work sponsored it kind of thing. And he, um, you know came up and grabbed my butt, 'Have you

---

Identify some of the connotations people associate with the word *flirting.*

How do you define *flirting*? Is it a way to let someone know you're interested in them romantically or sexually? Is it a way to interact with someone in a playful manner? Is it a threat to your romantic partner if you flirt with someone else?

How do you feel about Cloud's behavior toward Susan? What would you do, if anything, if someone you worked with behaved this way?

What does the phrase *sexual harassment* mean to you? In your opinion, is Susan's experience an example of sexual harassment?

How would you define the concept of *othering*? Can you think of examples in which you have experienced or engaged in *othering*?

ever had Cloud love?' I said, 'No.' He goes 'Well do you want some?' kind of thing."

The interviewer asked Susan three times if this was really an example of flirting. Didn't she mean it was sexual harassment? This woman momentarily contemplated this possibility, but then confirmed that she did not consider it to be sexual harassment because it was normal behavior in her workplace. For this woman, normal behavior could not be sexual harassment.

Now contrast Susan's story with Elaine's story . . . Elaine described a situation in which she felt that the main character on the television show *Blue's Clues* was flirting with the children in the audience when he said, "Oh, I'm going to play, that game with the ball and you know, uh, you shoot it through something, and there's a net on it. What do you call that? Oh, right, basketball. You are so smart." For Elaine, flirting is nonsexual, playful banter.

Although both of these women use the word *flirting*, their examples make it clear that their meanings for this term are radically different. Examples like these seem to represent very different understandings of a common language. To describe this phenomenon, we propose a communication theory of language convergence/meaning divergence (LC/MD). Simply put, the theory suggests that people often reach agreement on language to describe or define a particular situation, concept, or plan of action, but the meanings they assign are different. These differences may be so great that it is difficult to imagine that the parties had participated in the same communication or used the same words.

So how do people respond when they use a shared language with different meanings? First, sharing a common language but with different meanings can create the illusion of shared meaning. People think they agree when they really don't. When this illusion of agreeing on meaning begins to fracture, people's natural tendency is to wonder what is wrong

with the other person. They might categorize the other person as crazy, not very bright, or morally questionable. This tendency is called *othering*. Othering is problematic because instead of trying to understand the other person so we can solve a problem or resolve a conflict, we assume that the other person *is* the problem.

LC/MD emphasizes an important misconception that is common in our understanding of communication. Generally, explanations of communication suggest that if we improve the clarity or precision of our communication, we will better understand each other. This study suggests that not only do we need to provide clear language, but we also need to check underlying meanings in order to increase the odds that similar understanding will occur.

This theory helps explain why men and women often evaluate sexual behavior in the workplace in significantly different ways. LC/MD would also be useful for exploring intercultural communication in which reaching language convergence is often challenging enough, but reaching meaning convergence is particularly difficult. Finally, LC/MD might be useful in understanding those conflicts we have with others, such as a friend or a spouse. By asking questions more often like "what do you mean by that?" perhaps we can begin fewer conversations with "But I thought we said. . ."

Is the woman's statement about what is normal another example of the authors' *language convergence; meaning divergence* theory? Could the authors' have misinterpreted the woman's meaning when she used this word?

ABOUT THE AUTHORS

Michael W. Kramer is Professor of Communication at the University of Oklahoma, Norman, Oklahoma, and **Debbie S. Dougherty** is Associate Professor of Communication at the University of Missouri, Columbia, Missouri. This essay is based on Dougherty, D.S., Kramer, M.W., Hamlett, S.R., & Kurth, T. (2009). "Language convergence and meaning divergence: An examination of language and meaning for social-sexual behaviors in organizations." *Communication Monographs,* 76, pp. 20–46. Communication Monographs, and Communication Currents are publications of the National Communication Association.

How, if at all, does this explanation of language convergence/meaning divergence theory differ from Haney's definition of bypassing, discussed on p. 93 of Chapter 5?

Relate this statement to Joann Keyton's claim that "We use words to create messages, and we create meanings from those messages" in her article "Examining Communication," on pp. 20–21.

NONVERBAL
Communication

In April 2009, the world met Susan Boyle, the unfashionable, unmarried, unemployed, 47-year-old church volunteer from Scotland who sang her way to instant fame on the television show *Britain's Got Talent*. When she walked onto the stage, the judges' faces registered skepticism. Camera pans of the audience revealed looks of disdain and disbelief. After Ms. Boyle announced that she would sing "I Dreamed a Dream," a song from the musical *Les Miserables*, the judges smirked and the audience snickered. When the music started, the judges sat back and braced themselves for what judge Simon Cowell would later describe as "something extraordinary."

And then Susan Boyle began to sing. The judges' skeptical gazes turned into expressions of delight; these, coupled with their hands held ready to applaud said it all. At the conclusion of her song, everyone rose in a standing ovation. The rest of Ms. Boyle's story is entertainment history.

Ms. Boyle's story teaches us that actions really *do* speak louder than words. What does a hug from a friend, a raised eyebrow from a coworker, tears from a child, or the applause of an audience tell you? The answer to this question depends on many factors—the communicators; their purpose; the context, content, and structure of a message; *and* how their nonverbal behavior expresses much or more than the words they say.

Communicating Without Words

What is nonverbal communication, and how does it affect your everyday life?

Nonverbal communication refers to message components other than words that generate meaning. Researchers estimate that 60 to 70 percent, or about two-thirds, of the meaning we generate may be conveyed through nonverbal behaviors.[1] Whereas verbal communication depends on words, nonverbal communication is more multidimensional, depending on such things as physical appearance, body movement, facial expressions, touch, vocal characteristics, and the communication context.

Everyone uses nonverbal communication. When you are aware of your own nonverbal behavior and are sensitive to others' unspoken messages, you are more likely to experience academic and occupational success, better social relationships (and, consequently, less loneliness, shyness, depression, and mental illness), a more satisfying marriage, and less stress, anxiety, and hypertension.[2]

Functions of Nonverbal Communication

Because nonverbal communication allows you to send and receive messages through all five of your senses, you have more information to draw on when generating or interpreting a message. You can achieve many communication goals through nonverbal behavior, ranging from creating a positive impression to detecting deception.

Create an Impression As soon as you walk into a room, your physical appearance, clothing, posture, and facial expression create an impression. When attorneys prepare witnesses to testify in court, they tell them how to dress and teach them how to look and sound sincere and confident. Experienced courtroom lawyers know that jurors begin forming their opinions of witnesses before witnesses utter a word. Whether it's a first date, a job interview, or a meeting with a new client, nonverbal messages create strong impressions.

Identify and Express Emotions We rely on nonverbal communication to identify and express the emotional components of a message. For example, if Jason says, "I'm angry," he simply labels an emotion, but his nonverbal behavior—vocal intensity, facial expression, and body movement—tell you how to interpret his anger. Expressing emotions by smiling, laughing, frowning, crying, grimacing, and even walking away from an encounter can make words unnecessary, provided the other person accurately interprets the meaning of the nonverbal cues they see or hear.

Define Relationships The nature of a relationship is often expressed nonverbally. For example, the closeness and duration of a hug can reveal the level of intimacy between friends. Or a group member may take a central position at the head of a conference table to establish leadership. The simple act of holding hands in public or a first kiss signifies "we are more than just friends."

Establish Power and Influence Do you know people who are powerful and persuasive? What kind of nonverbal characteristics do they display? Powerful people often take up more space by having a bigger office or desk. They often touch others more than they are touched. They look at others less frequently unless they want to stare someone down. By using a powerful voice and confident posture, they command attention and influence.

Interpret Verbal Messages Non-verbal communication provides us with a message about a message, or a **metamessage**, by offering important clues about

how to interpret its verbal aspects. For example, you may doubt a person who says he's feeling fine after a fall if he winces when he walks. If someone says she's glad to see you but is looking over your shoulder to see who else is in the room, you may distrust her sincerity.

Deceive Others and Detect Deception Have you ever tried to hide your feelings from others—whether you're denying wrongdoing or keeping a secret? Of course you have.

> **"He that has eyes to see and ears to hear may convince himself that no mortal can keep a secret. If his lips are silent, he chatters with his fingertips; betrayal oozes out of him at every pore."**
> —Sigmund Freud[3]

Great poker players have mastered this skill. However, most of us are amateurs. Our "innocent" smile may seem false, our gestures may look awkward, our voice may sound shaky, and our persistent toe tapping or knee jiggling may broadcast our anxiety.

STOP&THINK

Can You Detect a Lie?

Most of us aren't very good at detecting a lie. According to Judee Burgoon, a noted researcher in human deception, most people's ability to detect deception accurately is equivalent to the flip of a coin: about 50/50.[4] Paul Ekman, another leading researcher in deception and nonverbal communication, points out that accurately identifying when someone is lying is further complicated by the fact that there is no single facial expression or body movement that serves as a reliable sign of deceit.[5]

Yet many liars do give themselves away by displaying **leakage cues**, unintentional nonverbal behaviors that may reveal deceptive communication. These cues, which fall into three categories, are what you need to look for when trying to detect a lie.

1. *Displays of nervousness*: More blinking, higher pitch speech, vocal tension, less gesturing, more fidgety movements, longer pauses, fewer facial changes
2. *Signs of negative emotions*: Reduced eye contact, fewer pleasant facial expressions, agitated vocal tone
3. *Incompetent communication*: More speech errors, physical rigidity, hesitations, exaggerated movements, lack of spontaneity[6]

Keep in mind that leakage cues are not the same for everyone. Rather than reduce or eliminate eye contact, a skillful liar may look you in the eye. Some nonverbal behaviors, however, are better lie indicators than others. For instance, since facial muscles are generally easier to control than other muscles in the body, facial expressions can be managed and therefore don't necessarily reveal a liar. But, vocal pitch is less controllable, so any noticeable changes may well give a liar away.

Mark Knapp, another prominent researcher in lying and deception, acknowledges that a small minority of people are highly skilled lie detectors. These human "lie detectors" pay close attention to what nonverbal communication tells them; they look for discrepancies between verbal and nonverbal behavior.[7] So pay attention to what people say as well as how they act. For example, researchers have noted that people telling the truth tend to add 20 to 30 percent more external detail to their stories and explanations than do those who are lying.[8]

THE NATURE OF
NONVERBAL COMMUNICATION

MORE CONVINCING
Nonverbal communication is more believable because it seems spontaneous and revealing. CAUTION: Perceptions can deceive. Think of the times you've heard, "He *seemed* so honest when I met him," or "She acted like she really cared."

HIGHLY CONTEXTUAL
The meaning of nonverbal messages depends on a situation's psychosocial, logistical, and interactional context. CAUTION: Depending on the context, a laugh can be interpreted as amusement, approval, contempt, scorn, or embarrassment.

CONTINUOUS
Whereas verbal communication may stop and start, nonverbal communication usually continues uninterrupted. CAUTION: People interpret your opinions and feelings even when you are not talking.

LESS STRUCTURED
Unlike verbal communication, nonverbal communication has few agreed-upon rules. CAUTION: Nonverbal behavior can communicate multiple and ambiguous meanings, and can be difficult to interpret.

LEARNED INFORMALLY
You learn to communicate nonverbally by watching others and interpreting feedback about your nonverbal behavior. CAUTION: Failure to learn appropriate nonverbal behavior can embarrass you and result in misunderstanding and confusion.

Is Your Teenage Brain to Blame?

For decades, parents, teachers, and psychologists "threw up their hands and cried, 'Hormones!' when asked why children become so nutty around the time of adolescence."[9] Scientists now claim that hormones are only part of the answer.

Using neuroimaging, neuropsychologist Deborah Yurgelun-Todd and her colleagues found that teenage brains work differently than adult brains when processing nonverbal emotional information.[10] Before explaining more about this research, look at the image above.

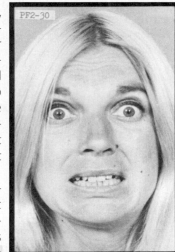

What emotion do you see on this person's face?

The answer is: fear. While 100 percent of adults who were shown this photo guessed this woman's emotion correctly, only 50 percent of teenagers got it right. Many teens identified the emotion as shock, confusion, or sadness.[11] It turns out that teens and adults use different part of their brains to identify emotions.

The results of these studies are significant for communicators of all ages. It means that what we see as teenage indifference to emotions is, in fact, an inability to recognize emotions correctly, particularly the feelings in an adult's face. According to Dr. Yurgelun-Todd,

[Teenagers] see anger when there isn't anger, or sadness when there isn't sadness. And if that's the case, then clearly their own behavior is not going to match that of the adult. So you'll see miscommunication, both in terms of what they think the adult is feeling, but also what the response should then be to that.[12]

In Chapter 2, we explained how effective self-monitoring helps you identify your own feelings and the feelings of others, particularly when they're expressed nonverbally. People who are high self-monitors astutely watch other people; correctly interpret the meaning of their facial expressions, body language, and tone of voice; and then appropriately respond to their behavior. Research on the teenage brain helps us understand why many teenage brains need to "grow up" and physically mature in order to develop and practice self-monitoring skills.

6.2
Linking Verbal and Nonverbal Communication

How do verbal and nonverbal communication interact to create meaning?

Verbal communication and nonverbal communication often rely on each other to generate and interpret the meaning of a message. When you verbally congratulate someone, you may smile, shake hands, or hug that person. When you verbally express anger, you may frown, stand farther away, or use a harsh voice.

Psychologist Paul Ekman notes that most nonverbal behaviors repeat, complement, accent, regulate, substitute for, and/or contradict verbal messages.[13]

Repeat

Repetitive nonverbal behaviors visually repeat a verbal message. For example, when a waiter asks if anyone is interested in dessert, Elaine nods as she says, "Yes." She then points at a selection on the dessert tray and says, "I want the cheesecake." Ralph says he would like

the same, so Elaine holds up two fingers and says, "Make it two pieces."

Complement

Complementary nonverbal behaviors are consistent with the verbal message. During a job interview, your words tell the interviewer that you are a confident professional, but what you say will be more believable if nonverbal elements such as posture, facial expressions, and vocal quality send the same message. Even the meaning of a simple *hello* can be strengthened if your facial expression and tone of voice communicate genuine interest and pleasure in greeting someone.

Accent

Accenting nonverbal behaviors emphasize important elements in a message by highlighting its focus or

emotional content. Saying the words "I'm angry" may fail to make the point, so you may couple this message with louder volume, forceful gestures, and piercing eye contact. Stressing a word or phrase in a sentence also focuses meaning.

Regulate

We use **regulating nonverbal behaviors** to manage the flow of a conversation. Nonverbal cues tell us when to start and stop talking, whose turn it is to speak, how to interrupt other speakers, and how to encourage others to talk more. If you lean forward and open your mouth as if to speak, you are signaling that you want a turn in the conversation. In a classroom or large meeting, you may raise your hand when you want to speak. When your friend nods her head as you speak, you may interpret her nod as a sign to continue what you're saying.

Substitute

Nonverbal behavior can take the place of verbal language. This is called **substituting nonverbal behaviors**. When we wave hello or good-bye, the meaning is usually clear even in the absence of words. Without saying anything, a mother may send a message to a misbehaving child by pursing her lips, narrowing her eyes, and moving a single finger to signal "stop."

Contradict

Contradictory nonverbal behaviors conflict with the meaning of spoken words. On receiving a birthday gift from a coworker, Sherry says, "It's lovely. Thank you." However, her forced smile, flat vocal expression, and lack of eye contact suggest that Sherry does not appreciate the gift. This is a classic example of a **mixed message**: a contradiction between verbal and nonverbal meanings. When nonverbal behavior contradicts spoken words, messages are confusing and difficult to interpret. Because nonverbal channels can carry more information than verbal ones, we usually rely on the nonverbal cues to determine the true meaning of a message.

FACTS **THINK** ABOUT THEORY
TEST IDEA PLAN EXPERIMENT METHOD

Expectancy Violation Theory

The following two scenarios are quite similar but may produce significantly different reactions.

Scenario 1. You stop at a local convenience store for a cup of coffee on your way to work, and you notice a poorly dressed man looking at you as you walk into the store. You've never seen him before. While you are preparing your coffee, he approaches and stands right next to you, smil-

ing. As he reaches for a cup, his hand brushes against your arm. You turn to leave. Now he is standing directly behind you to pay for the coffee—and smiles again. As you leave, he follows you out the door.

Scenario 2. You stop at the office snack bar to get a cup of coffee, and you notice a well-dressed man looking at you. He's a valued friend and colleague you've worked with for many years. While you are preparing your coffee, he approaches and stands right next to you, smiling. As he reaches for a cup, his hand brushes against your arm. You turn to leave. Now he is standing directly behind you to pay for the coffee—and smiles again. As you leave, he follows you out the door.

Both scenarios are similar. Yet in the first case, you probably react with suspicion and disapproval, whereas in the second case you may feel more relaxed and positive. According to **Expectancy Violation Theory**, your expectations about nonverbal behavior have a significant effect on how you interact with others and how you interpret the meaning of nonverbal messages. When you enter an elevator, you probably conform to nonverbal expectations: You turn around and face front, avoid eye contact with others, avoid movement, refrain from talking or touching others, and stare at the numbers as they go up or down. But how would you react if someone en-

tered a cramped elevator with three unruly dogs and lit a cigar? You'd most likely disapprove or object because this is not the kind of behavior you'd expect in a confined public space.

At least three characteristics influence your expectations and reactions to the nonverbal behavior of another person.[14] Think of the previous two scenarios as you consider these characteristics.

1. *Communicator Characteristics.* Personal characteristics, such as age, gender, ethnicity, and physical appearance, as well as personality and reputation
2. *Relational Characteristics.* Level of familiarity, past experiences, relative status, and type of relationship with others, such as close friend, romantic partner, business associate, service provider, or stranger
3. *Contextual Characteristics.* Physical, social, psychological, cultural, and professional settings and occasions, such as football games, stores, religious services, classrooms, or business meetings

Clearly, the first scenario highlights differences in communicator, relational, and contextual characteristics, whereas the second scenario highlights similarities. In the first scenario, the man violates a number of nonverbal expectations: don't stare, follow, or touch strangers. In the second scenario, the man is "allowed" to violate the same nonverbal "rules" because you know him well.

6.3
Types of Nonverbal Communication

What types of nonverbal communication should you pay attention to when interacting with others?

Nonverbal communication is undeniably complex. To interpret nonverbal meaning accurately, you must pay attention to multiple nonverbal dimensions. To be an effective communicator you must consider the totality of your own and others' nonverbal behavior.

Physical Appearance

When you first meet someone, you automatically analyze a person's physical appearance to form an impression. Although it seems unfair to judge a person's personality and character based on physical characteristics such as weight, attractiveness, clothing,

Types of NONVERBAL CUES

Physical Appearance

Body Movement and Gestures

Touch

Facial Expressions

Eye Behavior

Vocal Expressiveness

Silence

Space and Distance

Time

Environment

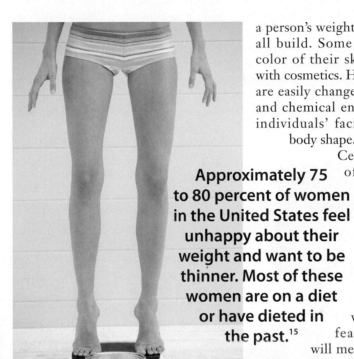

Approximately 75 to 80 percent of women in the United States feel unhappy about their weight and want to be thinner. Most of these women are on a diet or have dieted in the past.[15]

and hairstyle, these factors strongly influence how we interact with others.

Attractiveness For better or worse, attractive people are perceived as kinder, more interesting, more sociable, more successful, and sexier than those considered less attractive. One study found that good-looking people tend to make more money and get promoted more often than those with average looks.[16]

In addition to weight, height influences how people perceive each other. Generally, taller people are viewed as more attractive, powerful, outgoing, and confident than shorter people. A 2009 study found that tall people report more enjoyment of life and less pain and sadness. These findings reflect the positive association between height and both income and education, both of which are positively linked to better lives.[17]

In their quest to be more attractive, many people try to change their physical appearance. Dieting, healthy eating, and fitness training can change

a person's weight, figure, and overall build. Some people alter the color of their skin by tanning or with cosmetics. Hair color and style are easily changed. Plastic surgery and chemical enhancements alter individuals' facial structure and body shape.

Certainly the images of attractive men and women on television and in popular magazines and film influence how we see others. Most of us were not born with movie-star features and never will meet those standards of "beauty." Yet there is no question that physical attraction plays a significant role in selecting romantic partners, getting and succeeding in a job, persuading others, and maintaining high self-esteem.

Clothing and Accessories Your clothing and accessories send messages about your economic status, education, trustworthiness, social position, level of sophistication, and moral character. For example, a person wearing a stylish suit and carrying an expensive leather briefcase suggests a higher income, a college education, and more status within a company than a person wearing a uniform and carrying a mop. Accessories such as a college ring, a wedding band, or a religious necklace reveal a great deal about another person.

However, judging others based on their clothing can lead to inaccurate assumptions. For example, what type of clothing does a millionaire wear? In their book *The Millionaire Next Door: The Surprising Secrets of America's Wealthy*, marketing researchers Thomas Stanley and William Danko note that the vast majority of

Can Tattooing and Body Piercing Hurt Your Image?

In many cultures, both past and present, people have pierced and tattooed their bodies. These markings often commemorated a rite of passage such as puberty, marriage, or a successful hunt. However, in most modern Western cultures, tattoos have been associated with people of lower social status, gangs, "bikers," and lower-ranked military personnel.

But in recent decades the popularity of tattoos has grown among all age groups. A 2007 Pew Research Center survey reported that 36 percent of those ages 18 to 25 and 40 percent of those ages 26 to 40 have at least one tattoo. Despite the increasing popularity of tattoos, the Pew Research Center notes that "the public is divided about the impact of more people getting tattoos: 45% say it has not made much of a difference, 40% think it has been a change for the worse, and only 7% say this has been a change for the better." Not surprisingly, 64 percent of those of people 65 and older and 51 percent of those ages 50 to 64 say that the increase in tattoos is a change for the worse.[18]

Interestingly and perhaps more surprising, a study at Texas State University found that "individuals of age 18–24, the age group with more body art than any other, tend to consider *visible* tattoos and piercings to be unacceptable at work, particularly when face-to-face customer contact or commission sharing goes with the job."

Many people are also divided about the social impact of body piercing, particularly piercings of ear edges as well as the nose, tongue, lips, face, nipples, naval, and genitals.

Ear gauging (stretching) is also popular despite the fact that many people (especially parents) find the practice appalling and even repulsive. When the mother of a 14-year-old inquired on an online chat whether she should let her son gauge his ears claiming she thought "ear gauging looks disgusting and weird," the answer voted as "best" by the blog visitors was "I definitely agree with you about ear gauging being disgusting. If I was a mother, I would NEVER let my child get their ears gauged."[20]

David Brooks, political and cultural commentator for the *New York Times*, observes that "a cadre of fashion-forward types thought they were doing something to separate themselves from the vanilla middle class but are now discovering that the signs etched into their skins are absolutely mainstream."[21] There's no question that "tattoos have become more acceptable for men and women of all socioeconomic classes in today's society."[22] Even so, some cities and public school systems force "employees to cover up tattoos if they want to keep their jobs."[23] Regardless of whether *you* like or dislike them, the popularity of tattoos has made it more difficult and often unfair to negatively stereotype those who tattoo and pierce their bodies.

> Contrary to what many people believe, it is not generally illegal for employers to ban visible body art in their dress code policies.[19]

millionaires do not wear expensive suits, shoes, or watches. "It is easier to purchase products that denote superiority than to actually be superior in economic achievement."[24]

Hair Hair is something of an obsession in the United States. In *Reading People*, jury consultant Jo-Ellan Dimitrius and attorney Mark Mazzarella use hair as a predictor of people's self-image and lifestyle. They claim that your hairstyle can reveal "how you feel about aging, how extravagant or practical you are, how much importance you attach to impressing others, your socioeconomic background, your overall emotional maturity, and sometimes even the part of the country where you were raised or now live."[25] If you doubt their claim, think about the ways in which very long hair on men communicated antiwar rebellion and hippie lifestyles in the late 1960s and early 1970s, what a multicolored mohawk said about a young person in the 1980s, or what a Justin Bieber flip meant in 2010.

In his recent documentary, *Good Hair*, comedian Chris Rock took a serious look at the high price that black women pay (in harsh chemical treatments, hours of tight braiding, and dollars) to have *good hair*, a colloquial phrase in the African American community that describes the straight or soft-curly hair of non-black women. Rock exposed a $90 billion (that's right, billion dollar) industry that profits by transforming "nappy" hair into hair more like that of European women or into elaborate weaves.[26] Darryl Owens, in a commentary for the *Orlando Sentinel*, notes that "For African Americans, nagging issues of self-identify, self-esteem, and self worth that step for our peculiar history in American are tangled up in our hair."[27] In an attempt to combat this negative view of "good hair" *Sesame Street* writer Joey Mazzarino, the white parent of an adopted Ethiopian girl, wrote "I Really Love My Hair," a celebration of natural hair sung by a brown-skinned Muppet. Here's a short excerpt:

Don't need a trip to the beauty shop,
'cause I love what I got on top.

It's curly and it's brown and it's right up there!
You know what I love? That's right, my hair![28]

Ultimately we should remember to be careful when drawing conclusions about others based on their hairstyle. A man who wears short hair may be an ultraconservative or a rebel, an athlete or a cancer patient, a police officer or a fashion model. A short and chic haircut on a woman can signify an artistic, creative, and expressive nature or may indicate a more practical nature.

Body Movement and Gestures

Jamal points to his watch to let the chairperson know that the meeting time is running short. Karen gives a thumbs-up gesture to signal that her friend's speech went well. Robin stands at attention as the American flag is raised. How you sit, stand, position the body, or move your hands generates nonverbal messages. Even your posture can convey moods and emotions. Slouching back in your chair may be perceived as lack of interest or dislike, whereas sitting upright and leaning forward communicates interest and is a sign of active listening.

Gestures are body movements that communicate an idea or emotion. They can emphasize or stress parts of a message, reveal discomfort with a situation, or convey a message without the use of words. The hands and arms are used most frequently for gesturing, although head and foot movements are also considered types of gestures.[29]

Many people have difficulty expressing their thoughts without using gestures. Why else would we gesture when speaking to someone on the phone? Gesturing can also ease the mental effort required when communication is difficult. For example, we tend to gesture more when using a language that is less familiar or when describing a picture that a listener cannot see. Paul Ekman and Wallace Friesen classify hand movements as **emblems**, **illustrators**, and **adaptors**.[30]

TYPES OF **GESTURES**

TYPE OF GESTURE	CHARACTERISTICS	EXAMPLES
EMBLEM	Expresses the same meaning as a word in a particular group or culture	• Forming a V with your index and middle finger as a sign of victory or peace • Raising your hand in class to indicate "I want to speak" • Placing your index finger over your lips to mean "be quiet" • Extending the middle finger to offend someone or declare "up yours"
ILLUSTRATOR	Used with a verbal message that would lack meaning without the words	• Pointing as a way of identifying an object or person. • Holding your hands two feet apart and saying, "The fish I caught was this big" • Counting out the steps of a procedure with your hand while orally describing each step • Snapping your fingers while saying, "It happened just like that," to indicate that an event occurred quickly
ADAPTOR	Habitual gestures that help manage and express emotions	• Scratching your head to signify confusion or an inability to answer. • Chewing your nails because you are worried or anxious • Drumming your fingers on a table because you are impatient • Wringing your hands because you are distressed • Playing with your hair or an object to relieve stress or impatience

COMMUNICATION & CULTURE

IS THE OK SIGN ALWAYS OK?

Keep in mind that the examples of emblems, illustrators, and adaptors discussed in this chapter are gestures commonly used in the United States and have very specific meanings. Therefore, before interacting with people from other countries and cultures, think before you gesture. For example, the emblem that means "OK" to most Americans (forming a circle with the thumb and index finger) is considered an obscene gesture to Brazilians and signifies money to the Japanese.[31] When describing the height of a person, we may hold an arm out, palm down, and say, "My friend is this tall." In some South American countries, this same gesture is fine for describing a dog but would not be used for describing a person. To designate a person's height, a South American would hold her arm out with her palm sideways. Even putting your hands in your pockets can offend others, as a professor friend of ours learned when he spent a year teaching in Indonesia.

Touch

Touch is one of the most potent forms of physical expression. It not only has the power to send strong messages, but it also affects your overall well-being. Being deprived of touch can have a negative effect on your physical and psychological health.[32] For example, we know that babies need human touch to survive and develop. When new parents and hospital nurses engage in more touching behavior, infant death rates decrease.

Many people have difficulty expressing their thoughts without using gestures. An encouraging pat on the shoulder from a coworker or a lover's embrace can convey encouragement, appreciation, affection, empathy, or sexual interest. Playful touches tend

Know Thy SELF

Are You Touchy?[33]

How touchy are you? Indicate the degree to which each statement below applies to you using the following rating scale: (5) strongly agree, (4) agree, (3) undecided or neutral, (2) disagree, or (1) strongly disagree.

_____ 1. I don't mind if I am hugged as a sign of friendship.

_____ 2. I enjoy touching others.

_____ 3. I seldom put my arms around others.

_____ 4. When I see people hugging, it bothers me.

_____ 5. People should not be uncomfortable about being touched.

_____ 6. I really like being touched by others.

_____ 7. I wish I were free to show my emotions by touching others.

_____ 8. I do not like touching other people.

_____ 9. I do not like being touched by others.

_____ 10. I find it enjoyable to be touched by others.

_____ 11. I dislike having to hug others.

_____ 12. Hugging and touching should be outlawed.

_____ 13. Touching others is a very important part of my personality.

_____ 14. Being touched by others makes me uncomfortable.

Scoring:

1. Add up the responses you put next to the following items: 1, 2, 5, 6, 7, 10, and 13. Your Step 1 score = _____.

2. Add up the responses you put next to the following items: 3, 4, 8, 9, 11, 12, and 14. Your Step 2 score = _____.

3. Complete the following formula: 42 + Step 1 score – Step 2 score = _____

Your score should be between 14 and 70 points. A score of more than 53 points suggests that you are a touch approacher. A score of less than 31 points indicates that you tend to avoid touch.

to lighten the mood without expressing a high degree of emotion. Lightly punching a friend in the arm or covering another's eyes and asking, "Guess who?" are forms of playful touch.

Touch is also used to express control or dominance. In some instances, only a minor level of control is needed, such as when we tap someone on the shoulder to get her or his attention. In other cases, touch sends very clear messages about status or dominance. Research shows that individuals with more power and status are more likely to touch someone of lesser status and subordinates rarely initiate touch with a person of higher status.[34]

Some people are more comfortable with touch than others as demonstrated in the *Know Thy Self: Are You Touchy?* feature on the previous page. **Touch approachers** are comfortable with touch and often initiate touch with others. A touch approacher is more likely to initiate a hug or a kiss when greeting a friend. Some touch approachers even touch or hug people

We use touch to express a wide range of emotions.

they don't know very well. At the extreme end of the continuum are touch approachers who touch too much and violate nonverbal expectations.

Touch avoiders are less comfortable initiating or being touched. They are also more conscious of when, how, and by whom they are touched. Extreme touch avoiders avoid any physical contact even with loved ones. Most of us are somewhere in the middle of the continuum. Obviously, misunderstandings can result when touch approachers and avoiders meet. Approachers may view avoiders as cold and unfriendly, and avoiders may perceive approachers as invasive and rude.

Not surprisingly, norms for touch depend on the context. For example, violating touch norms in the workplace can result in misunderstandings or allegations of sexual harassment. Norms for touch also vary according to gender and culture. Most North American men tend to avoid same-sex touch except for the hugging and high-fiving we see on sports teams.

Facial Expression

Your face is composed of complex muscles capable of displaying well over a thousand different expressions. Facial expressions let you know if others are interested in, agree with, or understand what you have said. Generally, women tend to be more facially expressive and smile more often than men. But although men are more likely to limit the amount of emotion they reveal, everyone relies on facial expressions to comprehend the full meaning of a message.

In order to add emotional flavor to online messages, some people use **emoticons**, typographical characters such as :-) or :-(that serve as substitutes for expressing emotions nonverbally. However, current research claims that emoticons have become less useful as nonverbal cues and have little or no effect on the interpretation of a typed message.[35]

We learn to manage facial expressions in order to convey or conceal an emotion and to adapt our facial expressions to particular situations. The most common techniques for adapting facial expressions are **masking**, **neutralization**, **intensification**, and **deintensification**.[36]

ADAPTING FACIAL EXPRESSIONS

TECHNIQUE	CHARACTERISTICS	EXAMPLES
Masking	Conceals true emotions by displaying expressions considered more appropriate in a particular situation	• Smiling and congratulating a colleague for getting a promotion you wanted • Looking stern when reprimanding a toddler who has dumped a bowl of spaghetti on his head
Neutralization	Eliminates all displays of emotions	• Avoiding any display of emotion when serving as a juror during a trial • Displaying a "poker face" during a card game
Intensification	Exaggerates expressions to meet other people's needs or to express strong feelings	• Hugging someone a few more seconds than usual to communicate how much you care • Pouting dramatically when you do not get your way
Deintensification	Reduces or downplays emotional displays to accommodate others	• Looking mildly disapproving when a committee member rudely interrupts another speaker during a meeting • Subduing smiles of happiness after defeating a highly competitive friend in a tennis match

Facial Expressions in CYBERSPACE

:)	Happiness, sarcasm, joking
:P	Sticking out your tongue
;)	Wink
:(	Unhappy or sad
:o	Surprise
:D	Laughing
XD	Hysterical laughter
:S	Indecision or disappointment
:3	coy/cutesy/self-conscious smile

Eye Behavior

Your eyes may be the most revealing and complex of all your facial features.

Our eyes can signify social position, express both positive and negative emotion, and indicate a willingness to relate.[37] When we try to understand what someone else is saying, most of us will look at a speaker more than 80 percent of the time. A group member who wants to be viewed as a leader may choose a seat at the head of the table to gain more visual attention. We tend to increase gaze in response to positive emotions such as surprise and avert our eyes in response to negative experiences like disgust or horror. We use eye contact to get a server's attention in a restaurant and avert our eyes when we don't want the instructor to call on us in class.

As with all nonverbal behavior, norms for eye contact vary according to gender and culture. Women tend to engage in more eye contact when listening than men. In North America, lack of eye contact is frequently perceived as rudeness, indifference, nervousness, or dishonesty. This is not true across all cultures. For example, "direct eye contact is a taboo or an insult in many Asian cultures. Cambodians consider direct eye contact an invasion of one's privacy."[38]

Vocal Expressiveness

How you *say* a word significantly influences its meaning. Your vocal quality also affects how others perceive you. For example, it can be difficult to listen to a person with a very high-pitched or monotone voice.

WHAT DO WE KNOW ABOUT **EYE BEHAVIOR?**

Researchers have arrived at several conclusions about eye behavior.[39] Rate each of the following behaviors as *generally* true or false. Keep in mind that factors such as personality, gender, culture, and context influence our eye behavior.

True/False

_____ 1. We look at people and things we like.

_____ 2. We avoid looking at people and things we do not like.

_____ 3. We look more at another person when seeking approval or wanting to be liked.

_____ 4. When we avert our gaze from someone, it's an intentional act.

_____ 5. Deception can rarely be detected by looking solely at another person's eye behavior.

_____ 6. Our pupils dilate when we look at someone or something that is appealing or interesting to us.

_____ 7. Our pupils constrict when we look at someone or something that is not appealing or interesting to us.

_____ 8. Women often look longer at their conversational partners than men do.

Correct answers: All of the statements are true.

Some of the most important vocal characteristics are volume, pitch, and word stress. **Volume** refers to the loudness of the voice. Whispering can indicate that the information is confidential; yelling suggests urgency or anger. **Pitch** refers to how high or low your voice sounds. In the United States, Americans seem to prefer low-pitched voices. Men and women with deeper voices are seen as more authoritative and effective. Men with a naturally high pitch may be labeled effeminate or weak, and women with very high pitches may be labeled as childish, silly, or anxious.

Rate is the speed at which you speak. A speaking rate that is too fast makes it difficult for others to understand your message. On the other hand, we become bored by or stop listening to a person who speaks to slowly.

When volume, pitch, and rate are combined, they can be used to vary the stress you give to a word or phrase. **Word stress** refers to the "degree of prominence given to a syllable within a word or words within a phrase or sentence."[40] Notice the differences in meaning as you stress the italicized words in the following sentences:

Is **that** the report you want me to read?

Is that the report you want **me** to read?

Is that the report you want me to **read**?

Although the same words are used in all three sentences, the meaning of each question is quite different.

In Chapter 14, "Language and Delivery," we will take a closer look at these and other vocal characteristics and see how they contribute to the success of a presentation.

Silence

The well-known phrase "silence is golden" may be based on a Swiss saying, "*Sprechen ist silbern; Swchweigen ist golden*," which means "speech is silver; silence is golden." This metaphor contrasts the value of speech and silence. Although speech is important, silence may be even more significant in certain contexts.

Silence is also speech. (African proverb)

A loud voice shows an empty head. (Finnish proverb)

Those who know, do not speak. Those who speak, do not know. Lao Tzu, *Tao Te Ching*

Silence is a friend who will not betray. (Confucius)

Understanding the value of silence is important because we use silence to communicate many things: to establish interpersonal distance, to put our thoughts together, to show respect for another person, or to modify others' behaviors.[41]

Space and Distance

The ways in which we claim, use, and interpret space and distance are significant dimensions of nonverbal communication.

In nonverbal terms, **territoriality** is the sense of personal ownership attached to a particular space. For instance, most classroom students sit in the same place every day. If you have ever walked into a classroom to find another person in *your* seat, you may have felt that your territory had been violated. Ownership of territory is often designated by objects acting as **markers** of territory. Placing a coat on a chair or books on a table can send a clear message that a seat is taken or saved.

ETHICAL COMMUNICATION

The Dark Side of Nonverbal Behavior

Just as a smile or a pat on the back can communicate, so too can an angry shove or a slap. Unfortunately, some people use violent nonverbal communication to express negative emotions or exert power over others. Each year, approximately 1.5 million women and more than 800,000 men are victims of violence from an intimate partner such as a husband, wife, boyfriend, girlfriend, or date.[42] Although female victims are more likely to need medical attention, research reveals that women hit men as often as men hit women.[43]

Violence also occurs in the workplace between coworkers and by frustrated customers.

Physical intimidation and violence includes acts such as hitting, restraining, and shoving as well as behavior that stops short of physical contact, such as throwing objects, pounding on a desk, or destroying property. Intimidating nonverbal communication can also take more subtle forms, such as physically blocking another's path, moving aggressively and too close, or creating a threatening presence. The use of unjustified physical aggression violates the National Communication Association's Credo for Ethical Communication, which specifically condemns communication that is intimidating, coercive, or violent.[45]

Fifteen percent of homicides in the workplace are committed by coworkers.[44]

Anthropologist Edward T. Hall uses the term **proxemics** to refer to the study of spatial relationships and how the distance between people communicates information about their relationship. Hall maintains that we have our own personal portable "air bubble" that we carry around with us. This personal space is culturally determined. For example, the Japanese, who are accustomed to crowding, need less space around them, whereas North Americans need "wide open spaces" around them to feel comfortable.[46]

Hall contends that most Americans interact within four spatial zones or distances: **intimate**, **personal**, **social**, and **public**.[47]

Not surprisingly, we reduce the distance between ourselves and others as our relationships become more personal. Intimate distance is usually associated with love, comfort, protection, and increased physical contact. In most situations, you encounter a mixture of distances. You may feel comfortable using an intimate or personal distance with a good friend at work but use social distance with other colleagues.

Time

In Chapter 3, we introduced the cultural dimension known as monochronic-polychronic time. We noted that people with these two time orientations may not be compatible. Monochronic people want things to run on schedule because time is valuable. They become frustrated by polychronic people who tolerate interruptions in a schedule.

Although researchers have studied how people make use of and respond to time, making rules about it proves difficult. For example, it's unforgivable to be late for a job interview but okay to be late for a party. And what, according to some research, do U.S. students see as the *most* disruptive thing in a classroom? The answer: students walking in after the class has begun.[48] As you pay attention and observe others' nonverbal behavior, try to learn what their attitudes are about time and punctuality and compare it to yours.

Hall's FOUR Spatial Zones

Intimate Distance
(0–18 inches)

Personal Distance
(18 inches–4 feet)

Social Distance
(4–12 feet)

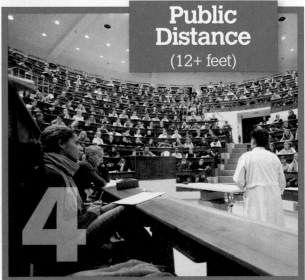

Public Distance
(12+ feet)

Environment

Do you behave the same way in the classroom as you do at work?

Context, or the environment, does more than influence nonverbal communication; it is a part of nonverbal communication. In other words, context alone can communicate a message. For example, an office with unorganized stacks of papers, a stale smell, uncomfortable chairs, and ugly orange walls may create a negative impression of the occupant. It also may also affect how comfortably you interact in that space. Environmental elements, such as furniture arrangement, lighting, color, temperature, and smell, communicate.

Most environments are designed with a purpose in mind. An expensive restaurant's dining room may separate tables at some distance to offer diners privacy. The restaurant's atmosphere may be comfortable, quiet, and only subject to the mouth-watering aroma of good food. How does this differ from the environment of your local fast-food restaurant?

6.4
Improving Nonverbal Skills

How can you improve your ability to recognize, use, and adapt to nonverbal communication?

Most people learn to communicate nonverbally by imitating others and by paying attention to and adapting to feedback. Thus, when someone responds positively to a particular nonverbal behavior, you tend to keep using it. If you receive negative reactions, you may choose a more effective behavior next time. Training and practice can help you develop more effective nonverbal communication skills.

Be Other Oriented

Other-oriented people are effective self-monitors and sensitive to others. They give serious, undivided attention to, feel genuine concern for, and focus on the needs of other communicators. For example, during a casual phone conversation, note whether your friend's tone of voice communicates more than the words you hear. During face-to-face encounters, observe and "listen" to the nonverbal messages; that is, *look* while you listen. The more of your five senses you use, the more nonverbal cues you will notice.

As you make your own observations of people as they communicate, ask yourself some of these questions:

- Does their nonverbal behavior repeat, complement, accent, regulate, or substitute for what they say, or does it contradict their verbal messages?

- How do use of emblems, illustrators, or adaptors affect the meaning of their messages?
- Do facial expressions mask, neutralize, intensify, or deintensify their thoughts and feelings?
- Do they maintain or avoid eye contact?
- Do they display leakage cues that may reveal a lie or deceptive communication?

Not only should you look at someone *while* you are listening, but you should also look as though you *are* listening. Nodding your head, leaning forward, and engaging in direct eye contact are just some of the nonverbal cues that indicate to others that you are paying attention and interested. Furthermore, your nonverbal feedback lets another communicator sense your response to a message. For example, if your nonverbal behaviors suggest you don't understand or that you disagree with what is being said, the other person may try to clarify information or present a better argument.

If, as you listen, you have difficulty interpreting the meaning of nonverbal behavior, ask for help. Describe the message as you understand it. For example, if someone tells you about a tragic event while smiling, you might say, "George, you don't seem very upset by this. Maybe your smile is just a sign of nervousness?" If you are having trouble setting up a meeting with someone and sense a problem, ask the person, "You seem to be avoiding me—or is it just my imagination?" In Chapter 7, "Understanding Interpersonal Relationships," we discuss several techniques for ensuring that you understand the meaning of verbal and nonverbal messages.

Use Immediacy Strategies

Generally, we avoid individuals who appear cold, unfriendly, or hostile. Similarly, we tend to feel more comfortable and want to approach people who seem warm and friendly. **Immediacy** is the degree to which a person seems approachable or likable. Imagine approaching a customer service counter where you see two workers, both available to help you. One of the workers leans away from the counter, does not make eye contact with you, and is frowning. The other

> Not only should you look at someone while you are listening, you should also look like you are listening

worker looks directly at you and smiles. The principle of immediate communication suggests that you will walk up to the worker who appears friendly.

A variety of nonverbal behaviors can promote immediacy.[49] Neat, clean, and pleasant-smelling people are, understandably, more approachable than those who are dirty, sloppy, and smelly. The degree to which you are perceived as likable and approachable may be the difference between a smile and a frown, leaning toward rather than away from another person, direct eye contact versus looking away, a relaxed rather than a rigid body posture, or animated instead of neutral vocal tones. When you use nonverbal immediacy behaviors, other people are more likely to want to communicate with you, and those interactions are warmer and friendlier for everyone involved.

STOP&THINK

How Immediate Are Your Teachers?

Think of your favorite and least favorite teachers—now or in the past. Which ones were most effective? Which teachers left the most indelible impressions? How would you describe their nonverbal behaviors? Were their bodies glued to their desk or lectern, or did they come from behind that barrier, gesture openly, and move closer to you and the other students? Did they smile and look at you directly, use an expressive voice, and listen actively? Did you like them more and learn more from them?[50]

Several studies find positive links between immediacy and learning. Teachers who are immediate generate more interest and enthusiasm about the subject matter.[51] Some of the nonverbal characteristics of high immediacy include the following:

- consistent and direct eye contact
- warm voice
- nods head approvingly
- uses expressive hand gestures
- smiling
- appropriate and natural body movement
- vocal variety
- maintaining closer physical distance[52]

Communication researchers conclude that "immediacy is the overriding factor in a teacher's overall effectiveness."[53] Now consider the following question: To what extent is immediacy a factor in a student's overall effectiveness? Unfortunately there hasn't been much research on this question. At the same time, you have many years of experience as a student and as an observer of other students. Consider the following list of student behaviors and the extent to which you could use such nonverbal immediacy behaviors to create a positive impression on your instructors:

1. Do you make direct eye contact when communicating with your instructors in or outside of class?
2. Do you smile at your instructors?
3. Do you nod your head thoughtfully as you listen to instructors?
4. Do you approach and stand at an appropriate distance from your instructors before or after class?
5. Do you participate in class using direct eye contact, a warm voice, vocal variety, and/or appropriate gestures?

If you answer yes to these questions, your nonverbal immediacy behavior have made a positive and lasting impression on your instructors.

COMMUNICATION **ASSESSMENT**

Read the items on Brian Spitzberg's **Conversational Skills Rating Scale.**[54] Check the items that describe verbal communication and those that describe nonverbal communication in face-to-face conversations. (Although most of the items depict either verbal or nonverbal communication, a few may warrant a check mark for both.) When you are finished, add up the number of items you checked as verbal and those you checked as nonverbal. Which category received the most checks? What does this tell you about the role of nonverbal communication in everyday interactions? To what extent do you skillfully employ these nonverbal communication behaviors when you are having a conversation with someone?

Conversational Skills Rating Scale

Verbal or Nonverbal	Communication Behavior
___ Verbal ___ Nonverbal	1. Speaking rate (neither too slow nor too fast)
___ Verbal ___ Nonverbal	2. Speaking fluency (pauses, silences, frequent "uhs")
___ Verbal ___ Nonverbal	3. Vocal confidence (neither too tense/nervous nor overly confident-sounding)
___ Verbal ___ Nonverbal	4. Articulation (clarity of individual sounds and words)
___ Verbal ___ Nonverbal	5. Vocal variety (neither overly monotone nor dramatic voice)
___ Verbal ___ Nonverbal	6. Volume (neither too loud nor too soft)
___ Verbal ___ Nonverbal	7. Posture (neither too closed/formal nor too open/informal)
___ Verbal ___ Nonverbal	8. Leaning toward partner (neither too forward nor too far back)
___ Verbal ___ Nonverbal	9. Shaking or nervous twitches (not noticeable or distracting)
___ Verbal ___ Nonverbal	10. Unmotivated movements (tapping feet, fingers, hair-twirling)
___ Verbal ___ Nonverbal	11. Facial expressiveness (neither neutral/blank nor exaggerated)
___ Verbal ___ Nonverbal	12. Nodding of head in response to partner statements
___ Verbal ___ Nonverbal	13. Using gestures to emphasize what is being said
___ Verbal ___ Nonverbal	14. Using humor and/or stories
___ Verbal ___ Nonverbal	15. Smiling and/or laughing
___ Verbal ___ Nonverbal	16. Using eye contact
___ Verbal ___ Nonverbal	17. Asking questions
___ Verbal ___ Nonverbal	18. Speaking about partner (involvement of partner as a topic of conversation)
___ Verbal ___ Nonverbal	19. Speaking about self (neither too much nor too little)
___ Verbal ___ Nonverbal	20. Encouragement or agreement (encouragement of partner to talk)
___ Verbal ___ Nonverbal	21. Personal opinion expression (neither too passive nor too aggressive)
___ Verbal ___ Nonverbal	22. Initiating new topics
___ Verbal ___ Nonverbal	23. Maintenance of topics and follow-up comments
___ Verbal ___ Nonverbal	24. Interrupting partner
___ Verbal ___ Nonverbal	25. Using more time speaking relative to partner

When you are finished, add up the number of items you checked as verbal and those you checked as nonverbal. Which category received the most checks? What does this tell you about the role of nonverbal communication in everyday interactions? To what extent do you skillfully employ these nonverbal communication behaviors when you are having a conversation with someone?

6.1
Communicating without Words

What is nonverbal communication, and how does it affect your everyday life?

- Nonverbal communication refers to message components other than words you use to generate and respond to meaning.

- Nonverbal communication accounts for between 60 and 70 percent of the meaning in a face-to-face message.

- In everyday life, you use nonverbal communication to express emotions, define relationships, establish power and influence, interpret verbal messages, deceive, and detect deception.

6.2
Linking Verbal and Nonverbal Communication

How do verbal and nonverbal communication interact to create meaning?

- Nonverbal communication differs from verbal communication in that it is more convincing, highly contextual, learned informally, less structured, and continuous.

- Nonverbal behavior can repeat, complement, accent, regulate, substitute, and/or contradict verbal messages.

- Expectancy violation theory demonstrates how your expectations about nonverbal behavior significantly affect how you interact with others and how you interpret the meaning of nonverbal messages.

6.3
Types of Nonverbal Communication

What types of nonverbal communication should you pay attention to when interacting with others?

- Nonverbal communication has many dimensions, including physical appearance, body movement and gestures, touch, facial expressions, eye behavior, vocal expressiveness, silence, space and distance, time, and environment.

- Physical appearance includes nonverbal elements such as attractiveness, the presence or absence of tattoos and body piercing, clothing and accessories, and hairstyles.

- Hand movement can be classified as emblems, illustrators, and adaptors.

- Facial expressions can function to mask, neutralize, intensify, or deintensify an emotion.

- *Proxemics* is the study of how the distance between people communicates information about the nature of their relationship.

- Edward Hall's four spatial zones—intimate, personal, social, and public distances—are culturally determined.

6.4
Improving Nonverbal Skills

How can you improve your ability to recognize, use, and adapt to nonverbal communication?

- By observing others' nonverbal behavior and confirming your interpretation of its meaning, you can become more other oriented.

- Nonverbal immediacy strategies such as maintaining eye contact, smiling, using vocal variety and appropriate body movements, and maintaining close physical distance can enhance your interactions with others.

MySearchLab®

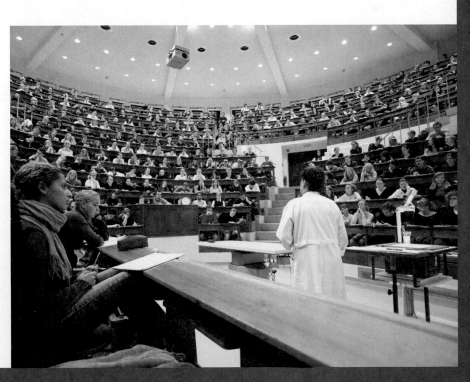

6.1 *What is nonverbal communication, and how does it affect your everyday life?*

1 The textbook defines *nonverbal communication* as message components other than words that generate meaning. Which of the following answers is *not* an example of nonverbal communication?

a. using :-) in an email to highlight your feelings

b. reading an old letter from a good friend who was living abroad

c. putting on perfume or cologne before going to a party

d. brightening up your apartment with flowers before your parents come over for dinner

e. sitting in a middle position at the side of a table during a staff meeting

2 Even though Fiona has nothing but good things to say about her boyfriend, her family can tell she's angry at him. Which nonverbal characteristic best explain this experience?

a. Nonverbal communication is more convincing.

b. Nonverbal communication is highly contextual.

c. Nonverbal communication is learned informally.

d. Nonverbal communication is less structured.

e. Nonverbal communication is continuous.

3 Which of the following nonverbal communication goals could Sigmund Freud have been describing when he wrote that "He who has eyes to see and ears to hear may convince himself that no mortal can keep a secret"?

a. to express emotions

b. to define relationships

c. to establish power and influence

d. to interpret verbal messages

e. to deceive and detect deception

4 Most people can detect deception accurately about_____ percent of the time.

a. 25   b. 30   c. 50   d. 75   e. 80

5 According to research reported by Mark Knapp, the small minority of people who are *highly* skilled lie detectors look for

a. higher voice pitch and vocal tension in a speaker.

b. exaggerated movements and longer pauses.

c. discrepancies between verbal and nonverbal behavior.

d. more blinking and less eye contact.

e. fidgety movements and less gesturing.

6.2 *How do verbal and nonverbal communication interact to create meaning?*

6 Which of the following nonverbal hand movements is an example of an illustrator?

a. Making a circle with your thumb and index finger to indicate "OK."

b. Holding your thumb and fingers about two inches apart as you describe how much shorter your hair was after your last haircut.

c. Putting your face in the palms of your hands when you realize that you've forgotten to buy your spouse a Valentine's present.

d. Raising your hand in class so the instructor will call on you.

e. Crossing your index and middle fingers as a good-luck signal.

6.3 *What types of nonverbal communication should you pay attention to when interacting with others?*

7 If one of your coworkers tells you that she got the promotion that both of you applied for, you may smile at the news even though you feel awful. Which technique for adapting facial expressions are you using?

a. masking

b. neutralizing

c. intensification

d. unmasking

e. deintensification

8 If the speaker stresses the word indicated in italics, which of the following statements means "I was born in New Jersey, not in New York as you seem to think."

a. "*I* was born in New Jersey."

b. "I *was* born in New Jersey."

c. "I was *born* in New Jersey."

d. "I was born *in* New Jersey."

e. "I was born in *New Jersey*."

9 According to anthropologist Edward Hall, how close to a good friend does the average person in the United States stand?

a. 0 to 6 inches

b. 6 to 18 inches

c. 18 inches to 4 feet

d. 4 feet to 12 feet

e. more than 12 feet

6.4 *How can you improve your ability to recognize, use, and adapt to nonverbal communication?*

10 _____ refers to the degree to which you seem approachable and likable.

a. Other oriented

b. Immediacy

c. Observant

d. Confirming

e. Conversational

Answers found on page 366.

Key Terms

Accenting nonverbal behavior	Immediacy	Public distance
Adaptors	Intensification	Rate
Complementary nonverbal behavior	Intimate distance	Regulating nonverbal behavior
Contradictory nonverbal behavior	Leakage cues	Repetitive nonverbal behavior
Deintensification	Marker	Social distance
Emblems	Masking	Substituting nonverbal behavior
Emoticons	Metamessage	Territoriality
Expectancy Violation Theory	Mixed message	Touch approachers
Gesture	Neutralization	Touch avoiders
Illustrators	Nonverbal communication	Volume
	Other oriented	Word stress
	Personal distance	
	Pitch	
	Proxemics	

Understanding
INTERPERSONAL
RELATIONSHIPS

7

What do most popular films, novels, and television series have in common? They tell stories. Now go one step further: What do these stories have in common? They are stories about interpersonal relationships. For example, are the Harry Potter books and films about wizards and magic, or are they about Harry's relationships with his friends, his foes, his teachers, and his dysfunctional Muggle family?

The close and supportive relationships Harry enjoys with his Hogwart classmates confirm psychologist David Myers's claim that "there are few stronger predictions of happiness than a close, nurturing, equitable, intimate, lifelong companionship with one's best friend."[1] Like all deeply satisfying stories with happy endings, from *The Wizard of Oz* and *Star Wars* to *Slumdog Millionaire* and *Avatar*, the films in the Harry Potter series reaffirm this universal truth: Interpersonal relationships—between friends, lovers, siblings, and colleagues—are central to the human condition.

7.1
Interpersonal Communication and Relationships

What are the characteristics and benefits of effective interpersonal communication?

Your ability to communicate effectively in close personal relationships influences your psychological and physical health, your identity and happiness, your social and moral development, your ability to cope with stress and misfortunes, and the quality and meaning of your life.[2] In this chapter and the two that follow, we examine the interpersonal communication theories, strategies, and skills that lead to healthy and satisfying relationships.

Interpersonal communication occurs when a limited number of people, usually two, interact and generate meaning through verbal and nonverbal messages. This interaction typically results in sharing information, achieving a goal, and/or maintaining a relationship. When we use the word **relationship** in this textbook, we are referring to a continuing and meaningful attachment or connection to another person. There are many types of interpersonal

relationships—perhaps as many as there are people you know.

In addition to the emotional connections and commitments you have in close **personal relationships** with friends, romantic partners, and family members, you also have work-based relationships. **Professional relationships** involve connections with people you associate and work with to accomplish a goal or perform a task. Many relationships fall into both categories. One of your best friends may also be a colleague at work.

John Gottman, who studies the value and consequences of close personal relationships and strong marriages, offers several conclusions drawn from his own and others' research:

- People with good friends usually have less stress and live longer.
- Longevity is determined far more by the state of people's closest relationships than by genetics.
- People who have good marriages live longer than those who don't.
- Loners are twice as likely to die from all causes over a five-year period as those who enjoy close friendships.[3]

Medical researchers have found "a link between relationships and physical health. . . . People with rich personal networks—who are married, have close family and friends, are active in social and religious groups—recover more quickly from disease and live longer."[4]

Some people mistakenly believe that Gottman is urging us to make as many friends as possible and (if not already married) to get married as soon as possible in order to live longer. But Gottman's essential point is that meaningful and lasting personal relationships lead to a happy life. Quality relationships do not just happen. *You* make them happen, and the success of those relationships depends largely on how well you communicate.

What Types of Relationships Are Shown in These Photos?

Schutz's Interpersonal Needs Theory

Psychologist William Schutz's **Fundamental Interpersonal Relationship Orientation (FIRO) Theory** asserts that people interact with others in order to satisfy one or all three basic interpersonal needs: the need for inclusion, the need for control, and the need for affection.[5]

The **inclusion need** represents a desire to belong, to be involved, and to be accepted. When inclusion needs are met, the result is what Schutz calls an *ideal social person*: someone who enjoys being with others but is also comfortable being alone.

If, however, your inclusion needs are *not* met, you may engage in undersocial or oversocial behavior. An *undersocial person* feels unworthy or undervalued. Such people often withdraw and become loners who avoid interpersonal relationships. An *oversocial person* also feels unworthy and undervalued but tries to compensate by attracting attention and impressing others with what and who they know. They dread being alone and do not actively seek companionship.

The **control need** refers to whether a person feels competent and confident. When control needs are met, the result is what Schutz calls a *democratic person*: someone who has no problems with power and control and who feels just as comfortable giving reasonable orders as taking them.

Unmet control needs can result in the emergence of an abdicrat or autocrat. The **abdicrat** wants control but

is reluctant to pursue it and therefore is often submissive. The **autocrat** also wants control but tries to take over or dominate others. Autocrats may criticize other people and force decisions on them.

The **affection need** refers to our desire to feel liked by others.[6] When we need affection, we seek close friendships, intimate relationships, and expressions of warmth from others. When affection needs are met, the result is what Schutz calls an *ideal personal type*: a person who wants to be liked but who also is secure enough to function in situations where

social interaction and affection are not high priorities.

According to Schutz, when affection needs are not met, people may develop underpersonal or overpersonal characteristics. *Underpersonal types* believe they are not liked and establish only superficial relationships with others. They rarely share their honest feelings and may appear aloof and uninvolved. *Overpersonal types* try to get close to everyone. They may seek an intimate relationship despite the disinterest of others.

Schutz's FIRO Theory

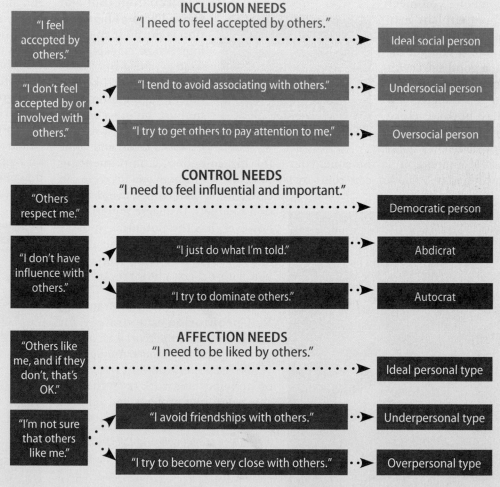

INCLUSION NEEDS
"I need to feel accepted by others."

"I feel accepted by others." ·······▶ Ideal social person

"I don't feel accepted by or involved with others." → "I tend to avoid associating with others." ··▶ Undersocial person

→ "I try to get others to pay attention to me." ··▶ Oversocial person

CONTROL NEEDS
"I need to feel influential and important."

"Others respect me." ·······▶ Democratic person

"I don't have influence with others." → "I just do what I'm told." ··▶ Abdicrat

→ "I try to dominate others." ··▶ Autocrat

AFFECTION NEEDS
"I need to be liked by others."

"Others like me, and if they don't, that's OK." ·······▶ Ideal personal type

"I'm not sure that others like me." → "I avoid friendships with others." ··▶ Underpersonal type

→ "I try to become very close with others." ··▶ Overpersonal type

Schutz's Fundamental Interpersonal Relationship Orientation (FIRO) Theory[7]

Developing Interpersonal Relationships

How do you form positive and lasting relationships with others?

Do you make a good impression on others? Do people seem to enjoy talking to you? Are you understood or misunderstood, seen as interesting or boring, and generally liked or merely tolerated?

The answers to these questions say a great deal about how you communicate, particularly when you want to initiate or further develop a relationship. Research tells us that significant and meaningful relationships develop when you make a positive impression and have satisfying conversations with others.

Impression Management

You know from experience that first impressions count. If you don't make a good impression on a first date, it may be your last with that person. Someone you meet on an airplane may eventually offer you a job. If you get off to a good start with someone sitting next to you in class, you may become close friends. And, once you've made a good initial impression on someone, your subsequent behavior can reinforce and maintain that impression or can weaken and even reverse it.

Sociologist Erving Goffman claims that we assume a social identity that others help us to maintain.[8] This perspective is useful in understanding **impression management**, the strategies we use to shape and control the way other people see us. These impressions affect how others perceive us in social interactions as well as how they interpret our ability to gain influence, power, sympathy, or approval.[9]

The section that follows presents five impression management strategies—ingratiation, self-promotion, exemplification, supplication, and intimidation—as related to a communicator's desired goal and the emotions sought in others.[10]

Ingratiation (But Not Phony Flattery) Ingratiation is the most common impression management strategy; the goal of integration is to be liked by others. Ingratiation skills include giving compliments, doing another person a favor, and comforting someone. Complimenting someone with whom you disagree can ease tensions and reopen communication channels. Insincere ingratiation, however, has the potential to damage rather than enhance your image. Whereas honest flattery ingratiates you with others, phony flattery can have the opposite effect.

Self-Promotion (But Not Bragging) Self-promotion is a strategy for being seen as competent. The goal is to be respected by others. Announcing "I'm a fast writer" can earn you a place on an important work team that has short-deadline projects and reports.

At the same time, over *self-promotion*—exaggerating your achievements and skills in order to impress others—may create a negative impression that is difficult to change. And if your actual performance does not live up to your self-promotion, you can create a bad, lasting impression. No one likes a braggart, so promote yourself honestly and appropriately.

Exemplification (But Not Just in Public) Exemplification entails offering yourself as a good example or a model of noteworthy behavior. The goal is to be seen as honest and moral. But make sure you practice what you preach. If you claim it's wrong to pirate CDs but you photocopy entire books rather than buy them, no one will believe your claims about honesty and moral values. Don't declare you're on a strict diet and then get caught with your hand in the cookie jar.

Supplication (But Not Endless Whining) Supplication describes a humble request or appeal for help. The goal of supplication is compassion from others. Appropriate supplication causes other people to feel resourceful and valued. But don't rely on supplication to get someone else to do your work or to earn eternal love and respect; if you cry out for help

Steve Jobs (co-founder and chief executive of Apple, Inc.) and Bill Gates (co-founder and chairman of Microsoft) created unique public images that differ from each other. What is your overall impression of each man?

> You don't get a second chance to make a first impression.

when you have the resources to handle something on your own, you will soon be ignored. In other words, don't cry "wolf" unless the wolf is knocking on your door.

Intimidation (But Not Brutality) The goal of **intimidation** is to provoke fear. In order to be seen as powerful, an intimidating person demonstrates a willingness and ability to cause personal harm. Intimidation strategies involve threats to subdue or control others. "If you speak to me that way again, I will file a formal grievance against you." We do not recommend using intimidation in most communication situations. In some instances, however, you may need to establish your authority and willingness to use power. If others are taking advantage of you, you may need to show them that you won't take it anymore—that you won't be intimidated.

Effective Conversations

A **conversation** is an interaction, often informal, in which we exchange speaking and listening roles with another person. In his book *A Good Talk*, Daniel Menakar regards conversation as a human art of great importance produced by all people everywhere.[11]

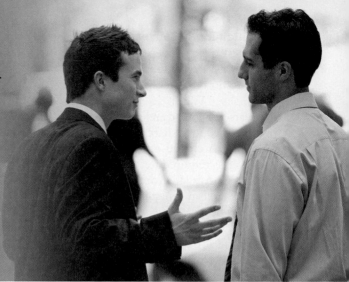

We negotiate conversational turn-taking primarily through our nonverbal behavior.

On any given day, you may have a conversation with a close friend from childhood on the phone, a classmate in the hallway, a coworker at the next desk, or someone you've just met at a party. Conversations differ depending on where they take place and the type of relationship. For example, you may wait until others aren't around or until a championship game on television is over to have a serious and private conversation with a close friend. You may discuss highly personal issues with your life partner, but you probably won't share as much with someone you've just met.

Starting a Conversation Introducing yourself and sharing some superficial information is the most obvious way to begin a conversation with someone you do not know: "I'm Ahmad; my family and I are here on vacation from Nebraska." The other person will usually reciprocate by offering similar information or following up on what you've shared: "I have cousins in Nebraska and visited them one summer when I was a kid." A second approach to opening a conversation is to ask simple questions: "Do you know anything about this movie?"

Cell Phone Conversations and Texting

Cell phone etiquette has been the subject of countless newspaper and magazine articles—and for good reasons. There is almost nothing as annoying and even embarrassing as being forced to listen in on someone else's cell phone conversation.[12] We're sure you have heard people complain to their spouses and colleagues or listened to boyfriends and girlfriends express their puppy love for one another. Surveys indicate that the majority of cell phone users believe that loud or private calls made in public settings are inappropriate. However, "that same majority indulges in such calls themselves."[13]

To avoid embarrassing yourself and annoying others nearby, follow a few simple rules when talking on a cell phone or texting in public:[14]

Loud/ Annoying Ring Tones.

- Do not make or take personal calls or text during business meetings, family celebrations, or class sessions.
- Maintain a distance from others of at least ten feet when talking on the phone.
- Avoid cell phone conversations in enclosed public spaces, such as elevators, waiting rooms, or buses and trains.
- Avoid cell phone conversations and texting in public places where side talk or disregarding others is considered bad manners, such as libraries, museums, theaters, restaurants, and places of worship.

- Control the volume of your voice. Tilt your chin downward so that you're speaking toward the floor. That way, your voice won't carry as far.
- Avoid cell phone conversations and texting when engaging in other tasks, such as driving, eating, or shopping.
- Do not talk on the phone or text someone while engaged in a face-to-face conversation or interaction with another person.
- Take advantage of your phone's features, such as vibrate mode and voice mail. When you step into your workplace or a classroom, put your cell phone on vibrate and let your calls roll to your voice mail.

developing interpersonal relationships

Maintaining a Conversation. One of the best ways to keep a conversation going is to ask **open-ended questions** that encourage specific or detailed responses. "What do you think of Dr. Pearson's course and assignments?" invites someone to share an observation or opinion. A **closed-ended question**, "Is this class required for your major?," requires only a short and direct response and can generally be answered with a yes or no.

When you answer questions during a conversation, give a response that provides the other person with more information about your thoughts or experiences. An engaging conversation requires the effort and commitment of two people. Without work, a conversation can quickly deteriorate into an awkward silence.

Finally, make sure you balance talking with listening. A successful conversationalist takes turns listening and speaking. Watch for nonverbal cues to find out when it's your turn to listen or speak. **Turn-requesting cues** are verbal and nonverbal messages that signal a desire to speak, such as leaning forward, providing direct eye contact, and lifting one hand as if beginning to gesture. **Turn-yielding cues** are verbal and nonverbal messages that signal that you are completing your comments and are preparing to listen, such as slowing down your speaking rate, relaxing your posture or gestures, and leaning slightly away. Good conversationalists are sensitive to turn-taking cues.

Listening in Conversations Effective listening promotes a genuine conversation rather than a one-way speech. In Chapter 3, "Listening and Critical Thinking," we introduced the Golden Listening Rule: Listen to others as you would have them listen to you. That rule is of utmost importance in every conversation.

In a good conversation, you must be able to suspend your own needs and opinions to listen to someone else's. Daniel Menaker explains that both parties in a conversation must "listen very closely, not only to the loud notes, but to the quiet one . . . as well—to what sounds as though it's being downplayed or skipped over. Such attention is, for one thing, flattering, but it also yields insights that the people we're talking to sometimes don't even know they have."[15] Review Chapter 3 to make sure that you listen to understand, remember, interpret, evaluate, and appropriately respond to what you hear.

Ending a Conversation Ending a conversation abruptly can send a rude message to the other person. Look for a moment in the conversation where an ending seems natural—either when the topic seems fully exhausted or when someone shifts to the edge of a chair, stands up, looks away, leans away, or picks up personal belongings.[16] Try to end every conversation on a positive and courteous note. If, however, your companion is ignoring your attempts to end the conversation, you may need to be direct but firm: "I hate to cut our conversation short, but I have to get going."

7.3
Strengthening Personal Relationships

How does interpersonal communication affect your relationships with friends and romantic partners?

Everyone has a multitude of personal relationships—with family members and friends, with teachers and students, with business associates and service providers, and with that special person who is your beloved partner or spouse. Unfortunately, we lack the space in this chapter and textbook to examine all these relationships in detail. Instead, we focus on two of the most significant personal relationships you develop in your lifetime: friends and lovers. The distinct context and importance of these relationships requires special communication strategies and skills to enhance their quality and longevity.

Friendship

Although just about everyone has friends, not all friendships are alike. Several factors influence the kind of friendship you have with another person. For example, for young children, a friend is simply someone with whom a child shares toys and plays; when these activities are absent, so is the friendship.[17]

In adolescence and young adulthood, we often establish enduring and intimate relationships with best friends. **Intimacy**, the feeling or state of knowing someone deeply, occurs in many forms. For example, in most romantic relationships, physical intimacy is a way of expressing affection and love. In romantic and friend relationships, intimacy takes a different form. It can be emotional (sharing private thoughts and feelings), intellectual (sharing attitudes, beliefs, and interests), and/or collaborative (sharing and achieving a common goal).[18]

Close friends learn that it's okay to share personal thoughts, secrets, hopes, and fears, but whether we do so depends on our ability (1) to disclose personal information in a way that maintains the relationship; (2) to recognize that most of these disclosures center on mundane, everyday

GIRL-FRIENDS AND BOY-FRIENDS DIFFER

In adolescence as well as in young, middle, and older adulthood, men report less intimacy, less complexity, and less contact in same-gender friendships. In contrast, women report greater continuity in their long-term, same-sex friendships than men and see these friendships as important in their lives over time. One interesting study notes that throughout middle and older adulthood, women often value talk with their friends more than talk with their husbands.[19]

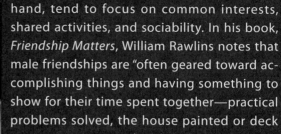

Mutual and confirming talk is both the substance and central feature of many women's friendships. Male friendships, on the other hand, tend to focus on common interests, shared activities, and sociability. In his book, *Friendship Matters*, William Rawlins notes that male friendships are "often geared toward accomplishing things and having something to show for their time spent together—practical problems solved, the house painted or deck completed . . . cars washed or tuned, poker, or music played, and so on."[20]

Despite these differences, both adult men and women view close friendship as a mutually dependent, accepting, confidential, and trusting relationship.

issues; and (3) to respect that some topics are taboo, such as negative life events and serious relationship issues.[21]

During late adolescence and young adulthood, most of us leave home—to work, to go to college, or to marry and raise a family. The dual tasks of developing new friendships while adapting to a new job, new living conditions, or new academic settings can take its toll. Although adolescents and young adults have more opportunities to make friends than any other age-group, this stage, more than at any other life stage, proves to be one of their loneliest times.[22]

Romance

Why do some people become romantically involved while others remain "just" friends? Learning how to develop and strengthen loving relationships is an important communication skill. Researchers confirm that people

STOP&THINK

Beware of Jealousy

Jealousy has the power to damage and end a relationship beyond repair. Although jealousy occurs among friends, it plays a much more significant role in romantic relationships. **Jealousy** is an intense feeling caused by a perceived threat to a relationship. In the eyes of a jealous partner, the perceived threat can take many forms—from a boyfriend spending time with other friends to a wife being honored for achievements at work. Highly jealous people may interpret an innocent look or a conversation with another person as signs of sexual unfaithfulness and may see other people as potential rivals, whether they are or not.

People express jealousy in a variety of ways: through accusations and sarcasm or depression and physical withdrawal (the "silent treatment"). Extremely jealous people are often aggressive, manipulative, or violent. Pathologically jealous individuals are highly sensitive to "every nuance in [their] environment that may hint of unfaithfulness." Jealousy taken to extremes can destroy relationships and lead to stronger feelings of resentment and inferiority.[23]

The following communication strategies can help address the negative effects of jealousy in a relationship, particularly if you are highly motivated to maintain the relationship:

- *Stay Calm, Cool, and Collected.* Provide direct but nonaggressive communication about jealousy in an effort to work things out. In other words, talk about it calmly and compassionately.
- *Defuse Jealous Feelings.* Work to improve the relationship or make yourself more desirable. Strategies such as sending flowers or a gift, demonstrating affection, and being extra nice can reduce or counteract jealous feelings.
- *Show How It Hurts.* Express yourself nonverbally so the jealous person can see how it affects you (e.g., appearing hurt, distressed, or crying).[24]

If someone's jealousy becomes extreme or is based on unfounded beliefs, none of the above strategies may help. When jealous people become cruelly aggressive, manipulative, or violent, professional counseling may be necessary.

who need others, and can admit to this, are the lucky ones.

How do you let another person know that you "like" her or him? How do you find out whether that person likes you? The process of romancing another person begins with generating and assessing *liking*, which can be communicated both nonverbally and verbally. In Chapter 6, "Nonverbal Communication," we introduced the concept of immediacy. Nonverbal cues, such as increased eye contact, touch, standing closer, and leaning forward, can signal romantic interest. When it comes to expressing interest verbally, most people don't take the direct route. We don't walk up to someone and say, "I like you." Instead, we tend to use more subtle strategies, such as inviting the other person to social activities; asking questions to encourage the other person to share personal information while also sharing our own when appropriate; presenting ourselves as positive, interesting, and dynamic; doing favors for or assisting the other person; and seeking and demonstrating similarities in tastes, interests, and attitudes.[25]

Taken one at a time, these strategies may not seem significant or romantic, but when combined, they let the other

RELATIONSHIP **STAGES**

Differentiating. Each person becomes distinct and different in character. More use of "I" and "you" than "we" and "our." There is more conflict.

"I don't like big social gatherings."

6

Circumscribing. There is a decrease in communication. Personal and important topics are no longer discussed.

"Did you have a good time on your trip?"

7

Stagnating. Communication shuts down. More time and attention is devoted to work and other friends.

"What's there to talk about?"

8

Avoiding. There is a lack of desire to spend time together. Communication may become antagonistic or unfriendly.

"I may not be around when you call."

9

Terminating. Psychological and physical barriers are created. Each person is more concerned about self.

"I'm leaving you . . . and don't bother trying to contact me."

10

Coming Apart

Bonding. The couple makes a public commitment to one another. The couple enjoys a stable relationship.

"I want to be with you always."

5

Integrating. Personalities, opinions, and behaviors join together. Individuals become a couple.

"What happens to you happens to me."

4

Intensifying. There is more intimate physical contact, more talk, and more self-disclosure.

"I . . . I think I love you."

3

Experimenting. The two people look for and learn about similarities and common interests. There is pleasant and casual small talk.

"Oh, so you like to ski . . . so do I."

2

Initiating. There is a cautious assessment of the other person and polite communication.

"Hi, how ya doin'?"

1

Coming Together

Figure 7.1 The Stages of a Relationship[26]

person see that the relationship is becoming closer and has the potential for future development.

Romantic relationships do not happen by chance, nor do they magically come into being. Rather, you start, develop, maintain, strengthen, and end romantic relationships. Communication scholars Mark Knapp and Anita Vangelisti describe ten predictable stages in intimate relationships.[27] Their model is heavily oriented toward male–female romantic couples, yet they also account for many child–parent relationships, close work relationships, and same-sex relationships. Knapp and Vangelisti divide relationship stages into two major processes: coming together and coming apart. Figure 7.1 describes the ten interaction stages using the example of a romantic relationship.

Knapp and Vangelisti's model only scratches the surface of each stage in

"People who are in loving relationships with another adult have better hormonal balance and better health, and are of course happier."[28]

— British Economist, Richard Layard

a relationship. Just because your partner doesn't like big social gatherings as much as you does not mean your relationship will come apart. "It is not necessarily 'bad' to terminate a relationship nor is it necessarily 'good' to become more intimate with someone. The model is descriptive of what seems to happen—not necessarily what should happen."[29]

STOP&THINK

Do Parents Really Matter?

Do parents make a major difference in the way children behave outside the home—and the way they grow up? Developmental psychologist Judith Rich Harris believes that parenting has almost no long-term effects on a child's personality, intelligence, or mental health. Instead she claims that children are most influenced by two other factors: their genes and their peers.[30] Harris points out that the children of immigrant parents (who speak English poorly) quickly learn to speak Standard English. They learn this from their peers, who have more influence on how they speak and sound.[31]

Same-age peers show children how to fit in and behave—in the classroom, on the ball field, or at parties. Children adopt certain behaviors in social settings to win acceptance from their peers, and it's those behaviors outside the home that remain steadfast through adulthood. Blame your peers, Harris says, not your parents.[32]

Judith Harris's research raises many questions and has created considerable controversy and debate among psychologists, communication scholars, and family members.[33] Now consider the popular *Battle Hymn of the Tiger Mother* written by Amy Chua, a Yale University professor and mother of two daughters. Her book has been criticized as "a diabolically well-packaged, highly readable screed [a long-essay or rant] ostensibly about the art of obsessive parenting." Chua uses the phrase "Chinese mother" to mean "driven, snobbish and hellbent on raising certifiably Grade A children."[34] Other detractors argue that Chua has deprived her daughters of many things young girls enjoy—texting and hanging out with girlfriends (rather than practicing the piano or violin for hours under Mom's stern gaze), staying up all night at sleepovers, going through phases with different clothing styles, and creating a "cool" Facebook page.

David Brooks, a columnist for *The New York Times,* claims that Chua's daughters have not learned hard, but critical lessons about deciding whom to trust beyond the family circle and about accurately interpreting and appropriately responding to nonverbal feedback.[35] In other words, they have not learned how to communicate interpersonally with skill and confidence.

More recently, we've read stories about "helicopter parents" who hover over their children and frequently intervene in all aspects of their children's lives—from who their friends are, how well or poorly their schools and teachers are, and even whether their doctor knows enough about their unique and precious child to make an accurate diagnosis. Even college students have had difficulty separating from what's called "Velcro parents" who call them to wake them up for class, complain to their colleges and professors about non-A grades, and review their major assignments and papers before giving their child "permission" to turn them in. Certainly all of these parents love their children and seek what is, in their opinion, best for them. Unfortunately, conclude some educators and psychologists, we are setting up such students for "long-term failure" because they haven't learned how to handle anything but parent-ensured success.[36]

What do you think? Do parents really matter? Do our childhood friends teach us more about getting along with others than our parents? Do demanding parents help or harm a child's development? How do you explain what happens when the child of two "good" parents turns out "bad"? Should parents be more concerned about the kind of school their sons and daughters attend than how they parent? Perhaps, when it comes to defining good parenting, there are more questions than answers?

7.4
Sharing Your Self with Others

How do self-disclosure and sensitivity to feedback affect personal relationships?

Sharing your self with others is essential for developing meaningful relationships. Whether you are talking about your favorite smartphone app with a new acquaintance or revealing your deepest fears to someone you love, both of you must be able and willing to share personal information and feelings.

Self-disclosure is the process of sharing with others personal information, opinions, and emotions that would not otherwise be known to them. This is *not* to say you should reveal the most intimate details of your life to everyone you meet. Rather, you must judge if and when sharing is appropriate by understanding and adapting to the other person's attitudes, beliefs, and values.[37] Deciding what, where, when, how, and with whom to self-disclose is one of the most difficult communication challenges you face in a personal relationship.

The Johari Window Model

Psychologists Joseph Luft and Harrington Ingham provide a useful model for understanding the connections between self-disclosure and feedback.[38] They use the metaphor of a window, calling their model the **Johari Window** (the name is a combination of their first names).[39] The model looks at two interpersonal communication dimensions: willingness to self-disclose and receptivity to feedback. *Willingness to self-disclose* describes the extent to which you are prepared to disclose personal information and feelings to other people. *Receptivity to feedback* describes your awareness, interpretation, and response to someone else's self-disclosure about you.[40] When these two dimensions are graphed against one another,

the result is a figure that resembles a four-paned window as shown below. Each pane means something different, and each pane can vary in size.

Four Different Panes The *open area* of your Johari Window contains information you are willing to share with others as well as information you have learned about yourself by accurately interpreting others' feedback. For example, suppose you wonder whether it's okay to tell an embarrassing but funny personal story to a group of new colleagues. You decide to take the risk. If your listeners laugh and seem to appreciate your sense of humor, you've learned two things: that it's safe to share personal stories with this group and that you are, in fact, funny.

The *hidden area* represents your private self, which includes information you know about yourself ("I am attracted to that person," "I was once arrested") but that you are not yet willing to share with others. The hidden area

contains your secrets. Some people retain a lot of personal information in this area that could enhance their personal relationships and likability if that information were shared.

The *blind area* contains information others know about you but that you do *not* know about yourself because you don't pay attention to or correctly interpret feedback from others. If you don't notice that someone disapproves of your behaviors or wants your praise for a job well done, you may not develop or maintain a close relationship with that person.

Information unknown to *both* you and others exists in the *unknown area*. For example, suppose you have always avoided doing any writing at work because you don't think you're a good writer. And yet, when working with a group of colleagues on an interesting project, you end up doing most of the writing. As time passes, you and your coworkers recognize and appreciate your writing talent. This "discovery" about yourself now moves from your unknown area to your open area.

Varying Size of Panes Depending on how willing you are to self-disclose and how receptive you are to feedback, each of the four panes in the Johari Window differs in size. Although this makes a very unusual-looking window, it does a good job of reflecting your level of self-awareness. As a relationship develops, you should disclose more, which enlarges your open area and reduces the amount of information in your hidden area. As you become more receptive to feedback, you reduce your blind area and enlarge your open area.[42] And as your open area expands, your unknown area gets smaller.

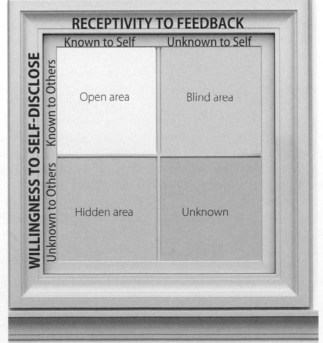

RECEPTIVITY TO FEEDBACK

	Known to Self	Unknown to Self
Known to Others	Open area	Blind area
Unknown to Others	Hidden area	Unknown

WILLINGNESS TO SELF-DISCLOSE

The Johari Window[41]

How Much Online Sharing Is Too Much?

"We are constantly Googling, Facebooking, and searching Blogger .com and other sites for applicants," says an admissions officer at the University of Connecticut.[43] And so do many other colleges and universities—as do businesses, corporations, and professional associations. The next time you are about to update your status or post a picture, here are a few questions to ask yourself:

- **Would you want a college dean, a potential or current employer, or your mother to see everything you post online?**
- **Would you share the same information with them face-to-face?**

Online providers can barely keep up as they scramble to fix security breaches that allow users to see other people's supposedly private information and personal chats. The problem of making private information public is not just the online provider's fault. Researchers in a study published in the *Journal of General Internal Medicine* looked up more than 800 medical students by name on Facebook. Although only 6 percent revealed their home address, "students were looser with lifestyle information including sexual orientation, relationship status, and political opinions and positions." Only 37 percent had made their Facebook entries private. Some profiles included photos of med students engaged in excessive or hazardous drinking behaviors. Others shared sexist and racist comments.[44] How would you like to see postings of your emergency room doctor or hospital intern bragging about binge drinking or writing sexist or racist statements?

Now transform the above examples into questions about *your* posting. If you answer *yes* to any of these questions, you should consider changing your posting habits and Web messages:

- **Do you post your home address and/or phone number?**
- **Do you post photos in which you're engaging in foolish, excessive, hazardous, or illegal behavior?**
- **Do you post comments that could be interpreted as offensive, racist, sexist, or exceptionally bizarre?**

Fortunately, the practice of "letting it all hang out" has begun to change on many social networking sites. Participants are becoming more cautious about what they disclose. An article in *The New York Times* reports that young people are finally learning when and when not to self-disclose online. For example, a University of California, Berkeley, study found that "more than half the young adults questioned had become more concerned about privacy than they were five years ago—mirroring the number of people their parents' age or older with that worry." Even more interesting, a study by the Pew Internet Project found that "people in their 20s exert more control of their digital reputation than older adults, more vigorously deleting unwanted posts and limiting information about themselves."[45]

Always remember that regardless of whether you are interacting face-to-face or via cyberspace, *you* are responsible for deciding what to share about your self with others. Later in this chapter, we recommend strategies and skills for making sure that your self-disclosures are appropriate and effective.

7.5
Expressing Your Self Appropriately

How should you express your personal thoughts and feelings to others?

As you get to know yourself and others better you may find yourself engaging in more intimate self disclosure and responding more to feedback. Both of these communication skills help to increase your self-awareness and the overall quality of your personal relationships. Social Penetration Theory (see p. 136) and the Johari Window Model help explain the need for appropriate self-disclosure and receptivity to feedback; this section describes communication strategies and skills that can help you express your self appropriately and thereby strengthen and preserve your relationships with others.

Effective Self-Disclosure

When you self-disclose, you reveal how you are reacting to a situation while sharing relevant information about yourself and your experiences.

STRATEGIES FOR **EFFECTIVE SELF DISCLOSURE**

STRATEGY	RATIONALE
Focus on the present, not the past.	Obsessing about past problems may not help or enlighten either person.
Be descriptive, not judgmental.	Criticizing someone's behavior can end up in a hostile argument.
Disclose your feelings, not just the facts.	Explaining how you feel about what is happening clarifies and justifies your reactions.
Adapt to the person and context.	Revealing intimate personal information to the wrong person at the wrong time in the wrong place benefits no one.
Be sensitive to others' reactions.	Modifying or discontinuing self-disclosure is essential if the other person's reaction is extreme (rage, crying, hysteria).
Engage in reciprocal self-disclosure.	Modifying or discontinuing self-disclosure is appropriate if the other person does not respond in kind.
Gradually move disclosure to a deeper level.	Increasing the breadth, depth, and frequency of your self-disclosure should occur as your level of comfort with the other person increases.

Social Penetration Theory

Social Penetration Theory, developed by Irwin Altman and Dalmas Taylor, describes the process of relationship bonding in which individuals move from superficial communication to deeper, more intimate communication.[46] According to Altman and Taylor, the process of developing an intimate relationship is similar to peeling an onion. The outer skin of the onion represents superficial and mostly public information about yourself. The inner layers—those closest to the core—represent intimate information.

Social Penetration Theory explains that self-disclosure has three interconnected dimensions: depth, breadth, and frequency.[47] *Deep* self-disclosure is intimate and near the core of the onion; for example, there's a big difference between telling someone "You're OK" and telling someone "I love you." When self-disclosure is *broad*, it covers many topic areas, some very personal, some impersonal. In addition to sharing information about your hobbies and job, you may also share your strong beliefs and values about family and religion. Self-disclosure becomes more *frequent* as the depth and breadth of your relationship expands.

The animated film *Shrek* captures the underlying premise of Social Penetration Theory. As Shrek, the large, lumbering, green ogre, and his hyperactive companion, Donkey, trek through fields and forests, Shrek tries to explain himself to Donkey:

Shrek:	For your information, there's a lot more to ogres than people think.
Donkey:	Example?
Shrek:	Example? Okay. Um. Ogres are like onions.
Donkey:	They stink?
Shrek:	No.
Donkey:	Oh, they make you cry?
Shrek:	No.
Donkey:	Oh, you leave them out in the sun and they get all brown and start sprouting little white hairs?
Shrek:	No! Layers. Onions have layers. Ogres have layers. You get it? We both have layers![48]

Social Penetration Theory contends that as two people get to know one another better, they reveal personal information, feelings, and experiences below the public image layer. Relationships develop when this process is reciprocal—that is, one person's openness leads to another's openness, and so on.

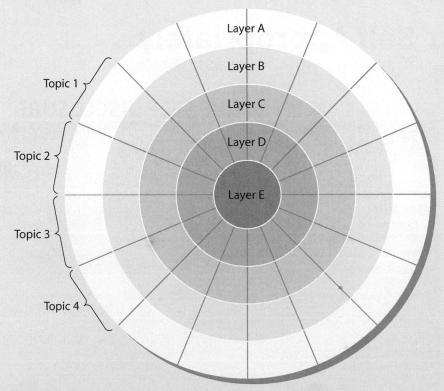

The Social Penetration Process

EXAMPLES OF LAYERS

Layer A: Most impersonal layer (music, clothing, food preferences)

Layer B: Impersonal layer (job, politics, education)

Layer C: Middle layer (religious beliefs, social attitudes)

Layer D: Personal layer (personal goals, fears, hopes, secrets)

Layer E: Most personal layer (inner core, self-concept)

EXAMPLES OF TOPICS

Topic 1: Leisure activities

Topic 2: Career

Topic 3: Family

Topic 4: Health

Successful self-disclosure is not a solo activity. If the other person does not self-disclose or respond to your self-disclosures, you may want to rethink the relationship or stop sharing your thoughts and feelings.[49]

> Although it can be painful and risky, when the emotional stakes are high, self-disclosure can benefit a relationship in significant ways.

Effective Feedback

Effective interpersonal communication relies on giving and receiving feedback from others. No matter where or when you provide feedback, it should not be threatening or demanding. At the same time, remember that there is only so much that you and another person can comprehend and process at one time. Too much personal information can overwhelm and overload the best of listeners.

Defensive and Supportive Communication

Communication scholar Jack Gibb asserts that there are six behaviors that create a supportive climate for communication and six that cause defensiveness.[50] **Defensive behaviors** reflect our instinct to protect ourselves when we are being physically or verbally attacked by someone. Even though such reactions are natural, they also discourage reciprocal self-disclosure. On the other hand, **supportive behaviors** create a climate in which self-disclosure and responsiveness to feedback benefit both parties.

The paired behaviors in Gibb's model are not necessarily "good" or "bad" behaviors. For example, you may behave strategically when you have important and strong personal motives.

You may behave with certainty when your expertise is well recognized and a critical decision must be made. And you may respond neutrally when the issue is of little consequence to you or others.[52]

Giving and Asking for FEEDBACK

- Focus on behavior, not on the person.
- Make it specific, not general or abstract.
- Use "I" rather than "you" statements.
- Focus on what was said and done, not on why it was said and done.
- Focus on current behavior, not behavior from the past.
- Share information, perceptions, and feelings, not advice.
- Provide feedback at an appropriate time and place.
- Focus on actions that both of you can change.[51]

DEFENSIVE BEHAVIORS

EVALUATION: Judges another person's behavior. Makes critical statements. "Why did you insult Sharon like that? Explain yourself!" "What you did was terrible."

CONTROL: Imposes your solution on someone else. Seeks control of the situation. "Give me that report and I'll make it better." "Since I'm paying for the vacation, we're going to the resort I like rather than the spa you like."

STRATEGY: Manipulates others. Hides or disguises personal motives. Withholds information. "Frankie's going to Florida over spring break." "Remember when I helped you rearrange your office?"

NEUTRALITY: Appears withdrawn, detached, indifferent. Won't take sides. "You can't win them all." "Life's a gamble." "It doesn't matter to me." "Whatever."

SUPERIORITY: Implies that you and your opinions are better than others. Promotes resentment and jealousy. "Hey—I've done this a million times—let me have it. I'll finish in no time." "Is this the best you could do?"

CERTAINTY: Believes that your opinion is the only correct one. Refuses to consider the ideas and opinions of others. Takes inflexible positions. "I can't see any other way of doing this that makes sense." "There's no point in discussing this any further."

SUPPORTIVE BEHAVIORS

DESCRIPTION: Describes another person's behavior. Makes understanding statements. Uses more I and we language. "When we heard what you said to Sharon, we were really embarrassed for her." "I'm sorry about that."

PROBLEM ORIENTATION: Seeks a mutually agreeable solution. "Okay. Let's see what we can do to get that report finished to specifications." "Let's figure out how both of us can enjoy our vacation."

SPONTANEITY: Makes straightforward, direct, open, honest, and helpful comments. "I'd like to go to Florida with Frankie over spring break." "Would you help me move some heavy boxes?"

EMPATHY: Accepts and understands another person's feelings. "I can't believe she did that. No wonder you're upset." "It sounds as though you're having a hard time deciding."

EQUALITY: Suggests that everyone can make a useful contribution. "If you don't mind, I'd like to explain how I've handled this before. It may help." "Let's tackle this problem together."

PROVISIONALISM: Offers ideas and accepts suggestions from others. "We have a lot of options here—which one makes the most sense?" "I feel strongly about this, but I would like to hear what you think."

Gibb's Defensive and Supportive Behaviors[53]

expressing your self appropriately

7.6

Expressing Emotions Appropriately

Why and how can you effectively manage your emotions and provide emotional support to others?

Emotions play a major role in all relationships. An **emotion** is the physical feeling you have when reacting to a situation. Emotions are fundamental to effective and ethical communication. They also play a significant role in how you develop, maintain, and strengthen interpersonal relationships.

The Basic Emotions

Everyone experiences basic, primary emotions, although researchers disagree on the number of such emotions. Robert Plutchik's **Psychoevolutionary Emotion Theory** illuminates the development and meaning of emotions.[54] According to this theory, each basic emotion has a range of feelings (from mild to intense). Plutchik further explains that some emotions blend two or more emotions. As the nearby figure shows, love is a combination of joy and acceptance. Contempt is a combination of anger and disgust.

Emotional Intelligence

Science writer Daniel Goleman defines **emotional intelligence** as "the capacity for recognizing our own feelings and those of others, for motivating ourselves, and for managing emotions well in ourselves and in our relationships."[55] His influential book *Emotional Intelligence: Why It Can Matter More Than IQ* credits two psychologists, Peter Salovey and John Mayer, who coined the term *emotional intelligence* in 1990. You can examine emotional intelligence as a set of interpersonal communication competencies summarized and described in Figure 7.2 on p. 139.[56]

What happens when people cannot make emotions work for them? Neurologist Antonio Damasio, who studies patients with damage to the emotional center of their brains, reports that these patients make terrible decisions even though their IQ scores stay the same. So even though they test as "smart," they "make disastrous choices in business and their personal lives, and can even obsess endlessly over a decision

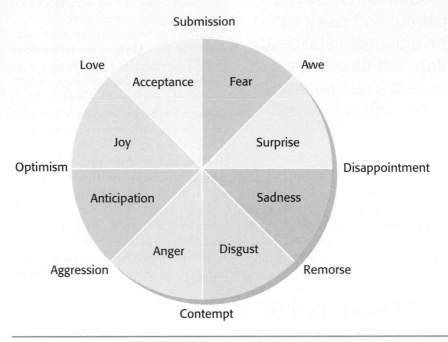

Plutchik's Primary and Compound Emotions[57]

as simple as when to make an appointment." Their decision-making skills are poor because they have lost access to their emotions.[58] Damasio's claims make sense when you consider whether you could answer any of the following questions without taking emotions into account: Whom should I marry? What career should I pursue? Should I buy this house? What should I say to a bereaved relative?

Emotional Support

Have you ever felt at a loss for words when someone needed emotional support and comfort? A colleague's home is seriously damaged by a fire. Your partner fails to get a "sure-thing" job she or he applied for. What do you say or do? As a concerned and compassionate person, you probably wanted to comfort your friend, colleague, partner, or family member. Unfortunately, many of us feel

inadequate to this task. We worry about saying the wrong thing. We search through racks of greeting cards to find a card that can "say it" better than we can.

As much as we may want to support and comfort a person in distress, many of us lack an understanding of the basic nature of emotional support as well as the communication skills needed to achieve its purpose. Communication scholar Brant Burleson defines **emotional support** as "specific lines of communicative behavior enacted by one party with the intent of helping another cope effectively with emotional distress." The distress can be acute (disappointment over not winning a contest or anxiety over an upcoming exam) or chronic (grief over the loss of a loved one or lingering depression over poor health) and may be mild or intense in character.[60]

> **" . . . feelings are *indispensable* for rational decision making."[59]**
>
> —Antonio Damasio, Neurologist

Communication Strategies	As an Emotionally Intelligent Communicator, You . . .
Intrapersonal Communication Strategies	
Develop Self-Awareness	Monitor and identify your feelings in order to guide your decision making. <u>Example:</u> Noticing whether you have raised your voice because you are angry or surprised.
Manage Your Emotions	Restrain or release your emotions when the situation is appropriate. Practice relaxation to recover from emotional distress. <u>Example:</u> Deciding whether expressing strong emotions will facilitate or interfere with your goals.
Motivate Yourself	Persevere in the face of disappointments and setbacks. Seek the support of friends, colleagues, and family members to stay motivated, improve your mood, and bolster your confidence. <u>Example:</u> Seeking help from a trusted mentor.
Interpersonal Communication Strategies	
Listen to Others	Engage effective listening skills to ensure you understand what another person means. Use effective, empathic listening. <u>Example:</u> Paraphrasing what you hear to make sure you understand someone before responding emotionally.
Develop Interpersonal Skills	Use self-disclosure, assertiveness, and appropriate verbal and nonverbal communication. Try to resolve conflicts. <u>Example:</u> Deciding whether and how to share your emotions with a close friend.
Help Others Help Themselves	Help others become more aware of their emotions. Help them speak and listen more effectively. <u>Example:</u> Providing emotional support to a distressed friend.

Figure 7.2 Emotionally Intelligent Communication

Constructing Emotionally Supportive Messages

Emotionally supportive communication strategies can help you comfort and support others. These strategies include being clear about your intentions, protecting the other person's self-esteem, and centering your messages on the other person.

Communicate Your Intentions Clearly When someone is in great distress, you may think this person knows you want to be helpful and supportive. You may assume that just "being there" tells the other person that you care. In some cases, your assumptions are correct. In other situations, a person in distress needs to know that you *want* to help or provide assistance.

You can enhance the clarity of your supportive messages by stating them directly ("I want to help you") and by making it clear you care ("I'm here for you"). You can also intensify the perceived sincerity of your response by emphasizing your desire to help ("I really want to help however I can"), by reminding the person of the personal history you share ("You know we've always been there for each other"), and

ETHICAL COMMUNICATION

The Ethics of Caring

The NCA Credo for Ethical Communication includes a principle that speaks directly to interpersonal relationships: "We promote communication climates of caring and mutual understanding that respect the unique needs and characteristics of individual communicators."[61] The ethical value of care focuses on the responsibilities we have for others in our interpersonal relationships.[62]

Philosopher and educator Nel Noddings believes we make moral choices based on an ethic of caring. For example, a mother picks up a crying baby, not because of a sense of duty or because she is worried about what others will say if she doesn't but because she cares about the baby. Relationship theorists emphasize that this is not a gender-based ethic. Rather, it is based on a way of thinking that honors two fundamental characteristics of ethical behavior: avoiding harm and providing mutual aid.[63]

In what way does this scene depict an ethic of caring, and how does such behavior promote effective communication?

expressing emotions appropriately

Comforting Message STRATEGIES

- Communicate Your Intentions Clearly
  "I'm here to help because I care."
- Protect the Other Person's Self-Esteem
  "I can see you're trying very hard to deal with this problem."
- Offer Person-Centered Messages
  "Tell me all about what happened and how you're feeling."

by indicating what you feel ("Helping you is important to me; I'd feel terrible if I weren't here to help").[64]

Protect the Other Person's Self-Esteem Make sure that your offer of help does not imply that the other person is incapable of solving the problem or dealing with the situation. Otherwise, you may damage someone's self-esteem. Even with the best of intentions, expressions of sympathy ("Oh, you poor thing . . .") can convey judgments about the person's lack of competence and lack of independence. Try to encourage and praise the other person.[65]

Offer Person-Centered Messages
Messages that reflect "the degree to which a helper validates [a] distressed person's feelings and encourages him or her to talk about the upsetting event" are **person-centered messages**.[66] Rather than focusing on helping someone feel better, your goal is helping the person develop a deeper understanding of the problem so that they may take on the task of solving or coping with it. You can help someone in distress understand the problem by encouraging her or him to tell an extended, personal story about the problem or upsetting event. People in need of emotional support may want nothing more than to share the details with a trusted friend.

While these communication strategies express your willingness to help, your supportive feelings, and your personal commitment, take care to avoid counterproductive strategies. For example, do not focus on or share *your* emotional experiences, as in "I know exactly how you feel. Last year, I went through a similar kind of problem. It all started when . . ." Not only does this stop the other person from sharing, but it also shifts the focus to yourself. You

Encourage Coping Through Storytelling

- Ask for your friend's version of the situation. ("What happened here?")
- Create a supportive environment and provide enough time for the person to talk. ("Take your time. I want to hear the whole story.")
- Ask about the person's feelings, not just the events. ("How did you feel when that happened?" "What was your reaction when she said that?")
- Legitimize the expression of feelings. ("I certainly understand why you'd feel that way.")
- Indicate that you connect with what the other person is saying. ("If that happened to me, I'd be furious too.")[67]

should also avoid messages that criticize or negatively evaluate another person because these can hurt more than help. Do not tell others that their feelings are wrong, inappropriate, immature, or embarrassing.

COMMUNICATION IN *ACTION*

The Comforting Touch

As a child you experienced nonverbal comforting well before you understood and communicated with language. "Not surprisingly, the nonverbal behaviors first used in infancy continue as expressions of emotional support throughout a lifetime. Hugs, touches and pats, hand-holding, focused looks and soothing sounds can be remarkably effective ways of expressing reassurance, love, warmth, and acceptance."[68] In terms of physical health, researchers note that a hospital patient's family and friends help just by visiting, regardless of whether they know what to say.[69] According to another study, a five-second touch can convey specific emotions, such as sympathy and sadness.[70]

Touch plays a significant role in comforting others. "Skin-on-skin touch is particularly soothing

because it primes oxytocin," a neurotransmitter that causes our body to undergo many healthy changes. Blood pressure lowers and we relax. Our pain threshold increases so that we are less sensitive to discomforts. Even wounds heal faster.[71]

How would you react nonverbally if a close same-sex friend told you that she or

Touch can be worth a thousand words.

he had just ended a serious romantic relationship? In one study, most college students ranked hugging as their number one response. Other high-ranking responses included being attentive, moving closer to the other person, using certain facial expressions, increasing touch, and making eye contact. Not surprisingly, men and women suggested different nonverbal responses. Men were less likely than women to hug their troubled friend; they were more likely to pat their friend on the arm or shoulder and to suggest going out and doing something to take their minds off the problem. Women were more likely to cry with their friend and to use a variety of comforting touches.[72]

Evacuees of Hurricane Katrina find consolation and comfort in the warm embrace of others.

How Emotionally Intelligent Are You?[73]

Daniel Goleman proposes five basic emotional competencies, expressed in the following headings.[74] Use the rating scale listed here to assess your level of competence for each question:

5 = Always,   4 = Usually,   3 = Sometimes,   2 = Rarely,   and   1 = Never.

Know Thy Self

_____ 1. Can you accurately identify the emotions you experience and why you experience them?

_____ 2. Do you have a strong self-concept?

_____ 3. Are you aware of your strengths and limitations?

Control Your Emotions and Impulses

_____ 4. Can you keep disruptive emotions under control?

_____ 5. Do you take responsibility for your emotions and resulting actions?

_____ 6. Are you open-minded and flexible in handling difficult situations?

Persevere

_____ 7. Do you strive to improve or meet high standards of excellence?

_____ 8. Do you persist in the face of obstacles and setbacks?

_____ 9. Can you postpone gratification and regulate your moods?

Empathize

_____ 10. Do you accurately interpret others' feelings and needs?

_____ 11. Do you provide appropriate emotional support to others?

_____ 12. Do you paraphrase appropriately?

Interact Effectively

_____ 13. Do you listen appropriately and effectively?

_____ 14. Do you make a positive social impression?

_____ 15. Do you work effectively with others to achieve shared goals?

Scoring: Add up your ratings. The higher your score, the more "emotionally intelligent" you are. Keep in mind that your ratings are only your *perceptions* of your feelings and behaviors. For example, despite what you think, you may not interpret others' feelings and needs accurately or persist in the face of obstacles. On the other hand, you may not recognize that you provide appropriate emotional support to others, even though your friends often turn to you when they need an empathetic ear.

7.1
Interpersonal Communication and Relationships

What are the characteristics and benefits of effective interpersonal communication?

- Good personal relationships positively affect your psychological and physical health, your happiness, your social and moral development, and your ability to cope with stress.

- William Schutz's Fundamental Interpersonal Relationship Orientation (FIRO) Theory identifies three interpersonal needs: inclusion, control, and affection.

7.2
Developing Interpersonal Relationships

How do you form positive and lasting relationships with others?

- Impression management strategies that help you shape your image in positive ways include ingratiation, self-promotion, exemplification, supplication, and intimidation.

- Effective communicators know how to initiate, maintain, and end conversations as well as how to listen with interest and empathy.

7.3
Strengthening Personal Relationships

How does interpersonal communication affect your relationships with friends and romantic partners?

- Strong friendships increase life satisfaction and help increase your life expectancy.

- There are ten common stages in most romantic relationships, divided into five coming-together steps and five coming-apart steps.

7.4
Sharing Yourself with Others

How does self-disclosure and sensitivity to feedback affect your personal relationships?

- Self-disclosure is the process of sharing personal information, opinions, and emotions.

- The Johari Window displays the extent to which you are willing to self-disclose and are receptive to feedback from others.

- Social Penetration Theory describes the process of relationship bonding in which individuals move from superficial communication to deeper, more intimate communication.

7.5
Expressing Yourself Appropriately

How should you express your personal thoughts and feelings to others?

- Effective self-disclosure requires the ability to focus on the present, be descriptive and understanding, respect and adapt to others, reciprocate self-disclosure, and move disclosure to deeper levels as appropriate.

- Effective feedback requires giving and asking for information about behavior, actions, perceptions and feelings, that you and others can change.

- Gibb's defensive-supportive communication behaviors are evaluation-description, control-problem orientation, strategy-spontaneity, neutrality-empathy, superiority-equality, and certainty-provisionalism.

7.6
Expressing Emotions Appropriately

Why and how should you manage your emotions and provide emotional support to others?

- Robert Plutchik's eight basic emotions are fear, acceptance, anger, disgust, joy, expectancy, sadness, and surprise.

- Emotional intelligence is the capacity for recognizing your own feelings and those of others, for motivating yourself, and for effectively managing your emotions in relationships.

- When comforting another person, you should make your intentions clear, protect the other person's self-esteem, and center your message on the other person, not on yourself.

MySearchLab®

7.1 What are the characteristics and benefits of effective interpersonal communication?

1 According to Schutz's FIRO Theory, an _____ is a submissive person who wants and needs control, but is reluctant to pursue it.
a. autocrat
b. abdicrat
c. democrat
d. undersocial type
e. underpersonal type

7.2 How do you form positive and lasting relationships with others?

2 What impression management strategy is Collette using if, in a conversation with a colleague, she says, "Let's work on your part of this report together so you can get home at a decent hour."
a. Ingratiation
b. Self-promotion
c. Exemplification
d. Supplication
e. Intimidation

7.3 How does interpersonal communication affect your relationships with friends and romantic partners?

3 According to Knapp and Vangelisti's Model of Relationship Stages, in which stage do the personalities, opinions, and behaviors of two people join together so that they become a couple rather than two separate individuals?
a. Intensification
b. Differentiation
c. Integration
d. Circumscribing
e. Initiation

7.4 How do self-disclosure and sensitivity to feedback affect your personal relationships?

4 In the Johari Window Model, the more receptive and adaptive you are to feedback from others, the larger your _____ window pane is.
a. open
b. hidden
c. blind
d. unknown
e. private

5 Social Penetration Theory explains that relationships are closest when communication is _____.
a. friendly, frequent, and fair
b. deep, broad, and frequent
c. open, hidden, and unknown
d. private, patient, and powerful
e. personal, social, and public

6 In terms of Gibb's categories of behavior for creating a positive communication climate, how would you classify the following statement? "Let's find a way for both of us to go where we want on our vacation."
a. Description
b. Strategy
c. Problem orientation
d. Empathy
e. Neutrality

7.5 How should you express your personal thoughts and feelings to others?

7 All of the following are effective ways to give and respond to feedback except _____.
a. focusing on behavior, not on the person
b. making your statements specific, not general or abstract
c. using "you" rather than "I" statements
d. focusing on what was said and done, not on why it was said and done
e. focusing on current rather than past behavior

8 All of the following behaviors are characteristics of effective self-disclosure except _____.
a. focusing on the person's past behavior
b. disclosing your feelings as well as facts
c. adapting to the person and context
d. describing rather than judging
e. engaging in reciprocal self-disclosure

7.6 Why and can you effectively manage your emotions and provide emotional support to others?

9 In Plutchik's Psychoevolutionary Emotion Theory, which two basic emotions combine to create the emotion of love?
a. Submission and surprise
b. Anticipation and awe
c. Acceptance and joy
d. Optimism and submission
e. Awe and envy

10 Which of the following statements communicates your desire to help and support a person dealing with emotional distress?
a. I'm here for you.
b. I really want to help however I can.
c. You know we've always been there for each other.
d. I'd feel terrible if I weren't here to help.
e. all of the above

Answers found on page 366.

Key Terms

Abdicrat	Orientation (FIRO)	Person-centered
Affection need	Theory	message
Autocrat	Impression management	Professional relationship
Closed-ended question	Inclusion need	Psychoevolutionary
Control need	Ingratiation	Emotion Theory
Conversation	Interpersonal	Relationship
Defensive behaviors	communication	Self-disclosure
Emotion	Intimacy	Self-promotion
Emotional intelligence	Intimidation	Social networking
Emotional support	Jealousy	Social Penetration Theory
Exemplification	Johari Window	Supplication
Fundamental	Open-ended question	Supportive behaviors
Interpersonal	Personal relationship	Turn-requesting cue
Relationship		Turn-yielding cue

THINK
COMMUNICATION

Communication
Knowledge for Communicating Well
Currents

N C A

A Publication of the National Communication Association

Volume 5, Issue 3 - June 2010

Stand by Me: Helping Bullied Victims

> Why has bullying become a big issue in the news? Is there more of it now than before or has it simply become more visible and more acceptable to discuss?

According to the *Indicators of School Crime and Safety 2009 Report*, 25 to 30% of students aged 12 to 18 in the U.S. have been bullied—physically, verbally, or relationally—at school. Similarly, the Ministry of Education, Culture, Sports, Science and Technology of Japan indicates that more than 20,000 cases of bullying were reported in 2007. Bullying is also reported in one out of every four companies in the U.S. according to the National Institute for Occupational Safety and Health. Not only employees but customers and supervisors can be targets of bullying at the workplace. Victims abound, and they need help.

Helping victims of bullying is a tricky business. Communication and culture play key roles in determine the effectiveness of efforts to help. An empathetic and caring interaction [may restore] victims' mental health and lead to constructive post-bullying adjustment. But not all messages are effective, and what counts as effective support varies across cultures. Messages intended to restore victims' self-esteem, for example, are not favored by victims in the U.S. On the other hand, victims in Japan find suggestions to contact a third party particularly objectionable. In fact, suggestions to talk to authorities or experts are likely to de-motivate Japanese victims to open up about bullying and even deteriorate their long-term psychological well-being.

> What do you know about the differences between U.S. and Japanese cultures that might explain this difference?

Data collected from young adults in the U.S. and Japan revealed that when victims indicate they are being bullied, their friends, family, or teachers exhibit a range of supportive behaviors. Some supporters express care and concern for the victims in a compassionate tone. Others try to re-establish the victims' self-esteem by reminding the victim of her or his good points and virtues. And some people (typically fathers and teachers) offer to connect victims to experts (such as school counselors) who might be able to help solve the problem, or trustworthy confidants with whom the victims can share their concerns. Interestingly, the last type of support—support that intends to connect a victim to a third party—is almost twice as likely to be used in the U.S. as it is in Japan. In contrast, the reported likelihood of using the other two types of support [expressing concern and re-establishing self-esteem] did not differ as much across cultures.

Cultural differences emerge even more clearly when it comes to how victims perceive those supportive messages. In the U.S., esteem support intended to directly restore or remind victims of their self-worth (such as, "You are still a good person even when you have a problem," or "Don't feel guilty") are not perceived favorably and victims who receive this type of supportive message are typically dissatisfied. Even if it is only to make a point that being a victim of bullying is not her or

> Read this paragraph, which previews what's to come in the rest of the article. Before reading any further consider how you would explain the authors' claims about why bullying in the U.S. and Japan differ. Then read the rest of the article. Did you and the author explain these results in similar of different ways—why or why not?

> A major section of Chapter 7 focuses on how to construct emotionally supportive messages including (a) Communicate Your Intentions Clearly, (b) Protect the Other Person's Self-Esteem, and (c) Offer Person-Centered Messages. To what extent does this article endorse these methods? Which strategies emerge as the most effective in both or either culture?

Would you be reluctant to see a therapist if you lived or worked with a tightly knit group and your need for a therapist would likely become known to others?

Do you agree with the author's claims that "bullying is a socially sanctioned experience" and that "victims avoid disclosing" that they've been bullied? Is this only true about bullying or does it apply to all physical and emotional abuse?

his fault, being identified with bullying is the last thing a victim wants. Bullying is a heavily stigmatized experience and typically victims make every effort to disassociate themselves from the experience. In the US, network support is favored over expressions of concern or efforts to boost victim self-esteem.

By contrast, for victims in Japan, network support turns out to be the worst type of message. Introducing a third-party expert or confidant resulted in a considerable drop in the satisfaction level of Japanese victims of bullying. There are several reasons that might account for this finding. First, seeking the advice of a third party is not customary in Japan. Seeing a therapist, for example, is still seen as equivalent to admitting to having psychological problems. A second reason may be the fear of information leakage. Japan is a tightly knit society. As a result, one's social network does not change often. Revealing the secret of bullying in such a closely tied society is a highly risky maneuver. Finally, suggesting to victims that they should see a third-party can be interpreted as an evasive answer, in essence saying: "I can't or don't want to deal with this issue. Go talk to someone else who is better capable of solving your problem."

Emotional support that conveys care, concern, and sympathy is found effective by victims in both cultures. Victims feel most satisfied when others encourage them to open up and express their emotions, show understanding of their suffering through attentive listening, and/or tell victims they can always find a shoulder to cry on with the recipient. Conceivably, emotional support seems appropriate to bullied victims because it alleviates their doubts about their own self-worth. Bullying causes more than stress; it also induces strong feelings of loneliness and self-doubt. Emotional support helps victims address those anxieties and realize that others love them.

Supportive communication affects victims' post-bullying adjustment, and this healing effect works similarly across cultures. Victims who are satisfied with the support they receive are more willing and comfortable to talk about bullying after the initial interaction. Bullying is a socially sanctioned experience and victims often avoid disclosing because they fear that revealing their victimhood might elicit accusation and finger pointing. Consequently, bullying becomes a hidden—and therefore untreatable—problem. Receiving sensitive support seems to break this cycle by reducing victims' anxiety and helping them realize the benefit of disclosure. Furthermore, those victims who have received quality support see their life as more satisfactory and meaningful. They are more psychologically healthy, emotionally stable, and well-adjusted.

From a practical point of view, these findings suggest the need to provide those who surround bullied victims with information on sound, supportive communication skills. Friends, family, and teachers can and do make a difference in victims' post-bullying adjustment process. These groups need to learn about effective, supportive communication for bullied victims because not all messages—even those meant to be supportive—are equally effective, and receiving sub-optimal support may impede victim readjustment. The importance of supportive communication illuminates a promising path for victims to escape from the iron claw of bullying.

ABOUT THE AUTHOR

Masaki Matsunaga, Assistant Professor of interpersonal and intercultural communication, Rikkyo University, Tokyo, Japan. This essay is based on Masaki Matsunaga (2010). "Testing a Meditational Model of Bullied Victims' Evaluation of Received Support and Post-Bullying Adaptation: A Japan-U.S. Cross-Cultural Comparison. *Communication Monographs*, 77, pp. 312–340. *Communication Monographs* and *Communication Currents* are publications of the National Communication Association.

In Chapter 7, we claim that "touch plays a significant role in comforting others" and that one study found that ". . . a five-second touch can convey specific emotions such as sympathy and sadness." Given what you've read in this article, do you think that touch is an appropriate and effective way to provide comforting and emotional support to victims of bullying regardless of their culture?

Chapter 8 devotes major sections to personality types, argumentativeness, assertiveness, anger, and conflict styles. When you read this material, consider whether any of these communication traits are characteristic of bullies or their victim. For example, in Myers-Briggs terms, are bullies more likely to be judgers and victims introverts? Are bullies more argumentative, aggressive, or assertive while victims are more passive? Do bullies see conflict as a competition while victims see it as something to avoid or accommodate?

Improving
INTERPERSONAL
COMMUNICATION

Why and when do couples break up? In *Uncoupling: How Relationships Come Apart*, sociologist Diane Vaughan notes that a couple's breakup is rarely sudden. It all begins with a secret. Usually, one of the partners starts to feel uncomfortable in the relationship—and keeps those thoughts, feelings, or actions to themselves. The world the two of them have built together no longer "fits."[1]

In some cases, the secret is huge and devastating, particularly when the secret goes public, as in the breakup and divorce of a high-profile couple such as Sandra Bullock and Jesse James. Shortly after winning the 2010 Academy Award for Best Actress, Sandra Bullock learned about her husband's affair with Michelle "Bombshell" McGee, a San Diego tattoo and fetish model who reportedly also worked as a stripper. The story was reported by public media ranging from *The New York Times* and major television networks to tabloid newspapers and celebrity gossip websites. So much for secrets!

The kinds of secrets that Diane Vaughan describes, however, are much less volatile. Typically, they concern one partner's feeling of dissatisfaction, discomfort, unhappiness, or fear about the relationship's future.[2]

THINK About… and ASK YOURSELF …

8.1
Balancing Interpersonal Tensions
How can you balance the inevitable tensions in interpersonal relationships?

All interpersonal relationships experience tensions. Romantic or married couples may experience tension when one person wants a quiet evening at home while the other person wants to go out and party. Work colleagues may experience tension when one coworker is driven to complete a project ahead of schedule while the other coworker would just as soon leave it to the last minute. Unresolved, these kinds of tensions

have the potential to damage relationships beyond repair. When, however, you understand and work to resolve interpersonal tensions, you have the potential to strengthen a valued relationship.

In this section, we examine two approaches to recognizing, respecting, and appropriately responding to the contradictory tensions in interpersonal relationships: relational dialectics and personal type indicators.

Relational Dialectics
The following pairs of common sayings illustrate several contradictory beliefs about personal relationships:

"Opposites attract" *but* "Birds of a feather flock together."
"To know him is to love him" *but* "Familiarity breeds contempt."
"Out of sight, out of mind" *but* "Absence makes the heart grow fonder."

FACTS TEST IDEA PLAN EXPERIMENT METHOD
THINK ABOUT THEORY
Relational Dialectics Theory

Leslie Baxter and Barbara Montgomery's Relational Dialectics Theory claims that personal relationships are characterized by **dialectics**, the interplay of opposing or contradictory forces. **Relational Dialectics Theory** focuses on the ongoing tensions between contradictory impulses in personal relationships.[3]

Rather than an "either/or" response to opposing tensions, relational dialectics takes a "both/and" approach. For example, two people in a romantic relationship seek togetherness, but they also need time to be alone—time to think about personal needs, to escape the daily routine, and to engage in personal interests not shared by the other person. In many close relationships, you want *both* intimacy *and* independence. You want *both* the comfort of a stable relationship *and* the excitement of change. You can

hear these dialectic tensions in the words a student wrote about her three-month romantic relationship: "Every relationship is a meeting of two people and however hard you try, you're not gonna form one sort of unified whole; you need the unity but there also has to be individuality for a relationship to be really close."[4]

Leslie Baxter and her colleagues identify three major dialectics in personal relationships: integration versus separation, stability versus change, and expression versus privacy.[5]

1 The Integration-Separation Dialectic.

Interpersonal relationships survive when we successfully negotiate our desire for *both* connection *and* independence. Generally, most of us want to be close to others without having to give up our separate selves. For example, as you grow up, you may want to remain closely connected to your parents but still live an independent life free from their intrusion. Or let's say you want to build a life with your partner, but you also want to maintain your own career and bank account. As much as you want to be close to others, you also need to be your separate self.

2 The Stability-Change Dialectic.

Most of us want the security of a stable relationship *and* the novelty and excitement of change, the predictability of day-after-day interactions *and* an occasional change in routine. For example, an engaged couple might decide to follow several wedding traditions—formal invitations, a wedding reception, flowers and traditional wedding music, and even the bride in white—but also decide to hold the wedding in a riding stable with the bride, groom, and presiding official on horseback. Another couple may share a stable, permanent home together in one city but rent an apartment in a different city or country every summer.[6]

3 The Expression-Privacy Dialectic.

Like most people, you may want to be open and honest with another person while also protecting your privacy. Do your best friends, romantic partner, and close family members know every secret you have? Should they? This dialectic addresses your conflicting urges to tell your secrets and to keep them hidden.[7] For example, when Jane tells Jack she'd like to rent an apartment in a building closer to where she works, he may say he wants to stay in the suburbs. In truth, he doesn't want to move to a building where a former girlfriend lives.

These contradictory folk sayings do not require an "either/or" verdict to determine which one is true or false. Rather, they demonstrate why these sayings survive: All of these sayings can be true depending on the circumstances, on the people involved, and on the nature of the interpersonal relationship.

Relational Dialectics Theory makes a strong case for a "both/and" focus when communicating with others rather than an either/or approach. Although the theory does not offer surefire guidelines for improving interpersonal relationships, it does help explain your experiences in new as well as ongoing relationships. It also suggests several strategies for negotiating tensions in close personal relationships.[8]

- Choose different options at different points in your life. **Example:** You may be close to siblings when you're young but less close when you're married and/or raising your own family.
- Choose different options in different contexts. **Example:** You may be less connected and open when interacting with a close friend in a work environment.
- Chose one option and ignore the other. **Example:** You may decide that being close to your family is more important at certain times than socializing with nonfamily friends.
- Chooses a compromise between opposite options. **Example:** You can invite relatives to join you on a vacation rather than only visiting them in their home
- Choose a new point of view that doesn't *appear* so opposite. **Example:** You may decide you can be close to someone if you occasionally put a little time and distance between you.
- Choose to avoid the topic in order to avoid the tension. **Example:** You may decide to be totally open with co-workers about all topics except sex, finances, and highly personal habits.

The integration-separation dialectic often surfaces when a child leaves home for college.

These options are not a "to-do" list for resolving dialectic tensions. Rather, they illustrate a range of options, the success of which depends on how your choice best meets the interpersonal needs of both communicators.

Meaningful and lasting interpersonal relationships do not just happen. *You* make them happen.

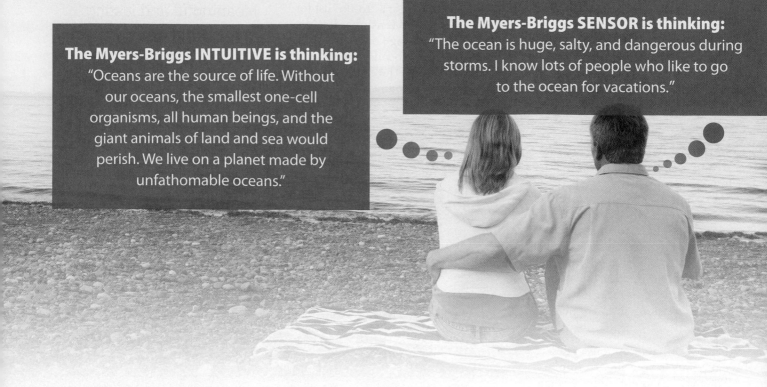

The Myers-Briggs INTUITIVE is thinking:
"Oceans are the source of life. Without our oceans, the smallest one-cell organisms, all human beings, and the giant animals of land and sea would perish. We live on a planet made by unfathomable oceans."

The Myers-Briggs SENSOR is thinking:
"The ocean is huge, salty, and dangerous during storms. I know lots of people who like to go to the ocean for vacations."

The Myers-Briggs Type Indicator

The psychological concept of **personality** represents the style in which we interact with the world around us and particularly with other people.[9] Understanding *and* appreciating your own and others' personality traits are central to improving the quality of interpersonal communication.

Isabel Briggs Myers and her mother, Katharine Briggs, developed the **Myers-Briggs Types Indicator**, a personality type assessment that examines the ways in which we perceive the world around us as well as how we reach conclusions and make decisions.[10] Thousands of corporations, including most Fortune 100 companies use the Myers-Briggs Type Indicator "to identify potential job applicants whose skills match those of their top performers," while others use it "to develop communication skills and promote teamwork among current employees."[11]

According to Myers-Briggs, all of us have preferred ways of thinking and behaving that can be divided into four categories, with two opposite preferences in each category, as indicated in the figure below. As you read about the types and their traits, ask yourself which preferences best describe how you communicate.[12]

> The Myers-Briggs Type Indicator tells us a great deal about how and why we get along with some people and have difficulty interacting with others.

Extrovert or Introvert Extrovert and introvert are two traits that describe where you focus your attention: outward or inward. **Extroverts** are outgoing; they talk more and gesture when they speak. They get their energy by being with people and enjoy solving problems in groups. They also have a tendency to dominate conversations without listening to others.

Introverts think before they speak and usually are not as talkative as extroverts. They prefer socializing with one or two close friends rather than spending time with a large group of people. Introverts recharge by being

The Myers-Briggs Personality Preferences

EXTROVERT Talkative, outgoing	⟷	**INTROVERT** Quieter, private
SENSOR Detail-oriented, precise	⟷	**INTUITIVE** Sees big picture, innovative
THINKER Task-oriented, objective	⟷	**FEELER** People-oriented, subjective
JUDGER Structured, punctual	⟷	**PERCEIVER** Flexible, spontaneous

alone and often prefer to work by themselves.

"Extroverts complain that introverts don't speak up at the right time in meetings. Introverts criticize extroverts for talking too much and not listening well."[13] In classrooms, extroverts like to participate in heated discussions, whereas introverts hate being put on the spot.

Sensor or Intuitive How do you look at the world around you? Do you see the forest (the big picture) or the trees (the details)? **Sensors** focus on details and prefer to concentrate on one task at a time. They may uncover minor flaws in an idea and like having detailed instructions for doing a task. **Intuitives** look for connections and concepts rather than rules and flaws. They come up with big ideas but are bored with details. Sensors focus on regulations, step-by-step explanations, and facts, whereas intuitives focus on outwitting regulations, supplying theoretical explanations, and skipping details.

Both personality types are needed in the workplace. Management communication experts Carl Larson and Frank LaFasto emphasize the importance of having a balance between the "nuts and bolts types" and those individuals who are capable of being creative and conceptual.[14]

Thinker or Feeler Thinker and feeler are two traits that explain how you go about making decisions. **Thinkers** are analytical and task-oriented people who take pride in their ability to make difficult decisions. They want to get the job done, even at the cost of others' feelings. **Feelers** are more people oriented. They want everyone to get along. Feelers will spend time and effort helping others.

Thinkers may appear unemotional and aggressive, whereas feelers may annoy others by "wasting time" with social chitchat. Although the thinker makes decisions and moves things forward, the feeler makes sure everyone gets along and works together harmoniously.

Each of the characters in the TV series *Modern Family* displays a distinct personality. Which Myers-Briggs traits would you assign to each of them?

The Myers-Briggs THINKER type: "I like this guy because he's smart, analytical, well organized, and takes a firm, but fair approach to grading."

The Myers-Briggs FEELER type: "I like this teacher because he takes an interest in every student, cares whether we learn or not, and never puts down anyone in class."

Judger or Perceiver Do you approach the world and its challenges in a structured and organized way? If so, you are most likely a judger. **Judgers** are highly structured people who plan ahead, are punctual, and become impatient with people who show up late or waste time. **Perceivers** are less rigid than judgers. Because they like open-endedness, being on time is less important than being flexible and adaptable. Perceivers are risk takers who are willing to try new options. They often procrastinate and end up in a frenzy to complete a task on time.

Judgers and perceivers often have difficulty understanding each other.

To a judger, a perceiver may appear scatterbrained. To a perceiver, a judger may appear rigid and controlling. Whereas judgers are prepared to make decisions and solve problems, perceivers "aren't comfortable with things being 'decided'; [they] want to reopen, discuss, rework, argue for the sake of arguing."[15] In classroom settings, judgers usually plan and finish class assignments well in advance, whereas perceivers may pull all-nighters to get their work done. It's important to note that both types get their work done—the difference is when and how they go about doing it.

balancing interpersonal tensions

What Is Your Personality Type?

Read the *pairs* of descriptions for each personality type and put a check mark next to the *one* phrase in each pair that *best* describes you.[16] When you have finished, add up the check marks in each column and note the personality type with the most check marks.

1. Are you an extrovert or an introvert?

_____ I am outgoing, sociable, and expressive.	**OR**	_____ I am reserved and private.
_____ I enjoy groups and discussions.	**OR**	_____ I prefer one-to-one interactions.
_____ I often talk first, think later.	**OR**	_____ I usually think first, then talk.
_____ I think out loud.	**OR**	_____ I think to myself.
_____ Other people give me energy.	**OR**	_____ Other people often exhaust me.

_____ **Total** (Extrovert)   _____ **Total** (Introvert)

2. Are you a sensor or an intuitive?

_____ I focus on details.	**OR**	_____ I focus on the big picture.
_____ I am practical and realistic.	**OR**	_____ I am theoretical.
_____ I like facts.	**OR**	_____ I get bored with facts and details.
_____ I trust experience.	**OR**	_____ I trust inspiration and intuition.
_____ I want clear, realistic goals.	**OR**	_____ I want to pursue a vision.

_____ **Total** (Sensor)   _____ **Total** (Intuitive)

3. Are you a thinker or a feeler?

_____ I am task oriented.	**OR**	_____ I am people oriented.
_____ I am objective, firm, analytical.	**OR**	_____ I am subjective, caring, appreciative.
_____ I value competence, reason, justice.	**OR**	_____ I value relationships and harmony.
_____ I am direct and firm-minded.	**OR**	_____ I am tactful and tenderhearted.
_____ I think with my head.	**OR**	_____ I think with my heart.

_____ **Total** (Thinker)   _____ **Total** (Feeler)

4. Are you a judger or a perceiver?

_____ I value organization and structure.	**OR**	_____ I value flexibility and spontaneity.
_____ I like having deadlines.	**OR**	_____ I dislike deadlines.
_____ I will work now, play later.	**OR**	_____ I will play now, work later.
_____ I adjust my schedule to complete work.	**OR**	_____ I do work at the last minute.
_____ I plan ahead.	**OR**	_____ I adapt as I go.

_____ **Total** (Judger)   _____ **Total** (Perceiver)

Summarize your decisions by indicating the letter that best describes your personality traits and preferences:

_____   _____   _____   _____
Extrovert (E)   Sensor (S)   Thinker (T)   Judger (J)
      or   or   or   or
Introvert (I)   Intuitive (N)   Feeler (F)   Perceiver (P)

8.2
Resolving Interpersonal Conflict

What communication strategies and skills help resolve interpersonal conflicts?

All healthy relationships, no matter how important or well managed, involve interpersonal conflict. Conflict is often associated with quarreling, fighting, anger, and hostility. Although these elements can be present, conflict does not have to involve negative emotions. We define **conflict** as the disagreement that occurs in relationships when differences are expressed.

Many people avoid conflict because they do not understand the differences between destructive and constructive conflict. **Destructive conflict** is the result of behaviors that create hostility or prevent problem solving. Constant complaining, personal insults, conflict avoidance, and loud arguments or threats all contribute to destructive conflict.[17] This kind of conflict has the potential to permanently harm a relationship.

In contrast, **constructive conflict** occurs when you express disagreement in a way that respects others' perspectives and promotes problem solving. Kenneth Cloke and Joan Goldsmith of the Center for Dispute Resolution explain that all of us have a choice about how to deal with conflict. We can treat conflict as dialectic experiences "that imprison us or lead us on a journey, as a battle that embitters us or as an opportunity for learning. Our choices between these contrasting attitudes and approaches will shape the way the conflict unfolds."[18]

Conflict Styles

When you are involved in a personal conflict, do you jump into the fray or run the other way? Do you marshal your forces and play to win, or do you work with everyone to find a mutually agreeable solution? Psychologists Kenneth Thomas and Ralph Kilmann claim that we use one or two of five conflict styles in most situations: avoidance, accommodation, competition, compromise, and collaboration.[19] These five styles represent the extent

DESTRUCTIVE CONFLICT

- Attacks others
- Insults others
- Defensive
- Inflexible
- Competitive
- Avoids or aggravates conflict

CONSTRUCTIVE CONFLICT

- Focuses on issues
- Respects others
- Supportive
- Flexible
- Cooperative
- Committed to conflict management

Constructive and Destructive Conflict.[20]

to which you focus on achieving personal needs or mutual needs. People who are motivated to fulfill their own needs tend to choose more competitive approaches, whereas collaborative people are more concerned with achieving mutual goals. Figure 8.1 illustrates the relationship of each conflict style to an individual's motivation.[21]

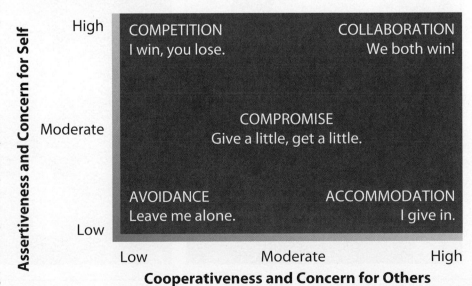

Figure 8.1 Conflict Styles

Avoidance If you are unable or unwilling to stand up for your own needs or the needs of others, you may rely on the **avoidance conflict style**. People who use this style often change the subject, sidestep a controversial issue, or deny that a conflict exists. Avoiding conflict can be counterproductive because you fail to address a problem and can increase tension in a relationship.

Ignoring or avoiding conflict does not make it go away.

However, in some circumstances, avoiding conflict is an appropriate response. Consider avoiding conflict when the issue is not important to you, when you need time to collect your thoughts or control your emotions, when the consequences of confrontation are too risky, or when the chances of resolution are unlikely.

Accommodation Do you give in to others during a conflict at the expense of meeting your own needs? If so, you use the **accommodating conflict style**. You may believe that giving in to others preserves peace and harmony, but frequently dealing with conflict by accommodating others may make you less influential in personal or professional relationships.

On the other hand, when the issue is very important to the other person but not very important to you, an accommodating conflict style may be appropriate and effective. Accommodation is also appropriate when it is more important to preserve harmony in a relationship than to resolve a particular issue, when realize you are wrong, or if you have changed your mind.

Competition If you are more concerned with fulfilling your own needs than with meeting the needs of others, you are using a **competitive conflict style**. Quite simply, you want to win because you believe that your ideas are better than anyone else's. When used inappropriately, the competitive style may result in hostility, ridicule, and personal attacks against others. Approaching conflict competitively tends to reduce people to winners or losers.

In certain situations, however, the competitive approach may be the most appropriate style. Approach conflict competitively when you have strong beliefs about an important issue or when immediate action is needed in an urgent situation. The competitive approach is particularly appropriate when the consequences of a bad decision may be harmful, unethical, or illegal.

Compromise The **compromising conflict style** is a "middle-ground" approach that involves conceding some goals to achieve others. Many people believe that compromise is an effective and fair method of resolving problems because, in theory, everyone loses and wins equally. However, if you are dissatisfied with the outcome or believe it is unfair, you may not do much to implement the solution or course of action.

The compromise approach should be used when you are unable to reach a unanimous decision or resolve a problem. Consider compromising when other methods of conflict resolution are not effective, when you have reached an impasse, or if there is not enough time to explore more creative options.

Constructive Conflict in Everyday Life

A husband and wife disagree about how to get from here to there, but are not having a hostile argument.

Friends disagree about something, but are not threatening or insulting one another.

How Argumentative Are You?[22]

Argumentativeness, your willingness to argue controversial issues with others, is a positive trait that does not promote hostility or anxiety. Argumentative people tend to focus on the most important issues and have no desire to make personal attacks.[23] This questionnaire assesses how you feel about arguing with others. Use the following ratings to respond to each statement: (1) almost never true, (2) rarely true, (3) occasionally true, (4) often true, (5) almost always true.

_____ 1. While in an argument, I worry that the person I am arguing with will form a negative impression of me.

_____ 2. Arguing over controversial issues improves my intelligence.

_____ 3. I enjoy avoiding arguments.

_____ 4. I am energetic and enthusiastic when I argue.

_____ 5. After I finish an argument, I promise myself that I will not get into another.

_____ 6. Arguing with a person creates more problems for me than it solves.

_____ 7. I have a pleasant, good feeling when I win a point in an argument.

_____ 8. When I finish arguing with someone, I feel nervous and upset.

_____ 9. I enjoy a good argument over a controversial issue.

_____ 10. I get an unpleasant feeling when I realize I am about to get into an argument.

_____ 11. I enjoy defending my point of view on an issue.

_____ 12. I am happy when I keep an argument from happening.

_____ 13. I do not like to miss the opportunity to argue a controversial issue.

_____ 14. I prefer being with people who rarely disagree with me.

_____ 15. I consider an argument an exciting intellectual challenge.

_____ 16. I find myself unable to think of effective points during an argument.

_____ 17. I feel refreshed after an argument on a controversial issue.

_____ 18. I have the ability to do well in an argument.

_____ 19. I try to avoid getting into arguments.

_____ 20. I feel excitement when I expect that a conversation I am in is leading to an argument.

Scoring:

1. Add your scores on items 2, 4, 7, 9, 11, 13, 15, 17, 18, and 20.

2. Add 60 to the sum obtained in step 1.

3. Add your scores on items 1, 3, 5, 6, 8, 10, 12, 14, 16, and 19.

4. To calculate your argumentativeness score, subtract the total obtained in step 3 from the total obtained in step 2.

Score Interpretation:

73–100 points = highly argumentive

56–72 points = Moderately argumentative

20–55 points = Not or mildly argumentative

Collaboration The **collaborative conflict style** searches for new solutions that will achieve both your goals and the goals of others. Also referred to as a *problem-solving* or *win–win approach*, the collaborative conflict style allows you to argue about whose ideas are superior. Instead, the parties collaborate and look for creative solutions that satisfy everyone.

There are two potential drawbacks to the collaborative approach. First, collaboration requires a lot of time and energy, and some issues may not be important enough to justify the extra time and effort. Second, in order for collaboration to be successful, everyone—even the avoiders and accommodators—must fully participate in the process. Collaboration works best when both parties welcome new and creative ideas and are committed to the resulting decision.

The AEIOU Model of Conflict Resolution

Assume the other person means well and wants to resolve the conflict. "I know that both of us want to do a good job and complete this project on time."

Express your feelings. "I'm frustrated when you ask me to spend time working on a less important project."

Identify what you would like to happen. "I want to share the responsibility *and* the work with you."

Outcomes you expect should be made clear. "If both of us don't make a commitment to working on this full time, we won't do a good job or get it done on time."

Understanding on a mutual basis is achieved. "Could we divide up the tasks and set deadlines for completion or bring in another person to help us?"

Conflict Resolution Strategies

Effective communicators are flexible and use a variety of approaches to resolving conflict. In this section we present two conflict resolution strategies: the A-E-I-O-U Model and the Six-Step Model.

The A-E-I-O-U Model of Conflict Resolution If you want to resolve a conflict, you should try to understand the attitudes, beliefs, and values of those involved in that conflict. The **A-E-I-O-U Model** of conflict resolution focuses on communicating personal concerns and suggesting alternative actions to resolve a conflict.[24]

The Six-Step Model of Conflict Resolution The Six-Step Model offers a series of steps to help you move a conflict toward successful resolution. The six steps illustrated in the figure below are neither simple, nor easy. They do, however, tell you "what to do and what not to do when confronting someone" in a conflict situation.[25]

The Six-Step Model of Conflict Resolution

	Step	Task	Strategies
1	Preparation	Identify the problem, issues, and causes of the conflict.	Analyze the conflict by asking yourself: Who is involved? What happened? Where, when, and why did the conflict occur. **Example:** Ask yourself: "Why and how did things go wrong?"
2	Initiation	Tell the person: "We need to talk."	Ask the other person to meet and talk about the problem. Provide some information about the subject. **Example:** "Can we get together for lunch and talk about the late report?"
3	Confrontation	Talk to the other person about the conflict and the need to resolve it.	Express your feelings constructively and describe, specifically, what you see as a solution. **Example:** "I want you to come to the family reunion with us."
4	Consideration	Consider the other person's point of view.	Listen, empathize, paraphrase, and respond with understanding. **Example:** "I didn't realize your mother was sick when I asked you to stay late."
5	Resolution	Come to a mutual understanding and reach an agreement.	Specify the outcome that both parties accept. **Example:** "Okay. I'll make sure I call you if they make me stay later than 6 P.M."
6	Reevaluation	Follow up on the solution.	Set a date for seeing whether the solution is working as hoped. **Example:** "Let's meet for lunch in two weeks to see if this is working as we hope it will."

Should You Apologize?

An apology can go a long way toward diffusing tension and hostility and opening the door to constructive conflict resolution. Yet, despite the importance and simplicity of an apology, many people find it difficult to say the words *I'm sorry*. Although you may "lose" a conflict or sacrifice some of your pride, an effective apology can earn the respect of others and help build trusting relationships. Consider the following guidelines for making an effective apology:[26]

- *Take responsibility for your actions with "I" statements.* "I paid the bills late."
- *Clearly identify the behavior that was wrong.* "I made a major commitment without talking to you about it first."
- *Acknowledge how the other person might feel.* "I understand that you are probably annoyed with me."
- *Acknowledge that you could have acted differently.* "I should have asked if you wanted to work together on this project."
- *Express regret.* "I'm upset with myself for not thinking ahead."
- *Follow through on any promises to correct the situation.* "I'll send an email message today acknowledging that your name should have been included on the report."
- *Request, but don't demand, forgiveness.* "I value our relationship and hope that you will to forgive me."

> When you say you are sorry, you take responsibility for your behavior and actions.

8.3
Developing Assertiveness

How can you assert yourself and also respect the rights and needs of others?

What should you do if your boss wants you to work longer hours, but you want more time with your family? What if your friend wants to go to a party, but you need to stay home and study? How do you balance these competing needs and resolve potential conflicts? The answer may lie in how ready you are to be assertive. **Assertiveness** is the willingness and ability to stand up for your own needs and rights while also respecting the needs and rights of others.

Passivity and Aggression

Assertiveness is best understood by considering three alternatives to assertiveness: passivity, aggression, and passive aggression. **Passivity** is characterized by giving in to others at the expense of your own needs in order to avoid conflict and disagreement. For example, Jackson's boss asks him to work over the weekend. Jackson agrees and says nothing about his plans to attend an important family event. Not surprisingly, passive individuals often feel taken advantage of by others and blame them for their unhappiness. As a result, they fail to take responsibility for their own actions and the consequences of those actions.[27]

The opposite of passive behavior is **aggression**, in which communicators put their personal needs first while violating someone else's needs and rights. Aggressive individuals demand compliance from others. Although aggressive behavior can be violent, it is usually displayed in more subtle behavior, such as a raised voice, rolled eyes, or a withering glance.[28]

THE BENEFITS OF ASSERTING YOURSELF

- **Expressing your feelings appropriately**
- **Accepting compliments graciously**
- **Speaking up for your rights when appropriate**
- **Enhancing your self-esteem and self-confidence**
- **Expressing disagreement on important issues**
- **Asking others to change their inappropriate or offensive behavior.**[29]

developing assertiveness

157

Sometimes people may *seem* passive when, in fact, their intentions are aggressive. Although **passive-aggressive** individuals may *appear* cooperative and willing to accommodate others and their needs, their behavior is a subtle form of aggressive behavior. Passive-aggressive communicators manipulate others to get what they want. For example, when you refuse to do a favor for your brother, he mopes around the house until you finally give in to his request. While aggressive, passive, and passive-aggressive behavior may initially seem effective, in the long run, they damage interpersonal and professional relationships.

Assertiveness Skills

Assertiveness can be difficult to learn, particularly if you become passive or aggressive when challenged or if you primarily rely on an avoiding, accommodating, competing, or compromising conflict style. Being assertive may involve breaking old communication habits while recognizing that in some contexts those styles may be appropriate. Initially, assertive behavior may feel strange or uncomfortable because asserting your rights can open the door to conflict.

Sharon and Gordon Bower, the authors of *Asserting Yourself*, have developed what they call a **DESC script**—a four-step process that relies on communication skills for becoming more assertive. DESC is an acronym for **D**escribe, **E**xpress, **S**pecify, and **C**onsequences. This scripting method can be used in both personal and professional relationships.[30] In some cases, you may want to write out your DESC script in advance and practice it before you have to confront someone. A DESC script can be used in both personal and professional relationships.

Assertive behavior can improve your self-esteem, your ability to resolve conflict, and the quality of your relationships.

COMMUNICATION IN *ACTION*

Just Say No.

Saying "no" to someone can very difficult—even scary. In his book *The Anxiety and Phobia Workbook*, Edmund Bourne, writes that "an important aspect of begin assertive is your ability to say no to requests you don't want to meet. Saying no means that you set limits on other people's demands for your time and energy when such demands conflict with your own needs and desires."[31]

In some cases, you may need to say no to a family member, good friend, or close colleague. Here are the four steps Bourne recommends:

- Acknowledge the other person's request by repeating it. "I'd love to have lunch with you tomorrow."

- Explain your reason for declining. "But, I have a deadline on Friday, so I have lots of work to do and can't take the time this week."

- Say no. "So I'll have to say no."

- (Optional) Suggest an alternative proposal in which both of your and the other person's needs will be met. "I'd love to do this another time. How about next Tuesday or Wednesday?"[32]

When there isn't a reasonable alternative proposal that works for both parties, leave out the fourth step. Bourne offers this example:

I hear that you need help with moving (acknowledgement). I'd like to help out but I promised my boyfriend we would go away this weekend (explanation), so I'm not going to be around (saying no). I hope you can find someone else.[33]

There are times, however, when you must say no to a person you don't want to be friends with, don't like, or who seems "unsafe." In such cases, simply say "No" or "No thank you" in a polite and firm manner. If the other person persists, say no again without apologizing.

Saying no means setting limits.

8.4
Managing Anger

Do you understand and manage your own anger and respond appropriately to anger in others?

Anger is a natural, human emotion. Everyone feels angry at some time. In many instances, anger may be fully justified. If a friend lies to you, a coworker takes credit for your work, or an intimate partner betrays you, **anger**—an emotional response to unmet expectations that ranges from minor irritation to intense rage—is a natural response. Effective anger management requires that you know how to communicate your angry feelings appropriately while treating others with respect.

> ## The issue is not whether you are angry but how well you understand and manage your anger.

Shouting may let others know you are angry, but calmly and assertively stating "I am angry" will let them know how you feel *and* pave the way for resolving conflict constructively. Furthermore, although you have a right to your feelings, screaming angrily at someone is disruptive and disrespectful and rarely solves anything. Try to avoid making personal attacks;

these only escalate a conflict. Use "I" statements ("I expected you to . . . ") instead of "you" statements ("You messed up when you . . . "). Finally,

THREE ANGER MYTHS[34]

1. **Anger and aggression are human instincts.** There is no scientific evidence to support the claim that humans are innately aggressive. Our survival depends on cooperation, not destructive conflict and aggression.[35]
2. **Anger is always helpful.** Anger can be beneficial when it warns you of danger or prepares your body for a fight-or-flight response. However, anger fueled by hostility to others (as opposed to anger that serves as a warning) is bad for your health, particularly for your heart.[36]
3. **Anger is caused by others**. When you're angry, you may say "She made me angry when she showed up late" or "The boss made me angry when he didn't give me credit for writing the report." By blaming others for your anger, you don't have to change your own behavior in any way. As a result, you stay angry.[37]

help others understand why you are angry: "Because the report isn't finished, I'm now in a bind with my supervisor." Social psychologist Carol Tavris writes that anger "requires an awareness of choice and an embrace of reason. It is knowing when to become angry—'this is wrong, this I will protest'—and when to make peace; when to take action, and when to keep silent; knowing the likely cause of one's anger and not berating the blameless."[38] In late fourth century B.C., Aristotle famously wrote that anyone can become angry—that is easy. But to be angry at the right things, with the right people, to the right degree, at the right time, for the right purpose, and in the right way—is worthy of praise.[39]

Strategies for EXPRESSING YOUR ANGER CONSTRUCTIVELY[40]

- State your anger verbally.
- Acknowledge your anger rather than venting it.
- Avoid expressing your anger as personal attacks.
- Identify the source of anger.

STOP&THINK

Should You Hold It in or Let It Out?

What's the best way to deal with anger—hold it in or let it out? Some people see anger as a destructive emotion that should be suppressed. However, when you suppress justified anger, it can fester or build while recurring problems go unresolved. Psychotherapist Bill DeFoore compares suppressed anger with a pressure cooker. "We can only suppress or apply pressure against our anger for so long before it erupts. Periodic eruptions can cause all kinds of problems."[41]

Other people believe in fully expressing their anger, regardless of how intense or potentially damaging it is. They

also believe that angry outbursts release tension and calm them down. Psychologists explain that venting anger to let off steam "is really worse than useless. Expressing anger does not reduce anger. Instead it functions to make you even angrier."[42] Moreover, people on the receiving end of angry outbursts usually get angry right back—which only makes the problem worse.

Both of these extreme views about anger can be counterproductive. Not only can they damage interpersonal relationships, but they may contribute to serious health problems, such as heart disease and hypertension.[43]

Strategies for Responding Effectively to Others' Anger[44]

- Acknowledge the other person's feelings of anger. *"I understand how angry you are."*
- Identify the issue or behavior that is the source of the anger. *"I don't believe I promised to work both your shifts next weekend, but you seem to think we made this agreement."*
- Assess the intensity of the anger and the importance of the issue. *"I know it's important for you to find someone to cover your shifts so you can attend your friend's wedding."*
- Encourage collaborative approaches to resolving the conflict. *"I can only cover one of your shifts this weekend. Why don't we work together to find someone else who will take the second shift?"*
- Make a positive statement about the relationship. *"I enjoy working with you and hope we can sort this out together."*

ETHICAL COMMUNICATION

Principles of Interpersonal Ethics

Ethical communication decisions can be challenging on a daily basis. When, however, conflict, anger, aggression, and passivity join the mix, the challenge of responding ethically may seem impossible. Are you more likely to want an eye for an eye and a tooth for a tooth rather than turning the other cheek? During a heated argument, are you more likely to flee or fight. If you're extremely angry, are you tempted to use words that hurt the other person so they feel as badly as you do? These dilemmas are more than communication challenges. They are ethical challenges as well.

In her book *Practicing Communication Ethics*, Paula Tompkins offers four principles for evaluating the ethical challenges you face in interpersonal encounters.[45]

1. **The Golden Rule:** Do unto others as you would have them do unto you. Is the communication response you want to use fair, honest, or caring?
2. **The Platinum Rule:** Do unto others as they wish to have done to themselves. Do you really know what others want or think, without asking or listening to them? Have you considered their age, culture, ethnicity, gender, status, education, and so on? In other words, what "you would have them do unto you" may well not be what they want done to themselves.
3. **The Principle of Generalizability:** Distinguish between what is momentary or limited and what is more enduring or broadly applicable. Are you using a different ethical value or principle with this particular person or in this particular situation? For example, would you let your best friend get away with an unethical act that you would condemn in others?
4. **The Test of Publicity:** Can you convince others that your communicative response is ethical and justified? What would a friend or colleague say? What would someone you don't know but who could ultimately be affected by your behavior say?[46]

An unresolved conflict or uncontrollable anger between two people can have far-reaching consequences. Unmanaged anger can escalate into violence. Failure to assert your own needs and rights can also compromise the needs and rights of others.

8.5
Adapting to Culture and Gender

How do cultural and gender differences affect conflict resolution?

Cultural values tell us a great deal about how people feel about conflict and the methods they use to resolve conflict. For example, collectivist cultures place a high value on "face." From a cultural perspective, **face** is the positive image you wish to create or preserve. Cultures that place a great deal of value on "saving face" discourage personal attacks and outcomes in which one person "loses." The figure below summarizes individualistic and collectivist perspectives about conflict.[47]

Gender roles vary across cultures, and as such, they add another level of complexity to the way individuals approach and attempt to resolve conflict. According to sociolinguist Deborah Tannen, men and women in the United States, in particular,

INDIVIDUALISTIC CULTURES

- Conflict is closely related to individual goals.
- Conflict should be dealt with openly and honestly.
- Conflict should result in a specific solution or plan of action.
- Conflict is addressed appropriately in terms of timing and situation.

COLLECTIVIST CULTURES

- Conflict is understood within the context of relationships and the need to preserve "face."
- Conflict resolution requires that "face" issues be mutually managed before a discussion of other issues.
- Conflict resolution is considered successful when both parties are able to save "face" and when both can claim they have "won."
- Conflict resolution requires attention to both verbal and nonverbal communication as well as the nature of the relationship.

Christine Ohuruogu of Great Britain wins an Olympic gold medal in Beijing, 2008.

A Zulu chief, his council, and tribal members collaborate to resolve conflict and make decisions.

COMMUNICATION & CULTURE

UNDERSTANDING DIVERSITY AND CONFLICT

Part of knowing how to manage conflict is recognizing and understanding that differences in culture and gender influence how people prefer to resolve both personal and professional altercations. For example, culture can determine the likelihood of whether we will express disagreement. Conformist cultures such as the Japanese, German, Mexican, and Brazilian are less likely to express disagreement than individualistic cultures such as the Swedish and French.[48]

Culture may also dictate *who* should argue. Many cultures give enormous respect to their elders. In these cultures, a young person arguing with an older adult is viewed as disrespectful. Among several Native American and African cultures, older adults are considered wiser and more knowledgeable, and young people are expected to accept the views of elders rather than challenge or rebel against them.

Companies that fail to respect and adapt to differences are likely to have more strikes and lawsuits, lower morale among workers, less productivity, and higher employee turnover.[49] Thus, when attempting to resolve conflict in personal or professional relationships, ignoring these cultural and gender differences can only worsen matters.

---

approach argument differently.[50] She contends that, in general, men tend to be competitive arguers, whereas women are more likely to seek consensus. Men tend to view issues as only two sided: for or against, right or wrong. Women are more likely to search out many perspectives on a subject. . . . two sided: for or against, right or wrong. Women are more likely to search out many perspectives on a subject.[51]

Researchers who study marriages, claim, "It is a biological fact: Men are more easily overwhelmed by marital conflict than their wives." As a result, a wife is more likely bring up a sensitive issue and want to talk about it, whereas a husband is more likely to avoid discussing the problem or become defensive and even belligerent in order to silence his spouse.[52] Marriage researcher Gottman notes that "Any conflict that begins with 'you always' or "you never' is likely to have a destructive effect" on a marriage and is even predictive of whether the couple is heading for a divorce.[53]

Gender differences in conflict styles, however, are generalizations. Overall, men and women are more similar in how they approach conflict than they are different. Both can and do use all five conflict resolution styles discussed in Section 8.2 of this chapter. In most cases, the context of the communication and the nature and history of the relationship will be just as influential in conflict resolution as any gender differences.

At the 2009 "beer summit," President Obama and Vice President Biden sought to resolve a dispute between Harvard Professor Henry Louis Gates Jr., (left) and police sergeant James Crowley (right). When called to investigate a potential burglary at Gates's house, Crowley arrested the confrontational professor for disorderly conduct. The case caused a national uproar over alleged race profiling. After the session, both parties expressed their understanding and respect for one another.

How Do *You* Respond to Conflict?[54]

The following 20 statements represent remarks made by a person a conflict situation. Consider each message separately and decide how closely it resembles *your* attitudes and behavior in a conflict situation, even if the language does not exactly echo the exact way you express yourself. Use the following numerical scale to rate the statements. Choose only one rating for each message.

5 = I always do this	4 = I usually do this	3 = I sometimes do this
2 = I rarely do this	1 = I never do this.	

When I'm involved in a conflict …

_____ 1. I try to change the subject when I face a conflict.

_____ 2. I play down the differences so the conflict doesn't become too serious.

_____ 3. I don't hold back in a conflict, particularly when I have something I really want.

_____ 4. I try to find a trade-off that everyone can agree to.

_____ 5. I try to look at a conflict objectively rather than taking it personally.

_____ 6. I avoid contact with the people when I know there's a serious conflict brewing.

_____ 7. I'm willing to change my position to resolve a conflict and let others have what they want.

_____ 8. I fight hard when an issue is very important to me and others are unlikely to agree.

_____ 9. I understand that I can't get everything I want when resolving a conflict.

_____ 10. I try to minimize status differences and defensiveness in order to resolve a conflict.

_____ 11. I put off or delay dealing with the conflict.

_____ 12. I rarely disclose much about how I feel during a conflict, particularly if it's negative.

_____ 13. I like having enough power to control a conflict situation.

_____ 14. I like to work on hammering out a deal among conflicting parties.

_____ 15. I believe that all conflicts have potential for positive resolution.

_____ 16. I give in to the other person's demands in most cases.

_____ 17. I'd rather keep a friend than win an argument.

_____ 18. I don't like wasting time in arguments when I know what we should do.

_____ 19. I'm willing to give in on some issues, but not on others.

_____ 20. I look for solutions that meet everyone's needs.

Conflict Style	**Avoid**	**Accommodate**	**Compete**	**Compromise**	**Collaborate**
Item Scores	1 = _____	2 = _____	3 = _____	4 = _____	5 = _____
	6 = _____	7 = _____	8 = _____	9 = _____	10 = _____
	11 = _____	12 = _____	13 = _____	14 = _____	15 = _____
	16 = _____	17 = _____	18 = _____	19 = _____	20 = _____
Total Scores	_____	_____	_____	_____	_____

Your scores identify which conflict style(s) you use most often. There are, however, no right or wrong responses. Your conflict style may differ depending on the issues, the people involved, and the situation's context.

8.1
Balancing Interpersonal Tensions

How can you balance the inevitable tensions in interpersonal relationships?

- Relational Dialectics Theory explains how the interplay of contradictory forces affects interpersonal relationships in three domains: integration-separate, stability-change, and expression-privacy.

- The Myers-Briggs Type Indicator helps you balance interpersonal tensions by understanding the extent to which you and others are extroverts or introverts, sensors or intuitives, thinkers or feelers, and judgers or perceivers.

8.2
Resolving Interpersonal Conflicts

What communication strategies and skills help resolve interpersonal conflicts?

- Conflict can be constructive or destructive depending on your intentions and how well you communicate.

- There are five conflict styles: avoidance, accommodation, competition, compromise, and collaboration.

- Determine how argumentative you are and how it affects the way you handle an interpersonal conflict

- The A-E-I-O-U Method and the Six-Step Method can help you resolve conflicts.

8.3
Developing Assertiveness

How can you assert yourself and also respect the rights and needs of others?

- Assertive communicators promote their own needs and rights while respecting the needs and rights of others

- Passivity is characterized by giving in to others at the expense of your own needs; aggression involves putting your own needs first often at the expenses of someone else's needs; passive aggression may appear to accommodate others but is a subtle form of aggressive behavior.

- DESC scripting is a four-step process (describe, express, specific, and consequences) for becoming more assertive.

8.4
Managing Anger

Do you understand and manage your own anger and respond appropriately to anger in others?

- Anger is a natural, human emotion that varies in terms of its causes and effects.

- There are several common myths about anger: anger is a human instinct, anger is always helpful, and my anger is caused by others.

- You can express anger appropriately by stating that you are angry without venting or exploding, by avoiding personal attacks, and by identifying the source of your anger.

8.5
Adapting to Culture and Gender

How do cultural and gender differences affect conflict resolution?

- Cultural values influence whether people are comfortable with conflict and how they resolve conflict.

- In general, men tend to be competitive arguers, whereas women are more likely to seek collaborative solutions. Overall women and men are more similar than different in terms of how they approach conflict.

MySearchLab®

TEST YOUR KNOWLEDGE

8.1 How can you balance the inevitable tensions in interpersonal relationships?

1 Which relational dialectic is involved when you're looking for some new excitement in your life while your partner is content to stay home, work on hobbies, and interact with lifelong friends?

   a. Integration versus separation
   b. Expression versus privacy
   c. Stability versus change
   d. Fight versus flight
   e. Individualism versus collectivism

2 Which Myers-Briggs personality trait is evident in the following description? "Carla is a risk taker who is willing to try new options. But she often procrastinates and end ups in a frenzy to complete a task on time."

   a. Extrovert
   b. Feeler
   c. Sensor
   d. Intuitive
   e. Perceiver

8.2 What communication strategies and skills help resolve interpersonal conflict?

3 In which of the following conflict styles do people respond by giving in to others at the expense of meeting their own needs?

   a. Avoidance
   b. Accommodation
   c. Competition
   d. Compromise
   e. Collaboration

4 Which word does the *I* in the A-E-I-O-U Model of Conflict Resolution stands for?

   a. Ignore
   b. Intimidate
   c. Identify
   d. Intuitive
   e. Initiation

5 Which step in the Six-Step Method of Conflict Resolution requires you to listen empathically, use paraphrases, and respond with understanding?

   a. Preparation
   b. Consideration
   c. Confrontation
   d. Reevaluation
   e. Resolution

8.3 How can you assert yourself and also respect the rights and needs of others?

6 Which of the following behaviors characterizes passive-aggressive behavior?

   a. You advance your own needs and rights while also respecting the needs and rights of others.
   b. You give in to others at the expense of your own needs in order to avoid conflict and disagreement.
   c. You put your personal needs first often at the expense of someone else.
   d. You appear to go along with others but sabotage their plans behind their backs.
   e. All of the above

7 The letters in DESC scripting are an acronym for

   a. Describe, Express, Specify, Consequence.
   b. Decide, Empathize, Self-Disclose, and Conflict.
   c. Dialectic, Expression, Separation, and Change.
   d. Decider, Extrovert, Sensor, and Controller.
   e. Decide, Explain, Sympathize, and Communicate.

8.4 Do you understand and manage your own anger and appropriately respond to anger in others?

8 All of the following are common myths about anger except —————.

   a. anger is a natural, human emotion
   b. anger and aggression are human instincts
   c. anger is always helpful
   d. anger is caused by what others do to you
   e. All of the above statements are true about anger.

9 Which of the following ethical principles asks the question: What would friends or colleagues say if I responded angrily?

   a. The Golden Rule
   b. The Platinum Rule
   c. The Principle of Generality
   d. The Test of Publicity
   e. The Test of Honesty

8.5 How do cultural and gender differences affect conflict resolution?

10 Which cultural group is most likely to show anger to others?

   a. Japanese
   b. German
   c. French
   d. Mexican
   e. German and Mexican

Answers found on page 366.

Key Terms

Accommodating conflict style	**Conflict**	**Judgers**
A-E-I-O-U Model of Conflict Resolution	**Constructive conflict**	**Myers-Briggs Type Indicator**
Aggression	**DESC script**	**passive agression**
Anger	**Destructive conflict**	**Passivity**
Argumentativeness	**Dialectic**	**Perceivers**
Assertiveness	**Expressive-privacy dialectic**	**Personality**
Avoidance conflict style	**Extroverts**	**Relational Dialectics Theory**
Collaborative conflict style	**Face**	**Six-Step Model of Conflict Resolution**
Competitive conflict style	**Feelers**	**Sensors**
Compromising conflict style	**Integration-separation dialectic**	**Stability-change dialectic**
	Introverts	**Thinkers**
	Intuitives	

PROFESSIONAL RELATIONSHIPS

"**D**o happier people work harder?" According to a recent study, the answer is yes. This outcome makes sense given that "working adults spend more of their waking hours at work than anywhere else."[1] Not surprisingly, if you work full-time, you probably spend more hours interacting with coworkers, managers, clients, or customers than you do with your family and friends. Whereas your personal relationships focus on private interactions with friends, romantic partners, and family members, your professional relationships focus on interactions with others to accomplish a goal or to perform a task in a workplace context.

Researchers who study the nature of professional relationships report a host of depressing statistics related to our interactions at work: 55 percent of managers are seen as unfit for their jobs,[2] 60 percent of employees consider dealing with a supervisor the most stressful part of their jobs,[3] and 85 percent of workers who quit their jobs report doing so because they are unhappy with their boss.[4] Recent surveys report that most U.S. workers feel worse about their jobs than ever before. The cost of such employee disengagement is $300 billion a year in lost productivity.[5]

Despite these distressing numbers, there is good news: Effective and ethical communication can create a more positive, productive, and (yes) happy work environment, reduce interpersonal conflicts, and help employees deal with work-related problems. Your professional relationships are among the most important in your life, and they present unique interpersonal communication challenges. This chapter focuses on communication strategies and skills that can enhance the quality of your professional relationships.

THINK About...

and ASK YOURSELF...

9.1 The Nature of Professional Relationships | *How can you improve your professional relationships?*

9.2 Professional Communication Challenges | *How should you deal with office rumors and gossip, workplace romances, working with friends, and leaving a job?*

9.3 Workplace and Job Interviews | *What are the most effective ways to prepare for, participate in, and follow up after workplace and job interviews?*

9.1
The Nature of Professional Relationships
How can you improve your professional relationships?

The nature of your professional relationships reflects your work responsibilities, the quality of your relationships with colleagues, and the organizational culture in which you work. You also have professional relationships beyond traditional workplace settings. For example, you may have professional interactions with the members of a labor union, an academic association, a community organization, a volunteer group, or a medical team.

Types of Professional Relationships

The quality and success of your professional relationships depend on how well you communicate with your boss, your coworkers, and your customers or clients. For example, a corporate attorney may communicate differently when interacting with a paralegal or assistant (superior–subordinate relationship), when resolving a dispute with a colleague (co-worker relationship), or when counselling a client (customer relationship).

Superior–Subordinate Relationships In **superior–subordinate relationships**, the superior (supervisor) has formal authority over the productivity and behavior of subordinates (workers).[6] Superiors direct activities, authorize projects, interpret policies, and assess subordinates' performance. Subordinates provide information about themselves, about coworkers, and about the progress of their work as well as "what needs to be done and how it can be done" to supervisors.[7]

Poor superior–subordinate relationships negatively affect productivity, job satisfaction, and employee retention. Recall some of the statistics presented at the beginning of this chapter. In addition to considering interactions with a supervisor the most stressful part of their jobs, the majority of employees who quit their jobs do so because they are unhappy with their boss.

For supervisors, success largely depends on their ability to establish trust with subordinates, convey immediacy and caring, and give useful feedback about work and progress.[8] Although some superior–subordinate

Can you tell who the supervisor is and who the subordinates are in this photo? What nonverbal cues might help you decide?

Supervisory Strategies for
PROMOTING TRUST AND OPENNESS[9]

- **Behave** in a consistent and predictable manner.
- Be **honest** and keep your promises.
- **Share** decision-making control.
- Clearly **explain** policies, procedures, and decisions.
- Express **concern** for employee well-being.

Difficult Behavior at Work

Supervisors and coworkers who are difficult to work with can negatively affect your ability to do your job and to enjoy what you're doing. They engage in counterproductive behaviors, such as chronic lateness, poor performance, derogatory emailing, persistent negativity, resisting needed change, shooting down new ideas, complaining constantly, and neglecting commitments, as well as more serious forms of behavior, such as harassment, work sabotage, and even physical abuse.[10]

Dealing with difficult behavior at work is, not surprisingly, difficult.

Failure to remedy such behavior, however, perpetuates a work environment that takes its toll on everyone. In his book *Dealing with Difficult People*, Hal Plotkin recommends a six-step approach to providing feedback to such people and to helping them realize their full potential:[11]

1. *Identify specific successes and failures.* Rather than saying, "You're always late," state the exact number of times the person has been late during a defined period of time. Be equally specific when offering praise.

2. *Stop talking and start listening.* Use all types of listening—hear, understand, remember, interpret, evaluate, and respond—to make sure you fully grasp the other person's point of view.

3. *Describe the implications of behavior.* Help others understand the consequences of their behavior—in both organizational and personal terms.

4. *Link past accomplishments to needed change.* Point out how the traits that have led to past successes can be applied to areas that need improvement.

5. *Agree on an action plan.* Work *together* to come up with a plan that has specific ideas or steps, clear timetables, and realistic standards for success.

6. *Follow up.* Stay engaged and set up times to meet often and regularly. Use follow-up sessions to help the other person deal with problems, provide personal support, and offer praise.

Finally, be aware of how you define the problem. If you refer to *people* as difficult, you are shifting attention from what they *do* to who they *are*. Rather, identify their *behavior* as the problem, and then maybe you can do something about it.[12]

relationships are formal and distant, others flourish in informal, friendly, and nonthreatening interactions without sacrificing respect and productivity.

Coworker Relationships Interactions among people who have little or no official authority over one another but who must work together

"Good relationships with coworkers are the primary source of most job satisfaction."[13]

to accomplish the goals of an organization are known as **coworker relationships**.

A coworker who won't share important information or who has a different work style can derail your performance. A colleague who does a poor job or is uncooperative won't be respected. Satisfying coworker relationships make the difference between looking forward to and dreading another day at work.

Customer Relationships The success of any business or organization depends on effective and ethical communication with customers and clients, particularly in the United States, where the average company loses half its customers within five years.[14] **Customer relationships**

Criteria for a **SATISFYING** Coworker Relationship[15]

- Individual Excellence. Do both of you perform well in the job?

- Interdependence. Do you have complementary skills and need one another to do the job?

- Investment. Do both of you devote time and resources to helping one another succeed?

- Information. Do both of you share information openly?

- Integration. Do you have compatible values about and styles of work?

- Integrity. Do you treat each other with respect?

Does *customer relationship* describe the interaction between teachers and students? Or are these relationships more like superior–subordinate or coworker relationships?

are interactions between someone communicating on behalf of an organization and an individual who is external to the organization. This category of relationships includes the way colleges treat students, the way medical professionals take care of patients, and the way police officers respond to crime victims.

Unfortunately, some employees lack appropriate training or have inaccurate assumptions about customer service. One study checked thousands of applications for grocery store workers and identified several false assumptions about customer service.[16] Almost half the applicants believed that customers should follow company policies if they want help and should be told when they are wrong. Approximately 10 percent of would-be employees would not help a customer if it was not part of their jobs and would not volunteer to assist a customer unless the customer asked for help.

Effective employees understand that, in a typical customer relationship, the customer has several basic communication needs.[17] First, the customer or client needs to feel welcome. Many retail staff members are trained to greet customers the moment they enter a store or business. Second, customers need enough information to make a decision or solve a problem regarding a service or product. Thus, sales and customer service representatives must be product experts who offer information and ask insightful questions. Finally, customers need to be treated with respect, especially because they have the power to take their business elsewhere and to encourage others to do the same.

> The quality of customer relationships affects the financial health of a business and employee job security.

STOP&THINK

Is the Customer Always Right?

Dealing with dissatisfied and angry customers can be difficult and stressful, especially when customers with legitimate complaints behave in inappropriate ways. When a customer is rude or disrespectful, you may become angry. Expressing your anger, however, may only escalate the conflict. The Better Business Bureau points out that even when a customer isn't happy with the solution, an employee who listens and attempts to help will be perceived as cooperative.[18] The following strategies can help calm an unruly customer and promote effective problem solving:[19]

- Don't take a complaint personally.
- Listen attentively and ask questions.
- Try to separate the issues from the emotions. A rude customer may have legitimate complaints and

may only be expressing well-founded frustrations inappropriately.

- Make statements that show you empathize: "I can understand why you're upset."
- Share information or explain the reasons for a decision but do not argue with a customer.
- If the company is at fault, acknowledge it and apologize.
- Ask the customer how she or he would like the problem to be resolved.

Customers may not always be right, but they should always be treated with courtesy and respect.

Organizational Culture Theory

Many workplaces are organized in a structured hierarchy that establishes levels of authority and decision-making power. That hierarchy may influence who talks to whom, about what, and in what manner. In large organizations, employees are often expected to convey information and voice concerns to their immediate supervisor. Only when a problem cannot be remedied at that level do employees have the "right" to speak to the next person up the hierarchy.

In general, the more levels within an organization's structure, the more likely it is that information will be distorted as communication goes up or down the "chain of command." The accuracy of information can be reduced by up to 20 percent every time a message passes through a different level.[20]

In addition to an organizational structure, every organization has a unique culture that influences member communication. According to Michael Pacanowsky and Nick O'Donnell-Trujillo, **Organizational Culture Theory**[21] describes the ways in which shared symbols, beliefs, values, and norms affect the behavior of people working in and with an organization. For example, one company may expect their employees to wear suits, spend much of their time working silently in their offices, arrive and leave promptly, and get together in small groups to socialize only after hours. Just as cultural beliefs, norms, and traditions change when you travel from one country to another, organizational culture can vary from job to job. Customs in an organizational culture include personal, celebratory, and ritual behaviors (responding to email, celebrating birthdays, attending department meetings), social behaviors (politeness, thanking customers, supporting worried colleagues), and communication behaviors (retelling legendary stories, using in-house-only jargon, giving colleagues nicknames).

Organizations also have subcultures. An **organizational subculture** consists of a group of people who engage in behaviors and share values that are, in part, different from that of the larger organizational culture. For example, the marketing department in an organization may develop different customs than the accounting department across the hall. The regional sales office in Texas may have different traditions than the Chicago office.

How would you describe the organizational culture being depicted in this photo of Google employees?

Classic Organizational Hierarchy

BOARD OF DIRECTORS
Makes policy and key decisions

UPPER MANAGEMENT
Senior executives who implement board policies and decisions

MIDDLE MANAGEMENT
Managers who link upper management to supervisors and their workers

LOWER MANAGEMENT
Supervisors or team leaders who have regular and direct contact with workers

SUPPORT STAFF
Secretaries, administrative assistants, project directors

FRONTLINE WORKERS
People who do the fundamental tasks of the organization

Professional Communication Challenges

How should you deal with office rumors and gossip, workplace romances, working with friends, and leaving a job?

Maria didn't want anyone at work to know that she was dating her coworker James. Unfortunately, her officemate overheard her talking with James on the phone and told several other people in the office about the relationship. Soon there was a buzz about it. Maria was worried that their boss would disapprove and that their coworkers would tease or harass them.

Ineffective and inappropriate communication in professional settings can result in serious consequences: tension in the workplace, limited advancement opportunities, and even job loss. In this section we examine some of the difficult communication situations that occur within organizations: office gossip, workplace romances, sexual harassment, working with friends, and quitting or losing a job.

Office Rumors and Gossip

Whereas a **rumor** is an unverified story or statement about the facts of a situation, **gossip** is a type of rumor that focuses on the private, personal, or even scandalous affairs of other people. Nicholas DiFonzo of the Rochester Institute of Technology describes gossip as a rumor that is "more

social in nature, usually personal and usually derogatory." When spreading "gossip, truth is beside the point. Spreading gossip is about fun."[22]

Most of us listen to rumors because we want to have as much information as everyone else. Typically, we spread gossip because we want to be perceived as "in the know."[23] In one survey of office workers, more than 90 percent of employees admitted to engaging in gossip.[24] The same study also found that after learning information about a colleague that was intended to be secret, 75 percent of employees revealed that secret to at least two other employees that same day.

While rumors and gossip have the potential to be harmful, they can also serve an important social function. Consultant Annette Simmons observes that "a certain amount of small talk—sharing small details of your life—helps people feel closer to co-workers. It is what humanizes the workplace and helps people bond."[25] However, unchecked or malicious gossip can have serious consequences. Private and potentially embarrassing information, even if untrue, can damage your professional credibility.

Strategies for MANAGING OFFICE GOSSIP

- Do not spread malicious rumors. If you don't know if the information is accurate or if someone else will be hurt if the information is shared, don't repeat it.
- Evaluate the reliability of a rumor or gossip by asking questions and checking facts.
- When others gossip, change the subject, tell them you prefer not to discuss certain topics, or say that you're too busy to talk at the moment.
- Consider the potential consequences of divulging confidential information or spreading a rumor.
- Before self-disclosing to a coworker, assume that your secret *will* be told to others.
- If you believe that gossip has created a serious problem, talk to someone with more power or influence.[26]

When organizations learn that misinformation is making its way through the rumor mill, they should address and correct it quickly before any more harm is done.

> In some workplaces, malicious gossip infects the workplace and creates a climate of hostility and distrust.

Divulging company secrets can get you fired. Time spent gossiping is time not spent doing your job.

An organization can take measures that prevent the *need* for gossip by keeping employees well informed.[27] For example, when a company is purchased by a larger corporation, many employees worry about losing their jobs and spend hours talking about who will stay and who will be asked to leave. If no personnel cutbacks are planned, employees should be told. When cutbacks are anticipated, an organization should inform everyone about how and when those decisions will be made—this way, everyone will have more accurate information.

STOP&THINK

Are You Twittering the Hours Away at Work?

Do you send and respond to personal emails at work? Do you tweet, text, or visit friends on Facebook while being paid to do a job? If your answer is *yes*, check the rules where you work before doing it again.

According to a study commissioned by Robert Half Technology, an information technology staffing firm, "54% of companies ban workers from using social networking sites like Twitter, Facebook, LinkedIn and MySpace while on the job. . . . Only 10 percent of the 1,400 surveyed companies said they allowed employees full access to social networks during work hours."[28]

Why such strict rules, you may wonder. Nucleus Research, an IT research firm, provides part of the answer: "nearly half of all online workers use Facebook at the office and one in every 33 employees has built their entire profile during work hours." The firm also reports that companies allowing unlimited employee "access to Facebook in the workplace lose an average of 1.5% in total employee productivity."[29]

The problem of on-the-job social networking involves more than concerns about employee productivity. What if employees use social media to send discriminatory statements, racial slurs, or sexually explicit messages to coworkers or clients? What if employees reveal, either intentionally or unintentionally, confidential company information? What should a company do if an information technology worker reports finding child pornography on a company computer they're servicing? Employees and corporate officers may be fired, the company may be sued, and/or law enforcement officials may prosecute.[30]

Most companies and organizations have formal or informal policies or guidelines to restrain social networking at work. At the same time, they may permit certain employees—depending on their job—to use social media during work hours. In either case, more and more companies are monitoring how you use computers at work.

Do you agree that your personal email, tweets, and social networking at work decrease your productivity? If your answer is *no*, you may like the results of a study by a university in Australia (a country with higher social media use rates than the United States). Researchers found "that 70% of office employees use the Internet at work for personal reasons. But of that group, 9% were more productive compared to employees that didn't use the web for fun." Brent Coker, one of the Australian researchers, explains that "short and unobtrusive breaks, such as a quick surf on the internet, enables the mind to rest itself, leading to a higher total net concentration for a day's work, and as a result, increased productivity." However, Coker also acknowledges that "those who behave with internet addiction tendencies will have a lower productivity than those without."[31]

> **Before deciding to redesign your Facebook page or get involved in a controversial political debate online, make sure you know the "rules."**

professional communication challenges

173

How Satisfied Are You with Your Job?

For each of the job-related items on the following list, rate your level of satisfaction with your current or most recent job:

1 = very dissatisfied   3 = somewhat satisfied
2 = somewhat dissatisfied   4 = very satisfied

How satisfied are you with . . .

_____ 1. your job responsibilities?
_____ 2. your workload?
_____ 3. your salary or hourly pay relative to your responsibilities and experience?
_____ 4. your level of job security?
_____ 5. how your work is evaluated and rewarded?
_____ 6. the extent to which the organization helps you grow professionally?
_____ 7. your relationship with your boss?
_____ 8. how your boss makes decisions?
_____ 9. the extent to which you are treated fairly?
_____ 10. your relationships with coworkers?
_____ 11. the overall quality of work by colleagues?
_____ 12. how well coworkers cooperate with one another?
_____ 13. your level of influence in decision making?
_____ 14. how information is shared within the organization?
_____ 15. how the organization handles dissent and disagreement?
_____ 16. the ethics of the organization's practices?

Review your responses to identify specific areas of dissatisfaction. You may enjoy your coworkers but dislike your boss. You may have a good relationship with your boss but be unhappy with organizational policies. You may enjoy a friendly work environment but believe that you are underpaid. Once you have identified the problems, you can then work to improve that area and your overall job satisfaction.

Add your responses to determine your total score.

16–27 points   Very dissatisfied
28–39 points   Somewhat dissatisfied
40–51 points   Somewhat satisfied
52–64 points   Very satisfied

Approximately one-third of all romantic relationships begin in the workplace.[34]

For example, a public display of affection in the workplace may be viewed as unprofessional and may make other colleagues feel uncomfortable. Coworkers may also suspect that a romantic partner receives preferential treatment. Romantically involved couples may find it difficult to separate issues at work from personal issues that arise after work. And if a romantic relationship ends, the professional relationship may become strained or awkward. Half the romantic relationships begun in the workplace also end there.[35]

Sexual Harassment

Workplace romances should not be confused with sexual harassment. Romance in the workplace involves two individuals who want a close, personal relationship, whereas **sexual harassment** is characterized by unwanted sexual advances for sexual favors, inappropriate verbal or physical conduct of a sexual nature, or an intimidating, hostile, or offensive work environment.[36] Sexual harassment is rarely an isolated incident. Usually, it is a pattern of offensive or unwelcome

Workplace Romances

In one study, 93 percent of people surveyed report that they have worked in places where colleagues had a romantic relationship,[32] and more than 60 percent say that they have been involved in at least one workplace romance.[33] Although some workplace romances result in long-lasting relationships and marriages, it can be difficult to manage the blurred distinction between private and professional lives.

The characters in *Glee* demonstrate how professional relationships can evolve into workplace romances.

Wall Street Journal columnist Sue Shellenbarger suggests that if you can answer *yes* to any of the following questions, your employer may be justified in warning, reprimanding, transferring, or even firing you:[37]

- Are you romantically involved with a subordinate or your boss?
- Are both of you assigned to the same team or division?
- Is the relationship negatively affecting your work?
- Will your work be negatively affected if the relationship ends?
- Could others perceive favoritism as a result of the relationship?

Shellenbarger also suggests that if you pursue an office romance, keep in mind that in all likelihood, it will eventually end. "If it does end, you have to be mature enough and professional enough to handle seeing the other person every day."[38]

behavior that takes place over a period of time. In many instances, sexual harassment involves a supervisor or colleague using power to demand sexual favors—from coercing a subordinate to perform sexually in order to guarantee her or his job to making sex a prerequisite for securing a promotion, a higher salary, or extra time off. Sexual harassment may also include demeaning or offensive communication in the form of emails containing sexually explicit messages and jokes, inappropriate comments made directly to a coworker, or postings of sexual images in staff rooms.

In some cases, romantic relationships that end badly result in sexual harassment. If, for example, an employee posts embarrassing photographs of an "ex" in the office lunchroom as a way of getting back for a hostile breakup, the person in those photos may feel humiliated, offended, and unable to work productively with colleagues. The distressed employee may also end up with grounds for a sexual harassment suit.

Research reports that many victims of sexual harassment experience "decreased work performance, anxiety, depression, self-blame, anger, feelings of helplessness, fear of further or escalating harassment, and fear of reporting the incident."[39] Although most workers say that they would immediately address or report harassment, research reveals that, when confronted with the situation, many people feel uncomfortable and fail to report the behavior.[40]

Most organizations have established policies against sexual harassment as well as grievance procedures for reporting such behavior. If you believe that you are the victim of sexual harassment, keep in mind that complaints are taken more seriously when brought to the attention of management immediately.[41]

Most organizations take allegations of sexual harassment very seriously—if for no other reason than to avoid costly lawsuits.

Workplace Friendships

Many coworker relationships are personal as well as professional. Mixing personal and professional relationships, however, can be difficult: You want your friend to like you, but you also need coworkers, superiors, and subordinates to respect you; you want approval from

COMMUNICATION & CULTURE

DIFFERING VIEWS ON SEXUAL HARASSMENT

Identifying sexual harassment is complicated by the fact that men and women often have different perceptions of similar behavior. Thus, telling a sexually explicit joke in the office may be viewed by women as harassment, whereas men may see it as harmless. Both men and women, however, judge overt behavior, such as demands for sexual favors, as harassment. According to the Equal Employment Opportunity Commission, approximately 15,000 complaints of sexual harassment are filed every year.[42] Thirteen percent of these are filed by men.[43]

How would you answer this question: Have any of the following incidents happened to you or someone you know in the workplace?

1. Unwanted and deliberate touching, leaning over, cornering, or pinching
2. Unwanted sexually suggestive looks or comments
3. Unwanted letters, telephone calls, or materials of a sexual nature
4. Unwanted pressure for dates
5. Unwanted sexual teasing, jokes, remarks, or questions

Now ask yourself this question: Are any of these incidents examples of sexual harassment? A large study asked these same questions to more than 8,000 federal government employees; the results indicated that women are more likely than males to view all these behaviors as sexually harassing. No one should have to tolerate a sexually hostile work environment.[44]

your friend, but you also must make objective decisions in the workplace; you hope for professional success but not at the expense of your friends' advancement.

In *Organizational Communication*, communication scholar Daniel Modaff and his colleagues recommend that you seek your most important relationships outside the workplace and that, if you do have a friend relationship at work, you should be prepared to manage the consequences.[45] Telling a best friend that he has not met expectations on a work team can be difficult and even impossible if you want to preserve the friendship. At the same time, letting a friend get away with less-than-excellent work can destroy the morale of a group and put your reputation and leadership at risk.

Leaving a Job

According to the Bureau of Labor Statistics, before the age of 32, the average American has had nine jobs and one-third of workers predict that they will probably change jobs again within five years.[46] There are many reasons for leaving a job or changing careers. Whatever your reason, always

try to depart on as good terms as possible and handle your resignation or exit with professionalism and courtesy. Just as you want to make a good first impression when interviewing and beginning a new job, it is equally important to leave a positive impression when departing from or ending a job.

Even when a resignation is the result of dissatisfaction with the job or a poor relationship with a boss or coworkers, leaving on good terms is important. After you resign, a supervisor or human resources manager may request an **exit interview**. Organizations gather information in exit interviews to develop strategies for retaining other employees and to improve the workplace for those who remain. Because you

STRAINS [47]

on FRIENDSHIPS

- Equal status in a friendship may be compromised by inequality at work.
- The need to withhold confidential work information may clash with the need for openness in a friendship.
- Collaboration may be impossible when one friend has more decision-making power at work.
- The friendship may be damaged by negative feedback given at work.
- Public expressions of friendship may need to be minimized in the workplace.

on PROFESSIONAL RELATIONSHIPS

- A friendship may make it difficult to manage unequal levels of power at work.
- It may be difficult to handle sensitive work information with discretion.
- Personal knowledge and feelings about a friend may compromise objectivity at work.
- A friend may be held to a higher performance standard at work.
- Socializing may adversely affect productivity and the quality of performance at work.

. . . the typical American will change *careers* approximately **7** times.[48]

— U.S. Department of Labor

LEAVING YOUR JOB
Best Practices[49]

- Follow company policies and procedures when resigning.
- Inform your immediate supervisor of your plans first.
- Resign in person but also write a brief resignation letter.
- Give the appropriate advance notice.
- Phrase explanations positively.

don't know how the information will be used or whether it will be treated confidentially, remain calm and communicate a positive attitude. Focus on issues, not people. An "exit interview is not the time to burn bridges. Most industries are small, and bad behavior is not something you want people remembering about you."[51]

Sometimes, leaving a job is not a decision you make by choice. As a stressful event, job loss ranks right up there with death in the family, divorce, and serious illness. Job loss can have a profound effect on your emotional well-being. Typically, most people experience a resulting cycle of denial, anger, frustration, and eventually

adaptation.[52] If you lose your job and your anxiety seems out of control, go back to the section on communication apprehension in Chapter 2. The relaxation strategies recommended there—cognitive restructuring, visualization, and systematic desensitization—can help you build confidence and reduce stress.

9.3
Workplace and Job Interviews

What are the most effective ways to prepare for, participate in, and follow up after workplace and job interviews?

When you hear the phrase "job interview," what comes to mind? Most people think of a job interview as one of the last steps in the job application process. However, interviews do not end once you get a job.

Workplace Interviews

You will encounter several types of interviews in the workplace, including selection interviews, appraisal interviews, information-gathering interviews, disciplinary interviews, and exit interviews. The table on p. 178 identifies the purpose and function of workplace interviews. Each type of interview has a unique purpose and process.

In the world of work, an **interview** is an interpersonal interaction between two parties in which at least

In terms of specific communication skills, how is this television interview similar to or different from other types of workplace interviews?

one party has a predetermined purpose and uses questions and answers to share information, solve a problem, or influence the other.[53]

Although a traditional job interview (a form of selection interview) can be a stressful communication situation, a good interview can land you the job of your dreams. Unfortunately, a poor interview can result in a major disappointment and the loss of a promising career opportunity.

The saying that you never get a *second* chance to make a *first* impression is especially true in job interviews.

In the following section, we focus on the communication skills needed to prepare for, participate in, and follow up on a job interview.

Before the Job Interview

In *What Color Is Your Parachute?*, the best-selling guidebook for career changers and job seekers, Richard Bolles recounts the story of an interview between an IBM recruiter and a college senior. The recruiter asked the student, "What does IBM stand for?" The student didn't know and thus ended the interview.[54] As with any important communication situation, a successful job interview requires careful preparation. In a survey of the most common job interview mistakes, senior executives identified three major errors, all of which related to poor interview preparation: (1) having little or no knowledge of the company, (2) being unprepared to discuss skills and experiences, and (3) being unprepared to discuss career plans and goals.[55] Before going to an interview, make sure you research the organization, assess your own strengths and weaknesses, and practice interviewing.

Research the Organization Learn as much as you can about the organization. As a first step, do a thorough search of the organization's website. A good website will tell you a great

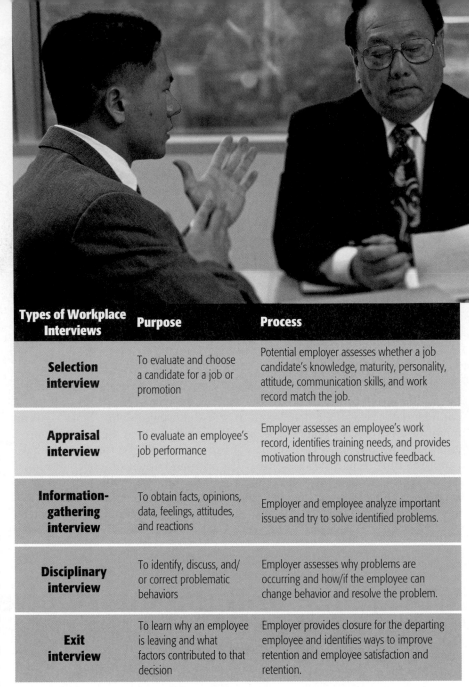

Types of Workplace Interviews	Purpose	Process
Selection interview	To evaluate and choose a candidate for a job or promotion	Potential employer assesses whether a job candidate's knowledge, maturity, personality, attitude, communication skills, and work record match the job.
Appraisal interview	To evaluate an employee's job performance	Employer assesses an employee's work record, identifies training needs, and provides motivation through constructive feedback.
Information-gathering interview	To obtain facts, opinions, data, feelings, attitudes, and reactions	Employer and employee analyze important issues and try to solve identified problems.
Disciplinary interview	To identify, discuss, and/or correct problematic behaviors	Employer assesses why problems are occurring and how/if the employee can change behavior and resolve the problem.
Exit interview	To learn why an employee is leaving and what factors contributed to that decision	Employer provides closure for the departing employee and identifies ways to improve retention and employee satisfaction and retention.

deal about the organization's mission, products and services, and achievements. If the website includes information about key employees, research the person or persons you will meet at the interview. You also may find news stories about the company or organization on other websites.

Given that other good candidates will be researching the website, go one step further. Contact the company or organization directly and request documents that they make available to the public, such as brochures,

catalogs, newsletters, and annual reports. If you know current or former employees, ask them about the organization. The more you know, the easier it is to explain how you can make a positive contribution. Research may also uncover reasons you don't want to work for that organization, ranging from a company's policy on unions or political issues to its health benefits or pension options.

Assess Your Strengths and Weaknesses Ron, a 32-year-old man with some sales experience, was preparing to interview for a sales director position at

Identify what you can bring to the job that will promote the organization's goals.

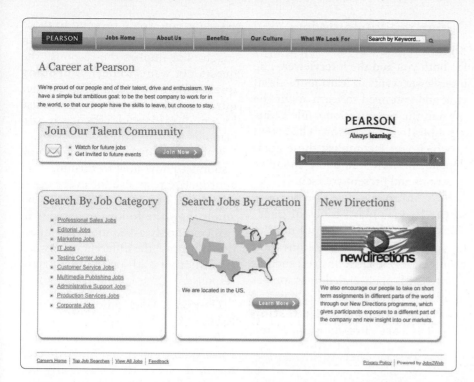

In addition to telling you about an organization's mission, products, services, and achievements, a website gives you a feel for the company's organizational culture and career opportunities.

a midsized company. He found a story on the Internet reporting that the company was considering restructuring its product pricing. Although the job description did not mention needing experience in this area, Ron decided to make a point of saying that his last job involved reevaluating product pricing. Using the information he unearthed about the organization helped Ron demonstrate why he was the best candidate for the position.

Be prepared to explain your weaknesses as well as your strengths. Plan how to address unexplained gaps of time on your résumé, several jobs in a short period of time, or the lack of a skill specifically mentioned in the job description. The time to develop an acceptable answer to such reasonable concerns is not in the middle of an interview. For example, Sharon quit her graphic design job when her first child was born and was a stay-at-home mother for seven years. When she decided to reenter the workplace, she knew she would have to address concerns about being up to date in her field. After careful consideration, she developed an answer that focused on refresher courses that she had taken during the past two years as well as the volunteer design work she had done for community groups. She also suggested that her design "eye" had matured and grown more sophisticated than it was when she was a younger artist. Whatever your weakness might be, don't assume that the interviewer hasn't noticed it on the application or résumé. Instead, be ready with a thoughtful response.

ETHICAL COMMUNICATION

Never Lie During a Job Interview

Approximately 20 to 45 percent of applicants lie on a résumé or in a job interview.[56] Another study reports that 11 percent of applicants do not tell the truth about why they left a previous job, and 9 percent lie about their education and responsibilities in previous jobs.[57] Not only is lying to a prospective employer unethical, but it can backfire and have serious personal consequences.

Most organizations have become much more rigorous when screening applicants. Private detective Fay Faron explains that many organizations conduct extensive background checks to avoid a lawsuit and ensure the safety of customers.[58] Count on being carefully screened, having your references checked, and being investigated for a criminal background. Furthermore, if your lie is discovered, your application will be rejected or, if you're already hired, you will be fired. A survey conducted by an executive search firm revealed that 95 percent of employers would reject applicants who lied about a college degree and that 80 percent would not hire someone who falsified previous job titles.[59]

Your goal is more than getting a job, it is getting a job that is right for you.[60] If you have to falsify your credentials or work experience, you are probably not qualified for the job. Moreover, the consequences of lying can be long lasting. If your lie is discovered, it can ruin your reputation for years to come.

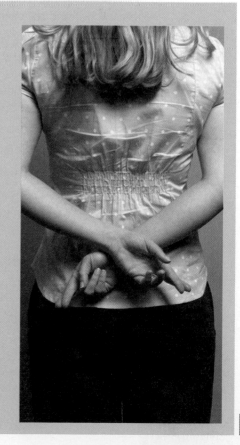

Practice Interviewing During a job interview, you have a limited amount of time to make a good impression in a fairly stressful communication situation. Doing a mock interview *before* the real thing will make a difference. Create a list of interview questions you might be asked (see the list of common questions below).

Because the interview will probably take place in a meeting room or office, sit at your desk or a table and practice your answers out loud and confidently. After you are comfortable with your responses, ask a few friends or family members to interview you. They can give you feedback on the quality of your answers and may suggest some additional questions to consider.

During the Job Interview

An interview is a golden opportunity for both you and the interviewer. The interviewer wants to learn more about you, and you need to learn about the job and the organization while creating a positive impression. The extent to which you accomplish these goals depends on how well you respond to questions and present yourself.

Most interviews use one or more of the five standard types of questions listed on p. 183. As we note in Chapter 7, a closed-ended question requires only a short answer, such as *yes* or *no*. An open-ended question requires or encourages a more detailed answer. A **hypothetical question** describes a set of circumstances and asks how you would respond to those circumstances. A **leading question** suggests or implies the response the questioner wants to hear. A **probing question** is used to follow up another question and/or a previous response by encouraging clarification and elaboration.

Regardless of the type of question, you must know how to formulate an appropriate response for every question asked of you. Consider, for example, how the following answers to two commonly asked interview questions illustrate the differences between an effective and an inappropriate response.

Question 1: Why did you leave your last job?

Inappropriate Response: My boss and I just didn't get along. She expected me to do work that was really her responsibility. They didn't pay me enough to do my job and someone else's. When I complained, nobody did anything about it.

Analysis: While honest, this is not a very effective or flattering response. Interviewers often ask questions like these to determine whether you had problems with a former employer and whether you will be just as troublesome in a new job. In this example, the interviewer could conclude that the applicant doesn't work well with others, resists doing required work, complains a lot, and evaluates work only in terms of a paycheck. A better approach is to focus on why a new job would offer more desirable opportunities and better match your values and goals. A job interview is not the time or place to vent frustrations about a former boss.

Question 2: What, in your opinion, is your greatest job-related weakness?

Effective Response: My natural tendency is to focus on one thing at a time until it's completed. However, most of my jobs have required me to manage several projects at once. I've had to learn how to juggle a variety of tasks, particularly when things get hectic. A couple of years ago I started using a project management software system to track projects and keep things organized. This has helped me shift attention back and forth among projects without losing track of priorities and deadlines.

COMMON Interview Questions[61]

1. Briefly, tell me about yourself.
2. What do you hope to be doing five years from now?
3. Where do you hope to be in ten years?
4. In terms of this job, what is your greatest strength?
5. What, in your opinion, is your greatest weakness?
6. What motivates you to work hard and do your best?
7. How well do you deal with pressure? Give an example.
8. What are the two or three characteristics you are seeking in a job?
9. Describe a major problem you encountered in a previous job. How did you deal with it?
10. What kind of relationship should be established between a supervisor and subordinates?
11. Why did you choose to pursue this particular career?
12. Why did you leave your last job(s)?
13. How can you contribute to our company?
14. How do you evaluate or determine success?
15. Given the fact that we have other applicants, why should we hire you?

STANDARD Interview Questions and Examples:[62]

Closed-ended question	Are you able to work on weekends?
Open-ended question	What do you view as the most significant challenges facing this industry over the next few years?
Hypothetical question	How would you handle an employee who does good work but, even after being warned, continues to arrive late?
Leading question	Do you think the ability to work well in a group is just as important as the ability to perform routine technical tasks?
Probing question	Could you explain what you mean by a "difficult client"?

Analysis: This answer is effective and strategic. When answering a question about a weakness, figure out how to acknowledge it while simultaneously demonstrating how you learned to deal with or overcome it. As a result, you transform the weakness into an example of your problem-solving abilities. But, don't exaggerate. When asked about your weakness, don't say, "I work too hard." We all do that. Working hard is usually considered a strength.

> **Never hesitate to ask for clarification before giving a response.**

In addition to preparing to answer questions, be prepared to ask some questions. Many interviewers assess your knowledge, interest, and communication skills based on the kinds of questions you ask. Use this opportunity to enhance your credibility and to learn more about the job, its employees, and the organization.

Interviews help employers decide whether you are the right person for a job, not just from your answers but also from the way you speak and behave during the interview. Remember that you are being observed from the moment you arrive until the time you leave the building. In fact, it's not unusual for an interviewer to ask receptionists or secretaries for their impressions of you.

In a survey conducted by Northwestern University, 153 companies were asked why they rejected job applicants.[64] Of the 50 reasons identified, almost half were related to lack of communication skills and failure to create a positive impression. One of the most common mistakes made by applicants is talking too much. If you talk *too* much, you may bore your listeners or may appear insensitive to the time limits of an interview. According to Richard Bolles, when it is your turn to speak or answer a question in an interview, try "not to speak any longer than two minutes at a time if you want to make the best impression."[65] Generally, it's better to leave interviewers hungry for more information about you rather than to overwhelm them with information.

After the Job Interview

Immediately after an interview, send a note thanking the interviewer for her or his time and consideration. The note should briefly refer to issues discussed in the interview and emphasize that you can perform the job and help the organization meet its goals. A brief but well-written letter (or, if appropriate, an email or text message) reinforces that you have a professional approach to and enthusiasm for the job.

Although it's natural to wonder how well you did during the interview, you may never learn how the interviewer evaluated you and your responses. An analytical self-evaluation may be more useful (See the Communication Assessment: Evaluating Your Interview Performance on p. 183).

Keep in mind that you can make an excellent impression during an interview and still not be hired because you may have been one of several outstanding candidates. Regardless of whether you are selected or not, view each interview as an opportunity to practice your skills.

Questions **TO ASK** During an Interview:[63]

- Can you tell me more about the specific, everyday responsibilities of this position?

- What, in your opinion, are the major challenges facing the organization?

- What is the most important characteristic you are looking for in an employee for this position?

- How would you describe the culture of your organization?

- How will success be measured for this position?

- What other people or departments will I be working with?

Strategies for ENHANCING YOUR FIRST IMPRESSION DURING AN INTERVIEW

- Arrive a few minutes early.

- Wear appropriate business attire.

- Make sure clothes, hair, and nails are clean and appropriate.

- Listen attentively.

- Use correct grammar and appropriate language.

- Smile and use direct eye contact.

- Maintain a posture that appears relaxed but not too informal.

- Try to appear calm and confident; avoid fidgeting.

- End the interview on a positive note.

> **"The more you practice answering possible questions, the more your interview skills will improve."**
>
> — Richard Bolles

Common Interview MISTAKES TO AVOID[66]

- Unprofessional appearance
- Aggressive or arrogant manner
- Poor grammar and vocal expression
- Lack of interest or enthusiasm
- Lack of confidence
- Evasiveness and tendency to make excuses
- Lack of tact

- Immaturity
- Poor manners
- Tendency to criticize past employers
- Lack of direct eye contact
- Weak or limp handshake
- Late to the interview
- Vague responses to questions

STOP & THINK

How Would You Handle Inappropriate Questions?

Federal and state laws prohibit discrimination in hiring. Generally, an interview should not include a discussion of race or ethnicity, gender, marital status, religion, sexual orientation, or disabilities. The best approach to answering inappropriate questions depends on the situation, what information you feel comfortable revealing, and your personal communication style. Consider the following questions; which, in your mind, are inappropriate during a job interview? Why?

_____ What does your husband or wife do?
_____ Do you plan to have children?
_____ How many more years do you plan to work before retiring?
_____ Which religious holidays will you take off from work?
_____ Do you have any disabilities?
_____ What country are your parents or grandparents from?

Answers: All of the above questions are inappropriate for a job interview.[67]

You have the right to refuse to answer a question you believe is inappropriate, but before you assume it is inappropriate, assess the purpose of the question. Once you've assessed the intent and decide you will respond, be as tactful as possible so as not to embarrass the interviewer and redirect the interview to a discussion of your qualifications. For example, "Do you have children?" may reflect the interviewer's concern that a busy parent won't work the number of hours necessary to demonstrate a full commitment to the job. An appropriate response might be, "If you're asking whether I can balance a demanding job with family obligations, I have always effectively done so in the past."

Furthermore, don't assume that the interviewer intends to discriminate. For instance, a hiring manager who asks whether you plan to have children may simply want to talk about the company's excellent maternity and child care benefits or brag about his or her own newborn child. These types of questions are often asked out of simple curiosity or an effort to engage in conversation.

Evaluating Your Job Interview Performance

Use this instrument to evaluate your performance in a past job interview, a classroom interview assignment, or a practice interview or to help prepare for an upcoming interview. Using criteria based on the seven key elements of communication discussed in Chapter 1, rate yourself as an interviewee with the following scores:

E = excellent; G = good; A = average; W = weak; P = Poor or N/A = not applicable.

Job Interview Competencies	E	G	A	W	P	N/A
Self: I was well prepared and confident.						
Others: I listened effectively and adapted to the interviewer or interviewers.						
Purpose: I could explain how hiring me would promote my personal and professional goals as well as the organization's mission.						
Context: I adapted to the logistics and psychosocial climate of the interview.						
Content: I included ideas and information relevant to and needed in the job or assignment; I asked good questions; I knew a great deal about the organization.						
Structure: I organized the content of my answers in a clear and memorable way. I asked questions at appropriate points in the interview.						
Expression: I used verbal and nonverbal behavior appropriately and effectively. I was dressed appropriately and professionally.						
Overall Assessment:						

Additional Assessment Questions:

1. Which questions did I answer best? What made my answers effective?

2. Which questions were the most difficult? Are these questions likely to be asked in future interviews? How could I answer such questions more effectively in the future?

3. Did I miss opportunities to emphasize particular strengths? How might I have incorporated those into my other answers?

4. What additional questions should I have asked?

5. What should I do differently in a future job interview?

9.1
The Nature of Professional Relationships

How can you improve your professional relationships?

- Superiors request work, supervise projects, and assess a subordinate's performance; subordinates provide information about themselves and coworkers as well as information about the progress of work, what needs to be done, and how to do it.

- Satisfying coworker relationships are characterized by individual excellence, interdependence, investment, information, integration, and integrity.

- Customers have three basic communication needs: to feel welcome, to have enough good information to make a decision, and to be treated with respect.

- When dealing with someone's difficult behavior at work, identify specific successes and failures, listen actively, explain the consequences of the behavior, call on the person's strengths, and mutually agree and follow up on an action plan.

9.2
Professional Communication Challenges

How should you deal with office rumors and gossip, workplace romances, working with friends, and leaving a job?

- Although rumors and gossip serve several social functions in an organization, self-serving rumors and malicious gossip can embarrass others, damage your credibility, waste time, and create a hostile and distrustful work environment.

- Many organizations disapprove of office romances because they can decrease productivity, make other colleagues feel uncomfortable, create suspicions that a romantic partner receives preferential treatment, and eventually end badly.

- Sexual harassment is characterized by unwanted sexual advances, inappropriate verbal or physical conduct of a sexual nature, or a hostile, or offensive work environment.

- Working with a close friend at work can put strains on the friendship and the professional relationship.

- Leaving a job—either voluntarily or involuntarily—requires communication strategies that leave a good impression with your former employer and create an equally good impression with your new or potential employer.

9.3
Job Interviews

What are the most effective ways to prepare for, participate in, and follow up after workplace and job interviews?

- Workplace interviews serve several purposes and come in many forms such as selection, appraisal, information-gathering, disciplinary, and exit interviews.

- Before going to a job interview, research the organization, assess your own strengths and weaknesses, and practice answering probable questions.

- During an interview, answer questions directly and concisely while presenting yourself and your skills positively.

- In addition to sending a follow-up note to the interviewer after an interview, assess your own performance and how you can do better in future interviews.

MySearchLab®

9.1 How can you improve your professional relationships?

1 According to a study quoted in this chapter, what percent of workers quit their jobs because they are unhappy with their bosses?

   a. 15%

   b. 30%

   c. 45%

   d. 60%

   e. 85%

2 In a superior–subordinate relationship at work, effective subordinates provide all of the following to their boss or manager except _____.

   a. information about themselves and coworkers

   b. information on the progress of work

   c. information on what needs to be done

   d. information about how to do the work more effectively

   e. Subordinates usually provide all of the above types of information

3 According to Organizational Culture Theory, the practice of giving colleagues nicknames is an example of a _____ behavior.

   a. ritual

   b. impersonal

   c. communication

   d. celebratory

   e. personal

9.2 How should you deal with office rumors and gossip, workplace romances, working with friends, and leaving a job?

4 Whereas a rumor is an unverified story or statement about the facts of a situation, gossip

   a. is a type of rumor that focuses on the private and personal interactions of other people.

   b. focuses on the scandalous affairs of other people.

   c. is more social in nature.

   d. is usually more personal and derogatory in nature.

   e. All of the above are characteristics of gossip.

5 All of the following answers represent reasons organizations and corporate executives disapprove of office romances except _____.

   a. office romances often result in long-lasting relationships and marriages

   b. most workplace romances end badly

   c. office romances may result in claims of sexual harassment

   d. office romances may result in retaliatory behavior after the relationship ends

   e. romantically involved employees may be less productive than other employees

6 Each of the following behaviors is an example of sexual harassment except _____.

   a. a supervisor demands sexual favors from a subordinate as a guarantee of keeping a job

   b. a supervisor demands sexual favors from a subordinate in order to earn a promotion

   c. a colleague passes around sexually explicit images and jokes via email

   d. a coworker makes sexually demeaning comments about another coworker

   e. All of the above are examples of sexual harassment.

9.3 What are the most effective ways to prepare for, participate in, and follow up after workplace and job interviews?

7 Which type of interview is conducted for the purpose of evaluating an employee's job performance?

   a. Selection interview

   b. Appraisal interview

   c. Information-gathering interview

   d. Disciplinary interview

   e. Exit interview

8 "What are the most significant challenges facing this industry in the current economic climate?" is what type of interview question?

   a. Closed-ended question

   b. Leading question

   c. Probing question

   d. Open-ended question

   e. Hypothetical question

9 Which of the following questions is technically inappropriate and illegal during a job interview?

   a. Do you plan to have children?

   b. Have you ever sought treatment for physical or mental disabilities?

   c. What country are your parents or ancestors from?

   d. Which religious holidays will you take off from work?

   e. All of the above are inappropriate and illegal questions.

10 Before ending an interview, interviewers often ask if you have additional questions. Which of the following questions would be an appropriate response?

   a. Do you have any disabilities?

   b. Will I be permitted to take off three very important holidays celebrated by my religion?

   c. What position does this company take on the abortion issue?

   d. How will my success be measured for this position?

   e. Will I be working with a culturally diverse group of people?

Answers found on page 366.

Key Terms

Coworker relationship	Leading question	Rumor
Customer relationship	Organizational Culture	Sexual harassment
Exit Interview	Theory	Superior–subordinate
Gossip	Organizational	relationships
Hypothetical question	subculture	
Interview	Probing question	

THINK
COMMUNICATION

This article from *Communication Currents* has been slightly edited and shortened with permission from the National Communication Association.

Communication
Knowledge for Communicating Well
Currents

N C A
A Publication of the National Communication Association

Volume 6, Issue 2 - April 2011

Making Sense of Workplace Deception

Peer coworker relationships between employees of the same rank are important elements in organizational processes and work-life wellness. Employees who enjoy positive and trusting peer coworker relationships report greater productivity and job satisfaction, making coworker relationships an important concern for organizations.

Unfortunately, deception is a common workplace occurrence that can disrupt peer coworker relationships. Deception refers to acts by which a person misrepresents information to communicate a false sense of reality to others. Deceptive behaviors range from outright lying to strategically omitting or altering details of information that is shared with others. Such behaviors are extremely common, with numerous studies revealing the average person uses some form of deception in one out of every five social interactions.

We conducted a study to examine how employees make sense of deception by peer coworkers. Individuals employed in various occupations were interviewed and asked to describe an incident in which they were deceived by a coworker. Our interviews revealed that deceived employees made sense of deceptive events by considering their co-workers' motives as well as the degree to which their organization may have influenced the situation.

We identified four distinct types of peer coworker deception:

Corrupt System Deception. Many participants blamed systemic company flaws for their co-workers' deceptive behavior, explaining that such organizations require employees to lie to survive. These companies were described as being cutthroat organizations in which deception was rampant. One participant reported lying because the manager encouraged workers to "give as little information as possible to the other departments" and "intentionally be vague when sending the messages to other departments so they can't trace it back to us if something goes wrong." Other examples involved employees who perceived deception as a way to earn bonuses. As one participant explained, "It's just the culture. So it's kind of like a survival of the fittest, but you've got to be a dirty dog to work there. In my opinion you can't be an honest person and survive." Such workplace climates were incredibly stressful for honest employees who survive by expecting that their coworkers will deceive them, adopting a deceptive work style in return, and simply grinding through their days without being invested in their work.

CYA Deception. Some participants reported their coworkers were deceptive as a defense mechanism or coping response. One person explained, "I don't

---

Chapter 9 cites several studies about employee satisfaction. One concludes that "60 percent of employees consider dealing with a supervisor the most stressful part of their jobs." Another claims that "Good relationships with co-workers are the primary source of most job satisfaction." Do you agree with the findings of these studies? Which is a greater challenge for you—dealing with a difficult boss or working with a difficult coworker?

How does this kind of organizational culture affect employee communication, productivity, and job satisfaction?

Why would an organization want to discourage CYA deception? What strategies could use to minimize this practice?

Several work challenges are discussed in Chapter 9 such as rumors and gossip, workplace romances, sexual harassment, and working with friends. How does workplace deception affect these challenges and employee morale?

What problems are likely to occur for honest employees in such cutthroat organizations? What are the ethical implications of these problems in terms of the survival of the organization? What is the impact on society?

The Ethical Communication feature in Chapter 9 on p. 179 notes that 20 to 45 percent of job applicants lie on their résumé and in a job interview. Moreover, 95 percent of employers say they would reject applicants who lie about a college degree and 80 percent would not hire someone who falsified previous job titles. Why then do you think employers often ignore on-job deception?

know if it's dishonesty, but people cover their ass, I mean they CYA. They may not necessarily do what they're supposed to, so they do things to cover up some of their lack of performance." Employees were somewhat sympathetic towards their coworkers who practice CYA deception and explained that these lies lacked malice and were simply an attempt to stay afloat and avoid getting in trouble due to an honest mistake. Employees also explained that CYA deception occurred because their coworkers felt they had no outlet to confess their mistakes without retribution, and therefore resorted to dishonesty. As such, the organizational structure received some degree of blame for CYA deception.

Personal Gain Deception. The most prevalent form of coworker deception involved employees who deceived for personal gain. Many employees explained that their coworkers used deception to discredit other employees and make themselves look better within the organization. Other employees told of coworkers who stole money and materials from the company, or inappropriately took clients from other workers via deceptive practices. Personal gain deception sometimes victimized the organization at large, such as when coworkers lied about the amount of hours they worked. Personal gain deception was most problematic, however, when employees felt targeted and were directly and negatively affected by their coworkers' gain. For example, one participant explained that a coworker wanted to get a promotion, so she attacked the participant's character and told lies to discredit her in front of the boss.

Personality Trait Deception. The final form of coworker deception was perceived to result from the coworkers' character or personality flaws. Some reported their coworkers possess avoidant communication styles and therefore tell white lies to avoid looking bad or upsetting someone. This form of deception was conceptualized as a mismatch of communication styles, and employees found it to be an unfortunate but unavoidable aspect of relational communication. Other coworkers were perceived to have seriously flawed morals and described as "lazy," "shady," "sneaky," and "unbalanced." Employees largely ignored the organizational climate when evaluating personality trait deception and instead focused on contextualizing

the vast history that proved their coworker was a liar. As one participant explained, "Personally, the guy really disgusts me and if I remember what he does I really don't want to talk to him."

The average person commits some form of deception in one out of every five interactions, yet these acts might be interpreted in different ways depending on other people's perceptions of the deception. Our study suggests that deception is viewed as an unavoidable aspect of all relationships; however, lies that maliciously target particular coworkers or reflect a destructive work environment are highly problematic. Indeed, peer coworker deception wreaks havoc when it hinders organizational members' ability to perform their jobs.

Organizations can minimize deception in several ways. First, employees are less likely to engage in CYA deception if they feel comfortable admitting to their mistakes. Training supervisors to communicate more effectively and more openly with employees could provide employees with an outlet to seek help and repair mistakes without fear of repercussions. However, many participants in our study asserted that coworker deception was a "survival of the fittest" behavior necessary to outperform coworkers, gain commissions, or be promoted. Notably, participants often blamed their company for either creating or fostering a competitive environment, which ultimately destroyed coworker trust and hindered productivity. Organizational leaders might help prevent coworker deception by facilitating a collaborative environment that rewards cooperative success over individual achievement. If workers personally benefit from lying, removing these individual benefits would also likely remove a common motive for deceptive workplace behavior and help shape a more honest and positive organizational climate.

ABOUT THE AUTHORS

Erin M. Bryant is a doctoral student in the Hugh Downs School of Human Communication at Arizona State University in Tempe, AZ, USA. **Patricia M. Sias** is a Professor in the Edward R. Murrow College of Communication at Washington State University in Pullman, WA. This essay is based on Erin M. Bryant and Patricia M. Sias (2011). "Sensemaking and Relational Consequences of Peer Coworker Deception. *Communication Monographs, 78,* 115–137. *Communication Monographs* and *Communication Currents* are publications of the National Communication Association.

hat communication strategies ould you mploy to eal with is kind of uation at ork? How ight assertiveness, ger management, pression manage-ent, and/ support-e mesges help?

Look at the strategies for managing office gossip in Chapter 9 on p. 172. Do any of those strategies have the potential to prevent or minimize coworker deceptions? Here are three examples: "Do not spread malicious rumors," "Before self-disclosing to a co-worker, assume that your secret will be told to others," and "If you believe that gossip has created a serious problem, talk to someone with more power or influence."

s this behavior characteristic of a communication style or a personality trait? Could it be both?

How can an organization help prevent coworker deception by creating a more collaborative environment? List some of the characteristics of a work environment you've experienced that rewards cooperation and teamwork rather than individual achievement and personal success.

making sense of workplace deception

10 Working in **GROUPS**

On August 5, 2010, the San Jose copper-gold mine in Chile collapsed, trapping 33 miners three miles below ground. All the miners were rescued on October 13, 2010. When the miners emerged from the tight capsule that brought them to the surface, they were joyous and, considering the conditions they'd lived in, a relatively healthy group of brave men.[1]

There were reasons these men dealt so well with the incredible adversity they faced. Immediately after the accident, even as the dust cleared from the mine collapse, the miners organized themselves into work groups and took on appropriate roles. At first, they rationed the little food they had to two spoonfuls of tuna, a sip of milk, and a morsel of peach each day. The shift foreman took on the role of leader, another miner organized fitness exercises, and a third became the group's "doctor." Two miners assumed more spiritual roles—as religious leaders and personal counselors—while two others maintained communication with the surface. In his book *Group Dynamics*, Donelson R. Forsyth concludes that groups respond to stressful environments like these "by becoming better groups—more organized, more cohesive, and more efficient."[2]

In this chapter, we look at the nature of groups: how they form and the communication challenges they face as they develop into productive teams.

The Challenges of Working in Groups

What are the pros and cons of working in groups?

All of us work in groups. We work in groups at school and on the job; with family members, friends, and colleagues; and in diverse locations, from sports fields and battlefields to courtrooms and classrooms. Whereas individual achievement was once the measure of personal success, success in today's complex world depends on the ability to work in groups. Researchers Steve Kozlowski and Daniel Ilgen describe our profound dependence on groups:

> Teams of people working together for a common cause touch all of our lives. From everyday activities like air travel, fire fighting, and running the United Way drive to amazing feats of human accomplishments like climbing Mt. Everest and reaching for the stars, teams are at the center of how work gets done in modern times.[3]

Working in groups may be the most important skill you learn in college. A comprehensive study commissioned by the Association of American Colleges and Universities asked employers to rank essential learning outcomes for college graduates entering the workplace. In two major categories—*intellectual and practical skills*, and *personal and social responsibility*—the top ranked outcome was "teamwork skills and the ability to collaborate with others in diverse group settings." Recent graduates ranked the same learning outcome as a top priority.[4]

The Nature of Group Communication

In 2009, the Educational Testing Service unveiled the Personal Potential Index, an evaluation instrument professors can use to rate students on their potential for success in graduate school. The instrument includes six critical traits, two of which are *communication skills* and *teamwork*. The teamwork trait specifies skills such as the abilities to work well in group settings, to behave in an open and friendly manner, to support the efforts of others, and to share ideas easily.[6] The American Management Association's "2010 Critical Skills Survey" found that 72 percent of top corporate managers rated the ability to work with others in groups as critical for career advancement.[7] These abilities characterize the nature of effective **group communication**—the interaction of three or more interdependent people working to achieve a common goal.[8]

> **❝I look for people [who] are good team people over anything else. I can teach the technical.❞**
>
> —Business executive[5]

Group Size The phrase "two's company; three's a crowd" recognizes that an interaction between two people is quite different from a three-person discussion. The ideal size for a problem-solving group is five to seven members. To avoid ties in decision making, an odd number of members is usually better than an even number. Groups larger than seven tend to divide into subgroups; talkative members may dominate or drown out quiet members.

Interaction and Interdependence Next time you're in a group, observe the ways members behave toward one another. A group member raises a controversial issue. In response, everyone starts talking at the same time. Later, the group listens intently to a member explain an important concept or describe a possible solution to a problem. When tensions arise, a funny comment eases the strain. Members exchange good cheer as they conclude their meeting or finalize a course of action. What you have just observed is group *interaction*—a necessity for effective

Members of a rafting group depend on one another to achieve a common goal—if one side were to paddle out of sync with the other, the chances of tipping over would increase.

Without a common goal, groups wonder: Why are we meeting? Why should we care or work hard?

Working in groups often leads to friendships, enhanced learning, and member satisfaction.

group communication in both face-to-face and virtual meetings.

Group members are *interdependent*—that is, the actions of an individual group member affect every other member. For example, if a member fails to provide needed background information, the group as a whole will suffer when it attempts to make an important decision or solve a significant problem.

Common Goal Group members come together for a reason: a collective purpose or goal that defines and unifies the group. A classic study by Carl Larson and Frank LaFasto concludes that "in every case, without exception, where an effectively functioning team was identified, it was described . . . as having a clear understanding of its objective."⁹

While some groups have the freedom to develop their own goals, other groups are assigned a goal. For example, a gathering of neighbors may meet to discuss ways of reducing crime in the neighborhood. Students may form a study group to prepare for an upcoming exam. On the other hand, a marketing instructor may assign a semester-long project to a group of students in which they must research, develop and present a marketing campaign. A manufacturing company may assemble a group of employees from various departments and ask them to develop recommendations for safer storage of hazardous chemicals. Whatever the circumstances, effective groups work to accomplish a common goal.

Advantages and Disadvantages of Working in Groups

If you're like most people, you have had to sit through some long and boring meetings. You may have lost patience (or your temper) in a group that couldn't accomplish a simple task you could have done better and more quickly by yourself. In the long run,

however, the advantages of working in groups usually outweigh the potential disadvantages.

Advantages In *The Wisdom of Teams*, Jon Katzenbach and Douglas Smith note that groups "outperform individuals acting alone . . . especially when performance requires multiple skills, judgments, and experiences."¹⁰ In general, the "approaches and outcomes

ETHICAL COMMUNICATION

Making *Good* Group Decisions

When you work closely with group members, not only do your choices affect the entire group, but the decisions and actions of the group have the potential to affect many others. Consider the unethical corporate officers who masked the financial losses and bad mortgages that triggered the 2008 economic crisis or how Bernard Madoff and associates conspired to cheat his once-wealthy investors out of nearly $3 billion. The consequences of these decisions were magnified well beyond the room in which they were made, affecting thousands of investors and employees.

Read the following scenarios and decide whether the behavior described in each is unethical or merely unpopular but justified.

1. A group member assigned to take notes at a meeting changes the wording of recommendations and motions so they reflect her personal preferences.
2. Although company employees are accustomed to lax rules and lush parties at the annual sales meeting, a new company president insists, on the penalty of fines, demotions, and even dismissal, that all members attend every work session.
3. Your group worked many months developing a plan that could revolutionize a challenging business practice. The group member assigned to write the report puts her name on it as the author and lists the other group members only at the end of the report document.
4. After you explain your recommendations to a group, members reject your ideas without discussion. You believe that your contributions were purposely ignored, so you share your ideas with your manager and explain why the group's decision and actions are flawed.
5. A group seeking funds to assist disadvantaged families inflates the program's success rate to justify its funding request.

of cooperating groups are not just better than those of the average group member, but are better than even the group's best problem solver functioning alone." Furthermore, the lone problem solver can't match the diversity of knowledge and perspectives of a group.[11]

Many of us also belong to and work in groups because we can make friends, socialize, and feel part of a successful team. Moreover, working in groups can enhance learning when members share information, stimulate critical thinking, challenge assumptions, and establish high standards of achievement.

Disadvantages Working in groups requires time, energy, and resources. For example, when 3M Corporation researchers calculated the hourly wages and overhead costs of workplace meetings, they concluded that meetings cost the company $78.8 million annually.[12] In addition to financial costs, there is also the potential for conflict among members.

As much as we may want everyone in a group to cooperate and work hard, the behavior of some members may create problems. They may talk too much, arrive late for meetings, and argue aggressively. However, these same members may also be excellent researchers, effective critical thinkers, and good friends.

Types of Groups

Groups are as diverse as the people in them and the goals they seek. Yet there are common characteristics that can be used to separate groups into several categories. These categories range from the most personal and informal types of groups to more professional and formal types. You can identify each type of group by noting its purpose (why the group meets) and by its membership (who is in the group).

The first six types of groups described in the figure below serve your personal needs and interests. In Chapter 8, we examined the importance of effective communication with family members, friends, and romantic partners—the people who belong to family and social groups. Self-help, learning, service, and civic groups are groups you join by choice because they offer support and encouragement, help you gain knowledge, and assist others. There are two types of groups—work groups and public groups—that serve the diverse interests of organizations and public audiences. Understanding your role in these types of groups requires more detailed information about their various forms, functions, and goals.

Work Groups Labor crews, sales staff, faculty, management groups, and research teams are all **work groups**—groups that are responsible for making decisions, solving problems, implementing projects, or performing routine duties in an organization. Committees and work teams are both types of work groups. **Committees** (social committees, budget committees, and awards committees) are created by a larger group or by a person in a position of authority to take on specific tasks. **Work teams** are usually given full responsibility and resources for their performance. Unlike committees, work teams are relatively permanent. They don't take time *from* work to meet—they unite *to* work.

TYPES OF GROUP

	PURPOSE	MEMBERSHIP
Primary	To provide members with affection, support, and a sense of belonging	Family members, best friends
Social	To share common interests in a friendly setting or participate in social activities	Athletic team members, hobbyists, sorority and fraternity members
Self-Help	To support and encourage members who want or need help with personal problems	Therapy group members, participants in programs such as Weight Watchers and Alcoholics Anonymous
Learning	To help members gain knowledge and develop skills	Classmates, book group members, participants in a ceramic workshop
Service	To assist worthy causes that help other people outside the group	Members of Kiwanis, Police Athletic League, charity groups
Civic	To support worthy causes that help people within the group or community	Members of a PTA, labor unions, veterans' groups, neighborhood associations
Work	To achieve specific goals on behalf of a business or organization	Committee members, employees, task force members, management teams
Public	To discuss important issues in front of or for the benefit of the public	Participants in public panel discussions, symposiums, forums, governance groups

VIRTUAL TEAM MEMBER **RESPONSIBILITIES**

When conducting or participating in a virtual team meeting, every group member should assume the following responsibilities:

■ Prepare for the meeting by reading the background material and becoming familiar with the technology

■ Speak out during the meeting (or respond using the available media)

■ Listen to and consider others' ideas

■ Make suggestions and decisions

■ Follow up on meeting actions[13]

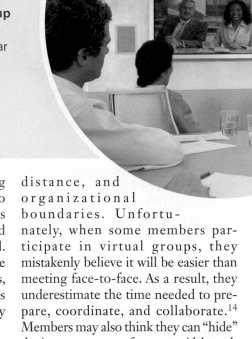

Public Groups Panel discussions, symposiums, forums, and governance groups are types of **public groups** that discuss issues in front of or for the benefit of the public. Their meetings usually occur in unrestricted public settings in front of public audiences. During a **panel discussion**, several people interact about a common topic to educate, influence, or entertain an audience. In a **symposium**, group members present short, uninterrupted presentations on different aspects of a topic for the benefit of an audience. Very often, a panel or symposium is followed by a **forum**, which provides an opportunity for audience members

to comment or ask questions. A strong moderator is needed in a forum to make sure that all audience members have an equal opportunity to speak and that the meeting is orderly and civil. **Governance groups** such as state legislatures, city and county councils, and governing boards of public agencies and educational institutions make policy decisions in public settings.

Virtual Groups In addition to face-to-face meetings with others, technology has made it possible to work in virtual groups. A **virtual group** relies on tools such as email, audioconferencing, videoconferencing, and Web conferencing to communicate across time,

distance, and organizational boundaries. Unfortunately, when some members participate in virtual groups, they mistakenly believe it will be easier than meeting face-to-face. As a result, they underestimate the time needed to prepare, coordinate, and collaborate.[14] Members may also think they can "hide" during remote conferences. Although you may not be in the same room or even on the same continent as the other members of a virtual group, you are just as personally responsible for being fully prepared to contribute to the group's work.

10.2

Balancing Individual and Group Goals

How can you balance individual and group needs in groups?

As groups form and develop, effective members learn how to balance individual and group goals. In the best of groups, your personal goals support the group's common goal. This balancing act, however, requires an understanding of two potential roadblocks to success: primary tension and hidden agendas.

Primary Tension

Group communication scholar Ernest G. Bormann describes **primary tension** as the social unease and inhibitions that accompany the getting-acquainted period in a new group.[15] Because most new group members want to create a good first impression, they tend to be overly polite with one another.

In most groups, primary tension decreases as members feel more

comfortable with one another. But if a group is bogged down in primary tension, you can and should intervene by talking about it and discussing how to break the cycle. Urge members to stick to the group's agenda and express opinions about relevant issues. When your group meets, be positive, energetic, patient, open-minded, and well-prepared.

> ### Characteristics of PRIMARY TENSION
>
> ■ Members rarely interrupt one another.
> ■ Long, awkward pauses often come between comments.
> ■ Members are soft-spoken and very polite.
> ■ Members avoid expressing strong opinions and emotions.

Hidden Agendas

Many (if not most) of us have personal goals we want to achieve in a group. As long as our personal goals support the group's goal, all is well. A **hidden agenda,** however, occurs when a member's private goals conflict with the group's goals. Hidden agendas represent what people *really* want rather than what they *say* they want. When hidden agendas become more important than a group's public agenda or goal, the result can be group frustration, unresolved conflicts, and failure.

Even when a group recognizes the existence of hidden agendas, some of them cannot and should not be shared because they may create an atmosphere of distrust. For instance, not many people would want to deal

Tuckman's Group Development Model

Most groups experience recognizable milestones. A "newborn" group behaves differently from an "adult" group that has worked together for a long time. In 1965, Bruce Tuckman, an educational psychologist, identified four discrete stages in the life cycle of groups—forming, storming, norming, and performing.[16] Since introducing his **Group Development Model**, more than 100 theoretical models have described how a group moves through several "passages" during its lifetime.[17] Tuckman's original four stages are, however, considered one of the most comprehensive models relevant to *all* types of groups.[18]

Stage 2: **STORMING**

During the **storming stage**, groups become more argumentative and emotional as they discuss important issues and vie for leadership. Some groups are tempted to suppress this stage in an effort to avoid conflict. However, conflict can help members develop relationships, decide who's in charge and who can be trusted, and clarify the group's common goal.

Stage 3: **NORMING**

During the **norming stage**, members define roles and establish norms. The group begins to work harmoniously as a cohesive team and makes decisions about the best ways to achieve a common goal. At this point in group development, members feel more comfortable with one another and are willing to disagree and express their

opinions. "Communication becomes more open and task oriented" as "members solidify positive working relationships with each other."[19]

Stage 4: **PERFORMING**

During the **performing stage**, members focus their energy on working harmoniously to achieve group goals. Roles and responsibilities change according to group needs. Decisions are reached, problems are solved, and ideas are implemented. When the performing stage is going well, members are highly energized, loyal to one another, and willing to accept every challenge that arises.

Tuckman's group development theory helps explain why and how groups and their members behave at different stages in their development. Understanding the natural development of a group can help explain, predict, and improve group productivity and member satisfaction.

Stage 1: **FORMING**

During the **forming stage**, group members may be more worried about themselves ("Will I be accepted and liked?") than about the group as a whole. Understandably, members are hesitant to express strong opinions or assert their personal needs during this phase until they know more about how other members think and feel about the task and about one another. Although little gets done during this stage, members need time to become acquainted with one another and define group goals.

Like people, groups move through stages as they develop and mature.

> # Dealing with hidden agendas means knowing that some of them can and should be confronted, whereas others cannot and should not be shared.

with the following revelation during a group discussion: "The reason I don't want to be here is that I don't want to work with Kenneth, who is untrustworthy and incompetent."

Sociologists Rodney Napier and Matti Gershenfeld suggest that discussing hidden agendas during the early stages of group development can counteract their disruptive power.[20]

Initial discussion could include some of the following questions:

- What are the group's goals?
- Do any members have any personal concerns or goals that differ from these?
- What outcomes do members expect?

Unrecognized and unresolved hidden agendas can permeate and infect *all* stages of group development.

10.3
Balancing Conflict and Cohesion
How can you balance conflict and cohesiveness in groups?

Conflict is valuable in groups because it forces us to analyze our opinions and decisions. As groups develop and begin discussing important issues, members become more argumentative and emotional. Many groups are tempted to discourage or avoid conflict. When conflict is accepted as normal and beneficial, it helps establish a climate in which members feel free to disagree with one another.[21] At the same time, groups also benefit from **cohesion**—the mutual attraction that holds the members of a group together.

> Effective groups learn to balance conflict and cohesion as they interact to achieve a common goal.

Secondary Tension

When a group moves from the polite interactions of the forming stage to the storming stage, confident members begin to compete with one another. They openly disagree on substantive issues. It is still too early in the group's existence to predict the outcome of such competition. At this point, a different kind of tension may emerge. **Secondary tension** describes the frustrations and personality conflicts experienced by group members as they compete for social acceptance, status, and achievement.[22] Regardless of the causes, a group cannot hope to achieve its goals if secondary tension is not managed effectively.

If you sense that your group cannot resolve its secondary tension, it is time to intervene. One strategy is to joke about the tension. The resulting laughter can ease individual and group stress. Another option is to work outside the group setting to discuss any personal difficulties and anxieties with individual group members.

Most groups experience some primary and secondary tension. A little bit of tension can motivate a group toward action and increase a group's sensitivity to feedback. As Donald Ellis and Aubrey Fisher point out, "The successful and socially healthy group is not characterized by an absence of social tension, but by successful management of social tension."[23]

Characteristics of SECONDARY TENSION

- Energy and alertness levels are high.
- The group is noisy and dynamic; members are loud and emphatic.
- Several members may speak at the same time.
- Members sit up, lean forward, and squirm in their seats.

Cohesive group members feel responsible for and take pride in their own work as well as the work of other members.

Group Cohesion

Group cohesion can be expressed as "All for one and one for all!" Cohesive groups are united and committed to a common goal, have high levels of interaction, and enjoy a supportive communication climate. Their members also share a sense of teamwork and pride in the group, want to conform to group expectations, and are willing to use creative approaches to achieve the group's goals.[24]

Cohesive groups are happier and get more done, and members use the terms *we* and *our* instead of *I* and *my*. Members of a cohesive group treat one another with respect, showing concern for members' personal needs, and appreciating the value of member diversity.

Cohesive groups create an encouraging climate that rewards praise-worthy contributions. Many groups use celebration dinners, letters of appreciation, certificates, and gifts to reward individual effort and initiative, although even a simple compliment can make a group member feel appreciated. And, rather than take personal and individual credit for success, members of a cohesive group emphasize the group's accomplishments.

10.4
Balancing Conformity and Nonconformity
How can you balance conformity and nonconformity in groups?

During the norming stage of group development, members define their roles and determine how the group will do its work. Effective groups learn to balance a commitment to group customs, rules, and standards (conformity) with a willingness to differ and change (nonconformity).

Group Norms

Communication scholar Patricia Andrews defines **norms** as "sets of expectations held by group members concerning what kinds of behavior or opinions are acceptable or unacceptable, good or bad, right or wrong, appropriate or inappropriate."[25] Group norms express the values of a group, help the group to function smoothly, define appropriate and inappropriate behavior, and facilitate group success.[26] Norms are the group's rules of behavior; they determine how members dress, speak, listen, and work. For example, one group may discourage interruptions, whereas another group may view interruptions and overlapping conversations as acceptable forms of interaction. Without norms, a group lacks agreed-on ways to organize and perform a task.

Group norms can have positive or negative effects on member behavior and group success. For example, if your group's norms place a premium on pleasant and peaceful discussions, members may be reluctant to voice disagreement or share bad news. If group norms permit members to arrive late and leave early, you may not have enough members to do the job. Norms that don't support your group's goals can prevent the group from succeeding. When this is the case, you are perfectly within your rights (in fact, it may be your duty) to engage in nonconforming behavior. **Constructive nonconformity** occurs when a member resists a norm while still working to promote the group goal.

> "I know we always have our annual retreat at a golf resort, but many of our new staff members don't play golf and may feel out of place or bored."

There are times when constructive nonconformity is needed and valued. Movies, television shows, and books champion the holdout juror, the stubbornly honest politician, and the principled but disobedient soldier or crew member. Sometimes there is so much pressure for group members to conform that they need a nonconformist to shake up the process, to provide critical feedback, and to create doubt about what had been a group-sanctioned but poor decision.

Group norms function only to the extent that members conform to them.

How does this parade of Marine Corps soldiers demonstrate the importance and value of group norms?

Effective groups appreciate constructive nonconformity.

Nonconformity can serve a group well if it prevents members from ignoring important information or making poor decisions.

Constructive nonconformity contributes to effective group decisions and more creative solutions because it allows members to voice serious and well-justified objections without fear of personal criticism or exclusion for taking a different position. In contrast, **destructive nonconformity** occurs when a member resists conformity without regard for the best interests of the group and its goal, such as by showing up late to attract attention or interrupting others to exert power.

When members do not conform to norms, a group may have to discuss the value of a particular norm and then choose to change, clarify, or continue to accept it. At the very least, nonconforming behavior helps members recognize and understand the norms of the group. For instance, if a member is reprimanded for leaving early, other members learn it is not acceptable to leave before a meeting is adjourned.

STOP&THINK

Can You Name Your Norms?

The left-hand column in the following table describes several types of group norms. In the middle column, list the related group norms in your classroom. In the right column, list the related group norms in a current or former workplace. Examine all these norms with a critical eye. Do they help the group achieve its common goal? If not, are you willing to challenge these norms for the good of the group?

Types of Group Norms	Classroom	Workplace
Verbal (e.g., formal, casual, jargon, profanity)		
Nonverbal (e.g., formal or informal attire, seating arrangements, activity level, appropriate touching, eye contact)		
Interactional (e.g., use of first or last names, nicknames, speaking turns, listening behavior, unruly behavior)		
Content (e.g., discussions are: serious, work related, social, intimate, humorous)		
Status (e.g., who makes decisions, who has influence, is disagreement allowed)		
Rewards (e.g., how success is determined, how achievement is rewarded)		

balancing conformity and nonconformity

10.5

Balancing Task and Maintenance Roles

How can you balance task and maintenance roles in groups?

Group members assume different roles depending on the nature of the group, its membership, and its goal. A **group role** is a pattern of behaviors associated with an expected function within a particular group context. For example, when someone asks, "Who will get the information we need for our next meeting?" all eyes turn to Zhu because researching and sharing information are tasks he performs well. If a disagreement between two group members becomes heated, the group may look to Alicia for help because she has a talent for resolving conflicts and mediating differences.

Every group member brings unique talents, preferences, and perspectives to a group.

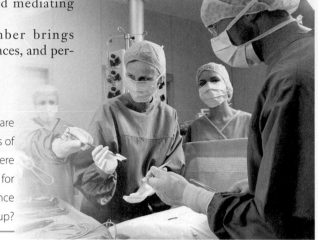

What task roles are critical to the success of a surgical team? Is there an appropriate place for maintenance roles in this group?

GROUP **TASK** ROLES [27]

ROLE	DESCRIPTION	EXAMPLE
INITIATOR/ CONTRIBUTOR	Proposes ideas; provides direction; gets the group started	"Let's begin by considering the client's point of view."
INFORMATION SEEKER	Asks for relevant information; requests explanations; points out information gaps	"How can we decide on a policy without knowing more about the cost and the legal requirements?"
INFORMATION GIVER	Researches, organizes, and presents relevant information	"I checked with human resources and they said . . ."
OPINION SEEKER	Asks for opinions; tests for agreement and disagreement	"Lyle, what do you think? Will it work?"
OPINION GIVER	States personal belief; shares feelings; offers analysis and arguments	"I don't agree that he's guilty. He may be annoying, but that doesn't constitute harassment."
CLARIFIER/ SUMMARIZER	Explains ideas and their consequences; reduces confusion; summarizes	"We've been trying to analyze this problem for two hours. Here's what I think we've agreed on."
EVALUATOR/ CRITIC	Assesses the value of ideas and arguments; diagnoses problems	"These figures don't consider monthly operating costs."
ENERGIZER	Motivates members; creates enthusiasm, and, if needed, a sense of urgency	"This is incredible! We've come up with a unique and workable solution to the problem."
PROCEDURAL TECHNICIAN	Helps prepare meetings; makes room arrangements; provides materials and equipment	"Before our next meeting, let me know if you will need a flip chart again."
RECORDER/ SECRETARY	Keeps accurate written records of group recommendations and decisions	"Maggie, please repeat the two deadline dates so I can get them into the minutes."

Group Task and Maintenance Roles

Group member roles are divided into two functional categories: task roles and maintenance roles. Group **task roles** focus on behaviors that help manage the task and complete the job. When members assume task roles, they provide useful information, ask important questions, analyze problems, and help the group stay organized. Group **maintenance roles** affect whether group members get along with one another while pursuing a common goal. Members who assume maintenance roles help to create a supportive communication climate, resolve conflicts, and encourage members or praise good work.

In addition to assuming roles on your own, analyze the group to determine whether important roles are missing. For example, if members are becoming frustrated because one or two people are doing all the talking, you might suggest that someone serve as a gatekeeper. If the group has trouble tracking its progress, suggest that someone take on the role of recorder/secretary. In highly effective the groups, all the task and maintenance roles are available to mobilize a group toward achieving its common goal.

Self-Centered Roles

Sometimes group members assume **self-centered roles** in which they put their own goals ahead of the group's goal and other member needs. Self-centered roles can disrupt the work of a group, adversely affect member relationships, and prevent the group from achieving its goals.

Three strategies can help you and your group deal with self-centered members: accept, confront, or even exclude the troublesome member. Acceptance is not the same as approval. A group may allow disruptive behavior

Common Self-Centered Roles:[29]

- **Aggressor.** Puts down other members, is sarcastic and critical, takes credit for someone else's work or ideas
- **Blocker.** Stands in the way of progress, presents uncompromising positions, uses delay tactics to derail an idea or proposal
- **Dominator.** Prevents others from participating, interrupts others, tries to manipulate others
- **Recognition Seeker.** Boasts about personal accomplishments, tries to be the center of attention, pouts if not getting enough attention
- **Clown.** Injects inappropriate humor, seems more interested in goofing off than working, distracts the group from its task
- **Deserter.** Withdraws from the group, appears "above it all" and annoyed or bored with the discussion, stops contributing
- **Confessor.** Shares very personal feelings and problems, uses the group for emotional support in ways that inappropriately distract members from the group's task

GROUP **MAINTENANCE** ROLES[28]

ROLE	DESCRIPTION	EXAMPLE
ENCOURAGER/ SUPPORTER	Praises and encourages group members; listens empathically	"Thanks for taking all that time to find the information we needed."
HARMONIZER	Helps resolve conflicts; mediates differences; encourages teamwork and group harmony	"I know we're becoming edgy, but we're almost done. Let's focus on the task, not our frustrations."
COMPROMISER	Offers suggestions that minimize differences; helps the group reach consensus	"Maybe we can improve the old system rather than adopting a brand-new way of doing it."
TENSION RELEASER	Uses friendly humor to alleviate tensions, tempers, and stress	"Can Karen and I arm-wrestle to decide who gets the assignment?"
GATEKEEPER	Monitors and regulates the flow of communication; encourages productive participation	"I think we've heard from everyone except Michelle, who has strong feelings about this issue."
STANDARD MONITOR	Reminds group of norms and rules; tests ideas against group-established standards	"We all agreed we'd start at 10 A.M. Now we sit around waiting for latecomers until 10:30."
OBSERVER/ INTERPRETER	Monitors and interprets feelings and nonverbal communication; paraphrases member comments	"Maybe we're not really disagreeing. I think we're in agreement that …"
FOLLOWER	Supports the group and its members; willingly accepts others' ideas and assignments	"That's fine with me. Just tell me when it's due."

to continue when it's not detrimental to the group's ultimate success or when the member's positive contributions far outweigh the inconvenience or annoyance of putting up with the negative behavior. For example, a "clown" may be disruptive on occasion but may also be the group's best report writer or a valued harmonizer.

When it becomes impossible to accept or ignore self-centered behavior, the group should take action. For instance, members can confront a member by making it clear that the group will progress despite that person's nonproductive behavior. "Ron, I think we fully understand your strong objections, but ultimately this is a group decision." In a moment of extreme frustration, one member may say what everyone is thinking—"Lisa, please let me finish my sentence!" Although such an outburst may make everyone uncomfortable, it can put a stop to disruptive behavior.

When all else fails, a group may ask disruptive members to leave the group and bar them from meetings; this is a humiliating experience that all but the most stubborn members would prefer to avoid.

Do You Disrupt Group Work?

Disruptive group behavior comes in all varieties. Do any of the following types describe the way you communicate in groups?[30] For each item, indicate how frequently you behave like the description: (1) usually, (2) often, (3) sometimes, (4) rarely, or (5) never.

—— **1.** *The Put-Downer.* Do you assume that members are wrong until they're proven right? Do you make negative remarks such as "That will never work," "Been there, done it, forget it," or "I don't like it" before the group has had time to discuss the issue in detail?

—— **2.** *The Interrupter.* Do you start talking before others are finished? Do you interrupt because you're impatient or annoyed?

—— **3.** *The Nonverbal Negative Naybobber.* Do you disagree nonverbally in a dramatic or disruptive manner? Do you frown or scowl, shake your head, roll your eyes, squirm in your seat, audibly sigh or groan, or madly scribble notes after someone has said something?

—— **4.** *The Laggard.* Are you late to meetings? Do you ask or demand to be told what happened before you arrived? Are you usually late in completing assigned tasks?

—— **5.** *The Chronic Talkaholic.* Talkaholics are compulsive communicators who have great difficulty (and often little desire for) being quiet in groups. Chronic talkaholics talk so much, they disrupt the group and annoy or anger other members. Do you ever talk when you know it would be much smarter to keep quiet? Do other group members often tell you that you talk too much?[31]

10.6

Developing Group Leadership

What are the characteristics of a successful group leader?

If you enter the word *leadership* into any major online bookseller's search engine, you will find thousands of books. And if you review these offerings, you'll see that most of them are written by highly respected scholars and well-regarded business leaders. Some unusual titles, demonstrate the range of leadership books. Here are just a few:

Popular Trade Books on Leadership

- *Leadership Secrets of Hillary Clinton*
- *Lincoln on Leadership*
- *Leadership Secrets of Colin Powell*
- *Jesus on Leadership*
- *Leadership Secrets of Attila the Hun*
- *The Leadership Secrets of Santa Claus*

Before you chuckle too much over *The Leadership Secrets of Santa Claus,* consider how you could translate some of his "secrets" into useful leadership tips: choose your reindeer wisely, make a list and check it twice, listen to the elves, find out who's naughty and nice, and be good for goodness' sake.[32]

Leadership is the ability to make strategic decisions and use communication to mobilize group members toward achieving a common goal.

Even though just about everyone recognizes the importance of leadership, it is not always easy to practice effectively. One review of leadership studies estimates that leadership incompetence is "as high as 60 to 75 percent—and that our hiring practices are so flawed that more than 50 percent of leaders hired by organizations are doomed to fail."[33]

In his book on leadership, Antony Bell describes communication as the mortar or glue that connects all leadership competencies. The abilities to think and act while remaining self-aware and self-disciplined are critical building blocks to leadership competency, but it takes communication to bind these blocks together.[34]

Three Approaches to Leadership

Leadership is a quality that defies precise measurement. However, three theories can help you understand your own and others' approaches to leadership: Trait Theory, Styles Theory, and Situational Theory.

Trait Theory Based on the belief that leaders are born, not made, the **Trait Theory of Leadership** identifies specific characteristics associated with leadership. Most of us can come up with a list of desirable leadership traits: intelligence, confidence, enthusiasm, organizational talent, and good listening skills. The weakness of Trait Theory is that it doesn't account for the fact that many effective leaders possess only a few of these traits. Just because you have most of these traits does not mean that you will be a great leader. At the same time, great leaders have emerged who have very few of these traits. For example, Harriet Tubman, an illiterate slave, did little talking but led hundreds of people from bondage in the South to freedom in the North.

Styles Theory The **Styles Theory of Leadership** examines a collection of specific behaviors that constitute three distinct leadership styles: autocratic, democratic, and laissez-faire. **Autocratic leaders** try to control the direction and outcome of a discussion, make many of the group's decisions, give orders, expect followers to obey orders, focus on achieving the group's task, and take credit for successful results. An autocratic style is often appropriate during a serious crisis when there may not be time to discuss issues or consider the wishes of all members. In an emergency, the group may want its leader to take total responsibility. However, too much control can lower group morale and sacrifice long-term productivity.

A **democratic leader** promotes the social equality and task interests of group members. This type of leader shares decision making with the group, helps the group plan a course of action, focuses on the group's morale as well as on the task, and gives the entire group credit for success. In groups with democratic leadership, members are often more satisfied with the group experience, more loyal to the leader, and more productive in the long run.

Laissez-faire is a French phrase that means "to let people do as they choose." A **laissez-faire leader** lets the group take charge of all decisions and actions. Such a leader may be a perfect match for mature and highly productive groups because a laid-back leadership style can generate a climate in which communication is encouraged and rewarded. Unfortunately, some laissez-faire leaders do little or nothing to help a group when it needs decisive leadership.

Situational Leadership Theory Rather than describing traits or styles, **Situational Leadership Theory** seeks an ideal fit between leaders and leadership roles.[35] The situational approach explains how leaders can become more effective by analyzing themselves, their group, and the context.

Situational Theory identifies two leadership styles: task motivated and relationship motivated. **Task-motivated leaders** want to get the job done. They gain satisfaction from completing a task even if it results in bad feelings between the leader and group members. As a result, task-motivated leaders are often criticized for being too focused on the job and overlooking group morale. **Relationship-motivated leaders** gain satisfaction from working well with other people even if the cost is failing to complete a task. Not surprisingly, they are sometimes criticized for paying too much attention to how members feel and for tolerating disruptive behavior.

Situational Theory requires you to match your leadership style to the situation in terms of three important dimensions: leader–member relations, task structure, and power. **Leader–member relations** can be positive, neutral, or negative. Are group members friendly and loyal to the leader and the rest of the group? Are they cooperative and supportive? **Task structure** can range from disorganized and chaotic to highly organized and rule driven. Are the goals and task clear? The third situational factor is the amount of power and control the leader possesses.

> **Without leadership,** a group may be nothing more than a collection of individuals lacking the coordination and will to achieve a goal.

Three THEORETICAL Approaches to Leadership

1 TRAIT THEORY ▶ You Have It or You Don't

2 STYLES THEORY ▶ Are Democracies Always Best?

3 SITUATIONAL THEORY ▶ Matching Leaders and Jobs

Relationship between leadership style and situational factors

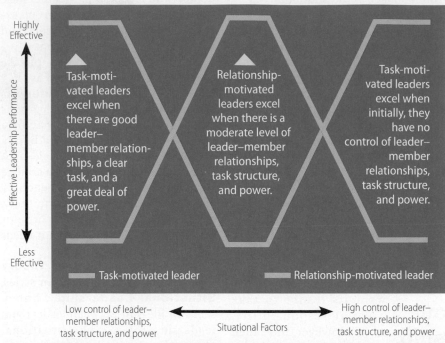

Effective Leadership Performance — Highly Effective / Less Effective

Task-motivated leaders excel when there are good leader–member relationships, a clear task, and a great deal of power.

Relationship-motivated leaders excel when there is a moderate level of leader–member relationships, task structure, and power.

Task-motivated leaders excel when initially, they have no control of leader–member relationships, task structure, and power.

▬▬ Task-motivated leader ▬▬ Relationship-motivated leader

Low control of leader–member relationships, task structure, and power ←— Situational Factors —→ High control of leader–member relationships, task structure, and power

The figure to the left shows that task motivated leaders perform best in extremes, such as when the situation requires high levels of leader control or when it is almost out of control. They excel when there are good or poor leader–member relationships, a clear or unclear task, and a great deal of or no power. Relationship-motivated leaders do well when in the middle ground where there is a mix of conditions, such as a semi-structured task or a group of interested but not eager followers.

COMMUNICATION IN *ACTION*

How to Become a Leader

Just about anyone can become a leader. Abraham Lincoln, Harry S. Truman, and Barack Obama rose from humble beginnings and hardship to become U.S. presidents. Corporate executives have worked their way up from the sales force and the secretarial pool to become chief executive officers.[36]

- Verizon chief executive officer (CEO) Ivan Seidenberg, the son of an electrical supply shop owner, started his business career as a telephone cable splicer's assistant.[37]
- Oprah Winfrey, born to an unwed teenager and raised on her grandmother's farm in Kosciusko, Mississippi, became a CEO and the richest self-made woman in the United States.[38]
- John Boehner, one of 12 children who worked in and then ran his father's bar, Andy's Café, in Cincinnati, became Speaker of the U.S. House of Representatives.[39]

The path to a leadership position can be as easy as being in the right place at the right time or being the only person willing to take on a difficult job.[40] Although there is no foolproof method, there are ways to improve your chances of becoming a group's leader.

- *Talk early and often (and listen).* The person who speaks first and most often is more likely to emerge as the group's leader.[41] How frequently you talk is even more important than what you say. The quality of your contributions becomes more significant *after* you become a leader.

- *Know more (and share it).* Leaders often are seen as experts. A potential leader can often explain ideas and information more clearly than other group members, and therefore be perceived as knowing more. While groups need well-informed leaders, they do not need know-it-alls who see their own comments as most important; effective leaders value everyone's contributions.

> The strategies for becoming a leader are *not* necessarily the same strategies for successful leadership.

- *Offer your opinion (and welcome disagreement).* Groups appreciate someone who offers valuable ideas and informed opinions. However, this is not the same as having your ideas accepted without question. If you are unwilling to compromise or listen to alternatives, the group may be unwilling to follow you. Effective leaders welcome constructive disagreement and discourage hostile confrontations.

After you become a leader, you may find it necessary to listen more than talk, welcome and reward better-informed members, and strongly criticize the opinions of others. Your focus should shift from *becoming* the leader to *serving* the group you lead.

Vice presidential candidate Sarah Palin talked a lot, claimed expertise, and expressed strong opinions. However, her credibility eroded when she seemed unwilling to listen and engaged in confrontations with opponents and the media. After the election, her poll numbers among Republicans dropped significantly.[42]

The 5-M Model of Leadership Effectiveness

Which communication strategies and skills characterize effective leadership?

As noted in the last section, thousands of books and articles have been published about leadership. To help you understand contributions made by these many approaches, we offer the **5-M Model of Leadership Effectiveness**,[43] an integrated model of leadership effectiveness that emphasizes specific communication strategies and skills and identifies five interdependent leadership functions: modeling, motivating, managing, making decisions, and mentoring.

Model Leadership Behavior

Model leaders project an image of confidence, competence, and trustworthiness. Model leaders publicly champion the group and its goals rather than their personal accomplishments and ego needs. They speak and listen effectively, behave consistently and assertively, confront problems head-on, and work to find solutions.

Motivate Members

Motivating others is a critical task for leaders. Effective leaders guide, develop, support, defend, and inspire group members. They develop relationships that meet the personal needs and expectations of followers. Motivational strategies include supporting and rewarding deserving members, helping members solve interpersonal problems, and adapting tasks and assignments to member abilities and expectations. Most important of all, motivating leaders give members the authority to make judgments about doing the group's work.

Mike Krzyzewski (Coach K), the highly successful men's basketball coach at Duke University, believes that motivating team members is the key to his success. "As a coach, leader, and teacher, my primary task is motivation. How do I get a group motivated, not only to be their individual best but also to become better as a team?"[44]

Manage Group Processes

From the perspective of group survival, managing group processes may be the most important function of leadership.[45] If a group is disorganized, lacks sufficient information to solve problems, or is unable to make important decisions when necessary, the group cannot be effective. Effective leaders are well organized and fully prepared for all group meetings and work sessions. They adapt to member strengths and weaknesses and help solve task-related and procedural problems. They also know when to monitor and intervene to improve group performance.

Make Decisions

An effective leader is willing and able to make appropriate, timely, and responsible decisions. When you assume or are appointed to a leadership role, you should accept the fact that some of your decisions may be unpopular, and some may even turn out to be wrong. But you still have to make them. It's often better for a group leader to make a bad decision than no decision at all, "for if you are seen as chronically indecisive, people won't let you lead them."[46]

In "Building the 21st Century Leader," Carol Tice reviews the evolution of corporate leadership, claiming that today's leaders must be able to do *both*—collaborate with others *and* be decisive.[47]

Several strategies can help a leader make decisions that help a group achieve its goal. First, make sure everyone has and shares the information needed to make a quality decision. If appropriate, discuss your pending decision and solicit feedback from members. Listen to members' opinions, arguments, and suggestions *before* making a

> **"The desire to reach consensus or get buy-in from all parties has to be curtailed at some point, and the leader has to** make a decision."[48]
>
> —Carol Tice

Model leadership behavior
Pope John Paul II

Motivate members
Martin Luther King, Jr.

Manage group processes
Nancy Pelosi

Make decisions
John F. Kennedy

Mentor members
Hillary Clinton

decision. When you make a decision, explain your reasons for doing so and communicate your decision to everyone.

Effective leaders intervene and tell members what to do when a group lacks the confidence, willingness, or ability to make decisions. However, when group members are confident, willing, and skilled, a leader can usually turn full responsibility over to the group and focus on helping members implement the group's decision.

Mentor Members

Good leaders are very busy people, particularly if they model leadership, motivate members, manage group process, and make decisions. Even so, great leaders find the time and energy to mentor others. They know that good mentoring does more than teach someone how to do a job—it also motivates that person to set high standards, seek advice when needed, and develop the skills characteristic of an excellent leader. In his book *Great Leadership*, Anthony Bell urges would-be leaders to find a mentor because a good "mentor will challenge you to ask (and answer) the tough questions."[49]

The following strategies can help a leader decide when and how to mentor group members:

1. *Be ready and willing to mentor every group member.* Although you cannot be a full-time mentor for everyone, you should be open to requests for advice. Eventually, you may develop a close relationship with a few mentees (that is, the people being mentored) who share your vision.

2. *Encourage and invite others to lead.* Look for situations in which group members can assume leadership responsibilities. Ask them to chair a meeting, take full responsibility for a group project, or implement a group's decision. And make sure they know you're there as backup.

3. *Inspire optimism.* When problems or setbacks occur, do not blame the group or its members. Instead, convert the situation into a teachable moment and make sure members learn to accept personal responsibility for a problem and its consequences.[50]

4. Effective mentors create appropriate balance and boundaries. They know when to intervene and when to back off. A mentor is neither a psychiatric counselor nor a group member's best friend. At some point, even the best mentors must let their mentees succeed or fail on their own.

COMMUNICATION&CULTURE

DIVERSITY AND LEADERSHIP

In the early studies of leadership, there was an unwritten but additional prerequisite for becoming a leader: be a man. Despite the achievements of exceptional female leaders, some people still question the ability of women to serve in leadership positions.

A summary of the research on leadership and gender concludes that "women are still less likely to be preselected as leaders, and the same leadership behavior is often evaluated more positively when attributed to a male than a female."[51]

Developing a leadership style is a challenge for most young managers but particularly for young women. If their behavior is similar to that of male leaders, they are perceived as unfeminine, but if they act "like a lady," they are viewed as weak or ineffective. One professional woman described this dilemma as follows:

I was thrilled when my boss evaluated me as "articulate, hard-working, mature in her judgment, and a skillful diplomat." What disturbed me were some of the evaluation comments from those I supervise or work with as colleagues. Although they had a lot of good things to say, a few of them described me as "pushy," "brusque," "impatient," "disregards social niceties," and "hard driving." What am I supposed to do? My boss thinks I'm energetic and creative while other people see the same behavior as pushy and aggressive.

Cultural differences also affect whether members become and succeed as leaders. For example, individualistic Western cultures (United States, Australia, Great Britain) assume that members are motivated by personal growth and achievement. However, a collectivist member might desire a close relationship with the leader and other group members rather than personal gain or growth. The same member may act out of loyalty to the leader and the group rather than for personal achievement or material gain.[52]

Group Member Participation and Leadership Evaluation

Evaluate the quantity and quality of participation by the members of a group to which you belong or have belonged by circling the number that describes its performance.

1. *Task Functions.* Members provide or ask for information and opinions, initiate discussion, clarify, summarize, evaluate, energize, and so on.

5	4	3	2	1
Excellent		Average		Poor

2. *Maintenance Functions.* One or more members serve as encourager, harmonizer, compromiser, tension releaser, gatekeeper, standard monitor, observer, follower, and so on.

5	4	3	2	1
Excellent		Average		Poor

3. *Group Processes.* Members avoid disruptive behavior, follow the agenda, adapt to group development stages and group norms, and so on.

5	4	3	2	1
Excellent		Average		Poor

4. *Manage Difficulties.* Members are ready, willing, and able to deal with difficult behavior and overall group problems.

5	4	3	2	1
Excellent		Average		Poor

5. *Leadership.* One or more members model leadership behavior, motivate others, help manage group processes, and make necessary decisions.

5	4	3	2	1
Excellent		Average		Poor

6. **Group's Overall Effectiveness**.

5	4	3	2	1
Excellent		Average		Poor

10.1
The Challenges of Working in Groups

What are the pros and cons of working in groups?

- Group communication refers to the interaction of three or more interdependent people working to achieve a common goal.
- In general, the advantages of working in groups far outweigh the disadvantages.
- Groups differ in terms of whether they are meeting personal goals, work goals, or public goals.
- Bruce Tuckman's Group Development stages include forming, storming, norming, and performing.

10.2
Balancing Individual and Group Goals

How can you balance individual and group needs in groups?

- During the forming stage of group development, most groups experience primary tension, the social unease and inhibitions that accompany the getting-acquainted period in a new group.
- Hidden agendas occur when a member's private goals conflict with the group's goals.

10.3
Balancing Conflict and Cohesion

How can you balance conflict and cohesiveness in groups?

- During the storming stage of group development, groups must resolve secondary tensions and personality conflicts in order to achieve cohesion.
- Cohesive groups share a sense of teamwork and pride.

10.4
Balancing Conformity and Nonconformity

How can you balance conformity and nonconformity in groups?

- Whereas constructive nonconformity is appropriate and helps a group achieve its goal, destructive nonconformity has no regard for the best interests of the group and its goal.

10.5
Balancing Task and Maintenance Roles

How can you balance task and maintenance roles in groups?

- Group task roles help a group achieve its goals. Group maintenance roles affect how group members get along.
- Self-centered roles adversely affect task and social goals.

10.6
Developing Group Leadership

What are the characteristics of a successful group leader?

- Leadership is the ability to make strategic decisions and use communication to mobilize group members toward achieving a common goal.

- The Trait Theory of Leadership identifies individual leadership characteristics.
- The Styles Theory of Leadership examines autocratic, democratic, and laissez-faire leadership.
- Situational Leadership Theory seeks an ideal fit between a leader's style and the leadership situation.

10.7
The 5-M Model of Leadership Effectiveness

Which communication strategies and skills characterize effective leadership?

- The 5-M Model of Leadership Effectiveness identifies five critical leadership tasks: (1) model leadership behavior, (2) motivate members, (3) manage group processes, (4) make decisions, and (5) mentor members.
- People become leaders by talking more, knowing more, and offering their opinions.
- Female and nonmajority group members are less likely to be preselected as leaders and are often evaluated less positively than are male leaders.

MySearchLab®

TEST YOUR KNOWLEDGE

10.1 What are the pros and cons of working in groups?

1 The ideal size for a problem-solving group is _____ members.
   a. 2–4
   b. 3–5
   c. 5–7
   d. 7–12
   e. 12–15

2 Which of the following best describes a forum?
   a. Several people interact about a common topic in front of an audience.
   b. Group members present short, uninterrupted presentations on different aspects of a topic for the benefit of an audience.
   c. Audience members comment or ask questions to a speaker or group of speakers.
   d. Elected officials and governing boards of public agencies conduct their meetings in public.
   e. None of the above is an example of a forum.

10.2 How can you balance individual and group needs in groups?

3 Which is the correct order for Tuckman's group development stages?
   a. Forming, storming, norming, performing
   b. Storming, forming, performing, norming
   c. Forming, norming, storming, performing
   d. Norming, forming, performing, storming
   e. Performing, norming, storming, forming

10.3 How can you balance conflict and cohesiveness in groups?

4 Which of the following is the best depiction of secondary tension in groups?
   a. The group resolves conflicts and establishes norms.
   b. The frustrations and conflicts experienced by group members as they compete for status, acceptance, and achievement.
   c. The social unease and inhibitions that accompany the getting-acquainted period in a new group.
   d. The social unease and inhibitions that accompany the process of competing for status, acceptance, and achievement in groups.
   e. The process during which group decisions are reached, problems are solved, and plans are implemented.

10.4 How can you balance conformity and nonconformity in groups?

5 Which answer best completes the following statement: Nonconformity _____
   a. will always undermine group performance.
   b. can improve group performance.
   c. occurs only when stubborn members are present.
   d. occurs under poor leadership.
   e. occurs only in the storming stage.

10.5 How can you balance task and maintenance roles in groups?

6 Which of the following represents a group task role?
   a. Tension releaser
   b. Compromiser
   c. Gatekeeper
   d. Encourager/supporter
   e. Clarifier/summarizer

7 Which of the following represents a self-centered group role?
   a. Evaluator/critic
   b. Opinion giver
   c. Gatekeeper
   d. Confessor
   e. Follower

10.6 What are the characteristics of a successful group leader?

8 Which leadership theory or model can be summarized as "either you have it or you don't"?
   a. Trait Theory
   b. Styles Theory
   c. Situational Theory
   d. The 5-M Model of Leadership
   e. The Styles and Situational Theories

9 According to Situational Leadership Theory, which style of leadership is most appropriate when a leader has poor leader–member relations, a highly organized task, and little or no power or control?
   a. A laissez-faire leader
   b. A task-motivated leader
   c. A democratic leader
   d. A relationship-motivated leader
   e. An autocratic leader

10.7 Which communication strategies and skills characterize effective leadership?

10 Which of the following strategies is most likely to help you *become* a leader?
   a. Talk early
   b. Talk often
   c. Know more
   d. Offer your opinion
   e. All of the above

Answers found on page 366.

Key Terms

Autocratic leader	Hidden agenda	Situational Leadership
Cohesion	Laissez-faire leader	Theory
Committee	Leader–member	Storming stage
Constructive	relations	Styles Theory of
nonconformity	Leadership	Leadership
Democratic leader	Maintenance role	Symposium
Destructive	Norming stage	Task-motivated leader
nonconformity	Norms	Task role
5-M Model of Leadership	Panel discussion	Task structure
Forming stage	Performing stage	Trait Theory of
Forum	Primary tension	Leadership
Governance group	Public group	Virtual group
Group communication	Relationship-motivated	Work group
Group Development	leader	Work team
Model	Secondary tension	
Group role	Self-centered role	

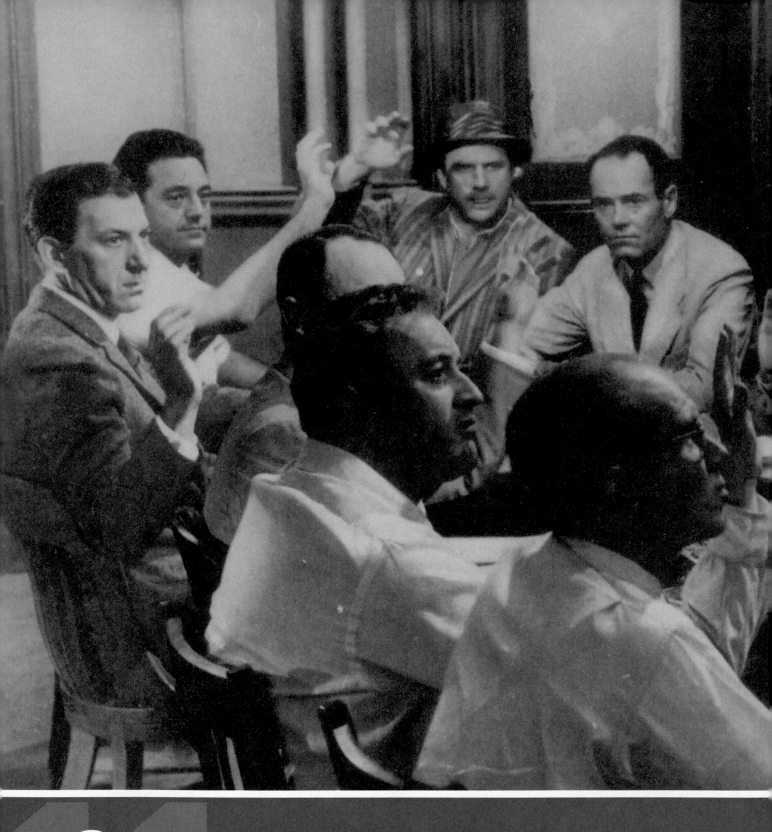

Group
DECISION MAKING and
PROBLEM SOLVING

11

The classic 1957 film *12 Angry Men* is a story about decision making and problem solving.[1] Twelve jurors (all male, mostly middle aged, white, and generally of middle-class status) must reach a verdict in a seemingly open-and-shut murder trial. The film examines how the jurors' deep-seated prejudices, flawed judgments, cultural differences, ignorance, and fears taint their decision-making abilities, cause them to ignore the real issues in the case, and potentially lead them to a miscarriage of justice. Fortunately, one brave dissenting juror votes "not guilty" because of his reasonable doubt. Persistently and persuasively, he compels the other men to slowly reconsider and review the shaky case.[2]

In all likelihood, you have been or will be called for jury duty. Like the characters in *12 Angry Men*, you will have to make a decision—guilty or not guilty, liable or not liable, severe or light sentence. The fairness of that decision will rely, in large part, on how well jury members communicate with one another and how well they employ critical thinking skills. Clearly, there is a world of difference between making any decision and making a good decision.[3]

THINK About... and ASK YOURSELF...

11.1 **Prerequisites for Group Decision Making and Problem Solving** | *What prerequisites help groups make good decisions and solve problems?*

11.2 **Effective Group Decision Making** | *What are the advantages and disadvantages of various decision-making methods?*

11.3 **Effective Group Problem Solving** | *Which problem-solving procedures help groups achieve their goals?*

11.4 **Effective Group Meetings** | *How should you plan and conduct an effective group meeting?*

Prerequisites for Group Decision Making and Problem Solving

What prerequisites help groups make good decisions and solve problems?

You make hundreds of decisions every day. You decide when to get up in the morning, what to wear, when to leave for class or work, and with whom to spend your leisure time. Many factors influence how you make these decisions—your culture, age, family, education, social status, and religion, as well as your dreams, fears, beliefs, values, interpersonal needs, and personal preferences.[4] Now take five people, put them in a room, and ask them to make a *group* decision. As difficult as it can be to make personal decisions, the challenge is multiplied many times over in groups.

Fortunately and in large part because of the many differences among members, effective groups have the potential to make excellent decisions because more minds are at work on the problem. As we noted in Chapter 10, groups have the potential to accomplish more and perform better than individuals working alone. So, while the road may be paved with challenges, group decision making and problem solving can be more satisfying, creative, and effective.

Although the terms *decision making* and *problem solving* are often used interchangeably, their meanings differ. **Decision making** refers to making a judgment, reaching a conclusion, or making up your mind. In a group setting, decision making results in a position, opinion, judgment, or action. For example, hiring committees, juries, and families decide which applicant is best, whether the accused is guilty, and whom they should invite to the wedding, respectively. Management expert Peter Drucker put it simply: "A decision is a judgment. It is a choice between alternatives."[5]

Most groups make decisions, but not all groups solve problems. **Problem solving** is a complex *process* in which groups make *multiple* decisions as they analyze a problem and develop a plan for solving the problem

> As difficult as it can be to make personal decisions, the challenge is multiplied many times over in groups.

or reducing its harmful effects. For instance, if student enrollment has significantly declined, a college faces a serious problem that must be analyzed and dealt with if the institution hopes to survive. Fortunately, there are decision-making and problem-solving strategies that can help a group "make up its mind" and resolve a problem.

However, before a group takes on such challenges, three prerequisites should be in place: a clear goal, quality content, and structured procedures.

A Clear Goal

The first and most important task for all groups is to make sure that everyone understands and supports the group's goal. One strategy to achieve this is to word the goal as a question.

In Chapter 4, we discussed the importance of critical thinking and how identifying claims of fact, conjecture, value, and policy helps you decide whether you should accept, reject, or suspend judgment about an idea, belief, or proposal. Groups face the same challenge when framing a discussion question.

A group may ask four types of questions to achieve its goal. **Questions of fact** investigate the truth, reliability, and cause of something using the best information available. **Questions of conjecture** examine the possibility of something happening in the future using valid facts and expert opinions to reach the most probable conclusion. **Questions of value** consider the worth or significance of something, and **questions of policy** investigate a course of action for implementing a plan.

Group members understand that the answers to each type of question will shape the discussions that ensue. In some group contexts, the questions are dictated by an outside group or authority. For example, a work group may be asked to find timesaving ways to process an order or contact a customer. A research group may be asked to test the durability of a new product.

STOP&THINK

Can You Identify the Question Type?

Each of the following examples represents a question members might address while trying to make a group decision. Identify the type of question (fact, conjecture, value, or policy).

1. What causes global warming?
2. Are community colleges a better place than a prestigious university to begin higher education?
3. Will company sales increase next quarter?
4. Which candidate should we support for president of the student government association?

Quality Content

Well-informed groups are more likely to make good decisions. The amount and accuracy of information available to a group are critical factors in predicting its success.

The key to becoming a well-informed group lies in the ability of members to collect, share, and analyze the information needed to achieve the group's goal. When a group lacks relevant and valid information, effective decision making and problem solving become difficult, even impossible. During an initial meeting, a group should discuss how to become better informed.

> "The ability of a group to gather and retain a wide range of information is the single most important determinant of high-quality decision making."[6]
>
> —Randy Hirokawa, group communication scholar

"Tribe" members on Survivor make strategic group decisions in order to win a team "challenge."

GROUP RESEARCH STRATEGIES

- Assess the group's current knowledge.
- Identify areas needing research.
- Assign research responsibilities.
- Set research deadlines.
- Determine how to share information effectively.

Structured Procedures

Groups need clear procedures that specify how they will make decisions and solve problems. Group communication scholar Marshall Scott Poole claims that structured procedures are "the heart of group work [and] the most powerful tools we have to improve the conduct of meetings."[7]

There are, however, many different kinds of procedures, including complex, theory-based problem-solving models designed to tackle the overall problem as well as decision-making methods designed for interim tasks such as idea generation and solution implementation. The next few sections of this chapter describe how various procedures can and should be used to improve group decision making and problem solving.

11.2

Effective Group Decision Making

What are the advantages and disadvantages of various decision-making methods?

All groups make decisions. Some decisions are simple and easy; others are complex and consequential. Regardless of the issue, effective groups look for the best way to reach a decision, one that considers the group's common goal and the characteristics and preferences of its members.

Decision-Making Methods

Although there are many ways to make decisions, certain methods work best for groups. Groups can let the majority have its way by voting, strive to reach consensus, or leave the final decision to a person in a position of authority. Each approach has its strengths, and an appropriate approach should be selected to match the needs and purpose of the group and its task.

Voting When a quick decision is needed, there is nothing more efficient and decisive than voting. Sometimes, though, voting may not be the best way to make important decisions. When a group votes, some members win, but others lose.

A **majority vote** requires that more than half the members vote in favor of a proposal. However, if a group is making a major decision, there may not be enough support if only 51 percent of the members vote in favor of

VOTING WORKS BEST WHEN . . .

- a group is pressed for time.
- the issue is not highly controversial.
- a group is too large to use any other decision-making method.
- there is no other way to break a deadlock.
- a group's constitution or rules require voting to make decisions.

FACTS **THINK** ABOUT THEORY
TEST IDEA PLAN EXPERIMENT METHOD

Groupthink

In his book *Group Genius,* Keith Sawyer retells a story about a group of 12 heavy smokers who signed up for a stop-smoking group at a local health clinic. One heavy smoker revealed that he had stopped smoking right after joining the group. His comment infuriated the other 11 members. They ganged up on him so fiercely that at the beginning of the next meeting, he announced that he'd gone back to smoking two packs a day. The entire group cheered. "Keep in mind," writes Sawyer, "that the whole point of the group was to reduce smoking!"[8]

What happened in the stop-smoking group is not unusual. Although conforming to group norms and promoting group cohesiveness benefit groups in many ways, too much of either is a bad thing. They can result in a phenomenon that Yale University psychologist Irving Janis identified as **groupthink**—the deterioration of group effectiveness as a consequence of in-group pressure.[9] It is "a mode of thinking that people engage in when they are deeply involved in a cohesive in-group, when the members' striving for unanimity overrides their motivation to realistically appraise alternative courses of action."[10]

> Groupthink stifles the free flow of information, suppresses constructive disagreement, and erects nearly impenetrable barriers to effective decision making and problem solving.

Janis's groupthink theory focuses on patterns of behavior in policy-making fiascos, such as the failed Bay of Pigs invasion in Cuba, decision errors during the Korean and Vietnam wars, the tragic *Challenger* space shuttle disaster, and the decision to invade Iraq in 2003, to name a few.

Groupthink tends to occur when one or more of three preconditions or causes are present in a group:

- The group is highly cohesive. Members overestimate their competence and perceptions of rightness. In order to maintain cohesiveness, the group may discourage disagreement in order to achieve total consensus.
- Structural flaws in the group process can "inhibit the flow of information and promote carelessness in the application of decision-making procedures."[12] For example, a leader or member may have too much influence, or the group's procedures may limit access to outside or contrary information.
- The situation is volatile. When a group must make a high-stakes decision, stress levels are high. Members may rush to make a decision that turns out to be flawed, and they may shut out other reasonable options.

Fortunately, there are ways to minimize the potential for groupthink. Every member should assume the role of critical evaluator and should ask questions, offer reasons for their positions, express disagreement, and evaluate one another's ideas.

Consider inviting an expert to your meeting and encourage constructive criticism. If nothing else, the group should discuss the potential negative consequences of any decision or action. Finally, before finalizing a decision, give members a second chance to express any lingering doubts.

Effective groups avoid groupthink by spending time and energy working through differences without sacrificing group cohesiveness in pursuit of responsible decisions. As an added and positive consequence, taking such "steps to minimize groupthink can turn a dysfunctional group into a highly competent one."[13]

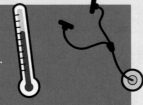

SYMPTOMS of Groupthink[11]

Irving Janis identified eight symptoms of groupthink. Each one can cause or be an indicator of flawed decision making.

SYMPTOMS	DESCRIPTION	EXAMPLE
Invulnerability	Group is overconfident; willing to take big risks	"We're right. We've done this before and nothing's gone wrong."
Rationalization	Group makes excuses; discounts warnings	"What does he know? He's only been here three weeks."
Morality	Group ignores ethical and moral consequences	"Sometimes the end justifies the means. Only results count."
Stereotyping Outsiders	Members believe opponents are too weak or unintelligent to make trouble	"Let's not worry about them—they can't get their act together."
Self-Censorship	Members doubt their own reservations; are unwilling to disagree	"I guess it's okay if I'm the only one who disagrees."
Pressure on Dissent	Members are pressured to agree	"Why are you holding this up? You'll ruin the project."
Illusion of Unanimity	Group believes that everyone agrees	"Hearing no objections, the motion passes."
Mindguarding	Group shields members from adverse information or opposition	"Tamela wanted to come to this meeting, but I told her that it wasn't necessary."

A decision-making group in action: The Senate Judiciary Committee discusses candidacy and confirmation of Judge Sonia Sotomayor as a member of the U.S. Supreme Court.

When a group votes, some members win, but others lose.

the project because the 49 percent who lose may resent working on a project they dislike. To avoid such problems, some groups opt for a two-thirds vote rather than majority rule. In a **two-thirds vote**, at least twice as many group members vote for a proposal as against it.

Consensus Because voting has built-in disadvantages, many groups rely on consensus to make decisions. **Consensus** is reached when "all members have a part in shaping and that all find at least minimally acceptable as a means of accomplishing some mutual goals."[14] Consensus does not work for all groups. Imagine how difficult it would be to achieve genuine consensus among pro-life and pro-choice or pro–gun control and anti–gun control group members. If your group seeks consensus when making decisions, follow the guidelines below.

Before choosing consensus as a decision-making method, make sure that group members trust one another and expect honesty, directness, and candor. Avoid rushing to achieve consensus—make sure that everyone's opinion is heard. Finally, be wary of a dominant leader or member who may make true consensus impossible. Sociologists Rodney Napier and Matti Gershenfeld put it this way: "A group that wants to use a consensual approach to decision making must be willing to develop the skills and discipline to take the time necessary to make it work. Without these, the group becomes highly vulnerable to domination or intimidation by a few and to psychological game playing by individuals unwilling to 'let go.'"[15]

Authority Rule Sometimes a single person or someone outside the group makes the final decision. When **authority rule** is used, groups may be asked to gather information for and recommend decisions to another person or larger group. For example, an association's nominating committee considers potential candidates and recommends a slate of officers to the association. Or a hiring committee screens dozens of job applications and submits a top-three list to the person or persons making the hiring decision.

If a leader or outside authority ignores or reverses group recommendations, members may become demoralized, resentful, and unproductive on future assignments. Even within a group, a strong leader or authority figure may use a group and its members to give the appearance of collaborative decision making. The group thus becomes a "rubber stamp" and surrenders its will to authority rule. Group scholars Randy Hirokawa and Roger Pace warn that "influential members [can] convince the group to accept invalid facts and assumptions, introduce poor ideas and suggestions, lead the group to misinterpret information presented to them, or lead the group off on tangents and irrelevant discussion."[16]

Guidelines for
ACHIEVING GROUP CONSENSUS

DO THIS:

- Listen carefully to and respect other members' points of view.
- Try to be logical rather than emotional.
- If there is a deadlock, work to find the next best alternative that is acceptable to all.
- Make sure that members not only agree but also will be committed to the final decision.
- Get everyone involved in the discussion.
- Welcome differences of opinion.

DON'T DO THIS:

- Don't be stubborn and argue only for your own position.
- Don't change your mind to avoid conflict or reach a quick decision.
- Don't give in, especially if you have a crucial piece of information to share.
- Don't agree to a decision or solution you can't possibly support.
- Don't use "easy" or arbitrary ways to reach a solution such as flipping a coin, letting the majority rule, or trading one decision for another.

STOP&THINK

Is There Consensus About Consensus?

Many groups fall short of achieving their common goals because they have complete faith in the virtues of achieving consensus. As a result, they believe the group *must* reach consensus on *all* decisions. The problem of false consensus haunts every decision-making group. **False consensus** occurs when members reluctantly give in to group pressures or an external authority. Rather than achieving consensus, the group agrees to a decision masquerading as consensus.[17]

In addition, the all-or-nothing approach to consensus "gives each member veto power over the progress of the whole group." In order to avoid impasse, members may "give up and give in" or seek a flawed compromise. This is much like the "illusion of unanimity" symptom of groupthink; members work hard to achieve total agreement even though the outcome may be a flawed decision. When this happens, the group will fall short of success as "it mindlessly pursues 100% agreement."[18]

In *The Discipline of Teams*, John Katzenbach and Douglas Smith observe that members who pursue complete consensus often act as though disagreement and conflict are bad for the group. Nothing, they claim, could be further from the reality of effective group performance. "Without disagreement, teams rarely generate the best, most creative solutions to the challenges at hand. They compromise . . . rather than developing a solution that incorporates the best of two or more opposing views. . . . The challenge for teams is to learn from disagreement and find energy in constructive conflict, not get ruined by it."[19]

The limited time and format of the television show *Top Chef* requires judges to reach consensus—even if it's false consensus.

One powerful but misguided member can be responsible for the poor quality of a group's decision.

Decision-Making Styles

In Chapter 8, we described the Myers-Briggs Type Indicator. Two traits—thinking and feeling—focus on how we make decisions. Thinkers are task-oriented members who prefer to use logic in making decisions. Feelers, on the other hand, are people-oriented members who want everyone to get along, even if it means spending more time on a task or giving in to some members to avoid interpersonal problems. Each type of decision making impacts a group's choice of decision-making methods and their outcomes.

In "Decision Making Style: The Development of a New Measure," Suzanne Scott and Reginald Bruce describe five decision-making styles, each of which has the potential to improve or impair member interaction and group outcomes.[20]

Rational decision makers carefully weigh information and options before making a decision. They claim, "I've carefully considered all the issues," and make decisions systematically using logical reasoning to justify their final decisions. This type

ETHICAL COMMUNICATION

Ethical Group Decision Making

Regardless of how contentious the discussion or controversial an issue, group members should always apply ethical standards to decision making. These standards include the following ethical responsibilities:[21]

1. **Research.** Group members are well informed and use what they know honestly.
   - Do not distort, suppress, or make up information.
   - Reveal the sources of information so others can evaluate them.

2. **Common Good.** Ethical group members are committed to achieving the group goal rather than winning a personal argument.
   - Consider the interests of those affected by group decisions.
   - Promote the group's goal ahead of personal goals.

3. **Reasoning.** Ethical group members avoid presenting faulty arguments; they build valid arguments and recognize fallacies.
   - Do not misrepresent the views of others.
   - Use sound critical thinking supported by evidence.
   - Avoid making fallacious arguments.

4. **The Social Code.** Group members promote an open, supportive, and group-centered climate for discussion.
   - Treat other group members as equals.
   - Do not insult or attack the character of group members.
   - Respect established group norms.

of person must be careful not to analyze a problem for so long that she or he never makes a decision. **Intuitive decision makers**, on the other hand, make decisions based on instincts, feelings, or hunches. They tend to say, "It just feels like the right thing to do." They may not always be able to explain the reasons for their decisions but know that their decisions "feel" right.

Dependent decision makers solicit the advice and opinions of others before making a decision: "If you think it's okay, then I'll do it." They feel uncomfortable making decisions that others disapprove of or oppose. They may even make a decision they aren't happy with just to please others. **Avoidant decision makers** feel uncomfortable making decisions. As a result, they may not think about a problem at all or will make a final decision at the very last minute: "I just can't deal with this right now." **Spontaneous decision makers** tend to be impulsive and make quick decisions on the spur of the moment: "Let's do it now and worry about the consequences later." As a result, they often make decisions they later regret.

Now consider what would happen if you had a group where half the members were rational decision makers and the other half were intuitive decision makers. Or what would happen if the group included *only* dependent or avoidant decision makers? Different decision-making styles can disrupt a group, but having only one type also has its pitfalls. The key is learning to recognize and adapt to different decision-making styles while pursuing a common goal.

Know Thy Self

What Is Your Decision-Making Style?[22]

Indicate the degree to which you agree or disagree with each of the statements below by circling the appropriate number: (1) strongly disagree, (2) disagree, (3) undecided (neither agree nor disagree), (4) agree, or (5) strongly agree. There are no right or wrong answers; answer as honestly as you can. Think carefully before choosing option 3 (undecided)—it may suggest you cannot make decisions.

1. When I have to make an important decision, I usually seek the opinions of others.	1	2	3	4	5
2. I tend to put off decisions on issues that make me uncomfortable.	1	2	3	4	5
3. I make decisions in a logical and systematic way.	1	2	3	4	5
4. When making a decision, I usually trust feelings or gut instincts.	1	2	3	4	5
5. When making a decision, I generally consider the advantages and disadvantages of many alternatives.	1	2	3	4	5
6. I often avoid making important decisions until I absolutely have to.	1	2	3	4	5
7. I often make impulsive decisions.	1	2	3	4	5
8. When making a decision, I rely on my instincts.	1	2	3	4	5
9. It is easier for me to make important decisions when I know others approve or support them.	1	2	3	4	5
10. I make decisions very quickly.	1	2	3	4	5

Scoring: To determine your score for each type of decision making, add the total of your responses to specific items as indicated below. Your higher scores identify your preferred decision-making styles.

Answers to items 3 and 5 = _____ (rational decision maker)
Answers to items 4 and 8 = _____ (intuitive decision maker)
Answers to items 1 and 9 = _____ (dependent decision maker)
Answers to items 2 and 6 = _____ (avoidant decision maker)
Answers to items 7 and 10 = _____ (spontaneous decision maker)

11.3
Effective Group Problem Solving

Which problem-solving procedures can groups use to achieve their goals?

Although there are several problem-solving methods, there is no "best" model or magic formula that ensures effective problem solving. However, as groups gain experience and succeed as problem solvers, they learn that some procedures work better than others and that some need modification to suit group needs. Here we present three problem-solving methods: Brainstorming, the Decreasing Options Technique (DOT), and the Standard Agenda.

Brainstorming

In 1953, Alex Osborn introduced the concept of brainstorming in *Applied Imagination*.[23] **Brainstorming**, a fairly simple and popular method, is used for generating as many ideas as possible in a short period of time. It assumes that postponing the evaluation of ideas improves the quality of participants' input. It also assumes that the quantity of ideas breeds quality, based on the notion that creative ideas will come

only after we have gotten the obvious suggestions out.[25] More than 70 percent of businesspeople claim that brainstorming is used in their organizations.[26] Unfortunately, many groups fail to use brainstorming effectively.

Brainstorming is a great way to tackle open-ended, unclear, or broad problems. If you're looking for lots of ideas, it is a very useful technique. But if you need a formal plan of action or you have a critical problem to solve that requires a single "right" answer, you may be better off trying another method.

There are several sure-fire ways to derail a productive brainstorming session.[27] If, for example, leaders or dominant members speak first and at length, they may influence and limit the direction and content of subsequent input and ideas. In an effort to be more democratic, some brainstorming groups require members to speak in turn. However, this approach prevents a group from building momentum and will probably result in fewer ideas. Finally, members who try to write down all of the group's ideas may end up being so focused on note taking that they rarely contribute ideas. It is better to have one person record all the ideas contributed by the group members.

Although many groups use brainstorming, their success depends on the nature of the group and the

Brainstorming Guidelines[24]

Sharpen the focus	• Start with a clear question or statement of the problem. • Give members a few minutes to think about possible ideas before brainstorming begins.
Display ideas for all to see	• Assign someone to write down the group's ideas. • Post the ideas where everyone can see them.
Number the ideas	• Numbering can motivate a group: for example, "Let's try to list 20 or 30 ideas." • Numbering makes it easier to jump back and forth among ideas.
Encourage creativity	• Announce that wild and crazy ideas are welcome. • Announce that quantity is more important than quality.
Emphasize input, prohibit put-downs	• Keep the ideas coming. • Evaluate ideas only *after* brainstorming is over.
Build and jump	• Build on, modify, or combine ideas offered by others to create new ideas.

characteristics of its members. If a group is self-conscious and sensitive to implied criticism, brainstorming can fail. However, if a group is comfortable with such a freewheeling process, brainstorming can enhance creativity and produce numerous ideas and suggestions.

Decreasing Options Technique

The **Decreasing Options Technique (DOT)** helps groups reduce and refine a large number of suggestions and ideas into a manageable set of options.[28] In our work as professional facilitators, we have used this technique to assist small and large groups facing a variety of decision-making tasks, such as creating an ethics credo for a professional association and drafting a vision statement for a college. The DOT method works best when a group needs to sort through a multitude of ideas and options.

Generate Individual Ideas At the beginning of the DOT process, group members generate ideas or suggestions related to a specific topic. Ideas can be single words or full-sentence suggestions. For example, when creating a professional association's ethics credo, participants contributed words such as *honesty*, *respect*, and *truth*.[29]

Post Ideas for All to See Each idea should be written on a separate sheet of thick paper in large, easy-to-read letters—only one idea per page. These pages are posted on the walls of the group's meeting room for all to see and consider. Postings should be

The Decreasing Options Technique (DOT)
✔ **Generate Ideas**   ✔ **Sort Ideas**

✔ **Post Ideas**   ✔ **Prioritize Ideas**

displayed only after all members have finished writing their ideas on separate sheets of paper.

Sort Ideas Not surprisingly, many group members will contribute similar or overlapping ideas. When this happens, sort the ideas and post similar ideas close to one another. For example, when facilitating the development of a college's vision statement, phrases such as *academic excellence*, *quality education*, and *high-quality instruction* were posted near one another. After everyone is comfortable with how the postings are sorted, give a title to each grouping of ideas. In the vision statement session, for instance, the term *quality education* was used as an umbrella phrase for nearly a dozen similar concepts.

Prioritize Ideas At this point, individual members decide which of the displayed ideas are most important: Which words *best* reflect the vision we have for our college? Which concepts *must* be included in our association's ethics credo?

In order to prioritize ideas efficiently, every member receives a limited number of colored sticker dots. They use their stickers to "dot" the most important ideas or options. In our example, each member of the vision statement group was given 10 dots and asked to "dot" the most important concepts from among the 25 phrases posted on the walls. After everyone has finished walking around

the room and posting dots, the most important ideas are usually very apparent. Some ideas will be covered with dots, others will be speckled with only three or four, and some will remain blank. After a brief review of the outcome, the group can eliminate some ideas, decide whether marginal ideas should be included, and end up with a limited and manageable number of options to consider and discuss.

Advantages of the DOT Method When a group generates dozens of ideas, valuable meeting time can be consumed by discussing every idea, regardless of its merit or relevance. The DOT method reduces the quantity of ideas to a manageable number.

Although the examples described focus on face-to-face interaction, the DOT strategy also works very well in virtual settings. A virtual group can follow the same steps by using email or networked software designed for interactive group work.

The Standard Agenda

The founding father of problem-solving procedures is a U.S. philosopher and educator named John Dewey. In 1910, Dewey wrote a book titled *How We Think* in which he described a set of practical steps that a rational person should follow when solving a problem.[30] These guidelines have come to be known as Dewey's *reflective thinking process*.

When to Use the DOT METHOD

- When the group is so large that open discussion of individual ideas is unworkable.
- When a significant number of competing ideas are generated that must be evaluated.
- When members want equal opportunities for input.
- When dominant members do not exert too much influence.
- When there is not enough time to discuss multiple or controversial ideas.

Dewey's step-by-step guidelines have been adapted for group problem solving. They begin with a focus on the problem itself and then moves to a systematic consideration of possible solutions. In this chapter, we offer one version of this process: the **Standard Agenda** involves clarifying the task at hand, understanding and analyzing the problem, assessing possible solutions, and implementing the decision or plan.[31]

Task Clarification: Make Sure That Everyone Understands the Group's Assignment The primary purpose of a group's first meeting is to determine what the group wants or needs to accomplish so that everyone is working to achieve a common goal. During this phase, group members should ask questions about their roles and responsibilities in the problem-solving process.

Problem Identification: Avoid Sending the Group in the Wrong Direction Once a group understands and supports a common goal, members should focus on understanding the problem and developing a set of key questions. Identifying questions of fact, value, conjecture, and/or policy can help focus and aim the group in the right direction.

COMMUNICATION IN *ACTION*

Decision Making and Problem Solving in Virtual Groups

The group decision-making and problem-solving methods in this chapter were designed for face-to-face meetings. These methods also work well in virtual groups using commonly available technology.

Additionally, specialized computer software, or groupware, can facilitate group collaboration, decision making, and problem solving.

Different types of technology, however, are not equally suited to all types of virtual groups. In *Mastering Virtual Teams*, Deborah Duarte and Nancy Tennant Snyder offer a matrix that rates the effectiveness of different types of technology in relation to the goals of a meeting.[32]

In this matrix, *Product Production* refers to a meeting in which group members work on a collaborative project such as analyzing complex data, developing a design, or drafting a policy. Electronic Meeting Systems are used in face-to-face settings and range from electronic voting systems to computer-aided systems in which members use a laptop computer to provide input into a central display screen.[33]

Meeting Selection Matrix for Virtual Groups

Type of Technology	Purpose of Meeting			
	Information Sharing	Discussion and Brainstorming	Decision Making	Product Production
Telephone or Computer Audioconference	Effective	Somewhat effective	Somewhat effective	Not effective
Email	Effective	Somewhat effective	Not effective	Not effective
Bulletin Board, Restricted Blog	Somewhat effective	Somewhat effective	Not effective	Not effective
Videoconference Without Shared Documents	Effective	Somewhat effective	Effective	Not effective
Videoconference with Text and Graphics	Effective	Effective	Effective	Effective
Electronic Meeting System with Audio, Video, and Graphics	Effective	Highly effective	Highly effective	Effective
Collaborative Writing with Audio and Video	Effective	Effective	Somewhat effective	Highly effective

Group experts John Katzenbach and Douglas Smith remind us that "whenever teams gather through groupware to advance, they need to recognize and adjust to key differences between face-to-face and groupware interactions."[34] In short, a virtual group should select the technology that is best suited to its problem-solving method.

Interestingly, virtual groups have the potential to stimulate more ideas and overall productivity with fewer blocking behaviors. Some studies have found that idea generation and consolidation using computers are more productive and satisfying than if done face-to-face.[35] However, most computer-linked groups require more time for task completion, and as a result, group members may become frustrated or bored.

The Seven Basic Steps in the Standard Agenda

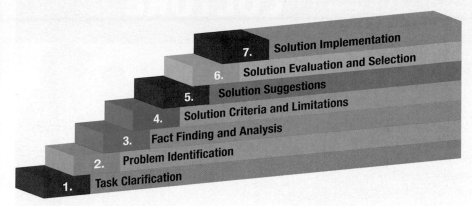

7. Solution Implementation
6. Solution Evaluation and Selection
5. Solution Suggestions
4. Solution Criteria and Limitations
3. Fact Finding and Analysis
2. Problem Identification
1. Task Clarification

Fact-Finding and Analysis: Ask Questions of Fact and Value The following questions require research and critical thinking about the facts, causes, and seriousness of a problem, as well as an analysis of the barriers that prevent a solution:

- What are the facts of the situation?
- What additional information or expert opinion do we need?
- How serious or widespread is the problem?
- What are the causes of the problem?
- What prevents or inhibits us from solving the problem?

Although carefully evaluating facts and opinions is critical to effective problem solving, groups must also avoid analysis paralysis.

Analysis paralysis occurs when groups are so focused on analyzing a problem that they fail to make a decision.[36] "Chances are you've been in [situations where] good ideas have been presented, but by the time enough people consider and reconsider the situation, it seems more complex, or not as great an idea as you originally thought. Or, in most cases, a conclusion about how to act is never reached."[37]

Rather than spending too much time arguing about the issue or giving up on finding the correct answer, a group may have to move on and begin its search for solutions.

Solution Criteria and Limitations: Set Standards for an Ideal Resolution Solution criteria are standards that should be met for an ideal resolution of a problem. A group can establish criteria by asking questions such as: Is the solution reasonable and realistic? Is it affordable? Do we have the staff, resources, and time to implement it? The development of solution criteria should also include an understanding of solution limitations, which may

be financial, institutional, practical, political, and legal in scope.

Solution Suggestions: Consider Multiple Solutions Without Judgment At this point in a group's deliberations, some solutions are probably obvious. Even so, the group should suggest or engage in brainstorming to identify as many solutions as possible without criticizing them. Having spent time analyzing the problem and establishing solution criteria, members should be able to offer numerous solutions.

Solution Evaluation and Selection: Discuss the Pros and Cons of Each Suggestion During this phase, a group should return to the solution criteria and use them to evaluate the strengths and weaknesses of each suggested solution. This stage of the Standard Agenda may be the most difficult and controversial. Discussion may become heated, and disagreements may grow fierce. If, however, the group has been conscientious in analyzing the problem and establishing criteria for solutions, some solutions will be rejected quickly, whereas others will swiftly rise to the top of the list.

Solution Implementation: Decide on a Plan of Action Having made a difficult decision, a group faces one more challenge: How should the decision be implemented? For all the time a group spends trying to solve a problem, it may take even more time organizing the task of implementing the solution. Brilliant solutions can fail if no one takes responsibility or has the authority to implement a group's decision.

11.4

Effective Group Meetings

How can you plan and conduct an effective group meeting?

More than 10 million business meetings occur daily in the United States,[38] and studies show that this is how managers spend 30 to 80 percent of their time.[39] Ninety percent report that half the meetings they attend are "either unnecessary or a complete waste of time."[40] How bad is this problem? The *Business Management Daily* reports that "too many meetings" is the second

biggest employee complaint, with "too much work" being the first.[41] However, when meetings are well planned and conducted, they build strong alliances and confer a sense of control. Members are more motivated to implement group ideas and actions when they have a real voice in the decision-making process.[42]

Before looking at how to plan and conduct a meeting, we should

specify what we mean by the word. A random gathering of people in one place does not constitute a meeting. Rather, a **meeting** is a scheduled gathering of group members for a structured discussion guided by a designated chairperson. The leader designated as a meeting's chairperson has a tremendous amount of influence over and responsibility for its success.

MOTIVATING MULTICULTURAL GROUP MEMBERS

In Chapter 3, we described five cultural dimensions, each of which has implications for motivating group members to fully participate in group decision making and problem solving.

- *Individualism–collectivism.* Individualistic members may need praise and seek public recognition for their personal contributions. Collectivistic members may be embarrassed by public praise and prefer being honored as a member of an outstanding group.

- *High power distance–low power distance.* Members from high-power-distance cultures value recognition by a leader and take pride in following instructions accurately and efficiently. Members from low-power-distance cultures prefer compliments from other group members and enjoy working in a collaborative environment.

- *Masculine–feminine.* Members—both male and female—who hold masculine values are motivated by competition, opportunities for leadership, and tasks that require assertive behavior. Members with more feminine values may be extremely effective and supportive of group goals but have difficulty achieving a respected voice or influence in the group. Such members are motivated by taking on group maintenance roles, such as encourager/supporter, harmonizer, or compromiser.

- *High context–low context.* Group members from high-context cultures do not need to *hear* someone praise their work—they are highly skilled at detecting admiration and approval because they are more sensitive to nonverbal cues. Members from low-context cultures often complain that they never receive praise or rewards when, in fact, other members respect them and value their contributions. Low-context members need to hear words of praise and receive tangible rewards.

- *Monochronic–polychronic.* Members from monochronic cultures are motivated in groups that concentrate their energies on a specific task and meeting deadlines. Members from polychronic cultures often find the single-mindedness of monochronic members stifling rather than motivating. The opportunity to work on multiple tasks with flexible deadlines can motivate polychronic members to work more effectively.

Planning the Meeting

Proper planning largely determines the success or failure of a meeting. To help make your meeting more efficient and effective and to decide whether one is even necessary, ask and answer the five W questions (see the feature on p. 221): Why are we meeting? Who should attend? When should we meet? Where should we meet? and What materials do we need?

Preparing the Agenda

The most important item to prepare and distribute to a group prior to a meeting is an **agenda**, an outline that puts the meeting topics in the order they will be discussed. A well-prepared agenda serves many purposes. First and foremost, the agenda is an organizational tool—a road map for the

> Careful planning can prevent at least 20 minutes of wasted time for each hour of a group's meeting.[43]

discussion that helps a group focus on its task and goal.

In *Meetings: Do's, Don'ts, and Donuts,* Sharon Lippincott uses a simile to explain why a well-planned agenda is essential for conducting effective meetings:

> Starting a meeting without an agenda is like setting out on a journey over unfamiliar roads with no map and only a general idea of the route to your destination. You may get there, but only after lengthy detours.

A good agenda defines the destination of the meeting, draws a map of the most direct route, and provides checkpoints along the way.[44]

When used properly, an agenda identifies what participants should expect and prepare for in a meeting. After a meeting, the agenda can be used to assess a meeting's success by determining the extent to which all items were addressed.

The following guidelines for agenda preparation can improve meeting productivity:

- Note the amount of time it should take to complete a discussion item or action. This lets the group see the relative importance of the item and help to manage the time available for discussion.

5 Ws of Planning a Meeting

Why Are We Meeting? The most important step in planning a meeting is defining its purpose and setting clear goals. Merely asking what a meeting is about only identifies the topic of discussion: "employer-provided day care." Asking why this topic is being discussed will lead you to the purpose: "to determine whether our employer-provided day care system needs to be expanded." Groups should be able to achieve their purpose by the end of a single meeting. However, if this is not possible, the purpose statement should be revised to focus on a more specific outcome. If many cases, a series of meetings are needed to achieve group goals.

Who Should Attend? Most group membership is predetermined. However, if a task requires input only from certain people, you should select only those participants who can make a significant contribution. Invite participants with special expertise, different opinions and approaches, and the power to implement decisions.

When Should We Meet? Seek input and decide on the best day and time for the meeting, as well as when a meeting should begin and end. Schedule the meeting when the most essential and productive members are free.

Where Should We Meet? Choose a location that is appropriate for the purpose and size of the meeting. Do your best to find a comfortable setting, making sure that the meeting room is free of distractions such as ringing phones and noisy conversations. An attractive and quiet meeting location will help your group stay motivated and focused.

What Materials Do We Need? The most important item to prepare and distribute to the group is the meeting's agenda. You may also need to distribute reports or other reading material for review before the meeting. Distribute all materials far enough in advance of the meeting so that everyone has time to prepare. In addition, make sure that supplies and equipment such as pens, paper, or computers and screens are available.

- Identify how the group will deal with each item. Will the group share information, discuss an issue, and/or make a decision? Consider putting the phrases *For Information*, *For Discussion*, and *For Decision* next to appropriate agenda items.
- Include the names of members responsible for reporting information on a particular item or facilitating a portion of the discussion. Such assignments remind members to prepare for participation.

After selecting the agenda items, carefully consider the order for discussing each topic. When a group must discuss several topics during a single meeting, put them in an order

> An agenda . . . is a road map for the discussion that helps a group focus on its task and goal.

SAMPLE AGENDAS

Sample Meeting Agenda

Complex III
987 So. Highland Street
Homegrown, USA 01234

"A" is for Apple
Produce Company

(777) 555-4119
cservice@aisforapple.com
www.aisforapple.com

RECYCLING TASK FORCE

Date: November 20th
Time: 1:00–3:00 pm
Place: Conference Room 352

Purpose: To recommend ways to increase the effectiveness of
and participation in the company's recycling program.

  I. What is the goal of this meeting? What have we been asked to do?

  II. How effective is the company's current recycling effort?

  III. Why has the program lacked effectiveness and full participation?

  IV. What are the requirements or standards for an ideal program?
    A. Level of participation
    B. Reasonable cost
    C. Physical requirements
    D. Legal requirements

  V. What are the possible ways in which we could improve the
recycling program?

  VI. What specific methods do we recommend for increasing the
recycling program's effectiveness?

  VII. How should the recommendations be implemented?
Who or what groups should be charged with implementation?

~ America's Oldest Producer of Quality Fruits and Vegetables ~

Sample discussion agenda for a group examining a specific issue: ways to improve a company's recycling program.

Standard Business Agenda

Complex III
987 So. Highland Street
Homegrown, USA 01234

"A" is for Apple
Produce Company

(777) 555-4119
cservice@aisforapple.com
www.aisforapple.com

AGENDA

Date: September 15th
Time: 12:30–3:45 pm
Place: Presidential Ballroom

  I. Call to order by president

  II. Approval of minutes and agenda

  III. Reports by officers and committees

  IV. Unfinished business

  V. New business

  VI. Announcements

  VII. Adjournment

~ America's Oldest Producer of Quality Fruits and Vegetables ~

Basic components of a standard business agenda that follows a traditional format for formal business meetings.

effective group meetings

that will maximize productivity and group satisfaction:

- Begin the meeting with simple business items and easy-to-discuss issues.
- Reserve important and difficult items for the middle portion of the meeting.
- Use the last third of the meeting for easy discussion items that do not require difficult decisions.

Taking Minutes

Most business and professional meetings require or benefit from a record of group progress and decision making. Responsible group leaders assign the important task of taking **minutes**—the written record of a group's discussion and activities—to a recorder, secretary, or a volunteer. The minutes cover discussion issues and decisions for those who attend the meeting and provide a way to communicate with those who do not attend. Most important, minutes help prevent disagreement about what was said or decided in a meeting and what tasks

individual members agreed to or were assigned to do.

Well-prepared minutes are brief and accurate. They are not a word-for-word record of everything that members say. Instead, they summarize arguments, key ideas, actions, and votes. Immediately after a meeting, minutes should be prepared for distribution to group members. The longer the delay, the more difficult it will be for members to recall the details of the meeting and the individual task assignments made at the meeting.

Chairing a Meeting

The responsibilities of planning a meeting, preparing an agenda, and making sure that accurate and useful minutes are recorded belong to the person with the title of *chair*. The person who chairs a meeting may be the group leader, a designated facilitator, or a group member who usually assumes that role.

The 3M Meeting Management Team describes the critical role of the chair as "a delicate balancing act" in which chairpersons must:

> ...influence the group's thinking —not dictate it. They must encourage participation but discourage domination of the discussion by any single member. They must welcome ideas but also question them, challenge them, and insist on evidence to back them up. They must control the meeting but take care not to overcontrol it.[45]

CLOSE TO HOME   JOHN McPHERSON

© 1994 John McPherson/Dist. by Universal Press Syndicate

8:45, 8:46, 8:47, 8:48, 8:49, 8:50, 8:51.....

McPHERSON   12-5

As soon as Mrs. Felster began to read the minutes of the last meeting, the board members knew she was not going to work out as the new secretary.

Group Problem-Solving Competencies

Use this assessment instrument to evaluate how well you or another group member participates in a problem-solving discussion. Rate yourself or another group member on each item by placing a check mark in the appropriate column, using the following scale:

1 = excellent   **2** = satisfactory   **3** = unsatisfactory

Group Problem-Solving Competencies	1	2	3
1. *Clarifies the task.* Helps clarify the group's overall goal as well as member roles and responsibilities.			
2. *Identifies the problem.* Helps the group define the nature of the problem and the group's responsibilities.			
3. *Analyzes the issues.* Identifies and analyzes several of the issues that arise from the problem. Contributes relevant and valid information.			
4. *Establishes solution criteria.* Suggests criteria for assessing the workability, effectiveness, and value of a solution.			
5. *Generates solutions.* Identifies possible solutions that meet the solution criteria.			
6. *Evaluates solutions.* Evaluates the potential solutions.			
7. *Plans solution implementation.* Helps the group develop a workable implementation plan that includes necessary resources.			
8. *Maintains task focus.* Stays on task and follows the agreed-on agenda. If responsible for taking or distributing minutes, makes sure the minutes are accurate.			
9. *Maintains supportive climate.* Collaborates with and appropriately supports other group members.			
10. *Facilitates interaction.* Communicates appropriately, manages interaction, and encourages others to participate.			

What makes this group effective or ineffective? _____

_____

_____

How could this group improve its problem-solving strategies and skills? _____

_____

_____

11.1
Prerequisites for Group Decision Making and Problem Solving

What prerequisites help groups make good decisions and solve problems?

- Whereas *decision making* refers to the passing of judgment or making up your mind, *problem solving* is a complex process in which groups make multiple decisions while trying to solve a problem.

- Groups should take steps to prevent groupthink, which results in the deterioration of group effectiveness as a consequence of in-group pressure.

- The first and most important task for all groups is to make sure that all members understand and support the group's common goal. Group members should determine whether they are trying to answer a question of fact, conjecture, value, or policy.

- In addition to being well-informed, groups need clear procedures that specify how they will make decisions and solve problems.

11.2
Effective Group Decision Making

What are the advantages and disadvantages of various decision-making methods?

- Although voting is the easiest way to make a group decision, some members win while others lose when a vote is taken.

- Consensus requires that all members agree to support a decision. Groups should look for and prevent false consensus.

- Authority rule occurs when a single person or someone outside the group makes the final decision.

- Different decision-making styles—rational, intuitive, dependent, avoidant, and spontaneous—have the potential to improve or impair group decision making.

11.3
Effective Group Problem Solving

Which problem-solving procedures can groups use to achieve goals?

- Brainstorming, a group technique for generating as many ideas as possible in a short period of time, works well when members are comfortable with the rules.

- The Decreasing Options Technique (DOT) helps groups reduce and refine a large number of suggestions or ideas into a manageable set of options.

- The Standard Agenda is based on Dewey's reflective thinking process and divides problem solving into a series of ordered steps: task clarification, problem identification, fact-finding and analysis, solution criteria and limitations, solution suggestions, solution evaluation and selection, and solution implementation.

11.4
Effective Group Meetings

How can you plan and conduct an effective group meeting?

- Before calling a meeting, make sure you decide or know why the group is meeting, who should attend, when and where the group should meet, and what materials are needed.

- An agenda—the outline of items to be discussed and the tasks to be accomplished at a meeting—should be prepared and delivered to all group members in advance of a meeting.

- The minutes of a meeting are the written record of a group's discussion, actions, and decisions.

- When chairing a meeting, begin and end on time, create a positive climate, delegate someone to take minutes, follow the agenda, and facilitate the discussion.

MySearchLab®

TEST YOUR KNOWLEDGE

11.1 What prerequisites help groups make good decisions and solve problems?

1 Which of the following groups is *primarily* responsible for solving a problem?
a. A jury
b. A hiring committee
c. A department's social committee
d. A toxic waste disaster team
e. None of the above is a problem-solving group.

2 Which of the following symptoms of groupthink is expressed by a member who says, "Let's not worry about how the other departments feel about this— they're so dumb they don't even know there's a problem"?
a. Invulnerability
b. Stereotyping others
c. Rationalization
d. Mindguarding
e. Illusion of unanimity

11.2 What are the advantages and disadvantages of various decision-making methods?

3 All of the following answers are guidelines for achieving consensus except _____.
a. use stress-free ways of achieving consensus, such as flipping a coin or letting the majority make the decision
b. try to be logical rather than highly emotional
c. welcome differences of opinion
d. listen carefully to and respect other members' points of view even if they are very different from your point of view
e. get everyone involved in the discussion

4 Which ethical responsibility are you assuming in a group if you treat other group members as equals and give everyone, including those who disagree, the opportunity to respond to an issue?
a. The research responsibility
b. The common good responsibility
c. The social code responsibility
d. The moral responsibility
e. The reasoning responsibility

11.3 Which problem-solving procedures can groups use to achieve goals?

5 Under which circumstances is brainstorming *not* very useful as a problem-solving method?
a. If there is a crisis in which the group needs rapid decisions and clear leadership
b. If you need to correct something and know how to fix the problem
c. If your group knows its goal and how to achieve it but needs a planning session to map out details
d. Brainstorming would *not* be very useful in all of the above situations.
e. Brainstorming would be very useful in all of the above situations.

6 Use the Decreasing Options Technique (DOT) when
a. the group is small and can discuss individual ideas openly.
b. the group must confront and discuss two competing ideas.
c. the group wants to prevent a dominant member from sharing ideas.
d. the group does not want to discuss controversial ideas.
e. ensuring equal opportunities for input by all members is important.

7 Which of the following answers presents the correct order for the first three steps in the Standard Agenda model of problem solving?
a. Fact-finding and analysis, problem identification, solution suggestions
b. Task clarification, problem identification, fact-finding and analysis
c. Solution suggestions, solution evaluation and selection, solution implementation

d. Problem identification, fact-finding and analysis, solution criteria and limitations
e. None of the above answers represents the first three steps.

8 If your group is using the Standard Agenda model to discuss a question (What is the best way to reduce domestic violence in our community?), in which agenda steps would you ask the following questions: "What are the causes of domestic violence?" and "How widespread and serious is the problem?"
a. Task clarification
b. Problem identification
c. Fact-finding and analysis
d. Solution suggestions
e. Solution evaluation and selection

11.4 How can you plan and conduct an effective group meeting?

9 Before calling a meeting, ask all of the following questions except _____.
a. why are we meeting?
b. who should attend?
c. when and where should we meet?
d. what materials do we need?
e. who will implement decisions?

10 All of the following responsibilities are essential for chairing an effective meeting except _____.
a. begin on time
b. create a positive communication climate and ground rules for member behavior
c. take the minutes
d. follow the agenda
e. provide closure and stop on time

Answers found on page 366.

Key Terms

Agenda	Dependent decision maker	Questions of conjecture
Analysis paralysis		Questions of fact
Authority rule	False consensus	Questions of policy
Avoidant decision maker	Groupthink	Questions of value
Brainstorming	Intuitive decision maker	Rational decision maker
Consensus	Majority vote	Spontaneous decision maker
Decision making	Meeting	
Decreasing Options Technique (DOT)	Minutes	Standard Agenda
	Problem solving	Two-thirds vote

Communication

Knowledge for Communicating Well

Currents

NCA

A Publication of the National Communication Association

Volume 4, Issue 2 - April 2009

Why Can't Groups Focus on New Information?

The roles of decision maker and advisor are not included in the list of positive group member roles in Chapter 10, pp. 198–199. After reading this article, do you think these roles should be added, or do the listed roles capture the functions of a decision maker and advisor? Which of the roles in Chapter 10—if any—encompass these functions?

In discussions, groups often fail to adequately use the unique information of their members. Rather, groups focus upon and repeat information that all group members know, even before the discussion began. That is, group members repeat what they know and every other group member knows, and fail to share new information with others. When this happens, the group cannot take advantage of the diverse informational perspectives available from its members. However, recent research has found that structuring group members into the roles of decision maker and advisor may increase the focus on unique information.

Imagine a group of three members (member A, member B, and member C) discussing whether to hire a job applicant. Assume all members of the hiring team have read the applicant's resume. This would be shared information. However, from individual interviews with the applicant, each learned information that the other two did not. For example, A may have had knowledge about the applicant's educational history that B and C did not have, and C may have talked to the applicant about a mutual professional interest, but A and B did not. According to research on the discussion of information in groups, members of the hiring team would probably mention and repeat more information about the applicant's resume—the shared information—in their discussion and fail to integrate the unshared information that each member has.

Does this conclusion seem warranted to you? Would you withhold information you know abut a job applicant? Does this example support Whittenbaum's research on mutual enhancement on the next page?

One reason shared information is mentioned more is that all group members have access to it. However, once shared information is mentioned, groups often keep repeating the same shared information.

To what extent can the tendency of members to keep repeating the same shared information increase the chance of groupthink? See Chapter 11, p. 212.

When unshared information is mentioned, groups often fail to repeat and integrate the unshared information into discussion. Thus, an opportunity

Whittenbaum (Michigan State University) explains that group members experience mutual enhancement when they evaluate one another's contributions and competencies more positively because they are discussing shared rather than unshared information.

Why would a group's decision makers conclude that members with more unshared information are more competent? And why wouldn't that be true in groups without a designated decision maker?

to gain a new perspective is lost. Research by Gwen Whittenbaum on *mutual enhancement* has helped shed light on why groups continue to focus on shared information. When shared information is first mentioned, other members can validate this information because they too are aware of it. They might respond by nodding their head or making comments affirming the information, such as "Yes, yes, I know." Group members observe this positive response to the shared information and may be more likely to then repeat that information later in the discussion. However, when unshared information is mentioned, other group members may not be able to respond to the information and cannot validate it. They may not completely trust the information since they are learning about it secondhand from another person. Therefore, members may respond less enthusiastically to unshared information. This can cause the member who mentioned the unique information to not repeat it. In support of mutual enhancement, it has been found that members who mention shared information are more influential and viewed as more competent in the group discussion.

Would the same pattern of information sharing hold true in groups that have differences in status and roles? What if one group member holds the decision-making power for the group? Imagine a group in which a cancer patient is meeting with a medical team to discuss treatment options, a congresswoman is meeting with constituents to get feedback about upcoming legislation that she needs to vote on, or a manager is meeting with subordinates to discuss reducing the budget. In each case there is a group discussion, but only one person will ultimately make the decision.

Research by Lyn Van Swol has found that in structured groups with one decision maker and multiple advisors, there is greater focus on unshared information. Moreover, members are more likely to repeat unshared information. For example, several studies have found that decision makers prefer to receive advice from group members who have more unshared information than those with shared information. Decision makers perceive group members with more unshared information as more competent. This is the opposite of studies about unstructured groups. In unstructured groups, members who shared information were more influential and perceived as more competent.

There are several reasons why structured groups may focus more on unshared information. Unstructured groups need to reach a group consensus. Because shared information influences everyone's opinion, it validates everyone's opinion and facilitates reaching consensus. When one person is the decision maker in a group, consensus is not necessary, so group members may be more open to new information and viewpoints and do not have to worry about the new information upsetting group agreement. Also, when put in the role of advisor, a group member may feel more responsible for providing a unique perspective than when a group member is in an unstructured group and has no assigned role. Decision makers may also try to pool more unique perspectives from their advisors and may expect advisors to provide new information as part of their role. These expectations may not exist for members of unstructured groups.

In conclusion, if your goal is to encourage your group or team members to share information that is unknown to others, then assigning members the roles of advisor and decision maker may help.

ABOUT THE AUTHOR

Lyn M. Van Swol is an Assistant Professor of Communication Arts at University of Wisconsin–Madison, Wisconsin. This essay is based on Van Swol, L. M. (2009). "Discussion and perception of information in groups and judge advisor systems." *Communication Monographs* 75,99–120. *Communication Monographs* and *Communication Currents* are publications of the National Communication Association.

y, in your opinion, would group members fail to respond to unshared information? Have you experienced this phenomenon in a group to which you belong or have belonged? What was the outcome of that behavior?

Think of the groups to which you now belong or have belonged. Did this tendency to focus on shared information occur when there was one decision maker or multiple advisors? If so, how did it affect group decision making?

The discussion of consensus in Chapter 11, pp. 213–214, explains that when group members reluctantly give in to group pressures, they may achieve a false consensus. To what extent—if at all—would Van Swol's recommendation to assign members the roles of advisor and decision maker help avoid this problem?

Planning Your
PRESENTATION

Effective presentations have enormous power. They can delight us, inspire us, even make us cry. You do not have to be famous or known for your eloquence to be a great speaker. What matters is that you have a compelling message worth sharing with others. What *also* matters is that you know *how* to share that message.

In his speech at the National Press Club in 2009, Nick Jonas, songwriter and lead singer of the Jonas Brothers, spoke clearly and honestly about how a diagnosis of diabetes changed his life. Since then, Jonas has traveled the country making speeches about juvenile diabetes to raise awareness and "help young people with diabetes feel supported and less alone."[1] Here is an excerpt from his speech:

I was diagnosed with type I diabetes in November 2005. My brothers were the first to notice that I'd lost a significant amount of weight, 15 pounds in three weeks. I was thirsty all the time, and my attitude had changed. I'm a really positive person, and it had changed during these few weeks. It would have been easy to blame my symptoms on a hectic schedule, but my family knew I had to get to a doctor. The normal range of a blood sugar is between 70 to 120. When we got to the doctor's office, we learned that my blood sugar was over 700. The doctor said that I had type I diabetes, but I had no idea what that meant. The first thing I asked was, "Am I going to die?" She looked back at me and said, "No, but this is something that you'll have to live with for the rest of your life."

12.1
The Speech Preparation Process
How does preparation help you create a more effective presentation?

Martin McDermott, author of *Speak with Courage*, writes, "A successful speech is not a matter of luck; it's a matter of preparation." He then describes watching *unprepared* students deliver speeches in classes. "It's like watching a deer in the headlights of an oncoming tractor trailer . . . in slow motion. Both speakers and audience feel grueling pain." To prevent such torment, he offers three important pieces of advice: "prepare, prepare, prepare."[2]

McDermott's students are not alone. Research conducted by John Daly and his colleagues conclude that anxious speakers are less likely to prepare effectively because, in short, they don't know *how*.[3] Rather than make orderly decisions about their purpose, audience, content, organization, and delivery, they become "lost" in the process.[4]

Martin McDermott also observes that we often put off what we don't like doing; we procrastinate about going to the dentist, tax preparation, and speechmaking. Although you don't have much control of what happens in the dentist's office or during encounters with the IRS, you can control how well you prepare and deliver a presentation. "Being prepared," writes McDermott, "will reduce your anxiety and increase the likelihood of a positive outcome. . . . Inadequate preparation often leads to a self-fulfilling prophecy: Speakers who don't prepare well don't do well and then 'hate' public speaking. Your fate is in your own hands."[5]

When discussing the wide variety of speaking opportunities and occasions, we use the phrase **presentation speaking** to describe the process of using verbal and nonverbal messages to generate meaning with audience members. Presentation speaking encompasses oral reports, informal talks, and business briefings in private settings as well as public speeches to small and large audiences. Regardless of its purpose, audience, or place, if

you know how to effectively plan and deliver a strong presentation, you are more likely to be noticed, believed, respected, and remembered.

Several years ago, we conducted two national surveys—one administered to working professionals and the other to students enrolled in public speaking courses in a variety of colleges and universities.[6] We asked respondents to identify the *most* important skills for effective presentations. For

the most part, student results were similar to those of the working professional respondents (see below), with two exceptions, which we'll discuss later in this and subsequent chapters.[7] Knowing how to prepare a presentation is the first step in mastering the top-ranked speaking skills the survey respondents identified. Effective preparation can also reduce your anxiety and increase your likelihood of delivering a successful speech.

TOP-RANKED SPEAKING SKILLS[8]

WORKING PROFESSIONALS

	COLLEGE STUDENTS
1 Keeping your audience interested	Keeping your audience interested
2 Beginning and ending your presentation	Organizing your presentation
3 Organizing your presentation	Deciding what to say; choosing a topic or approach to your presentation
4 Selecting ideas and information for your presentation	Using your voice effectively
5 Deciding what to say; choosing a topic or an approach	Selecting ideas and information for your presentation
6 Understanding and adapting to your audience	Determining the purpose of your presentation
7 Determining the purpose of your presentation	Overcoming/reducing nervousness/stage fright
8 Choosing appropriate and effective words	Understanding and adapting to your audience
9 Enhancing your credibility	Beginning and ending your presentation
10 Using your voice effectively	Choosing appropriate and effective words

Without a purpose, it is difficult to decide what to say, what materials to include, and how to deliver your presentation.

First Lady Michelle Obama had a clear and worthy purpose when she announced the expansion of the Initiative for Military Families at the 2011 National Math and Science competition, part of a White House Joining Forces project.

12.2
Determining Your Purpose and Topic

How does your purpose and topic affect the presentation planning process?

Determining your purpose is the most important decision you have to make as you begin the speech preparation process. To determine your purpose, ask yourself: What do I want my audience to know, think, feel, or do as a result of my presentation? Purpose focuses on *why*: Why am I speaking, and what outcome do I want?

Presentation Goals

Having a clear purpose does not guarantee you will achieve it. But without a purpose, it is difficult to decide what to say, what materials to include, and how to deliver your presentation. Begin your search for a purpose by deciding whether you want to inform, persuade, entertain, inspire, or combine all four of these goals.

Speaking to Inform An **informative presentation** is designed to instruct, enlighten, explain, describe, clarify, correct, remind, and/or demonstrate. Teachers spend most of their lecture time informing students. Sometimes, an informative presentation explains a complex concept, demonstrates a complicated process, or clears up misunderstandings. Informative presentations may take the form of class reports, committee updates, and formal lectures. (See Chapter 15, "Speaking to Inform.")

Speaking to Persuade A **persuasive presentation** is designed to change or influence audience opinions and/or behavior. Advertisements persuade customers to buy products. Political candidates persuade audiences to elect them. Persuasive presentations occur in courtrooms and classrooms, as well as during religious services, around the dinner table, and in daily conversations. (See Chapter 16, "Speaking to Persuade.")

Speaking to Entertain **Entertainment speaking** amuses, interests, diverts, or "warms up" an audience. Stand-up comedy is a form of entertainment speaking. After-dinner speakers amuse audiences too full to move or absorb serious ideas and complex information. At a retirement party, friends may "roast" a retiree. (For more details on using humor in a presentation, see Chapter 15.)

Speaking to Inspire **Inspirational speaking** brings like-minded people together, creates social unity, builds goodwill, or celebrates by arousing audience emotions. Inspirational speaking occurs in special contexts, takes many forms, and can tap a wide range of emotions by appealing to societal and cultural values.

EXAMPLES OF PERSUASIVE TOPICS

IDEA
Anger is *not* caused by others.

PEOPLE
Susan B. Anthony was the most influential advocate for women's rights in the U.S.

OBJECT
Electric cars help save the planet.

Think Blue.
blue-e-motion

ACTION
Register to vote.

REGISTER TO VOTE HERE

Choose an Appropriate Topic

Your topic is the subject matter of your presentation. A topic is often a simple word or phrase: *rap music*. Yet two presentations on the same topic can have very different purposes. Look at the differences between these two purpose statements:

"I want my audience to understand and appreciate rap and hip-hop music."

"I want my audience to boycott recording companies that promote rap music with violent and offensive lyrics."

When looking for a good topic, start with these questions: (1) What interests you and takes up your free time? (2) What do you value? and (3) What's new and interesting on the Web?

What Interests You or Takes Up Your Free Time? If you are called on to make a presentation, but find it difficult to decide on a topic, consider any hobbies, special expertise, unusual jobs, unique experiences, or causes you support. If you still have difficulty identifying a topic, complete the Know Thy Self: What Inspires You? exercise below.

Or create a chart in which you list potential topics under broad headings—sports, food, hobbies, places

Inspirational speaking is also more common than you may think. Examples include motivational speeches, toasts at weddings and anniversaries, eulogies to honor the dead and comfort the grieving, commencement addresses, dedications, and tributes, as well as award presentations and acceptances. (For more on inspiring an audience, see Chapter 16.)

Inform, Persuade, Entertain, *and* Inspire Presentations that only inform, persuade, entertain, or inspire are rare. You can make your presentation more compelling by doing all four. A professor's lecture may inform students about intercultural communication theories as well as persuade students that understanding cultural differences will improve communication in their daily lives and careers. To entertain them, the professor might use humorous examples of cultural misunderstandings and include stories about other cultures to inspire students to travel abroad.

Know Thy Self

What Inspires You?

Directions: Completing the following statements may help you find topics worth researching and developing into a presentation that reflects your personal interests and values.

1. I have always wanted to know more about . . .

2. If I were to read one book of nonfiction, it would be about . . .

3. If I had an unexpected week off, I would . . .

4. I have always wanted to be able to . . .

5. If I had a million dollars to give away, I would . . .

6. If I could make one new law, I would . . .

7. If I could travel back in time, the one person I would like to meet is . . .

8. If I could travel anywhere in the world, I would go to . . .

9. The thing that would be the most difficult or inconvenient to do without is . . .

10. My favorite vacation was . . .

11. My life would be better if only I could . . .

12. My ideal job would be . . .

13. I am afraid of . . .

14. If I could cure one disease, it would be . . .

15. I get angry when I see or hear . . .

16. At work, I have to know how to . . .

17. My favorite book is . . .

18. My favorite topic of conversation is . . .

19. My most cherished possession is . . .

20. The world would be a better place if . . .

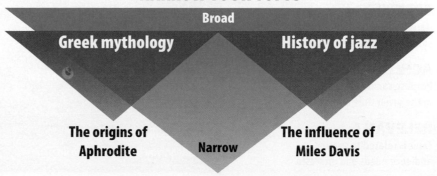

Value + Issue = Topic

The Institute for Global Ethics identified eight universal values: love, truthfulness, fairness, freedom, unity, tolerance, responsibility, and respect for life.[9] Next to each value, we've listed a related issue. Fill in the blank with a presentation topic for this value and issue.

Example: *Love* + Marital infidelity = <u>How to save a marriage if your spouse has been unfaithful.</u>

- *Truthfulness* + Plagiarism = Presentation topic: _____

- *Fairness* + Gender biases = Presentation topic: _____

- *Freedom* + Gun control = Presentation topic: _____

- *Unity* + Labor unions = Presentation topic: _____

- *Tolerance* + Hate speech = Presentation topic: _____

- *Responsibility* + Parental accountability = Presentation topic: _____

- *Respect for life* + Human cloning = Presentation topic: _____

Student-Selected SPEECH TOPICS

Blogging

Closing a sale

Alternative energy sources

Afro-Cuban jazz

Stricter or less strict gun laws

Exercise and long life

Investment strategies

Interpretation of dreams

Genealogy and your family tree

Becoming a Big Brother/Big Sister

Internet addiction

Banning homework for kids

Therapeutic massage

Vaccines

Weight lifting

The truth about Cleopatra

Brewing bear

Myths about Mormons

The new Digital Divide

Swimming with Diana Nyad

Save the U.S. Post Office

The Neanderthal in us

Body piercing

and destinations, famous people, music, important events, personal goals, community issues, and so on.

What Do You Value? Values are beliefs that guide your ideas about what is right or wrong, good or bad, just or unjust, and correct or incorrect. If you examine the values that are most important to you, you may find a speech topic that's right and appropriate for you and your audience.

Be cautious when you search your personal values for a topic; they may not align with those of your audience. For example, you may strongly support gun control, but audience members may consider gun ownership a basic freedom. Also, remember that cultures often differ in what they value. Although most Americans value individualism, other cultures may place greater value on community and group goals.

What's Interesting on the Web? The World Wide Web is a wonderful resource for finding interesting presentation topics. Major search engines have subject directories that suggest numerous topics, within which are dozens of subtopics. For example, the Health and Fitness directory on one site begins with Alternative Medicine and ends with Women's Health—with dozens of topics in between.

> **Values also trigger emotions and guide your actions.**[10]

NARROW YOUR TOPIC

Broad

Greek mythology

History of jazz

The origins of Aphrodite

Narrow

The influence of Miles Davis

The web organized by topic into categories.

Arts
Music, Movies, Performing Arts, ...

Business
Industrial Goods and Services, Finance, ...

Computers
Software, Internet, Programming, ...

Games
Video Games, Roleplaying, Board Games, ...

Health
Conditions and Diseases, Medicine, Animal, ...

World
Deutsch, Español, Français, Italiano, Japanese, Korean, Nederlands, Polski, Svenska, ...

Home
Cooking, Family, Gardening, ...

Kids and Teens
International, School Time, Games, ...

News
Newspapers, Media, Colleges and Universities, ...

Recreation
Pets, Outdoors, Food, ...

Reference
Education, Biography, Museums, ...

Regional
North America, Europe, Oceania, ...

Science
Biology, Social Sciences, Technology, ...

Shopping
Home and Garden, Crafts, Sports, ...

Society
Religion and Spirituality, Law, Issues, ...

Sports
Soccer, Equestrian, Football, ...

Major search engines such as Google offer a rich source of presentation topics.

Narrow Your Topic

Make sure that you appropriately narrow or modify your topic to achieve your purpose and adapt to listeners' needs and interests. Select the most important and interesting ideas and information for your presentation rather than telling your audience everything you know about a topic.

Although *you* may be an expert on your topic, your audience may be hearing about it for the first time. Don't bury them under mounds of information. Ask yourself, "If I only have time to tell them one thing about my topic, what would it be?" Chances are that conveying a single important idea is enough to achieve your purpose.

Develop a Purpose Statement

When you know *why* you are speaking (your purpose) and *what* you are speaking about (your topic), develop a clear **purpose statement**, a specific, achievable, and relevant sentence that identifies the purpose and main ideas of your presentation. It is not enough to say, "My purpose is to tell my audience about my job as a phone solicitor." This statement is too general and probably an impossible goal to achieve in a time-limited presentation. Instead, your purpose statement must convey the specific focus of your presentation, such as "I want my audience to recognize two common strategies used by effective phone solicitors to overcome listener objections."

A purpose statement is similar to a writer's thesis statement, which identifies the main idea you want to communicate to your reader.

A purpose statement guides how you **research, create, organize,** and **present** your message.

Characteristics of an EFFECTIVE PURPOSE STATEMENT

	EFFECTIVE	NOT EFFECTIVE
SPECIFIC Narrows a topic to content appropriate for your purpose and audience.	I want my audience to understand how to use the government's new food group recommendations as a diet guide.	The benefits of good health.
ACHIEVABLE Purpose can be achieved in the given time limit.	There are two preferred treatments for mental depression.	Be able to identify all the the causes, symptoms, treatments, and preventions of mental depression.
RELEVANT Topic is related to specific audience needs and interests.	Next time you witness an accident, you'll know what to do.	Next time you encounter an exotic Australian tree toad, you'll appreciate its morphology.

12.3
Analyzing and Adapting to Your Audience
What strategies and skills can help you adapt to your audience?

Audience analysis refers to the ability to understand, respect, and adapt to audience members before and during a presentation. It involves researching your audience, interpreting those findings, and selecting appropriate strategies to achieve your purpose. The examples in your presentation, the words you choose, and even your delivery style should be adapted to your audience's interests and needs.

> The examples in your presentation, the words you choose, and even your delivery style should be adapted to your audience's interests and needs.

Know Your Audience

Knowing your audience means asking questions about audience members' characteristics, attitudes, values, backgrounds, and needs as well as what they may and may not know about your topic. The answers to these questions will help you understand your audience and help you to decide what to include in your presentation.

Who Are They? Gather as much general **demographic information** (information about audience characteristics such as age, gender, marital status, race, religion, place of residence, ethnicity, occupation, education, and income) as you can about the people who will be watching and listening to you. If the audience is composed of a particular group or is meeting for a special reason, gather more specific demographic information as well. (See the figure to the right.)

Avoid "one-size-fits-all" conclusions about audience members based on visible or obvious characteristics, such as age, race, gender, occupation, nationality, or religion. As you know from Chapter 3, "Adapting to Others," oversimplified conclusions are stereotypes that can distort your perceptions. In addition, remember that *your* age, nationality, race, gender, educational level, and

socioeconomic background may be just as critical in determining how well an audience listens to you.

Why Are They Here? Audiences attend presentations for many reasons. They may need to satisfy a class requirement or have nothing better to do. They may attend presentations because they are interested in the speaker, for example, a candidate running for office or a celebrity writer giving a public talk. Audience members who are interested in your topic or who stand to benefit from attending a presentation will be different from those who don't know why they are there or who are required to attend. Each type of audience presents its own unique challenges. A highly interested and well-informed audience demands a compelling, knowledgeable, well-prepared speaker. An audience required or reluctant to attend may be pleasantly surprised and influenced by a dynamic speaker who gives them a good reason to listen. Entire audiences rarely fit into one type or group. Your audience may include people with many diverse reasons for attending.

What Do They Know? Almost nothing is more boring to an audience than hearing a speaker talk about a subject audience members know more about than the speaker. Almost as frustrating is listening to a speaker talk over your head. To ensure that your presentation matches your audience's level of understanding about the topic, ask questions to assess their level of knowledge when you are preparing your presentation: How much do they know about this topic? How much

Age	Cultural background	Place of residence	Education
Race	Marital status	Income level	Parental status
Occupation	Religion	Gender	Disabilities

GENERAL

AUDIENCE DEMOGRAPHICS

SPECIFIC

Political affiliations	Professional memberships
Employment positions	Career goals
Military experience	Individual and group achievements

Do You Honor the Audience's Bill of Rights?

In his book *Say It with Presentations*, Gene Zelazny proposes an Audience's Bill of Rights.[11] Here we present a modified version of Zelazny's rights. Review each of the audience's rights listed in the left-hand column. In the right-hand column, describe a speaking strategy you can use to ensure this right.

Audience Rights	Speaker Strategies
1. The right to receive value for the time you spend attending a presentation.	I can _____
2. The right to be spoken to with respect for your experience, intelligence, knowledge, and culture; the right to ask questions and expect answers.	I can _____
3. The right to know what the speaker wants you to do or think as a result of a presentation.	I can _____
4. The right to have a presentation start and stop on time and to know, in advance, how much time it will take.	I can _____
5. The right to know the speaker's position, the rationale for that position, and the evidence that supports the position; the right to have complex charts explained.	I can _____
6. The right to know where the speaker is going and how the presentation will progress.	I can _____
7. The right to hear and see a speaker from anywhere in a room; the right to be able to read every word on every visual no matter where you sit.	I can _____

background material should I cover? Will they understand topic-related terms or jargon?

What Are Their Interests? Find out if audience members have interests that match your purpose and topic. Consider two types of interests: self-centered interests and topic-centered interests.

Self-centered interests are aroused when a presentation can result in personal gain. Some audience members are enthralled by a speaker who teaches them how to earn or save money. Others will be riveted by ways to improve their appearance or health. In all these cases, the listener stands to gain something as a result of the presentation and its outcome.

Audiences also have **topic-centered interests**—subjects they enjoy hearing and learning about. Topic-centered interests include hobbies, favorite sports or pastimes, or subjects loaded with intrigue and mystery. Topic-centered interests tend to be personal. A detailed description of a Civil War battle may captivate Civil War history buffs but bore other audience members. Whether self-centered or topic-centered, listener interests have a significant effect on how well an audience pays attention to you and your message.[12]

What Are Their Attitudes? When assessing **audience attitudes**, you are asking whether they agree or disagree with you as well as how strongly they agree and disagree. Some audience members will already agree with you, others will disagree no matter what you say, and others will be undecided or have no opinion.

> **There can be as many opinions in your audience as there are people.**

Modifying Your Purpose to Suit the Audience

Preliminary Purpose. To describe journalism in the twenty-first century.

Who Are They? They are 10 women and four men; some are 18 to 20 years old; others appear to be in their late 30s, early 40s.

Why Are They Here? They are students in an intro to mass communication course.

What Do They Know? They already know that the face of journalism is changing—that many, if not most, people get their news from online sources; they know that many print-only newspapers are in financial trouble.

What Are Their Interests? Some are more interested in public relations; others want to know about specific types of journalism; many are concerned about future job opportunities.

What Are Their Attitudes? Some think that, armed with a video phone, Internet access, and writing ability, anyone can become a journalist.

Revised Purpose. To explain recent trends in journalism—backpack journalism and citizen journalism—and their uncertain potential as career paths.

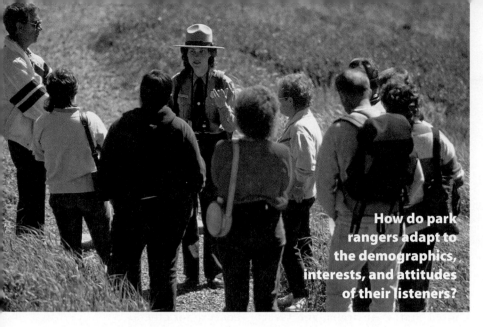

How do park rangers adapt to the demographics, interests, and attitudes of their listeners?

seem restless or hostile? How can you adjust? What if you must shorten your 20-minute presentation to 10 minutes to accommodate another speaker?

Adapting to your audience *during* a presentation requires you to do three things at once: deliver your presentation, correctly interpret audience feedback as you speak, and successfully modify your message. Interpreting audience responses involves looking at your audience members, reading their nonverbal signals, and sensing their moods. If audience feedback suggests that you're not getting through, don't be afraid to stop and ask comprehension questions such as, "Would you like more detail on this point before I go on to the next one?"

Think about adjusting your presentation in the same way you adjust your conversation with a friend. If your friend looks confused, you might ask what's unclear. If your friend interrupts with a question, you probably will answer it or ask if you can finish your thought before answering. If your friend tells you that he has a pressing appointment, you are likely to shorten what you have to say. The same adaptations work just as well when speaking to an audience.

Adapt to Your Audience

Everything you learn about your audience tells you something about how to prepare and deliver your presentation. Depending on the amount of audience research and analysis you do, you can adapt your presentation to your audience as you prepare it. In other cases, you may use audience feedback to modify your presentation as you speak.

Prepresentation Adaptation After researching and analyzing information about your audience's characteristics and attitudes, go back to your purpose statement and apply what you've learned. Answers to the five basic audience questions discussed on the previous two pages can help you modify your preliminary purpose into one that better suits your audience.

Midpresentation Adaptation No matter how well you prepare for an audience, you must expect for the unexpected. What if audience members

---

COMMUNICATION & CULTURE

ADAPT TO NONNATIVE SPEAKERS OF ENGLISH

Have you studied a foreign language in school? If so, what happens when you listen to a native speaker of that language? Do you understand every word? Probably not. Such an experience can be difficult and frustrating. Imagine what it must be like for a nonnative speaker of English to understand a presentation in English. The following guidelines are derived from general intercultural research and from observations of international audiences, both at home and abroad.[13]

- *Speak slowly and clearly.* Many nonnative speakers of English need more time because they translate your words into their own language as you speak. But don't shout at them; they are not hearing impaired.
- *Use visual aids.* Most nonnative speakers of English are better readers than listeners. Use slides or provide handouts for important information. Give the audience time to read and take notes.

- *Be more formal.* In general, use a more formal style and dress professionally when speaking to international audiences.

- *Adapt to contextual perspectives.* If you are addressing an audience from a high-context culture (see Chapter 3), be less direct. Let them draw their own conclusions. Give them time to get to know and trust you.

- *Avoid humor and clichés.* Humor rarely translates into another language and can backfire if misunderstood. Avoid clichés—overused expressions familiar to a particular culture—or obscure idioms. Will a nonnative speaker of English understand "Cool as a cucumber" or "Shop 'til you drop"?

237

Adapt to Cultural Differences

Respecting and adapting to a diverse audience begins with understanding the nature and characteristics of various cultures. Two of the cultural dimensions we examined in Chapter 3 are especially critical for presentations: power distance and individualism/collectivism.

Power Distance As we indicated in Chapter 3, *power distance* refers to varying levels of equality and status among the members of a culture. In the United States, a low-power-distance culture, authority figures often play down status differences. American presidents are often photographed wearing casual clothes, corporate executives may promote an open-door policy, and college freshmen and full professors may interact on a first-name basis.

If most of your audience members are from a low-power-distance culture, you can encourage them to challenge authority and make independent decisions. However, if many audience members come from high-power-distance culture *and* if you also command authority and influence, you can tell them exactly what you want them to do—and expect compliance.

Individualism and Collectivism When speaking to individualistic audiences (e.g., listeners from the United States, Australia, and Great Britain), you can appeal to their sense of adventure, their desire to achieve personal goals, and their defense of individual rights. When speaking to a collectivist audience (e.g., listeners from most Asian and Latin American countries), you may want to demonstrate how a particular course of action will benefit their company, family, or community. If you are an individualistic American who feels comfortable drawing attention to your own or your organization's accomplishments in your presentation, you may find a collectivist audience disturbed by your seeming arrogance and lack of concern for others.

12.4

Enhancing Your Credibility

How does your credibility affect the success of a presentation?

Speaker credibility represents the extent to which an audience believes a speaker and the speaker's message. The dictionary defines credibility as the "quality, capability, or power to elicit belief."[14] The more credible you are in the eyes of your audience, the more likely it is that you will achieve the purpose of your presentation. If your audience rates you as highly credible, they may excuse poor delivery. They are so ready to believe you that the presentation doesn't have to be perfect.[15]

> The more credible you are in the eyes of your audience, the more likely it is that you will achieve the purpose of your presentation.

Components of Speaker Credibility

Researchers identify three major components of speaker credibility that have a strong impact on the believability of a speaker: character, competence, and charisma.[16] The speaker credibility chart on the next page summarizes the distinct characteristics that personify each of these three components.

Character Of the three components of speaker credibility, **character**—a speaker's perceived honesty and goodwill—may be the most important. A speaker of good character is seen as a good person—trustworthy, sincere, and fair. Is your evidence valid and your claims warranted? Are you doing what is right and ethical? If an audience doesn't trust you, it won't matter if you are an expert speaker or an electrifying performer.

Competence Competence refers to a speaker's perceived expertise and abilities. Proving that you are competent can be as simple as mentioning your credentials and experience. An audience is unlikely to question a recognized brain surgeon, a professional baseball player, or famous fashion designer as long as they stick to brain surgery, baseball, and fashion, respectively. An auto mechanic, a waitress, a parent of six children, a nurse, and a government employee can all be experts in their own right. Such speakers rely on their life experiences and opinions to demonstrate competence.

But what happens when you are not an expert? How can you demonstrate that you know what you're talking about? The answer lies in one word: *research*. If you don't have firsthand experience or cannot claim to be an expert, let your audience know how well prepared you are: "I conducted a phone survey of more than 30 individuals and found . . ." or "After reviewing the top ten textbooks on this subject, I was surprised that only one author addresses . . ."

Charisma Your perceived level of energy, enthusiasm, vigor, and commitment reflects your **charisma**. A speaker with charisma is seen as dynamic, forceful, powerful, assertive, and intense. When running for

> **Researching and sharing up-to-date information helps establish your competence as a conscientious and knowledgeable speaker.**

Aristotle's Ethos

The concept of speaker credibility is more than 2,000 years old. Aristotle's *Rhetoric*, written during the late fourth century B.C., established many of the public-speaking strategies we use today. His definition of **rhetoric** as the ability to discover "in the particular case what are the available means of persuasion"[17] focuses on strategies for selecting the most appropriate persuasive arguments for a particular audience in a particular circumstance. His division of proof into logical arguments (*logos*), emotional arguments (*pathos*), and arguments based on speaker credibility (*ethos*) remains a basic model for teaching the principles of persuasive speaking.

Here we focus on Aristotle's **ethos**, a Greek word meaning *character*. "The character [ethos] of the speaker is a cause of persuasion when the speech is so uttered as to make him worthy of belief. . . . His character [ethos] is the most potent of all the means to persuasion."[18]

> Aristotle's concept of ethos evolved into what we now call *speaker credibility*.

We want to emphasize that a speaker's ethos varies with audiences and varies over time. "That is to say, a speaker may have a positive ethos with one set of listeners and a negative ethos with another; a speaker who is highly regarded at one time may be considered a has-been ten years later."[19] For example, when campaigning for public office, Republican candidates usually have higher ethos when speaking to conservative audiences than to liberal audiences.

Aristotle confines his discussion of ethos to what a speaker does *during* a speech because what people think of a speaker *before* a speech is not related to the three modes of persuasion.[20] Later in our discussion of speaker credibility, we examine the ways in which an audience's previous knowledge and beliefs about a speaker affect ethos or, as it's now called, speaker credibility.

president, Barack Obama is a charismatic speaker who motivated and energized audiences when he was campaigning for office. John F. Kennedy and Senator Barbara Jordan were charismatic, and Supreme Court Justice Sonia Sotomayor is as well. Charisma has more to do with how you deliver a presentation than with what you have to say; in that regard, Adolf Hitler was also a charismatic speaker.

Speakers with strong and expressive voices are seen as more charismatic than speakers with hesitant or unexpressive voices. Speakers who gesture naturally and move gracefully are viewed as more charismatic than those who look uncomfortable and awkward in front of an audience. Speakers who look their audiences in the eye are thought of as more charismatic than those who avoid eye contact with members of the audience. Practicing and developing your performance skills enhances your charisma in the same way that preparation helps you to be seen as a competent speaker.

> Credibility does not exist in an absolute sense; it is solely based on the attitudes and perceptions of the audience.

Developing Speaker Credibility

Credibility does not exist in an absolute sense; it is solely based on the attitudes and perceptions of the audience. Thus, even if you are the world's greatest expert on your topic and deliver your presentation with skill, the ultimate decision about your credibility lies with your audience.

COMPONENTS OF SPEAKER CREDIBILITY

Character	Competence	Charisma
Honest	Experienced	Active
Kind	Well prepared	Enthusiastic
Friendly	Qualified	Energetic
Fair	Up to date	Confident
Respectful	Informed	Stimulating
Caring	Intelligent	Dynamic

What makes Holocaust survivor and Nobel Peace Prize winner Elie Wiesel a credible speaker when speaking out against hatred, racism, and genocide?

Credibility is "like the process of getting a grade in school. Only the teacher (or audience) can assign the grade to the student (or speaker), but the student can do all sorts of things—turn in homework, prepare for class, follow the rules—to influence what grade is assigned."[21] So what can you do to influence your audience's opinion of you and your presentation? Find out what you have to offer to your audience, prepare an interesting presentation, and show your audience why you're uniquely qualified to deliver it. In other words, do a personal inventory and toot your own horn.

Do a Personal Inventory Each of us can do something that sets us apart from most other people. It's just a matter of discovering what that something is. A personal inventory is a way of identifying the unique gifts and talents that contribute to your credibility. Begin your self-inventory by answering three questions: (1) What are your experiences? (2) What are your achievements? and (3) What are your skills and traits?

An experience that seems routine to you may be a new experience for your listeners. You don't have to land on the moon to achieve something important. Consider how you might answer the following questions: Have you lived or worked in another town, city, state, or country? Do you have or have you had an unusual job? What experiences have had a big impact on your life (childbirth, a visit to a foreign country, combat experience)? What can you do that most of your peers cannot (play the cello, write a song or short story, speak Turkish)?

Toot Your Own Horn A presentation lets you show an audience that your ideas and opinions are based on more than good preparation. They are based on personal experiences, accomplishments, and special skills. There is nothing wrong with using words such as *I* and *my* and *me* if they are appropriate; overuse, however, can sound boastful. For example, at an honors awards ceremony for students, one faculty member talked more about herself than about the student who was being honored: "As chairman of the department and an expert in this field of study, I decided. . . ." By using the awards presentation to spotlight herself, the speaker undermined her credibility.

If you're an expert, find a way to tell the audience: "In my 10 years of leading . . ." or "When my partner and I won the state's debate championship. . . ." In neither case would you be exaggerating or boasting. Rather, you would be explaining how and why you know what you're talking about.

The Ethical Speaker

The words *ethos* and *ethics* come from the Greek word meaning *character*. As we indicated in our discussion of character, the apparent "goodness" of a speaker is important in determining whether an audience believes a speaker. Audiences are also more likely to believe you if they see you as an ethical speaker. *Ethos* and *ethics*, however, are not the same. As we've noted, ethos, or speaker credibility, relies on the perceived character, competence, and charisma of the speaker. The audience determines a speaker's ethos, but a speaker's beliefs about what is right or wrong, moral or immoral, good or bad determine her or his *ethics*. Ethics is a set of personal principles of right conduct, a system of moral values.[22] Only you can determine how ethical you are.

ETHOS determined by the audience

ETHICS determined by the speaker

The Perils of Plagiarism

Any discussion of speaker ethics must address the perils of plagiarism. The word **plagiarism** comes from the Latin, *plagium*, which means "kidnapping." Simply put, if you include a quotation or idea from another source and pretend it's your idea and words, you are plagiarizing. Some speakers believe that plagiarism rules don't apply to them. Others think they can get away with it. Still others plagiarize without knowing they are doing it. Ignorance, however, is no excuse.

Although most speakers don't intend to kidnap or steal another person's work, plagiarism occurs more frequently than it should, often with serious consequences. Students have failed classes, been expelled from programs and schools, or been denied degrees when caught plagiarizing in college. In the publishing business, authors have been sued by other writers who claim that their ideas and words were plagiarized. The careers of well-respected scientists, politicians, university officials, and civic leaders have been tarnished and even ruined by acts of plagiarism.

- **High school student Blair Hornstine's** admission to Harvard University was revoked when it was discovered that she had passed off speeches and writings by famous people as her own in articles she wrote as a student journalist for a local newspaper.[23]
- **The Beatles' George Harrison** was successfully challenged in a prolonged suit for plagiarizing the Chiffons' "He's So Fine" for the melody of his own "My Sweet Lord."[24]
- **Author Alex Haley** settled a lawsuit with Harold Courlander for $650,000 in 1978, when Courlander claimed that a passage in Haley's novel *Roots* imitated Courlander's novel *The African*.[25]

For many students and speakers, the Web has become the primary source for plagiarism. In an article in *Prism*, a publication of the American Society of Engineering Education, author Julie Ryan describes the problem of Web plagiarism:

> When you plagiarize, you are stealing or kidnapping something that belongs to someone else.

> *A few words typed into a Web search engine can lead a student to hundreds, sometimes thousands, of relevant documents, making it easy to "cut and paste" a few paragraphs from here and a few more from there until the student has an entire paper-length collection. Or a student can find a research paper published in one of the hundreds of new journals that have gone online over the past few years, copy the entire text, turn it into a new document, and then offer it up as original work without having to type anything but a cover page. Even recycling efforts and ghost writers have gone global with Web sites offering professionally or student-written research papers for sale, some even with a money-back guarantee against detection.*[26]

We extend Julie Ryan's examples to visual resources too. Given how easy it is to find good photographs, graphics, and PowerPoint slides on the Web, plagiarists may download someone else's visual and treat it as if it were their original work. Fortunately, the Web also provides instructors with the same access to information so they can check the originality of the material submitted by students. With time and a good search engine, many would-be plagiarizers have been caught *and* appropriately punished.

One of the best reasons to refrain from plagiarizing comes from students who responded the question "How Do Teachers Check for Plagiarism?" on the Yahoo Answer site.[27] One respondent wrote:

> PLAGIARISM IS NOT JUST UNETHICAL; IT IS ILLEGAL.

> *Lots of ways: By using various computer programs or by googling portions of the paper; by comparing your paper to your past performance; by asking you to define words you've used in your paper; by seeing all the links you've forgotten to convert to black (duh); by seeing the web address where you got the paper printed at the bottom of the paper (duh).*

The key to avoiding plagiarism and its consequences is identifying the sources of your information in your presentation. Changing a few words of someone else's work is not enough to avoid plagiarism. Some of our students have told us that plagiarism occurs *only* if they use an entire article or someone else's written presentation. Some also believe that it's okay to "borrow" a few phrases or someone else's idea. We quickly tell them that this behavior is plagiarism—no matter how small the amount you are stealing, it is still stealing. If they're not your original ideas, and most of the words are not yours, you are ethically obligated to tell your audience who wrote or said them and where they came from.

The following guidelines can help you avoid plagiarism:

- If you include an identifiable phrase or an idea that appears in someone else's work, always acknowledge and document your source.
- Do not use someone else's sequence of ideas and organization without acknowledging and citing the similarities in structure.
- Tell an audience exactly when you are citing someone else's exact words or ideas in your presentation.
- Never buy or use someone else's speech or writing and claim it as your own work.

Remember that ethical speakers are liked and respected by their audiences because they are honest, fair, caring, informed, and justifiably confident. Do not use what you know about the audience, the occasion, the setting, or the time limits to take unfair advantage of the audience or to achieve unethical goals. Make sure that both you and the audience benefit from your purpose. Always check that your content and your sources of information are truthful and qualified. Furthermore, if you present an argument, acknowledge both sides.

The Ethical Audience

Ethical audience members listen for ideas and information with open minds. They withhold evaluation until they comprehend what a speaker means. Ethical audiences are active listeners; they listen to understand, to empathize, to evaluate, and to appreciate. They think critically about a speaker's message. Unfortunately, some audience members may lack these skills. Even worse, they may not listen because they have decided, even before the presentation begins, that they don't like the message or the speaker. An audience with open, unprejudiced minds is essential for a genuine transaction to occur between speakers and listeners.

While the audience has the final say, they also have an ethical responsibility to do unto the speaker as they would have the speaker do unto them.

12.5

Adapting to the Context

What strategies and skills can help you adapt to the context of a presentation?

Whether you are preparing a presentation for a public speaking course or formal banquet, a prayer meeting, or a retirement party, take time to analyze the context of the situation.

Analyze and Adapt to the Logistics

Logistics refers to strategic planning—adapting a presentation to the audience size, the physical location, the equipment, and the amount of time you have.

Audience Size Knowing the size of your audience helps you choose appropriate audio and visual aids. For example, if there are hundreds of people in your audience, plan to use a microphone and make sure it's supported by a good sound system. If you expect 500 people in your audience, projecting images onto a large screen is more effective than using a small chart or demonstrating a detailed procedure.

Facilities Make sure you know as much as you can about where you will be speaking. Will audience members be seated in a theater-style auditorium, around a long conference table, or at round tables scattered throughout a seminar room? If you are in an auditorium that seats 800 people and you expect only 100 listeners to attend, consider closing off the balcony or side sections so that the audience will sit in front of you.

Equipment Computer-generated slide presentations are the norm in many speaking situations. Wireless microphones and sophisticated sound systems enable speakers to address large audiences with ease. Make sure you know in advance what is—and what isn't—available at the location where you will be speaking.

ASSESS the Facilities

- **What is the size, shape, and decor of the room?**
- **Does the room have good ventilation, comfortable seating, distracting sights or sounds?**
- **What are the seating arrangements (rows, tables)?**
- **What kind of lighting will there be? Can it be adjusted for the presentation?**
- **Will you speak from a stage or platform?**
- **Is there a good sound system?**

ASSESS the Equipment

- **What equipment, if any, do you need to be seen and/or heard?**
- **What equipment, if any, do you need for your audio or visual aids?**
- **Is there a lectern (adjustable, with a built-in light or microphone, space enough to hold your notes)?**
- **Do you need to make any special arrangements (a timer, water, special lighting, wireless microphone, a media technician)?**

Arrive at least 45 minutes before you speak. Check that everything you need is in the room, that the equipment works, and that you know how to dim or brighten the lights if needed. Allow enough time to find equipment if something is missing or to make last-minute changes.

Time The most important thing to consider about time is how long you are *scheduled* to speak. Plan your presentation so that it fits well within your time limit. Put a watch next to you when you speak or ask someone to give you a signal when it's time to begin your conclusion. And when that signal comes, don't ignore it, even if it means skipping major sections of your presentation. Audiences rarely like, appreciate, or return to hear a long-winded speaker.

Consider the following questions in relationship to your time limit: At what hour will you be speaking? For how long are you scheduled to speak? What comes before or after your presentation (other speakers, lunch, entertainment, a question-and-answer session)?

Analyze and Adapt to the Occasion

What's the occasion of your presentation? Will you be speaking at a celebration? Or is the occasion an oral class assignment, a memorial service, a convention keynote address, or testimony before a government agency? Make sure that your presentation suits the **occasion**—the reason an audience has assembled at a particular place and time. As is the case with setting, there are important questions to respond to as you prepare a presentation.

adapting to the context

243

How Long *Should* You Speak?

We often hear two questions about the time limit for a presentation: "What if I'm not given a time limit?" and "What if I have something *really* important to say and I have to talk longer?"

If you are not given a time limit, we recommend keeping your presentation under 20 minutes. Peggy Noonan, former President Reagan's speechwriter, recommends a 20-minute limit.[28] Granville Toogood, author of *The Articulate Executive*, reports the results of a study conducted by the U.S. Navy in which they tried to determine how long people can listen and retain information. The answer: 18 minutes.[29]

Of course, there are times when the circumstances or content requires that you speak longer than 20 minutes. In such cases, you have several options. You can cover the basics in 20 minutes and then set aside time for a question-and-answer session. You can use presentation aids or a video to break up your talk. You may also want to insert short personal stories or anecdotes to help drive home your point and give the audience a pleasant respite.[30]

Finally, don't fall into the ego trap of thinking that what you have to say is *so* important that it deserves more time. Your audience may not share this belief—no matter how long you take to convince them. Demonstrate respect for your audience's time and they will appreciate your self-discipline and consideration.

If you plan to speak for longer than 20 minutes ... Change the medium to break the tedium.

Remember, your presentation should be the center of an audience's attention. If something in your appearance could distract listeners, FIX IT.

What Is Your Relationship to the Occasion? When you are invited to make a presentation, ask yourself: Why have *I* been invited to speak to *this* audience in *this* place on *this* occasion? Speakers are not picked randomly. Make sure you understand how you are personally connected to the occasion.

What Does the Audience Expect? The nature of an occasion creates audience expectations about the way a presentation will be prepared and delivered. Business audiences may expect well-qualified speakers to pepper their presentations with sophisticated, computer-generated graphics. Audiences at political events are accustomed to sound bites on television and expect to hear short, crisp phrases. Audiences expect an uplifting tone at a graduation ceremony and a more raucous tone at a football pep rally. At a funeral, a eulogy may be touching or funny, but it's almost always very respectful and short. Do your best to match your speaking style and content to audience expectations.

What Should You Wear? Long before an audience hears what you say, they will see you, so wear something that matches the purpose and tone of your presentation. Your clothes don't have to be expensive or make a fashion statement. What matters is that they are appropriate for the situation. Common sense dictates our number-one piece of advice: Wear comfortable clothes. Presentations are stressful enough without worrying about your clothing. When selecting appropriate clothes for a presentation, dress as key members of your audience would.

Nothing on your body (clothes, grooming, accessories) should draw attention to itself. Clanging bracelets or earrings or ties featuring big patterns or cartoon characters may not be appropriate. Take items out of your pockets, whether they're pens in your shirt pocket or the change and keys in your pants pockets. Remember, your presentation should be the center of an audience's attention.

What's Your Preparation Plan?

Before you determine the content and structure of your message or practice your delivery, make sure you have made appropriate decisions about the four elements involved in presentation planning: purpose and topic, audience analysis, speaker credibility, and context. The following checklist will help determine whether you are ready to take the next steps in preparing your presentation.

Purpose and Topic

_____ 1. I know my purpose will inform, persuade, entertain, and/or inspire.

_____ 2. I have developed a specific, achievable, and relevant purpose statement.

_____ 3. My topic area reflects my interests, values, and/or knowledge.

Audience Analysis

_____ 1. I have researched, analyzed, and planned ways of adapting to audience characteristics, knowledge, and interests.

_____ 2. I have researched, analyzed, and planned ways of adapting to audience attitudes.

_____ 3. I have researched, analyzed, and planned ways of adapting to cultural differences in my audience.

Speaker Credibility

_____ 1. I have assessed my potential credibility by identifying my strengths, talents, achievements, and positive character traits.

_____ 2. I will demonstrate my competence and good character.

_____ 3. I have made ethical decisions about myself, others, purpose, context, content, structure, and expression.

Context

_____ 1. I have researched, analyzed, and planned ways of adapting to the logistics of the presentation (audience size, facilities, equipment, time).

_____ 2. I have researched, analyzed, and planned ways of adapting to the psychosocial context and occasion.

_____ 3. I have researched, analyzed, and planned ways of adapting to the cultural context.

Preparation Notes

Ways to Improve My Preparation

_____

_____

_____

_____

_____

_____

_____

_____

_____

_____

12.1
The Speech Preparation Process

How does preparation help you produce a more effective presentation?

- Being well prepared for a presentation will reduce your anxiety and increase the likelihood of a positive outcome.

- Many speakers identify "keeping your audience interested" as the *most* important speaking skill.

12.2
Determining Your Purpose and Topic

How does your purpose and topic affect the presentation planning process?

- Determining the purpose of a presentation helps you decide what you want your audience to know, think, feel, or do.

- Decide whether you want to inform, persuade, entertain, inspire, or a combination of all four goals in your presentation.

- When choosing a presentation topic that suits you and your purpose, consider your interests, values, knowledge, and what's interesting on the Web.

- Develop a specific, achievable, and relevant purpose statement to guide your preparation and narrow your topic appropriately.

12.3
Analyzing and Adapting to Your Audience

What strategies and skills can help you analyze and adapt to your audience?

- Audience analysis requires that you understand, respect, and adapt to listeners before and during a presentation.

- Answer the following questions about your audience: (1) Who are they? (2) Why are they here? (3) What do they know? (4) What are their interests? and (5) What are their attitudes?

- Adapt your presentation to what you know about your audience as you prepare it and use audience feedback to modify your presentation as you speak.

- As a speaker, honor the Audience's Bill of Rights. As an audience member, defend and stand up for your rights.

12.4
Enhancing Your Credibility

How does your credibility affect the success of a presentation?

- Speaker credibility (Aristotle's *ethos*) represents the extent to which an audience believes you and your message.

- The three major components of speaker credibility are character, competence, and charisma.

- Credibility is solely based on the attitudes and perceptions of the audience.

- You can improve your credibility by doing a personal inventory and tooting your own horn.

- Whereas the *audience* determines your credibility (*ethos*), *you* determine your ethics—your beliefs about what is right or wrong, moral or immoral, good or bad.

- The key to avoiding plagiarism and its consequences is identifying the sources of your information in your presentation.

12.5
Adapting to the Context

What strategies and skills can help you adapt to the context of a presentation?

- Adapt to the logistics of a presentation by analyzing and adjusting to the audience's size, the facilities, the equipment, and the time (time of day and length) of the presentation.

- Adapt to the occasion of the presentation by clarifying your relationship to the situation and by identifying and adapting to audience expectations.

- Make sure you dress comfortably and appropriately for the logistics and occasion of a presentation.

MySearchLab®

TEST YOUR KNOWLEDGE

12.1 How does preparation help you produce a more effective presentation?

1 According to research by John Daly and colleagues, anxious speakers are less likely to prepare effectively for making a presentation because
- a. their nervousness disrupts their thinking ability.
- b. they don't know *how* to prepare an effective presentation.
- c. they worry more about *choosing* a topic than achieving their purpose.
- d. they confuse ethics and ethos.
- e. they already know what they want to say.

2 Which of the following answers was ranked first in a survey of college students asking them to identify the speaking skills most important for improving their presentations?
- a. Selecting good ideas and information
- b. Keeping your audience interested
- c. Deciding what to say; choosing a good topic
- d. Organizing a presentation
- e. Reducing nervousness and stage fright

12.2 How does your purpose and topic affect the presentation planning process?

3 Which type of presentation seeks to instruct, enlighten, explain, describe, and/or demonstrate?
- a. Informative presentation
- b. Persuasive presentation
- c. Entertainment presentation
- d. Inspirational presentation
- e. Manuscript presentation

12.3 What strategies and skills can help you analyze and adapt to your audience?

4 Which of the five basic questions you should ask about your audience is answered in this response: "My audience wants to hear *me* speak because of my work in Darfur on behalf of Doctors without Borders"?
- a. Who are they?
- b. Why are they here?
- c. What are their interests?
- d. What are their attitudes?
- e. What are their values?

5 Which key element of human communication is aligned with "The right to have a presentation start and stop on time and to know, in advance, how much time it will take" in the Audience's Bill of Rights?
- a. Content
- b. Others
- c. Purpose
- d. Credibility
- e. Context

12.4 How does your credibility affect the success of a presentation?

6 The Institute for Global Ethics identified eight universal values. Which value would be addressed in a presentation on avoiding the pitfalls of plagiarism?
- a. Freedom
- b. Unity
- c. Love
- d. Truthfulness
- e. Unity

7 Which component of speaker credibility (*ethos*) is reflected in a speaker's level of energy, enthusiasm, vigor, and commitment?
- a. Character
- b. Charity
- c. Competence
- d. Charisma
- e. Caring

8 Whereas ethos is determined by the audience, ethics is determined by the
- a. content.
- b. speaker.
- c. others.
- d. structure.
- e. context.

12.5 What strategies and skills can help you adapt to the context of a presentation?

9 Logistical questions about a presentation's context focus on
- a. audience size.
- b. facilities.
- c. time.
- d. equipment.
- e. all of the above

10 This chapter advises you to remember this saying: "Change the medium to break the tedium." Under what circumstances should you apply this advice?
- a. If the audience knows nothing about your topic
- b. If your purpose is not clear
- c. If you plan to speak more than 20 minutes
- d. If there are more than 50 people in the audience
- e. If you don't have PowerPoint slides

Answers found on page 366.

Key Terms

Audience analysis	Ethos	Presentation speaking
Audience attitudes	Informative	Purpose statement
Character	presentation	Rhetoric
Charisma	Inspirational speaking	Self-centered interests
Competence	Logistics	Speaker credibility
Demographic	Occasion	Topic-centered
information	Persuasive presentation	interests
Entertainment speaking	Plagiarism	Values

CONTENT and ORGANIZATION

13

A student speaker created the following compelling introduction for a speech for her communication class:

On June 23, 2001, at 7:43 P.M., a smoldering car was found twisted around a tree. Two dead bodies. One adult. One baby. Why did this happen? Was it drunk driving? No. Adverse road conditions? No. A defect in the car? No. Something else took the life of my best friend and her baby brother. Something quite simple, quite common, and deadly: my best friend fell asleep at the wheel.

This student understood that a good introduction was only a small component of an effective presentation. She also needed content that was clear, interesting, valid, and persuasive.

After just an hour of research, she found the next sentence for her introduction: "Falling asleep accounts for 100,000 car accidents and 1,500 deaths every year." The more she researched, the more relevant information she discovered from sources such as the National Sleep Foundation, a book on healthy living, and several print and online articles describing the effects of sleep deprivation.

A good introduction is only a part of an effective presentation. Recall from Chapter 12 that you also must consider your purpose, your audience, your credibility, and the speaking context. Once you have addressed these essential elements, you then face the "What should I say?" dilemma. Cicero, the great Roman senator and orator, used the Latin word *inventio* to describe the speaker's attempt "to find out what he should say." He also identified a subsequent step, *dispositio*, as the task of arranging ideas and information for a presentation in an orderly sequence.[1] In this chapter, we examine both *inventio* and *dispositio*.

Researching and Selecting Your Content
How do you find good information for a presentation?

The **content** of your presentation consists of the ideas, information, and opinions you include in your message. As soon as you know you will be speaking, you should begin searching for and collecting **supporting material**, content that explains and/or advances your presentation's purpose and key points. Although you may have general ideas about the content and the types of supporting material you need, you should also do extensive research to find more. Even if you are an expert or have a unique background or life experience related to your topic, good research can help you support, verify, and reinforce the content of your message.

Gathering Supporting Material

Supporting material comes in many different forms from many different sources: definitions in dictionaries, background and historical information in encyclopedias, facts and figures online and in almanacs, true-life stories in magazines and on personal websites, and editorial opinions in newspapers, newsletters, and online sources. The best presenters use a mix of supporting material; they don't rely on just one type. Why? Different types of material have different strengths and weaknesses. Most audiences find an unending list of statistics boring. A speaker who tells story after story frustrates listeners if there's no clear reason for telling the stories.

Facts A **fact** is a verifiable observation, experience, or event known to be true. For example, the statement *"The King's Speech* won the 2011 Academy Award for Best Picture" is a fact, but the statement "I think *The Social Network* should have won" is not a fact—it is an opinion. Facts can be personal ("I went to the 2011 Super Bowl") or the official record of an event ("The Green Bay Packers won the 2011 Super Bowl"). Facts appear in headlines around the world ("In 2010—and for the first time in the company's 102-year history—General Motors sold more cars and trucks in China than it did in the United States.").[2]

Sometimes, an unknown or unusual fact can spark audience interest: "By testing water from a city's sewage-treatment plant, researchers can determine what illicit drugs are being used by the population of a specific city on a daily basis."[3] Regardless of their purpose, most presentations are supported by facts, which serve to remind, illustrate, demonstrate, and clarify.

Statistics **Statistics** is a branch of mathematics concerned with collecting, summarizing, analyzing, and interpreting numerical data. Statistics are used for many purposes—from describing the characteristics of a specific population to predicting events ranging from economic trends to football games.

In a 2010 speech to UNESCO (the United Nations Educational, Scientific, and Cultural Organization), Secretary of Education Arne Duncan used statistics to highlight the plight of failing high schools in the United States.[4]

> Fewer than 2,000 high schools in the United States—a manageable number—produce half of all its dropouts. These "dropout factories" produce almost 75 percent—three-fourths—of our dropouts from the minority community, our African American and Latino boys and girls.

Although audiences often equate statistics with facts, statistics are factual only if they are collected and analyzed fairly.

Testimony **Testimony** refers to statements or opinions that someone has spoken or written. You can support a presentation with testimony from books, speeches, plays, magazine articles, radio or television, courtrooms, interviews, or Web pages. Here's an excerpt from a student presentation:

> In her book, *Mommy, I'm Scared*, Professor Joanne Cantor writes: "From my 15 years of research on mass media and children's fear, I am convinced that TV programs and movies are the number-one preventable cause of nightmares and anxiety in children."

The believability of testimony depends on the credibility of the speaker or writer.

Definitions **Definitions** explain or clarify the meaning of a word, phrase, or concept. A definition can explain what *you* mean in a word or be as detailed as an encyclopedia definition. In the following example, in a presentation explaining the differences between jazz and the blues, a speaker used two types of definitions:

> The technical definition of the blues is a vocal and instrumental music style that uses a three-line stanza and, typically, a 12-measure form in which expressive inflections—blues notes—are combined with uniquely African American tonal qualities. Or according to an old bluesman's definition: The blues ain't nothin' but the facts of life.

> Use definitions if your presentation includes words or phrases that your audience may not know or may misunderstand.

Descriptions **Descriptions** create mental images for your listeners. They provide more details than definitions by offering causes, effects, historical background information, and characteristics. In an address about the Civil Rights Memorial in Atlanta,

Different types of information give a presentation added life and vitality.

ETHICAL COMMUNICATION

Don't Take It Out of Context

When you "take words out of context," you select isolated statements from a source and distort or contradict the speaker or writer's intended meaning. **When you take words out of context, you do harm to the writer, the audience, and eventually yourself.**

Words taken out of context resulted in a political uproar in 2010. Shirley Sherrod, an African American, was fired from her position as Georgia state director of rural development for the U.S. Department of Agriculture (USDA) after Andrew Breitbart, a politically conservative blogger, posted a two-and-a-half-minute video excerpt of a speech by Sherrod. The short clip showed Sherrod admitting that race made her question whether she should help a white farmer. On his cable television show, Bill O'Reilly called for Sherrod's resignation in response to the blog posting. The National Association for the Advancement of Colored People (NAACP) condemned her comments.

But Breitbart's chosen clip took Sherrod's words out of context. The comments that Sherrod made immediately after the statement excerpted in the clip explained that it was not so much about white and black but "about poor versus those who have." She talked about the white farmer and said, "I didn't let [race] get in the way of trying to help" him and that "in the end, we became very good friends, and that friendship has lasted for some time." In a subsequent interview, Roger Spooner, the farmer in question, said that Sherrod did everything she could for his family.

Unfortunately, those who read about or watched Breitbart's video excerpt failed to get a copy of the speech in its entirety. When it was discovered that her remarks were taken out of context, White House officials, the NAACP, and the secretary of agriculture apologized. The USDA offered Sherrod her job back. She refused it. When Bill O'Reilly learned about the rest of the speech, he said, "I owe Ms. Sherrod an apology for not doing my homework, for not putting her remarks into the proper context.[5]

Unethical speakers, audience members, and reporters often take testimony out of context in order to attack an author, discredit an idea, or gain credibility for something that is not supported by the full context.[6]

> **"When context is misplaced, so is the truth."**[7]
> —Dan Le Batard, columnist for the *Miami Herald*

---

a complex process or relating a new concept to something that the audience understands well.

Poets use analogies, as in "Memory is to love what the saucer is to the cup" (Elizabeth Bowen, *The House in Paris*, 1949). Comedians use analogies, as in "MTV is to music as KFC is to chicken" (Lewis Black). So do good speakers.

Use analogies to describe a complex process or to relate a new concept to something the audience already understands. Here's an example of an analogy that uses a computer to explain how our brain processes memories.

> Your short-term memory is like the RAM on a computer: it records the information in front of you right now. Some of what you experience seems to evaporate—like words that go missing when you turn off your computer without hitting SAVE. But other short-term memories . . . [are] downloaded onto the hard drive. These long-term memories, filled with past loves and losses and fears, stay dormant until you call them up.[9]

Examples An **example** refers to a specific case or instance. Examples make a large or abstract idea concrete and understandable; they can be facts, brief descriptions, or detailed stories. When someone says, "Give me an example," it's natural to reply with an

A speech on female blues singers from the 1920s is strengthened by specific examples. Playing a song by Bessie Smith (shown here) can make a good speech even better.

Carole Blair describes the architecture of the memorial. Here is an excerpt from that description:

> Immediately in front of the wall . . . is an off-center, black granite pedestal . . . the top of which forms a circle of about 12 feet in diameter. Water bubbles up from a well near the center of the structure and flows slowly and smoothly across its surface. Around the circumference of the tabletop is a . . . time line, marking 53 events of the civil

rights movement, beginning with the *Brown* v. *Board of Education* decision in 1954 and ending with the assassination of Dr. King in 1968.[8]

Analogies Analogies compare two things in order to highlight some point of similarity. They can identify the similarities in things that function in different contexts—for example, "If a copilot must be qualified to fly a plane, a U.S. vice president should be qualified to govern the country." Analogies are a useful way of describing illustration or instance that explains your idea. When asked for examples of individualistic cultures, you might list the United States, Australia, Great Britain, and Canada. Or, if you were making a presentation on female blues singers from the 1920s, you might name Ma Rainey, Bessie Smith, Victoria Spivey, and Alberta Hunter.[10]

Stories Real stories about real people in the real world can arouse attention, create an appropriate mood, and reinforce important ideas. **Stories** are accounts or reports about something that happened.

In the following example, a successful attorney with an incapacitating physical disability uses her brief, personal story to emphasize the importance of hope, hard work, and determination:

I was in an automobile accident just after high school, which left me in a wheelchair for life. I was trying to deal with that, a new marriage, and other personal problems, not the least of which was uncertainty about what I could do—about the extent of my own potential.[11]

> Audiences often remember a good story even when they can't remember much else about a presentation.

Documenting Your Sources

Documentation is citing the sources of your supporting material. You should document all supporting material (including information from Internet sources and interviews) in writing and then orally in your presentation.

Unlike writers, speakers rarely display complete footnotes during a presentation. Of course, they don't recite every detail such as the publisher, publisher's city, and page number of a citation. In speaking situations, citations must be oral. Your spoken citation—sometimes called an **oral footnote**—should include enough information to allow an interested listener to find the original sources you're citing. Generally, it's a good idea to provide the name of the person (or people) whose work you are citing, to say a word or two about that person's credentials, and to mention the source of the information. If you want the audience to have permanent access to the information you use, provide a handout listing your references with complete citations.

In a delicious speech about the benefits of drinking chocolate milk after strenuous exercise a student provided

> Documentation enhances your credibility as a speaker while assuring listeners of the validity of your content.

all the information anyone would need to find and verify his statement:

According to a 2011 press release from the University of Texas, a study led by Dr. John Ivy found that "serious and amateur athletes alike enjoyed physical recovered benefits when they drank low-fat chocolate milk after a vigorous workout."

Imagine how cumbersome it would have been to say, "According to a June 22, 2011 press release from the University of Texas Office of the President titled "Chocolate Milk Gives Athletes Leg-up After Exercises, Says University of Texas at Austin study," posted on http://www.utexas.edu/news/2011/06/22/milk_studies, Dr. John Ivy. . . .

Evaluating Your Supporting Material

Many speakers rely on researched information to support their claims and enhance their credibility. It is important that you evaluate every piece of supporting material before you use it. Make sure your information is **valid**—that the ideas, information, and opinions you include are well founded, justified, and accurate. The questions described in the sections that follow

COMMUNICATION & CULTURE

LINEAR VERSUS SPIRAL THINKING

Low-context cultures like the United States tend to use a linear style of thinking when developing a message—moving from facts, evidence, and proof to drawing logical conclusions. Other cultures use a more spiral style of thinking when developing a message—moving from dramatic supporting material to subtle conclusions. For example, members of many Arab and African cultures use detailed metaphors, similes, stories, and parables to reinforce or dramatize a point. The final message may be quite subtle or even

elusive. It's up to the audience to draw the intended conclusion.[12]

Because this textbook is primarily written for U.S. speakers and audiences, we focus on a more linear thinking style in which speakers use clear supporting material to back up their claims and outlines to map the content of their messages. When speaking to an audience that prefers a more spiral style of thinking, consider ways to use supporting material more dramatically and to present your conclusions in a less direct style.

The bold headline, "My Steamy Nights with Hillary in UFO Love Nest," is as comical as it is absurd. Why would anyone believe anything written in these kinds of publications?

will help you test the validity of your supporting material.

Is the Source Identified and Credible? Are the author and publisher identified? Are they reputable? For example, the sensational and often bizarre articles in the *National Enquirer* may be fun to read, but *The New York Times* and the *Wall Street Journal* are more likely to contain reliable information because their worldwide reputations depend on publishing accurate information. Ask yourself whether the source you are quoting is a recognized expert,

a firsthand observer, a respected journalist, or an informed blogger.

Is the Source Primary or Secondary? When researching and selecting supporting material, determine whether you are using a primary or secondary source of information. A **primary source** is the document, testimony, or publication in which information first appears. For example, an academic journal article that contains the results of an author's original research is a primary source. And don't overlook the most obvious

primary source of all—you. If you interview an expert or conduct a survey, you are the primary source when reporting the results.

A **secondary source**, such as an encyclopedia or Wikipedia, reports, repeats, or summarizes information from many sources. Look carefully at secondary sources of information to uncover, if possible, the primary source of the information.

Is the Source Biased? A source is **biased** when it states an opinion so slanted in one direction that it may not be objective or fair. If the source has a very strong opinion or will benefit from your agreement, be cautious. For years, tobacco companies publicly denied that cigarette smoking was harmful, even though their own research confirmed that it was. Even not-for-profit special-interest groups

COMMUNICATION IN *ACTION*

Evaluating Internet Information

In addition to the general tests of supporting material, you will want to apply special criteria to the information and opinions you find on websites. Ask the following questions to assess the validity and reliability of online supporting material:[13]

Criteria #1: Source Credibility

1 Is the author's or sponsor's identity and qualifications evident?

2 Have you checked other websites or sources to determine whether the

author's or sponsor's credentials are legitimate and/or reflect a particular bias?

3 Does the author or sponsor provide a contact email or address/phone number?

Criteria #2: Accuracy

1 Are the sources of factual information clearly listed so that you can verify them in another source?

2 Are there statements indicating where data from charts and graphs were gathered?

3 Is the information free of grammatical, spelling, and typographical errors that would indicate a lack of quality control?

Criteria #3: Objectivity

1 Is information represented as fact, or is it a mask for advertising and biased opinions?

2 Is the sponsor's point of view expressed clearly with well-supported arguments?

3 If the site is not objective, does it account for opposing points of view?

Criteria #4: Currency

1 When was the information produced or updated?

2 Is the material recent enough to be accurate and relevant?

3 Are there any indications that the material is kept up to date?

researching and selecting your content

such as the National Rifle Association, pro-choice or pro-life groups, or the American Association of Retired Persons have biases. The information they publish may be true, but the conclusions they draw from that information may be biased.

Is the Information Recent? Always note the date of the information you want to use. When was the information collected? When was it published? In this age of rapidly changing information, your information can become old news in a matter of hours. For current events or scientific breakthroughs, use magazines, journals, newspaper articles, or reliable Web sources. Look for the date indicating when the page was written or revised. If a website makes it difficult to locate this information, this may be a sign that the site is not credible and reliable.

Is the Information Consistent? Check whether the information you want to use reports facts and findings similar to information on the same subject from other reputable sources. Does the information make sense based on what you know about the topic? For example, if most doctors and medical experts agree that penicillin will *not* cure a common viral cold, why believe an obscure source that recommends it as a treatment?

Are the Statistics Valid? Good statistics can be informative, dramatic, and convincing. But statistics also can mislead, distort, and confuse. Make sure your statistics are well founded, justified, and accurate. Closely consider whether the statistics are believable and whether the researcher who collected and analyzed the data is a well-respected expert. Confirm who is reporting the statistics as well—is it the researcher or a reporter?

COMMUNICATION IN *ACTION*

Hoaxes, Rumors, Myths, Lies, and Urban Legends on the Web

Don't trust or believe everything you read online. In *Human Communication on the Internet*, Leonard Shedletsky and Joan Aitken note that misinformation on the Internet is a serious problem, particularly given that many disreputable sites appear valid and legitimate.[14] To make matters worse, Internet hoaxes, rumors, myths, and urban legends are often repeated over and over, making them appear to come from credible sources.

Several respected websites have taken up the challenge of identifying false rumors and legends. For example, the *St. Petersburg Times* website, polifact.com, won a Pulitzer Prize for helping readers separate political fact from fiction. Other websites focus on urban legends and myths, including snopes.com, urbanlegends.about.com, urbanmyths.com, suite101.com, and truthorfiction.com. Here are just a few examples found on these sites:

FALSE: President Obama's birth certificate is a forgery and proves that he was not a natural-born U.S. citizen.

FALSE: Bill O'Reilly's claim that the majority of Americans do "not support Obamacare" is false. The truth is that the public is evenly split on the health care bill.

FALSE: During the 2008 presidential campaign, Sarah Palin said, "I can see Russia from my house." The line was said by comedian Tina Fey in a satire of Palin's foreign policy credentials on *Saturday Night Live*.

At the same time, you may learn that some urban legends are true, such as the following: When first developed in the nineteenth century, Coca-Cola did, in fact, include cocaine in its formula.[15] Generally, though, urban legends are usually so far-fetched that they have been called a "cultural epidemic" and "thought contagion." Thus, before you include anything you find on the Web in your presentation, we urge you to identify the sources, analyze whether the sources are biased or hoaxes, and consult reputable sites for verification.

13.2
Organizing Your Presentation
What strategies should you use to organize the content of a presentation?

Michael Kepper, a marketing communication specialist, compares the need for organizing a presentation's content with the needs of a human body:

> A speech without structure is like a human body without a skeleton. It won't stand up. Spineless. Like a jellyfish. . . . Having structure won't make the speech a great one, but lacking structure will surely kill all the inspired thoughts . . . because listeners are too busy trying to find out where they are to pay attention.[16]

Organization refers to the way you arrange the content of your presentation into a clear and appropriate format. Organization helps you focus on the purpose of your presentation while

Research confirms that audiences react positively to well-organized presentations and negatively to poorly organized ones.[17]

deciding what to include and how to maximize the impact of your message.

As an audience member, you know that organization matters. It is difficult to understand and remember the words of a speaker who rambles and doesn't connect ideas. In fact, you may never want to hear that speaker again.

Identifying Your Central Idea

The **central idea** is a sentence that summarizes the key points of your presentation. Your central idea provides a brief preview of the organizational pattern you will follow to achieve your purpose.

The following example illustrates how topic area, purpose, and central idea are different but closely linked to one another:

Topic area   Traveling abroad

Purpose   To prepare travelers for a trip abroad

Central idea   Before visiting a foreign country, research the culture and the places you will visit, make sure you have the required travel documents, and get any immunizations and medicines you might need.

Determining the key points of your presentation is like fitting together the pieces of a puzzle—if one point doesn't fit or follow, the rest may not work.

Determining Your Key Points

Begin organizing your presentation by determining your key points. **Key points** represent the most important issues or the main ideas you want your audience to understand and remember about your message.

Look for a pattern or natural groups of ideas and information as the basis for key points. Depending on your purpose and topic area, this can be an easy task or a daunting puzzle. Inexperienced speakers often feel overwhelmed by what seems to be mountains of unrelated facts and figures. Don't give up!

Before creating an outline, consider using two other techniques to identify your key points and build a preliminary structure for your message: mind mapping and the Speech Framer.

Mind Mapping Mind mapping encourages the free flow of ideas and lets you define relationships among those ideas. It harnesses the potential of your whole brain while it's in a highly creative mode of thought to generate ideas.[18] On this page, for instance, you will see the mind map that one student created for a presentation on Muzak, that ever-present background music you often hear in stores, elevators, and offices.[19]

This mind map for a speech on Muzak demonstrates one method of determining key points and establishing relationships among ideas.

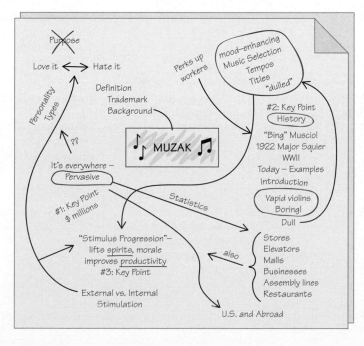

organizing your presentation

255

The mind map is a hodgepodge of words, phrases, lists, circles, and arrows. Certainly it contains more concepts than should be included in a single presentation. After completing such a mind map, you can label circled ideas as key points and put them in a logical order.

Mind maps allow you to see your ideas without superimposing a predetermined organizational pattern on them. They also let you postpone the need to arrange your ideas in a pattern until you collect enough information to organize the content. Use mind mapping when you have lots of ideas and information but are having trouble deciding how to select and arrange the materials for a presentation.

The Speech Framer The **Speech Framer** is a visual model for organizing presentation content that provides a place for every component of a presentation while encouraging experimentation and creativity.[20] Below is an example of a Speech Framer based on our student's speech from the chapter-opening story on the dangers of driving while sleep deprived.

The Speech Framer lets you experiment with a variety of organizational formats. For example, if you have four key points, you merely add a column to the frame. If you think you have three key points but find that you don't have good supporting material for the second key point, you might consider deleting that point. If you only have three types of supporting material for one key point and two for the others, that's okay—just make sure all the supporting material is strong. If you notice that several pieces of supporting material apply to two key points, you can combine them into a new key point. And if you must have five or more key points, use only one or two pieces of supporting material for each point to control the length of your presentation.

In addition to helping you organize the content of your presentation, you can use the single-page Speech Framer as your speaking notes. It allows you to see the presentation laid out entirely before you practice or deliver it.

Select an Organizational Pattern

Even the most experienced speakers may find it difficult to see how their ideas and information fall into a clear structure. Fortunately, there are several commonly used organizational patterns that can help you clarify your central idea and find an effective format for your presentation.[21]

THE SPEECH FRAMER: ASLEEP AT THE WHEEL

Introduction: Story about my best friend's death in a car accident.

Central Idea: Falling asleep accounts for 100,000 car accidents and 1,500 deaths every year. Everyone knows about the dangers of drunk driving, but very few of us know about the dangers of sleep deprivation—and what to do about it.

Key Points	#1 Why we need sleep. Transition: What happens when you don't get enough sleep?	#2 Sleep deprivation affects your health, well-being, and safety. Transition: So how can you ease your tired body and mind?	#3 Three steps can help you get a good night's sleep.
Support	Would you drive home from class drunk? 14 hrs w/o sleep = .1 blood alcohol level Very long day = .05 blood alcohol level	Lack of sleep affects your attitude and mood (results of study)	1 Decide how much sleep is right for you: a Keep a sleep log. b Most people need 8 or more hours a night.
Support	Circadian clock controls sleep & also regulates hormones, heart rate, body temperature, etc.	Lack of sleep affects your health. Most important sleep is between 7th and 8th hour of sleep.	2 Create a comfy sleep environment. a Don't sleep on a full or empty stomach. b Cut back on fluids. c No alcohol or caffeine before sleep.
Support	Things that rob you of sleep: 24-hour stores; Internet; television; studying; homework	Symptoms: • Crave naps or doze off? • Hit snooze button a lot? • Hard to solve problems? • Feel groggy, lethargic?	3 Don't take your troubles to bed. a Can't sleep, get up. b Soothing music. c Read.

Conclusion: Summarize the Three Key Points. Final line: There is so much in life to enjoy. Sleep longer, live longer.

For a presentation about facial expressions in different cultures, a topical arrangement works well.

Topic area   Brain structure

Purpose   To explain how major sections of the brain are responsible for different functions

Central idea   A guided tour of the brain begins in the hindbrain, moves through the midbrain, and ends in the forebrain, with side trips to the right and left hemispheres.

Key points

   A   The hindbrain

   B   The midbrain

   C   The forebrain

   D   The right and left hemispheres

ARRANGE BY SUBTOPICS

Topical arrangement involves dividing a large topic into smaller subtopics. Subtopics can describe reasons, characteristics, or techniques. Use a topical arrangement if your ideas and information can be divided into discrete categories of relatively equal importance.

Topic area   Facial expressions in different cultures

Purpose   To appreciate that some facial expressions don't always translate between cultures

Central idea   Americans and native Japanese often misinterpret facial expressions depicting fear, sadness, and disgust.

Key points

   A   Fear

   B   Sadness

   C   Disgust

SEQUENCE IN TIME

Time arrangement orders information according to time or calendar dates. Most step-by-step procedures begin with the first step and continue sequentially (or chronologically) through the last step. Use a time arrangement when your key points occur in time relative to each other, as in recipes, assembly instructions, technical procedures, and historical events.

Topic area   Making vanilla ice cream

Purpose   To explain how to make custard-based vanilla ice cream

Central idea   To make homemade vanilla ice cream, make sure that you combine and heat the ingredients properly, know when the custard is thick enough, and correctly churn the ice cream.

Key points

   A   Warm up and whisk in the first ingredients.

   B   Cook the custard slowly.

   C   Cool and add final ingredients.

   D   Refrigerate before churning.

POSITION IN SPACE

Use a **space arrangement** if your key points can be arranged in terms of their location or physical relationship to one another.

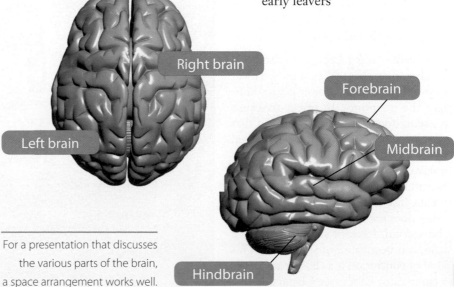

For a presentation that discusses the various parts of the brain, a space arrangement works well.

PRESENT A PROBLEM AND A SOLUTION

Use a **problem–solution arrangement** to describe a harmful or difficult situation (the problem) and then offer a plan to solve the problem (the solution). Problems can be as simple as a squeaky door or as significant as world famine.

Topic area   Behavioral problems in groups

Purpose   To provide suggestions for solving common behavioral problems that occur in group discussions and meetings

Central idea   Learning how to deal with three common behavioral problems in groups will improve a group's performance.

Key points

   A   Dealing with nonparticipants

   B   Dealing with disruptive behavior

   C   Dealing with latecomers and early leavers

organizing your presentation

257

STOP&THINK

The Organizational Jigsaw Puzzle

Develop a purpose statement, central idea, and list of key points for a presentation on "The Care and Treatment of Shoulder Problems" using any of the subtopics provided. You may delete or add subtopics to create an effective organizational pattern.

Topic: Care and Treatment of Common Shoulder Problems

Anatomy of the shoulder	Oral medication
Arthroscopic surgery	Prevention of shoulder problems
Causes of shoulder injuries	Physical therapy
Cold treatment	Shoulder exercises
Cortisone injections	Shoulder injury symptoms
Diagnosing shoulder injuries	Shoulder separations
Heat treatment	Shoulder sprains
How the shoulder moves	Torn rotator cuff
Need for early treatment	

SHOW CAUSE AND EFFECT

Use a **cause-and-effect arrangement** either to present a cause and its resulting effects or to detail the effects that result from a specific cause.

Topic area   Children and television

Purpose   To describe the harmful effects that television has on children

Central idea   Watching too much television negatively affects children and their families because it uses time that could be spent on more important activities.

Key points

A Television has a negative effect on children's physical fitness.

B Television has a negative effect on children's school achievement.

C Television watching may become a serious addiction.

In cause-and-effect presentations, speakers may claim that eating red meat causes disease or that lower taxes stimulate the economy. In effect-to-cause presentations, speakers may claim that sleepiness or lack of energy can be caused by an iron deficiency or that a decrease in lake fish is caused by global warming. Be careful with cause-and-effect arrangements. Just because one thing follows another does not mean that the first causes the second. Lack of sleep, not lack of iron, can be a cause of sleepiness. This kind of conclusion is a classic example of a faulty cause fallacy (see Chapter 4).

TELL STORIES AND SHARE EXAMPLES

A series of well-told stories or dramatic examples can be so compelling and interesting that they become the organizational pattern for a presentation.

Topic area   Leaders and adversity

Purpose   To convince listeners that disabilities are not barriers to success

Central idea   Many noteworthy leaders have lived with disabilities.

Key points

A Franklin D. Roosevelt, president of the United States, had polio

B Jan Scruggs, disabled soldier and Vietnam Memorial founder

C Helen Keller, deaf and blind advocate

COMPARE AND CONTRAST

Use a **comparison–contrast arrangement** to demonstrate how two things are similar or different. This pattern works well in two situations: (1) when an unfamiliar concept can be explained by comparing it with a familiar concept or (2) when you are demonstrating the advantages of one alternative over another. Comparisons can be real (comparing products or contrasting medical treatments) or fanciful (comparing student success to racehorse success).

Topic area   Gas-powered cars versus gas–electric hybrid cars

Purpose   To recommend ways of evaluating gas-powered and gas–electric hybrid cars

Central idea   Comparing performance, fuel economy, and reliability can help you decide whether to purchase a gas-powered or gas–electric hybrid car.

Key points

A Performance

B Fuel economy

C Predicted reliability and battery life

For a presentation about the advantages of fuel-efficient vehicles, consider using the comparison–contrast arrangement.

Know Thy Self

How Creative Are You?

If you want your presentation to be interesting and memorable, think creatively about its structure. Lee Towe, president of Innovators International, defines creativity as consisting of two parts: creative thinking and creative output.[22] *Creative output* consists of connecting and combining previously unrelated elements. For example, the circles and arrows you draw on a mind map allow you to combine ideas from various places on the page.

For example, Patricia Phillips, a customer service expert, used excerpts from popular songs to begin each major section of her training seminar in a creative way: "I Can't Get No Satisfaction" by the Rolling Stones, "Help" by the Beatles, "Respect" by Aretha Franklin, and "Don't You Come Back No More" by Ray Charles.

Creativity, however, runs some risks. Some audience members may be unfamiliar with the songs chosen by a speaker. Or, the audience may have expected or wanted a more technical presentation. **If you want to use creative patterns, make sure your audience will understand and appreciate your creativity.**

So how creative are you? In three minutes, list all of the uses you can imagine for a balloon. When you finish your three minutes of thinking, rate the creativity of your answers based on the following criteria:

- **Quantity:** Did you come up with more than 24 ideas?
- **Variety:** Did you come up with at least five categories of answers? For example, birthday decorations and prom decorations would be the same category—decorations.
- **Uniqueness:** Did you have unusual items on your list? For example, most people would say that a balloon can be used as decoration. A more creative person might suggest using blown-up balloons to fill empty space when packing a box for shipment.[23]

13.3
Outlining Your Presentation

How can outlining help you structure a presentation?

Outlines—just like presentations and speakers—come in many shapes and forms. Here we look at three types of outlines and how they can help you organize the content of a presentation.

Preliminary Outlines

Outlines begin in a preliminary form with a few basic building blocks. You can use a **preliminary outline** to put the major pieces of almost any presentation in order, modifying it on the basis of the number of key points and the types and amount of supporting material. Aim for at least two pieces of supporting material under each key point—facts, statistics, testimony, definitions, descriptions, analogies, examples, or stories.

After you identify the key points that will support your central idea and after you choose an organizational pattern to structure your message, determine which key points go first, second, or last. In many cases, the organizational pattern you choose dictates the order. For example, if you use time arrangement, the first step in a procedure comes first. If your format

Preliminary OUTLINE FORMAT

Topic Area

I Introduction

  A Purpose/topic

  B Central idea

  C Brief preview of key points

    1 Key point #1

    2 Key point #2

    3 Key point #3

II Body of the presentation

  A Key point #1

    1 Supporting material

    2 Supporting material

  B Key point #2

    1 Supporting material

    2 Supporting material

  C Key point #3

    1 Supporting material

    2 Supporting material

III Conclusion

Strategies for ORDERING KEY POINTS[24]

■ **STRENGTH AND FAMILIARITY.** Place your strongest points first and last and your weakest or least familiar idea in the middle position so that you start and end with strength.

■ **AUDIENCE NEEDS.** If your audience needs current information, satisfy that need early. Background information can come later. If you are speaking about a controversial topic, begin with a point that focuses on the background of an issue or on the reasons for a change.

■ **LOGISTICS.** If you're one of a series of presenters, you may end up with less time to speak than was originally scheduled. Plan your presentation so that the strongest key points come first in case you need to cut your presentation short.

Brief Outline

I Introduction: Story of Best Friend's Death in Car Accident

II Central idea: Stay Longer, Drive Safer, Live Longer

III Key Points

  A Importance and Need for Sleep

    1 Lack of sleep = alcohol-impaired effects

    2 Things that rob our sleep: media, work hours, study and homework, etc.

    3 Circadian clock regulates body functions

  B Sleep Deprivation

    1 Influences attitudes and moods

    2 Symptoms of sleep deprivation: dozing, groggy, flawed thinking, etc.

  C How to Get a Good Night's Sleep

    1 Decide how much sleep you need

    2 Create a comfy sleep environment

    3 Don't take trouble to bed

IV Conclusion: Recognize the symptoms; alter your habits. Sleep Longer, Live Longer

COMPREHENSIVE OUTLINE

"What's Fair Is Fair" by Regina Smith

I Introduction

  A Americans love fairness.

  B Many Americans oppose affirmative action for minority students because it seems unfair.

  C There are other preferences for college admission that are just as unfair.

(*Transition:* Let's start with the oldest type of preference.)

II Body

  A Legacy Admissions

    1 Legacy admissions began in the 1920s to give the children of wealthy white alumni preference over the children of Jews and immigrants.

    2 Legacy students' SATs and GPAs are lower than nonlegacy students.

    3 Percent of legacy students: U. of Penn, 41%; U. of Virginia, 52%; Notre Dame U., 57%.

  B Athletic Scholarships

    1 National Collegiate Athletic Association college admissions standards:

      a Combined SAT score of 1010 with a 2.0 high school GPA.

      b Combined SAT score of 850 with a 2.5 high school GPA.

    2 Athletes get special treatment: special advisors, paid tutors, easier classes.

    3 Poor graduation rates:

      a Division I football players: 51% rate.

      b Division I basketball players: 40% rate.

      c Of 3,700 athletes, 50% earn degrees.

      d Exception at Duke University: 90% graduation rate for scholarship athletes.

    4 Reason for athletic preferences is money:

      a $6 billion for NCAA television contracts.

      b $187 million to Division 1 schools.

      c Low-income scholarships

    5 U. of California grants scholarships to "socioeconomically disadvantaged" students.

    6 What about blue-collar and middle-class students who struggle to pay tuition?

  C Affirmative Action

    1 Why is affirmative action singled out as unfair?

    2 Universities relax standards for alumni children, for athletes, and for poor students—why not African American students?

    3 Quote from Ron Wilson, African American representative from Texas.

III Conclusion

  A Either stop giving preferences to legacy students, athletes, and poor students, or continue affirmative action programs.

  B Do what is fair.

does not dictate the order of key points, place your best ideas in strategic positions.

If you use mind mapping or the Speech Framer to generate key points, you have everything you need to develop a preliminary outline for your presentation. Take another look at the student Speech Framer for the student speech *Asleep at the Wheel* on p. 256. Notice how easily it serves as the basis for the brief outline shown above.

Comprehensive Outline

A **comprehensive outline** is an all-inclusive presentation framework that follows established outlining rules. A preliminary outline helps you plan your presentation; a comprehensive outline creates the first draft of your presentation. There are two very basic rules for comprehensive outlining: (1) use numbers, letters, *and* indentations and (2) divide your subpoints logically.

Use Numbers, Letters, and Indentations Like most good outlines, a comprehensive outline uses a system of indenting and numbers and letters.

Roman numerals (I, II, III) signify the major divisions such as the introduction, body, and conclusion. Indented capital letters (A, B, C) are used for key points. Additional indents use Arabic numbers (1, 2, 3) for more specific points and supporting material. If you need a fourth level, indent again and use lowercase letters (a, b, c).

Divide Your Subpoints Logically Each major point should include at least two subpoints indented under it, or none at all. If there is an A, there must be a B; for every 1, there must be a 2.

Wrong: I.

        A.

      II.

Right: I.

        A.

        B.

      II.

As much as possible, try to keep your key points consistent in terms of grammar and format; for example, if you begin each subpoint with a verb, then each subpoint that follows should also begin with a verb and so forth. The comprehensive outline on the previous page for "What's Fair Is Fair," by Regina Smith, was developed for her class presentation on affirmative action and college admissions.

Speaking Outline

For the actual delivery of your presentation, you may need to create a **speaking outline**—either a short outline that includes little more than a list of key points and reminders of supporting material or a more complex and detailed outline that includes numerous quotations, statistics, or other data. Some speaking outlines may also include notes on when to introduce and remove a visual aid or provide a handout.

13.4
Connecting Your Key Points

How do connectives make a presentation more coherent?

An outline shows your structure and your key points and supporting material, but it's missing the "glue" that attaches the key points to one another and makes your presentation a coherent whole. **Connectives** are this glue, and they include internal previews and summaries as well as transitions and signposts.[25]

Internal Previews and Internal Summaries

An **internal preview** identifies, in advance, the key points of a presentation or section in a specific order. It tells audience members what you are going to cover and in what order. For example,

> How do researchers and doctors explain obesity? Some offer genetic explanations; others psychological ones. Either or both factors can be responsible for your never-ending battle with the bathroom scale.

Internal summaries are a useful way to end a major section and to reinforce important ideas. They also are an opportunity to repeat critical ideas or information. For example,

> So remember, before spending hundreds of dollars on diet books and exercise toys, make sure that your weight problem is not influenced by the number and size of your fat cells, your hormone level, your metabolism, or the amount of glucose in your bloodstream.

Transitions

The most common type of connective is the **transition**—a word, number, brief phrase, or sentence that helps you move from one key point or section to another. Transitions act like lubricating oil to keep a presentation moving smoothly. In the following examples, the transitions are underlined:

<u>Yet</u> it's important to remember . . .

<u>In addition</u> to metabolism, there is . . .

<u>On the other hand</u>, some people believe . . .

<u>Finally</u>, a responsible parent should . . .

Transitions also function as minipreviews and minisummaries that link the conclusion of one section to the beginning of another. For example,

> After you've eliminated these four genetic explanations for weight gain, it's time to consider several psychological factors.

Signposts

A fourth type of connective is **signposts**—short phrases that, like signs on the highway, tell or remind listeners where you are in the organizational structure of a presentation. If you are discussing four genetic explanations for weight gain, begin each explanation with numbers—first, second, third, and fourth: "Fourth and finally, make sure your glucose level has been tested and is within normal levels." For example,

> Even if you can't remember all of his accomplishments, please remember one thing: Alexa Curry is the only candidate who has been endorsed by every newspaper and civic association in the county.

13.5
Beginning Your Presentation

What strategies will help you begin a presentation successfully?

Introductions capitalize on the power of first impressions. First impressions can create a positive, lasting impression and pave the way for a highly successful presentation. A weak beginning gives audience members a reason to tune out or remember you as a poor speaker. Effective introductions give your audience time to adjust, to block out distractions, and to focus attention on you and your message.

There are many strategies for beginning a presentation effectively. The following methods represent just a handful of the more common introductory strategies that can be used separately or in combination: statistics and examples; quotations; stories; metaphors; questions; references to places; occasions; incidents and events; and addressing audience needs.

GOALS OF THE INTRODUCTION

Focus Audience Attention and Interest
Gain audience attention by using compelling supporting material, involving them actively, and speaking expressively.

Connect to Your Audience
Find a way to connect your message to audience interests, attitudes, beliefs, and values.

Put You in Your Presentation
Link your expertise, experiences, and personal enthusiasm to your topic or purpose. Personalize your message.

Set the Emotional Tone
Make sure the introduction sets an appropriate emotional tone that matches its purpose. Use appropriate language, delivery styles, and supporting material.

Preview the Message
Give your audience a sneak preview about the subject. State your central idea and *briefly* list the key points you will cover.

Use a Statistic or Example

Sometimes, your research turns up a statistic or example that is unusual or dramatic. If you anticipate a problem in gaining and keeping audience attention, an interesting statistic or example can do it for you:

> The statistics are appalling: More than 5,000 juveniles and 35,000 adults die each year from gunshot wounds. Since 1984, the homicide rate for males has tripled. This is an epidemic! An epidemic that is about 10 times as big in terms of lives lost as the great polio epidemic of the first half of the twentieth century.[26]

Quote Someone

A dramatic statement or eloquent phrase written by someone else can make an ideal beginning. A good quotation helps an audience overcome their doubts, especially when the quotation is from a writer or speaker who is highly respected or an expert source

of information. Remember to give the writer or speaker of the quotation full credit.

We need more money, high-quality instruction, and better equipment in all of our science classes. Here is how Arne Duncan, the Secretary of Education, put it in a 2009 address to the National Science Teachers Association: "America won the space race but, in many ways, American education lost the science race. A decade ago . . . our best districts could compete with anyone in the world, but our worst districts—which, of course, were in low-income communities— were on a par with third-world countries."[27]

> [Effective introductions] . . . establish a relationship among three elements: you, your message, and your audience.[28]

Tell a Story

Audiences will give you their undivided attention if you tell a good story and tell it well. Consider using a story about a personal hardship, a triumph, or even an embarrassment. Remember that the purpose of using a story is to illustrate a concept or idea. The following example is from a student presentation:

> When I was 15, I was operated on to remove the deadliest form of skin cancer, a melanoma carcinoma. My doctors injected 10 shots of steroids into each scar every three weeks to stop the scars from spreading. I now know that it wasn't worth a couple of summers of being tan to go through all that pain and suffering. Take steps now to protect yourself from the harmful effects of the sun.

Use a Metaphor

Dr. Ralph Bunche, grandson of a former slave, earned a PhD from Harvard, was a member of the UN

Dr. Ralph Bunche

Secretariat, and later won the Nobel Peace Prize. In June 1949, Dr. Bunche began a speech at Brandeis University with a "road to peace" metaphor that explains what must be done to achieve a more peaceful world:

> There is no road in the world today more important than the road to peace. It is, to date, insufficiently traveled, and indeed, not at all clearly charted. The United Nations is attempting both to chart it and to guide the nations and people of the world along it.[29]

This metaphor is an eloquent way of beginning a presentation.

Ask a Question

Asking a question attracts your audience's attention because it challenges them to think about an answer. One of the best kinds of questions elicits a response such as "I had no idea!" A student speaker used this technique in a series of questions:

> What do China, Iran, Saudi Arabia, and the United States have in common? Nuclear weapons? No. Abundant oil resources? No. What we have in common is this: Last year, these four countries accounted for nearly all the executions in the world.[30]

Refer to the Current Place or Occasion

A simple way to begin a presentation is to refer to the place in which you are speaking or the occasion for the

The Primacy and Recency Effects

As predicted by Hermann Ebbinghaus, a German psychologist who spearheaded the research on memory and recall, the parts of a presentation audiences most remember are the beginning and the end. Ebbinghaus, who is best known for his discovery of the *forgetting curve* and the *learning curve*, also discovered the *serial position effect*, which explains that "for information learned in a sequence, recall is better for items at the beginning (**primacy effect**) and the end (**recency effect**) than for items in the middle of the sequence."[31]

Interestingly, the primacy and recency effects link up with what we know about listening and memory. We are more likely to recall the last thing we hear because the information is still in our short-term memory. In contrast, we are likely to remember the first thing we hear because the information has had time to become part of our long-term memory. The poorest recall of information is in the middle of a sequence "because the information is no longer in short-term memory and has not yet been placed in long-term memory."[32]

Originally, the primacy and recency effects evolved from studies of what people remember after hearing a list of words or numbers. Today, it has been applied to studying how first and last impressions affect how we react to and feel about other people. It also has found its way into the study of presentations, specifically to emphasize the critical importance of a presentation's introduction and conclusion.

---

gathering. Your audience's memories and feelings about a specific place or occasion conjure up the emotions needed to capture their attention and interest.

When Dr. Martin Luther King Jr. made his famous "I Have a Dream" presentation on the steps of the Lincoln Memorial, his first few words echoed Abraham Lincoln's famous Gettysburg Address ("Four score and seven years ago"):

> Five score years ago, a great American, in whose symbolic shadow we stand, signed the Emancipation Proclamation.[33]

Address Audience Needs

When there is a crisis, address the problem at the outset. If budget cuts require salary reductions, audience members are not interested in clever questions or dramatic statistics:

> As you know, the state has reduced our operating budget by 2.7 million dollars. It is also just as important that you know this: All of you will have a job here next year—and the year after. There will be no layoffs. Instead, there will be cutbacks on nonpersonnel budget lines, downsizing of programs, and possibly short furloughs.

TIPS FOR STARTING STRONG

- PLAN THE BEGINNING AT THE END. Don't plan your introduction until you have developed the content of your presentation.

- DON'T APOLOGIZE. Don't use your introduction to offer excuses or apologize for poor preparation, weak delivery, or nervousness.

- AVOID BEGINNING WITH "MY SPEECH IS ABOUT . . ." Boring beginnings do not capture audience attention or enhance a speaker's credibility. Be original and creative.

13.6

Concluding Your Presentation

What strategies will help you end a presentation effectively?

Just as audiences remember things that are presented first (the primacy effect), they also remember information that comes last (recency effect). Your final words have a powerful and lasting effect on your audience members and determine how they think and feel about you and your presentation.[34] Like the introduction, a conclusion establishes a relationship among you, your topic, and your audience.

Some methods of concluding your presentation reinforce your message; others strengthen the audience's final impression of you. Use any of the following approaches separately or in combination: summarize, quote someone, tell a story, use poetic language, call for action, or refer to the beginning.

Summarize

One of the best and most direct ways of concluding a presentation is to provide a succinct summary that reinforces your key points. Summaries should be memorable, clear, and brief. Here, a student speaker uses questions to emphasize his central idea and key points:

> Now, if you hear someone ask whether more women should serve in the U.S. Congress, ask and then answer the two questions I discussed today: Can women and their issues attract big donors? And, are

women too nice to be "tough" in politics? Now that you know how to answer these questions, don't let doubters stand in the way of making a woman's place in the House.

Summarizing your key points is an effective way of concluding most presentations. If, however your key points have been laid out clearly *and* you want to conclude by motivating, inspiring, arousing emotions, or moving your audience to action, you will need to consider other or additional concluding strategies.

Quote Someone

Concluding a presentation with a quotation can be as effective and appealing as quoting someone in your introduction. Because quotations are memorable, clear, and brief, speakers often use them to conclude their presentations. Good research can provide a quotation with a dramatic effect.

Tell a Story

End with a story when you want the audience to visualize the central idea of your presentation. Marge Anderson, chief executive of the Mille Lacs Band of Ojibwe Indians, concluded a presentation with a story. (See the complete speech in Chapter 16.)

> Years ago, white settlers came to this area and built the first European-style homes. When Indian People walked by these homes and saw [windows], they looked through them to see what the strangers inside were doing. The settlers were shocked, but it made sense when you think about it: Windows are made to be looked through from both sides. Since then, my People have spent many years looking at the world through your window. I hope today I've given you a reason to look at it through ours.[35]

Use Poetic Language

Being poetic doesn't necessarily mean ending with a poem. Rather, it means using language that inspires and creates memorable images. In her tribute to the late Coretta Scott King, poet Maya Angelou concluded with poetic, prayerlike phrases:

> I pledge to you, my sister, I will never cease.
>
> I mean to say I want to see a better world.
>
> I mean to say I want to see some peace somewhere.
>
> I mean to say I want to see some honesty, some fair play.
>
> I want to see kindness and justice. This is what I want to see and I want to see it through my eyes and through your eyes, Coretta Scott King.[36]

Call for Action

A challenging but effective way to end a presentation is to call for action. Use a call for action when you want your audience to do more than merely listen—when you want them to *do* something. A call to action might mean rallying an audience to remember something important, to think about the relevance of a story you told, or to ask themselves a significant question.

Dr. Robert M. Franklin, president of Morehouse College, ended remarks delivered to a town hall meeting of students on his campus as follows:

> Morehouse is your house. You must take responsibility for its excellence. . . . If you want to be part of something rare and noble, something that the world has not often seen—a community of educated, ethical, disciplined black men more powerful

than a standing army—then you've come to the right place. . . . Up, you mighty men of Morehouse, you aristocrats of spirit, you can accomplish what you will![37]

> **Don't end by demanding something from your audience unless you are reasonably sure you can get it.**

Refer to the Beginning

Consider ending your presentation with the same technique you used to begin it. If you began with a quotation, end with the same or a similar quotation. If you began with a story, refer back to that story. Audiences like this concluding method because it returns to something familiar and "bookends" the content of your presentation:

> Remember the story I told you about two-year-old Joey, a hole in his throat so he can breathe, a tube jutting out of his stomach so he can be fed. For Joey, an accidental poisoning was an excruciatingly painful and horrifying experience. For Joey's parents, it was a time of fear, panic, and helplessness. Thus, it is a time to be prepared for, and even better, a time to prevent.

Knowing that you have a well-prepared and strong ending for your presentation can calm your nerves and inspire your audience. The most effective endings match the mood and style of the presentation, and make realistic assumptions about the audience.

GOALS of the Conclusion

Be Memorable

Give the audience a reason to remember you and your presentation. Show how your message affected you and how it affects them.

Be Clear

Repeat the one thing you want your audience to remember at the end of your presentation.

Be Brief

The announced ending of a presentation should never go beyond one or two minutes.

Can You Match the Organizational Patterns?

Each of the following examples demonstrates how to use one (or more) of the organizational patterns listed below. Try to match each outline with a pattern.

Organizational Patterns

A   Topical arrangement   E   Causes and effects
B   Time arrangement   F   Stories and examples
C   Space arrangement   G   Comparison–contrast
D   Problem–solution

Outline Examples

——— 1. The Three Stages of Pregnancy

First trimester
Second trimester
Third trimester

——— 2. Four Basic Techniques Used to Play Volleyball

Setting
Bumping
Spiking
Serving

——— 3. The Richest Sources of Diamonds

South Africa
Tanzania
Murfreesboro, Arkansas

——— 4. The Legacies of Presidents Reagan, Bush Sr., and Clinton

Domestic politics
International politics
Party politics

——— 5. Homeless Shelters and Homeless Families

The Khoo family
The Taylor family
The Arias family

——— 6. Slowing the AIDS Epidemic

AIDS is a devastating disease.
A cure has not been found.
New drug "cocktails" can slow the onset of AIDS.

——— 7. Aspirin and Heart Attacks

Does research verify that aspirin prevents heart attacks?
Who should follow the aspirin prescription?
Are there potential, dangerous side effects of aspirin therapy?

13.1
Researching and Selecting Your Content

How do you find good information for a presentation?

- Effective speakers use several forms of supporting material: facts, statistics, testimony, definitions, descriptions, analogies, examples, and stories.

- Document your supporting material in writing and then orally in your presentation.

- Make sure your source is identified, credible, and unbiased.

- Test the validity of your supporting material by determining whether the information comes from a primary or secondary source and whether it's recent and consistent.

- Evaluate the validity of statistics by making sure they are well founded, justified, and accurate.

13.2
Organizing Your Presentation

What strategies should you use to organize the content of a presentation?

- The first step in organizing the content of a presentation is to identify your central idea and your key points. Make sure your key points reflect your central idea.

- Mind mapping and the Speech Framer can help you identify key points and organize your message.

- Common organizational patterns include topical, time, space, problem–solution, causes and effects, stories and examples, and comparison–contrast arrangements.

13.3
Outlining Your Presentation

How can outlining help you structure a presentation?

- Use a preliminary outline to identify the basic building blocks of a presentation.

- When preparing a comprehensive outline, use numbers, letters, and indentation; divide your subpoints logically; and keep the outline consistent in style.

13.4
Connecting Your Key Points

How do connectives make a presentation more coherent?

- Connective phrases are the "glue" that links the key points to one another and makes your presentation a coherent whole.

- Connective phrases include internal previews, internal summaries, transitions, and signposts.

13.5
Beginning Your Presentation

What strategies will help you begin a presentation successfully?

- The primacy effect explains our tendency to recall the introduction of a presentation better than the middle.

- Presentation introductions should attempt to focus attention and interest, connect with the audience, enhance your credibility, set the emotional tone, and preview the message.

- Methods of beginning a presentation include using a statistic or example, quoting someone, telling a story, using a metaphor, asking a question, referring to the current place or occasion, and addressing audience needs.

- Your introduction will be more effective if you plan the beginning at the end, do not apologize, and avoid beginning with "*My speech is about . . .*"

13.6
Concluding Your Presentation

What strategies will help you end a presentation effectively?

- The recency effect explains our tendency to recall the conclusion of a presentation.

- Presentation conclusions should be memorable, clear, and brief.

- Methods of concluding a presentation include summarizing, quoting someone, telling a story, using poetic language, calling for action, and referring back to your beginning.

- Your conclusion will be more effective if you make sure that the mood and style are consistent with the presentation and if you have realistic expectations about audience reactions.

MySearchLab®

TEST YOUR KNOWLEDGE

13.1 How do you find good information for a presentation?

1 What kind of supporting material is used in the following excerpt from a student's presentation? *Ron Wilson, an African American representative in Texas, argues that it's a great hypocrisy when courts allow selective universities to relax their academic standards for athletes and children of alumni but not for African Americans.*

   a. Fact
   b. Statistics
   c. Testimony
   d. Description
   e. Story

2 What kind of supporting material is used in the following example? *One way to understand neuroplasticity (how the brain creates mind-sets) is by comparing it to snow skiing. Plasticity is like snow on a hill in winter. Because it is pliable we can take many paths if we choose to ski down that hill. But because it is pliable, if we keep taking the same path, we develop tracks, and then ruts, and get stuck in them.*

   a. Description
   b. Analogy
   c. Example
   d. Story
   e. Definition

3 You need to ask all of the questions that test supporting material for the following example except one. Which test is not needed for this example? *Joseph Farah, editor of* World News Daily, *the politically conservative, conspiracy-theory website, writes that "Obama is choreographing a top-down revolution in America—one from which it may take generations to extricate ourselves. It will be a shame if we learn he was ineligible to serve in the office of president only after he's gone."*

   a. Is the source credible?
   b. Is the source biased?
   c. Is the source identified?
   d. Is the information valid?
   e. Is the information recent?

13.2 What strategies should you use to organize the content of a presentation?

4 All of the following answers are good rules for outlining a presentation except _____.

   a. use numbers and letters
   b. leave the introduction and conclusion out of the outline
   c. divide subpoints logically
   d. keep the outline consistent in design and grammatical structure
   e. use indentations in the outline

13.3 How can outlining help you structure a presentation?

5 Which of the following answers constitutes the best example of a central idea for a presentation on the different meanings of facial expressions in other cultures?

   a. Facial expressions differ across cultures.
   b. The meaning of some facial expressions differs from culture to culture.
   c. Facial expressions for fear, sadness, and disgust are the same across cultures.
   d. Although many facial expressions are the same in different cultures—such as smiling—other facial expressions differ.
   e. Americans and native Japanese often misinterpret facial expressions depicting fear, sadness, and disgust.

6 Which organizational pattern works best for explaining to an audience how to bake a cake?

   a. Time
   b. Topical
   c. Space
   d. Causes and effects
   e. Stories and examples

13.4 How do connectives make a presentation more effective?

7 Which kind of connective is used in the following example? *Once you've collected all of your ingredients, you can begin the process of putting the recipe together.*

   a. Internal preview
   b. Internal outline
   c. Internal summary
   d. Transition
   e. Signpost

13.5 What strategies will help you begin a presentation successfully?

8 What introductory technique did Abraham Lincoln use when he started the Gettysburg Address with these words? *Four score and seven years ago, our fathers brought forth on this continent, a new nation, conceived in liberty, and dedicated to the proposition that all men are created equal.*

   a. Refer to a current place or occasion.
   b. Refer to a well-known incident or event.
   c. Use a metaphor.
   d. Quote someone.
   e. Address audience needs.

9 The primacy effect explains why

   a. an effective introduction is so important at the beginning of a presentation.
   b. an effective conclusion is so important at the end of a presentation.
   c. transitions are so important in the middle of a presentation.
   d. presentations should "end with a bang."
   e. a presentation's key points should be determined before looking for supporting material.

13.6 What strategies will help you end a presentation effectively?

10 What concluding technique did Abraham Lincoln use when he ended the Gettysburg Address with these words? *. . . that this nation, under God, shall have a new birth of freedom—and that government of the people, by the people, for the people, shall not perish from the earth.*

   a. Summarize
   b. Quote someone
   c. Tell a story
   d. Use poetic language
   e. Call for action

Answers found on page 366.

Key Terms

Analogy	Fact	Signpost
Biased	Internal preview	Space arrangement
Cause-and-effect arrangement	Internal summary	Speaking outline
Central idea	Key points	Speech Framer
Comparison–contrast arrangement	Mind mapping	Statistics
Comprehensive outline	Oral footnote	Stories
Connectives	Organization	Supporting material
Content	Preliminary outline	Testimony
Definition	Primacy effect	Time arrangement
Description	Primary source	Topical arrangement
Documentation	Problem–solution arrangement	Transition
Example	Recency effect	Valid
	Secondary source	

LANGUAGE and DELIVERY

14

A presidential candidate's language and delivery can determine who "wins" and "loses" televised presidential debates—as well as who wins the presidency.

Televised presidential debates began in 1960 when Richard Nixon (Republican vice president) accepted a challenge from John Kennedy (junior Democratic senator from Massachusetts). The
confident, witty, good-looking Kennedy outdebated an awkward, seemingly insincere, and unappealing
Nixon. Although Nixon's performance improved in three subsequent debates, "what happened in the
first was what lingered in the public consciousness."[1] According to Dr. Rick Shenkman, historian and
editor of George Mason University's History News Network, "The perceived winners of presidential
debates, in every case since the first one . . . have always gone on to win the presidency."[2]

In this chapter, we focus on two performance components of presentation speaking—language
and delivery. How you use words, your voice, your body, and presentation aids to express yourself
and communicate your message are irreversible components in every presentation. If your language
is bland and boring or your eye contact never strays from your notes, you can't recapture your audience to do a better job. If, for example, you use inappropriate words or speak in a voice that cannot
be heard, you can't undo what you've said or how you've said it.

14.1

The CORE Language Styles

How do you choose appropriate language for a presentation?

Carefully chosen words can add power and authority to a presentation and transform good speeches into great ones. Your speaking style can add a distinct flavor, emotional excitement, and brilliant clarity.

Speaking style refers to how you use vocabulary, sentence structure and length, grammar and syntax, and rhetorical devices to express a message.[3] In this section, we describe four **CORE speaking styles**: **c**lear style, **o**ral style, **r**hetorical style, and **e**loquent style. Your task is to decide which style or styles suit you, your purpose, your audience, the setting and occasion of your presentation, and your message.

The four CORE speaking styles are often most effective when used in combination. Once you become capable and comfortable using the clear and oral styles, you are on "firm ground" to use the rhetorical and eloquent styles to persuade and inspire your audience. While you may use all four styles, we recognize that some

> **"** Nobody has time to try and figure out what you're trying to say, so you need to be direct. Most great advertising is direct. That's how people talk. That the style they read. That's what sells products and services or ideas. **"**[4]
>
> —Jerry Della Femina, marketing expert

speakers are more comfortable using only the clear and oral styles whiles others prefer the added intensity of the rhetorical and eloquent styles. Depending on your purpose, audience, setting, and occasion, use the styles that best match you and your messages.

Clear Style

Clarity always comes first. If you aren't clear, your audience won't understand you or your message. The **clear style** uses short, simple, and direct words and phrases as well as active verbs, concrete words, and plain language.

Oral Style

In Chapter 5, "Verbal Communication," we emphasize the importance of using oral language when interacting with others. Recall the features of the **oral style**: short, familiar words; shorter, simpler, and even incomplete sentences; and more personal pronouns and informal colloquial expressions. (For an example of both clear and oral styles, see John Sullivan's informative presentation, "Cliff's Notes" on pp. 303–305.)

> **When using an oral style, say what you mean by speaking the way you talk, not the way you write.**

Rhetorical Style

The **rhetorical style** uses language designed to influence, persuade, and/ or inspire. Vivid and powerful words enhance the intensity of a persuasive presentation. **Language intensity** refers to the degree to which your language deviates from bland, neutral terms.[5] For example, instead of using a word like *nice*, try *delightful* or *captivating*. *Disaster* is a much more intense word than *mistake*. A *vile* meal sounds much worse than a *bad* meal.

The rhetorical style often relies on **rhetorical devices**, word strategies designed to enhance a presentation's impact and persuasiveness. Two

The **CORE** Speaking Styles

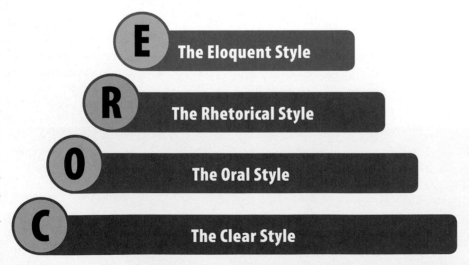

The CORE speaking styles build on a foundation that uses the clear and oral styles as firm ground for enlisting the rhetorical and eloquent speaking styles.

Differences in Written and Oral Styles[6]

EXCERPTS FROM AN ESSAY ON NEUROMUSICOLOGY	EXCERPTS FROM A PRESENTATION ON NEUROMUSICOLOGY

EXCERPTS FROM AN ESSAY ON NEUROMUSICOLOGY

"I haven't understood a bar of music in my entire life, but I have felt it" (qtd. in Peter, p. 350). These words were spoken by Igor Stravinsky, who composed some of the most complex and sophisticated music of his century. If the great Stravinsky can accept the elusive nature of music, and still love it, why can't we? Why are we analyzing it to try to make it useful?

Ours is an age of information—an age that wishes to conquer all the mysteries of the human brain. Today there is a growing trend to study music's effects on our emotions, behavior, health, and intelligence. Journalist Alex Ross reports how the relatively new field of neuromusicology (the science of the nervous system and its response to music) has been developed to experiment with music as a tool and to shape it to the needs of society. Observations like these let us know that we are on the threshold of seeing music in a whole new way and using music to achieve measurable changes in behavior. However, this new approach carries dangers, and once we go in this direction, there can be no turning back. How far do we want to go in our study of musical science? What effects will it have on our listening pleasures?

A short history lesson reveals that there has been an awareness that music affects us, even if the reasons are not clear. Around 900 B.C., the Bible's King David played the harp "to cure Saul's derangement" (Gonzalez-Crussi, p. 69).

Ann Raimes, *Keys for Writers: A Brief Handbook,* 3rd ed. (Boston: Houghton Mifflin, 2004), pp. 152–158.

EXCERPTS FROM A PRESENTATION ON NEUROMUSICOLOGY

[Note: As an opening, the speaker plays an excerpt from "God Bless America" followed by an excerpt from *Sesame Street*'s theme music.]

What did you think of or feel when you heard "God Bless America"? What about the *Sesame Street* theme? I'm sure that you're not surprised to learn that "God Bless America" reminds many people of the September 11th tragedy, the War in Iraq, and patriotism. And the theme from *Sesame Street* probably put a smile on your face as you revisited the world of Kermit the Frog, Miss Piggy, and Big Bird.

Why were your responses so predictable and so emotional? The answer lies in a new brain science—a science that threatens to control you by controlling the music you hear. Is resistance futile?

In the next few minutes, we'll take a close look at the field of neuromusicology. What? *Neuro*, meaning related to our brain and nervous system. And *musicology*—the historic and scientific study of music.

Journalist Alex Ross put it this way: By understanding the nervous system and its response to music, neuromusicologists study music as a tool and shape it to the needs of society.

As New Age as all this may sound, there's plenty of history to back up the claims of neuromusicologists. For example, those of you who know your Bible know that King David played the harp to "cure Saul's derangement."

---

rhetorical devices work particularly well in presentations: repetition and metaphors.

Repetition Because your listeners can't rewind and immediately rehear what you've just said, use repetition to highlight the sounds, words, ideas, and phrases you want your audience to remember. Repetition can be as simple as beginning a series of words (or words placed closely together) with the same sound. This type of repetition is called **alliteration**. For example, the first part of Lincoln's Gettysburg Address—"*F*our score and seven years ago our *f*athers brought *f*orth"—includes three words beginning with the letter *f*.

Repetition can be extended to a word, a phrase, or an entire sentence. Dr. Martin Luther King Jr. used the phrase "I have a dream" nine times in his famous 1963 speech in Washington, D.C. He used "let freedom ring" 10 times. Repetition can drive home an idea and provoke action. Audience members anticipate and remember repeated phrases.

Metaphors Metaphors and their cousins—similes and analogies—are powerful rhetorical devices. Shakespeare's famous line "All the world's a stage" is a classic metaphor. The world is not a theatrical stage, but we do assume many roles during a lifetime. Author Isabel Allende's colorful

description of art is another potent metaphor: "*Art is a rebellious child, a wild animal that will not be tamed.*" Metaphors leave it to the audience to get the point for themselves.[7]

Many linguists claim that metaphors are the most powerful figures of speech. Some researchers believe that metaphors are windows into the workings of the human mind.[8]

Eloquent Style

The **eloquent style** uses poetic and expressive language in a way that makes thoughts and feelings clear, inspiring, *and* memorable. Eloquent language does not have to be flowery or grand; it can use an oral style, personal pronouns, and repetition or metaphors. Statements such as Abraham Lincoln's "government of the people, by the people, for the people shall not perish from the earth" are memorable and inspiring because (in addition to the alliteration and despite myths to the contrary) Lincoln spent considerable time and effort searching for the best words to communicate his thoughts and feelings.[9]

In *Eloquence in an Electronic Age: The Transformation of Political Speechmaking*, Kathleen Jamieson notes that eloquent speakers comfortably disclose personal experiences and feelings. Rather than explaining the lessons of the past or creating a public sense of ethics, today's most eloquent speakers often call on their own past or their own sense of ethics to inspire an audience.[10] Consider the words

POETIC LANGUAGE has the remarkable ability to capture profound ideas and feelings in a few simple words.

Barack Obama used in his "A More Perfect Union" speech in Philadelphia on March 18, 2008:[11]

> I am the son of a black man from Kenya and a white woman from Kansas. I was raised with the help of a white grandfather who survived a Depression to serve in Patton's Army during World War II and a white grandmother who worked on a bomber assembly line at Fort Leavenworth while he was overseas. I've gone to some of the best schools in America and lived in one of the world's poorest nations. I am married to a black American who carries within her the blood of slaves and slaveowners—an inheritance we pass on to our two precious daughters. I have brothers, sisters, nieces, nephews, uncles and cousins, of every race and every hue, scattered across three continents, and for as long as I live, I will never forget that in no other country on Earth is my story even possible.

14.2
Modes of Delivery

How do you choose an appropriate delivery style for a presentation?

The term **delivery** describes the ways in which you use your voice, body, and presentation aids to express your presentation's message. You should begin planning how to deliver your presentation by deciding which delivery mode to use: impromptu, extemporaneous, manuscript, memorized, or a combination of forms. But, before you do, decide which of these modes best suits your purpose.

Impromptu

Impromptu speaking occurs when you speak without advanced preparation or practice. For example, you may be called on in class or at work to answer a question or share an opinion. You may be inspired to get up and speak on an important issue at a public meeting. Even in those instances when you don't have a lot of time to prepare,

you can quickly think of a purpose and a way to organize and adapt your message to the audience.

ADVANTAGES AND DISADVANTAGES OF IMPROMPTU DELIVERY
ADVANTAGES
• Natural and conversational speaking style
• Maximum eye contact
• Freedom of movement
• Easier to adjust to audience feedback
• Demonstrates speaker's knowledge and skill
DISADVANTAGES
• Limited time to make basic decisions about purpose, audience adaptation, content, and organization
• Speaker anxiety can be high
• Speaker may be at a "loss for words"
• Delivery may be awkward and ineffective
• Difficult to gauge speaking time
• Limited or no supporting material
• Speaker may have nothing to say on such short notice

Extemporaneous

Extemporaneous speaking is the most common form of delivery and occurs when you use an outline or a set of notes to guide you through a well-prepared presentation. Your notes can be a few words on a card or a detailed, full-sentence outline. Classroom lectures, business briefings, and courtroom arguments are usually delivered extemporaneously.

Extemporaneous speaking is easiest for beginners to do well and the method preferred by professionals. No other form of delivery gives you as much freedom and flexibility with preplanned material. A well-practiced extemporaneous presentation seems spontaneous and has an ease to it that makes the audience and speaker feel comfortable.

Manuscript

Manuscript speaking involves writing your presentation in advance and reading it out loud. For very nervous speakers, a manuscript may *seem* like a lifesaving document, keeping them afloat when they feel as though they're drowning. However, manuscript speeches are difficult to deliver for all but the most skilled speakers, and we strongly discourage speakers from using manuscript delivery. When, however, an occasion is a major public

event after which your words will be published word for word, you may have no choice but to use a manuscript for at least part of your presentation. And if an occasion is highly emotional—such as delivering a eulogy—you may need the support of a manuscript.

Using a manuscript allows you to choose each word carefully. You can plan and practice every detail. It also ensures that your presentation will fit within your allotted speaking time.

If you must use a manuscript, focus on maintaining an oral style when you write your speech: *Write as though you are speaking.*

ADVANTAGES AND DISADVANTAGES OF EXTEMPORANEOUS DELIVERY

ADVANTAGES	DISADVANTAGES
• More preparation time than impromptu delivery • Seems spontaneous but is actually well prepared • Speaker can monitor and adapt to audience feedback • Allows more eye contact and audience interaction than manuscript delivery • Audiences typically respond positively to extemporaneous delivery • Speaker can choose concise language for central idea and key points • With practice, it becomes the most powerful form of delivery	• Speaker anxiety can increase for content not covered by notes • Language may not be well chosen or eloquent • Can be difficult to estimate speaking time

ADVANTAGES AND DISADVANTAGES OF MANUSCRIPT DELIVERY

ADVANTAGES	DISADVANTAGES
• Speaker can pay careful attention to all the basic principles of effective speaking • Speaker can choose concise and eloquent language • Speaker anxiety may be eased by having a "script" • Speaker can rehearse the same presentation over and over • Ensures accurate reporting of presentation content • Speaker can stay within time limit	• Delivery can be dull • Difficult to maintain sufficient eye contact • Gestures and movement are limited • Language can be too formal, lacking oral style • Difficult to modify or adapt to the audience or situation

Memorized

Memorized speaking requires a speaker to deliver a presentation from recall with very few or no notes. A memorized presentation offers one major advantage and one major disadvantage. The major advantage is physical freedom. You can gesture freely and look at your audience 100 percent of the time. The disadvantage, however, outweighs any and all advantages. If you forget the words you memorized, it is more difficult to recover your thoughts without creating an awkward moment for both you and your audience.

Rarely do speakers memorize an entire presentation. However, there's nothing wrong with memorizing your introduction or a few key sections as long as you have your notes to fall back on.

Mix and Match Modes of Delivery

Learning to mix and match modes of delivery appropriately lets you select the method that works best for you and your purpose. An impromptu speaker may recite a memorized statistic or a rehearsed argument in the same way that a politician responds to press questions. An extemporaneous speaker may read a lengthy quotation or a series of statistics and then deliver a memorized ending.

Speaking Notes

Effective speakers use their notes efficiently. Even when your presentation is impromptu, you may use a few quick words jotted down just before you speak. Speaking notes may appear on index cards and outlines or as a manuscript.

Index Cards and Outlines A single card can be used for each component of your presentation; for example, you can use one card for the introduction, another card for each key point, and one card for your conclusion. Record key words rather than complete sentences; use only one side of each index card. To help you organize your presentation and

ADVANTAGES AND DISADVANTAGES OF MEMORIZED DELIVERY

ADVANTAGES

- Incorporates the preparation advantages of manuscript delivery and the delivery advantages of impromptu speaking
- Maximizes eye contact and freedom of movement

DISADVANTAGES

- Requires extensive time to memorize
- Disaster awaits if memory fails
- Can sound stilted and insincere
- Very difficult to modify or adapt to the audience or situation
- Lacks a sense of spontaneity unless expertly delivered

Bruce Springsteen uses a lectern and manuscript during his tribute to U2 at the Rock and Roll Hall of Fame Induction Ceremony.

rearrange key points at the last minute, number each of the cards. If you have too many notes for a few index cards, use an outline on a full sheet of paper.

Manuscript When preparing a speech manuscript, double space each page and use a 14- to 16-point font size. Use only the top two-thirds of the page to avoid having to bend your head to see the bottom of each page and lose eye contact with your audience or constrict your windpipe. Set wide margins so that you have space on the page to add any last-minute changes. Remember to number each page so that you can keep everything in order and do not staple your pages together. Instead, place your manuscript to one side of the lectern and slide the pages to the other side when it's time to go on to the next page.

14.3
Confident Delivery
How can you reduce presentation anxiety?

When we begin the section of our course on presentation speaking, we often ask students to complete the sentence: "Giving a speech makes me feel . . ." Their responses range from feelings of empowerment to total terror. Here are some examples:

- "Giving a speech makes me feel powerful. Although nervousness enters the picture, so does a feeling of power. The thought of having everybody's full attention and being able to convey my point of view makes me feel as though I'm in charge."

- "Giving a speech makes me feel uncomfortable. I'm very quiet and shy in front of most people, especially people I don't know. Because I'm a quiet person, I'm not comfortable with just coming out and speaking to someone—which is just like giving a speech because you are speaking to people you've never met."

- "Giving a speech makes me feel like I'm going to lose control—my heart starts to race, my body starts to tremble. I've tried taking deep breaths to calm myself down when I feel this way. I've also tried medication, but it doesn't work. The last time I enrolled in a speech class, I dropped out because I was so nervous about giving a speech and embarrassing myself."

All three of these students did quite well in their presentations, especially after realizing they were not alone in their fears. Nervousness is inevitable but certainly not fatal. In fact, a little bit of anxiety can keep you on your toes and motivate you to spend the time and effort needed to both develop and deliver an effective presentation.

Before reviewing specific strategies for reducing speaking anxiety, let's examine some of the so-called facts that people have long held to be true. Researchers know that people often fear things they don't understand. Here, we use contemporary research to examine and correct two common misconceptions about speaking anxiety:

- "I am more nervous than most people."
- "Reading about speaking anxiety makes me more nervous."

Are You More Nervous Than Most People?

When we ask students about their presentation speaking goals, they tell us that they want to "gain confidence," "overcome anxiety," "stop being nervous," "get rid of the jitters," and "calm down." No other answer comes close in terms of frequency. Most of these students also believe they are more nervous than other speakers are.

Successful presenters know two very important facts about speaking anxiety: They know that it's very common and that it's usually invisible. As speakers—experienced or otherwise—we all share many of the same worried thoughts, physical discomforts, and psychological anxieties. This means that most audience members understand your feelings, don't want to trade places with you, and may even admire your courage for being up there.

If you still believe that you are more nervous than anyone else is, make an appointment with your instructor to discuss your concerns. Many colleges and departments offer special assistance to students who feel disabled by their level of fear and anxiety associated with speaking to others.

> Despite most people's worst fears, audiences are usually kind to speakers. They are willing to forgive and forget an honest mistake.

Know Thy Self

Will the Audience Know I'm Nervous?

Many speakers fear that audience members know they're anxious. Although there are some signs of nervousness that an audience can see or hear, most signs are invisible. Use the following table to make a list of your own symptoms of speaking anxiety or symptoms you have seen or heard in others. In the left-hand column, list symptoms the audience *can* see or hear. In the right-hand column, list symptoms the audience *cannot* see or hear. An example is provided for each type of symptom.

Here's the good news: In most cases, speaking anxiety is invisible. Audiences cannot see a pounding heart, an upset stomach, cold hands, or worried thoughts. They do not notice small changes in your vocal quality or remember occasional mistakes. Although you may feel as though your legs are quivering and quaking uncontrollably, the audience will rarely see any movement.

Most speakers who describe themselves as being nervous appear confident and calm to their audiences. Even experienced communication instructors, when asked about how anxious a speaker is, seldom accurately estimate the speaker's anxiety.[12] Now recheck the symptoms you believe the audience *can* see or hear in the chart you just filled out. In all probability, you will want to move some of those symptoms to the list of symptoms that listeners *cannot* see or hear.

Symptoms the audience *can* see or hear	Symptoms the audience *cannot* see or hear
Example: Shaking hands	*Example:* Upset stomach
1.	1.
2.	2.
3.	3.
4.	4.
5.	5.

confident delivery

Will Reading About Speaking Anxiety Make You *More* Nervous?

You may think that the more you learn about speaking anxiety, the more nervous you'll become. Just the opposite is true: The more accurate information and sound advice you read about speaking anxiety, the more likely you are to build confidence. In his study on reading about public speaking apprehension, Michael Motley had one group of college students read a booklet that discussed the nature and causes of, as well as strategies for minimizing, speaking anxiety. A second group either viewed relaxation tapes, read an excerpt from a popular self-help book on reducing fears, or received no treatment at all. The greatest decrease in speaking anxiety occurred in the group that read the booklet on speaking anxiety.[13] Similarly, reading this textbook can help you understand why you become anxious when you have to make a presentation and help calm your fears, expose you to techniques for dealing with those fears, and increase your speaking confidence.

COMMUNICATION IN *ACTION*

Communicating with Confidence

Section 2.4 of Chapter 2, "Understanding Your Self," addresses communication apprehension, the fear or anxiety associated with communicating in group discussions, meetings, interpersonal conversations, and public speaking. If you haven't completed and scored the Personal Report of Communication Apprehension (PRCA) on p. 39, do so now. You can compare your public speaking anxiety to the average score for most people. You may find that you are not alone in your level of apprehension.

In addition to explaining the major sources of communication apprehension in Chapter 2, we noted that when American adults were asked what they feared the most, 51 percent chose snakes. Public speaking came in second (40%), and heights earned third place (36%).[14]

Speaking anxiety is prevalent but there are many effective strategies for becoming a more confident communicator. Review the strategies in Chapter 2 as well as the presentation planning tools in Chapter 12. Then read on—the rest of this chapter focuses on learning delivery skills that will not only help you sound and look confident but also reduce your level of speaking anxiety.

14.4
Vocal Delivery

What are the components of effective vocal delivery?

Developing an effective speaking voice requires the same time and effort that you would devote to mastering any skill. You can't become an accomplished carpenter, pianist, swimmer, writer, or speaker overnight. Because only a few lucky speakers are born with beautiful voices, the majority of us must work at sounding clear and expressive. Fortunately, there are ways to improve the characteristics and quality of your voice. Begin by focusing on the basics: breathing, volume, rate, pitch, fluency, articulation, and pronunciation.

Breathing

Effective breath control enables you to speak more loudly, say more in a single breath, and reduce the likelihood of vocal problems such as harshness or breathiness. Thus, the first step in learning how to breathe for presentation speaking is to note the differences between the shallow, unconscious breathing you do all the time and the deeper breathing that produces strong, sustained sound quality. Many speech coaches recommend the exercise below to learn deep, abdominal breathing.

Exercise for Deep Breathing

1. Lie flat on your back. Support the back of your knees with a pillow.

2. Place a moderately heavy, hardbound book on your stomach, right over your navel.

3. Begin breathing through your mouth. The book should move up when you breathe in and sink down when you breathe out.

4. Place one of your hands on the upper part of your chest in a "Pledge of Allegiance" position. As you inhale and exhale, this area should not move in and out or up and down.

5. Take the book away and replace it with your other hand. Your abdominal area should continue to move up when you breathe in and sink down when you breathe out.

6. After you're comfortable with step 5, try doing the same kind of breathing while sitting up or standing.

7. Add sound. Try sighing and sustaining the vowel *ahh* for five seconds with each exhalation. Then try counting or reciting the alphabet.

Activist and politician Harvey Milk was well known for his dynamic speeches, which he would often deliver without the aid of a microphone.

Volume

Volume measures the loudness level of your voice. The key to producing adequate volume is adapting to the size of the audience and the dimensions of the room in which you will be speaking. If there are only five people in an audience and they are sitting close to you, speak at a normal, everyday volume. If there are 50 people in your audience, you need more energy and force to support your voice. When your audience exceeds 50, you may be more comfortable with a microphone. However, a strong speaking voice can project to an audience of a thousand people without electronic amplification. Professional actors and classical singers do it all the time.

Practice your presentation in a room about the same size as the one in which you will be speaking, or, at least, imagine speaking in such a room. Ask a friend to sit in a far corner and report back on your volume and clarity. Also note that a room full of people absorbs sound; you will have to turn up your volume another notch when your audience is present. Speakers who cannot be heard are a common problem. It's very rare, though, for a speaker to be too loud.

> Remember that audiences can listen faster than you talk, so it's better to keep the pace up than speak at a crawl.

Rate

Your speaking **rate** refers to the number of words you say per minute (wpm). Generally, a rate less than 125 wpm is too slow, 125 to 145 wpm is acceptable, 145 to 180 wpm is better, and 180 wpm or more exceeds the speed limit. But these guidelines are not carved in stone. Your preferred rate depends on you, the nature and mood of your message, and your audience. If you are explaining a highly technical process or expressing personal sorrow, your rate may slow to 125 wpm. On the other hand, if you are telling an exciting, amusing, or infuriating story, your rate may hit 200 wpm. For maximum effectiveness, speakers vary their rate. Martin Luther King Jr.'s "I Have a Dream" speech opened at a slow 90 wpm but ended at 150 wpm.[15]

Listeners perceive presenters who speak quickly *and* clearly as energized, motivated, and interested. Given the choice, we'd rather be accused of speaking too quickly than run the risk of boring an audience. Too slow a rate suggests that you are unsure of yourself or, even worse, that you are not very bright.

COMMUNICATION IN ACTION

Master the Microphone

If your speaking situation requires a microphone, make the most out of this technology. Unless a sound technician is monitoring the presentation, your microphone will be preset for one volume. If you speak with too much volume, it may sound as though you are shouting at your audience. If you speak too softly, the microphone may not pick up everything you have to say. The trick is to go against your instincts. If you want to project a soft tone, speak closer to the microphone and lower your volume. Your voice will sound more intimate and will convey subtle emotions. If you want to be more forceful, speak farther away from the microphone and project your voice.

Most important, familiarize yourself with the specific microphone and system you will be using. For example, when placed on a lapel, a microphone faces outward rather than upward. As a result, it receives and sends a less direct sound than a handheld microphone.[16] Here are some tips to follow for all microphones:

- Test the microphone ahead of time.
- Determine whether the microphone is sophisticated enough to capture your voice from several angles and distances or whether you will need to keep your mouth close to it.
- Place the microphone about 5 to 10 inches from your mouth. If you are using a handheld microphone, hold it below your mouth at chin level.

Experienced speakers make the adjustments they need during the first few seconds that they hear their own voices projected through an amplification system.

- Focus on your audience, not the microphone. Stay near the mike but don't tap it, lean over it, keep readjusting it, or make the p-p-p-p-p "motorboat sounds" as a test.
- Keep in mind that a microphone will do more than amplify your voice; it will also amplify other sounds—coughing, clearing your throat, shuffling papers, or tapping a pen.
- If your microphone is well adjusted, speak in a natural, conversational voice.

vocal delivery

Pitch

Pitch is how high or low your voice sounds—just like the notes on a musical scale. Anatomy determines pitch (most men speak at a lower pitch than women and children). Your **optimum pitch** is the pitch at which you speak most easily and expressively. If you speak at your optimum pitch, you will not tire as easily; your voice will sound stronger and will be less likely to fade at the end of sentences. It will also be less likely to sound harsh, hoarse, or breathy.

To find your optimum pitch, sing up the musical scale from the lowest note you can sing. By the fifth or sixth note, you should have reached your optimum pitch. Test your optimum pitch to see if your voice is clear and whether you can increase its volume with minimal effort. Finding your optimum pitch does *not* mean using that pitch for everything you say in your presentation. Think of your optimum pitch as "neutral" and use it as your baseline, then increase the expressiveness of your voice through **inflection**—the changing pitch within a syllable, word, or group of words. Lack of inflection results in a monotone voice. A slight change, however, even just a fraction, can change the entire meaning of a sentence or the quality of your voice:

I was born in New Jersey. (You, on the other hand, were born in Texas.)

I *was* born in New Jersey. (No doubt about it!)

I was *born* in New Jersey. (So I know my way around.)

I was born in *New Jersey*. (Not in New York.)

Fluency

When you speak with **fluency**, you speak smoothly without tripping over words or pausing at awkward moments. The more you practice your presentation, the more fluent you will become. Practice will alert you to words, phrases, and sentences that may look good in your notes but sound awkward or choppy when spoken. You'll also discover words that you have trouble pronouncing or notice **filler phrases**—*you know, uh, um, okay,* and *like*—that can break up your fluency and annoy your audience. There is nothing wrong with an occasional filler phrase, particularly when you're speaking informally or impromptu. What you want to avoid is excessive use. Try recording your practice sessions and listening for filler phrases as you play back the recording. To break the filler-phrase habit, slow down and listen to the words you use. To break the habit, you must work on it all the time, not just when you are speaking in front of an audience.

Articulation

A strong, well-paced, optimally pitched voice that is also fluent and expressive may not be enough to ensure the successful delivery of a presentation. Proper **articulation**—clearly making the sounds in the words of a language—is just as important as your volume, rate, pitch, and fluency. Poor articulation is often described as sloppy speech, poor diction, or mumbling. Fortunately, you can improve and practice your articulation by speaking more slowly, speaking with a bit more volume, and opening your mouth wider when you speak.

COMMUNICATION&**CULTURE**

ADAPT YOUR GESTURES TO CULTURAL DIFFERENCES

People all over the world "talk" with their hands. The meanings of gestures, however, may be quite different in different cultures and cultural contexts—both domestic and international. Everett Rogers and Thomas Steinfatt share a story about a U.S. professor teaching at Bangkok University in Thailand. The professor frequently put his hands in his pockets or held them behind his back while lecturing to his class. At the end of the semester, his polite Thai students gently informed him that he should hold his hands in front of himself. They had been embarrassed and distracted when he broke the cultural norm of keeping your hands visible when communicating.[17]

Most of our hand gestures are culturally determined. One of the best examples is a gesture in which you touch the tips of your thumb to index finger to form a circle. In the United States, this gesture usually means that everything is "A-okay." The same gesture, however, can be a sign for the sex act in some Latin American nations. To the French, the sign may indicate that someone is a "zero," and to people in Malta, it is an invitation to have homosexual sex.[18]

In most speaking situations—both inside and outside the United States—certain gestures can trigger negative responses from an audience. Pointing or wagging the index finger at your audience, for example, may be seen as rude and offensive because it is associated with parental scolding. Instead of pointing your index finger at your audience, try gesturing with an open hand—fingers together, palm and inner wrist turned slightly toward the audience, and forearm slightly bent and extended at about a 45-degree angle to the side (not aimed directly *at* the audience).[19] The photo on p. 274 shows a speaker in this position.

Certain sounds account for most articulation problems: combined words, "-ing" endings, and final consonants. Many speakers combine words—"what's the matter" becomes "watsumata." Some speakers shorten the "ing" sound to an "in" sound: "sayin" instead of "saying." The final consonants that get left off most often are the ones that pop out of your mouth. Because these consonants—*p*, *b*, *t*, *d*, *k*, and *g*—cannot be hummed like an "m" or hissed like an "s," it's easy to lose them at the end of a word. Usually you can hear the difference between "Rome" and "rose," but poor articulation can make it difficult to hear the difference between "hit" and "hid" or "tap" and "tab."

Pronunciation

Proper **pronunciation** involves putting all the correct sounds of a word in the correct order with the correct stress. In a presentation speaking situation, poor pronunciation can result in misunderstanding and embarrassment. For example, we once heard a speaker undermine her credibility in a talk about effective communication when she repeatedly said the word "pro*noun*ciation" instead of "pro*nun*ciation."

Pronunciations can and do change. According to most dictionaries, the word *often* should be pronounced "awfen," but many people now put the "t" sound in the middle and pronounce it the way it's spelled. The word *a* should be pronounced "uh," not rhymed with *hay*, but many people now use both versions. Even the word *the* is often mispronounced. When *the* appears before the sound of a consonant as in "the dog" or "the paper," it should be pronounced "thuh." When *the* comes before the sound of a vowel as in "the alligator" or "the article," it should be pronounced "thee."

14.5

Physical Delivery
What are the components of effective physical delivery?

The key to effective physical delivery is naturalness. However, being natural doesn't mean "letting it all hang out." Rather, it means being so well prepared and well practiced that your presentation is an authentic reflection of you.

> **Your delivery tells an audience a great deal about who you are and how much you care about reaching them.**

After all, if you don't look at your audience, why should they look at you?

Audience members jump to conclusions about speakers based on first impressions of appearance and behavior. The way you stand, move, gesture, and make eye contact has a significant impact on your presentation.

Eye Contact

Eye contact, establishing and maintaining direct, visual links with individual audience members, may be the most important component of effective physical delivery. Generally, the more eye contact you have with your audience, the better. Try to maintain eye contact during *most* of your presentation. If you are using detailed notes or a manuscript, use a technique called *eye scan*. **Eye scan** involves glancing at a specific section of your notes or manuscript and then looking up at your audience to speak. Begin by placing your thumb and index finger on one side of the page to frame the section of the notes you are using. Then, as you approach the end of a phrase or sentence within that section, glance down again and visually grasp the next phrase to be spoken. This allows you to maintain maximum eye contact without losing your place.

Eye contact does more than ensure that you are looking in the direction of your audience. It also helps you to initiate and control communication, enhance your credibility, and interpret valuable audience feedback.

Control Have you ever noticed a teacher "catch the eye" of a student or "give the eye" to an inattentive student? When you establish initial eye contact with your audience, you indicate that you are ready to begin speaking and that they should get ready to listen. Lack of eye contact communicates a message, too: It says that you don't care to connect with your audience.

Credibility Direct eye contact says, "I'm talking to *you*; I want *you* to hear this." In Western cultures, such directness positively affects your credibility.[20] It says, "I'm of good character (I care enough to share this important message with you)," "I'm competent (I know this subject so well I can leave my notes and look at you)," and "I'm charismatic (I want to energize and connect with everyone in this room)."

> ### Strategies for
> ### MAINTAINING EYE CONTACT
>
> - Talk to your audience members and look at them the same way you would talk and look at a friend, coworker, or customer
>
> - Move your gaze around the room, occasionally settle on someone, and establish direct eye contact
>
> - Don't move your eyes in a rigid pattern; try to establish eye contact with as many individual people as you can

Feedback Eye contact is the best way to gauge audience feedback during a presentation. At first, looking audience members in the eye may distract you. Some people smile, others may look bored or confused, and some may be looking around the room or passing notes to their friends. With all this going on in the audience, it's easy to become sidetracked. However, these different responses are also the very reason you must establish and maintain eye contact. Speakers who don't look directly at audience members rarely have a clue about why their presentations succeed or fail.

Facial Expression

Your face reflects your attitudes and emotional states, provides nonverbal feedback, and, next to the words you speak, is the primary source of information about you.[21]

Despite the importance of facial expressions, they are difficult to control. Most of us tend to display a particular style of facial expression. Some people show little expression—they have a stoic, poker face most of the time. Others are as open as a book—you have little doubt about how they feel. It's very difficult to change a "poker face" into an "open book" or vice versa. A nervous speaker may be

Your face . . .

. . . is the primary source of information about you.

— Mark Knapp and Judith Hall

too distracted to smile, too frightened to stop smiling, or too giddy to register displeasure or anger when appropriate.

Audiences will direct their eyes at your face, so unless your topic is very solemn or serious, try to smile. A smile shows your listeners that you are comfortable and eager to share your ideas and information. Audience members are more likely to smile if you smile. However, if you do not feel comfortable smiling, don't force it. Let your face communicate your feelings; let your face do what comes naturally. If you speak honestly and sincerely, your facial expression will be appropriate and effective.

Gestures

As Chapter 6, "Nonverbal Communication," explains, a gesture is a body movement that conveys or reinforces a thought or an emotion. Most gestures are made with your hands and arms, but shrugging a shoulder, bending a knee, and tapping a foot are gestures, too. Gestures can clarify and support your words, relieve nervous tension, and arouse audience attention.

Repetitive movements such as constantly pushing up your eyeglasses, tapping on a lectern, or jingling change or keys in your pocket can distract and eventually annoy an audience. One of the best ways to eliminate unwanted gestures is to video and then watch a practice session. Once you see how often you fidget, you'll work even harder to correct your behavior.

STOP&THINK

What Should You Do with Your Hands?

We hear this question all the time, and our answer is always the same: Do what you normally do with your hands. If you gesture a lot in conversations with other people, keep doing what comes naturally. If you rarely gesture, don't try to invent new and unnatural hand movements.

Peggy Noonan, former speechwriter for President Ronald Reagan, describes a whole industry that exists to tell people how to move their hands when giving a presentation. It's one of the reasons, she maintains, why so many politicians and television journalists look and gesture alike. "You don't have to be smooth; your audience is composed of Americans, and they've seen smooth. Instead, be you. They haven't seen that yet."[22] In other words, effective gestures are a natural outgrowth of what you feel and what you have to say. If you start thinking about your gestures, you are likely to appear awkward and unnatural. Rather than thinking about your hands, think about your audience and your message. In all likelihood, your gestures will join forces with your emotions in a spontaneous mixture of verbal and nonverbal communication.

Posture and Movement

Posture and movement involve how you stand and move and whether your movements add or detract from your presentation. If you stand comfortably and confidently, you will radiate alertness and control. If you stoop or look unsure on your feet, you will communicate anxiety or disinterest. Try to stand straight but not rigid. Your feet should be about a foot apart. If you stand tall, lean forward, and keep your chin up, you will open your airways and help make your voice clear and your volume appropriate.

Your posture communicates.

In general, a purposeful movement can attract attention, channel nervous energy, or support and emphasize a point you are making. Movement allows for short pauses during which you can collect your thoughts or give the audience time to ponder what you have said.

If your presentation is formal or your audience large, you will probably have a lectern. Learn how to take advantage of a lectern without allowing it to act as a barrier. First, don't lean over your lectern. It may look as though you and the lectern are about to come crashing down into the audience. Second, avoid hitting the lectern or tapping it with a pen or pointer while you speak. Given that a microphone is often attached to the lectern, the tapping can become a deafening noise.

Lecterns provide a place to put your notes, a spot to focus audience attention, and even an electrical outlet for a light and microphone. When possible *and* appropriate, come out from behind the lectern and speak at its side. In this way, you can remain close to your notes but also get closer to the audience.

14.6
Presentation Aids

What guidelines should you follow when designing and displaying presentation aids?

We use the term **presentation aids** to refer to the many supplementary resources—most often visual—for presenting and highlighting key ideas and supporting material.

Although it's tempting to use computer-generated slides for every presentation, remember that you and your presentation come first. Prepare visuals only after deciding what you want to say and what you want audience members to understand and remember.

Don't let your presentation aids and their technical razzle-dazzle steal the show.

Functions and Types of Presentation Aids

Presentation aids are more than pretty pictures or a set of colorful computer graphics. They serve specific functions, namely, to attract audience attention and to enhance the comprehension of ideas through clarification and reinforcement. Presentation aids can also save you time and help audiences remember your message.

There are as many different types of presentation aids as there are people to imagine them. The key to selecting an appropriate type requires a thoughtful answer to the following question: Which type of aid will help you achieve your purpose? Review the different types of presentation aids and their functions on p. 282 to decide which ones best support your message.

Choosing the Media

Selecting the right media is one of the first challenges you face when preparing presentation aids. Consider your purpose, the audience, the setting, and the logistics of the situation. You may want to do a multimedia presentation, but the place where you're scheduled to speak cannot be darkened or the facility doesn't have the equipment you need. Writing detailed notes on a board or flip chart for an audience of hundreds will frustrate listeners in the back rows.

A predesigned flip chart with one- or two-word messages in huge lettering on each page would work in front of an audience of 300 people, whereas a PowerPoint slide with too much data or too-small type would not.

"It's about design, not software."[23]
—Janet Bozarth, *Better than Bullet Points*

STRATEGIES FOR USING PRESENTATION AIDS

- **Begin with you, not your visual.** Establish rapport with your audience before you start using presentation aids.

- **Touch, turn, talk.** Touch your aid (or refer to it with your hand or a pointer), turn to your audience, then talk.

- **Pick the right time to display your aids.** Display aids for at least the length of time it takes an average reader to read them twice. When you're finished talking about a presentation aid, remove it.

- **Be prepared to do without.** Can you deliver your presentation without your presentation aids? It's always a good idea to have a "plan B" in case something goes wrong.

- **Practice before you present.** Rehearse as you would in an actual presentation. Don't sit at your computer mouthing the words as you scroll through your visuals.

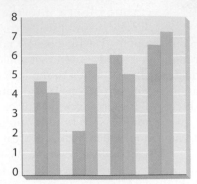

Graphs show *how much* by demonstrating comparisons. They can illustrate trends and show increases or decreases by using bars or lines to represent countable things.

Media	Small Audience (50 or fewer)	Medium Audience (50–150)	Large Audience (150 or more)
Chalk/white board	✓		
Flip chart	✓		
Hand held object	✓	✓	
Overhead transparencies	✓	✓	✓
Presentation software slides	✓	✓	✓
Videotapes/DVDs	✓	✓	✓
Multimedia	✓	✓	✓

Tables *summarize and compare* data. When graphs aren't detailed enough and descriptions require too many words, tables are an effective alternative for showing numeric values. Tables also summarize and compare key features.

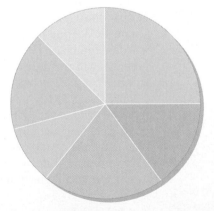

Pie charts show *how much* by identifying proportions in relation to a whole. Each wedge of the pie usually represents a percentage. Most audiences comprehend pie charts quickly and easily.

Maps show *where* by translating data into spatial patterns. Maps give directions, compare locations, or link statistical data to population characteristics.

Source   Receiver

Diagrams and illustrations show *how things work*. They take many forms: flowcharts, organizational diagrams, time lines, floor plans, and even enlargements of physical objects so that you can see the inside of an engine, a heart, or a flower.

Group Advantages	**Group Disadvantages**
• Groups generally accomplish more and perform better than individuals working alone. • Groups provide members with an opportunity to socialize and create a sense of belonging. • Collaborative group work promotes learning.	• Group work requires a lot of time, energy, and resources. • Conflict among group members can be frustrating and difficult to resolve. • Working with members who are unprepared, unwilling to work, or have difficult personalities can be aggravating.

Text charts *list ideas or key phrases*, often under a title or headline. They depict goals, functions, types of formats, recommendations, and guidelines. Items listed on a text chart may be numbered, bulleted, or set apart on separate lines.

Photographs *portray reality*—a real face or place is easily recognized and can capture emotions.

Note: Other forms of presentation aids include audio and video recordings, objects, handouts, and physical demonstration.

DESIGN PRINCIPLES FOR PRESENTATION AIDS

Preview and Highlight	Presentation aids should preview your key points and highlight important facts and features.
Headline Your Visuals	Clear headlines reduce the risk that readers will misunderstand your message.
Exercise Restraint	Avoid using too many graphics, fonts, colors, and other visual elements and effects.
Choose Readable Type and Suitable Colors	Don't use more than two different fonts on a slide, a font size smaller than 24 points, or illegible colors.
Use Appropriate Graphics	Make sure your graphics are essential and support your purpose.

Using Design Principles

Even with the best intentions, equipment, and cutting-edge software, presentation aids can fail to have an impact. They can be dull, distracting, and difficult to follow. Regardless of what type of supporting materials or in which medium you choose to display them, the basic visual design principles shown above can help you create aids that inform and please the eye without distracting or detracting from your presentation.

Keep the basic design principles in mind but remember not to be too rigid. Although these rules are based on sound principles, they are often misunderstood or followed blindly.

Because strict design principles may not apply in every situation, in some cases, you may need to break the "rules." For example, we are reluctant to give you a rule for the maximum number bullet points on a slide and the number of words per bullet point. Different sources inform us that three words, five words, and seven words per line are ideal. But there are times when you should use more than seven words and times

when you should highlight one word. In general, there's nothing wrong with following a reasonable standard—such as the "six-by-six" rule (six bullets per slide and six words per bullet)—to make sure that you don't end up with too many bullet points or full paragraphs on your slides. However, in *The Non-Designer's Presentation Book*, Robin Williams cautions us to be skeptical about most of the slide rules we hear or read. She offers more reasonable advice: Although "it's okay to put five bullet points on

(For more instruction how to *design* presentations aids effectively—including a special focus on computer-generated slides—see "Effective Presentation Aids" at http://www.thethinkspot.com.)

every slide," you're much better off putting the right number of lines and words on slides based on the needs of your speech.[24] To that she adds, "Make every word count, be as succinct as possible, but don't arbitrarily limit the number of words because of [a] rule. Be clear."[25]

Handling Presentation Aids

After you invest time, effort, and significant resources to plan and prepare presentation aids, make sure you handle your aids smoothly and professionally by following several general rules of thumb: Don't turn your back to the audience or stand in front of your screen or flip chart while speaking. Decide when to introduce your aids, how long to leave them up, and when to remove them. Even if you have numerous presentation aids to display, always start and end your presentation by making direct and personal contact with your audience.

Remember that presentation aids are not the presentation; they are only there to assist you. You and your message should always come first.

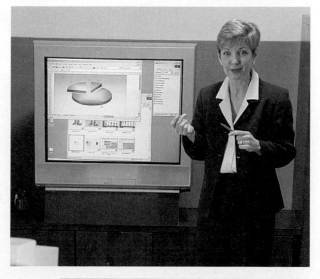

In light of what you've just read about using design principles and handling presentation aids, evaluate the design and presentation of the slide that the speaker in the photo is using.

Cognitive Science Meets Presentation Aids

Cognitive science is the interdisciplinary study of the mind and intelligence that focuses on how people process information. Cognitive science can also help you design visuals that adapt to your audience members' perception, thinking, and learning.

Here we present two significant cognitive science principles based on a synthesis of Stephen Kosslyn's study of PowerPoint presentations and Richard Mayer's broader research on multimedia learning using both verbal forms (written and spoken words) and images (illustrations, graphs, photos, maps, and animation or video).[26] These two principles—coherence and contrast—are described in the nearby table.

Cognitive science explains why emotionally interesting but irrelevant pictures actually *reduce* learning and comprehension. The term **seductive details** describes elements that attract audience attention but do not support a writer's or speaker's key points. Instead of learning, audience members are "seduced" and distracted by seductive details, such as interesting scenes, dramatic graphics, vivid colors, and engaging motion. They can confuse audience members about the meaning or purpose of a message.[27]

When you design or view a computer-generated slide, ask yourself: Is the slide coherent and does it use contrast to focus audience attention? Look at the two slides shown below. Which is the most coherent and which uses contrast more effectively? The second slide exhibit coherence and contrast principles better than the first. The section on visual design principles in this section of the text can help you integrate these key principles into the preparation of your presentation aids.

Cognitive Principle	Research Finding	Practical Application
Coherence	Irrelevant words, pictures, sounds, and music compete for cognitive resources in our working memory *and* divert our attention.	Cut or exclude extraneous material. Focus on and highlight only essentials ideas and items.
Contrast	Contrast reduces extraneous processing and directs our attention to important information.	Use visual contrast to guide listeners' attention to key elements and the connections between them.

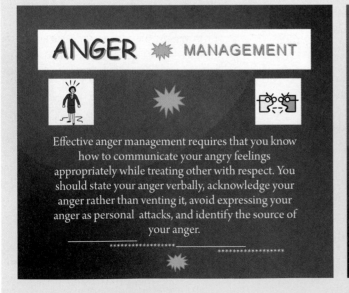

Plagiarism Plagues Presentation Aids

When the creation of visuals or audio is a person's livelihood, the uncompensated use of such works raises ethical questions about applying federal copyright laws.

To respond to this concern, companies such as Microsoft have developed online banks of clip art, clip video, and clip audio for fair use. For instance, Microsoft's Design Gallery Live site offers more than 250,000 graphics. The U.S. Library of Congress's own online catalog offers more than 7 million images, many of which are in the public domain and no longer protected by copyright. If you purchase a graphics package, you have the right to make copies of the images and use them in your presentations.

If, however, you use a photo scanned from a photographer's portfolio, an audio clip copied from a CD, or a graph downloaded from the Internet without giving these works proper attribution, you are plagiarizing.

14.7

Practicing Your Presentation

Why is practice essential for effective presentations?

In *Present Like a Pro*, Cyndi Maxey and Kevin E. O'Connor describe a study of the National Speakers Association's nearly 4,000 professional members who were asked for their top tips for a successful speech. *Practice* received more than 35 percent of the vote, making it first in importance.[28]

Effective practice sessions require more than repeating your presentation over and over again. Practice lets you know whether there are words you have trouble pronouncing or sentences that are too long to say in one breath. In addition, you may discover when you practice that what you thought was a 10-minute talk takes 30 minutes to deliver. Practicing with presentation aids is critical, as anyone can tell you who has seen the embarrassing results that befall speakers

> To put it another way, "give your speech *before* you give it."[29]

who don't have their visuals in order. Practicing is the only way to make sure that you sound and look good in a presentation.

Practice can take many forms. It can be as simple as closing your door and rehearsing your presentation in private or as complex as an onstage, videotaped dress rehearsal in front of a volunteer audience.

At the same time, don't get carried away with excessive practicing. Exercise restraint. Too much practice can make you sound canned, a term used to describe speakers who have practiced so much or given the same speech so many times that they no longer sound spontaneous, sincere, or natural. Our advice: Keep practicing until you feel satisfied. Then, practice with the goal of improving the fine points of your presentation. Practice until you feel confident. Then, stop.

Know Thy Self

Do You Practice Your Presentations?

Be honest. Do you devote significant time to practicing a presentation before you deliver it? Take a few seconds to answer the following questions:

1. Do you practice your entire presentation several different times rather than devoting one long single session to the process?

2. Do you divide each practice session into manageable, bite-sized chunks?

3. Do you practice in at least three complete run-through sessions?

4. Do you make changes to your notes or presentation as you practice?

5. Do you practice using an audio or video recorder, or do you ask someone to listen to you?

6. Do you believe that practice helps you gain confidence?

- **Do not memorize your presentation.** Not only do such presentations sound memorized, but you run the risk of forgetting. If you want to memorize a few key portions of a presentation, practice those sections so they sound natural.

- **Practice wherever and whenever you can.** If you have a long commute to work or school, turn off the radio and practice portions of your presentation out loud. Practice while you exercise, while you shower, when there's no one around to interrupt or distract you.

- **Time your practice session and understand that your actual presentation will take longer.** So if you are scheduled for a 10-minute speech, make sure it only takes 8 minutes in a practice session.

- **Audio record and, if possible, video your practice sessions.**

- **Practice in front of a friend or a small volunteer audience.** Listen carefully to their comments and decide which ones can help you improve your presentation.

- **Practice your entire presentation at several different times rather than devoting one long session to the process.**

- **Schedule brief 5- to 10-minute sessions of small segments.** "If you divide your practice time into manageable, bite-sized chunks, you'll find yourself practicing more often and building confidence for each segment."[30]

- **Schedule at least three—but no more than five—complete run-through sessions.** If you rehearse too much, you may sound dull or bored.

As you practice and deliver a presentation, remember that there are very few "must do" rules for effective speaking. Although this book is filled with good advice, successful speakers adapt that advice to their purpose, their audience, and the situation. Is it sometimes all right to put your hands in your pockets while speaking? Yes. Is it acceptable, in some situations, to sit down rather than to stand when speaking? Sure. Will the audience protest if you occasionally say "um" or "uh"? Nope.

Delivery and practice "rules" are guidelines, not commandments. Sometimes breaking a commonly accepted rule can make your presentation more interesting and memorable. Smart speakers use rules when they improve their presentations and dismiss them when they get in the way. For example, if everyone around you is using dozens of complex PowerPoint slides, consider using just a few or even none. If your audience seems resigned to sitting in silence as they listen, sprinkle your speech with a few questions. If there is one cardinal rule, it's this: Rules only work when they help you achieve your purpose.

Evaluate *Their* Speaking Style and *Your* Delivery

Read the brief excerpts from the following presentations:

1. Senator Hillary Clinton's Concession Speech, June 7, 2008[31]
2. President George W. Bush's Speech to a Joint Session of Congress, September 20, 2001[32]
3. Nick Jonas's speech on "Diabetes Awareness" at the National Press Club, August 24, 2009[33]

Review each speaker's style and language strategies. Which CORE language style (or styles) predominates? What language strategies do these speakers use? How well do they use them? What are the similarities and differences in these speakers' styles? Then be prepared to read each excerpt out loud and to deliver each one in a way that expresses the speaker's intentions, mood, and message most effectively. You may find this task difficult until you have practiced them at length.

When you listen to other class members read these excerpts, note the ways in which they use their voices and bodies to emphasize words and phrases. Also note how reading from a manuscript affects each speaker's delivery.

Excerpt from Senator Hillary Clinton's Concession Speech, June 7, 2008

We all want an economy that sustains the American Dream, the opportunity to work hard and have that work rewarded, to save for college a home and retirement, to afford that gas and those groceries, and still have a little left over at the end of the month.

We all want a health care system that is universal high quality and affordable so that parents no longer have to choose between care for themselves or their children or be stuck in dead-end jobs simply to keep their insurance. This isn't just an issue for me, it is a passion and a cause and it is a fight I will continue until every single American is insured no exceptions no excuses.

We all want an America defined by deep and meaningful equality from civil rights to labor rights, from women's rights to gay rights, from ending discrimination to promoting unionization, to providing help for the most important job there is, caring for our families.

Excerpt from President George W. Bush's Speech to a Joint Session of Congress, September 20, 2001

Americans are asking, "How will we fight and win this war?" We will direct every resource at our command—every means of diplomacy, every tool of intelligence, every instrument of law enforcement, every financial influence, and every necessary weapon of war—to the destruction and to the defeat of the global terror network.

Now, this war will not be like the war against Iraq a decade ago, with a decisive liberation of territory and a swift conclusion. It will not look like the air war above Kosovo two years ago, where no ground troops were used and not a single American was lost in combat.

Excerpt from Nick Jonas's speech on "Diabetes Awareness" at the National Press Club in Washington, DC, August 24, 2009

I was diagnosed with type I diabetes in November, 2005. My brothers were the first to notice that I'd lost a significant amount of weight, 15 pounds in three weeks. I was thirsty all the time, and my attitude had changed. I'm a really positive person, and it had changed during these few weeks. It would have been easy to blame my symptoms on a hectic schedule, but my family knew I had to get to a doctor. The normal range of a blood sugar is between 70 to 120. When we got to the doctor's office, we learned that my blood sugar was over 700. The doctor said that I had type I diabetes, but I had no idea what that meant. The first thing I asked was, "Am I going to die?"

14.1
The CORE Language Styles

How do you choose appropriate language for a presentation?

- Choose an appropriate language style from among the CORE speaking styles: **c**lear style; **o**ral style, **r**hetorical style, and **e**loquent style.

- The clear style uses short, simple, and direct words.

- The oral style employs familiar words; short sentences, personal pronouns, and colloquial expressions.

- The rhetorical style features vivid and powerful language.

- The eloquent style includes poetic and persuasive language in inspiring and memorable ways.

14.2
Modes of Delivery

How do you choose an appropriate delivery style for a presentation?

- Impromptu speaking occurs without advance preparation or practice.

- Extemporaneous speaking involves using an outline or a set of notes.

- Manuscript speaking involves reading a written presentation out loud.

- Memorized speaking is delivering a presentation without notes.

14.3
Confident Delivery

How can you reduce presentation anxiety?

- Although all speakers experience speaking anxiety, it is usually invisible. Audiences cannot see or hear your fear.

- When you read accurate information about speaking anxiety, you build confidence rather than increase your fear.

- To relax and reduce speaking anxiety, know your audience, focus on your message, and be well prepared.

14.4
Vocal Delivery

What are the components of effective vocal delivery?

- Effective breath control enables you to speak more loudly and say more in a single breath.

- Adapt your volume to the size of the audience and the dimensions of the room.

- Your speaking rate depends on your speaking style, the nature of your message, and your audience.

- Optimum pitch is the pitch at which you speak most easily and expressively.

- Frequent use of filler phrases can annoy your audience.

- Articulation involves clearly making the sounds in words; pronunciation refers to whether you say a word correctly.

14.5
Physical Delivery

What are the components of effective physical delivery?

- Direct effective eye contact helps you control communication, enhance your credibility, and interpret audience feedback.

- Speak naturally to ensure that your facial expressions and gestures support your message.

- Speakers who stand and move confidently radiate alertness and control.

14.6
Presentation Aids

What guideline should you follow when designing and displaying presentation aids?

- Choose media and presentation aids appropriate for your purpose, context, audience, and content.

- Five basic design principles for creating presentations aids include (1) preview and highlight, (2) headline your visuals, (3) exercise restraint, (4) choose readable type and suitable colors, and (5) use appropriate graphics.

- When handling presentation aids, focus on your audience (not the aids or yourself), begin with you, not your aids, and be prepared to do without your aids.

14.7
Practicing Your Presentation

Why is practice essential for effective presentations?

- Practicing ensures you sound and look good.

- Practice your entire presentation several different times by dividing each practice session into bite-sized chunks.

MySearchLab®

TEST YOUR KNOWLEDGE

14.1 How do you choose appropriate language for a presentation?

1 In a speech on "Diabetes Awareness" at the National Press Club in Washington, D.C., Nick Jonas said: *And at times . . . it would be a lot easier to throw in the towel and say, "Enough's enough, I'm done, and I'd like to just have a day off from having diabetes." But it just doesn't work like that.* Which speaking style was Nick Jonas using?
   a. Clear style
   b. Oral style
   c. Rhetorical style
   d. Eloquent style
   e. Academic style

2 In Abraham Lincoln's first inauguration address (1861), he concluded by imploring his mostly Southern audience not to go to war: *"The mystic chords of memory, stretching from every battlefield and patriot grave to every living hearth and hearth stone all over this broad land, will yet swell the chorus of the Union when again touched, as surely they will be by the better angels of our nature."* Which presentation speaking style was Lincoln using?
   a. Clear style
   b. Oral style
   c. Rhetorical style
   d. Eloquent style
   e. Academic style

14.2 How do you choose an appropriate delivery style for a presentation?

3 Which is the most common mode of presentation delivery?
   a. Impromptu
   b. Extemporaneous
   c. Manuscript
   d. Memorized
   e. None of the above

14.3 How can you reduce presentation anxiety?

4 Which of the following statements is *NOT* a myth about speaking anxiety?
   a. Reading about speaking anxiety will make you more nervous.
   b. Americans are more afraid of snakes than public speaking.
   c. Speaking anxiety is usually invisible to audience members.
   d. All of the above are myths about public speaking.

14.4 What are the components of effective vocal delivery?

5 What, in general, is the most effective rate of delivery?
   a. 100–125 words per minute
   b. 125–145 words per minute
   c. 145–180 words per minute
   d. 180–200 words per minute
   e. 200–250 words per minute

14.5 What are the components of effective physical delivery?

6 Which component of physical delivery is the most important for a successful presentation?
   a. Eye contact
   b. Facial expression
   c. Gestures
   d. Posture
   e. Movement

14.6 What guideline should you follow when designing and displaying presentation aids?

7 The phrase *seductive details* refers to
   a. the tendency of some speakers to focus on the personal details of their lives.
   b. a presentation speaking style that uses very vivid and intense language.
   c. the tendency of some speakers to hold an audience member's eye contact too long.
   d. using PowerPoint slides when other media would be more successful for sharing visual aids with an audience.
   e. elements in presentation aids that attract audience attention but do not support a speaker's key points.

8 Which presentation aid design principle advises speakers to avoid using too many graphics, fonts, colors, and other visual elements and effects?
   a. Use appropriate graphics
   b. Headline your visuals
   c. Exercise restraint
   d. Select appropriate media
   e. Preview and highlight

9 Which presentation aid design principle advises speakers to avoid more than two different fonts on a slide as well as font sizes smaller than 24 points?
   a. Preview and highlight
   b. Exercise restraint
   c. Choose readable type and suitable colors
   d. Use appropriate graphics
   e. Headline your visuals

14.7 Why is practice essential for effective presentations?

10 All of the following recommendations for practicing a presentation can help improve your delivery and confidence when speaking except _____.
   a. practicing until you have memorized your presentation
   b. practicing several times
   c. practicing using a voice or video recorder
   d. practicing in front of someone and ask for feedback
   e. practicing by dividing each session into manageable, bite-sized chunks

Answers found on page 366.

Key Terms

Alliteration	Eye scan	Presentation aids
Articulation	Filler phrases	Pronunciation
Clear style	Fluency	Rate
Cognitive science	Impromptu speaking	Rhetorical devices
CORE speaking styles	Inflection	Rhetorical style
Delivery	Language intensity	Seductive details
Eloquent style	Manuscript speaking	Speaking style
Extemporaneous speaking	Memorized speaking	Volume
Eye contact	Optimum pitch	
	Pitch	

SPEAKING to INFORM 15

For many college students, the most familiar type of informative presentation is the classroom lecture. In recent years, however, the traditional lecture has fallen out of favor. Researchers have found that if a professor speaks 150 words per minute, students hear only about 50 of them.[1] Most students tune out of a 50-minute lecture around 40 percent of the time.[2]

In *Teaching Tips*, Wilbert McKeachie notes that the typical attention span of students peaks within the first ten minutes of a class session and then decreases after that point.[3] As a result, you might expect McKeachie to recommend abandoning lectures in favor of other teaching methods. Not so. Rather, he sees lectures as a very efficient and effective teaching method if the instructor knows how to gain and maintain attention, if the lecture is well-planned and well-organized, if the body of the lecture includes various types of supporting material and clear transitions, and if the instructor actively involves students.[4] Essentially, McKeachie's description of a successful lecture captures the characteristics of a successful informative presentation.

THINK About...

and ASK YOURSELF...

15.1 The Purpose of Informative Speaking | *Why is informative speaking important?*

15.2 Informative Communication Strategies | *Which communication strategies work best for different types of informative presentations?*

15.3 Generating Audience Interest | *Which communication strategies effectively generate audience interest?*

15.4 Informative Speaking in Action | *What are the characteristics of an effective informative presentation?*

The Purpose of Informative Speaking

Why is informative speaking important?

Informative speaking is the most common type of presentation. Students use informative speaking to present oral reports, to share research with classmates, and to explain group projects. Beyond the classroom, business executives use informative presentations to orient new employees, to present company reports, and to explain new policies.

The primary purpose of an informative presentation is to instruct, enlighten, explain, describe, clarify, correct, remind, and/or demonstrate (see also Chapter 12, "Planning Your Presentation"). Informative presentations can present new information, explain complex concepts and processes, and clarify and correct misunderstood information. You will be asked to prepare and deliver informative presentations throughout your lifetime and career, so learning how to do it well can give you a competitive edge.[5]

Sometimes it's difficult to determine where an informative presentation ends and a persuasive presentation begins. Most informative presentations contain an element of persuasion. For example, an informative presentation explaining the causes of global warming may convince an audience that the problem is serious and requires stricter controls on air pollution. Even demonstrating how to sew on a button properly can persuade some listeners to change the way they've been doing it for years. It may also persuade other to do it themselves rather than giving it to mom or paying to have it done at the cleaner. Your purpose signifies the difference between informative and persuasive presentations. When you ask listeners to change their opinions or behavior, your presentation becomes persuasive.

Informative presentations can cover a wide range of topics—from the commonplace to the exotic.

COMMUNICATION IN *ACTION*

Focus on What's Valuable to Your Audience

Just because *you* love banjo music, bowling, or bidding on eBay doesn't mean audience members share your enthusiasm. How, then, do you give them a reason to listener? The answer is: Include a value step in your introduction to capture their attention. A **value step** explains how the information can enhance their success and personal well being. While this step may not be necessary in all informative presentations, it can motivate a disinterested audience to listen to you.

When looking for a value step, ask yourself whether your presentation will benefit your audience in any of the following ways:

- *Socially*. Will your presentation help listeners interact with others, become more popular, or throw a great party?
- *Physically*. Will your presentation offer advice about improving physical health, treating common ailments, or losing weight?

- *Psychologically*. Will your presentation help audience members feel better about themselves or help them cope with common psychological problems?
- *Intellectually*. Will your presentation explain intriguing and novel discoveries in science? Will you satisfy listeners' intellectual curiosity?
- *Financially*. Will your presentation help audience members make, save, or invest money wisely?
- *Professionally*. Will your presentation help audience members succeed and prosper in a career or profession?

If there's a good reason for you to make a presentation, there should be a good reason for your audience to listen.

15.2
Informative Communication Strategies

Which communication strategies should you use for different types of informative presentations?

In her **Theory of Informatory and Explanatory Communication**, Katherine Rowan explains how to make strategic decisions about the content and structure of an informative presentation. Her two-part theory focuses on the differences between informatory and explanatory communication. **Informatory communication** seeks to create or increase audience awareness about a topic by presenting the latest information—much like news reporting. **Explanatory communication** seeks to enhance or deepen an audience's understanding about a topic so that listeners can understand, interpret, and evaluate complex ideas and information. Good explanatory presentations answer such questions as "Why?" or "What does that mean?"[6]

Not surprisingly, different types of informative messages have different purposes and require different communication strategies. Rowan offers one set of strategies for informatory communication and then further divides explanatory communication into three different types of explanatory functions, as shown in the Classifications of Informative Communication graphic to the left.

Report New Information

Reporting new information is what most journalists do when they answer *who, what, where, when, why,* and *how* questions. New information is published in newspapers, popular magazines, and online.

You face two challenges when reporting new information. First, when information is new to an audience, it must be presented clearly and in a well-organized manner. Second, you may need to give audience members a reason to listen, learn, and remember. Rowan recommends four strategies for reporting new information as shown below.

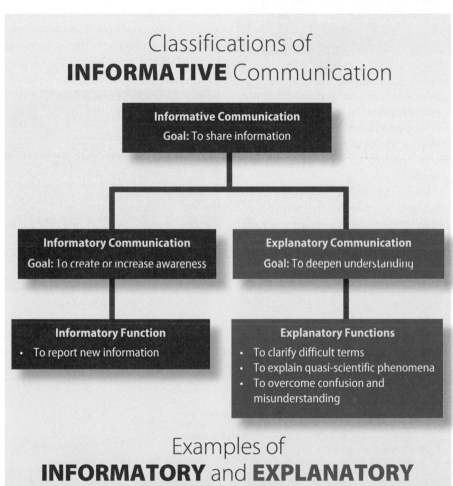

Classifications of
INFORMATIVE Communication

Informative Communication
Goal: To share information

Informatory Communication
Goal: To create or increase awareness

Explanatory Communication
Goal: To deepen understanding

Informatory Function
- To report new information

Explanatory Functions
- To clarify difficult terms
- To explain quasi-scientific phenomena
- To overcome confusion and misunderstanding

Examples of
INFORMATORY and **EXPLANATORY**
Communication[7]

INFORMATORY Creates Awareness	EXPLANATORY Deepens Understanding
• Cake recipes • Simple directions • Brief news story • Sports trivia • Biographies	• Baking principles • Academic lectures • In-depth news story • Game analysis • Philosophies

Strategies for
REPORTING NEW INFORMATION

- Include a value step in the introduction.
- Use a clear, organizational pattern.
- Use a variety of supporting materials.
- Relate the information to audience interests and needs.

Topic area Fire ants

Purpose To familiarize audience members with the external anatomy of a fire ant

Central idea A tour of the fire ant's external anatomy will help you understand why these ants are so hard to exterminate.

Value step In addition to inflicting painful and sometimes deadly stings, fire ants can eat up your garden, damage your home, and harm your pets and local wildlife.

Organization Space arrangement—a visual tour of the fire ant's external anatomy

Key points
A. Integument (exoskeleton)
B. Head and its components
C. Thorax
D. Abdomen

Clarify Difficult Terms

Understanding a difficult term is just that—difficult. Unlike an object, person, procedure, or event, a difficult term is often abstract—rarely can you touch it, demonstrate it, or explain it with a short and simple definition.

Explaining a difficult concept requires more than reporting. It requires explanatory communication in which you help audience members understand and separate essential characteristics from nonessential features. For example, what is the difference between *validity* and *reliability* or *ethos* and *ethics*? Why are corals classified as *animals* and not *plants*?[8]

In the outline on the next page, the meaning of *heuristics* is explained using four strategies Rowan recommends for clarifying difficult terms as shown below.

Informatory strategies work best when reporting new, uncomplicated information about objects, people, procedures, and events. Keep in mind, however, that an object, person, procedure, or event is not a purpose statement or central idea, so you need to develop one, as the above example on fire ants shows.

Informatory presentations often describe simple procedures that focus on how to do something. When informing an audience about a procedure or how something works, consider demonstrating the process. Through a series of well-ordered steps, **demonstration speeches** show an audience how to do something and/or how to understand how something works. These presentations can range from signing for the deaf or washing clothes properly to making guacamole or doing a magic trick. Obvious organizational patterns for such presentations include topical, time, and space arrangement, often along with effective visual aids.

A physician friend of ours who works at a large medical school and teaching hospital advises his students to "Tell, Show, Do." First, he *tells* students how to carry out a medical procedure by providing oral and/ or written instructions and advice. Then he *shows* them how to perform the procedure on a patient or volunteer medical student. Finally, he allows students to *do* the procedure under strict supervision. The "Tell, Show, Do" technique can help you inform an audience about any basic procedure— from boiling an egg to installing software.

When informing about an event such as the race to the moon or a presidential campaign, remember that the *purpose* of your presentation will determine how you will talk about that event—regardless of the date, size, or significance of the event.

Strategies for CLARIFYING DIFFICULT TERMS

- Define the term's essential features.
- Use various and typical examples.
- Contrast examples and nonexamples.
- Quiz the audience.

"Tell, Show, Do"

TELL	SHOW	DO
In American Sign Language "hello" is signed by moving the hand away from the forehead in a forward and downward motion, similar to a salute.	Watch me as I show you how to make the motions that signify the word "hello" in American Sign Language.	Now you try it!

PRESENTATION OUTLINE: Clarifying Difficult Terms

Topic area Heuristics

Purpose To explain how heuristics affect persuasion

Central idea Understanding heuristics will help you analyze the validity of persuasive arguments.

Value step Understanding heuristics can improve your ability to persuade others and to reject invalid arguments.

Organization Topical plus questions to audience

Key points

A. The essential features of heuristic messages

B. Common heuristics

  1 Longer messages are stronger.

  2 Confident speakers are more trustworthy.

  3 Celebrity endorsements sell products.

C. Contrast heuristic messages with valid arguments

D. Quiz the audience about heuristic messages

Heuristic: Celebrity Endorsement. Superstar Jennifer Lopez announces her new clothing line for Kohl's. The company hopes to persuade women that buying these clothes will make them more stylish and alluring.

Explain Quasi-Scientific Phenomena

The phrase *quasi-scientific phenomena* requires clarification. The key word here is *quasi*. *Quasi* (pronounced *kwah-zee*) means "having a likeness to something; resembling."[9] When you explain a **quasi-scientific phenomenon**, you look for a way to enhance audience understanding without using complex scientific terms, data, and methodologies.

Unlike difficult terms, quasi-scientific phenomena are complex, multidimensional processes. You are asking audience members to unravel something that is complicated, and that may require specialized knowledge to understand. The biggest challenge when making this kind of explanatory presentation is identifying the key components.

The presentation outline for "Breathing for speech" below is designed to teach audience members how to improve the quality of their voices. By comparing something well known (breathing for life) with something less well known (breathing for speech), the speaker helps the audience understand this anatomical process. Rowan recommends four strategies for explaining quasi-scientific phenomena as shown below.

Strategies for EXPLAINING QUASI-SCIENTIFIC PHENOMENA

- Provide clear key points.
- Use analogies and metaphors.
- Use presentation aids.
- Use frequent transitions, previews, summaries, and signposts.

PRESENTATION OUTLINE: Explaining Quasi-Scientific Phenomena

Topic area Breathing for speech

Purpose To explain how to breathe correctly for speech

Central idea The ability to produce a strong and expressive voice requires an understanding and control of the inhalation/exhalation process.

Value step Learning to breathe for speech will make you a more effective, expressive, and confident speaker.

Organization Compare and contrast three components of the breathing process

Key points

A. Active versus passive exhalation

B. Deep diaphragmatic versus shallow clavicular breathing

C. Quick versus equal time for inhalation

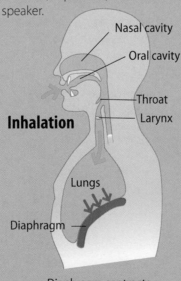

Diaphragm contracts and flattens during inhalation.

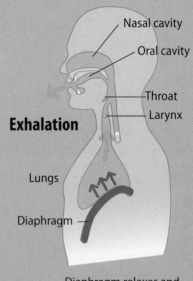

Diaphragm relaxes and moves upward during exhalation.

Overcome Confusion and Misunderstanding

Audience members sometimes cling to strong beliefs, even when those beliefs have been proved false. As a result, informative speakers often face the challenge of replacing old, erroneous beliefs with new, more accurate ones. As long as your overriding purpose is to instruct, explain, clarify, or correct—rather than persuade—your presentation is informative. Rowan recommends four strategies for overcoming confusion and misunderstanding as shown below.

Strategies for OVERCOMING CONFUSION AND MISUNDERSTANDING

1. State the belief or theory.

2. Acknowledge its believability and the reason(s) it is believed.

3. Create dissatisfaction with the misconception or explain the misconception by providing contrary evidence.

4. State and explain the more acceptable or accurate belief or theory.

In the example below, the speaker dispels misconceptions about the fat content in our diets.

ETHICAL COMMUNICATION

Trust Me ... I'm Just Informing You

The long infomercials on television are not presented for your enjoyment. They have only one purpose: To persuade you to buy a product. When a salesperson says (and yes, we've actually heard this line), "I'm not here to sell you anything. I only want to let you in on a few facts," we know the opposite is true.

On June 28, 2009, Billy Mays ("Hi, Billy Mays here!"), the millionaire TV pitchman, died. Although you may not know his name, his face will probably be familiar to you. As-seen-on-TV commercials like the ones starring Mays are part of a $150 billion industry.[10] Were it not for his over-the-top enthusiastic pitches, none of us would know much about the "amazing, " and "you-won't-believe-your-eyes" benefits of Oxi-Clean, Mighty Putty, or Tool Band-It.

When considering the purpose of any informative presentation, remember the first principle in the National Communication Association's Credo for Ethical Communication: "We advocate truthfulness, accuracy, honesty, and reason as essential to the integrity of communication."[11] Claiming to inform when your real purpose is to persuade violates this ethical principle.

Whether you love or hate infomercials, never doubt that the "information" in them is designed to persuade you.

PRESENTATION OUTLINE: Overcome Confusion and Misunderstanding

Topic area Fat in food

Purpose To explain that fat is an important element in everyone's diet

Central idea Our health-conscious society has all but declared an unwinnable and unwise war on any and all food containing fat.

Value step Eliminating all fat from your diet can hurt you rather than help you lose weight.

Organization Problem (misinformation)—solution (accurate information)

Key points

A. Many people believe that eliminating all fat from their diet will make them thinner and healthier.

B. This belief is understandable given that fat is the very thing we're trying to reduce in our bodies.

C. Fat is an essential nutrient.

D. Fats are naturally occurring components in all foods that, in appropriate quantities, make food tastier and bodies stronger.

At first, an explanatory presentation designed to overcome confusion and misunderstanding may seem more persuasive than informative Yet, it clearly fits within our definition of an informative presentation: one that seeks to instruct, enlighten, explain, describe, clarify, correct, remind, and/or demonstrate. If it's successful, a presentation about fat in the diet will encourage listeners to rethink what they believe. The primary purpose of presentations is to provide accurate information in the hope that a misunderstanding will be corrected. To that end, instructors correct mistaken beliefs about theories, physicians explain why penicillin doesn't cure the common cold, and nutritionists enlighten dieters about the need for fat in food.

Generating Audience Interest

Which communication strategies effectively generate audience interest?

In Chapter 12, we described two surveys that identified the most important skill for becoming a better speaker according to working adults and college students. In both cases, the top-rated skill was "keeping your audience interested."[12] Thus, it's not surprising that many of our students ask, "How can I make sure I'm not boring?" Novice speakers often *assume* they're not interesting; they can't imagine why an audience would want to listen to them. Or they have heard lots of boring presentations and fear they are doomed to the same fate. Rarely is either assumption true. Fortunately, three strategies can help keep your audience interested: tell stories, use humor, and involve your audience.

This Tlingit storyteller of Haines, Alaska, wears the traditional storytelling regalia to enhance his credibility and audience interest as he tells his tale.

Tell Stories

Throughout history, storytellers have acted as the keepers of tradition and held honored places in their societies.[13] All of us respond to stories, whether they are depicted in prehistoric cave paintings, portrayed in a film, or read to us.[14]

Stories are accounts of real or imagined events. They can be success stories, personal stories, humorous stories, and even startling stories.

Members of the clergy use parables, or stories with a lesson or moral, to apply religious teachings to everyday life.

Joanna Slan, author of *Using Stories and Humor*, claims that the ability to tell stories separates great presenters from mediocre ones.[15] Audiences remember stories because they have the power to captivate, educate, and create lasting images.

STORYTELLING
Best Practices

- **Use a simple story line.** Long stories with complex themes are hard to follow and difficult to tell. If you can't summarize your story in less than 25 words, don't tell it.[17]

- **Limit the number of characters.** Unless you're an accomplished actor or storyteller, limit the number of characters in your story. If your story has more than three or four characters, look for another story.

- **Connect to the audience.** Make sure that your story is appropriate for your audience.

- **Exaggerate effectively.** You can exaggerate both content and delivery when telling a story. Exaggeration makes a story more vivid and helps you highlight its message. The tone of your voice, the sweep of your gestures, and your facial expression add a layer of meaning and emphasis to your story.

- **Practice.** Practice telling your story to others—your friends, colleagues, or family members. Practice until you can tell a planned story without notes.

STOP&THINK

Can You Keep It Short?

In Chapter 12, we recommended 20 minutes as the maximum length for most presentations. If you realize that your presentation will run long, how will you shorten it? If you don't have a good answer to this question, you run the risk of losing your audience's attention and interest. Alan M. Perlman, a professional speechwriter, recommends answering three questions to find an appropriate way to shorten a presentation:

1. **Will audience members be able to reach this conclusion without my help?** If the answer is *yes*, don't overburden them with unnecessary explanations, stories, visuals, or evidence.

2. **Does the audience already know this information?** Don't spend a lot of time on a point if the audience already knows or understands the point.

3. **Does the audience really need to know this?** If the answer is *no*, delete or shorten any material that isn't directly relevant to your purpose.[16]

Storytelling also benefits speakers. If you're anxious, it can reduce your nervousness. Stories are easy to remember and usually easy to tell, particularly when they relate to events that you experienced personally.

Where to Find Stories Stories are everywhere, from your favorite children's book to your local news. To find the "right" story for your presentation, consider three rich sources: you, your audience, and other people.

You are a living, breathing collection of stories. The origin of your name, for example, might produce a fascinating narrative. Personal incidents or events that changed your life can lead to a good story. Or consider your family's roots, a place that holds significant meaning for you, your successes or failures, and your values.[18]

Your *audience* is also a rich source of stories. Tap into their interests, beliefs, and values. If your audience is deeply religious, you may share a story about a neighbor who gave up her worldly goods to work on a

mission. If your audience loves sports, you may share a story about your own triumphs or trials as an athlete. If your audience is culturally diverse, you may share a story about how you, a friend, or colleagues succeeded in bridging cultural differences.

Finally, stories about *other people* can help you connect with your audience. Think about people you know or people you have read about. Consider interviewing friends or family to uncover relevant stories about their life and knowledge. If you are going to tell a story about someone you know, make sure you have that person's permission. Don't embarrass a good friend or colleague by divulging a private story.

> Regardless of the type, stories must have a point that relates to your purpose, a reason for being told; otherwise, you run the risk of annoying your audience.[19]

The Structure of a Story Most good stories, no matter how short or how simple, follow the structure illustrated by the Story-Building Chart on p. 299. Not only can this chart help you develop a good, original story, it can also be used as speaking notes.

Use Humor

Humor in a presentation can capture an audience's attention and help them remember your presentation. Audience members tend to remember humorous speakers positively, even when they are not enthusiastic about the speaker's message. Humor can generate audience respect for the speaker, hold listeners' attention, and help an audience remember your main points.

Typically, the best source of humor is *you*. **Self-effacing humor**—directing humor at yourself—is usually much more effective than funny stories you've made up or borrowed from a book. But be careful that you don't poke too much fun at yourself. If you begin to look foolish or less than competent, you will damage your credibility.

FACTS **THINK** ABOUT THEORY

TEST IDEA PLAN EXPERIMENT METHOD

Narrative Theory

Walter R. Fisher, a respected communication scholar, studies the nature of **narratives**, a term that encompasses the process, art, and techniques of storytelling. Fisher sees storytelling as an essential aspect of being human. We experience life "as an ongoing narrative, as conflict, characters, beginnings, middles, and ends."[20] Good stories, he claims, have two essential qualities: probability and fidelity.[21]

Story probability refers to the formal features of a story, such as the consistency of characters and actions, and whether the elements of a story "hang together" and make sense. Would it, for example, seem right if Harry Potter double-crossed his best friends and teachers (unless, of course, he was under some diabolical spell)? Stories that make sense have a clear and coherent structure—one event leads logically to another. When trying to assess a story's probability, ask yourself the following questions:

- **Does the story make sense?** Can you follow the events as they unfold?

- **Do the characters behave in a consistent manner?** Do you wonder "Why did he do that?" or "How could she do that given everything else she's said and done?"

- **Is the plot plausible?** Do you find yourself saying "That just couldn't happen?"

Story fidelity refers to the apparent truthfulness of a story. Whereas story probability investigates the formal storytelling rules related to plot and characters, story fidelity focuses on the story's relationships to the audience's values and knowledge.[22] According to Walter Fisher, when you evaluate a story's fidelity, you try to determine whether the audience's experience rings true "with the stories they know to be true in their lives."[23] To assess the fidelity of a story, ask the following questions:

- **Do the facts and incidents in the story seem realistic?**

- **Does the story reflect your personal values, beliefs, and experiences?**

STORY-BUILDING CHART[24]

	STORY-BUILDING GUIDELINES	STORY EXAMPLE
TITLE OF THE STORY	Title of the Story	The Three Little Pigs[25]
BACKGROUND INFORMATION	• Where and when does the story take place? What's going on? • Did anything important happen before the story began? • Provide an initial buildup to the story. • Use concrete details. • Create a vivid image of the time, place, and occasion of the story.	Once upon a time, three little pigs set off to seek their fortune. . . .
CHARACTER DEVELOPMENT	• Who is in the story? • What are their backgrounds? • What do they look and sound like? • How do you want the audience to feel about them? • Bring them to life with colorful and captivating words.	Each little pig built a home. One was made of straw and one was made of sticks. The most industrious pig built a house of bricks. . . .
ACTION OR CONFLICT	• What is happening? • What did you or a character see, hear, feel, smell, or taste? • How are the characters reacting to what's happening? • Let the action build as you tell the story.	Soon, a wolf came along. He blew down the houses made of straw and sticks, but both pigs ran to the house of bricks. At the house of bricks the wolf said, "Little pig, little pig, let me come in." All three pigs said, "No, no, not by the hair of our chinny chin chin." So the wolf huffed and puffed but could not blow the house in. . . .
HIGH POINT OR CLIMAX	• What's the culminating event or significant moment in the story? • What's the turning point in the action? • All action should lead to a discovery, decision, or outcome. • Show the audience how the character has grown or has responded to a situation or problem.	The wolf was very angry. "I'm going to climb down your chimney and eat all of you up," he laughed, "including your chinny chin chins." . . .
PUNCH LINE	• What's the punch line? • Is there a sentence or phrase that communicates the climax of the story? • The punch line pulls the other five elements together. • If you leave out the punch line, the story won't make any sense.	When the pigs heard the wolf on the roof, they hung a pot of boiling water in the fireplace over a blazing fire. . . .
CONCLUSION OR RESOLUTION	• How is the situation resolved? • How do the characters respond to the climax? • Make sure that you don't leave the audience wondering about the fate of a character. • In some cases, a story doesn't need a conclusion—the punch line may conclude it for you.	When the wolf jumped down the chimney, he landed in the pot of boiling water. The pigs quickly put the cover on it, boiled up the wolf, and ate him for dinner. And the three little pigs lived happily ever after.
THE CENTRAL POINT OF THE STORY	The Central Point of the Story	The time and energy you use to prepare for trouble will make you safe to live happily ever after.

President Ronald Reagan was well known for making fun of his age, an approach that also defused campaign controversy about him being the oldest president in U.S. history:

> There was a very prominent Democrat who reportedly told a large group, "Don't worry. I've seen Ronald Reagan, and he looks like a million." He was talking about my age.[26]

There are, however, some approaches to humor that audiences will not and should not tolerate. Offensive humor—swearing, jokes that make fun of any group of people, references to private body functions—tops the list because it insults your audience and can damage your credibility.

> "Humor can generate audience respect for the speaker, **hold listeners' attention,** and help an audience remember your main points."[27]
>
> —Gene Perret, *Using Humor for Effective Business Speaking*

Know Thy SELF

Are You Funny?

Every month, *The New Yorker* magazine conducts its popular cartoon caption contest. The magazine displays the illustrated part of a cartoon and invites readers to write a funny caption. If you want to try your hand as a contestant, register at http://www.newyorker.com/captioncontest.

Here we present a cartoon that's popular in our classes. It comes from a 2001 drawing by Frank Cotham that asks the question, "Why would a man drive a car in circles in front of a couple of guys seated by a garage?"[28] Just to get you started, here's a sample caption submitted by a student: "That's not what we meant by rotate your tires."

What caption would you submit? The editors look for a caption that is simple, elegant, and, of course, funny.

As a word of warning, avoid singling out audience members for ridicule, unless you are speaking at a roast—an event at which a series of speakers warmheartedly tease an honored guest. And, although it should go without saying, avoid ethnic or religious jokes. Even if everyone in the audience shares your ethnicity and religion, don't assume they will appreciate your humor. Don't let the prospect of arousing audience laughter distract you from your purpose. You are a presenter, not a comedian. Humor counts, but too much humor can be counterproductive.

To ensure you are using humor effectively, make sure that your humor is relevant—that it supports the central idea and key points of your presentation. Then use the kind of humor that comes naturally to you—be it jokes, stories, puns, imitations. Also remember that humorous speaking requires more than knowing the witty content. It also requires effective delivery and comic timing—knowing when and how to say a line, when to pause, and when to look at the audience members for their reactions.

How does a two-time Grammy award–winning comedian like Lewis Black use strategies such as personal storytelling, self-effacing humor, and exaggerated delivery to engage his audiences?

7 Tips for USING HUMOR in a Presentation[29]

1. Focus your humor on the message.
2. Make sure the humor suits you.
3. Practice, practice, practice.
4. Avoid offensive humor such as talking about body functions.
5. Don't tease anyone in your audience.
6. Avoid ethnic or religious humor, unless you are making fun of yourself in an inoffensive way.
7. Limit your funny content.

When audience members are encouraged to speak, raise their hands, write, or interact with one another, they become involved in the speechmaking process.

What does the raised hand in this photo reveal about the way the speaker has involved the audience in his presentation?

Involve the Audience

One of the most powerful ways to keep audience members alert and interested is to ask them to participate actively in your presentation. When audience members are encouraged to speak, raise their hands, write, or interact with one another, they become involved in the speechmaking process. You can involve the audience by using several strategies: ask questions, encourage interaction, do an exercise, ask for volunteers, and invite feedback.

Ask Questions Involve audience members by asking questions, posing riddles, or soliciting reactions during or at the end of your presentation. Even if your listeners do little more than nod their heads in response, they will be involved in your presentation. Audience members will be more alert and interested if they know that they will be quizzed or questioned during or after a presentation.

Encourage Interaction Something as simple as asking audience members to shake hands with one another or to introduce themselves to the people sitting on either side of them generates more audience attention and interest. If you are addressing a professional or business audience, ask them to exchange business cards. If you're addressing young college students, ask them to tell each other their majors or career aspirations.

Do an Exercise Simple games or complex training exercises can involve audience members in your presentation and with one another. Bookstores sell training manuals describing ways to involve groups in games and exercises. Interrupting a presentation for a group exercise gives the audience and the speaker a break during which they can interact in a different but equally effective way.

Ask for Volunteers If you ask for volunteers from the audience, someone will usually offer to participate. Volunteers can help you demonstrate how to perform a skill or how to use a piece of equipment. Some can even be persuaded to participate in a funny exercise or game. Most audiences love to watch a volunteer in action.

Invite Feedback Invite questions and comments from your audience. If audience members seem reluctant to participate, don't badger or embarrass them. If no one responds, continue your presentation. It takes a skillful presenter to encourage and respond to feedback without losing track of a prepared presentation. The more you speak, the easier and more useful feedback is.

ADAPT TO DIFFERENT LEARNING STYLES

From an audience's perspective, informative presentations are learning experiences. The most effective speakers understand that audience members differ in terms of how they learn. Each of us has a unique **learning style**, the strengths and preferences that characterize the way we take in and process information. If you understand the ways in which audience members learn, you can adapt your message and its delivery to three basic learning styles: visual, auditory, and kinesthetic/tactile.

Visual learners use their eyes to learn. They learn by reading, seeing information displayed on a word chart, and using flash cards or their notes to study. If they can't see it, they won't learn it well. **Auditory learners** learn by listening. In class, they may ask if they can record an instructor's lecture. Books on tape delight auditory learners. The third type of learning style, **kinesthetic/tactile**, is a hands-on approach. These learners may squirm in their seats if someone talks too long. They want to "do it" rather than listen or read.

Take your audience's styles into account as you prepare and deliver a presentation. Auditory learners may need nothing more than your spoken words, but visual learners may need to see words on a slide or through a physical demonstration. Consider breaking up a presentation with audience questions or activities for those who learn by doing. A variety of approaches can make your presentation more dynamic and accommodate the range of learning styles in an audience.[30]

15.4
Informative Speaking in Action
What are the characteristics of an effective informative presentation?

"For all the trust I put in *CliffsNotes*, I don't know one thing about them" was the sentence that inspired the informative presentation on *CliffsNotes* that begins on the following page.[31] Our former student John Sullivan, who is now the director of information technology at a large nonprofit organization, translated his likable speaking style into a delightful and memorable presentation. The presentation included most types of supporting material: facts, statistics, testimony, descriptions, analogies, examples, and stories from a variety of sources. When John discovered that very little was written about the history of *CliffsNotes*, he phoned the company's headquarters and interviewed the managing editor, Gary Carey.

The information in this presentation has been updated but has not changed the speaker's style. Use the *Preparation and Content* section of the Information Presentation Assessment instrument on p. 307 to see how well this speech and the outline that follows meet the criteria for an effective informative presentation.

Cliff's Notes

John Sullivan

John's simple, opening story uses short sentences as well as grammatically incomplete sentences. His *clear* and *oral style* immediately engage listeners who can relate to pulling an all-nighter before an exam.

Eight o'clock Wednesday night. I have an English exam bright and early tomorrow morning. It's on Homer's *Iliad*. And I haven't read page one. I forgo tonight's beer drinking and try to read. Eight forty-five. I'm only on page 12. Only 482 more to go. Nine thirty, it hits me. Like a rock. I'm not going to make it.

Throughout this presentation, John uses *I*, *me*, and *my* to make his presentation personal, engaging, and enjoyable. In this paragraph he uses the word *I* nine times.

The way I see it I have three options. I can drop the class, cheat, or go ask Cliff. Because I'm not a quitter, and because I don't think cheating is the right thing to do, I borrow a copy of the *CliffsNotes* from my roommate. Yes, I know, I could have used *SparkNotes* or *Shmoop*, but at 9:30 at night, with a copy of *CliffsNotes* close at hand, I wasn't going to comparison shop online.

Humor helps the audience remember that there is a real person named Cliff behind *CliffsNotes*.

So I put my trust in *CliffsNotes* that night, even though I couldn't have told you one thing about the origins or quality of these yellow and black booklets. The time had come to learn more. After an exhaustive but not too productive search through sources as diverse as *People Magazine*, the *Omaha World-Herald*, and *Forbes Magazine* as well as almost a hundred websites, I turned to Cliff himself to get the real story. Yes, there is a Cliff behind *CliffsNotes* and no, his last name is not Notes. After two phone interviews with the managing editor of *CliffsNotes*, it became clear to me that *CliffsNotes* was truly an American success story. Whereas newcomers like *SparkNotes* and *Shmoop* keep the market humming, the history of *CliffsNotes* helps explain the long-term success of these study guides.

Conducting a personal interview with the editor of *CliffsNotes* demonstrates the speaker's success in finding credible *information* from a *primary source*. John's purpose is primarily *informatory* (creates awareness) rather than *explanatory* (deepens understanding)

In the last sentence of this paragraph, John *reviews* the three *key points* of his presentation. Notice how well he systematically covers each of these points in the body of the presentation

At one time, the notes were nothing more than simple plot summaries. But today, they offer the reader much more in terms of character analysis and literary criticism. To better appreciate this unique publishing phenomenon, it is necessary to trace the history of *CliffsNotes* along with some of the changes the company has undergone, the growth of its competitors, and finally, to understand why study guides get put down by teachers and praised by students.

Mr. Cliff Hillegass, owner and founder of *CliffsNotes*, literally started the business in the basement of his home as a mail-order company. As an employee of the Nebraska Book Company, he happened upon a Canadian publisher who had a full line of study guides. Upon returning home from a trip to Canada, he brought with him the notes to sixteen plays by Shakespeare and the rights to publish them in the United States. He immediately produced three thousand copies of each and sent them throughout the U.S. Bookstore managers were very receptive to the idea and quickly put the first *Notes* on sale.

The *descriptive story* of how *CliffsNotes* started includes details that humanize the founder and share relevant facts about the company.

When *CliffsNotes* first splashed onto the scene in 1958, 18,000 copies were sold. By 1960 sales had increased to 54,000 per year. By the mid-'60s, the magic number was two million and soon everyone wanted a piece of the action. By 1968, no less than thirteen other companies were in the market. Mr. Hillegass was confident through it all that none could overtake him. He told his sales staff not to worry. He said, "I believe most of our competitors are large publishers for whom the study guides would never be more than one item in their line." He couldn't have been more correct. By 1968, just two years later, only three competitors were left. And as the competition went down, sales figures for *CliffsNotes* went up.

A direct *quotation* from Cliff Hillegass adds a personal touch and *credibility* to the *story*.

Because *CliffsNotes* has been so successful for so long, it holds a rare honor: it's become a common noun and frequently used adjective. For example, when the Financial Crisis Inquiry Commission report was published in 2011, a *The New York Times* reporter began her summary of the study by writing "For those who might find the report's 633 pages a bit daunting … we offer a Cliff Notes version." A simple web search can put you in touch with "Health Care Reform: The Cliff's Notes Version," "Wikileaks: Cliff Notes Version," and my personal favorite, "Cliffs Notes Version: Seven Psychological Principles Con Artists Exploit."

Despite its long and profitable history, *CliffsNotes* now faces its greatest challenge from both print and online competitors. A review of what a *The New York Times* article calls "on-line cheat sheets" reports that *CliffsNotes* publishes 159 literature booklets and provides more than 250 study guides online. They also have free podcasts called *CramCasts*, the "literature light" versions with little more than three to five minute overviews and plot summaries. *SparkNotes*—who cleverly decided to substitute *Spark* for *Cliffs*—is the major competitor with similar booklets and online resources. The *SparkNotes* website claims they are "Today's Most Popular Study Guides." New online sites are emerging to join the competitive fray.

Even with hundreds of titles, a few dozen dominate most of *CliffsNotes* sales. Obviously certain titles have remained relatively constant through the years. Here are the top-ten *CliffsNotes* sold in 1992. As I list them in descending order, guess which book might be number one. And, as a hint, keep in mind that most *CliffsNotes* are sold to high school juniors and seniors.

10. *To Kill a Mockingbird*	5. *The Great Gatsby*
9. *The Scarlet Letter*	4. *Julius Caesar*
8. *Great Expectations*	3. *Macbeth*
7. *A Tale of Two Cities*	2. *The Adventures of Huckleberry Finn*
6. *Romeo and Juliet*	1. *Hamlet*

Now let's jump ahead almost 20 years and look at the 2010 top-sellers in two categories: Shakespeare's plays and other literary classics.

The top-three Shakespearean plays from *CliffsNotes* and *SparkNotes* are *Romeo and Juliet*, *Hamlet*, and *Macbeth*. Alas, poor Hamlet is no longer number one. In terms of other classics, *CliffsNotes* lists *To Kill a Mockingbird*, *The Scarlet Letter*, and *The Adventures of Huckleberry Finn* as the top three. Whereas *To Kill a Mockingbird* came in tenth on the best-seller list in 1992, it now rules the roost as number one. I guess not much has changed in the list of books we read *and* the study guides we rely on.

Although study guides—in a variety of formats—are here to stay, many educators are seriously concerned about quality of their quality. There have also been claims of copyright infringements as well as questions about the ethics of using a study guide rather than reading the real thing.

Quality control issues abound even though study guide authors are PhDs, literature instructors, or graduate students who have experience with the literary work. Dr. Carl Fisher, chair of the comparative world literature and classics department at California State University, Long Beach, reviewed samples from a variety of study guide publishers

In several sections of his presentation, John adds an aside that is usually humorous and personal. In this way, he is a friendly and often amusing presence in the speech.

Does Gary Carey's admission about the questionable quality of CliffsNotes 20 years ago help or hurt his credibility.

to evaluate their quality. Much to my relief, *CliffsNotes* and *SparkNotes* got high grades. Although *Shmoop* claims their writers come from graduate students at top universities, their guides contain misspellings of authors' names and other errors. Three guides—*Pink Monkey*, *Book Rags*, and *Bookwolf*—"did not make the grade at all." With those names, I'm not surprised.

In the early days, *CliffsNotes* saw its share of problems. In 1966 Random House filed suit against *CliffsNotes* for quoting too extensively from some of its copyrighted works by William Faulkner. Both sides had lawyers poised and ready to do combat. It could have become a landmark case. Instead Cliff and Random House solved their problems out of court. Cliff saw this as a turning point for both himself and his company. It forced them to take a fresh look at the notes. As a result, the classic guides were revamped to the point that they are now approximately 50 percent text summary and 50 percent critical analysis.

Although study guide publishers have learned lessons about quality control and copyright laws, academic critics are still at their door. I'm sure you have heard (or can easily imagine) teacher complaints that study guides allow students to avoid reading the original text.

Gary Carey, a former managing editor for *CliffsNotes*, countered such criticism in the same article by stating: "Teachers' apprehensions concerning *CliffsNotes* may have been well founded twenty years ago when they were simple plot summaries. But, today, they are mainly composites of mainstream literary criticism that are of little value to students who have not read the book." An informal survey at Creighton University and the University of Nebraska found that Mr. Carey may be correct. Where students' older brothers and sisters may have used *CliffsNotes* in place of the real thing, more than 80 percent of those students interviewed said they never used *CliffsNotes* by themselves. They only used them to accompany the reading of the required text.

However, another survey, this time of students at the University of Missouri-Columbia found that "one-third of the respondents admitted reading the 'cliffs notes' rather than the actual work." As one educator said, "Reading *CliffsNotes* is like letting someone else eat your dinner. They deprive students of the pleasure of discovering literature for themselves."

As for me … I did pass my exam, and I have yet to read *The Iliad*. And I'm sure there are plenty of students out there who have missed the delights of *Huckleberry Finn* or the pathos of *The Grapes of Wrath*. And "To be or not to be," "Friends, Romans, countrymen," and "Out, damned spot" very well could be the only lines of Shakespeare that some students know despite their passing grades.

So the controversy continues. But at least now you know that, unlike Ronald McDonald, Cliff was a real person who began a major industry and who did not dodge the issues. *CliffsNotes* and its competitors will continue explaining the finer points of literature to students around the globe. Because as long as teachers assign the classics of literature, the study guides will continue to grow and prosper.

How would you explain the differences in survey results at different universities?

John returns to his *personal experience* and acknowledges that many students miss the delights of reading literature by solely relying on *CliffsNotes*

Once again, John uses *humor*, this time as a way to effectively conclude his presentation

Cliff's Notes: Basic Outline

I. Introduction	I. Introduction
	Eight o'clock Wednesday night. . . .
A. Purpose/Topic	A. Study guides help students understand great literature and succeed in literature courses.
B. Central Idea	B. Study guides are a unique publishing phenomenon often criticized by instructors and praised by students.
C. Brief Preview of Key Points	C. Preview
1. Key Point #1	1. History of *CliffsNotes*
2. Key Point #2	2. Competition and comparisons of study guides
3. Key Point #2	3. Criticism of study guides
II. Body of the Presentation	II. Body of the Presentation
A. Key Point #1	A. History of *CliffsNotes*
1. Supporting Material	1. Story of Cliff Hillegass, owner and founder of *CliffsNotes*
2. Supporting Material	2. Growth and success of *CliffsNotes*
3. Supporting Material	3. *CliffsNotes* becomes a common noun/adjective.
B. Key Point #2	B. Competition and Comparisons
1. Supporting Material	1. Competition of *CliffsNotes* and *SparkNotes*
2. Supporting Material	2. Comparisons of best-selling titles
C. Key Point #3	C. Criticism of Study Guides
1. Supporting Material	1. Questions about the quality of content
2. Supporting Material	2. Copyright issues
3. Supporting Material	3. Overreliance on Study Guides
III. Conclusion	III. Conclusion
	I passed the exam without reading *The Iliad.* . . .
	Study guides will continue to grow and prosper.

Informative Presentation Assessment

Use the following ratings to assess each of the competencies on this assessment instrument for a presentation you are preparing or for one you watch, listen to, and/or read.

E = excellent; G = good; A = average; W = weak; M = missing; N/A = not applicable.

COMPETENCIES	E	G	A	W	M	N/A
Preparation and Content						
Purpose and topic						
Audience adaptation						
Adaptation to context						
Introduction						
Organization						
Supporting material						
Transitions						
Conclusion						
Language						
Interest factors						
Informative strategies						
Delivery						
Extemporaneous mode						
Vocal delivery						
Physical delivery						
Presentation aids, if used						
Other Criteria						
Outline/written work						
Bibliography						
Other: _____						
Overall Assessment (circle one)	E	G	A	W	M	N/A
Comments:						

15.1
The Purpose of Informative Speaking
Why is informative speaking important?

- An effective informative presentation can instruct, inspire, explain, describe, clarify, correct, remind, and/or demonstrate.

- The dividing line between informing and persuading is the speaker's purpose.

- When speaking to inform, include a value step that explains why the information is valuable to audience members and how it can enhance their success or well-being.

15.2
Informative Communication Strategies
Which communication strategies should you use for different types of informative presentations?

- Classify your informative presentation in terms of whether its purpose is informatory (reports new information) or explanatory (clarifies difficult terms, explains quasi-scientific phenomena, or overcomes confusion and misunderstanding).

- Strategies for reporting new information include beginning with a value step, using a clear organizational pattern, including various types of supporting material, and relating the information to audience interests and needs.

- Strategies for clarifying difficult terms include defining the term's essential features, using various examples, discussing nonexamples, and quizzing the audience to ensure comprehension.

- Strategies for explaining quasi-scientific phenomena include providing clear key points, using analogies and metaphors, using presentation aids, and using transitions, previews, summaries, and signposts to connect key points.

- Strategies for overcoming confusion and misinformation include stating the belief or theory, acknowledging its believability, creating dissatisfaction with the misconception, and stating and explaining the more acceptable belief or theory.

15.3
Generating Audience Interest
Which communication strategies effectively generate audience interest?

- In order to tell stories that captivate and educate your audience, look for good sources of stories, structure the story effectively, check the story for fidelity and probability, and use effective storytelling skills.

- In order to use humor to generate audience interest, avoid offensive humor, be prepared to direct humor at yourself, and avoid inappropriate humor.

- Involve audience members in your presentation by asking questions, encouraging interaction, doing exercises, asking for volunteers, and inviting feedback.

- Analyze and adapt to your audience's learning styles: visual, auditory, and/or kinesthetic/tactile.

15.4
Informative Speaking in Action
What are the characteristics of an effective informative presentation?

- Effective informative speakers use a clear and oral speaking style, adapt to audience experiences and needs, generate interest by using stories, humor, and audience involvement, and promote their own credibility.

MySearchLab®

TEST YOUR KNOWLEDGE

15.1 Why is informative speaking important?

1 If you ask yourself, "Will my presentation explain intriguing and novel discoveries in science?" when searching for a value step, which audience benefit are you trying to achieve?

a. Social benefit

b. Psychological benefit

c. Physical benefit

d. Intellectual benefit

e. Professional benefit

2 Which of the following constitutes a value step for a presentation on cooking hard-boiled eggs?

a. Hard-boiled eggs are easy to make.

b. I will teach you how to make foolproof hard-boiled eggs.

c. There are four steps—cold-water start, stopping the boiling, the 15-minute stand, and cold-water rinse—for cooking perfect hard-boiled eggs.

d. You won't have cracked or leaky eggs if you use this method for making perfect hard-boiled eggs.

e. Use the cold-water method to cook perfect hard-boiled eggs.

15.2 Which communication strategies should you use for different types of informative presentations?

3 All of the following topics are appropriate for an *informatory* type of informative presentation except ——.

a. learning how to bake bread recipes

b. learning how to change gears on a bicycle

c. giving directions for sewing on a button

d. understanding the chemistry of yeast in bread baking

e. highlighting Michael Jackson's greatest hits

4 When clarifying a difficult term in an informative presentation, which of the following strategies should you use?

a. Use analogies and metaphors

b. Use various examples

c. Use presentation aids

d. Explain the theory

e. Quiz the audience

5 When explaining a quasi-scientific phenomenon, which of the following strategies should you include?

a. Use analogies and metaphors

b. Use various examples

c. Use nonexamples

d. Create dissatisfaction with the theory

e. Quiz the audience

15.3 Which communication strategies effectively generate audience interest?

6 According to Fisher's narrative theory, which of the following questions tests a story's probability?

a. Do the facts and incidents in the story ring true?

b. Do the characters behave in a consistent manner?

c. Does the story reflect my personal values, beliefs, and experiences?

d. Does the story address or support the speaker's point?

e. Does the story omit or distort any key facts or events?

7 Which of the following is the third step in the story-building chart?

a. High point or climax

b. Action or conflict

c. Background information

d. Punch line

e. Character development

8 All of the following statements are good tips for using humor except ——.

a. do not tease anyone in your audience.

b. focus your humor on the message.

c. do not direct humor at yourself.

d. be wary of telling stories about body functions.

e. avoid ethnic or religious humor.

9 Which of the following strategies does your textbook recommend for involving the audience in your presentation?

a. Ask questions

b. Encourage interaction

c. Do an exercise

d. Invite feedback

e. All of the above

10 Which of the following learning styles might account for audience members who tend to squirm in their seats?

a. Visual learners

b. Auditory learners

c. Oral learners

d. Kinesthetic learners

e. Quantitative learners

Answers found on page 366.

Key Terms

Demonstration speeches	Learning style	Theory of Informatory
Explanatory	Narratives	and Explanatory
communication	Self-effacing humor	Communication
Informatory	Story fidelity	Value step
communication	Story probability	

In 2010, Apple launched its official sales of iPads in Moscow, much to the delight of young Russian customers.

SPEAKING to PERSUADE

16

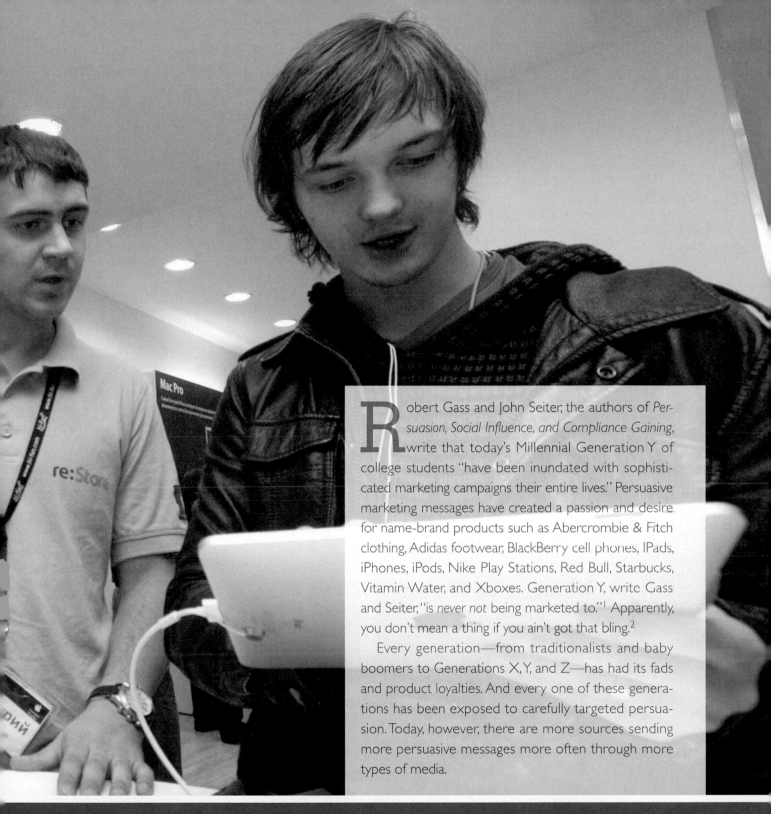

obert Gass and John Seiter, the authors of *Persuasion, Social Influence, and Compliance Gaining*, write that today's Millennial Generation Y of college students "have been inundated with sophisticated marketing campaigns their entire lives." Persuasive marketing messages have created a passion and desire for name-brand products such as Abercrombie & Fitch clothing, Adidas footwear, BlackBerry cell phones, IPads, iPhones, iPods, Nike Play Stations, Red Bull, Starbucks, Vitamin Water, and Xboxes. Generation Y, write Gass and Seiter, "is *never not* being marketed to."[1] Apparently, you don't mean a thing if you ain't got that bling.[2]

Every generation—from traditionalists and baby boomers to Generations X, Y, and Z—has had its fads and product loyalties. And every one of these generations has been exposed to carefully targeted persuasion. Today, however, there are more sources sending more persuasive messages more often through more types of media.

The Nature of Persuasion

What is the goal of a persuasive presentation?

Persuasive messages bombard us from the time we wake up until the moment we end each day. Sometimes persuasion is obvious—a sales call, a political campaign speech, or a television commercial. At other times it's more subtle—a sermon, an investment newsletter, a product sample in the mail.[3]

Businesses use persuasion to sell products. Colleges use persuasion to recruit students and faculty. Children persuade parents to let them stay up late or to buy the newest toy. And speakers use persuasion in everyday presentations and in major public speeches. In this chapter, we explain how and why persuasion works. Then we show you how to use these persuasive strategies and skills to develop effective persuasive presentations.

Persuasion seeks to change audience opinions (what they think) or behavior (what they do). Your purpose determines whether you will speak to inform or to persuade. Whereas informative presentations *tell* audiences something by *giving* them information or explanations, persuasive presentations *ask* for something *from* audiences—their agreement or a change in their opinions or behavior.

PERSUASION CHANGES
OPINIONS AND BEHAVIOR

OPINIONS
- Your family is more important than your job.
- Japan makes the best automobiles.
- Vegetarian diets are good for your body and good for the planet.

BEHAVIOR
- Eat dinner with your family at least five times a week.
- Buy a Japanese-made car.
- Stop eating meat.

PERSUASIVE PRESENTATIONS *ask* for something *from* audience members—their agreement or a change in their opinions or behavior.

16.2
Persuading Others

How can you adapt to different audience attitudes?

If you want to change audience members' opinions or behavior, you need to understand why they resist change. Why don't people vote for the first candidate who asks for their support? Why don't we run out and buy every cereal a sports star recommends? Why don't workers quit their job if they dislike their boss? All these questions have good answers—and that's the problem. Most audience members know why they *won't* vote, buy, quit, or do any of the things you ask them to do. It's up to you to determine what the reasons are and address them.

Classifying Audience Attitudes

The more you know about audience members and their attitudes, the more effectively you can adapt your message to them. For example, an audience of homeowners may strongly agree that their property taxes are too high, but a group of local college students may support more taxes for higher education. If you're scheduled to talk to a group of avid gun collectors or hunters, you can probably assume that they are resistant to stricter gun control legislation.

Review what you know about your audience's demographic characteristics and attitudes. Then place your audience along a continuum such as the one shown below that measures the extent to which *most* members will agree or disagree with you. When you understand where audience members stand, you can begin the process of adapting your message to the people you want to persuade.

Persuading Audience Members Who Agree with You

When audience members already agree with you, you don't have to *change* their way of thinking. Rather, your goal is to strengthen their attitudes and encourage behavioral change.

When audience members agree with you, consider giving them an **inoculation**. According to social psychologist William McGuire, protecting audience attitudes from counterpersuasion by the "other side" is like inoculating the body against disease.[4] You can build up audience resistance by exposing flaws in the arguments of the opposition *and* showing your audience how to refute them. This strategy creates a more enduring change in attitudes or behavior.

> **Inoculation** works best when audience members are involved in and care about an issue because it makes them aware that their attitudes are vulnerable to attack and then provides ammunition against or resistance to the attack.[5]

Apple keeps its devoted fans all over the globe happy by preaching to the faithful and, as a result, keeps them coming back for the newest versions and upgrades.

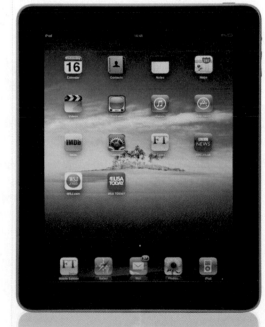

CONTINUUM OF AUDIENCE ATTITUDES

| Strongly agree with me | Agree | Undecided | Disagree | Strongly disagree with me |

Persuading Audience Members Who Disagree with You

Disagreement does not mean that audience members will be hostile or rude. It does mean, however, that changing their opinions is more challenging. In the face of audience disagreement, don't try to change the world. Focus on what can reasonably be changed.

Finding **common ground**—a place where both you and your audience can stand without disagreement—is often the key to persuading an audience that disagrees with you. Identify and discuss a position or behavior that you share with your audience. For example, smokers and nonsmokers may both agree that smoking should be prohibited in and around schools.

If you find common ground, your audience is more likely to listen to you when you move into less friendly territory.

Persuasive Strategies FOR AUDIENCES THAT DISAGREE WITH YOU

- **Set reasonable goals.** Do not expect audience members to change their opinions or behavior radically. Even a small step taken in your direction can eventually add up to a big change.

- **Find common ground.** Find a belief, value, attitude, or opinion that you and your audience have in common before moving on to areas of disagreement.

- **Accept and adapt to differences of opinion.** Acknowledge the legitimacy of audience opinions and give them credit for defending their principles. Demonstrate respect for their viewpoint.

- **Cite fair and respected evidence.** Make sure your supporting material is flawless. Choose evidence from respected, unbiased sources.

- **Build your personal credibility.** Present yourself as credible. Positive feelings about you enhance your persuasiveness.

Persuading Indecisive Audience Members

Some audience members may not have an opinion about your topic because they are uninformed, unconcerned, or undecided. Knowing which type of persuasive strategy to apply in each case depends on audience members' reasons for indecision. In the following example, a college student begins her presentation on the importance of voting by getting the attention of the undecided students and giving them a reason to care.

How many of you applied for some form of financial aid for college? [More than half the class raised their hands.] How many of you got the full amount you applied for or needed? [Less than one-fourth of the class raised their hands.] I have some bad news for you. Financial aid may be even more difficult to get in the future. But the good news is that there's something you can do about it.

In the real world of persuasive speaking, you are likely to face audiences with some members who agree with your message, others who don't, and still others who are indecisive. In such cases, you can focus on just one group—the largest, most influential, or easiest to persuade—or appeal to all three types of audiences by providing new information from highly respected sources.

STOP&THINK

Can You Find Common Ground?

Below are two controversial topics often chosen by students for class presentations that are just as often unsuccessful in achieving their purpose. Complete each sentence by stating an issue on which a speaker and audience might find common ground. For example, "Free speech advocates and anti-pornography groups would *probably* agree that … pornography should not be available to young children." Note that the word *probably* is written in italics. Audience members at extreme ends of any position or belief may not make exceptions and may not be willing to stand on common ground with you.

1. Pro–capital punishment and anti–capital punishment groups would *probably* agree that

_____

_____

2. People who are for and against gay marriages would *probably* agree that

_____

_____

Strategies for PERSUADING INDECISIVE AUDIENCE MEMBERS

For the Uninformed
- Gain their attention and interest.
- Provide new information.

For the Unconcerned
- Gain their attention and interest.
- Give them a reason to care.
- Present relevant information and evidence.

For the Adamantly Undecided
- Acknowledge the legitimacy of different viewpoints.
- Provide new information.
- Emphasize or reinforce the strength of arguments on your side of the issue.

Psychological Reactance Theory

Psychologist Jack W. Brehm explains why telling an audience what *not* to do can produce the exact opposite reaction. His **Psychological Reactance Theory** suggests that when you perceive a threat to your freedom to believe or behave as you wish, you may go out of your way to *do* the forbidden behavior or rebel against the prohibiting authority.[6]

Children react this way all the time. You tell them, "Don't snack before dinner!" or "Don't hit your brother!" or "Stop texting, now!" so they hide their snacks, sneak in a few punches, and spend more time texting. Consider this interesting fact: Although legally designated "coffee shops" in Amsterdam sell marijuana, only about 15 percent of Dutch people older than 12 years have ever used marijuana, whereas 33 percent of Americans have used it illegally.[7] Because the drug is strictly prohibited by law in the United States, it may be more attractive as an outlet of rebellion.[8]

> If you tell an audience
> "Do this" or
> "Don't believe that,"
> you may run into
> strong resistance.

If you believe that your audience may react negatively to your advice or directions, use the following strategies to reduce the likelihood of a reactance response:

- Avoid strong, direct commands such as "don't," "stop," and "you *must*."
- Avoid extreme statements depicting terrible consequences such as "You will die," or "You will fail," or "You will be punished."
- Avoid finger-pointing—literally and figuratively. Don't single out specific audience members for condemnation or harsh criticism.
- Advocate a middle ground that preserves audience members' freedom and dignity while moving them toward attitude or behavior change.
- Use strategies that are appropriate for audience members who disagree with you.
- Respect your audience's perspectives, needs, and lifestyles.

16.3
Building Persuasive Arguments

Which strategies can help you develop effective arguments?

Some people think of an *argument* as a dispute or hostile confrontation between two people. In this textbook however, we define an **argument** as a claim supported by evidence and reasoning for or against a claim. For example, if a student speaker says, "The Latino/Latina Heritage Club should be given more funds next year," there is no argument because there is no evidence or reasons supporting the statement. To turn this statement into an argument, we would say, "The Latino/Latina Heritage Club should be given more funds next year because it has doubled in size; without an increase in funding, it cannot provide its members the same number or quality of programs." The statement now includes a claim supported by evidence and reasoning.

Toulmin Model of an Argument

To help understand the essential structure of an argument, we turn to the **Toulmin Model of an Argument**, which was developed by Stephen Toulmin, a British philosopher. Toulmin's model maintains that a complete argument requires three essential components: a claim, evidence, and a warrant. In many speaking situations, three supplementary components—backing for the warrant, reservations, and qualifiers—are also necessary.[9] Regardless of whether you are putting together an argument for a speech or you are an audience member listening to a speaker make an argument, you should think critically about all of Toulmin's components to determine whether the argument is worthy of belief.

Claim, Evidence, and Warrant. A **claim** is the conclusion of an argument or the overall position you advocate in a presentation. Claims answer the question, *What is the argument trying to prove?* Stating a claim, however, is not an argument—it is only the starting point. "Where an argument starts is far less important than where it finishes because the logic and evidence in between [are] crucial."[10]

In a complete argument, you support and prove the claim you advocate by providing relevant evidence. **Evidence** answers the question, *How do you know that?* A sound argument relies on strong evidence, which can range from statistics and multiple examples to the advice of experts and generally accepted audience beliefs.

Without the support of good evidence, your audience may be reluctant to accept your claims.

For example, if you claim that keeping a food-intake diary is the best way to monitor a diet, you might share the results of a study conducted at a major medical school, which concluded that food-intake diaries produce the best results. Alternatively, you might tell stories about how your attempts to lose weight failed until you spent two months keeping a food-intake diary. You might even distribute examples of food-intake diaries to the audience to show them how easy it is to surpass a 30-gram fat allowance during a "day of dieting."

The **warrant** explains why the evidence is relevant and why it supports the claim. For example, the warrant might say that the author of the article on food-intake diaries is one of the country's leading nutrition experts. Rather than asking, *How do you know that?* the warrant asks, *How did you get there? What gives you the right to draw that conclusion?* In their book *The Well-Crafted Argument*, Fred White and Simone Billings write that "compelling warrants are just as vital to the force of an argument as compelling evidence because they reinforce they validity and trustworthiness of both the claim and evidence."[11]

Figure 16.1 shows how the "Basic T" of the Toulmin Model represents the three components—claim, evidence, and warrant—of an argument. The argument advocating food diaries might sound something like this:

> Want to lose those extra pounds for good? Keep a food-intake diary. Dr. Nathan Carter, the lead researcher in a medical school study, reports that patients who kept food-intake diaries were twice as likely to lose weight as were patients who used any other method.

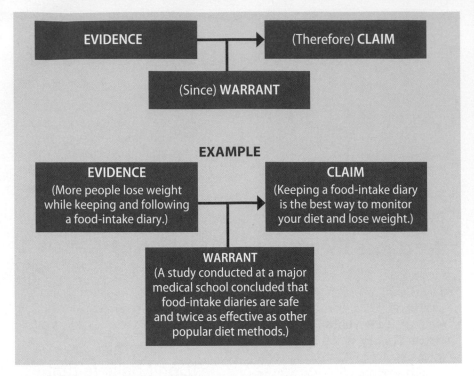

Figure 16.1 The Basic "T" of the Toulmin Model of Argument

Backing, Reservation, and Qualifier. In addition to the three essential elements of an argument, there are three supplementary components of the Toulmin Model: backing, reservation, and qualifier.

Backing provides support for the argument's warrant. Backing is not needed in all arguments, but it can be crucial if an audience questions why the warrant should be accepted as the link between the evidence and the claim. While the warrant answers the question, *How did you get there?* the backing answers the question, *Why is this the right way to get there?* Backing can be in the form of more information about the credibility of a source: "Dr. Nathan Carter and his colleagues received two national awards for their contributions to weight-loss research." Backing can also describe the methodology used in the weight-loss study that determined the effectiveness of food-intake diaries.

Not all claims are true all the time. The **reservation** component of the Toulmin Model recognizes exceptions to an argument or indications that a claim may not be true under certain circumstances.

For example, a food-intake diary is only as good as the limits placed on daily food intake. Setting a limit of 4,000 calories and 100 fat grams a day for

sedentary person whose ideal weight is 125 pounds won't result in weight loss. In addition, some people have weight problems with hormonal or genetic causes that do not respond to typical diets. The reservations could be stated this way: "Food-intake diaries must be well calibrated and may not work if there are genetic or hormonal causes of obesity. In such cases, keeping a standard food-intake diary may not be sufficient."

When an argument contains reservations, the speaker should qualify the claim. The **qualifier** states the degree to which a claim appears to be true. Qualifiers usually include the words *probably*, *possibly*, or *likely*. Consider this claim with a qualifier: "Unless there are medical reasons for seeking other therapies, using and following a food-intake diary calibrated to your own dietary goals is *probably* the best way to lose weight."

Speakers need qualifiers when the evidence or warrant is less than certain and when audience members are likely to have doubts. Qualifiers soften a claim and therefore can make an argument more acceptable to a skeptical audience. Figure 16.2 on the next page maps out a complete argument.

In the next section, we take a closer look at the strategies and skills needed to prove that your arguments are worthy of belief.

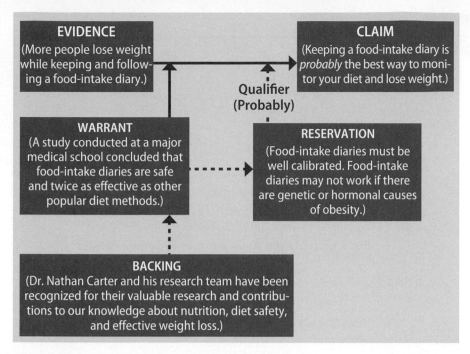

| EVIDENCE (More people lose weight while keeping and following a food-intake diary.) | → | CLAIM (Keeping a food-intake diary is *probably* the best way to monitor your diet and lose weight.) |

Qualifier (Probably)

WARRANT (A study conducted at a major medical school concluded that food-intake diaries are safe and twice as effective as other popular diet methods.)

RESERVATION (Food-intake diaries must be well calibrated. Food-intake diaries may not work if there are genetic or hormonal causes of obesity.)

BACKING (Dr. Nathan Carter and his research team have been recognized for their valuable research and contributions to our knowledge about nutrition, diet safety, and effective weight loss.)

Figure 16.2 The Complete Toulmin Model of Argument

Choosing Persuasive Claims

A good way to start building a persuasive argument is by listing all the possible claims you could use—all the reasons why the audience should agree with you. For example, a student speaker planning a presentation on hunting as a means of controlling the growing deer population listed several reasons:

The enormous deer population …

… is starving and dying of disease.

… is eating up crops, gardens, and forest seedlings.

… is carrying deer ticks that cause Lyme disease in people.

… is causing an increase in the number of highway accidents.

… is consuming the food needed by other forest animals.

Although there were many arguments for advocating hunting to reduce the deer population, the speaker had to choose the arguments that, based on his analysis of the audience, were most likely persuade his audience in the amount of time he was scheduled to speak.

Whatever arguments you choose, make sure you know whether you are advocating claims of fact, conjecture, value, or policy (see Chapter 4, "Listening and Critical Thinking"). Understanding the type of claim will help

you "make your case." Many effective speakers use several types of claims in a single presentation. For example, a persuasive presentation on capital punishment—regardless of your position on the issue—might start with facts that answer questions, such as, How many people are executed in the United States each year? Which state leads the nation in executions? Then you might move on to value claims that answer questions, such as, Is it right for a state to take the life of a prisoner regardless of the seriousness of the crime? Is capital punishment cruel or immoral?

Choosing Persuasive Proof

Like lawyers before a jury, persuasive speakers must prove their case. Lawyers decide what evidence to use when in court, but it's up to the jury or judge to determine whether the evidence is valid and persuasive. When trying to persuade an audience, your success depends on the quality and validity of your **proof**, the arguments and evidence you use to support and strengthen a persuasive claim. Because audiences and persuasive situations differ, so should your proof.[12]

During the early fourth century B.C., Aristotle developed a multidimensional theory of persuasion as we noted in Chapter 12, "Planning Your Presentation." More than 2,000 years later, his conclusions continue to influence the way we study persuasion. In *Rhetoric*, Aristotle identifies three major types of proof: *logos* (message logic), *pathos* (audience emotions), and *ethos* (the personal nature of the speaker). To that list we add a fourth type of proof—*mythos* (social and cultural values often expressed through narratives).

Four Forms of PERSUASIVE PROOF

LOGOS	Logical Proof
PATHOS	Emotional Proof
ETHOS	Personal Proof
MYTHOS	Narrative Proof

building persuasive arguments

Logos: Logical Proof Arguments that rely on reasoning and analysis are using **logos** or logical proof. Logical proof relies on an audience's ability to think critically and arrive at a justified conclusion or decision. Note how the speaker quoted below uses facts and statistics to prove logically that health care is too expensive for many Americans:

> Many hard-working Americans cannot afford the most basic forms of health care and health insurance. Some 50 million Americans—about 16.3 percent of the population—live without health insurance. In 2000, 64 percent received health insurance from their employers; today only 55 percent do.[13]

Pathos: Emotional Proof Pathos is aimed at deep-seated, emotional feelings about justice, generosity, courage, forgiveness, and wisdom.[14] Many television commercials succeed because they understand the power of emotional proof.

Commercials succeed because they understand the power of emotional proof.

Notice, for instance, how this student speaker uses testimony as emotional proof to evoke the audience's sympathies and fears:

> Kevin was 27 years old and only two months into a new job when

he began to lose weight and feel ill. After weeks of testing and finally surgery, he was found to have colon cancer. The bills were more than $100,000. But soon after his release from the hospital, he found out that his insurance benefits had run out. Kevin's reaction: "At one point in the middle of the whole thing, I hit bottom; between having cancer and being told I had no insurance, I tried to commit suicide."[16]

Rather than using logos to prove that many Americans suffer because they do not have dependable health insurance, the speaker highlights one person's suffering. Stories like these tap the audience's sympathies *and* fears. When fear appeals consider the context, are well crafted and well delivered, and used for a good reason (for example, when you believe that audience members are putting themselves or their loved ones in harm's way), it can change audience attitudes and behavior. Think of how many advertisements use this approach. Life insurance ads suggest that you invest not for yourself but for those you love.

"It's tough to scare people effectively ... it can be done."
—Richard Perloff[17]

Ethos: Personal Proof Recall from Chapter 12 that **ethos** (speaker credibility) has three major dimensions: competence, character, and charisma. Each of these dimensions can serve as a form of personal proof in a persuasive

President Barack Obama awards the 2010 Presidential Medal of Freedom to basketball great Bill Russell. The Medal of Honor winners often exemplify all three dimensions of *ethos*.

presentation. To demonstrate that you are a competent speaker of good character, deliver your presentation with conviction. Audiences are more likely to be persuaded when a speaker seems committed to the cause.

In his *Rhetoric*, Aristotle claims that the speaker's personal character "may almost be called the most effective means of persuasion he possesses."[18] Consider how ethos operates in your everyday life. Do you believe what your favorite professors tell you? If, in your opinion, they are of good character and are experts in their field of study, you probably do. Ethos is a powerful form of proof—but you have to *earn* it from your audience if you expect it to help you achieve your persuasive purpose.

Mythos: Narrative Proof During the second half of the twentieth century, *mythos*, or narrative proof, emerged as a fourth and significant form of persuasive proof. According to communication scholars Michael and Suzanne Osborn, **mythos** is a form of proof that addresses the values, faith, and feelings that make up our social character and is most often expressed in traditional stories, sayings, and symbols.[19]

Americans are raised on mythic stories that teach patriotism, freedom, honesty, and national pride. For instance, President George Washington's statement "I cannot tell a lie" after cutting down the family's cherry tree may be a myth, but it has helped teach millions of young Americans about the value of honesty. The civil rights refrain "We shall overcome" also informs American beliefs and values. Speakers who tap into the *mythos* of an audience form a powerful identification with their listeners.

MYTHOS can connect your message with your audience's social and cultural identity, and give them a reason to listen carefully to your ideas.[20]

One of the best ways to enlist mythos in persuasion is through storytelling. Religions, for example, teach many values through parables. (For more on storytelling, see Chapter 15, "Speaking to Inform.")

Choosing Persuasive Evidence

In Chapter 13, "Content and Organization," we describe how to gather and use supporting material to explain and/or advance your central idea and key points. Here we examine how to choose strong evidence that justifies and strengthens your claim and choice of proof.

For example, if you argue that responsible environmentalists support deer hunting, use a highly reputable quotation or survey to prove your point. If you advocate early testing for diabetes, tell two contrasting stories—one about a person who was diagnosed early and one who wasn't diagnosed until the disease had ravaged her body.

Lady Liberty's invitation from Emma Lazarus's poem, "Give me your tired, your poor …" taps into the mythos that drew thousands of immigrants to the United States in search of freedom and a better life.

ETHICAL COMMUNICATION

Reject Fallacies

In Chapter 4, we identified six common fallacies of argument. There are, in fact, hundreds of potential fallacies waiting to distort persuasive messages. **Fallacies can mislead and misinform listeners, rob audiences of their precious time and well-founded convictions, and permanently damage your reputation and credibility.**

Every communicator has an ethical obligation to recognize and reject the fallacies in persuasive arguments. Three factors lead to most mistakes in reasoning:[21]

- **Intentional and unintentional fallacies.** Unethical speakers may intentionally use fallacies to deceive or mislead audience members. Ethical, well-intentioned speakers may use fallacious reasoning without knowing it. Ignorance—as the old saying goes—is no excuse. Every speaker has an ethical obligation to avoid fallacies.

- **Careless listening and reasoning.** Inattentive listeners can fall prey to deceptive arguments and claims that evoke strong emotions. Poor critical thinking can lead speakers and listeners to accept fallacies as true.

- **Different worldviews.** Your worldview—developed over many years of life experiences—affects how you determine what you believe is reasonable and unreasonable. Prejudices may lead some people to see the misbehavior by a handful of immigrants, police officers, or basketball players as typical of everyone in that population. A politically conservative speaker or listener may automatically ignore or dismiss an argument made by a liberal speaker and vice versa. Ethical communicators consider how culture, language, gender, religion, politics, and social and economic status affect the way they and their audiences see the world.

Be strategic. Select your evidence based on the types of argument you are trying to prove and the attitudes and needs of your audience. Then make sure that your evidence is novel, believable, and/or dramatic.

Novel Evidence Effective persuaders look for new or novel evidence to support their arguments. Overly familiar evidence doesn't work that well and may not succeed in justifying your claim.

Believable Evidence Even if your evidence is easily understood and novel, it will not be persuasive if people don't believe it is true. If your audience appears to doubt the believability of your evidence, take time to explain why it's true, or provide other sources that reach the same conclusion. If the source of your evidence has high credibility, mention the source *before* presenting your evidence. On the other hand, if naming the source will not add to the evidence's believability, mention it *after* you present the evidence.

Although stories serve as powerful forms of evidence, several studies conclude that arguments using statistical evidence can be *more* persuasive than those using narratives (storytelling)—but only if used effectively.[22]

Communication researchers Lisa Massi Lindsey and Kimo Ah Yun describe three factors that affect the persuasiveness of statistics: sample size, perceived validity, and message credibility.[23] When statistics are based on large sample sizes, they

Iowa Senator Tom Harkin learned that the U.S. government was paying $2.32 for surgical gauze when it could have been bought wholesale for 19 cents. How well did he dramatize his evidence?

are more believable. For example, if statistics report that 90 percent of 20,000 doctors recommend, or 75 percent of *all* the college professors on your campus claim, your audience is more likely to believe the results—and be persuaded.

STATISTICAL APPEALS can enhance message and speaker credibility.

Dramatic Evidence To make your evidence memorable, find ways to dramatize that evidence. Rather than saying that your proposal will save the organization $250,000 in the next year, say that it will save a quarter of a million dollars—the equivalent of the entire travel budgets of the three largest divisions of the company. Here's another comparison: The Bill and Melinda Gates Foundation has assets larger than the gross national production of 104 countries. Comparing such statistical evidence, rather than merely reporting it, heightens its impact on the audience.

COMMUNICATION IN *ACTION*

Watch out for Heuristics

Heuristics help explain our susceptibility to claims that rely on questionable evidence and warrants. **Heuristics** are cognitive thinking shortcuts we use in decision making because they are correct often enough to be useful. Unfortunately, unethical persuaders sometimes use them to win agreement from their audiences even though their arguments are flawed.[24]

When audience members are not very interested or motivated to listen or when they are not thinking critically,

they are more likely to believe arguments that lack valid evidence or that offer evidence unrelated to a speaker's claim. The following brief list includes common heuristics we see and hear in everyday life:

- The quality of an item correlates with its price.
- We should believe likable people.
- The behavior of others is a good guide as to how *we* should behave.
- Confident speakers know what they are talking about.

- Something that is scarce is also valuable.
- Longer messages are strong messages; vivid examples are strong evidence.

Successful salespeople often use heuristics. They appear confident, likable, and trustworthy. They also give you multiple reasons for purchasing expensive, high-quality, limited-edition products that are very popular with discerning customers. When you hear a message that is loaded with heuristics, be cautious. Analyze the arguments carefully before you succumb to their persuasive power.

Persuasive Organizational Patterns

Which organizational patterns are particularly suited for persuasive presentations?

You have a topic you care about; a list of potential arguments; an understanding of how your arguments present claims of fact, value, conjecture, and policy; and good evidence to support your arguments. You've reached a key decision-making point. It's time to put these elements together into an effective persuasive message. In addition to the organizational patterns discussed in Chapter 13, there are several strategic organizational formats particularly suited to persuasive presentations.

Problem/Cause/Solution

As its name implies, the **problem/cause/solution pattern** describes a serious problem, explains why the problem continues (the cause), and offers a solution. This organizational pattern works best when you are proposing a specific course of action.

In the following outline, the speaker uses a problem/cause/solution organizational pattern to propose a national health-care system for all U.S. citizens:

A. Americans are not getting needed medical care. (*Problem*)
  1. Serious diseases such as (cancer, heart disease, and diabetes) go undetected and untreated.
  2. Millions of Americans do not get regular checkups.
B. The high costs of health care and health insurance prevent a solution. (*Cause*)
C. A national health care system can guarantee affordable medical care for those in need without eliminating private care for those who want it. (*Solution*)
  1. This plan works well in other modern, industrialized countries.
  2. This plan will not result in low-quality care or long waiting lines.

Comparative Advantage

When your audience is aware of a problem and recognizes that a solution is necessary, the **comparative advantage pattern** may help you make your case. In this pattern, you present a plan that will improve a situation and help to solve a problem while acknowledging that a total solution may not be possible. In the following outline, the speaker contends that increased hunting is a more advantageous way of reducing the serious problems caused by the growing deer population.

A. There is a plan that will help reduce the deer population. (*Plan*)
  1. Extend the deer-hunting season.
  2. Permit hunters to kill more female than male deer.
B. This plan will reduce the severity of the problem. (*Comparative Advantages*)
  1. It will reduce the number of deer deaths from starvation and disease.
  2. It will save millions of dollars now lost from crop, garden, and forest seedling damage.
  3. It will reduce the number of ticks carrying Lyme disease.
  4. It will reduce the number of automobile deaths and injuries caused by deer crossing highways.

Refuting Objections Pattern

Sometimes, audience members agree that there is a problem and even know what should be done to solve it, yet they do not act because the solution is objectionable, frightening, expensive, or difficult to understand or implement. In other situations, an audience disagrees with a speaker and comes prepared to reject the message even before hearing it. With both types of audiences, you should try to overcome these objections by using appropriate forms of proof and persuasive evidence. The **refuting objections pattern** allows you to refute and disprove each point that stands in opposition to your own.

In the following outline, the speaker employs the refuting objections organizational pattern to encourage listeners to donate blood:

A. People should give blood but often don't. (*Problem*)
  1. Most people approve of and support donations.
  2. Most people don't give blood.
B. There are several reasons people don't give blood. (*Objections*)
  1. They fear needles and pain.
  2. They fear they could get a disease from giving blood.
  3. They claim they don't have time or know where to give blood.
C. These objections are poor excuses. (*Refutation*)
  1. There is little or no pain in giving blood.
  2. You can't get a disease by *giving* blood.
  3. The Red Cross makes it easy and convenient to give the gift of life.

Monroe's Motivated Sequence

In the mid-1930s, communication professor Alan Monroe took the basic functions of a sales presentation (attention, interest, desire, and action) and transformed them into a step-by-step method for organizing persuasive speeches. This became known as **Monroe's Motivated Sequence**.[25]

The unique visualization step in Monroe's Motivated Sequence (D in the outline) makes this organizational pattern useful for audience members who are uninformed, unconcerned, and unmotivated to listen, or for listeners who are skeptical of or opposed to the proposed course of actions.

persuasive organizational patterns

In the following outline, note how the speaker uses Monroe's Motivated Sequence to organize a presentation on how to liberate women suffering from brutality and injustice in poor countries.[26]

A. The Attention Step. Stories about abused women in Pakistan and Rwanda.
   1. Saima Muhammad, Pakistan, was beaten and starved by her husband.
   2. Claudine Mukakarisa, Rwanda, was imprisoned in a rape house.
B. The Need Step
   1. Millions of women in poor countries are beaten, disfigured, raped, murdered, or sold into slavery or brothels.
   2. Millions of girls in poor countries are denied medical care, education, and civil rights.
   3. Countries that suppress women's rights are often poor and torn apart by religious fundamentalism and civil war.
C. The Satisfaction Step
   1. Focus private and government aid on women's health and education.
   2. Grant small microfinance loans to women.
   3. Advocate for women's rights through organizations and government agencies.
D. The Visualization Step
   1. Saima Muhammad's embroidery business now supports her family and employs 30 other families.
   2. Claudine Mukakarisa was "adopted" by a U.S. woman who helped her start a business.
E. The Action Step
   1. Contribute to legitimate organizations dedicated to helping women.
   2. "Adopt" a woman by lending money to support a business.
   3. Become an advocate for change by joining the CARE Action Network.

The visualization step (D in the outline) intensifies the audience's motivation to believe, feel, or act. By encouraging listeners to "see" the result of taking or failing to take action, you can strengthen the impact of your message.

COMMUNICATION & CULTURE

TALL POPPIES AND BIG BRITCHES

In a highly individualistic culture like the United States, many audience members will value individual achievement and personal freedom. In collectivist cultures (Asian and Latin American countries as well as in co-cultures in the United States), audience members are more likely to value group identity, selflessness, and collective action. Audiences in collectivist cultures place less importance on the opinions and preferences of the individual than do audiences in individualistic cultures.[27] In the United States, appeals that benefit individuals—personal wealth, personal success, personal health and fitness—may be highly persuasive, while appeals that benefit society at large and other families may be less effective.

In low-context cultures such as those of the United States, England, and Germany, audiences expect messages to be clear, factual, and objective. In the United States, persuasive appeals are often direct—do this; buy that; avoid that; just do it! In advertising, this would be termed a *hard-sell* approach to persuasion.

In contrast, high-context cultures such as those of Japan, China, and Mexico expect messages that are implied and situation specific. A soft-sell approach would be a better persuasive strategy. When addressing a high-context audience, encourage listeners to draw their own conclusions. Demonstrate benefits and advantages rather than advocating action.

Differences among cultures are very real. At the same time, be cautious about how you interpret and use this information. Are all Japanese collectivist and high-context? Many young Japanese business professionals are learning and embracing American ways that include a more direct and self-centered approach to communication. Are all Australians individualistic? Although Australians are very independent and value personal freedom, they also live in a culture in which power distance is minimal. Public displays of achievement or wealth are frowned upon.[28]

One of your authors lived in Australia for a year and was introduced to the *tall poppy syndrome*. If, in a field of poppies, one red blossom grows higher than the others, you chop it off. When people show off or try to rise above others, you cut them down to size, too. "He thinks he's a tall poppy," describes someone who—in American terms—is "too big for his britches."

A persuasive speech can motivate audience members to take actions such as joining the CARE Action Network to help women in Afghanistan.

16.5
Persuasive Speaking in Action

What are the characteristics of an effective persuasive presentation?

"Looking through Our Window" by Ms. Marge Anderson, chief executive of the Mille Lacs Band of Ojibwe Indians, includes both informative strategies for generating audience interest *and* persuasive strategies that use different types of proof.[29]

Chief Anderson's speech also shows the power of language as described in Chapter 14, "Language and Delivery," as well as the value of storytelling, humor, and audience involvement as described in Chapter 15, "Speaking to Inform." As you read Ms. Anderson's presentation, notice how she:

- adapts to her audience's interests, attitudes, and beliefs about Indian people;

- adapts to the audience's level of motivation and listening habits;

- uses clear, oral, rhetorical, and eloquent language;

- tells two stories—one real, one mythic;

- cites novel, believable, and dramatic evidence;

- relies on her competence, character, and charisma to enhance her credibility;

- uses informative speaking strategies to persuade by explaining "what it means to be Indian" and "how my People experience the world"

to help them understand why they "should care about all this."

- uses the audience-centered example of St. Thomas Aquinas and the story of Jacob wrestling with the angel as a theme and a form of mythos (narrative proof);

- includes logical, emotional, personal, and narrative persuasive proof;

- acknowledges and respects differences between Indians and non-Indians;

- employs a modified version of Monroe's Motivated Sequence.

Looking through Our Window: The Value of Indian Culture
Address by Marge Anderson, Chief Executive, Mille Lacs Band of Ojibwe

Delivered to the First Friday Club of the Twin Cities Sponsored by the St. Thomas Aquinas College Alumni Association in St. Paul, Minnesota

Aaniin. Thank you for inviting me here today. When I was asked to speak to you, I was told you are interested in hearing about the improvements we are making on the Mille Lacs Reservation, and about our investment of casino dollars back into our community through schools, health care facilities, and other services. And I do want to talk to you about these things, because they are tremendously important, and I am very proud of them.

Anderson warmly greets audience members and acknowledges their interests in Indian casino income during the attention step of Monroe's Motivated Sequence.

Chief Anderson uses the word *Indian* to refers to herself and her People. Why doesn't she use the phrase *Native American*? Research both terms and decide which term you think is most appropriate.

Here, the speaker presents a *need* step by describing the misunderstandings about the Indian culture and practices that lead to problems and conflict.

Anderson attempts to overcome *audience disagreement* through identification with St. Thomas Aquinas, a European who is the namesake of the university alumni association she is addressing.

To *counter audience expectations*, she assures the audience that she will not read a long list of complaints about the mistreatment of Indians.

Here the speaker seeks *common ground* by describing Indian efforts to take the best of American culture into their own.

Here the speaker identifies the *satisfaction* step by advocating better understanding, mutual respect, and appreciation between Indians and non-Indians.

But before I do, I want to take a few minutes to talk to you about something else, something I'm not asked about very often. I want to talk to you about what it means to be Indian. About how my People experience the world. About the fundamental way in which our culture differs from yours. And about why you should care about all this.

The differences between Indians and non-Indians have created a lot of controversy lately. Casinos, treaty rights, tribal sovereignty—these issues have stirred such anger and bitterness.

I believe the accusations against us are made out of ignorance. The vast majority of non-Indians do not understand how my People view the world, what we value, what motivates us.

They do not know these things for one simple reason: They've never heard us talk about them. For many years the only stories that non-Indians heard about my People came from other non-Indians. As a result, the picture you got of us was fanciful or distorted or so shadowy it hardly existed at all.

It's time for *Indian* voices to tell *Indian* stories.

Now, I'm sure at least a few of you are wondering, "Why do I need to hear these stories? Why should I care about what Indian People think, and feel, and believe?"

I think the most eloquent answer I can give you comes from the namesake for this university, St. Thomas Aquinas. St. Thomas wrote that dialogue is the struggle to learn from each other. This struggle, he said, is like Jacob wrestling the angel—it leaves one wounded and blessed at the same time.

Indian People know this struggle very well. The wounds we've suffered in our dialogue with non-Indians are well documented; I don't need to give you a laundry list of complaints.

We also know some of the blessings of this struggle. As *American* Indians, we live in two worlds—ours and yours. In the five hundred years since you first came to our lands, we have struggled to learn how to take the best of what your culture has to offer in arts, science, technology, and more, and then weave them into the fabric of our traditional ways.

But for non-Indians, the struggle is new. Now that our People have begun to achieve success, now that we are in business and in the headlines, you are starting to wrestle with understanding us.

Your wounds from this struggle are fresh, and the pain might make it hard for you to see beyond them. But if you try, you'll begin to see the blessings as well—the blessings of what a deepened knowledge of Indian culture can bring you. I'd like to share a few of those blessings with you today.

Earlier I mentioned that there is a fundamental difference between the way Indians and non-Indians experience the world. This difference goes all the way back to the Bible, and Genesis.

In Genesis, the first book of the Old Testament, God creates man in his own image. Then God says, "Be fruitful, multiply, fill the earth and conquer it. Be masters of the fish and the sea, the birds of the heaven, and all living animals on the earth."

Masters. Conquer. Nothing, *nothing* could be further from the way Indian People view the world and our place in it. Here are the words of the great

Anderson identifies her *central idea*: Non-Indians should care about what it means to be Indian in the United States. Note her *effective oral style* in this section—simple words, short sentences, active voice, personal pronouns, and repetition.

Anderson carefully chooses her words, using *they* to refer to people who do not understand Indians, rather than *you*. You would carry a more accusatory tone.

This *transition* attempts to acknowledge the audience difficulty with understanding the Indian struggles. Anderson *repeats a variation* her central idea.

This section *compares and contrasts* non-Indian and Indian perspectives by using a *familiar quotation* from Genesis (a non-Indian source) and quotation from Chief Seattle (an Indian source).

Who is Chief Seattle? Is it important that the audience know what he did to be called *great*? Or is this a subtle way of showing the audience that they need to know more about Indian culture? You can learn about and read Chief Seattle's famous speech online at http://www.chiefseattle.com/history/chiefseattle/speech/speech.htm.

nineteenth-century Chief Seattle: "You are a part of the earth, and the earth is a part of you. You did not weave the web of life, you are merely a strand in it. *Whatever you do to the web, you do to yourself*." In our tradition, there is no mastery.

When you begin to see the world this way—through Indian eyes—you will begin to understand our view of land, and treaties, very differently. You will begin to understand that when we speak of Father Sun and Mother Earth, these are not New Age catchwords—they are very real terms of respect for very real beings.

And when you understand this, then you will understand that our fight for treaty rights is not just about hunting deer or catching fish. It is about teaching our children to honor Mother Earth and Father Sun. It is about teaching them to respectfully receive the gifts these loving parents offer us in return for the care we give them. And it is about teaching this generation and the generations yet to come about their place in the web of life. Our culture and the fish, our values and the deer, the lessons we learn and the rice we harvest—everything is tied together. You can no more separate one from the other than you can divide a person's spirit from his body.

When you understand how we view the world and our place in it, it's easy to appreciate why our casinos are so important to us. The reason we defend our businesses so fiercely isn't because we want to have something that others don't. The reason is because these businesses allow us to give back to others—to our People, our communities, and the Creator.

I'd like to take a minute and mention just a few of the ways we've already given back:

- We've opened new schools, new health care facilities, and new community centers where our children get a better education, where our elders get better medical care, and where our families can gather to socialize and keep our traditions alive.
- We've created programs to teach and preserve our language and cultural traditions.
- We've created a small Business Development Program to help band members start their own businesses.
- We've created more than twenty-eight hundred jobs for band members, People from other tribes, and non-Indians.
- We've generated more than fifty million dollars in federal taxes, and more than fifteen million dollars in state taxes through wages paid to employees.
- And we've given back more than two million dollars in charitable donations.

The list goes on and on. But rather than flood you with more numbers, I'll tell you a story that sums up how my People view business through the lens of our traditional values.

Last year, the Woodlands National Bank, which is owned and operated by the Mille Lacs Band, was approached by the city of Onamia and asked to forgive a mortgage on a building in the downtown area. The building had been abandoned and was an eyesore on Main Street. The city planned to renovate and sell the building, and return it to the tax rolls.

Anderson begins the process of *linking* the Indian worldview with Indian struggles for treaty rights. Although listeners may not believe in Father Sun and Mother Earth, they may share a respect for and concern about the environment.

Notice how Anderson repeats the word *about* in a series of similarly constructed sentences.

Here, she identifies the *visualization step* by *addressing her audience directly* and describing how casinos not only preserve the Indian way of life, but also give back to non-Indians.

Chief Anderson provides *multiple examples* (actual and statistical) of the benefits of casino income. She begins each example with the word *we*, a *stylistic device* that helps her focus on Indian contributions.

Anderson concludes her list with a factual story (*narrative proof/mythos*) that reflects Indian values such as caring for others and the environment in which they live.

Although the bank would lose money by forgiving the mortgage, our business leaders could see the wisdom in improving the community. The opportunity to help our neighbors was an opportunity to strengthen the web of life. So we forgave the mortgage.

Now, I know this is not a decision everyone would agree with. Some people feel that in business, you have to look out for number one. But my People feel that in business—and in life—you have to look out for *every* one.

And this, I believe, is one of the blessings that Indian culture has to offer you and other non-Indians. We have a different perspective on so many things, from caring for the environment to healing the body, mind, and soul.

But if our culture disappears, if the Indian ways are swallowed up by the dominant American culture, no one will be able to learn from them. Not Indian children. Not your children. No one. All that knowledge, all that wisdom, will be lost forever.

The struggle of dialogue will be over. Yes, there will be no more wounds. But there will also be no more blessings.

There is still so much we have to learn from each other, and we have already wasted so much time. Our world grows smaller every day. And every day, more of our unsettling, surprising, wonderful differences vanish. And when that happens, part of each of us vanishes too.

I'd like to end with one of my favorite stories. It's a funny little story about Indians and non-Indians, but its message is serious: You can see something differently if you are willing to learn from those around you.

This is the story: Years ago, white settlers came to this area and built the first European-style homes. When Indian People walked by these homes and saw see-through things in the walls, they looked through them to see what the strangers inside were doing. The settlers were shocked, but it makes sense when you think about it: Windows are made to be looked through from both sides.

Since then, my People have spent many years looking at the world through your window. I hope today I've given you a reason to look at it through ours. *Mii gwetch.*

Notice how Anderson acknowledges and respects the differences between Indians and non-Indian views of business practices and beliefs.

The speaker describes what will happen if the Indian culture disappears, and reuses words from the earlier cited Aquinas quote—*struggle, dialogue, wounds, blessing.*

Here Anderson's message becomes more urgent and *rhetorical in style.* She talks about wasting time, a world growing smaller, and the risk that Indian culture will vanish.

In this final *action step*, Chief Anderson relies on *metaphor* to ask the audience to continue a productive dialogue with the Indian people.

The Ojibwas word for thank you becomes a "bookend" conclusion to a speech that begins with *aaniin.*

Her final story is a good example of *mythos.* She *previews* the story moral, which her return to her *central idea.*

Persuasive Presentation Assessment

Use the following ratings to assess each of the competencies on this assessment instrument for a presentation you are preparing or for one you watch, listen to, and/or read.

E = excellent;   G = good;   A = average;   W = weak;   M = missing;   N/A = not applicable.

COMPETENCIES	E	G	A	W	M	N/A
Preparation and Content						
Purpose and topic						
Audience adaptation						
Adaptation to the context						
Introduction						
Organization						
Supporting material						
Transitions						
Conclusion						
Language						
Persuasive strategies						
Delivery						
Delivery mode						
Vocal delivery						
Physical delivery						
Presentation aids, if used						
Other Criteria						
Outline or manuscript						
Bibliography						
Other: _____						
Overall Assessment (circle one)	E	G	A	W	M	N/A

Comments:

16.1
The Nature of Persuasion
What is the goal of a persuasive presentation?

- Persuasion seeks to change audience members' opinions (what they think) or behavior (what they do).
- Whereas informative presentations *give* audience members, advice or explanations, persuasive presentations *ask* for their agreement or a change in their opinions or behavior.

16.2
Persuading Others
How can you adapt to different audience attitudes?

- When audience members agree with you, present new information, strengthen audience resistance to persuasion, excite emotions, provide a personal role model, and advocate a course of action.
- When audiences disagree with you, set reasonable goals, find common ground, adapt to differences of opinion, use evidence, and build your personal credibility.
- When audience members are (1) undecided: gain their attention and provide relevant information; (2) unconcerned: gain their attention, give them a reason to care, and use strong evidence; (3) adamantly undecided: acknowledge their opinions and strengthen the arguments on your side of the issue.
- Psychological Reactance Theory explains why telling an audience what *not* to do can produce the exact opposite reaction.

16.3
Building Persuasive Arguments
Which strategies can help you develop effective arguments?

- Include persuasive claims that, based on audience analysis, will most likely persuade that audience.
- The Toulmin Model of an Argument requires three major components: a claim, evidence, and a warrant. In many speaking situations, three additional components—backing for the warrant, reservations, and qualifiers—are also necessary to build a strong argument.
- Whichever arguments you choose, make sure you know whether they are advocating claims of fact, conjecture, value, or policy.
- Effective persuaders often use logical proof (*logos*), emotional proof (*pathos*), personal proof (*ethos*), and narrative proof (*mythos*) in presentations.
- Use novel, believable, dramatic, and valid evidence to persuade.
- When fear appeals are well crafted and well delivered, they can influence audience attitudes.

- *Heuristics* (cognitive shortcuts that are correct often enough to be useful when we make decisions) help explain why we believe arguments that rely on questionable claims, evidence, and warrants.

16.4
Persuasive Organizational Patterns
Which organizational patterns are particularly suited for persuasive presentations?

- Organizational patterns particularly suited for persuasive speaking include problem/cause/solution, comparative advantage, refuting objections, and Monroe's Motivated Sequence.

16.5
Persuasive Speaking in Action
What are the characteristics of an effective persuasive presentation?

- Effective persuasive speakers adapt their content to the characteristics and attitudes of audience members and to the context of the presentation.

MySearchLab®

16.1 What is the goal of a persuasive presentation?

1 Given that persuasion seeks to change audience opinions and/or behavior, which of the following examples represents an appeal to audience opinion?

a. Eat dinner with your family at least five times a week.

b. Vegetarian diets are good for you and the planet.

c. Buy a gas–electric hybrid car.

d. Vote!

e. Choose a college that matches your interests, personality, and needs.

16.2 How can you adapt to different audience attitudes?

2 Which persuasive strategy is likely to be more effective when speaking to an audience that disagrees with you?

a. Excite audience emotions

b. Provide a personal role model

c. Set reasonable goals

d. Give them a reason to care

e. Emphasize the arguments on your side of an issue

3 With which kind of audience should you try to find common ground?

a. An audience that agrees with you

b. An audience that disagrees with you

c. An audience that is uninformed

d. An audience that is unconcerned

e. An audience that is undecided

4 You can reduce the likelihood of a reactance response to a persuasive presentation by heeding all of the following strategies except _____.

a. avoid strong direct commands such as "you must" or "stop"

b. avoid finger-pointing, literally and figuratively

c. advocate a middle ground that preserves audience freedom

d. avoid extreme statements depicting horrible consequences such as "you will die"

e. use fear appeals to scare them into action

16.3 Which strategies can help you develop effective arguments?

5 Which form of proof relies on touching audience emotions—fear, anger, pride, love, jealousy, or envy?

a. Mythos

b. Ethos

c. Logos

d. Pathos

e. Samos

6 In terms of Toulmin's Model of an Argument, which statement is the claim of this argument? "John is coughing, has a lot of chest congestion, been throwing up and has had a temperature of 102 degrees for several days. Given that all of these symptoms are signs of the flu, he probably has the flu."

a. John is coughing with a lot of chest congestion.

b. He probably has the flu.

c. He has had a temperature of 102 degrees for several days.

d. He has been throwing up.

e. All of these symptoms are signs of the flu.

7 All of the following examples are common heuristics used to persuade audiences except _____.

a. think critically about source biases

b. longer messages are stronger messages

c. quality products cost more

d. all experts should be trusted

e. confident speakers know what they're talking about

16.4 Which organizational patterns are particularly suited for persuasive presentations?

8 Which persuasive organizational pattern features the following three sections? (1) People should do X, (2) People don't do X for several reasons, (3) These reasons should not stop you from doing X.

a. Problem/cause/solution

b. Comparative advantage

c. Refuting objections

d. Monroe's Motivated Sequence

e. Comparison-contrast

9 Which step in Monroe's Motivated Sequence is most useful for audience members who are uninformed, unconcerned, skeptical, or opposed to the proposed course of action?

a. Attention step

b. Need step

c. Satisfaction step

d. Visualization step

e. Action step

16.5 What are the characteristics of an effective persuasive presentation?

10 What kind of audience was Chief Marge Anderson seeking to persuade when she said the following?

Now, I'm sure at least a few of you are wondering, "Why do I need to hear these stories? Why should I care about what Indian People think, and feel, and believe?" I think the most eloquent answer I can give you comes from the namesake for this university, St. Thomas Aquinas. St. Thomas wrote that dialogue is the struggle to learn from each other. This struggle, he said, is like Jacob wrestling the angel—it leaves one wounded and blessed at the same time.

a. An audience that agrees with her

b. An audience that disagrees with her

c. An audience that is uninformed

d. An audience that is unconcerned

e. An audience that is undecided

Answers found on page 366.

Key Terms

Argument	Logos	Psychological Reactance
Backing	Monroe's Motivated	Theory
Claim	Sequence	Qualifier
Common ground	Mythos	Refuting objections
Comparative advantage	Persuasion	pattern
pattern	Problem/cause/solution	Reservation
Ethos	pattern	Toulmin Model of an
Evidence	Proof	Argument
Heuristics		Warrant

glossary

A

Abdicrat   A type of leader who emerges when control needs are unmet. The abdicrat wants control but is reluctant to pursue it and therefore is often submissive.

Abstract word   Word that refers to ideas or concepts that cannot be observed or touched and often require interpretation.

Accenting nonverbal behavior   Nonverbal behavior that emphasizes important elements in a message by highlighting its focus or emotional content.

Accommodating conflict style   A conflict style in which you give in to others for the purpose of preserving peace and harmony.

Active voice   A sentence in which the subject performs the action. Example: *Erin read the book*.

A-E-I-O-U Model of Conflict Resolution   A model of conflict resolution that focuses on communicating personal concerns and suggesting alternative actions.

Adaptors   Habitual gestures that help manage and express emotions.

Affection need   The need to feel liked by others.

Agenda   An outline that puts meeting topics in the order in which they will be discussed.

Aggression   Behavior in which communicators put their personal needs first and demand compliance of others, often at the expense of someone else's needs and rights.

Alliteration   A type of repetition in which a series of words with the same sound are placed together or very near one another.

Analogy   Comparison of two things in order to highlight a point of similarity.

Analysis paralysis   A crippling situation where group members are so focused on analyzing a situation that they fail to make a decision.

Anger   An emotional response to unmet expectations that ranges from minor irritation to intense rage.

Appeal to authority   A fallacy of argument in which the opinion of a supposed expert who has no relevant experience on the issues being discussed is solicited.

Appeal to popularity   A fallacy of argument in which an action is deemed acceptable or excusable because many people are doing it.

Appeal to tradition   A fallacy of argument in which a certain course of action is recommended because it has always been done that way in the past.

Argument   A claim supported by evidence and reasons for accepting the claim.

Argumentativeness   Willingness to argue controversial issues with others.

Articulation   The process of clearly making the sounds in the words of a language.

Assertiveness   The willingness and ability to stand up for your own needs and rights while also respecting the needs and rights of others.

Attacking the person   A fallacy of argument in which irrelevant or untrue attacks are made against a person rather than the substance of that person's argument.

Audience analysis   The process of understanding, respecting, and adapting to audience members before and during a presentation.

Audience attitudes   The degree or extent to which the audience agrees or disagrees with the speaker.

Authority rule   A decision making method in which the leader or an authority outside the group makes the final decision.

Autocrat/Autocratic Leader   A type of leader who emerges when control needs are unmet. The autocrat wants control but tries to take over or dominate others by criticizing members and forcing decisions on them. An autocratic leader tries to control the direction and outcome of a discussion, makes many of the group's decisions, gives orders, expects people to obey orders, and takes credit for successful results.

Avoidance conflict style   A conflict style in which people change the subject, sidestep a controversial issue, or deny that a conflict exists because they are unable or unwilling to stand up for their own needs or the needs of others.

Avoidant decision maker   A person who is uncomfortable making decisions, may not think about a problem at all, or who makes a decision at the last minute.

B

Backing   A component of the Toulmin model of an argument that provides support for the argument's warrant.

Basic terms   General words that come to mind when you see an object, such as *car* or *cat*.

Biased   Statement of opinion so slanted in one direction that it may not be objective or fair.

Brainstorming   A simple and popular problem solving method in which group members generate as many ideas as possible in a short period of time.

Bypassing   A form of miscommunication that occurs when people "miss each other with their meanings."

C

Cause and effect arrangement   An organizational pattern that presents a cause and its resulting effects or details the effects that result from a specific cause.

Central idea   A sentence that summarizes the key points of a presentation.

Channels   The various physical and electronic media through which we express messages.

Character   A component of speaker credibility that focuses on the speaker's perceived honesty and goodwill.

Charisma   A component of speaker credibility that focuses on the speaker's levels of energy, enthusiasm, vigor, and commitment.

Claim   The conclusion of an argument or the overall position advocated in a presentation or discussion.

Claims of Conjecture   Statements that something will or will not happen in the future.

Claims of Fact   Statements that can be proved true or false.

Claims of Policy   Statements that recommend a course of action or solution to a problem.

Claims of Value   Statements that assert the worth of something—good or bad, right or wrong, best, average, or worst.

Clear style   A speaking style that features short, simple, and direct words and phrases as well as active verbs, concrete words, and plain language.

Closed-ended question   A question that requires only a short and direct response and can generally be answered with a yes or no.

Closure principle   Filling in missing elements to form a more complete impression of an object, person, or event.

Co-cultures   A group of people who coexist within the mainstream society yet remain connected to one another through their cultural heritage.

Code switching   The process of modifying the use of verbal and nonverbal communication in different contexts.

Cognitive restructuring   A method for reducing communication anxiety by replacing negative, irrational thoughts with more realistic, positive self-talk.

Cognitive science   The interdisciplinary study of the mind and intelligence that focuses on how people process information.

Cohesion   The mutual attraction that holds the members of a group together.

Collaborative conflict style   An approach to conflict resolution in which people search for new solutions that will achieve both personal goals and the goals of others.

Collectivism   A cultural dimension that emphasizes the views, needs, and goals of the group rather than focusing on the individual.

Committee   A group created by a larger group or by a person in a position of authority to take on specific tasks.

Common ground   A place where you and your audience can stand without disagreement, often in terms of shared beliefs, values, attitudes, or opinions.

Communication   The process of using verbal and nonverbal messages to generate meaning within and across various contexts, cultures, and channels.

Communication Accommodation Theory   A theory that claims that when we believe others have more power or have desirable characteristics, we may adopt their accepted speech behaviors and norms.

Communication apprehension   An individual's level of fear or anxiety associated with real or anticipated communication with another person or persons.

Communication channels   The various physical and electronic media through which we express messages.

Communication models   Illustrations that simplify and present the basic elements and complex interaction patterns in the communication process.

Communication skills   The ability to accomplish communication goals through interactions with others.

Communication source   A person or group of people who create messages that generate meaning.

Comparative advantage pattern   A persuasive organizational pattern that proposes a plan for improving a situation or helping solve a problem while acknowledging that a total solution may not be possible.

Comparison-contrast arrangement   An organizational pattern that demonstrates how two things are similar or different.

Competence   A component of speaker credibility that focuses on the speaker's perceived expertise and abilities.

Competitive conflict style   A conflict style in which people are more concerned with fulfilling their own needs than with meeting the needs of others.

Complementary nonverbal behavior   Nonverbal behavior that is consistent with the verbal message being expressed at the same time.

Comprehensive outline   An all-inclusive presentation framework that follows established outlining rules.

Compromising conflict style   A "middle-ground" approach to conflict resolution that involves conceding some goals to achieve others.

Concrete word   Words that refer to specific things you can perceive with your senses—smell, taste, touch, sight, or hearing.

Conflict   A disagreement that occurs in relationships when differences are expressed.

Connectives   The internal previews, summaries, transitions, and signposts that help connect key components of a presentation.

Connotation   The emotional responses or personal thoughts connected to the meaning of a word.

Consensus   A group agreement, which all members have a part in shaping and that all find at least minimally acceptable as a means of accomplishing mutual goals.

Constructive conflict   A conflict style in which people express disagreement in a way that respects others' perspectives and promotes problem solving.

Constructive nonconformity   A situation that occurs when someone resists a group norm while still working to promote the group goal.

Content   The ideas, information, and opinions included in a message.

Context   The circumstances and settings in which communication takes place.

Contradictory nonverbal behavior   Nonverbal behavior that conflicts with the meaning of spoken words.

Control need   The need to feel influential, competent, and confident.

Conversation   An interaction, often informal, in which a person exchanges speaking and listening roles with another person.

CORE speaking styles   Four basic speaking styles – Clear Style, Oral Style, Rhetorical Style, and Eloquent Style – used to express a message.

Coworker relationship   A relationship characterized by interactions among people who have little or no official authority over one another but who must work together to accomplish the goals of an organization.

Critical thinking   The thought process you use to analyze what you read, see, or hear to arrive at a justified conclusion or decision.

Culture   A learned set of shared interpretations about beliefs, values, norms, and social practices that affect the behaviors of a relatively large group of people.

Customer relationship   Professional interactions between someone communicating on behalf of an organization and an individual who is external to the organization.

D

Decision making   The process of making a judgment, reaching a conclusion, or making up your mind.

Decoding   The decision-making process used to interpret, evaluate, and respond to the meaning of verbal and nonverbal messages.

Decreasing Options Technique (DOT)   A problem-solving method which helps groups reduce and refine a large number of suggestions or ideas into a manageable set of options.

Defensive behaviors   Behaviors that reflect our instinct to protect ourselves when we are being physically or verbally attacked by someone.

Definition   A statement that explains or clarifies the meaning of a word, phrase, or concept.

Deintensification   The process of displaying facial expressions that reduce or downplay emotional displays in an effort to accommodate others.

Delivery   The various ways in which you use your voice, body, and presentation aids to express a message.

Democratic leader   A leader who promotes the social equality and task interests of group members.

Demographic information   Information about audience characteristics such as age, gender, marital status, race, religion, place of residence, ethnicity, occupation, education, and income.

Demonstration speeches   Speeches that show an audience how to do something and/or how something works.

Denotation   The specific and objective dictionary-based meaning of a word.

Dependent decision maker   A person who solicits the advice and opinions of others before making a decision.

DESC script   A four-step assertiveness process (describe, express, specify, consequences) that provides an appropriate way of addressing another person's objectionable behavior.

Description   An explanation that creates a mental image in the minds of listeners by providing details about causes, effects, historical background information, and characteristics.

Destructive conflict   The result of behaviors such as constant complaining, personal insults, conflict avoidance, and aggressive arguments that create hostility or prevent problem solving.

Destructive nonconformity   A situation that occurs when a group member resists conformity without regard for the best interests of the group and its goal, such as by showing up late to attract attention or interrupting others to exert power.

Dialectic   The interplay of opposing or contradictory forces.

Discrimination   Behavior that expresses and manifests prejudice.

Documentation   The practice of citing the sources of supporting material in writing or orally in a presentation.

E

Eloquent style   A speaking style that features poetic and expressive language used in a way that makes thoughts and feelings clear, inspiring, and memorable.

Emblems   Gestures that express the same meaning as a word in a particular group or culture.

Emoticons   Typographical characters such as :-) or :-(that serve as substitutes for expressing emotions verbally.

Emotion   The feeling you have when reacting to a situation; it is often accompanied by physical changes.

Emotional intelligence   The capacity for recognizing our own feelings and those of others, for motivating ourselves, and for managing emotions in ourselves and in our relationships.

Emotional support   Specific communication behaviors enacted by one person with the intent of helping another person cope effectively with emotional distress.

Empathic listening   The ability to understand and identify with someone's situation, feelings, or motives when you hear what they say.

Encoding   The decision-making process you use to create and send messages that generate meaning.

Entertainment speaking   A presentation designed to entertain, amuse, interest, drive, or warm-up an audience.

Ethics   Agreed-on standards of right and wrong.

Ethnocentrism   The mistaken belief that your culture is a superior culture with special rights and privileges that are or should be denied to others.

Ethos (personal proof)   A Greek word for speaker credibility that refers to the perceived character, competence, and charisma of a speaker; also a form of persuasive proof.

Euphemism   A bland, mild, vague, or unobjectionable word or phrase that substitutes for indecent, harsh, offensive, or hurtful words.

Evidence   The component of the Toulmin model of argument that answers the question, how do you know that? Evidence can range from facts, statistics, and multiple examples to the advice of experts and generally accepted audience beliefs.

Example   A word or phrase that refers to a specific case or instance in order to make large or abstract ideas concrete and understandable.

Exemplifiation   An impression management strategy that entails offering yourself as a good example or a model of noteworthy behavior.

Exclusionary language   Words that reinforce stereotypes, belittle other people, or exclude others from understanding an in-group's message.

Exit Interview   An interview conducted after an employee resigns in order to learn why the employee is leaving and what factors contributed to the decision to leave.

Expectancy Violation Theory A theory that explains how your expectations about nonverbal behavior significantly affect how you interact with others and how you interpret the meaning of nonverbal messages.

Explanatory communication Communication that seeks to enhance or deepen an audience's understanding about a topic so listeners can understand, interpret, and evaluate complex ideas and information.

Expression -privacy dialectic The relational tension between wanting both openness and privacy.

Extemporaneous speaking The most common form of delivery, which occurs when you use an outline as a guide for delivering a prepared presentation.

External noise Physical elements in the environment that interfere with effective communication.

Extroverts People who are outgoing. They talk more and gesture when they speak and enjoy interacting with others and solving problems in groups. Also a Myers-Briggs personality type.

Eye contact The practice of establishing and maintaining direct, visual links with individual audience members.

Eye scan The practice of glancing at a specific section of your speaking notes or manuscript and then looking at your audience.

F

Face The positive image you wish to create or preserve when interacting with others.

Fact A verifiable observation, experience, or event known to be true.

Fallacy An error in thinking that leads to false and invalid claims and has the potential to mislead or deceive others.

False consensus A state of agreement in a group when members reluctantly give in to group pressures or an external authority in order to make a decision masquerading as consensus.

Faulty cause A fallacy of argument that claims a particular situation or event is the cause of another event before ruling out other possible causes.

Feedback Any verbal or nonverbal response you can see or hear from others.

Feelers A Myers-Briggs personality type; Feelers want to get along with others and will spend time and effort helping others and creating a supportive communication climate.

Feminine societies Societies in which gender roles overlap; both men and women are expected to be modest, tender, and concerned with the quality of life.

Figure–ground principle A perception principle that explains why people focus on certain features (the figure) while deemphasizing less relevant background stimuli (the ground).

Filler phrases Frequently overused and usually unnecessary words, phrases, or sounds such as *you know, uh, um, okay,* and *like* that break up a speaker's fluency and that can also annoy listeners.

5-M Model of Leadership An integrated model of leadership effectiveness that emphasizes specific communication skills and identifies five interdependent leadership functions: modeling, motivating, managing, making decisions, and mentoring.

Fluency The ability to speak smoothly without tripping over words.

Forming stage A group development stage in which group members are becoming acquainted with each other and may be more worried about themselves ("Will I be accepted and liked?") than about the group as a whole.

Forum An opportunity for audience members to comment or ask questions after a public discussion or presentation.

Fundamental Interpersonal Relationship Orientation (FIRO) Theory A theory that asserts that people interact with others to satisfy their own needs for inclusion, control, and affection.

G

Gesture A body movement that communicates an idea or emotion.

Gobbledygook The result of using many words in place of one or using a multi syllable word where a single-syllable word would suffice.

Golden listening rule An ethical listening practice- "Listen to others as you would have them listen to you."

Gossip A type of rumor that focuses on the private, personal, or even scandalous affairs of other.

Governance group An elected or appointed group that makes public policy decisions in public settings.

Group communication The interaction of three or more interdependent people who interact for the purpose of achieving a common goal.

Group Development Model A model that identifies four discrete stages in the life cycle of groups—forming, storming, norming, and performing.

Group role A pattern of behaviors associated with an expected function within a particular group context.

Groupthink The deterioration of group effectiveness as a consequence of in-group pressure.

H

Hasty generalization A fallacy argument that claims something is true based on too little evidence or too few experiences.

Hearing The ability to make clear, aural distinctions among the sounds and words in a language.

Heuristics Cognitive thinking shortcuts we use in decision making because they are correct often enough to be useful.

Hidden agenda Occurs when a member's private goals conflict with the group's goals.

High power distance A cultural dimension in which people accept differences in power as normal.

High-context culture A cultural dimension in which very little meaning is expressed through words.

Hypothetical question A question that describes a set of circumstances and asks how you would respond to those circumstances.

I

I language Taking responsibility for one's own feelings and actions by using the word *I* rather than *you* or *they*.

Illustrators Gestures used with a verbal message that would lack meaning without the words.

Immediacy   The degree to which a person seems approachable or likable.

Impression management   The strategies people use to shape and control the way other people see them.

Impromptu speaking   The practice of speaking without advanced preparation or practice.

Inclusion need   The need to belong, to be involved, and to be accepted.

Individualism   A cultural dimension that emphasizes the values of independence, personal achievement, and individual uniqueness.

Inference   A conclusion based on claims of fact.

Inflection   The changing pitch within a syllable, word, or group of words during a presentation that makes speech expressive.

Informative presentation   A presentation designed to instruct, enlighten, explain, describe, clarify, correct, remind, and/or demonstrate.

Informatory communication   Communication that seeks to create or increase audience awareness about a topic by presenting the latest information.

Ingratiation   The most common impression management strategy; the goal of integration is to be liked by others. Ingratiation skills include giving compliments, doing another person a favor, and comforting someone.

Inspirational speaking   Presentations that bring like-minded people together, create social unity, build goodwill, or celebrate by arousing audience emotions.

Integration-separation dialectic   The relational tension between wanting both interpersonal dependence and independence.

Intensification   The process of exaggerating facial expressions in an effort to meet other people's needs or to express strong feelings.

Interactional context   Refers to whether the interaction is between two people, among group members, or between a presenter and an audience.

Interactive Communication Model   This model includes the concepts of noise and feedback to show that communication is not an unobstructed or one-way street.

Intercultural dimension   An aspect of a culture that can be measured relative to other cultures.

Internal noise   Thoughts, feelings, and attitudes that interfere with your ability to communicate and understand a message as it was intended.

Internal preview   A connective that identifies, in advance, the key points of a presentation or section in a specific order.

Internal summary   A connective that signals the end of a major section of a presentation and reinforces important ideas.

Interpersonal communication   Communication that occurs when a limited number of people, usually two, interact for the purpose of sharing information, accomplishing a specific goal, or maintaining a relationship.

Interview   An interpersonal interaction between two parties in which at least one party has a predetermined purpose and uses questions and answers to share information, solve a problem, or influence the other.

Intimacy   The feeling or state of knowing someone deeply in physical, psychological, emotional, intellectual, and/or collaborative ways because that person is significant in your life.

Intimate distance   One of four spatial zones or distances, intimate distance is usually 0 to 18 inches and is associated with love, comfort, protection, and increased physical contact.

Intimidation   An impression management strategy, the goal of which is to provoke fear.

Introverts   People who think before speaking, are not very talkative, and often prefer to work alone. Also, a Myers-Briggs personality type.

Intuitive decision maker   A person who makes decisions based on instincts, feelings, or hunches.

Intuitives   People who look for connections, overall concepts, and basic assumptions rather than focussing on details and procedures. Also, a Myers-Briggs personality type.

J

Jargon   The specialized or technical language of a profession or homogeneous group that allows members to communicate with each other clearly, efficiently, and quickly.

Jealousy   An intense feeling caused by a perceived threat to a relationship.

Johari Window   A model for understanding the connections between willingness to self-disclose and receptivity to feedback.

Judgers   People who are highly structured, plan ahead, are punctual, and become impatient with those who show up late or waste time. Also, a Myers-Briggs personality type.

K

Key points   Points that represent the most important issues or main ideas in the message.

L

Laissez-faire leader   A leader who lets the group take charge of all decisions and actions.

Language   A system of arbitrary signs and symbols used to communicate thoughts and feelings.

Language intensity   The degree to which one's language deviates from bland, neutral terms.

Leader–member relations   A situational leadership factor that assesses how well a leader gets along with group members and whether the group is cooperative and supportive.

Leadership   The ability to make strategic decisions and use communication to mobilize group members toward achieving a common goal.

Leading question   A question that suggests or implies the response the questioner wants to hear.

Leakage cues   Unintentional nonverbal behavior that may reveal deceptive communication.

Learning style   The strengths and preferences that characterize the way we take in and processes information.

Leet   Also known as eleet or leetspeak, a way of communicating online that uses an alternative alphabet to create words.

Linear Communication Model   The earliest type of communication model that addresses communication that functions in only one direction: a source creates a message and sends it through a channel to reach a receiver.

Listening   The process of receiving, constructing meaning from, and responding to a spoken and/or nonverbal message.

Listening to Evaluate   The ability to analyze and make judgments about the validity of someone's spoken and nonverbal messages.

Listening to Hear   The ability to make clear, aural distinctions among the sounds and words in a language.

Listening to Interpret   The ability to empathize with another person's feelings without judging the message

Listening to Remember   The ability to store, retain, and recall information you have heard.

Listening to Respond   The ability to respond in a way that indicates you fully understand someone's meaning.

Listening to Understand   The ability to accurately grasp the meaning of someone's spoken and nonverbal messages.

Logistical context   The physical characteristics of a particular communication situation—focuses on a specific time, place, setting, and occasion.

Logistics   The strategic planning and arranging of people, facilities, time, and materials relevant to a presentation.

Logos (logical proof)   A Greek word for a form of proof that relies on reasoning and analysis and an audience's ability to think critically and arrive at a justified conclusion or decision.

Low power distance   A cultural dimension in which power distinctions are minimized: supervisors work with subordinates; professors work with students; elected officials work with constituents.

Low-context culture   A cultural dimension in which meaning is expressed primarily through language; low-context speakers talk more, speak directly, and may fail to notice or correctly interpret nonverbal messages.

M

Maintenance role   A member role that positively affects how group members get along with one another while pursuing a common goal.

Majority vote   A vote in which more than half the members of the group vote in favor of a proposal.

Manuscript speaking   A form of delivery in which a speaker writes a presentation in advance and reads it out loud.

Marker   The placement of an object to establish nonverbal "ownership" of an area or space.

Masculine societies   Societies in which men are supposed to be assertive, tough, and focused on material success, whereas women are supposed to be more modest, tender, and concerned with the quality of life.

Masking   The process of changing your facial expressions to conceal true emotions by displaying expressions considered more appropriate in a particular situation.

Mass communication   Forms of mediated communication that occur between a person and large, often unknown audiences; radio, television, film, publications, and computer-based media are all forms of mass communication.

Media Richness Theory   A theory that examines how the qualities of different media affect communication and helps explain why your physical presence makes a significant difference in communication situations.

Mediated context   Any form of communication in which something (usually technology) exists between communicators; telephone, email.

Meeting   A scheduled gathering of group members for a structured discussion guided by a designated chairperson.

Memorized speaking   The practice of delivering a presentation from recall with very few or no notes.

Messages   Verbal and nonverbal contents that generate meaning.

Metamessage   A message about a message.

Mind mapping   An organizing technique that uses a hodgepodge of words, phrases, lists, circles, and arrows in order to encourage the free flow of ideas and help define the relationships among ideas.

Mindfulness   The ability to be fully aware of the present moment without making hasty judgments.

Mindlessness   A state that occurs when people allow rigid categories and false distinctions to become habits of thought and behavior.

Minutes   The written record of a group's discussion and activities.

Mixed message   A contradiction between the verbal and nonverbal meanings of a message.

Mnemonic   A memory aid based on similarities in the beginning letters of words, acronyms, or rhyme.

Monochronic time   A cultural dimension (also referred to as M-time) in which people emphasize promptness and schedule events as separate items—one thing at a time.

Monroe's Motivated Sequence   An organizational pattern for persuasive presentations that follows five steps: attention, need, satisfaction, visualization, and action.

Muted Group Theory   A theory, which claims that powerful, wealthy groups at the top of a society determine and control who will communicate and be listened to.

Myers-Briggs Type Indicator   A theory about personality types that examines the ways in which we perceive the world around us as well as how we reach conclusions and make decisions.

Mythos (narrative proof)   A Greek word for persuasive proof that addresses the values, faith, and feelings that make up our social character and is most often expressed in traditional stories, sayings, and symbols.

N

Narratives   The process, art, and techniques of storytelling.

Netlingo   A variety of language forms used in Internet communication.

Netspeak   Typographic strategies used to achieve a sociable, oral, and interactive communication style on the Internet.

Neutralization   The process of controlling your facial expressions in order to eliminate all displays of emotions.

Noise   Internal and external obstacles that can prevent a message from reaching its receivers as intended.

Nonverbal communication   Message components other than words that generate meaning; nonverbal communication encompasses physical appearance, body movement, facial expressions, touch, vocal characteristics, and the communication context.

Norming stage   A group development stage in which members define their roles, establish norms, and determine how the group will do its work.

Norms   Sets of expectations held by group members concerning what kinds of behavior or opinions are acceptable or unacceptable.

O

Occasion   The reason an audience has assembled at a particular place and time.

Open-ended question   A question that encourages specific or detailed responses.

Optimum pitch   The pitch at which you speak most easily and expressively.

Oral footnote   A spoken citation that includes enough information for listeners to find the original sources.

Organization   The way you arrange the content of your presentation into a clear and appropriate format.

Organizational Culture Theory   A theory which describes the ways in which shared symbols, beliefs, values, and norms affect the behavior of people working in and with an organization.

Organizational subculture   A group of people who engage in behaviors and share values that are, in part, different from that of the larger organizational culture.

Other oriented   People who are effective self-monitors and who give serious, undivided attention to, feel genuine concern for, and focus on the needs of other communicators.

P

Panel discussion   A type of public discussion in which several people interact about a common topic to educate, influence, or entertain an audience.

Paraphrasing   The ability to restate what people say in a way that indicates you understand them.

Passive aggression   Behavior that appears to accommodate another person's needs, but actually represents subtle aggressive behavior.

Passive voice   A sentence in which the subject receives the action. Example: *The book was read by Erin*.

Passivity   Behavior characterized by giving in to others at the expense of your own needs in order to avoid conflict and disagreement.

Pathos (emotional proof)   A Greek word for a form of persuasive proof that appeals to deep-seated feelings and emotions.

Perceivers   People who are flexible and adaptable thinkers and are likely to take risks, act spontaneously, and procrastinate. Also, a Myers-Briggs personality type.

Perception   The process we use to select, organize, and interpret sensory stimuli in the world around us.

Perception checking   A method for testing the accuracy of your perceptual interpretations.

Performing stage   A group development stage in which members focus their energy on working harmoniously to achieve group goals.

Personal distance   One of four spatial zones or distances, personal distance is 18 inches to 4 feet.

Personal integrity   Behaving in ways that are consistent with your values and beliefs while also understanding and respecting others.

Personal relationship   A relationship characterized by a high level of emotional connection and commitment.

Personality   The style in which each of us interacts with the world around us and particularly with other people.

Person-centered message   A message that reflects the degree to which a helper validates a distressed person's feelings and encourages the person to talk about the upsetting event.

Persuasion   Messages that seek to change audience members' opinions (what they think) or behavior (what they do).

Persuasive presentation   A presentation designed to change or influence audience members' opinions and/or behavior.

Pitch   How high or low your voice sounds in terms of the notes on a musical scale.

Plagiarism   Using a quotation or idea from another source and passing it as your own.

Polychronic time   A cultural dimension, also referred to as P-time, in which schedules are not as important and are frequently broken; P-time people are often late and are easily distracted and tolerant of interruptions.

Power distance   A cultural dimension in which there is a large physical and psychological gap between those who have power and those who do not.

Prejudices   Positive or negative attitudes about an individual or cultural group based on little or no direct experience with that person or group.

Preliminary outline   A first-draft outline that puts the major pieces of a presentation in a clear and logical order.

Presentation aids   Supplementary aids – most often visual – used for presenting and highlighting key ideas and supporting material.

Presentation speaking   The process of using verbal and nonverbal messages to generate meaning with audience members.

Presentational communication   Communication that occurs between speakers and their audience members.

Primacy effect   Our tendency to recall the first item in a sequence; the reason why audiences often recall a presentation's introduction.

Primary source   The document, testimony, or publication in which new information first appears.

Primary tension   The social unease and inhibitions that accompany the getting-acquainted period in a new group.

Probing question   A question used to follow up another question or a response by encouraging clarification and elaboration.

Problem-solution arrangement   An organizational pattern that describes a harmful or difficult situation (the problem) and then offers a plan (the solution) to solve the problem.

Problem solving   A complex process in which groups make multiple decisions as they analyze a problem and develop a plan for solving the problem or reducing its harmful effects.

Problem/cause/solution pattern   An organizational pattern often used in persuasive presentations that describes a serious problem, explains why the problem continues (the cause), and offers a solution.

Professional relationship   A relationship characterized by connections with people with whom you associate and work to accomplish a goal or perform a task.

Pronunciation   The process of putting all the correct sounds of a word in the correct order with the correct stress.

Proof   The arguments and evidence used to support and strengthen a persuasive claim.

Proxemics   The study of spatial relationships and how the distance between people communicates information about the nature of their relationship.

Proximity principle   A perception principle that explains why objects, events, or people that are physically closer to one another are more likely to be perceived as belonging together.

Psychoevolutionary Emotion Theory   A theory that explains the development and meaning of emotions.

Psychological Reactance Theory   A theory that claims that when people perceive a threat to their freedom to believe or behave as they wishes, they may go out of their way to do the forbidden behavior or rebel against the prohibiting authority.

Psychosocial context   The psychological and cultural environment in which you live and communicate.

Public distance   One of four spatial zones or distances, public distance is 12 plus feet.

Public group   A group that discusses issues in front of or for the benefit of public audiences.

Purpose statement   A specific, achievable, and relevant sentence that identifies the purpose and main ideas of your presentation.

Q

Qualifier   A component of the Toulmin model of an argument that states the degree to which a claim appears to be true using terms such as *probably*, *possibly*, *certainly*, *likely*, and *unlikely*.

Questions of conjecture   Questions that ask whether something will or will not happen in the future.

Questions of fact   Questions that ask whether something is true or false.

Questions of policy   Questions that ask whether and/or how a specific course of action should be taken.

Questions of value   Questions that ask whether something is worthy—good or bad, right or wrong, ethical or unethical, best, average, or worst.

R

Race   A socially constructed concept (not a scientific classification) that is the outcome of ancient population shifts which left their mark in our genes.

Racism   The assumption that people with certain characteristics (usually superficial characteristics such as skin color) have inherited negative traits that are inferior to those of other races; the culminating effect of ethnocentrism, stereotyping, prejudice, and discrimination.

Rate   The number of words a person says each minute (wpm).

Rational decision maker   A person who carefully weighs information and options before making a decision.

Receiver   The person or group of people who interpret and evaluate messages.

Recency effect   Our tendency to recall the last item in a sequence; the reason why audiences often recall a presentation's conclusion.

Reference groups   Groups with whom you identify and who influence your self-concept.

Refuting objections pattern   An organizational pattern in a persuasive presentation in which you refute and/or disprove each point that stands in opposition to your own.

Regulating nonverbal behavior   Nonverbal behavior used to manage the flow of a conversation.

Relational Dialectics Theory   A theory which explains how the interplay of contradictory forces affects interpersonal relationships in three domains: integration-separate, stability-change, and expression-privacy.

Relationship   A continuing and meaningful attachment or connection to another person.

Relationship-motivated leader   A leader who gets satisfaction from working well with other people even if the group's task or goal is neglected.

Religious literacy   The ability to understand and use the religious terms, symbols, images, beliefs, practices, scripture, heroes, themes, and stories central to American public life.

Repetitive non verbal behavior   Nonverbal behavior that visually repeats a verbal message.

Reservation   A component of the Toulmin model of an argument that recognizes exceptions to an argument or concedes that a claim may not be true under certain circumstances.

Rewards   Recognitions received from others at home, at school, on the job, or in a community for good work (academic honor, employee-of-the-month award, job promotion, community service prize).

Rhetoric   The ability to discover the available means of persuasion appropriate for a particular audience in a particular circumstance or setting.

Rhetorical devices   Word strategies designed to enhance a presentation's impact and persuasiveness.

Rhetorical style   A speaking style that features language designed to influence, persuade, and/or inspire.

Role   Adopted patterns of behaviors associated with an expected function in a specific context or relationship.

Rumor   An unverified story or statement about the facts of a situation.

S

Secondary source   Sources that report, repeat, or summarize information from one or more other sources.

Secondary tension   The frustrations and personality conflicts experienced by group members as they compete for social acceptance, status, and achievement.

Seductive details   Elements in a visual text or presentation aid that attract audience attention but do not support a writer's or speaker's key points.

Self-acceptance   Recognizing, accepting, and "owning" your thoughts, feelings, and behavior.

Self-appraisals   Evaluations of your self-concept in terms of your abilities, attitudes, and behaviors.

Self-awareness   An understanding of your core identity that requires a realistic assessment of your traits, thoughts, and feelings.

Self-centered interests   Interests aroused when a presentation can result in personal gain.

Self-centered role   A role assumed by group members who put their own goals ahead of the group's goal; can adversely affect member relationships and prevent the group from achieving its goals.

Self-concept   The sum total of beliefs you have about yourself.

Self-disclosure   The process of sharing personal information, opinions, and emotions with others that would not otherwise be known to them.

Self-effacing humor   Humor directed at yourself rather than at others.

Self-esteem   Your positive and negative judgments about yourself.

Self-fulfilling prophecy   An impression formation process in which an initial impression elicits behavior that conforms to the impression.

Self-monitoring   A sensitivity to your own behavior and others' reactions as well as the ability to modify how you present yourself.

Self-promotion   An impression management strategy for being seen as competent. The goal is to be respected by others.

Self-responsibility   Taking responsibility and being accountable for your own happiness and fulfillment of your own goals without trying to control others.

Self-talk   The silent statements you make to yourself about yourself.

Sensors   People who focuses on details and prefers to concentrate on one task at a time. Also, a Myers-Briggs personality type.

Sexual harassment   Unwanted sexual advances or inappropriate verbal or physical conduct of a sexual nature, which creates an intimidating, hostile, or offensive work environment.

Short-term memory   The limited capacity to remember content immediately after listening to a series of numbers, words, sentences, or paragraphs.

Sign   Something that stands for or represents a specific thing and often looks like the thing it represents.

Significant others   People whose opinions you value, such as family members, friends, coworkers, and mentors.

Signpost   A type of connective consisting of short phrases that, like signs on the highway, tell or remind listeners where a speaker is in the organizational structure of a presentation.

Similarity principle   A perception principle that explains why similar items or people are more likely to be perceived as a group.

Simplicity principle   A perception principle that explains why we tend to organize information in a way that provides the simplest interpretation.

Situational Leadership Theory   A theory that explains how leaders can become more effective by analyzing themselves, their group, and the context in order to find or create an ideal match between leaders and leadership roles.

Six-Step Model of Conflict Resolution   A model which offers six steps (preparation, initiation, confrontation, consideration, resolution, and reevaluation) that help you move through a conflict toward successful resolution.

Skills   Your acquired ability to accomplish communication goals when interacting with others.

Slang   A short-lived, group-related, ever-changing, creative and innovative, often playful and metaphorical, colloquial language variety that is below the level of stylistically neutral language.

Social comparison   The process of evaluating yourself in relation to others in your reference groups.

Social distance   One of four spatial zones or distances, social distance is 4 to 12 feet.

Social identity   Your self-concept as derived from the social categories to which you see yourself belonging.

Social Penetration Theory   A theory that describes the process of relationship bonding in which individuals move from superficial communication to deeper, more intimate communication.

Source   A person or group of people who create a message intended to produce a particular response.

Space arrangement   An organizational pattern in which key points are arranged in terms of their location or physical relationship to one another.

Speaker credibility   The characteristics of a speaker that determine the extent to which an audience believes the speaker and the speaker's message.

Speaking outline   The outline used by a speaker to deliver a presentation; it may be short and simple or a complex and detailed outline including significant supporting material.

Speaking style   The manner in which you use vocabulary, sentence structure and length, grammar and syntax, and rhetorical devices to express a message.

Speech Framer   A visual model for organizing presentation content that provides a place for every component of a presentation while encouraging experimentation and creativity.

Spontaneous decision maker   A person who tends to be impulsive and make quick decisions on the spur of the moment.

Stability-change dialectic   The relational tension between wanting both a stable relationship and the novelty and excitement of change.

Standard Agenda   A procedure that guides a group through problem solving by using the following steps: clarify the task, understand and analyze the problem, assess and choose solutions, and implement the decision or plan.

Statistics   Supporting material that requires collecting, summarizing, analyzing, and interpreting numerical data.

Stereotypes   Generalizations about a group of people that oversimplify the group's characteristics.

Stories Accounts or reports about something that happened.

Storming stage A group development stage in which members become more argumentative and emotional as they discuss important issues and vie for leadership.

Story fidelity The apparent truthfulness of a story and whether it accurately reflects audience values and knowledge.

Story probability The formal features of a story, such as the consistency of characters and actions, and whether the elements of a story "hang together" and make sense.

Strategies Specific plans of action that help you achieve your communication goals.

Structure The organization of message content into a coherent and purposeful message.

Styles Theory of Leadership A theory which examines three distinct leadership styles: autocratic, democratic, and laissez-faire.

Subordinate terms The most concrete words that provide specific descriptions.

Substituting nonverbal behavior Nonverbal behavior that replaces verbal language; for example, waving hello instead of saying "hello".

Superior–subordinate relationships Professional relationships in which the superior (supervisor) has formal authority over the productivity and behavior of subordinates (workers).

Superordinate terms Words that group objects and ideas together very generally.

Supplication An impression management strategy that often involves a humble request or appeal for help. The goal of supplication is compassion from others.

Supporting material Ideas and information that help explain and/or advance a presentation's purpose and key points.

Supportive behaviors Actions that create an encouraging and caring climate in which self-disclosure and responsiveness to feedback benefit both communicators.

Swearing Using words that are taboo or disapproved of in a culture, but that may not be meant literally and are used to express strong emotions and attitudes.

Symbol An arbitrary collection of sounds or letters that in certain combinations stands for a concept but does not have a direct relationship to the thing it represents.

Symposium A public group in which group members present short, uninterrupted presentations on different aspects of a topic for the benefit of an audience.

Systematic desensitization A relaxation and visualization technique that helps reduce communication apprehension.

T

Task role A group member role that positively affects the group's ability to manage a task and achieve its common goal.

Task structure A situational leadership factor that assesses how a group organizes or plans a specific task.

Task-motivated leader A leader who gains satisfaction from completing a task even at the expense of group relationships.

Territoriality The sense of personal ownership attached to a particular space.

Testimony Supporting material that consists of statements or opinions that someone has spoken or written.

Theories Statements that explain how the world works; they describe, explain, and predict events and behavior.

Theory of Informatory and Explanatory Communication A theory that explains the differences between and the communication strategies needed for presenting informatory and explanatory information to an audience.

Thinkers People who are analytical, objective, and task-oriented and who take pride in making difficult decisions. Also, a Myers-Briggs personality type.

Thought speed The speed (words per minute) at which most people can think compared with the speed at which they can speak.

Time arrangement An organizational pattern that arranges key points and message content according to time or calendar dates.

Topical arrangement An organizational pattern that divides a large topic into smaller subtopics in order to describe specific reasons, characteristics, or techniques.

Topic-centered interests Subjects audience members enjoy hearing and learning about.

Touch approachers People who are comfortable with touch and often initiate touch with others.

Touch avoiders People who are not comfortable initiating touch or being touched.

Toulmin Model of an Argument A model of an argument in which a complete argument requires three major components: a claim, evidence, and a warrant and, in some cases, backing, a reservation, and/or a qualifier.

Trait Theory of Leadership A theory which identifies specific characteristics and behaviors associated with effective leadership.

Transactional Communication Model A communication model that shows how we send and receive messages simultaneously within specific contexts.

Transition A connective that uses a word, number, brief phrase, or sentence to help a speaker move from one key point or section of a presentation to another.

Turn-requesting cue Verbal and nonverbal messages that signal a desire to speak, such as leaning forward, providing direct eye contact, and lifting your hand as if beginning to gesture.

Turn-yielding cue Verbal and nonverbal messages that signal that you are completing your comments and are prepared to listen; for example, you may slow down your speaking rate, relax your posture or gestures, or lean slightly away.

Two-thirds vote A vote in which at least twice as many group members vote for a proposal as against it.

V

Valid Well founded, justified, and accurate.

Value step A step that captures audience attention by explaining how the message can enhance the success and personal well being of audience members.

Values Beliefs that guide your ideas about what is right or wrong, good or bad, just or unjust, and correct or incorrect.

Verbal communication   The ways in which we use the words in a language to generate meaning.

Virtual group   A group that relies on technology to communicate across time, distance, and organizational boundaries. A virtual group does not typically meet face-to-face.

Visualization   A method for reducing communication apprehension and for building confidence by imagining what it would be like to communicate successfully.

Volume   A measure of loudness in a person's voice.

W

Warrant   A component of the Toulmin model of an argument that explains how and why the evidence supports the claim.

Whorf Hypothesis   A hypothesis that claims that language influences how we see, experience, and interpret the world around us.

Word stress   The degree of prominence given to a syllable within a word or words within a phrase or sentence.

Work group   Groups that are responsible for making decisions, solving problems, implementing projects, or performing routine duties in an organization.

Work team   A group given full responsibility and resources for its performance.

Working memory   The memory subsystem we use when trying to understand information, remember it, and use it to solve a problem or communicate with others; working memory allows us to shift message content from and into long-term memory.

Working Memory Theory   A theory that explains the dual-task system of working memory, which involves information processing and storage functions as well as creating new meanings.

Writing apprehension   The fear or anxiety associated with writing situations and topic-specific writing assignments.

Y

You language   Language that may be interpreted as expressing negative judgments about others.

Chapter 1

[1]Marilyn H. Buckley, "Focus on Research: We Listen to a Book a Day; Speak a Book a Week: Learning from Walter Loban," *Language Arts* 69 (1992): 101–9.

[2]In association with the National Communication Association, the Association for Communication Administration's 1995 Conference on Defining the Field of Communication produced the following definition: "The field of communication focuses on how people use verbal and nonverbal messages to generate meanings within and across various contexts, cultures, channels, and media. The field promotes the effective and ethical practice of human communication." See http://www.natcom.org.

[3]See Sherwyn P. Morreale, Michael M. Osborn, and Judy C. Pearson, "Why Communication Is Important: A Rationale for the Centrality of the Study of Communication," *Journal of the Association for Communication Administration* 29 (2000): 1–25. The authors of this article collected and annotated nearly 100 articles, commentaries, and publications that call attention to the importance of studying communication in contemporary society.

[4]Robert M. Diamond, "Designing and Assessing Courses and Curricula," *Chronicle of Higher Education*, August 1, 1997, p. B7.

[5]Jerry L. Winsor, Dan B. Curtis, and Ronald D. Stephens, "National Preferences in Business and Communication Education: A Survey Update," *Journal of the Association for Communication Administration* 3 (September 1997): 170–79. The authors conclude that a stronger emphasis should be given to training in listening and interpersonal communication in addition to developing competencies in group communication and presentation speaking.

[6] "Graduates Are Not Prepared to Work in Business," *Association Trends*, June 1997, p. 4.

[7]Business-Higher Education Forum in affiliation with the American Council on Education, *Spanning the Chasm: Corporate and Academic Cooperation to Improve Work-Force Preparation* (Washington, DC: American Council on Education, 1997).

[8]For a historical review of communication studies, see James A. Herrick, *The History and Theatre of Rhetoric: An Introduction*, 3rd ed. (Boston: Allyn and Bacon, 2005), and James L. Golden, Goodwin F. Berquist, and William E. Coleman, *The Rhetoric of Western Thought*, 4th ed. (Dubuque, IA: Kendall/Hunt, 1978).

[9]David Berlo, *The Process of Communication: An Introduction to Theory and Practice* (New York: Holt, Rinehart and Winston, 1960), p. 24.

[10]Myron W. Lustig and Jolene Koester, *Intercultural Competence: Interpersonal Communication Across Cultures*, 5th ed. (Boston: Pearson/Allyn and Bacon, 2010), p. 25.

[11]In this textbook, we prefer and use the broader term *presentational communication* rather than *public speaking* to describe the act of speaking before an audience. Public speaking is one type of presentational communication that occurs when a speaker addresses a public audience. See Isa N. Engleberg and John A. Daly, *Presentations in Everyday Life*, 3rd ed. (Boston: Pearson/Allyn and Bacon, 2009), p. 4.

[12]See Richard L. Daft and Robert H. Lengel, "Information Richness: A New Approach to Managerial Behavior and Organizational Design," in *Research in Organizational Behavior*, ed. Barry M. Staw and Larry L. Cummings (Greenwich, CT: JAI Press, 1984), pp. 355–66; Richard L. Daft, Robert H. Lengel, and Linda K. Trevino, "Message Equivocality, Media Selection, and Manager Performance: Implications for Information Systems," *MIS Quarterly* 11 (1987): 355–66; and Linda K. Trevino, Robert H. Lengel, and Richard L. Daft, "Media Symbolism, Media Richness, and Media Choice in Organizations," *Communication Research* 14 (5, 1987): 553–74.

[13]John McWhorter, *The Power of Babel: A Natural History of Language* (New York: A.W.H. Freeman, 2001), p. 5.

[14]Nielsen.com, "Twitter's Tweet Smell of Success," http://blog.nielsen.com/nielsenwire/online_mobile/twitters-tweet-smell-of-success.

[15]Mike Musgrove, "Twitter Is a Player in Iran's Drama," *Washington Post*, http://www.washingtonpost.com/wp-dyn/content/article/2009/06/16/AR2009061603391.html, June 17, 2009.

[16]Quoted in Malcolm Gladwell, "Why the Revolution Will Not Be Tweeted," *The New Yorker*, October 4, 2010, p. 44.

[17]Darren Rowse, "Twitter Is a Complete Waste of Time," http://www.problogger.net/archives/2008/06/06/twitter-is-a-waste-of-time.

[18]http://www.tumblr.com/about.

[19]Rob Anderson and Veronica Ross, *Questions of Communication: A Practical Introduction to Theory*, 3rd ed. (New York: St. Martin's Press, 2002), p. 69.

[20]Karl R. Popper, *The Logic of Scientific Discovery* (New York: Basic Books, 1959), p. 59.

[21]Excerpt from Stephen R. Covey, *The 7 Habits of Highly Effective People* (New York: Simon and Schuster, 1989), pp. 46–48.

[22]Rob Anderson and Veronica Ross, *Questions of Communication: A Practical Introduction to Theory*, 3rd ed. (New York: St. Martin's Press, 2002), p. 301.

[23]Richard L. Johannesen, *Ethics in Human Communication*, 5th ed. (Prospect Heights, IL: Waveland Press, 2002), p. 1.

[24]National Communication Association Credo for Ethical Communication, http://www.natcom.org/aboutNCA/Policies/Platform.html.

Chapter 2

[1]David Gates, "Finding Neverland," *Newsweek* (July 13, 2009), http://www.newsweek.com/id/204296.

[2]Hanish Babu, "How Did Michael Jackson's Skin Turn White?," http://skindisease.suite101.com/article.cfm/how_did_michael_jackson_skin_turn_white#ixzz0K6jQnBBy&D.

[3]hysperia, "On Michael Jackson," *mirabile dictu*, http://alterwords.wordpress.com/2009/06/26/on-michael-jackson. The blogger hysperia is a Canadian who was "once a lawyer, once a law professor, now a poet and a Feminist for forty years."

[4]Sharon S. Brehm, Saul M. Kassin, and Steven Fein, *Social Psychology*, 6th ed. (Boston: Houghton Mifflin, 2005), p. 57.

[5]"Self-Awareness," http://en.wikipedia.org/wiki/Self-awareness.

[6]Daniel Goleman, *Emotional Intelligence* (New York: Bantam, 1995), pp. 43, 47.

[7]Ibid., p. 43.

[8]"Self-Monitoring Behavior," http://changingminds.org/explanations/theories/self-monitoring.htm.

[9]Daniel Goleman, *Emotional Intelligence* (New York: Bantam, 1995), p. 43.

[10]Sharon S. Brehm, Saul M. Kassin, and Steven Fein, *Social Psychology*, 6th ed. (Boston: Houghton Mifflin, 2005), p. 65.

[11]Anthony G. Greenwald, "The Totalitarian Ego: Fabrication and Revision of Personal History," *American Psychologist* 35 (1980): 603–18.

[12]Min-Sun Kim, *Non-Western Perspectives on Human Communication* (Thousand Oaks, CA: Sage, 2002), p. 9.

[13]Richard E. Boyatzis, "Developing Emotional Intelligence Competencies," in *Applying Emotional Intelligence: A Practitioner's Guide*, ed. Joseph Ciarrochi and John D. Mayer (New York: Psychology Press, 2007), p. 42.

[14]Nathaniel Branden, http://www.nathanielbranden.com.

[15]David Nyberg, *The Varnished Truth: Truth Telling and Deceiving in Ordinary Life* (Chicago: University of Chicago Press, 1993), p. 81.

[16]Mark L. Knapp, *Lying and Deception in Human Interaction* (Boston: Pearson/Allyn and Bacon, 2008), p. 122.

[17]Albert Bandura, *Social Foundations of Thought and Action: A Social Cognitive Theory* (Englewood Cliffs, NJ: Prentice Hall, 1986), pp. 399–408. Quoted in William Crain, *Theories of Development: Concepts and Applications*, 4th ed. (Upper Saddle River, NJ: Prentice Hall, 2000), p. 203.

[18]Leon Festinger, "A Theory of Social Comparison Processes," *Human Relations*, 7 (1954): 117–140.

[19]Susan B. Barnes, *Online Connections: Internet Interpersonal Relationships* (Cresskill, NJ: Hampton Press, 2001), p. 234.

[20]Ibid., p. 91.

[21]Jeffrey Hall, Namkee Park, Ha Yeon Song, and Michael Cody, "Strategic Misrepresentation in Online Dating: The Effects of Gender, Self-Monitoring, Personality, and Demographics," paper presented at the National Communication Association Convention, 2008.

[22]Rebecca McCarthy, "Conviction Is Tossed Out in MySpace Suicide Case," *The New York Times*, July 3, 2009, p. A12.

[23]Several news outlet websites chronicle the events leading up to Clementi's suicide and the arrest and trial of Dharun Ravi. Jesse Solomon, "Roommate Indicted in Rutgers University Suicide Case," *CNN Justice*, April 21, 2011, http://www.cnn.com/2011/CRIME/04/20/new.jersey.rutgers.indictment/index.html; Brendan Davis, "The Glaad Daily: Dharun Ravi in Court," *glaad*, September 9, 2011, http://www.glaad.org/2011/09/09/the-glaad-daily-dharun-ravi-in-court-8-sentence-for-stonewall-attackers-and-more; Also see, http://abcnews.go.com/US/victim-secret-dorm-sex-tape-commits-suicide/story?id=11758716, http://www.nytimes.com/2010/09/30/nyregion/30suicide.html.

[24]Nathaniel Branden, http://www.nathanielbranden.com.

[25]Roy F. Baumeister, Jennifer D. Campbell, Joachim I. Krueger, and Kathleen D. Vohs, "Exploding the Self-Esteem Myth," *Scientific American.com* (January 2005), http://www.papillonsartpalace.com/exSplodin.htm; http://cranepsych.edublogs.org/files/2009/06/Self_esteem_myth.pdf.

[26]Morris Rosenberg, *Society and the Adolescent Self-Image* (Princeton, NJ: Princeton University Press, 1965).

[27]Nathaniel Branden, *The Art of Living Consciously: The Power of Awareness to Transform Everyday Life* (New York: Fireside Books/Simon and Schuster, 1999), pp. 168–69.

[28]See Nathaniel Branden, *The Power of Self-Esteem* (Deerfield Beach, FL: Health Communications, 1992), pp. 168–69.

29"Women's Math Scores Affected by Suggestions," *Washington Post*, October 20, 2006, p. A11. This article summarizes a study published in the October 2006 issue of *Science*.

30Sam Dillon, "Praise, Advice and Reminders of the Sour Economy for Graduates," *The New York Times*, June 14, 2009, p. A18.

31Roy F. Baumeister, Jennifer D. Campbell, Joachim I. Krueger, and Kathleen D. Vohs, "Exploding the Self-Esteem Myth," *Scientific American.com* (January 2005) http://www.papillonsartpalace.com/exSplodin.htm; http://cranepsych.edublogs .org/files/2009/06/Self_esteem_myth.pdf.

32Roy F. Baumeister, "Violent Pride," *Scientific American* 284 (2001): 96–101.

33Douglas A. Bernstein, Louis A. Penner, Alison Clarke-Stewart, and Edward Roy, *Psychology*, 7th ed. (Boston: Houghton Mifflin, 2006), p. 161.

34Ibid., p. 172.

35Lila Guterman, "Do You Smell What I Hear? Neuroscientists Crosstalk among the Senses," *Chronicle of Higher Education*, December 14, 2001, pp. 17–18.

36Holly St. Lifer, "Fear Factor: What We Touch Can Change How We Think," *AARP The Magazine* (November/December 2010), http://www.aarp.org/health/medical-research/info-09-2010/feel-factor.print.html.

37Douglas A. Bernstein, Louis A. Penner, Alison Clarke-Stewart, and Edward Roy, *Psychology*, 7th ed. (Boston: Houghton Mifflin, 2006), p. 162.

38Ibid.

39Richard E. Nisbett, *The Geography of Thought: How Asians and Westerners Think Differently … and Why* (New York: Free Press, 2003), p. 87.

40J. Richard Block and Harold Yuker, *Can You Believe Your Eyes?* (New York: Gardner Press, 1989), p. 239.

41Ronald B. Adler, Lawrence B. Rosenfeld, and Russell F. Proctor II, *Interplay: The Process of Interpersonal Communication*, 8th ed. (Fort Worth, TX: Harcourt Brace, 2001), p. 114.

42"The Golden Rule is found in the New Testament (Matthew 7:12, NIV) but is often confused with the related admonition to 'love your neighbor as yourself,' which appears repeatedly in both the Hebrew Bible and the New Testament… . The Golden Rule has also been attributed to other religious leaders, including Confucius, Muhammad, and the first-century rabbi Hillel." Stephen Prothero, *Religious Literacy: What Every American Needs to Know—And Doesn't* (New York: HarperSanFrancisco, 2007), pp. 182–83.

43George Bernard Shaw, *Maxims for a Revolutionist* (1903).

44The discussion of communication apprehension is based on Chapter 2 of Isa Engleberg and John Daly, *Presentations in Everyday Life*, 3rd ed. (Boston: Pearson/Allyn and Bacon, 2009), and Chapter 3 of Isa Engleberg and Dianna Wynn, *Working in Groups: Communication Principles and Strategies*, 5th ed. (Boston: Pearson/Allyn and Bacon, 2010).

45Virginia P. Richmond and James C. McCroskey, *Communication: Apprehension, Avoidance, and Effectiveness*, 4th ed. (Scottsdale, AZ: Gorsuch, Scarisbrick, 1995), p. 32.

46Virginia P. Richmond and James C. McCroskey, *Communication: Apprehension, Avoidance, and Effectiveness*, 4th ed. (Scottsdale, AZ: Gorsuch, Scarisbrick, 1995), p. 41.

47James C. McCroskey, "Oral Communication Apprehension: Summary of Recent Theory and Research," *Human Communication Research* 4 (1977): 80.

48Michael J. Beatty and James McCroskey with Kristin M. Valencic, *The Biology of Communication: A Communibiological Perspective* (Cresskill, NJ: Hampton, 2001), p. 80.

49Virginia P. Richmond and James C. McCroskey, *Communication: Apprehension, Avoidance, and Effectiveness*, 4th ed. (Scottsdale, AZ: Gorsuch, Scarisbrick, 1995), p. 108.

50Sharon S. Brehm, Saul M. Kassin, and Steven Fein, *Social Psychology*, 6th ed. (Boston: Houghton Mifflin, 2005), p. 525.

51Peter Desberg, *Speaking Scared, Sounding Good* (Garden City Park, NY: Square One Publishers, 2007), pp. 101–10. Desberg describes several effective relaxation exercises that readers can practice. Desberg notes that "Fortunately, it feels great to practice them" (p. 100).

52See John A. Daly and James C. McCroskey, eds., *Avoiding Communication: Shyness, Reticence, and Communication Apprehension* (Thousand Oaks, CA: Sage, 1984); Virginia P. Richmond and James C. McCroskey, *Communication: Apprehension, Avoidance, and Effectiveness*, 4th ed. (Scottsdale, AZ: Gorsuch, Scarisbrick, 1995); Karen Kangas Dwyer, *Conquer Your Speechfright*, 2nd ed. (Belmont, CA: Thomson Wadsworth, 2005); and Michael T. Motley, *Overcoming Your Fear of Public Speaking: A Proven Method* (Boston: Houghton Mifflin, 1997).

53Karen Kangas Dwyer, *Conquer Your Speechfright*, 2nd ed. (Belmont, CA: Thomson Wadsworth, 2005), p. 23.

54Peter Desberg, *Speaking Scared, Sounding Good* (Garden City Park, NY: Square One Publishers, 2007), p. 60.

55As cited in Virginia P. Richmond and James C. McCroskey, *Communication: Apprehension, Avoidance, and Effectiveness*, 4th ed. (Scottsdale, AZ: Gorsuch, Scarisbrick, 1995), pp. 97, 101. For more on systematic desensitization, see ibid., pp. 97–102; and Karen Kangas Dwyer, *Conquer Your Speechfright*, 2nd ed. (Belmont, CA: Thomson Wadsworth, 2005), pp. 95–103, 137–41.

56Daniel Goleman, *Social Intelligence* (New York: Bantam, 2006), pp. 41–42.

57From Virginia P. Richmond and James C. McCroskey, *Communication: Apprehension, Avoidance, and Effectiveness*, 5th ed. (Boston: Allyn and Bacon, 1998). Copyright © 1998 by Pearson Education. Reprinted by permission of the publisher.

58Virginia P. Richmond and James C. McCroskey, *Communication: Apprehension, Avoidance, and Effectiveness*, 4th ed. (Scottsdale, AZ: Gorsuch, Scarisbrick, 1995), pp. 129–30. Reprinted by permission of the authors and publisher.

Chapter 3

1In 1967, the Supreme Court overturned the conviction of Richard and Mildred Loving, a young interracial couple from Caroline County, Virginia. "Richard Loving was white; his wife, Mildred, was black. In 1958, they went to Washington, D.C.—where interracial marriage was legal—to get married. But when they returned home, they were arrested, jailed and banished from the state for 25 years for violating the state's Racial Integrity Act." When they challenged the law in Virginia, "the original judge in the case upheld his decision [and wrote] 'Almighty God created the races white, black, yellow, Malay and red, and he placed them on separate continents. . . . The fact that he separated the races shows that he did not intend for the races to mix'" (National Public Radio, "Loving Decision: 40 Years of Legal Interracial Unions," *All Things Considered*, June 11, 2007, http://www.npr.org/templates/story/story.php?storyId=10889047).

2Karen R. Humes, Nicholas A. Jones, and Roberto R. Ramirez, *Overview of Race and Hispanic Origin: 2010 Census Brief* (U.S. Census Bureau, March 2011), pp. 3, 4–5, 17, 22. http://www.census.gov/prod/cen2010/briefs/c2010br-02.pdf.

3U.S. Census Bureau, www.census.gov/population.

4Myron W. Lustig and Jolene Koester, *Intercultural Competence: Interpersonal Communication across Cultures*, 6th ed. (Boston: Pearson/Allyn and Bacon, 2010), p. 25.

5Intercultural authors use a variety of terms (*co-cultures*, *microcultures*) to describe the cultural groups that coexist within a larger culture. Using either of these terms is preferable to using the older, somewhat derogatory term *subcultures*.

6Based on Myron W. Lustig and Jolene Koester, *Instructor's Manual to Accompany Intercultural Competence*, 2nd ed. (New York: HarperCollins, 1996), pp. 72–74.

7Data from Patricia G. Devine and A. J. Elliot, "Are Racial Stereotypes Really Fading? The Princeton Trilogy Revisited," *Personality and Social Psychology Bulletin* 21 (1995), pp. 1139–50.

8Stella Ting-Toomey and Leeva C. Chung, *Understanding Intercultural Communication* (Los Angeles: Roxbury, 2005), pp. 236–39.

9Based on Lustig and Koester, *Instructor's Manual to Accompany Intercultural Competence*, p. 151.

10Nicholas Wade, *Before the Dawn: Recovering the Lost History of Our Ancestors* (New York: Penguin, 2006), p. 183.

11Mark P. Orbe and Tina M. Harris, *Interracial Communication: Theory into Practice* (Belmont, CA: Wadsworth/Thomson Learning, 2001), p. 31.

12Nicholas Wade, *Before the Dawn: Recovering the Lost History of Our Ancestors* (New York: Penguin, 2006), p. 188.

13National Communication Association, "National Communication Association Policy Platform," http://www.natcom.org/index.asp?bid=510.

14Shankar Vedantam, "For Allen and Webb, Implicit Biases Would Be Better Confronted," *Washington Post*, October 9, 2006, p. A2. See also http://www.washingtonpost.com/science and http://implicit.harvard.edu.

15Allan Johnson, *Privilege, Power, and Difference* (Mountain View, CA: Mayfield Publishing, 2006), pp. 104–105.

16Ibid., p. 104.

17http://www.washingtonpost.com/wp-dyn/content/article/2009/06/10/AR2009061001768.html; Associated Press, "Guard Dies after Holocaust Museum Shooting," MSNBC.com, June 10, 2009, http://www.msnbc.msn.com/id/31208188.

18Several websites describe the massacre and the online manifesto: See "Norway—Breivik Attacks, July 2011," *The New York Times*, Updated August 25, 2001, http://topics.nytimes.com/top/news/international/countriesandterritories/norway/index.html, as well as http://www.abacusnews.com/news/11/004-anders-breivik-latest-update.php; http://www.cbsnews.com/stories/2011/08/04/501364/main20088232.shtml; http://www.telegraph.co.uk/news/worldnews/europe/norway/8655175/Norway-shooting-live.html.

19Judith Warner, "The Wages of Hate," Judith Warner Blog, *New York Times*, June 11, 2009, http://warner.blogs.nytimes.com/2009/06/11/the-wages-of-hate.

20Brenda J. Allen, *Difference Matters: Communicating Social Identity* (Long Grove, IL: Waveland Press, 2004), p. 10.

21Rita Hardiman, "White Racial Identity Development in the United States," in *Race, Ethnicity and Self: Identity in Multicultural Perspective*, ed. Elizabeth Pathy Salett and Dianne R. Koslow (Washington, DC: National MultiCultural Institute, 1994), pp. 130–31.

22Ibid.

23J. Richard Hoel. "Developing Intercultural Competence," in *Intercultural Communication with Readings*, ed. Pamela J. Cooper, Carolyn Calloway-Thomas, and Cheri J. Simonds (Boston: Allyn and Bacon, 2007), p. 305.

24Stephen Prothero, *Religious Literacy: What Every American Needs to Know—And Doesn't* (New York: HarperSanFrancisco, 2007), p. 11. See also Prothero's religious literacy quiz, pp. 27–28, 235–39.

25Statements are based on three sources: Robert Pollock, *The Everything World's Religions Book* (Avon, MA: Adams Media, 2002); Leo Rosen, ed., *Religions of America: Fragment of Faith in an Age of Crisis* (New York: Touchstone, 1975); and *Encyclopedia Britannica Almanac 2004* (Chicago: Encyclopedia Britannica, 2003).

[26]According to Richard L. Evans, a former member of the Council of Twelve of the Church of Jesus Christ of Latter-day Saints, "Strictly speaking, 'Mormon' is merely a nickname for a member of the Church of Jesus Christ of Latter-day Saints." When asked whether Mormons are Christians, he answered, "Unequivocally yes." See "What Is a Mormon?" in Leo Rosen (Ed.), *Religions of America: Fragment of Faith in an Age of Crisis* (New York: Touchstone, 1975), p. 187; Robert Pollock describes Mormonism as a "prevalent Christian faith" in Robert Pollock, *The Everything World's Religions Book* (Avon, MA: Adams Media, 2002), pp. 49–51.

[27]Geert Hofstede, *Cultures and Organizations: Software of the Mind* (New York: McGraw-Hill, 1997), p. 14. See also Geert Hofstede, *Culture's Consequences: Comparing Values, Behavior, Institutions and Organizations across Nations*, 2nd ed. (Thousand Oaks, CA: Sage, 2001), p. 29. In addition to the three intercultural dimensions included in this chapter, Hofstede identifies several other dimensions: long-term versus short-term time orientation, uncertainty avoidance, indulgence versus restraint, and monumentalism versus self-effacement. For a summary of these additional dimensions, see Lustig and Koester, *Intercultural Competence*, pp. 113–24.

[28]William B. Gudykunst and Carmen M. Lee, "Cross-Cultural Communication Theories," in *Handbook of International and Intercultural Communication*, 2nd ed., ed. William B. Gudykunst and Bella Mody (Thousand Oaks, CA: Sage, 2002), p. 27.

[29]Harry C. Triandis, "The Self and Social Behavior in Different Cultural Contexts," *Psychological Review* 96 (1989), pp. 506–20. See also Harry C. Triandis, *Individualism and Collectivism* (Boulder, CO: Westview, 1995), p. 29. Data from Geert Hofstede, *Cultural Consequences: Comparing Values, Behavior, Institutions and Organizations across Nations*, 2nd ed. (Thousand Oaks, CA: Sage, 2001), p. 215.

[30]Data from Hofstede, *Cultural Consequences*, p. 215.

[31]Ibid., p. 53.

[32]Geert Hofstede, *Cultures and Organizations: Software of the Mind* (New York: McGraw-Hill, 1997), p. 28.

[33]Triandis, *Individualism and Collectivism*.

[34]Harry C. Triandis, "Cross-Cultural Studies of Individualism and Collectivism," in *Cross-Cultural Perspectives*, ed. J. J. Berman (Lincoln: University of Nebraska Press, 1990), p. 52.

[35]Data from Hofstede, *Culture's Consequences*, p. 87.

[36]Ibid., pp. 81–82, p. 96.

[37]Data from ibid., p. 286.

[38]Edward T. Hall, "Context and Meaning," in *Beyond Culture* (Garden City, NY: Anchor, 1997).

[39]Peter Andersen et al., "Nonverbal Communication across Cultures," in *Handbook of International and Intercultural Communication*, 2nd ed., ed. William B. Gudykunst and Bella Mody (Thousand Oaks, CA: Sage, 2002), p. 99.

[40]Shirley van der Veur, "Africa: Communication and Cultural Patterns," in *Intercultural Communication: A Reader*, 10th ed., ed. Larry A. Samovar and Richard E. Porter (Belmont, CA: Wadsworth, 2003), p. 84.

[41]Edward T. Hall, *The Silent Language* (Garden City, NY: Doubleday, 1959). See also Lustig and Koester, *Intercultural Competence*, p. 226.

[42]Edward T. Hall and M. R. Hall, *Understanding Cultural Differences: Germans, French and Americans* (Yarmouth, ME: Intercultural Press, 1990), p. 6.

[43]Dean Allen Foster, *Bargaining across Borders* (New York: McGraw-Hill, 1992), p. 280.

[44]Richard West and Lynn H. Turner, *Introducing Communication Theory*, 3rd ed. (Boston: McGraw-Hill, 2007), pp. 515–32. See Cheris Kramarae, *Women and Men Speaking: Framework for Analysis* (Rowley, MA: Newbury House, 1981).

[45]Edward T. Hall, *The Dance of Life: Other Dimensions of Time* (New York: Anchor/Doubleday, 1983), p. 42.

[46]http://www.users.vioicenet.com/~howard/mindful.html.

[47]Ellen J. Langer, *Mindfulness* (Cambridge, MA: Da Capo, 1989), p. 11.

[48]Based on examples in Ellen J. Langer, *Mindfulness* (Cambridge, MA: Da Capo, 1989), p. 12.

[49]http://www.users.vioicenet.com/~howard/mindful.html.

[50]Richard Boyatzis and Annie McKee, *Resonant Leadership* (Boston: Harvard Business School Press, 2005), p. 112.

[51]Richard Nisbett, *The Geography of Thought: How Asians and Westerners Think Differently . . . and Why* (New York: Free Press, 2003), p. xiii.

[52]Langer, *Mindfulness*, p. 69.

[53]Marvin Harris, *Cows, Pigs, Wars, and Witches: The Riddles of Culture* (New York: Vintage Books, 1975), pp. 11–34.

[54]Ibid., p. 30.

[55]See the following references: Howard Giles et al., "Speech Accommodation Theory: The First Decade and Beyond," in *Communication Yearbook*, ed. Margaret L. McLaughlin (Newbury Park, CA: Sage, 1987), pp. 13–48; Howard Giles et al., "Accommodation Theory: Communication, Context, and Consequence," in *Contexts of Accommodation: Developments in Applied Sociolinguistics*, ed. Howard Giles et al. (Cambridge: Cambridge University Press, 1991), pp. 1–68.

[56]Mary M. Dwyer and Courtney K. Peters, "The Benefits of Study Abroad," http://www.transitionsabroad.com/publications/studyabroadmagazine/2007Spring/lasting_benefits_of_study_abroad.shtml.

[57]James Leigh, "Teaching Content and Skills for Intercultural Communication: A Mini Case Studies Approach," *The Edge: The E-Journal of Intercultural Relations* 2 (Winter 1999), http://www.interculturalrelations.com/v2i1Winter1999leigh.htm.

[58]The GENE Scale, developed by James Neuliep and James C. McCroskey. See James W. Neuliep, *Intercultural Communication: A Contextual Approach*, 2nd ed. (Boston: Houghton Mifflin, 2003), pp. 29–30.

Chapter 4

[1]Don Gabor, *How to Start a Conversation and Make Friends* (New York: Fireside, 2001), pp. 66–68.

[2]Phillip Emmert, "A Definition of Listening," *Listening Post* 51 (1995), p. 6.

[3]Richard Emanuel et al., "How College Students Spend Their Time Communicating," *International Journal of Listening* 22 (2008), pp. 13–28.

[4]Lynn O. Cooper and Trey Buchanan, "Listening Competency on Campus: A Psychometric Analysis of Student Learning, *The International Journal of Listening*, 24 (2010), pp. 141–163.

[5]Andrew D. Wolvin and Carolyn G. Coakley, *Listening*, 5th ed. (Madison, WI: Brown and Benchmark, 1996), p. 15.

[6]Reported in Sandra D. Collins, *Listening and Responding Managerial Communication Series* (Mason, OH: Thomson, 2006), p. 21.

[7]Michael P. Nichols, *The Lost Art of Listening* (New York: Guildford, 1995), p. 11.

[8]Ralph G. Nichols, "Listening Is a 10-Part Skill," *Nation's Business* 75 (September 1987), p. 40.

[9]S. S. Benoit and J. W. Lee, "Listening: It Can Be Taught," *Journal of Education for Business* 63 (1986), pp. 229–32.

[10]Florence I. Wolff and Nadine C. Marsnik, *Perceptive Listening*, 2nd ed. (Fort Worth, TX: Harcourt Brace Jovanovich, 1992), pp. 9–16.

[11]The numerical ranges in Figure 4.1 summarize research on communication and listening time studies. See Andrew Wolvin and Carolyn Gwynn Coakley, *Listening* (Madison, WI: Brown & Benchmark, 1996), pp. 13–15; Laura A. Janusik and Andrew D. Wolvin, "24 Hours in a Day: A Listening Update to the Time Studies," *The International Journal of Listening*, 23 (2009), pp. 104–120; Emanuel et al., "How College Students Spend Their Time Communicating."

[12]Nichols, M. P., *The Lost Art of Listening*, pp. 196, 221.

[13]Tony Alessandra and Phil Hunsaker, *Communicating at Work* (New York: Fireside, 1993), p. 55.

[14]Jim Collins, *Good to Great* (New York: Harper Collins, 2001), p. 14.

[15]Lynn O. Cooper and Trey Buchanan, "Listening Competency on Campus: A Psychometric Analysis of Students Listening," *International Journal of Listening* 24 (2010), p. 157.

[16]Many sources substantiate this list of poor listening habits including Judi Brownell, *Listening: Attitudes, Principles, and Skills*, 4th ed. (Boston: Pearson/Allyn and Bacon, 2010); Madelyn Burley-Allen, *Listening: The Forgotten Skill*, 2nd ed. (New York: Wiley, 1995); Ralph G. Nichols, "Do We Know How to Listen? Practical Helps in a Modern Age," *Speech Teacher* 10 (1961); Nichols, R. G., "Listening Is a 10-Part Skill"; and Wolvin and Coakley, *Listening*.

[17]Judi Brownell, *Listening: Attitudes, Principles, and Skills*, 4th ed. (Boston: Pearson/Allyn and Bacon, 2010), p. 14.

[18]Ibid., p. 16.

[19]Ibid., pp. 16–17.

[20]Ibid., p. 73.

[21]National Institute on Deafness and Other Communication Disorders, "Quick Statistics," http://www.nidcd.nih.gov/health/statistics/quick.htm, June 16, 2010.

[22]Gallaudet Research Institute, Gallaudet University, "A Brief Summary of Estimates for the Size of the Deaf Population in the USA Based on Available Federal Data and Published Research," http://research.gallaudet.edu/Demographics/deaf-US.php, June 6, 2010.

[23]Based on Alessandra and Hunsaker, *Communicating at Work* (New York: Fireside, 1993), pp. 76–77.

[24]Samuel E. Wood, Ellen Green Wood, and Denise Boyd, *The World of Psychology*, 6th ed. (Boston: Pearson/Allyn and Bacon, 2008), p. 199.

[25]Alan D. Baddeley and Robert H. Logie, "Working Memory: The Multiple-Component Model," in *Models of Working Memory*, ed. Akira Miyake and Priti Shah (Cambridge: Cambridge University Press, 1999), pp. 28–61; see also http://cogweb.ucla.edu/Abstracts/Miyake_Shah_99.html#intro.

[26]Laura Ann Janusik, "Building Listening Theory: The Validation of the Conversational Listening Span," *Communication Studies* 58 (2007), p. 142.

[27]Ibid.

[28]Peter Desberg, *Speaking Scared Sounding Good* (Garden City Park, NY: Square One, 2007), p. 127.

[29]Don Gabor, *How to Start a Conversation and Make Friends*, pp. 66–68.

[30]Brownell, *Listening*, p. 168.

[31]Nichols, M. P., *The Lost Art of Listening*, pp. 36–37.

[32]Based on Wolff and Marsnik, *Perceptive Listening*, p. 100.

[33]Ibid., pp. 101–2.

[34]Isa Engleberg and Dianna Wynn, *Working in Groups: Communication Principles and Strategies*, 5th ed. (Boston: Pearson/Allyn and Bacon, 2010), p. 196.

[35]National Communication Association Credo for Ethical Communication, http://www.natcom.org/aboutNCA/Policies/Platform.html.

[36]Nichols, M. P., *The Lost Art of Listening*, pp. 42–43.

[37]Wolvin and Coakley, *Listening*, pp. 135–38.

[38]Based on Wolff and Marsnik, *Perceptive Listening*, pp. 94–95.

[39]Nichols, M. P., *The Lost Art of Listening*, p. 126.

⁴⁰Based on David W. Johnson's Questionnaire on Listening and Response Alternatives in *Reaching Out: Interpersonal Effectiveness and Self-Actualization*, 7th ed. (Boston: Allyn and Bacon, 2000), pp. 234–39.

⁴¹Nichols, M. P., *The Lost Art of Listening*, p. 126.

⁴²Nichols, R. G., "Listening Is a 10-Part Skill," p. 40.

⁴³Mark Knapp and Judith A. Hall, *Nonverbal Communication in Human Interaction*, 6th ed. (Belmont, CA: Thomson/Wadsworth, 2006), p. 296.

⁴⁴Sindya N. Bhanoo, "Ability Seen in Toddlers to Judge Others' Intent," *The New York Times*, November 16, 2010. http://www.nytimes.com/2010/11/16/science/16obchildren.html?_r=1&sq=toddlers%20intention&st=cse&scp=1&pagewanted=print.

⁴⁵Kittie W. Watson, Larry L. Barker, and James B. Weaver, "The Listening Styles Profile (LSP-16): Development and Validation of an Instrument to Assess Four Listening Styles," *International Journal of Listen*ing, 9 (1995), pp. 1–13; Also see Kittie W. Watson, Larry L. Barker, and James B. Weaver, *Listening Styles Profile*, http://www.flipkart.com/listening-styles-profile-combo-package-book.

⁴⁶Graham Bodie and Debra Worthington, "Revisiting the Listening Styles Profile (LSP-16): A Confirmatory Factor Analytic Approach to Scale Validation and Reliability Estimation," *International Journal of Listening* 24 (2010), p. 84; Debra Worthington, Graham D. Bodie, Christopher Gearhart, "The Listening Styles Profile Revised (LSP-R): A Scale Revision and Validation, paper presented at the Eastern Communication Convention, April 15, 2011; personal email exchanges with Bodie and Worthington in April 2011.

⁴⁷Nichols, R. G., "Do We Know How to Listen?," p. 121.

⁴⁸Burley-Allen, *Listening*, pp. 68–70.

⁴⁹Paul J. Kaufmann, *Sensible Listening: The Key to Responsive Interaction*, 5th ed. (Dubuque, IA: Kendall/Hunt, 2006), p. 115.

⁵⁰Nichols, R. G., "Do We Know How to Listen?," p. 122.

⁵¹Deborah Tannen, *You Just Don't Understand: Women and Men in Conversation* (New York: Ballantine Books, 1990), pp. 141–42.

⁵²Ibid., pp. 142–43.

⁵³See ibid., pp. 123–48; see also Diana K. Ivy and Phil Backlund, *Exploring GenderSpeak* (New York: McGraw-Hill, 1994), pp. 224–25.

⁵⁴See Tannen, *You Just Don't Understand*, pp. 149–151; Ivy and Backlund, *Exploring GenderSpeak*, pp. 206–8, 224–25; and Teri Kwal Gamble and Michael W. Gamble, *The Gender Communication Connection* (Boston: Houghton Mifflin, 2003), pp. 122–28.

⁵⁵Elizabeth A. Tuleja, *Intercultural Communication for Business* (Mason, OH: Thomson Higher Education, 2005), p. 43.

⁵⁶For other definitions and discussions of critical thinking, see Brooke Noel Moore and Richard Parker, *Critical Thinking*, 5th ed. (Mountain View, CA: Mayfield, 1998); John Chaffee, *Thinking Critically*, 6th ed. (Boston: Houghton Mifflin, 2000); Richard W. Paul, *Critical Thinking: How to Prepare Students for a Rapidly Changing World* (Santa Rosa, CA: Foundation for Critical Thinking, 1995); and Vincent Ryan Ruggero, *Becoming a Critical Thinker*, 4th ed. (Boston: Houghton Mifflin, 2002).

⁵⁷Robert H. Ennis, "Critical Thinking Assessment," *Theory into Practice* 32 (1993), p. 180.

⁵⁸Isa N. Engleberg and John A. Daly, *Presentations in Everyday Life*, 3rd ed. (Boston: Pearson/Allyn and Bacon, 2009), p. 59.

⁵⁹William V. Haney, *Communication and Interpersonal Relationships: Text and Cases* (Homewood, IL: Irwin, 1992), pp. 231–32, 241.

⁶⁰Antonio R. Damasio, *Descartes' Error: Emotion, Reason, and the Human Brain* (New York: Penguin U.S.A., 1994), and *The Feeling of What Happens: Body and Emotion in the Making of Consciousness* (San Diego, CA: Harvest/Harcourt, 1999).

⁶¹Based on Andrew Wolvin and Laura Janusik, "Janusik/Wolvin Student Listening Inventory," in *Instructor's Manual for Communicating: A Social and Career Focus*, 9th ed., ed. Roy M. Berko, Andrew D. Wolvin, and Darlyn R. Wolvin (Boston: Houghton Mifflin, 2004), pp. 129–131.

Chapter 5

¹Maureen O'Conner, "All the Terrible Things Mel Gibson Has Said on the Record," *Gawker*, July 8, 2010, http://gawker.com/5582644/all-the-terrible-things-mel-gibson-has-said-on-the-record.

²Isa N. Engleberg and John A. Daly, *Presentations in Everyday Life*, 3rd ed. (Pearson/Allyn and Bacon, 2009), p. 261. Survey responses were received from more than 600 students enrolled in a basic communication course at geographically dispersed institutions of higher education (community colleges, liberal arts colleges, and large universities).

³William O' Grady et al., *Contemporary Linguistics: An Introduction*, 4th ed. (Boston: Bedford/St. Martin's, 2001), p. 659.

⁴Mark Twain, Letter to George Bainton, October 15, 1888, http://www.twainquotes.com/Lightning.html.

⁵Nicholas Wade, *Before the Dawn: Recovering the Lost History of Our Ancestors* (New York: Penguin, 2006), pp. 36–37.

⁶John H. McWhorter, *The Power of Babel: A Natural History of Language* (New York: Times Books/Henry Holt, 2001), pp. 4–5.

⁷Nicholas Wade, *Before the Dawn: Recovering the Lost History of Our Ancestors* (New York: Penguin, 2006), p. 226.

⁸Geoffrey Finch, *Word of Mouth: A New Introduction to Language and Communication* (New York: Palgrave, 2003), pp. 5–10; William O'Grady, Michael Dobrovolsky, and Mark Aronoff, *Contemporary Linguistics*, 2nd ed. (New York: St. Martin's Press, 1993), p. 9.

⁹See Bart G. de Boer, "Modelling Vocal Anatomy's Significant Effect on Speech," *Journal of Evolutionary Psychology*, 2010, 8(4), pp. 351–366. http://uvafon.hum.uva.nl/bart/papers/deBoerJEP2010.pdf; http://www.babelsdawn.com/babels_dawn/2010/10/the-evolution-of-the-vocal-tract.html.

¹⁰Joann S. Lubin, "To Win Advancement, You Need to Clean up Any Bad Speech Habits," *Wall Street Journal*, October 5, 2004, p. B1.

¹¹William O'Grady et al., *Contemporary Linguistics: An Introduction*, 5th ed. (Boston: Bedford/St. Martin's, 2005), p. 2.

¹²Victoria Fromkin and Robert Rodman, *An Introduction to Language*, 6th ed., (Fort Worth: Harcourt Brace, 1998), p. 3.

¹³Anne Donnellon, *Team Talk: The Power of Language in Team Dynamics* (Boston: Harvard Business School Press, 1996), p. 6.

¹⁴Nelson W. Francis, *The English Language: An Introduction* (London: English University Press, 1967), p. 119.

¹⁵Geoffrey Finch, *Word of Mouth: A New Introduction to Language and Communication* (New York: Palgrave, 2003), p. 1.

¹⁶Ibid., p. 11.

¹⁷S. I. Hayakawa and Alan R. Hayakawa, *Language and Thought in Action*, 5th ed. (San Diego, CA: Harcourt Brace Jovanovich, 1990), p. 39.

¹⁸Adapted from Ogden and Richards, *The Meaning of Meaning* (New York: Harcourt Brace, 1936).

¹⁹Hayakawa and Hayakawa, *Language and Thought in Acti*on, p. 43.

²⁰Geoffrey Finch, *Word of Mouth: A New Introduction to Language and Communication* (New York: Palgrave, 2003), p. 28.

²¹Permission granted by Lilian I. Eman, November 26, 1999.

²²Isa N. Engleberg and Dianna R. Wynn, *Working in Groups: Communication Principles and Strategies*, 5th ed. (Boston: Houghton Mifflin, 2010), p. 164.

²³Vivian J. Cook, *Inside Language* (London: Arnold, 1997), p. 91.

²⁴Geoffrey Finch, *Word of Mouth: A New Introduction to Language and Communication* (New York: Palgrave, 2003), p. 2.

²⁵See Geoffrey Finch, *Word of Mouth: A New Introduction to Language and Communication* (New York: Palgrave, 2003); http://www.aber.ac.uk/media/Documents/short/whorf.html; http://www.users.globalnet.co.uk/~skolyles/swh.htm.

²⁶Marcel Danesi and Paul Perron, *Analyzing Cultures: An Introduction and Handbook* (Bloomington, IN: Indiana University Press, 1999), p. 61.

²⁷Tony Hillerman, *The Wailing Wind* (New York: HarperTorch, 2002), p. 126.

²⁸William O'Grady et al., *Contemporary Linguistics: An Introduction*, 5th ed. (Boston: Bedford/St. Martin's, 2005), p. 509.

²⁹Myron W. Lustig and Jolene Koester, *Intercultural Competence: Interpersonal Communication across Cultures*, 6th ed. (Boston: Pearson/Allyn & Bacon, 2010), pp. 183–184.

³⁰Ibid., p. 184.

³¹Larry A. Samovar and Richard Porter, *Communication between Cultures*, 5th ed. (Belmont, CA: Wadsworth, 2004), pp. 146–147.

³²*Washington Post*, April 6, 2002, p. A1, http://www.whitehouse.gov/news/release/2002/04/print/20020406-3.html.

³³Geoffrey Finch, *Word of Mouth: A New Introduction to Language and Communication* (New York: Palgrave, 2003), p. 134.

³⁴Ibid., p. 135.

³⁵Ibid., p. 136.

³⁶M. Schultz, "The Semantic Derogation of Woman," in *Language and Sex: Difference and Dominance*, ed. B. Thorne and N. Henley (Rowley, MA: Newbury House, 1975), as quoted in Geoffrey Finch, *Word of Mouth: A New Introduction to Language and Communication* (New York: Palgrave, 2003), p. 137.

³⁷Robin Lakoff, *Language and Woman's Place* (New York: HarperCollins, 1975).

³⁸Janet Holmes, "Myth 6: Women Talk Too Much," in *Language Myths*, ed. Lauri Bauer and Peter Trudgill (London: Penguin, 1998), p. 41.

³⁹David Brown, "Stereotypes of Quiet Men, Chatty Women Not Sound Science," *The Washington Post*, July 6, 2007, p. A2. See also Donald G. McNeill, "Yada, Yada, Yada. Him? Or Her?" *The New York Times*, July 6, 2007, p. A13.

⁴⁰Janet Holmes, "Myth 6: Women Talk Too Much," in *Language Myths*, ed. Lauri Bauer and Peter Trudgill (London: Penguin, 1998), pp. 42–47.

⁴¹Ibid., pp. 48–49.

⁴²John McWhorter, *Word on the Street: Dubunking the Myth of a "Pure" Standard English* (Cambridge, MA: Perseus, 1998), p. 143.

⁴³Ibid., pp. 145–146.

⁴⁴William V. Haney, *Communication and Interpersonal Relations: Text and Cases*, 6th ed. (Homewood, IL: Irwin, 1992), p. 269.

⁴⁵Randy Cohen, "The Ethicist," *The New York Times Magazine*, July 26, 2009, p. 17.

⁴⁶William O'Grady, Michael Dobrovolsky, and Mark Aronoff, *Contemporary Linguistics*, 2nd ed. (New York: St. Martin's Press, 1993), pp. 235–236.

⁴⁷"The Leaked Memos: Did the White House Condone Torture?" *The Week*, June 25, 2004, p. 6.

⁴⁸Anna-Britta Stenstrom, "Slang to Language: A Description Based on Teenage Talk," in *i love english language*, http://aggslanguage.wordpress.com/slang-to-slanguage/.

[49]Shirley Johnson, "What Is Slang?" Modern America, 1914-Present, http://www.uncp.edu/home/canada/work/allam/1914-/language/slang.htm.

[50]Brian Jones, Jr., "Sir John Harrington—Inventor of 'The John'," Ezine, http://ezinearticles.com/?Sir-John-Harrington—Inventor-of-The-John&id=3570402.

[51]Kathryn Lindskoog, Creating Writing: For People Who Can't Write (Grand Rapids, MI: Zondervan Publishing, 1989), p. 66.

[52]Jerkeshea Morris, "A UNC-P Campus Survey," Modern America, 1914-Present, http://www.uncp.edu/home/canada/work/allam/1914-/language/slang.htm.

[53]Quoted in David Crystal, The Cambridge Encyclopedia of the English Language (NY: Cambridge University Press, 2003), p. 182.

[54]William V. Haney, Communication and Interpersonal Relations: Text and Cases, 6th ed. (Homewood, IL: Irwin, 1992), p. 290.

[55]Tom Diemer, "West Virginia Democrat Strikes Back at GOP 'Hick' Ad: 'It's Insulting'," Politics Daily/AOL News, October 10, 2010. http://www.politicsdaily.com/2010/10/09/west-virginia-democrat-strikes-back-at-gop-hick-ad-its-insu/.

[56]William Lutz, Doublespeak (New York: HarperPerennial, 1990), p. 3.

[57]Lyn Miller, "Quit Talking Like a Corporate Geek," USA Today, March 21, 2005, p. 7B.

[58]James V. O'Conner, Cuss Control: The Complete Book on How to Curb Your Cursing (New York: Three Rivers Press, 2000), p. 3.

[59]Natalie Angier, "Almost Before We Spoke, We Swore," Science Times in The New York Times, September 20, 2005, p. D6.

[60]Lars Andersson and Peter Trudgill, "Swearing," in A Cultural Approach to Interpersonal Communication: Essential Readings, ed. Leila Monaghan and Jane Goodman (Malden, MA: Wiley-Blackwell, 2007), p. 195.

[61]Natalie Angier, "Almost Before We Spoke, We Swore," Science Times in The New York Times, September 20, 2005, p. D6.

[62]James V. O'Conner, Cuss Control: The Complete Book on How to Curb Your Cursing (New York: Three Rivers Press, 2000), pp. 18–27; Timothy Jay, Why We Curse: A Neuro-Psycho-Social Theory of Speech (Amsterdam/Philadelphia: John Benjamins Publishing, 2000), p. 328.

[63]David Crystal, Language and the Internet (Cambridge: Cambridge University Press, 2001), pp. 238–39, cited in Crispin Thurlow, Laura Lengel, and Alice Tomic, Computer Mediated Communication: Social Interaction and the Internet (London: Sage, 2004), p. 123.

[64]Crispin Thurlow, Laura Lengel, and Alice Tomic, Computer Mediated Communication: Social Interaction and the Internet (London: Sage, 2004), pp. 124–125.

[65]"Leet," Urban Dictionary, http://www.urbandictionary.com/define.php?term=netspeak. Use "It's a variation of the word Elite" as search terms.

[66]Matt Richtel, "In Youthful World of Messaging, E-Mail Gets Instant Makeover," The New York Times, December 21, 2010, p. B4.

[67]For additional examples and warnings about overuse of symbols, see Deborah Jude-York, Lauren D. David, and Susan L. Wise, Virtual Teams: Breaking the Boundaries of Time and Place (Menlo Park, CA: Crisp Learning, 2000), pp. 91–92.

[68]"Cleaning Up Potty-Mouths," The Week, August 18, 2006, p. 35.

[69]Natalie Angier, "Almost Before We Spoke, We Swore," p. D6.

[70]R. L. Trask, Language: The Basics, 2nd ed. (London: Routledge, 1995), p. 170, 179.

[71]Based on Melinda G. Kramer, Glenn Leggett, and C. David Mead, Prentice Hall Handbook for Writers, 12th ed. (Englewood Cliffs, NJ: Prentice Hall, 1995), p. 272.

[72]Robert Mayer, How to Win Any Argument (Franklin Lakes, NJ: Career Press, 2006), p. 187.

[73]Stuart Chase, quoted in Richard Lederer, "Fowl Language: The Fine Art of the New Doublespeak," AARP Bulletin (March 2005), p. 27.

[74]Rudolf Flesch, Say What You Mean (New York: Harper and Row, 1972), p. 70.

[75]Excerpts from Jonathan Pitts, "At a D.C. Workshop, Participants in the Plain Language Conference Plead for End to Convoluted Communication," The Sun, November 7, 2005, p. 1C, 6C.

[76]Ibid.

[77]Joel Saltzman, If You Can Talk, You Can Write (New York: Time Warner, 1993), pp. 48–49.

[78]Virginia Richmond and James C. McCroskey, Communication Apprehension, Avoidance and Effectiveness, 5th ed. (Boston: Allyn and Bacon, 1998). © 1998 by Pearson Education. Reprinted by permission of the publisher. See also John Daly and Michael Miller, "The Empirical Development of an Instrument to Measure Writing Apprehension," Research in the Teaching of English 12 (1975), pp. 242–249.

Chapter 6

[1]Nina-Jo Moore, Mark Hickson, III, and Don W. Stacks, Nonverbal Communication, Studies and Application, 6th ed. (New York: Oxford, 2010), p. 4.

[2]Judee K. Burgoon and Aaron E. Bacue, "Nonverbal Communication Skills," in Handbook of Communication and Social Interaction Skills, ed. John O. Greene and Brant R. Burleson (Mahwah, NJ: Lawrence Erlbaum, 2003), pp. 208–209.

[3]From Sigmund Freud, Fragment of Analysis of a Case of Hysteria, Standard Edition, Volume 7, 1905, Chapter 2: The First Dream. See Psychoanalytical Electronic Publishing, http://www.pep-web.org/document.php?id=se.007.0001a.

[4]Judee Burgoon, "Truth, Lies, and Virtual Worlds," The National Communication Association's Carroll C. Arnold Distinguished Lecture, 2005 annual convention of the National Communication Association, Boston, November 2005.

[5]Paul Ekman, Telling Lies: Clues to Deceit in the Marketplace, Politics, and Marriage (New York: W.W. Norton, 1992), p. 80.

[6]H. Dan O'Hair and Michael J. Cody, "Deception," in The Dark Side of Interpersonal Communication, ed. William R. Cupach and Brian H. Spitzberg (Hillsdale, NJ: Lawrence Erlbaum Associates, 1994), p. 190.

[7]Mark L. Knapp, Lying and Deception in Human Interaction (Boston: Pearson Education, 2008), pp. 217–218.

[8]Benedict Carey, "Judging Honesty By Words, Not Fidgets," The New York Times, May 12, 2009, p. D4.

[9]Judith Newman "Inside the Teenage Brain," Parade Magazine, November 28, 2010, http://www.parade.com/news/2010/11/28-inside-the-teenage-brain.html; See also National Institute of Mental Health, "Teenage Brain: A Work in Progress (Fact Sheet), http://www.nimh.nih.gov/health/publications/teenage-brain-a-work-in-progress-fact-sheet/index.shtml.

[10]William D. S. Killgore and Deborah A. Yurgelun-Todd, "Neural Correlates of Emotional Intelligence in Adolescent Children, Cognitive, Affective and Behavioral Neuroscience, 2007, 7 (2), pp. 140–151; Deborah A. Yurgelun-Todd and William D. Killgore, "Fear-related Activity in the Prefrontal Cortex Increases with Age During Adolescence: A preliminary MRI Study. Neuroscience Letters, 2006, 406, pp. 194–199.

[11]Interview: Deborah Yrgelun-Todd, Frontline, January 31, 2002, http://www.pbs.org/wgbh/pages/frontline/shows/teenbrain/interviews/todd.html.

[12]Ibid.

[13]Paul Ekman, "Communication through Nonverbal Behavior: A Source of Information about an Interpersonal Relationship," in Affect, Cognition and Personality, ed. Silvan S. Tompkins and C. E. Izard (New York: Springer, 1965), pp. 390–442.

[14]Judee K. Burgoon, David B. Buller, and W. Gill Woodall, Nonverbal Communication: The Unspoken Dialog (New York, McGraw-Hill, 1996), 286. See also Richard West and Lynn H. Turner, Introducing Communication Theory (Boston: McGraw Hill, 2007), pp. 152–153.

[15]Virginia P. Richmond and James C. McCroskey, Behavior in Interpersonal Relationships, 5th ed. (Boston: Allyn and Bacon, 2004), p. 33.

[16]From the Federal Reserve Bank of St. Louis, The Regional Economist (April 2005), quoted in "Good Looks Can Mean Good Pay, Study Says," The Sun, April 28, 2005, p. D1.

[17]Angus Deaton, "Life at the Top: The Benefits of Height," http://www.princeton.edu/~deaton/downloads/life_at_the_top_benefits_of_height_final_june_2009.pdf.

[18]"Dress Codes, Tatoos and Piercings, June 4, 2008, Employee Rights Blog, http://employeeissues.com/blog/body-art-dress-code.

[19]The Pew Research Center, "45%–40% – The Tattoo Divide," February, 2010, http://pewresearch.org/databank/dailynumber/?NumberID=927.

[20]Son wants to gauge his ears? http://answers.yahoo.com/question/index?qid=20070913141142AAKPdRk.

[21]David Brooks, "Nonconformity Is Skin Deep," The New York Times, August 27, 2006, p. WK11.

[22]Moore, Hickson, and Stacks, Nonverbal Communication: Studies and Applications, p. 170.

[23]Oren Dorell, "Cover Up Your Tattoos, Some Employees Told," USA Today, October 31, 2008, p. 3A.

[24]Thomas J. Stanley and William D. Danko, The Millionaire Next Door: The Surprising Secrets of America's Wealthy (Atlanta, GA: Longstreet Press, 1996), pp. 28, 31–35.

[25]Jo-Ellan Dimitrius and Mark Mazzarella, Reading People: How to Understand People and Predict Their Behavior—Anytime, Anyplace (New York: Ballantine, 1999), p. 52.

[26]Jeannette Catsoulis, "Look but Don't Touch: It's All About the Hair," The New York Times, October 8, 2009, http://movies.nytimes.com/2009/10/09/movies/09hair.html; Also see "Chris Rock, Official Trailer, Good Hair," YouTube, July 31, 2009, http://www.youtube.com/watch?v=1m-4qxz08So&noredirect=1.

[27]Darryl E. Owens, "Still Locked into 'Good Hair' Image?" The Orlando Sentinel, October 31, 2009, http://www.orlandosentinel.com/news/local/orl-darryl-owens-good-hair-103109,0,4483022.column.

[28]Freezy, "Video: Sesame Street Makes 'I Love My Hair' for Young Black Girls." FREESWORLD (Marie 'Free' Wright), October 18, 2010, http://www.freesworld.com/2010/10/18/video-sesame-street-makes-i-love-my-hair-for-young-black-girls/.

[29]Mark L. Knapp and Judith A. Hall, Nonverbal Communication in Human Interaction, 4th ed. (Fort Worth, TX: Harcourt Brace, 1997), p. 229.

[30]Paul Ekman and Wallace V. Friesen, "Hand Movements," in The Nonverbal Communication Reader: Classic and Contemporary Readings, 2nd ed., ed. Laura K. Guerrero, Joseph A. DeVito, and Michael L. Hecht (Long Grove, IL: Waveland Press, 2008), 105–108. The original article, "Hand Movements," was published in the Journal of Communication 22 (1972), pp. 353–374.

[31]Roger E. Axtell, Do's and Taboos Around the World, 2nd ed. (New York: John Wiley and Sons, 1990), p. 47.

[32]Laura K. Guerrero, Joseph A. DeVito, and Michael L. Hecht, "Section D. Contact Codes: Proxemics and Haptics," in The Nonverbal Communication Reader: Classic and Contemporary Readings, 2nd ed., ed. Laura K. Guerrero, Joseph A. DeVito, and Michael L. Hecht (Long Grove, IL: Waveland Press, 2008), p. 174.

[33]Richmond, *Nonverbal Behavior in Interpersonal Relations*, p. 151.

[34]Larry Smeltzer, John Waltman, and Donald Leonard, "Proxemics and Haptics in Managerial Communication" in *The Nonverbal Communication Reader: Classic and Contemporary Readings*, 3rd ed., ed. Laura K. Guerrero and Michael L. Hecht (Long Grove, IL: Waveland Press, 2008), p. 190.

[35]Joseph B. Walther and Kyle P. D'Addario, *The Impacts of Emoticons on Message Interpretation in Computer-Mediated Communication* (paper presented at the meeting of the International Communication Association, Washington, DC, May 2001), p. 13.

[36]Richmond and McCroskey, *Nonverbal Behavior in Interpersonal Relationships*, pp. 75–77. Based on Paul Ekman and W. V. Frie, *Face*, 2nd ed., ed. Paul Ekman (Cambridge: Cambridge University Press, 1982), pp. 7–21.

[37]Gerald W. Grumet, "Eye Contact: The Core of Interpersonal Relatedness," in *The Nonverbal Communication Reader: Classic and Contemporary Readings*, 3rd ed., Laura K. Guerrero and Michael L. Hecht (Long Grove, IL: Waveland Press, 2008), pp. 125–126.

[38]Guo-Ming Chen and William J. Starosta, *Fundamentals of Intercultural Communication* (Boston: Allyn & Bacon, 1998), p. 91.

[39]Summary of eye behavior research from Virginia P. Richmond, James C. McCroskey, and Mark L. Hickson, *Nonverbal Behavior in Interpersonal Relations* (Boston: Pearson/Allyn and Bacon, 2008), pp. 95–96.

[40]Lyle V. Mayer, *Fundamentals of Voice and Diction*, 13th ed. (Boston: McGraw Hill, 2004), p. 229.

[41]Richmond and McCroskey, *Nonverbal Behavior in Interpersonal Relationships*, p. 103.

[42]Centers for Disease Control and Prevention, *Intimate Partner Violence: Fact Sheet*, http://www.cdc.gov/violenceprevention/pdf/IPV_factsheet-a.pdf.

[43]ABC News, "Battle of the Sexes: Spousal Abuse Cuts Both Ways," February 7, 2004, http://abcnews.go.com/sections/2020/dailynews/2020_ batteredhusbands030207.html.

[44]Eric F. Sygnatur and Guy A. Toscano, "Work-Related Homicides: The Facts," in *Compensation and Working Conditions* (Spring 2000), http://bls.gov/opub/cwc/ archive/spring2000art1.pdf.

[45]National Communication Association, Credo for Ethical Communication, 1999, http://www.natcom.org/nca/Template2.asp?bid=374.

[46]Allan Pease and Barbara Pease, *The Definitive Book of Body Language* (New York: Bantam, 2004), pp. 193–194.

[47]Edward T. Hall, *The Hidden Dimension* (Garden City, NY: Doubleday, 1966).

[48]Moore, Hickson, and Stacks, *Nonverbal Communication: Studies and Applications*, p. 293.

[49]Richmond and McCroskey, *Nonverbal Behavior in Interpersonal Relationships*, pp. 199–212.

[50]Isa N. Engleberg and John A. Daly, *Presentations in Everyday Life*, 3rd ed. (Boston: Houghton Mifflin, 2009), p. 138.

[51]John A. Daly and Anita Vangelisti, "Skillfully Instructing Learners: How Communicators Effectively Convey Messages," in *Handbook of Communication and Social Interaction Skills*, ed. John O. Greene and Brant R. Burleson (Mahwah, NJ: Lawrence Erlbaum, 2003), pp. 892–894.

[52]Timothy G. Plax and Patricia Kearney, "Classroom Management: Contending with College Student Discipline," in *Teaching Communication: Theory, Research, and Methods*, 2nd ed., ed. Anita L. Vangelisti, John A. Daly, and Gustav W. Friedrich (Lea's Communication Series) (Mahwah, NJ: Lawrence Erlbaum, 1999), p. 276.

[53]Moore, Hickson, and Stacks, *Nonverbal Communication: Studies and Applications*, p. 375.

[54]Brian H. Spitzberg, "CSRS: The Conversational Skills Rating Scale—An Instructional Assessment of Interpersonal Competence," in the *NCA Diagnostic Series*, 2nd ed. (Washington, D.C.: National Communication Association, 2007). See applications to nonverbal communication in Brian H. Spitzberg, "Perspectives on Nonverbal Communication Skills," in *The Nonverbal Communication Reader: Classic and Contemporary Readings*, 3rd ed., ed. Laura K. Guerrero and Michael L. Hecht (Long Grove, IL: Waveland Press, 2008), pp. 21–26.

Chapter 7

[1]Jerry Lopper, "The Six Life Benefits of Happiness," November 19, 2007, http://personaldevelopment.suite101.com/article.cfm/the_six_life_benefits_of_ happiness#ixzz0JqwpOgDk&D.

[2]David W. Johnson, *Reaching Out: Interpersonal Effectiveness and Self-Actualization*, 7th ed. (Boston: Allyn & Bacon, 2000), p. 12.

[3]John M. Gottman with Joan De Claire, *The Relationship Cure* (New York: Three Rivers Press, 2001), p. 23.

[4]Daniel Goleman, "'Friends for Life': An Emerging Biology of Emotional Healing," *The New York Times*, October 10, 2006, p. D5. For a more detailed examination of this phenomenon, see Daniel Goleman, *Social Intelligence* (New York: Bantam, 2006), p. 10.

[5]William Schutz, *The Human Element: Productivity, Self-Esteem, and the Bottom Line* (San Francisco: Jossey-Bass, 1994).

[6]In his more recent works, Schutz refers to this need as *openness*. However, we find that students understand this concept better when we use Schutz's original term—*affection*.

[7]Based on material in Isa Engleberg and Dianna Wynn, *Working in Groups: Communication Principles and Strategies*, 5th ed. (Boston: Houghton Mifflin, 2010), pp. 82–85.

[8]Erving Goffman, *The Presentation of Self in Everyday Life* (New York: Doubleday, 1959).

[9]Based on Edward E. Jones and Thane S. Pittman, "Toward a General Theory of Strategic Self-Presentation," in Jerry M. Suls (Ed.), *Psychological Perspectives on the Self*, Vol 1(Hillsdale, N.J.: Erlbaum, 1982), pp. 231–262; see also Sandra Metts and Erica Grohskopf, "Impression Management: Goals, Strategies, and Skills," in *Handbook of Communication and Social Interaction Skills*, ed. John O. Greene and Brant Burleson (Mahwah, NJ: Lawrence Erlbaum, 2003), pp. 358–359. Hans Grietens, *Attitudes Towards Social Limits, Undersocialized Behavior, and Self-Presentation in Young People* (Leuven, Belgium: Leuven University Press, 1999), p. 44.

[10]We have added the parenthetical cautions to the Jones and Pittman taxonomy of impression formation strategies.

[11]Daniel Menaker, *A Good Talk: The Story and Skill of Conversation* (NY: Hatchette Book Groups, 2010), p. 1.

[12]"What Drives Co-Workers Crazy," *The Week*, February 23, 2007, p. 40.

[13]Ibid.

[14]Ibid. See also "Proper Cell Phone Etiquette," www.cellphonecarriers.com/ cell-phone-etiquette.html.

[15]Daniel Menaker, *A Good Talk: The Story and Skill of Conversation*, p. 182.

[16]Maria J. O'Leary and Cynthia Gallois, "The Last Ten Turns in Conversations between Friends and Strangers," in *The Nonverbal Communication Reader: Classic and Contemporary Readings*, 2nd ed., ed. Laura K. Guerrero, Joseph A. DeVito, and Michael L. Hecht (Prospect Heights, IL: Waveland Press, 1999), pp. 415–421.

[17]Wendy Samter, "Friendship Interaction Skills across the Life Span," in *Handbook of Communication and Social Interaction Skills*, ed. John O. Greene and Brant R. Burleson (Mahwah, NJ: Lawrence Erlbaum, 2003), p. 641.

[18]Sandra Petronio, *Boundaries of Privacy: Dialectics of Disclosure* (Albany: State University of New York Press, 2003), pp. 5–6.

[19]Wendy Samter, "Friendship Interaction Skills across the Life Span," in *Handbook of Communication and Social Interaction Skills*, ed. John O. Greene and Brant R. Burleson (Mahwah, NJ: Lawrence Erlbaum, 2003), p. 662.

[20]William K. Rawlins, *Friendship Matters: Communication, Dialects, and the Life Course* (New York: Aldine De Gruyter, 1992), p. 181.

[21]Wendy Samter, "Friendship Interaction Skills across the Life Span," p. 661.

[22]William K. Rawlins, *Friendship Matters: Communication, Dialects, and the Life Course*, p. 105.

[23]Laura K. Guerrero and Peter A. Andersen, "The Dark Side of Jealousy and Envy: Desire, Delusions, Desperation, and Destructive Communication," in Brian H. Spitzberg and William R. Cupach (Eds.), *The Dark Side of Close Relationships* (Mahwah, NJ: Lawrence Erlbaum Associates, 1998), p. 55 and p. 66.

[24]Based on Laura K. Guerrero et al., "Coping with the Green-Eyed Monster: Conceptualizing and Measuring Communicative Responses to Romantic Jealousy," *Western Journal of Communication* 59 (1995), pp. 270–304; Laura K. Guerrero and Walid Afifi, "Toward a Goal-Oriented Approach for Understanding Communicative Responses to Jealousy," *Western Journal of Communication* 63 (1999), pp. 216–248. The three communication strategies are labeled as follows in these articles: Integrative Communication, Compensatory Restoration, and Negative Affect Expression.

[25]Kathryn Dindia and Lindsay Timmerman, "Accomplishing Romantic Relationships," in *Handbook of Communication and Social Interaction Skills*, ed. John O. Greene and Brant R. Burleson (Mahwah, NJ: Lawrence Erlbaum, 2003), pp. 694–697.

[26]Knapp and Vangelisti, *Interpersonal Communication and Human Relationships*, pp. 34–35.

[27]Mark C. Knapp and Anita L. Vangelisti, *Interpersonal Communication and Human Relationships* (Boston: Allyn & Bacon, 1996), pp. 33–44.

[28]Richard Layard, *Happiness: Lessons from a New Science* (New York: Penguin Books, 2005), p. 66.

[29]Mark C. Knapp and Anita L. Vangelisti, *Interpersonal Communication and Human Relationships* (Boston: Allyn & Bacon, 1996), p. 34.

[30]Judith R. Harris as quoted in several online chats and interviews. See the Washington Post's online chat, September 30, 1998, http://discuss.washingtonpost. com/wp-srv/zforum/98/harris093098.html; and *Edge 58*, June 29, 1999, www.edge. org/documents/archive/edge58.html.

[31]Judith Rich Harris, "Where Is the Child's Environment? A Group Socialization Theory of Development," *Psychological Review*, 102 (1995), p. 462, p. 469.

[32]"Blame Your Peers, Not Your Parents, Authors Says," *APA Monitor* (October 1998), www.snc.edu/psych/korshavn/peer01.html.

[33]For analysis and criticism of Harris's research, see Craig H. Hart, Lloyd D. Newell, and Susanne Frost Olsen, "Parenting Skills and Social–Communicative Competences in Childhood," in *Handbook of Communication and Social Interaction Skills*, ed. John O. Greene and Brant R. Burleson (Mahwah, NJ: Lawrence Erlbaum, 2003), pp. 774–776.

[34]Janet Maslin, "But Will It All Make 'Tiger Mom' Happy?" *The New York Times*, January 20, 2011, http://www.nytimes.com/2011/01/20/books/20book.html?_r=1.

[35]David Brooks, "Amy Chua Is a Wimp," *The New York Times*, January 17, 2011, http://www.nytimes.com/2011/01/18/opinion/18brooks.html.

[36]Paul Tough, "The Character Test," *The New York Times Magazine*, September 18, 2011, p. 40.

[37]Malcolm R. Parks, "Ideology in Interpersonal Communication: Off the Couch and into the World," in *Communication Yearbook 5*, ed. Michael Burgoon (New Brunswick, NJ: Transaction Books, 1982), pp. 79–107.

[38]Joseph Luft, *Group Process: An Introduction to Group Dynamics*, 3rd ed. (Palo Alto, CA: Mayfield, 1984).

[39]Ibid.

[40]David W. Johnson, *Reaching Out: Interpersonal Effectiveness and Self-Actualization*, 7th ed. (Boston: Allyn & Bacon, 2000), p. 47.

[41]Luft, *Group Process: An Introduction to Group Dynamics*, 3rd ed.

[42]Ibid., pp. 58–59.

[43]Michael Daniels, "Facebook Profile: Will They 'Like' What They See?" http://www.bschooladmissionsformula.com/law-school-administrators-are-looking-at-your-facebook-profile.

[44]Tim Lockette, "Future Doctors Share Too Much Information on Facebook," http://news.ufl.edu/2008/07/10/facebook.

[45]Reported in Laura M. Holson, "Tell-All Generation Learns to Keep Things Offline," May 8, 2010, http://www.nytimes.com/2010/05/09/fashion/09privacy.html

[46]Irvin Altman and Dalmas Taylor, *Social Penetration: The Development of Interpersonal Relationships* (New York: Holt, Rinehart, and Winston, 1973).

[47]Walid A. Afifi and Laura K. Guerrero, "Motivations Underlying Topic Avoidance in Close Relationships," in *Balancing the Secrets of Private Disclosure*, ed. Sandra Petronio (Mahwah, NJ: Lawrence Erlbaum, 2000), p. 168.

[48]*Shrek*, DreamWorks, 2003.

[49]For more information on self-disclosure skills, see David W. Johnson, *Reaching Out: Interpersonal Effectiveness and Self-Actualization*, 7th ed. (Boston: Allyn & Bacon, 2000), pp. 59–61.

[50]Jack R. Gibb, "Defensive Communication," *Journal of Communication* 2 (1961), pp. 141–148.

[51]David W. Johnson, *Reaching Out: Interpersonal Effectiveness and Self-Actualization*, 7th ed., p. 61.

[52]The original Gibb article was published in 1961 with no references or explanations of his research methodology. Although Gibb's climate categories are interesting, researchers have concluded that "the confidence placed in Gibb's theory of supportive and defensive communication as currently construed has been facile and empirically unwarranted." See Gordon Forward and Kathleen Czech, "Why (Most) Everything You Think You Know About Gibb's Supportive and Defensive Communication Climate May be Wrong and What To Do About It," Paper presented to the Small Group Communication Division at the National Communication Association Convention, San Diego, 2008, p. 16.

[53]Based on Jack R. Gibb, "Defensive Communication," pp. 141–148; also see http://lynn_meade.tripod.com/id61_m.htm.

[54]Robert Plutchik, *Emotions: A Psychoevolutionary Synthesis* (New York: Harper and Row, 1980).

[55]Daniel Goleman, *Working with Emotional Intelligence* (New York: Bantam Books, 1998), p. 317.

[56]See Daniel Goleman, *Emotional Intelligence: Why It Can Matter More Than IQ* (New York: Bantam, 1995); Goleman, 1998; Hendrie Weisinger, *Emotional Intelligence at Work* (San Francisco: Jossey-Bass, 1998).

[57]Robert Plutchik, "Emotions: A General Psychoevolutionary Theory," in *Approaches to Emotion*, ed. K.R. Scherer and Paul Ekman (Mahwah, NJ: Lawrence Erlbaum, 1984), p. 203.

[58]Goleman, *Emotional Intelligence: Why It Can Matter More Than IQ*, pp. 27–28. See also Antonio R. Damasio, *Descartes' Error: Emotion, Reason, and the Human Brain* (New York: Quill, 2000).

[59]Ibid.

[60]Brant R. Burleson, "Emotional Support Skills," in *Handbook of Communication and Social Interaction Skills*, ed. John O. Greene and Brant R. Burleson (Mahwah, NJ: Lawrence Erlbaum, 2003), p. 552.

[61]National Communication Association Credo for Ethical Communication, www.natcom.org/aboutNCA/Policies/Platform.html.

[62]Paula S. Tompkins, *Practicing Communication Ethics* (Boston: Allyn & Bacon, 2011), p. 83.

[63]Elaine E. Englehardt, "Introduction to Ethics in Interpersonal Communication," in *Ethical Issues in Interpersonal Communication*, ed. Elaine E. Englehardt (Fort Worth, TX: Harcourt, 2001), pp. 1–25; Carol Gilligan, "Images of Relationship," and Nel Noddings, "An Ethics of Care," in *Ethical Issues in Interpersonal Communication*, ed. Elaine E. Englehardt (Fort Worth, TX: Harcourt, 2001), pp. 88–96 and 96–103.

[64]Brant R. Burleson, "Emotional Support Skills," pp. 589–681.

[65]Brant R. Burleson, Amanda J. Holmstrom, and Cristina M. Gilstrap, "Guys Can't Say *That* to Guys: Four Experiments Assessing the Normative Motivation Account for Deficiencies in the Emotional Support Provided by Men," *Communication Monographs* 72 (2005), p. 582.

[66]Susan M. Jones and John G. Wirtz, "How Does the Comforting Process Work? An Empirical Test of an Appraisal-Based Model of Comforting," *Human Communication Research* 32 (2006), p. 217.

[67]Brant R. Burleson, "Emotional Support Skills," p. 553.

[68]Ibid., p. 583.

[69]Daniel Goleman, "Friends for Life: An Emerging Biology of Emotional Healing," *The New York Times*, October 10, 2006, p. D5. Also see, Daniel Goleman, *Social Intelligence* (New York: Bantam, 2006).

[70]Nicholas Bakalar, "Five-Second Touch Can Convey Specific Emotions, Study Finds," *The New York Times*, August 11, 2009, p. D3.

[71]Daniel Goleman, *Social Intelligence* (New York: Bantam, 2006), p. 243.

[72]Martin S. Remland, *Nonverbal Communication in Everyday Life*, 2nd ed. (Boston: Houghton Mifflin, 2003), p. 330.

[73]Based on Daniel Goleman, *Emotional Intelligence*; Daniel Goleman, *Working with Emotional Intelligence*; Hendrie Weisinger, *Emotional Intelligence at Work* (San Francisco: Jossey-Bass, 1998).

[74]Based on Daniel Goleman, *Working with Emotional Intelligence*, pp. 26–27.

Chapter 8

[1]Diane Vaughan, *Uncoupling: How Relationships Come Apart* (New York: Vintage Books, 1986), p. 3.

[2]Ibid., p. 6.

[3]Leslie A. Baxter and Barbara M. Montgomery, *Relating: Dialogues and Dialectics* (New York: Guilford Press, 1996), p. 19.

[4]Ibid., p. 5.

[5]See Leslie A. Baxter, "A Dialectical Perspective on Communication Strategies in Relationship Development," in Steve Duck (Ed.), *Handbook of Personal Relationships* (New York, Wiley, 1990), pp. 257–273.

[6]Lawrence B. Rosenfeld, "Overview of the Ways Privacy, Secrecy, and Disclosure Are Balanced in Today's Society," in *Balancing the Secrets of Private Disclosures*, ed. Sandra Petronio (Mahwah: NJ: Lawrence Erlbaum, 2000), p. 5.

[7]Richard West and Lynn H. Turner, *Introducing Communication Theory*, 3rd ed. (New York: McGraw-Hill, 2007), p. 203.

[8]Based on Richard West and Lynn H. Turner, *Introducing Communication Theory*, 2nd ed. (New York: McGraw-Hill, 2004), p. 215. Also see Dominic A. Infante, Andrew S. Rancer, and Deanna F. Womack, *Building Communication Theory*, 4th ed. (Prospect Heights, IL: Waveland, 2003), pp. 212–214; Leslie A. Baxter, "Dialectical Contradictions in Relationships Development," *Journal of Social and Personal Relationships* 6 (1990), pp. 69–88.

[9]Abigail A. Baird, *THINK Psychology* (Upper Saddle River, NJ: Prentice Hall, 2010), p. 4.

[10]Isabel B. Myers with Peter B. Myers, *Gifts Differing: Tenth Anniversary Edition* (Palo Alto, CA: Consulting Psychologists, 1990).

[11]Annie Murphy Paul, *The Cult of Personality* (New York: Free Press, 2004), pp. 125–127.

[12]Exercise caution in accepting and applying psychological theories as "laws" of interpersonal communication. Also note that, "Most people's personalities, psychologists note, do not fall neatly into one category or another, but occupy some intermediate zone. . . . [Nor are these traits necessarily] inborn or immutable types." Annie Murphy Paul, *The Cult of Personality*, pp. 125–127.

[13]Robert E. Levasseur, *Breakthrough Business Meetings: Shared Leadership in Action*. (Holbrook, MA: Bob Adams, 1994), p. 79.

[14]Carl E. Larson and Frank M. J. LaFasto, *TeamWork: What Must Go Right/What Can Go Wrong* (Newbury Park, CA: Sage), p. 63.

[15]Otto Kroeger and Janet M. Thuesen, *Type Talk: Or How to Determine Your Personality Type and Change Your Life* (New York: Delacorte, 1988), p. 80.

[16]This non-validated instrument is a compilation of Myers-Briggs Type Indicator traits based on Isa N. Engleberg's analysis, background, and experience as a certified Myers-Briggs Type Indicator® trainer and a synthesis of MBTI resources (© Isa N. Engleberg). The authorized Myers-Briggs Type Indicator® instrument is for licensed use only by qualified professionals whose qualifications are on file and have been accepted by Consulting Psychologists Press, Inc.

[17]Ronald T. Potter-Efron, *Work Rage: Preventing Anger and Resolving Conflict on the Job* (New York: Barnes and Noble Books, 2000), pp. 22–23.

[18]Kenneth Cloke and Joan Goldsmith, *Resolving Conflicts at Work: A Complete Guide for Everyone on the Job* (San Francisco: Jossey-Bass, 2000), p. 23.

[19]See Kenneth W. Thomas and Ralph W. Kilmann, "Developing a Forced-Choice Measure of Conflict-Handling Behavior: The MODE Instrument," *Educational Psychological Measurement* 37 (1977), pp. 390–395; William W. Wilmot and Joyce L. Hocker, *Interpersonal Conflict*, 7th ed. (New York: McGraw-Hill, 2007), pp. 130–175.

[20]Isa N. Engleberg and Dianna R. Wynn, *Working in Groups: Communication Principles and Strategies*, 5th ed. (Boston: Pearson, Allyn and Bacon, 2010), pp. 214–215, by permission of the publisher and authors.

[21]Ibid., p. 216. Based on Kenneth W. Thomas, *Intrinsic Motivation at Work: Building Energy and Commitment* (San Francisco: Berret-Koehler, 2000), p. 94.

[22]Dominic A. Infante and Andrew S. Rancer, "A Conceptualization and Measure of Argumentativeness," *Journal of Personality Assessment* 46 (1982), pp. 72–80. Reproduced by permission of Society for Personality Assessment. www.personality.org.

[23]Daniel J. Canary and William R. Cupach, *Competencies in Interpersonal Conflict* (New York: McGraw-Hill, 1997), p. 58.

[24]Jerry Wisinski, *Resolving Conflicts on the Job* (New York: American Management Association, 1993), pp. 27–31.

[25]Adapted from Dudley D. Cahn and Ruth Anna Abigail, *Managing Conflict through Communication*, 3rd ed. (Boston: Pearson/Allyn & Bacon, 2007), pp. 97–104.

[26]Cloke and Goldsmith, *Resolving Conflicts at Work: A Complete Guide for Everyone on the Job*, pp. 109–110; *When and How to Apologize*, University of Nebraska Cooperative Extension and the Nebraska Health and Human Services System http://extension.unl.edu/welfare/apology.htm.

notes

[27]Sharon Anthony Bower and Gordon H. Bower, *Asserting Yourself: A Practical Guide to Positive Change* (Cambridge, MA: Perseus Books, 1991), p. 9.

[28]Madelyn Burley-Allen, *Managing Assertively: How to Improve Your People Skills* (New York: John Wiley, 1983), p. 45.

[29]Bower and Bower, *Asserting Yourself: A Practical Guide to Positive Change*, pp. 4–5.

[30]Bower and Bower, *Asserting Yourself: A Practical Guide to Positive Change*, p. 90. See also, "Assertiveness," athealth.com, January 6, 2010, http://www.athealth.com/Consumer/disorders/assertiveness.html

[31]Edmund J. Bourne, *The Anxiety and Phobia Workbook*, 5th ed. (Oakland, CA: Harbinger, 2010), p. 306.

[32]Ibid., p. 307. The example is adapted and written by the textbook authors.

[33]Ibid., p. 307.

[34]Georg H. Eifert, Matthew McKay, and John P. Forsyth, *ACT on Life Not on Anger* (Oakland, CA: New Harbinger, 2006).

[35]Ibid., pp. 15, 16.

[36]Ibid., pp. 19, 20.

[37]Ibid., p. 21.

[38]Carol Tavris, *Anger: The Misunderstood Emotion* (New York: Simon and Schuster, 1982), p. 253.

[39]Aristotle, *Nicomachean Ethics*, translated by W. D. Ross; revised by J. O. Urmson, in *The Complete Works of Aristotle: The Revised Oxford Translation*, ed. Jonathan Barnes. (Princeton, NJ: Princeton University Press, 1984), p. 1776.

[40]Based on studies suggesting guidelines for expressing anger reasonably: See William W. Wilmot and Joyce L. Hocker, *Interpersonal Conflict*, 5th ed. (New York: McGraw Hill, 1998), p. 227.

[41]Bill DeFoore, *Anger: Deal with It, Heal with It, Stop It from Killing You* (Deerfield Beach, FL: Health Communications, 1991), p. viii.

[42]Eifert, McKay, and Forsyth, *ACT on Life Not on Anger*, p. 19.

[43]Canary and Cupach, *Competencies in Interpersonal Conflict*, p. 78.

[44]William W. Wilmot and Joyce L. Hocker, *Interpersonal Conflict*, 5th ed. (New York: McGraw Hill, 1998), p. 228.

[45]Paula S. Tompkins, *Practicing Communication Ethics: Development, Discernment, and Decision Making* (Boston: Allyn & Bacon, 2011), pp. 56–57.

[46]Based on Sissela Bok, *Lying: Moral Choice in Public and Private Life* (New York: Vintage Books, 1978) in Paula S. Tompkins, *Practicing Communication Ethics: Development, Discernment, and Decision Making*, pp. 56–57.

[47]Canary and Cupach, *Competencies in Interpersonal Conflict*, p. 133.

[48]Russell Copranzano, Herman Aguinis, Marshall Schminke, and Dina L. Denham, "Disputant Reactions to Managerial Conflict Resolution Tactics: A Comparison among Argentina, the Dominican Republic, Mexico, and the United States" *Group and Organization Management* 24 (1999), p. 131.

[49]Bren Ortega Murphy, "Promoting Dialogue in Culturally Diverse Workplace Environments," in *Innovation in Group Facilitation: Applications in Natural Settings*, ed. Larry R. Frey (Creskill, NJ: Hampton, 1995), pp. 77–93.

[50]Deborah Tannen, *You Just Don't Understand: Women and Men in Conversation* (New York: William Morrow, 1990).

[51]William W. Wilmot and Joyce L. Hocker, *Interpersonal Conflict*, 5th ed. (New York: McGraw Hill, 1998), p. 25.

[52]Ibid., p. 26.

[53]John Gottman and Nan Silver, *Seven Principles for Making Marriages Work* (New York: Three Rivers Press, 1999), pp. 38–39.

[54]© Isa N. Engleberg, 2010.

Chapter 9

[1]Teresa Amabile and Steven Kramer, "Do Happier People Work Harder?" *The New York Times*, September 4, 2011, p. SR 7.

[2]James M. Kouzes and Barry Z. Posner, *Encouraging the Heart: A Leader's Guide to Rewarding and Recognizing Others* (San Francisco: Jossey-Bass, 1999), p. 4.

[3]Matthew Gilbert, *Communication Miracles at Work: Effective Tools and Tips for Getting the Most from Your Work Relationships* (Berkeley, CA: Conari Press, 2002), p. 112.

[4]Ibid., p. 198.

[5]Based on a Gallup Poll reported in Amabile and Steven, "Do Happier People Work Harder?" 2011, p. SR 7.

[6]Daniel P. Modaff, Sue DeWine, and Jennifer A. Butler, *Organizational Communication: Foundations, Challenges, Misunderstandings* (Los Angeles, CA: Roxbury, 2008), p. 197.

[7]Ibid., p. 198.

[8]Ibid., p. 206.

[9]Ibid., p. 207.

[10]Hal Plotkin, "Introduction," *Dealing with Difficult People* (Boston: Harvard Business School Press, 2005), p. 1.

[11]Hal Plotkin, "Feedback in the Future Tense," *Dealing with Difficult People* (Boston: Harvard Business School Press, 2005), pp. 132–137.

[12]Ken Cloke and Joan Goldsmith, "How to Handle Difficult Behaviors," in *Dealing with Difficult People* (Boston: Harvard Business School Press, 2005), pp. 66–67.

[13]Robert Longley, "Labor Studies of Attitudes toward Work and Leisure: U.S. Workers Are Happy and Stress Is Over-stressed," August 1999, http://usgovinfo.about.com/od/censusandstatsitics/a/labordaystudy.htm.

[14]Gilbert, *Communication Miracles at Work: Effective Tools and Tips for Getting the Most from Your Work Relationships*, p. 153.

[15]Modaff, DeWine, and Butler, *Organizational Communication: Foundations, Challenges, Misunderstandings*, pp. 236–237.

[16]Ibid., p. 157.

[17]Based on Carley H. Dodd, *Managing Business and Professional Communication* (Boston: Allyn & Bacon, 2004), pp. 169–170.

[18]Council of Better Business Bureaus, "Dealing with Unruly Customers." http://www.bbb.org/alerts/article.asp?ID=370.

[19]John Tschohl, Service Quality Institute, "Service, Not Servitude: Common Sense Is Critical Element of Customer Service," 2004, http://www.customer-service.com/articles/022502.cfm.

[20]Dodd, *Managing Business and Professional Communication*, p. 40.

[21]Michael E. Pacanowsky and Nick O'Donnell-Trujillo, "Communication and Organizational Cultures," *Western Journal of Speech Communication*, 46 (1982), pp. 115–130; Michael E. Pacanowsky and Nick O'Donnell-Trujillo, *Communication Monographs* 50 (1983), pp. 127–130.

[22]Joel Lovell, "Workplace Rumors Are True," *The New York Times*, December 10, 2006. http://www.nytimes.com/2006/12/10/magazine/10section4.t-9.html.

[23]Ibid.

[24]Rachel Devine, "Work and Career: Gossip Galore," *iVillage Work & Career*, http://www.ivillage.co.uk/workcareer/survive/opolotics/articles/#0,,156475_164246,00.html.

[25]Quoted in Samuel Greengard, "Gossip Poisons Business: HR Can Stop It," *Workforce* (July 2001), http://www.findarticles.com/p/articles/mi_m0FXS/is_7_80/ai_76938891.

[26]Devine, "Work and Career: Gossip Galore,"; Carl Skooglund and Glenn Coleman, "Advice from the Ethics Office at Texas Instruments Corporation: Gossiping at Work" *Online Ethics Center for Engineering and Science* (2004), http://onlineethics.org/corp/gossip.html; Muriel Solomon, *Working with Difficult People* (New York: Prentice Hall, 2002), pp. 125–126.

[27]Samuel Greengard, "Gossip Poisons Business: HR Can Stop It," *Workforce* (July 2001), http://www.findarticles.com/p/articles/mi_m0FXS/is_7_80/ai_76938891. "Rumor Has It—Dealing with Misinformation in the Workplace," *Entrepreneur* (September 1, 1997), http://www.findarticles.com/p/articles/mi_m0DTI/is_n9_v25/ai_19892317.

[28]"Study: 54 Percent of Companies Ban Facebook, Twitter at Work, *Wired.Com*, October 9, 2009. http://www.wired.com/epicenter/2009/10/study-54-of-companies-ban-facebook-twitter-at-work.

[29]Sharon Gaudin, "Study: Facebook Use Cuts Productivity at Work, *Computerworld*, July 22, 2009. http://www.computerworld.com/s/article/print/9139020/Study_54_of_companies_ban_Facebook_Twitter_at_work?taxonomyName=Web+2.0+and+Web+Apps&taxonomyId=16.

[30]Association of Corporate Counsel, "Workplace Challenges Associated with Employees' Social Media Use," *Legal Resources QuickCounsel*, http://www.acc.com/legalresources/quickcounsel/wcawesmu.cfm.

[31]Carrie-Ann Skinner, "Twitter, Facebook Can Improve Work Productivity," *PCWorld*, April 2, 2009. http://www.pcworld.com/businesscenter/article/162478/twitter_facebook_can_improve_work_productivity.html.

[32]Ibid.; "Working It—L.A. Stories—Survey Data on Office Romances," *Los Angeles Business Journal* (May 27, 2002), http://www.findarticles.com/p/articles/mi_/5072/is_21_24/ai_91233190.

[33]Ed Piantek, "Flirting with Disaster," *Risk and Insurance* (May 1, 2000), http://www.findarticles.com/p/articles/mi_m0BJK/is_200_May/ai_62408701.

[34]Bill Leonard, "Workplace Romances Seem to Be Rule, Not Exception," *HR Magazine* (April 2001), http://www.findarticles.com/p/articles/mi_m3495/is_4_46/ai_73848276.

[35]Piantek, "Flirting with Disaster," *Risk and Insurance*.

[36]U.S. Equal Employment Opportunity Commission, "Facts about Sexual Harassment" (June 27, 2002), http://www.eeoc.gov/facts/fs-sex.html.

[37]Quoted in *HaLife*, "Be Cautious with a Workplace Romance" (2004), http://halife.com/business/mayromance/html.

[38]Ibid.

[39]Deborah Ware Balogh, "The Effects of Delayed Report and Motive for Reporting on Perceptions of Sexual Harassment," *Sex Roles: A Journal of Research* (April 2003), http://www.findarticles.com/p/articles/mi_m2294/is_2003_April/ai_101174064.

[40]Julie A. Woodzicka and Marianne LaFrance, "Real Versus Imagined Gender Harassment," *Journal of Social Issues* (Spring 2001), http://www.findarticles.com/p/articles/mi_m0341/is_1_57/ai_75140959.

[41]Balogh, "The Effects of Delayed Report and Motive for Reporting on Perceptions of Sexual Harassment."

[42]Piantek, "Flirting with Disaster." *Risk and Insurance*.

[43]Nichole L. Torres, "Boys Will Not Be Boys: Lewdness and Rudeness Can Be a Mess for Your Business—Even Without Mixed Company," *Entrepreneur* (November 1, 2001), http://www.findarticles.com/p/articles/mi_m0DTI/is_11_29/ai_83663647.

[44]Rebecca A. Thacker and Stephen F. Gohmann, "Male/Female Differences in Perceptions and Effects of Hostile Environment Sexual Harassment: 'Reasonable' Assumptions?" *Public Personnel Management*, September 22, 1993, http://www.allbusiness.com/human-resources/workforce-management/401746-1.html. See also Maria Rotundo, Dung-Hanh Nguyen, and Paul R. Sacket, "A Meta-analytic Review of Gender Differences in Perceptions of Sexual Harassment," *Journal of Applied Psychology* 86, no. 5 (October 2001), pp. 914–922.

[45] Modaff, DeWine, and Butler, *Organizational Communication: Foundations, Challenges, Misunderstandings*, p. 236.

[46] Cited in Gilbert, *Communication Miracles at Work: Effective Tools and Tips for Getting the Most from Your Work Relationships*, p. 10; See also Humphrey Taylor, "The Mood of American Workers" *Harris Interactive*, January 19, 2000, http://www.harrisinteractive.com/harris_poll.

[47] Based on Daniel P. Modaff and Sue DeWine, *Organizational Communication: Foundations, Challenges, Misunderstandings* (Los Angeles, CA: Roxbury, 2002), p. 202.

[48] Marky Stein, "89-Day Career Change Media Challenge," July 29, 2004. http://ca.preweb.com/releases./2004/7/preweb144867.htm.

[49] Virginia Galt, "When Quitting a Job, Discretion Is the Better Part of Valor," http://globeandmail.workopolis.com/servlet/Content/fasttrack/2004041; Peggy Post, "Rules to Live By: Quitting Your Job," http://magazines.ivillage.com/goodhousekeeping/print/0,,636770,00.html.

[50] Based on How to Cope With Job Loss, *eHow*, http://www.ehow.com/how_2084091_cope-job-loss.html.

[51] Matt Villano, "What to Tell the Company as You Walk out the Door," *The New York Times*, November 27, 2005, p. BU8. Quoting Jim Atkinson, regional vice president, Right Management Consultants.

[52] Dawn Rosenberg McKay, "Job Loss: How to Cope" (2009), http://careerplanning.about.com/od/jobloss/a/job_loss.htm.

[53] This definition is a composite of components found in most academic definitions of an interview. See, for example, Larry Powell and Jonathan Amsbary, *Interviewing: Situations and Contexts* (Boston: Pearson/Allyn & Bacon, 2006), p. 1; Charles Stewart and William B. Cash, *Interviewing: Principles and Practices*, 10th ed. (New York: McGraw-Hill, 2003), p. 4; Jeanne Tessier Barone and Jo Young Switzer, *Interviewing Art and Skill* (Boston: Allyn & Bacon, 1995), p. 8.

[54] Richard Nelson Bolles, *What Color Is Your Parachute? A Practical Manual for Job-Hunters and Career-Changers* (Berkeley: Ten Speed Press, 2007), p. 78.

[55] Accountemps study displayed in *USA Today* Snapshots, "Most Common Job Interview Mistakes Noticed by Employers," *USA Today*, October 17, 2006, p. B1.

[56] "Lying: How Can You Protect Your Company?" http://www.westaff.com/yourworkplace/ywissues37_full.html.

[57] Daryl Koehn, University of St. Thomas Center for Business Ethics, "Rewriting History: Resume Falsification More Than a Passing Fiction," http://www.stthom.edu/cbes/resume.html.

[58] Donna Hemmila, "Tired of Lying, Cheating Job Applicants, Employers Calling in Detectives," *San Francisco Business Times* 12, no. 29 (February 27–March 5, 1998), http://www.esrcheck.com/articles/Tired-of-lying-cheating-job-applicants-employers-calling-in-detectives.php.

[59] Barbara Mende, "Employers Crack down on Candidates Who Lie," *Wall Street Journal Career Journal*, http://www.careerjournal.com/jobhunting/resumes/20020606-mende.html.

[60] Wallace V. Schmidt and Conaway, *Results-Oriented Interviewing: Principles, Practices, and Procedures* (Boston: Allyn & Bacon, 1999), p. 84.

[61] Powell and Amsbary, *Interviewing: Situations and Contexts*, p. 47; Schmidt and Conaway, *Results-Oriented Interviewing: Principles, Practices, and Procedures*, p. 107; Stewart and Cash, *Interviewing: Principles and Practices*, p. 245; Job Link USA, "Interview," http://www.joblink-usa.com/interview.htm; CollegeGrad.Com, "Candidate Interview Questions," http://www.collegegrad.com/jobsearch/16-15.shtml.

[62] Schmidt and Conaway, *Results-Oriented Interviewing: Principles, Practices, and Procedures*, pp. 34–37.

[63] Stewart and Cash, *Interviewing: Principles and Practices*, pp. 254–255; "Candidate Interview Questions," http://www.collegegrad.com/jobsearch/16-15.shtml.

[64] Schmidt and Conaway, *Results-Oriented Interviewing: Principles, Practices, and Procedures*, pp. 100–111.

[65] Bolles, *What Color Is Your Parachute? A Practical Manual for Job-Hunters and Career-Changers*, p. 82.

[66] Schmidt and Conaway, *Results-Oriented Interviewing: Principles, Practices, and Procedures*, pp. 100–111.

[67] Mary Heiberger and Julia Miller Vick, "How To Handle Difficult Interview Questions," *Chronicle of Higher Education*, January 22, 1999, http://chronicle.com/jobs/v45/i21/4521career.htm; Allison Doyle, "Illegal Interview Questions: Illegal Interview Question Samples," http://jobsearch.about.com/library/weekly/aa0224032/htm.

Chapter 10

[1] Many web sites provide detailed information about the ways in which the Chilean miners organized themselves into an effective group. For examples, see Alonso Soto and Irene Klotz, "Space, Oceans Hold Clues to Chile Miners' Survival," *Reuters*, http://www.reuters.com/assets/print?aid=USTRE67O05Q20100825, 2010; Chilean Miners' Survival 'May Provide a Lesson in Human Resilience,'" NewKerala, http://www.newkeraqla.com/news/world/fullnews-64474.html; 2010 Copiapo Mining Accident, http://en.wikipedia.org/wiki/2010_Copiap%C3%B3_mining_accident.

[2] Donelson R. Forsyth, *Group Dynamics*, 5th ed. (Belmont, CA: Wadsworth/Cengage Learning, 2010), p. 470.

[3] Steve W. J. Kozlowski and Daniel R. Ilgen (2006). "Enhancing the Effectiveness of Work Groups and Teams," *Psychological Science in the Public Interest*, 7 (3), p. 77.

[4] Peter D. Hart Research Associates, *How Should Colleges Prepare Students to Succeed in Today's Global Economy?* (Washington, D.C.: Peter D. Hart Research Associates, December 28, 2006), p. 2; See also Association of American Colleges and Universities, *College Learning for the New Global Age* (Washington, D.C.: Association of American Colleges and Universities, 2007).

[5] Peter D. Hart Research Associates, *How Should Colleges Prepare Students to Succeed in Today's Global Economy?* p. 7.

[6] Patrick C. Kyllonen, *The Research Behind the ETS Personal Potential Index (PPI)* (2008), Background Paper from the Educational Testing Service, http://www.ets.org/Media/Products/PPI/10411_PPI_bkgrd_report_RD4.pdf. See also Daniel S. de Vise, "New Index Will Score Graduate Students' Personality Tests," *The Washington Post*, July 10, 2009, p. A11.

[7] American Management Association "2010 Critical Skills Survey," quoted in Elaine Pofeldt, "Put Some Punch Into Your Career," *Money*, May 2011, p. 24.

[8] This definition is modified from Isa N. Engleberg and Dianna R. Wynn, *Working in Groups: Communication Principles and Strategies*, 5th ed. (Boston: Pearson/Allyn & Bacon, 2010), p. 4.

[9] Carl E. Larson and Frank M. J. LaFasto, *TeamWork: What Must Go Right/What Can Go Wrong* (Newbury Park, CA: Sage, 1989), p. 27.

[10] Jon R. Katzenbach and Douglas K. Smith, *The Wisdom of Teams: Creating the High-Performance Organization* (New York: HarperBusiness, 1999), p. 9.

[11] Robert B. Cialdini, "The Perils of Being the Best and the Brightest," *Becoming an Effective Leader* (Boston: Harvard Business School Press, 2005), pp. 174, 175.

[12] 3M Meeting Management Team with Jeannine Drew, *Mastering Meetings: Discovering the Hidden Potential of Effective Business Meetings* (New York: McGraw-Hill, 1994), p. 12.

[13] Deborah L. Duarte and Nancy Tennant Snyder, *Mastering Virtual Teams*, 3rd ed. (San Francisco: Jossey-Bass, 2007), pp. 21, 158.

[14] Engleberg and Wynn, *Working in Groups: Communication Principles and Strategies*, 5th ed., pp. 203–207.

[15] Ernest G. Bormann, *Small Group Communication: Theory and Practice*, 3rd ed. (Edina, MN: Burgess, 1996), pp. 132–135, 181–183.

[16] Bruce W. Tuckman, "Developmental Sequence in Small Groups," *Psychological Bulletin* 63 (1965), pp. 384–399. Tuckman's 1965 article is reprinted in *Group Facilitation: A Research and Applications Journal* 3 (Spring 2001), http://dennislearningcenter.osu.edu/references/Group%20DEV%20ARTICLE.doc. Note: Tuckman and Jensen identified a fifth stage—adjourning—in the 1970s. There is little research on the characteristics and behavior of members during this stage other than a decrease in interaction and, in some cases, separation anxiety. See Bruce Tuckman and Mary Ann Jensen, "Stages of Small-Group Development Revisited," *Group and Organization Studies* 2 (1977), pp. 419–427.

[17] Artemis Change, Julie Duck, and Prashant Bordia, "Understanding the Multidimensionality of Group Development," *Small Group Research* 37 (2006), p. 329.

[18] Ibid., pp. 331, 337–338.

[19] Susan Wheelan and Nancy Brewer Danganan, "The Relationship Between the Internal Dynamics of Student Affairs Leadership Teams and Campus Leaders' Perceptions of the Effectiveness of Student Affairs Divisions," *Journal of Student Affairs Research and Practice*, 40 (2002), p. 27

[20] Rodney W. Napier and Matti K. Gershenfeld, *Groups: Theory and Experience*, 7th ed. (Boston: Houghton Mifflin, 2004), p. 182.

[21] Wheelan and Danganan, "The Relationship Between the Internal Dynamics of Student Affairs Leadership Teams and Campus Leaders' Perceptions of the Effectiveness of Student Affairs Divisions," p. 96.

[22] Ernest G. Bormann, *Small Group Communication Theory and Practice*, 6th ed. (Edina, MN: Burgess International, 1996), pp. 134–135.

[23] Donald G. Ellis and B. Aubrey Fisher, *Small Group Decision Making: Communication and the Group Process*, 4th ed. (New York: McGraw-Hill, 1994), pp. 43–44.

[24] Marvin E. Shaw, "Group Composition and Group Cohesiveness" in *Small Group Communication: A Reader*, 6th ed., ed. Robert S. Cathcart and Larry A. Samovar (Dubuque, IA: Wm. C. Brown, 1992), pp. 214–220.

[25] Patricia H. Andrews, "Group Conformity," in *Small Group Communication: Theory and Practice*, 7th ed., ed. Robert S. Cathcart, Larry A. Samovar, and Linda D. Henman (Madison, WI: Brown and Benchmark, 1996), p. 185.

[26] Nicky Hayes, *Managing Teams: A Strategy for Success* (London: Thomson, 2004), p. 31.

[27] Kenneth D. Benne and Paul Sheats, "Functional Roles of Group Members," *Journal of Social Issues* 4 (1948), pp. 41–49. We have modified the original Benne and Sheats list by adding or combining behaviors that we have observed, as well as roles identified by other writers and researchers.

[28] Ibid.

[29] Ibid.

[30] Based on Michael Doyle and David Straus, *How to Make Meetings Work* (New York: Jove, 1976), pp. 107–117. Several titles and behaviors are original contributions by the authors.

[31] James C. McCroskey and Virginia P. Richmond, "Correlates of Compulsive Communication: Quantitative and Qualitative Characteristics," *Communication Quarterly* 43 (1995), pp. 39–52.

[32] Eric Harper, David Cottrell, Al Lucia, and Mike Hourigan, *The Leadership Secrets of Santa Claus: How to Get Big Things Done in YOUR "Workshop" . . . All Year Long* (Dallas, TX: The Walk the Talk Company, 2003), pp. 78–79.

[33]Isa N. Engleberg and Dianna R. Wynn, *Working in Groups: Communication Principles and Strategies*, 3rd ed. (Boston: Houghton Mifflin, 2004), p. 207.

[34]Antony Bell, *Great Leadership: What It Is and What It Takes in a Complex World* (Mountain View, CA: Davies-Black, 2006), pp. 87, 91.

[35]Fred E. Feidler and Martin M. Chemers, *Improving Leadership Effectiveness: The Leader Match Concept*, 2nd ed. (New York: Wiley, 1984).

[36]See Joseph R. Santo, Where the Fortune 50 CEIOs Went to College, *Time*, August 15, 2006, http://www.time.com/time/printout/0,8816,1227055,00.html.

[37]Ivan G. Seidenberg, Reference for Business, *Encyclopedia of Business*, 2nd edition, http://www.referenceforbusiness.com/biography/S-Z/Seidenberg-Ivan-G-1946.html.

[38]*Forbes Magazine*, 2010, http://www.forbes.com/2009/05/06/richest-black-americans-business-billionaires-richest-black-americans.html; http://billionaires.forbes.com/article/0eAPBmrcJhaSj/articles?q=billionaire+OR+billionaires+OR+billionaire%27s.

[39]"John Boehner, U.S. House Majority Leader," Encyclopedia of World Biography, http://www.notablebiographies.com/newsmakers2/2006-A-Ec/Boehner-John-A.html.

[40]Based on material in Engleberg and Wynn, *Working in Groups: Communication Principles and Strategies*, 5th ed., pp. 113–114.

[41]Edwin P. Hollander, *Leadership Dynamics: A Practical Guide to Effective Relationships* (New York: Macmillan, 1978), p. 53. Also see a meta-analysis of this variable in Marianne Schmid Mast, "Dominance as Expressed and Inferred through Speaking Time," *Human Communication Research* 28 (2002), pp. 420–450.

[42]CNN 2012 Poll: Obama and Palin Going in Different Directions? December 28, 2010 http://politicalticker.blogs.cnn.com/2010/12/28/cnn-2012-poll-obama-palin-going-in-different-directions/.

[43]The 5-M Model of Effective Leadership© is based, in part, on Martin M. Chemers's integrative theory of leadership, which identifies three functional aspects of leadership: image management, relationship development, and resource utilization. We have added two more functions—decision making and mentoring—and have incorporated more of a communication perspective into Chemers's view of leadership as a multifaceted process. See Martin M. Chemers, *An Integrative Theory of Leadership* (Mahwah, NJ: Lawrence Erlbaum, 1997), pp. 151–173.

[44]Mike Krzyzewski, "Coach K on How to Connect," *The Wall Street Journal*, 16–17 July 2011, p. C12.

[45]Martin M. Chemers, *An Integrative Theory of Leadership* (Mahwah, NJ: Lawrence Erlbaum, 1997), p. 160.

[46]Harvey Robbins and Michael Finley, *The New Why Teams Don't Work: What Goes Wrong and How to Make It Right* (San Francisco: Berrett-Koehler, 2000), p. 107.

[47]Carol Tice, "Building the 21st Century Leader," *Entrepreneur* (February 2007), pp. 66, 67.

[48]Ibid., p. 68.

[49]Bell, *Great Leadership: What It Is and What It Takes in a Complex World*, p. 67.

[50]James M. Kouzes and Barry Z. Posner, *Credibility: How Leaders Gain and Lose It, Why People Demand It* (San Francisco: Jossey-Bass, 1993), pp. 230–231.

[51]Susan B. Shimanoff and Mercilee M. Jenkins, "Leadership and Gender: Challenging Assumptions and Recognizing Resources," in *Small Group Communication: Theory and Practice*, 7th ed., ed. Robert S. Cathcart, Larry A. Samovar, and Linda D. Henman (Madison, WI: Brown and Benchmark, 1996), p. 327.

[52]Chemers, *An Integrative Theory of Leadership*, p. 126.

Chapter 11

[1]Tim Dirks, *12 Angry Men* (1957), http://www.filmsite.org/twelve.html; *12 Angry Men* was remade for television in 1997. In this production, the judge is a woman and four of the jurors are African American. The producers decided against putting a woman in the jury because they didn't want to change the title. Still, most of the action and dialogue of the film is identical to the original. Modernizations include a prohibition on smoking in the jury room, the changing of references to income and pop culture figures, more dialogue relating to race, and profanity.

[2]Tim Dirks, *12 Angry Men*.

[3]Marshall Scott Poole and Randy Y. Hirokawa, "Introduction: Communication and Group Decision Making," in *Communication and Group Decision Making*, 2nd ed. ed. Randy Y. Hirokawa and Marshall Scott Poole (Thousand Oaks, CA: Sage, 1996), p. 1.

[4]Rodney W. Napier and Matti K. Gershenfeld, *Groups: Theory and Experience*, 7th ed. (Boston: Houghton Mifflin, 2004), p. 291.

[5]Peter R. Drucker, *The Effective Executive* (New York: HarperBusiness, 1967), p. 143.

[6]Randy Y. Hirokawa, "Communication and Group Decision-Making Efficacy," in *Small Group Communication: Theory and Practice*, 7th ed., ed. Robert S. Cathcart, Larry A. Samovar, and Linda D. Henman (Madison, WI: Brown and Benchmark, 1996), p. 108.

[7]Marshall Scott Poole, "Procedures for Managing Meetings: Social and Technological Innovation," in *Innovative Meeting Management*, ed. Richard A. Swanson and Bonnie Ogram Knapp (Austin, TX: 3M Meeting Management Institute, 1990), pp. 54–55.

[8]Keith Sawyer, *Group Genius: The Creative Power of Collaboration* (New York: Basic Books, 2007), pp. 66–67. Sawyer attributes the story to Dale Carnegie.

[9]Irving L. Janis, *Groupthink*, 2nd ed. (Boston: Houghton Mifflin, 1982), p. 9.

[10]Ibid.

[11]John Gastil, *The Group in Society* (Los Angeles: Sage, 2010), p. 82.

[12]Ibid.

[13]Donelson R. Forsyth, *Group Dynamics*, 5th ed. (Belmont, CA: Wadsworth/Cengage, 2010), p. 342.

[14]Julia T. Wood, "Alternative Methods of Group Decision Making," in *Small Group Communication: A Reader*, 6th ed., ed. Robert S. Cathcart and Larry A. Samovar (Dubuque, IA: Wm. C. Brown, 1992), p. 159.

[15]Napier and Gershenfeld, *Groups: Theory and Experience*, 7th ed., p. 337.

[16]Randy Hirokawa and Roger Pace, "A Descriptive Investigation of the Possible Communication-Based Reasons for Effective and Ineffective Group Decision Making," *Communication Monographs* 50 (1983): p. 379.

[17]Donald G. Ellis and B. Aubrey Fisher, *Small Group Decision Making* (New York: McGraw-Hill, 1994), p. 142

[18]John R. Katzenbach and Douglas K. Smith, *The Discipline of Teams* (New York: Wiley, 2001), p. 112.

[19]Ibid., p. 113.

[20]Suzanne Scott and Reginald Bruce "Decision Making Style: The Development of a New Measure," *Educational and Psychological Measurements* 55 (1995): 818–831.

[21]Adapted from Karyn C. Rybacki and Donald J. Rybacki, *Advocacy and Opposition: An Introduction to Argumentation*, 4th ed. (Boston: Allyn & Bacon, 2000), pp. 11–15.

[22]Scott and Bruce, "Decision Making Style: The Development of a New Measure." Reginald A. Bruce and Susanne G. Scott, "The Moderating Effective of Decision-Maling Style on the Turnover Process: An Extension of Previous Research," http://cobweb2.louisville.edu/faculty/regbruce/bruce//research/japturn.htm; Decision Making Styles, UCD Career Development Center, 2006, http://www.ucd.ie/careers/cms/decision/student_skills_decision_styleex.html;

[23]Alex F. Osborn, *Applied Imagination*, rev. ed. (New York: Scribner, 1957).

[24]Based, in part, on Tom Kelley with Jonathan Littman, *The Art of Innovation: Lessons in Creativity from IDEO, America's Leading Design Firm* (New York: Currency, 2001), pp. 56–59. Also see Napier and Gershenfeld, *Groups: Theory and Experience*, 7th ed., p. 321.

[25]3M Meeting Management Team with Jeannine Drew, *Mastering Meetings: Discovering the Hidden Potential of Effective Business Meetings* (New York: McGraw-Hill, 1994), p. 59.

[26]Kelley with Littman, *The Art of Innovation: Lessons in Creativity from IDEO, America's Leading Design Firm*, p. 55.

[27]Ibid pp. 64–66.

[28]Isa N. Engleberg and Dianna R. Wynn, *Working in Groups: Communication Principles and Strategies*, 5th ed. (Boston: Pearson/Allyn & Bacon, 2010), pp. 256–258.

[29]See Kenneth E. Andersen, "Developments in Communication Ethics: The Ethics Commission, Code of Professional Responsibilities, and Credo for Ethical Communication," *Journal of the Association for Communication Administration* 29 (2000): 131–144. The Credo for Ethical Communication is also posted on the NCA Website (http://www.natcom.org).

[30]John Dewey, *How We Think* (Boston: Heath, 1910).

[31]Based on Kathryn Sue Young, Julia T. Wood, Gerald M. Phillips, and Douglas J. Pedersen, *Group Discussion: A Practical Guide to Participation and Leadership*, 3rd ed. (Prospect Heights, IL: Waveland Press, 2001), pp. 8–9. The authors present six steps in their standard-agenda model by combining solution suggestions and solution selection into one step. We have divided this step into separate functions given that the solution suggestion step may require creative thinking and brainstorming. Given that the solution evaluation and selection step may be the most difficult and controversial, it deserves a separate focus as well as different strategies and skills.

[32]Deborah L. Duarte and Nancy Tennant Snyder, *Mastering Virtual Teams*, 3rd ed. (San Francisco: Jossey-Bass, 2006), p. 171.

[33]Ibid., pp. 33–34, 168.

[34]Katzenbach and Smith, *The Discipline of Teams*, p. 167.

[35]Napier and Gershenfeld, *Groups: Theory and Experience*, 7th ed., p. 327.

[36]Edward De Bono, *New Thinking for the New Millennium* (New York: Viking, 1999) quoted in Darrell Man, "Analysis Paralysis: When Root Cause Analysis Isn't the Way," *The TRIZ-Journal*, 2006, http://www.triz-journal.com.

[37]"Avoid Analysis Paralysis," Infusion Insight, http://www.infusionsoft.com/articles/65-infusion-insight/615-avoid-analysis-paralysis.

[38]Edward D. McDonald, "Chaos or Communication: Technical Barriers to Effective Meetings," in *Innovative Meeting Management*, ed. Richard A. Swanson and Bonnie Ogram Knapp (Austin, TX: Minnesota Mining and Manufacturing, 1991), p. 177.

[39]Poole, "Procedures for Managing Meetings: Social and Technological Innovation," p. 53.

[40]Dave Wiggins, "How to Have a Successful Meeting," *Journal of Environmental Health* 60 (1998): 1, http://db.texshare.org/ovidweb/ovidweb.cgi.

[41]"Office Communication Toolkit: 7 Common Employee Gripes," Special Report from *Business Management Daily*, September 22, 2009.

[42]Tyler Cowen, "On My Mind: In Favor of Face Time," October 1, 2007, www.members.forbes.com/forbes/2007/1001/030.html.

[43]Karen Anderson, *Making Meetings Work: How to Plan and Conduct Effective Meetings* (West Des Moines, IA: American Media Publishing, 1997), p. 17.

[44]Sharon M. Lippincott, *Meetings: Do's, Don'ts, and Donuts* (Pittsburgh, PA: Lighthouse Point Press, 1994), p. 172.

[45]3M Meeting Management Team with Jeannine Drew, *Mastering Meetings: Discovering the Hidden Potential of Effective Business Meetings* (New York: McGraw-Hill, 1994), p. 78.

[46]Engleberg and Wynn, *Working in Groups: Communication Principles and Strategies*, 5th ed., pp. 299–300; Lippincott, *Meetings: Do's, Don'ts, and Donuts*, pp. 89–90.

Chapter 12

[1]Nicholas Jonas, "Diabetes Awareness," National Press Club, August 24, 2009, http://www.press.org/members/transcriptview.cfm?pdf=20090824_jonas.pdf.

[2]Martin McDermott, *Speak with Courage: 50 Insider Strategies for Presenting with Ease and Confidence* (CreateSpace/Amazon: Martin McDermott, 2010), p. 52, 54. See www.martinmcdermott.com.

[3]John A. Daly, Anita L. Vangelisti, and David J. Weber (1995), "Speech Anxiety Affects How People Prepare Speeches: A Protocol Analysis of the Preparation Process of Speaking," *Communication Monographs* 62, pp. 283–398.

[4]Ibid., p. 396.

[5]McDermott, *Speak with Courage: 50 Insider Strategies for Presenting with Ease and Confidence*, p. 53, 54.

[6]The complete, 24-item survey is available in the *Instructor's Manual* that accompanies this textbook. Class results can be compared to those of both types of survey respondents: book buyers who speak professionally and students enrolled in a college public speaking course.

[7]We conducted the survey of book buyers in collaboration with the Market Research Department at Houghton Mifflin, a former publisher. Survey items included traditional topics usually covered in public speaking textbooks. Approximately two thousand copies of a two-page questionnaire were mailed to individuals who had recently purchased a commercially available public speaking book and who had used a business address to secure the purchase. We received 281 usable questionnaires, resulting a response rate of 11 percent. Respondents were geographically dispersed. Twenty-five percent worked in industry. Workers in government (10 percent), health (10 percent) and nonprofit organizations (10 percent) made up 30 percent of respondents. Nine percent came from the financial industry; another 9 percent worked in technology related industries. Approximately 25 percent of the respondents, including business owners and independent contractors, worked in "other" occupations. More recently, we administered a similar survey to 600 college students enrolled in a basic public speaking course. Respondents attended various types of geographically dispersed institutions of higher education (community colleges, liberal arts colleges, and large universities). We received more than six hundred usable questionnaires.

[8]Isa N. Engleberg and John A. Daly, *Presentations in Everyday Life*, 3rd ed. (Boston: Pearson/Allyn & Bacon, 2009), p. 3 and Note 5 on p. 21.

[9]Milton Rokeach, *The Nature of Human Values* (New York: Free Press, 1973), p. 3.

[10]Rushworth M. Kidder, "Trust: A Primer on Current Thinking," Institute for Global Ethics, 7, http://www.globalethics.org/files/wp_trust_1222960968.pdf/21/.

[11]Gene Zelazny, *Say It with Presentations*, Revised (New York: McGraw-Hill, 2006), pp. 4–6.

[12]Engleberg and Daly, *Presentations in Everyday Life*, 3rd ed., p. 113.

[13]Ibid., p. 126.

[14]*The American Heritage Dictionary of the English Language*, 4th ed. (Boston: Houghton Mifflin, 2000), p. 427.

[15]Malcolm Kushner, *Successful Presentations for Dummies* (Foster City, CA: IDG Books Worldwide, 1997), p. 21.

[16]The earliest and most respected source describing the components of a speaker's credibility is Aristotle's *Rhetoric*, trans. Lane Cooper (New York: Appleton-Century-Crofts, 1932), p. 92. Aristotle identified "intelligence, character, and good will" as "three things that gain our belief." Aristotle's observations have been verified and expanded. In addition to those qualities identified by Aristotle, researchers have added variables such as objectivity, trustworthiness, co-orientation, dynamism, composure, likability, and extroversion. Research has consolidated these qualities into three well-accepted attributes: competence, character, and dynamism. We have used the term *charisma* in place of dynamism.

[17]Lane Cooper, *The Rhetoric of Aristotle* (New York: Appleton-Century-Crofts, 1932), p. 7.

[18]Ibid., p. 8,9.

[19]Lester Thonssen and A. Craig Baird, *Speech Criticism: The Development of Standards for Rhetorical Appraisal* (New York: The Ronald Press, 1948).

[20]James R. Andrews, Michael C. Leff, and Robert Terrill, *Reading Rhetorical Texts: An Introduction to Criticism* (Boston: Houghton Mifflin, 1998), p. 59.

[21]Kushner, *Successful Presentations for Dummies*, p. 21.

[22]*The American Heritage Dictionary of the English Language*, 4th ed., p. 611.

[23]"Blair Hornstine: "Stories, Essays Lack Attribution," *The Courier Post*, June 3, 2003; http://www.newworldencyclopedia.org/entry/Plagiarism#Famous_examples_and_accusations_of_plagiarism.

[24]Joseph C. Self, "The 'My Sweet Lord/He's So Fine' Plagiarism Suits," *The 901 Magazine*, 2003, http://abbeyrd.best.vwh.net/mysweet.htm; http://www.newworldencyclopedia.org/entry/Plagiarism#Famous_examples_and_accusations_of_plagiarism.

[25]Esther B. Fein, Book Notes, The New York Times, March 3, 1993, http://select.nytimes.com/gst/abstract.html?res=F00613FC3E580C708CDDAA0894DB494D81&pagewanted=print=Fhttp; http://www.newworldencyclopedia.org/entry/Plagiarism#Famous_examples_and_accusations_of_plagiarism.

[26]Julie J. C. H. Ryan, "Student Plagiarism in an Online World," *Prism*, December 1998, http://www.prism-magazine.org/december/html/student_plagiarism_in_an_onlin.htm.

[27]"How Do Teachers Check for Plagiarism," *Yahoo Answers*, 2007, 2011. http://answers.yahoo.com/question/index?qid=20080210172831AAb1tP5.

[28]Peggy Noonan, *Simply Speaking* (New York: HarperCollins, 1998), p. x.

[29]Granville N. Toogood, *The Articulate Executive* (New York: McGraw-Hill, 1996), p. 93.

[30]Ibid., pp. 94–95.

Chapter 13

[1]One of the best overviews of Cicero's contributions to rhetoric appears in Lester Thonssen and A. Craig Baird, *Speech Criticism: The Development of Standards for Rhetorical Appraisal*. (New York: The Ronald Press, 1948), pp. 78–91. Also see James L. Golden, Goodwin F. Berquist, and William E. Coleman, *The Rhetoric of Western Thought*, 4th ed. (Dubuque, IA: Kendall/Hunt, 1989).

[2]Associated Press, "GM's China Sales Pass U.S. for First Time in History," National Public Radio, January 24, 2001, http://www.npr.org/templates/story/story.php?storyId=133176256.

[3]Clive Thompson, "Community Urinalysis," *The New York Times Magazine* (December 8, 2007), p. 62.

[4]Arne Duncan, "The Vision of Education Reform in the United States: Secretary Arne Duncan's Remarks to United Nations Educational, Scientific and Cultural Organization (UNESCO)," U.S. Department of Education, November 4, 2010, http://www.ed.gov/news/speeches/vision-education-reform-united-states-secretary-arne-duncans-remarks-united-nations-ed.

[5]Bill O'Reilly, *The O'Reilly Factor*, Fox News, July 21, 2010 edition, *Media Matters for America*, July 21, 2010. http://mediamatters.org/iphone/research/201007210079.

[6]Matthew S. McGlone, "Contextomy: The Art of Quoting Out of Context," *Media Culture and Society* 27 (2005), pp. 511–522.

[7]See www.miami.com/mld/miamiherald/sports/columnists/dan_le_batard/9745974.htm, September 24, 2004.

[8]Carole Blair, "Civil Rights/Civil Sites: '. . . Until Justice Rolls Down Like Waters,'" *The Carroll C. Arnold Distinguished Lecture*, National Communication Association Convention, November 2006 (Boston: Pearson/Allyn & Bacon, 2008), p. 2.

[9]"To Pluck a Rooted Sorrow," *Newsweek*, April 27, 2009, as quoted in Richard Nordquist, "What Is an Analogy," *About.com* (2009), http://grammar.about.com/od/rhetoricstyle/f/qanalogy07.htm.

[10]Daphne Duval Harrison, *Black Pearls: Blues Queens of the 1920s* (New Brunswick, NJ: Rutgers University Press, 1988).

[11]Vivian Hobbs, Commencement Address at Prince George's Community College, Largo, Maryland, 1991. See full manuscript in Isa N. Engleberg, *The Principles of Public Presentations* (New York: HarperCollins, 1994), pp. 339–341.

[12]Stella Ting-Toomey and Leeva C. Chung, *Understanding Intercultural Communication* (Los Angeles: Roxbury, 2005), pp. 189–190.

[13]Based on John Chafee with Christine McMahon and Barbara Stout, *Critical Thinking, Thoughtful Writing*, 2nd ed. (Boston: Houghton Mifflin, 2002), pp. 534–536, 614; Jim Kapoun "Teaching Undergrads Web Evaluation: A Guide for Library Instruction," *C&RL News* (July/August, 1998), pp. 522–523 cited in "Five Criteria for Evaluating Web Pages," Cornell University, http://olinuris.library.cornell.edu/print/4499 and http://olinuris.library.cornell.edu/ref/research/webcrit.html, Minor textual corrections, May 10, 2010. For more criteria questions and a worksheet see, Isa Engleberg and Dianna R. Wynn, "Assessing a Web Site Worksheet," *Instructor's Manual for THINK Communication* (Boston: Pearson/Allyn and Bacon, 2010).

[14]Leonard J. Shedletsky and Joan E. Aitken, *Human Communication on the Internet* (Boston: Pearson/Allyn & Bacon, 2004), pp. 100–101.

[15]"Cocaine-Cola," http://www.snopes.com/cokelore/cocaine.asp.

[16]Michael M. Kepper with Robert E. Gunther, *I'd Rather Die Than Give a Speech* (Burr Ridge, IL: Irwin, 1994), p. 6.

[17]Some of the best research on the value of organizing a presentation was conducted in the 1960s and '70s. See Ernest C. Thompson, "An Experimental Investigation of the Relative Effectiveness of Organizational Structure in Oral Communication," *Southern Speech Journal* 26 (1960), pp. 59–69; Ernest C. Thompson, "Some Effects of Message Structure on Listeners' Comprehension," *Speech Monographs* 34 (1967), pp. 51–57; James C. McCroskey and R. Samuel Mehrley, "The Effects of Disorganization and Nonfluency on Attitude Change and Source Credibility," *Communication Monographs* 36 (1969), pp. 13–21; Arlee Johnson, "A Preliminary Investigation of the Relationship between Organization and Listener Comprehension," *Central States Speech Journal* 21 (1970), pp. 104–107; and Christopher Spicer and Ronald E. Bassett, "The Effect of Organization on Learning from an Informative Message," *Southern Speech Communication Journal* 41 (1976), pp. 290–299.

[18]Tony Buzon, *Use Both Sides of Your Brain*, 3rd ed. (New York: Plume, 1989).

[19]An annotated manuscript of Julie Borchard's "The Sound of Muzak" speech is available in Engleberg and Daly, *Presentations in Everyday Life*, 3rd ed., pp. 251–253. Ms. Borchard was a student and forensics team member at Prince George's Community College.

[20]The Speech Framer was developed by Isa N. Engleberg as an alternative or supplement to outlining. See Engleberg and Daly, *Presentations in Everyday Life*, 3rd ed., pp. 217–218. © Isa N. Engleberg, 2003.

[21]Ibid., pp. 199–207.

[22]Lee Towe, *Why Didn't I Think of That? Creativity in the Workplace* (West Des Moines, IA: American Media, 1966), p. 7.

[23]Ibid., pp. 9–11.

[24]Engleberg and Daly, *Presentations in Everyday Life*, 3rd ed., p. 216.

[25]Ibid., pp. 219–221.

[26]Bob Herbert, "Gun Violence Is Becoming an Epidemic," in *Guns and Violence: Current Controversies*, ed. Henry H. Kim (San Diego, CA: Greenhaven Press, 1999), p. 20.

[27]Arne Duncan, National Science Teachers Association Conference, March 20, 2009. http://www.ed.gov/print/news/speeches/2009/03/03202009.html.

[28]Ibid., pp. 228–229.

[29]Quoted in Engleberg, *The Principles of Public Presentation*, p. 160.

[30]Based on information in Anna Quindlen, "The Failed Experiment," *Newsweek* (June 26, 2006), p. 64.

[31]Samuel E. Wood, Ellen Green Wood, and Denise Boyd, *The World of Psychology*, 6th ed. (Boston: Pearson/Allyn & Bacon, 2008), p. 204.

[32]Ibid., 204–205.

[33]For the complete text of King's "I Have a Dream" speech plus commentary, see James R. Andrews and David Zarefsky, *Contemporary American Voices: Significant Speech in American History, 1945–Present* (New York: Longman, 1992), pp. 78–81; See also Martin Luther King, Jr., "I Have a Dream," *American Rhetoric: Top 100 Speeches*, http://www.americanrhetoric.com/top100speechesall.html.

[34]Engleberg and Daly, Presentations in Everyday Life, 3rd ed., pp. 251–256.

[35]Marge Anderson, "Looking through Our Window: The Value of Indian Culture," *Vital Speeches of the Day* 65 (1999): pp. 633–634.

[36]Maya Angelou. Remarks at the Funeral Service for Coretta Scott King in Atlanta, Georgia, delivered February 7, 2006, http://www.americanrhetoric.com/speeches/mayaangeloueulogyforcorettaking.htm.

[37]Robert M. Franklin, "The Soul of Morehouse and the Future of the Mystique," President's Town Meeting, Morehouse College, April 21, 2009, http://themaroontiger.com/attachments/329_The%20Soul%20of%20Morehouse%20and%20the%20Future%20of%20the%20Mystique%20-%20abridged.pdf.

Chapter 14

[1]Rick Shenkman, "History Proves that Presidential Debates Matter," George Mason University's History News Network, September 22, 2004, http://hnn.us/articles/7478.html.

[2]Ibid.

[3]Lani Arredondo, *The McGraw-Hill 36-Hour Course: Business Presentations* (New York: McGraw-Hill, 1994), p. 147.

[4]Jerry Della Femina, quoted in *Creative Strategy in Advertising*, 2nd ed., ed. A. Jerome Jewler (Belmont, CA: Wadsworth, 1985), p. 41.

[5]John W. Bowers, "Some Correlates of Language Intensity," *Quarterly Journal of Speech* 50 (1964), pp. 415–420.

[6]Based on Isa Engleberg and Ann Raimes, *Pocket Keys for Speakers* (Boston: Houghton Mifflin, 2004), pp. 191–193.

[7]Max Atkinson, *Lend Me Your Ears* (New York: Oxford, 2005), p. 221.

[8]Marcel Danesi and Paul Perron, *Analyzing Cultures: An Introduction and Handbook* (Bloomington, IN: Indiana University Press, 1999), p. 174.

[9]Engleberg and Raimes, pp. 94–95.

[10]Kathleen Hall Jamieson, *Eloquence in an Electronic Age: The Transformation of Political Speechmaking* (New York: Oxford University Press, 1988), p. 81, 84.

[11]Read and watch Obama's entire speech on "Obama Race Speech: Read the Full Text," *The Huffington Post*, Updated, November 17, 2008, http://www.huffingtonpost.com/2008/03/18/obama-race-speech-read-th_n_92077.html.

[12]Lori J. Carrell and S. Clay Willmington, "The Relationship between Self-Report Measures of Communication Apprehension and Trained Observers' Ratings of Communication Competence," *Communication Reports* 11 (1998), pp. 87–95.

[13]Michael T. Motley and Jennifer L. Molloy, "An Efficacy Test of New Therapy ("Communication-Orientation Motivation") for Public Speaking Anxiety, *Journal of Applied Communication Research*, 22 (1994), pp. 44–58.

[14]Geoffrey, Brewer, "Snakes Top List of Americans' Fears," *Gallup News Service*, March 19, 2001, http://www.gallup.com/poll/1891/snakes-top-list-americans-fears.aspx.

[15]Susan D. Miller, *Be Heard the First Time: A Woman's Guide to Powerful Speaking* (Herndon, VA: Capital Books, 2006), p. 100.

[16]Ty Ford, *Ty Ford's Audio Bootcamp Field Guide* (Baltimore: Technique, Inc., 2004), p. 19.

[17]Everett M. Rogers and Thomas M. Steinfatt, *Intercultural Communication* (Prospect Heights, IL: Waveland Press, 1999), p. 174.

[18]Rogers and Steinfatt, p. 172; Guo-Ming Chen and William J. Starosta, *Foundations of Intercultural Communication* (Boston: Allyn and Bacon, 1998), pp. 81–92.

[19]Arredondo, p. 238.

[20]Steven A. Beebe, "Eye Contact: A Nonverbal Determinant of Speaker Credibility," *The Speech Teacher* 23 (1974), pp. 21–25.

[21]Mark L. Knapp and Judith A. Hall, *Nonverbal Communication in Human Interaction*, 5th ed. (Belmont, CA: Wadsworth/Thomson Learning, 2006), p. 295.

[22]Peggy Noonan, *Simply Speaking: How to Communicate Your Ideas with Style, Substance, and Clarity* (New York: HarperCollins, 1998), p. 206.

[23]Janet Bozarth, *Better than Bullet Points: Creating Engaging e-Learning with PowerPoint®* (San Francisco: Pfeiffer/Wiley, 2008), p. 3.

[24]Robin Williams, *The Non-Designer's Presentation Book: Principles for Effective Presentation Design* (Berkeley, CA: Peachpit Press, 2010), p. 136.

[25]Ibid., p. 137.

[26]Stephen M. Kosslyn, *Clear and to the Point: 8 Psychological Principles for Compelling PowerPoint Presentations* (New York: Oxford University Press, 2007), pp. 4–12; Richard E. Mayer, *Multimedia Learning*, 2nd ed. (New York: Cambridge University Press, 2009).

[27]John Daly and Anita Vangelisti, "Skillfully Instructing Learners: How Communicators Effectively Convey Messages," in *Handbook of Communication and Social Interaction*, ed. John O. Greene and Brant R. Burleson (Mahwah, NJ: Lawrence Erlbaum Associates, 2003), p. 878.

[28]Cyndi Maxey and Kevin E. O'Connor, *Present Like a Pro* (New York: St. Martin's Griffin, 2006), p. 49.

[29]Noonan, p. 9.

[30]Thomas K. Mira, *Speak Smart: The Art of Public Speaking* (New York: Random House, 1997), p. 91.

[31]Read Hillary Clinton's concession speech on "Hillary Clinton Endorses Barack Obama," *The New York Times*, June 7, 2008, http://www.nytimes.com/2008/06/07/us/politics/07text-clinton.html. Watch and listen to Clinton's speech on YouTube at http://www.youtube.com/watch?v=zgi_kIYx_bY

[32]Read George W. Bush's speech to a Joint Session of Congress on "Text: President Bush Addresses the Nation," *The Washington Post*, September 20, 2001, http://www.washingtonpost.com/wp-srv/nation/specials/attacked/transcripts/bushaddress_092001.html; Watch and listen to the speech on "G.W.Bush Declares "Freedom and Fear Are at War," *YouTube*, September 20,2001, http://www.youtube.com/watch?v=ZMj9g6WRLfQ.

[33]Read a transcript of the Nick Jonas speech on "Diabetes Awareness" at the National Press Club, August 24, 2009 at http://www.press.org/members/transcriptview.cfm?pdf=20090824_jonas.pdf; Watch and listen to the Nick Jonas speech on "Nick Jonas discusses juvenile diabetes at the National Press Club, August 24, 2009," *YouTube*, http://www.youtube.com/watch?v=DyYOxzrJB4Y.

Chapter 15

[1]James M. Lang, "Beyond Lecturing," *The Chronicle of Higher Education*, September 9, 2006, p. C4.

[2]Ibid.

[3]Wilbert J. McKeachie, *Teaching Tips: Strategies, Research, and Theory for College and University Teachers*, 10th ed. (Boston: Houghton Mifflin, 1999), p. 70.

[4]Ibid., pp. 69–84.

[5]Sections of Chapters 12 through 16 are based on Isa N. Engleberg and John A. Daly, *Presentations in Everyday Life*, 3rd ed. (Boston: Pearson/Allyn & Bacon, 2009); Isa N. Engleberg and Ann Raimes, *Pocket Keys for Speakers* (Boston: Houghton Mifflin, 2004); Isa N. Engleberg and John A. Daly, *Think Public Speaking* (Boston: Pearson/Allyn & Bacon, 2013), Chapter 15.

[6]This section is based on the research and theory-building of Katherine E. Rowan, professor of communication at George Mason University. See Katherine E. Rowan, "Informing and Explaining Skills: Theory and Research on Informative Communication," in *Handbook of Communication and Social Interaction Skills*, ed. John O. Greene and Brant R. Burleson (Mahwah, NJ: Lawrence Erlbaum Associates, 2003), pp. 403–438; Katherine E. Rowan, "A New Pedagogy for Explanatory Public Speaking: Why Arrangement Should Not Substitute for Invention," *Communication Education* 44 (1995), pp. 236–250.

[7]Rowan, "A New Pedagogy for Explanatory Public Speaking: Why Arrangement Should Not Substitute for Invention," p. 242; Rowan, "Informing and Explaining Skills: Theory and Research on Informative Communication," p. 411.

[8]Rowan, "A New Pedagogy for Explanatory Public Speaking: Why Arrangement Should Not Substitute for Invention," p. 241.

[9]*The American Heritage Dictionary of the English Language* (Boston: Houghton Mifflin, 2000), pp. 1433–1434.

[10]Al Tompkins, "Bill Mays: the Death of a TV Pitchman," *PoynterOnline*, June 29, 2009, http://www.poynter.org/column.asp?id=2&aid=165905.

[11]http://www.natcom.org/index.asp?bid=510.

[12]Engleberg and Daly, *Presentations in Everyday Life*, pp. 3–4.

[13]Rives Collins and Pamela J. Cooper, *The Power of Story: Teaching through Storytelling*, 2nd ed. (Boston: Allyn & Bacon, 1997), p. 2.

[14]Walter R. Fisher, *Human Communication as Narration: Toward a Philosophy of Reason, Value, and Action* (Columbia, SC: University of South Carolina Press, 1987), p. 64, 65.

[15]Joanna Slan, *Using Stories and Humor: Grab Your Audience* (Boston: Allyn & Bacon, 1998), pp. 5–6.

[16]Alan M. Perlman, *Writing Great Speeches: Professional Techniques You Can Use* (Boston: Allyn & Bacon, 1998), p. 52.

[17]William Hendricks et al., *Secrets of Power Presentations* (Franklin Lakes, NJ: Career Press, 1996), p. 79.

[18]Malcolm Kushner, *Successful Presentations for Dummies* (Foster City, CA: IDG Books, 1997), p. 79.

[19]Collins and Cooper, pp. 24–28; Engleberg and Daly, *Presentations in Everyday Life: Strategies for Effective Speaking*, pp. 292–294.

[20]Fisher, *Human Communication as Narration: Toward a Philosophy of Reason, Value, and Action*, p. 24.

[21]Ibid., p. 68.

[22]Candace Spigelman, "Argument and Evidence in the Case of the Personal," *College English* 64. 1 (2001), pp. 80–81.

[23]Walter Fisher, "Narrative as Human Communication Paradigm," in *Contemporary Rhetorical Theory*, ed. John Louis Lucaites, Celeste Michelle Condit, and Sally Caudill (New York: The Guilford Press, 1999), p. 272.

[24]Based on Slan, pp. 89–95, 116. See also Engleberg and Daly, *Presentations in Everyday Life*, pp. 296–298.

[25]Based on Paul Galdone, *The Three Little Pigs* (New York: Houghton Mifflin, 1970).

[26]Kushner, p. 350.

[27]Gene Perret, *Using Humor for Effective Business Speaking* (New York: Sterling, 1989), pp. 19–26.

[28]Frank Cotham cartoon, Published in *The New Yorker*, February, 18, 2002, http://www.cartoonbank.com/2002/at-what-point-does-this-become-our-problem/invt/122039.

[29]Summary of tips for using humor from Isa N. Engleberg and Dianna R. Wynn, *The Challenge of Communicating: Guiding Principles and Practices* (Pearson/Allyn & Bacon, 2008), p. 408; Slan, pp. 170–172.

[30]Engleberg and Daly, *Presentations in Everyday Life*, pp. 110–111.

[31]Since developing this presentation, *CliffsNotes* has gone through several changes and traumas. In 1998, Cliff Hillegass sold Cliff'sNotes, Inc., to John Wiley & Sons, Inc. In May 2001, Mr. Hillegass passed away at the age of 83. In 2007, CliffsNotes.com was relaunched with an updated design and notes for school subjects such as math, science, writing, foreign languages, history, and government. "A Brief History of CliffsNotes," http://www.cliffsnotes.com/WileyCDA/Section/A-Brief-History.id-305430.html.

Chapter 16

[1]Robert H. Gass and John S. Seiter, *Persuasion, Social Influence, and Compliance Gaining*, 4th ed. (Boston: Allyn & Bacon, 2011), Preface, p. xiii.

[2]A variation on the 1931 jazz standard "It Don't Mean a Thing (If It Ain't Got That Swing)" by Duke Ellington with lyrics by Irving Mills.

[3]Sections of this chapter are based on Isa N. Engleberg and John A. Daly, *Presentations in Everyday Life*, 3rd ed. (Boston: Pearson/Allyn & Bacon, 2009), Chapter 5; Isa N. Engleberg and Ann Raimes, *Pocket Keys for Speakers* (Boston: Houghton Mifflin, 2004), Part 8: Sections 25 and 26; Isa N. Engleberg and John A. Daly, *Think Public Speaking* (Boston: Pearson/Allyn & Bacon, 2013), Chapter 16.

[4]William J. McGuire, "Inducing Resistance to Persuasion: Some Contemporary Approaches," in *Advances in Experimental Psychology*, ed. Leonard Berkowitz (New York: Academic Press, 1964), pp. 192–229.

[5]Gass and Seiter, p. 198.

[6]Jack W. Brehm, *A Theory of Psychological Reactance* (New York: Academic Press, 1966). Also see Michael Burgoon et al., "Revisiting the Theory of Psychological Reactance," in *The Persuasion Handbook: Development in Theory and Practice*, ed.

James Price Dillard and Michael Pfau (Thousand Oaks, CA: Sage, 2002), pp. 213–232; James Price Dillard and Linda J. Marshall, "Persuasion as a Social Skill," in *Handbook of Communication and Social Interaction Skills*, ed. John O. Greene and Brant R. Burleson (Mahwah, NJ: Lawrence Erlbaum, 2003), pp. 500–501.

[7]Don Levine, "Booze Barriers," *Boulder Weekly*, September 7, 2000, http://www.boulderweekly.com/archive/090700/coverstory.html, p. 4.

[8]Ibid.

[9]Stephen Toulmin, *The Uses of Argument* (London: Cambridge University Press, 1958). See also Stephen Toulmin, Richard Rieke, and Allan Janik, *An Introduction to Reasoning* (New York: Macmillan, 1979).

[10]Thomas Sewell, "I Beg to Disagree: The Lost Art of Logical Arguments," *Naples Daily News*, January 14, 2005, p. 9D.

[11]Fred D. White and Simone J. Billings, *The Well-Crafted Argument: A Guide and Reader*, 2nd ed. (Boston: Houghton Mifflin, 2005), p. 93.

[12]Charles U. Larson, *Persuasion: Reception and Responsibility*, 11th ed. (Belmont, CA: Thomson/Wadsworth, 2007), p. 185.

[13]Les Christie, "Number of People Without Health Insurance Climbs," *CNN Money* (A Service of CNN, Fortunate, and Money) September 13, 20011, http://money.cnn.com/2011/09/13/news/economy/census_bureau_health_insurance/index.htm

[14]Larson, p. 58.

[15]Richard M. Perloff, *The Dynamics of Persuasion: Communication and Attitudes in the 21st Century*, 4th (New York: Routledge/Taylor & Francis, 2010), pp. 204–206.

[16]Student speech from Authors' files.

[17]Perloff, p. 207.

[18]Aristotle, *Rhetoric*, in *The Complete Works of Aristotle: The Revised Oxford Translation*, vol. 2, ed. Jonathan Barnes (Princeton, NJ: Princeton University Press, 1995), p. 2155.

[19]Michael Osborn, Suzanne Osborn, and Randall Osborn, *Public Speaking*, 8th ed. (Boston: Pearson/Allyn & Bacon, 2009), p. 380.

[20]Ibid., p. 376.

[21]Based on Patrick J. Hurley, *A Concise Introduction to Logic*, 8th ed. (Belmont, CA: Wadsworth Thomson Learning, 2003), pp. 172–174.

[22]Mike Allen and Raymond W. Preiss, "Comparing the Persuasiveness of Narrative and Statistical Evidence Using Meta-Analysis," *Communication Research Reports* 14 (1997), pp. 125–131.

[23]Lisa L. Massi Lindsey and Kimo Ah Yun, "Examining the Persuasive Effects of Statistical Messages: A Test of Mediating Relationships," *Communication Studies* 54 (2003), pp. 306–321.

[24]See Alexander Todorov, Shelley Chaiken, and Marlone D. Henderson, "The Heuristic-Systematic Model of Social Information Processing," in *The Persuasion Handbook: Developments in Theory and Practice*, ed. James Price Dillard and Michael Pfau (Thousand Oaks, CA: Sage, 2002), pp. 195–211; Dillard and Marshall, pp. 494–495.

[25]Alan H. Monroe, *Principles and Types of Speech* (Chicago: Scott, Foresman, 1935).

[26]Based on Nicholas D. Kristof and Sheryl WuDunn, "The Women's Crusade," *The New York Times Magazine*, August 23, 2009, pp. 28–39. Kristof is an international journalist and advocate for women's rights.

[27]Sharon Shavitt and Michelle R. Nelson, "The Role of Attitude Functions in Persuasion and Social Judgment," in *The Persuasion Handbook: Developments in Theory and Practice*, ed. James Price Dillard and Michael Pfau (Thousand Oaks, CA: Sage, 2002), p. 150.

[28]Ibid.

[29]This presentation appeared in *Vital Speeches of the Day* 65 (August 1, 1999), pp. 633–634.

Text Credits

Chapter 1
p. 15: Stephen R. Covey, *The 7 Habits of Highly Effective People*, New York: Simon and Schuster, 1989.

p. 16: From the National Communication Association Credo for Ethical Communication, www.natcom.org. Reprinted by permission.

p. 20: "Examining Communication" from *Communication Currents*, Volume 5, Issue 3, June 2010. By permission of the National Communication Association, www.natcom.org.

Chapter 2
p. 28: From Rosenberg "Self-Esteem Scale," Rosenberg, Morris. 1989. *Society and the Adolescent Self-Image*. Revised edition. Middletown, CT: Wesleyan University Press. By permission.

p. 31: Adapted from "Fear Factor: What We Touch Can Change How We Think," *AARP The Magazine*, Nov/Dec 2010 Edition. Author: Holly St. Lifer, © 2010.

pp. 35–36: Virginia P. Richmond and James C. McCroskey, *Communication: Apprehension, Avoidance, and Effectiveness*, 5th ed. © 1998 by Pearson Education, Inc. Reproduced by permission of Pearson Education, Inc.

p. 38: Virginia P. Richmond and James C. McCroskey, *Communication: Apprehension, Avoidance, and Effectiveness*, 5th ed. © 1998 by Pearson Education, Inc. Reproduced by permission of Pearson Education, Inc.

p. 39: Virginia P. Richmond and James C. McCroskey, *Communication: Apprehension, Avoidance, and Effectiveness*, 5th ed., p. 133. © 1998 by Pearson Education, Inc. Reproduced by permission of Pearson Education, Inc., Upper Saddle River, NJ.

Chapter 3
p. 57: The "Generalized Ethnocentrism (GENE) Scale" from James Neuliep, *Intercultural Communication: A Contextual Approach*, 4th ed., pp. 30–31. Copyright 2009 by Sage Publications Inc. Permission conveyed via Copyright Clearance Center.

p. 60: K. Kam et al., "Culture and Deception: Moral Transgression or Social Necessity?" from *Communication Currents*, Volume 3, Issue 1, February 2008. By permission of the National Communication Association, www.natcom.org.

Chapter 4
p. 65: Judi Brownell, *Listening: Attitudes, Principles, and Skills*, 4th ed. © 2010. Printed and electronically reproduced by permission of Pearson Education, Inc., Upper Saddle River, NJ.

p. 68: Don Gabor, *How to Start a Conversation and Make Friends*. New York: Fireside, 2001.

p. 77: From William V. Haney, *Communication and Interpersonal Relationships: Text and Cases*, 1992, pp. 231–232. By Permission of the author.

p. 79: Roy M. Berko, Andrew D. Wolvin, and Darlyn R. Wolvin, *Communicating: A Social and Career Focus*, 9th ed., "Student Listening Inventory," pp. 129–131, © 2004. Reprinted by permission of Pearson Education, Inc., Upper Saddle River, NJ.

Chapter 5
p. 84: Joann S. Lubin, "To Win Advancement, You Need to Clean up Any Bad Speech Habits," *Wall Street Journal*, October 5, 2004, p. B1.

p. 99: Virginia P. Richmond and James C. McCroskey, *Communication: Apprehension, Avoidance, and Effectiveness*, 5th ed., p. 133. © 1998 by Pearson Education, Inc. Reproduced by permission of Pearson Education, Inc., Upper Saddle River, NJ.

p. 102: Michael W. Kramer and Debbie S. Dougherty, "Language Convergence; Meaning Divergence" from *Communication Currents*, Volume 4, Issue 2, April 2009. By permission of the National Communication Association, www.natcom.org.

Chapter 6
p. 114: Virginia P. Richmond and James C. McCroskey, *Nonverbal Behavior in Interpersonal Relations*, 5th ed., © 2004. Reprinted by permission of Pearson Education, Inc., Upper Saddle River, NJ.

p. 121: Adapted from Brian Spitzberg, "CSRS: The Conversational Skills Rating Scale--An Instructional Assessment of Interpersonal Competence," in the *NCA Diagnostic Series*, 2nd ed., 2007. By permission of the National Communication Association, www.natcom.org.

Chapter 7
p. 127: Isa Engleberg and Dianna Wynn, *Working in Groups: Communication Principles and Strategies*, 5th ed., pp. 82–85. © 2010. Reprinted by permission of Pearson Education, Inc., Upper Saddle River, NJ.

p. 132: Mark C. Knapp and Anita L. Vangelisti, *Interpersonal Communication and Human Relationships*, 5th ed., Figure 7.2 "Staircase Model of Interaction Stages," p. 49 excerpt from pp. 48–49, © 2005. Reprinted by permission of Pearson Education, Inc., Upper Saddle River, NJ.

p. 134: Reprinted with permission from Joseph Luft, *Group Process: An Introduction to Group Dynamics*, 3rd ed. (Palo Alto, CA: Mayfield, 1984). Copyright ©1984 The McGraw-Hill Companies, Inc.

p. 137: Reprinted with permission from Jack R. Gibb, "Defensive Communication," *Journal of Communication* 2 (1961), pp. 141–148. Copyright © John Wiley & Sons.

p. 144: Masaki Matsunaga, "Stand by Me: Helping Bullied Victims" from *Communication Currents*, Volume 5, Issue 3, June 2010. By permission of the National Communication Association, www.natcom.org.

Chapter 8
p. 155: Dominic A. Infante and Andrew S. Rancer, "A Conceptualization and Measure of Argumentativeness," *Journal of Personality Assessment* 46 (1982), pp. 72–80. Reproduced by permission of Society for Personality Assessment. www.personality.org.

p. 156: Dudley D. Cahn and Ruth Anna Abigail, *Managing Conflict through Communication*, 3rd ed., "Six-Step Model of Conflict Resolution," pp. 97–104. © 2007. Reprinted by permission of Pearson Education, Inc., Upper Saddle River, NJ.

Chapter 9
p. 186: Erin M. Bryant and Patricia M. Sias, "Making Sense of Workplace Deception" from *Communication Currents*, Volume 6, Issue 2, April 2011. By permission of the National Communication Association, www.natcom.org.

Chapter 11
p. 214: Karyn C. Rybacki and Donald J. Rybacki, *Advocacy and Opposition: An Introduction to Argumentation*, 4th ed., © 2000. Reprinted by permission of Pearson Education, Inc., Upper Saddle River, NJ.

p. 226: Lyn M. Van Swol, "Why Can't Groups Focus on New Information?" from *Communication Currents*, Volume 4, Issue 2, April 2009. By permission of the National Communication Association, www.natcom.org.

Chapter 12
p. 241: Julie J. C. H. Ryan, "Student Plagiarism in an Online World," *Prism*, December 1998. Reprinted with permission.

Chapter 14
p. 271 (left): From Ann Raimes, *Pocket Keys for Writers MLA UPD*, 3E. © 2010 Heinle/Arts & Sciences, a part of Cengage Learning, Inc. Reproduced by permission. www.cengage.com/permissions.

p. 271 (right): From Isa Engleberg and Ann Raimes, *Pocket Keys for Speakers*. © 2004 Heinle/Arts & Sciences, a part of Cengage Learning, Inc. Reproduced by permission. www.cengage.com/permissions.

Chapter 15
pp. 303–306: John Sullivan, student presentation, "Cliff's Notes." Reprinted by permission.

Chapter 16
pp. 323–326: Marge Anderson, from "Looking through Our Window: The Value of Indian Culture," a speech delivered to the First Friday Club of the Twin Cities, March 5, 1999. Reprinted by permission of Marge Anderson, Chief Executive of the Mille Lacs Band of Ojibwe.

Photo Credits

Front Matter
vi: (top, left) Stockbyte/Thinkstock; (top, right) MEGAN LEWIS/El Tiempo de Colombia/Newscom; vii: (top, left) U.S. Air Force photo/Tech. Sgt. Shane A. Cuomo; (top, right) Stockbyte/Jupiter Images; viii: (top, left) AP Photo/Damian Dovarganes; (top, right) HO/AFP/Getty Images/Newscom; ix: (top, left) Warner Bros. Ent. All rights reserved./Courtesy Everett Collection; (top, right) REUTERS/Lucas Jackson; x: (top, left) Chris Haston / NBC / Everett Collection; (top, right) EPA/JOSE MANUEL DE LA MAZA / CHILEAN PRESIDENTIAL OFFICE / HANDOUT /Landov; xi: (top, left) Photos 12 / Alamy; (top, right) CD1 WENN Photos/Newscom; xii: (top, left) FancyVeerSet8/Fancy/Alamy; (top, right) UPPA/Photoshot; xiii: (top, left) Noel Hendrickson/Getty Images; (top, right) ZUMA Press/Newscom; xv: (top) Isa Engleberg; (bottom) Dianna Wynn

Chapter 1
2–3: Stockbyte/Thinkstock; 6: Ben Cooper/Alamy; 7: (left) Lara Jo Regan/Liaison/Getty Images; (center) Allison Michael Orenstein/Photodisc/Getty Images; (right) Ciaran Griffin/Lifesize/Getty Images; 8: (left, top) Ryan McVay/Getty Images; (left, center) Garry Wade/Getty Images; (left, bottom) Randy Faris/Corbis; (right, top) Iain Masterton/Alamy; (right, top, inset) ICP/Alamy; 9: John Giustina/Stone/Getty Images; 10, 18: MANDY GODBEHEAR/Shutterstock; 11: NOAH BERGER/The New York Times/Redux Pictures; 12: (left, right) Stockbyte/Jupiter Images; (background) Losevsky Pavel/Shutterstock; 13: (top, background) Losevsky Pavel/Shutterstock; (bottom) Poulsons Photography/Shutterstock; 14: (clockwise, from top center) Courtesy, Peace Corps; Radius Images/Alamy; Monkey Business

THINK COMMUNICATION FEATURES

ANSWERS to test your knowledge questions

Chapter 1
Answers: 1-e; 2-a; 3-a; 4-d; 5-c; 6-b; 7-e; 8-d; 9-d; 10-d

Chapter 2
Answers: 1-d; 2-d; 3-d; 4-e; 5-b; 6-d; 7-e; 8-e; 9-c; 10-b

Chapter 3
Answers: 1-c; 2-a; 3-d; 4-e; 5-b; 6-e; 7-a; 8-b; 9-b; 10-e

Chapter 4
Answers: 1-d; 2-d; 3-e; 4-b; 5-e; 6-c; 7-b; 8-a; 9-e; 10-a

Chapter 5
Answers: 1-b; 2-b; 3-a; 4-c; 5-a; 6-e; 7-e; 8-a; 9-d; 10-e

Chapter 6
Answers: 1-b; 2-a; 3-e; 4-c; 5-c; 6-b; 7-a; 8-e; 9-c; 10-b

Chapter 7
Answers: 1-b; 2-a; 3-c; 4-a; 5-b; 6-c; 7-c; 8-a; 9-c; 10-e

Chapter 8
Answers: 1-c; 2-e; 3-b; 4-c; 5-b; 6-d; 7-a; 8-a; 9-d; 10-c

Chapter 9
Answers: 1-e; 2-e; 3-c; 4-e; 5-a; 6-e; 7-b; 8-d; 9-e; 10-d

Chapter 10
Answers: 1-c; 2-c; 3-a; 4-b; 5-b; 6-e; 7-d; 8-a; 9-b; 10-e

Chapter 11
Answers: 1-d; 2-b; 3-a; 4-c; 5-d; 6-e; 7-b; 8-c; 9-e; 10-c

Chapter 12
Answers: 1-b; 2-b; 3-a; 4-d; 5-e; 6-d; 7-d; 8-c; 9-e; 10-c

Chapter 13
Answers: 1-c; 2-b; 3-c; 4-b; 5-e; 6-a; 7-a; 8-b; 9-a; 10-d

Chapter 14
Answers: 1-b; 2-d; 3-b; 4-a; 5-c; 6-a; 7-e; 8-c; 9-c; 10-a

Chapter 15
Answers: 1-d; 2-d; 3-d; 4-b; 5-a; 6-b; 7-b; 8-c; 9-e; 10-d

Chapter 16
Answers: 1-b; 2-c; 3-b; 4-c; 5-d; 6-b; 7-a; 8-c; 9-d; 10-d